Fascism and Pre-Fascism in Europe, 1890–1945

Fascism and Pre-Fascism in Europe, 1890–1945:

A Bibliography of the Extreme Right

Philip Rees *Dip. Lib.,*

Head of Acquisitions
University of York Library

THE HARVESTER PRESS · SUSSEX

BARNES & NOBLE BOOKS · NEW JERSEY

First published in Great Britain in 1984 by
THE HARVESTER PRESS LIMITED
Publisher: John Spiers
16 Ship Street, Brighton, Sussex

and in the USA by
BARNES & NOBLE BOOKS
81 Adams Drive, Totowa, New Jersey 07512

© Philip Rees, 1984

British Library Cataloguing in Publication Data
Rees, Philip
    Fascism and pre-fascism.
    1. Fascism—Europe—History—Bibliography
    I. Title
    016.3356′094   Z2361.F2

    ISBN 0-7108-0372-9

Library of Congress Cataloging in Publication Data
Rees, Philip.
    Fascism and pre-fascism in Europe, 1890–1945.

    1. Fascism—Europe—History—Bibliography.
    I. Title.
    Z2000.7.R44 1984   016.3205′33′094   84-433
    [D726.5]

    ISBN 0-389-20472-2

Photoset in 10 point Baskerville by Photobooks (Bristol) Ltd
Printed and bound in Great Britain by
Biddles Ltd, Guildford and King's Lynn

CONTENTS

vii

PREFACE

To compile a bibliography covering the extreme right in Europe from 1890 to 1945 may appear to be a foolhardy enterprise not least because of the vast body of literature which has been generated since 1890. However, the central concern of this volume is to present a representative selection of the most cited and the most significant writings on the ideology and practice of the extreme right; it is of necessity highly selective. Certain areas and topics have been omitted almost totally due entirely to the limitations of space. The major omissions include the extreme right in Britain which has already been covered in my *Fascism in Britain: an Annotated Bibliography*,[1] the foreign and external policies of the states in which the extreme right took power, and the various anti-fascist and resistance movements and activities. Some aspects of the subject are already so well under bibliographical control, for example, the nazi concentration camp system and the Holocaust, that I have felt it unnecessary to duplicate the effort in the present work. In these cases it is, perhaps, enough to list only the basic texts and the relevant bibliographical and reference works. In fact, it is a feature of the following pages to concentrate in particular on the wide array of reference and bibliographical tools available.

There are few limitations on either form or language of the material, although the great majority of the entries are either books, unpublished dissertations or periodical articles. In general the bibliography is weighted towards post-1945 and especially more recent contributions. I have been inclined to exclude general historical surveys in favour of works of more particular application. Readers may also detect a tendency to give more detailed attention to the less well-known countries and movements.

The title of the bibliography refers to fascism and the extreme right as though the two terms are synonymous and co-extensive. I should make it clear that the terms are used *faute de mieux* and that I do not accept that fascism can necessarily be identified with the category of the extreme right. Gilbert Allardyce refers to the difficulty inherent in comprehending through generic concepts or ideological abstractions the species of 'fascism' which arose as a result of defections from the left; fugitives from that direction found a place in 'virtually every reputed fascist organization'. He alludes to the 'independent quality of Doriot's "fascism"'. It should come as no surprise that I include a section on Hendrik de Man, the Belgian socialist, who though a man of the left, was a great influence on Marcel Déat and came to admire German National Socialism. Aware of the ultimate tyranny of concepts, I have eschewed any exact definition of fascism, authoritarian nationalism, or the radical right. I am concerned with bibliographical taxonomy rather than with any scientific comparative typological classification but, at the same time, I am conscious of Professor Stanley Payne's suggestion that authoritarian nationalism can be divided into three categories: fascist, radical right, and conservative right.[2] This bibliography concentrates most extensively on the obviously 'fascist' movements and on the radical right but does include certain phenomena of the conservative right, which adopted a certain fascisant colouring and accoutrements while remaining ideologically conservative. This principle has allowed the appearance of the Franco, Salazar, and Vichy regimes, the Croix de Feu in France, and the Fatherland Front in Austria.

The use of the term pre-fascism is a convenience and implies no necessary influential or precursory connection between the groups subsumed under this category and any later groups or movements. Yet clearly, fascism like other similar phenomena did not spring spontaneously and fully armed from the void; it was the progeny of complicated but surely discernible processes which had been taking place well before the First World War, however much its subsequent form may have been determined by the War and its aftermath. These processes are succinctly described by Professor Payne:

> The roots of the new forms of the authoritarian right in the late nineteenth century and early twentieth centuries may be found in at least four different areas: the growth of corporatist doctrine, primarily in Catholic circles, and the ambiguous development of certain new forms of political Catholicism, the transformation of moderate or conservative liberalism, by degrees, in an overtly authoritarian direction, especially in southern Europe; the transformation of previously traditionalist, anti-liberal and monarchist forces in various countries from the Latin West to Russia; and the emergence of an instrumental, modernizing, and imperialist new kind of radical right in Italy.[3]

Whether these movements can be regarded as precursors of fascism, or are taken synchronically as discrete, autochthonous phenomena, the important consideration is that in the literature they have often been treated as forming an 'extreme right' continuum with later movements or viewed as merely part of the amorphous roots of the later 'fascist' movements. The purpose of this bibliography is to present a one volume survey of the literature illustrating the broad sweep of the new authoritarian right as it formed in the late nineteenth century (1890 is an arbitrary but justifiable starting point) and subsequently developed up to 1945. I hope it is as mindful of difference as it is of the artificial need for conceptual unity.

Notes

1. Philip Rees. *Fascism in Britain: an Annotated Bibliography*. Hassocks: Harvester Press, 1979. See also Philip Rees. 'Changing interpretations of British fascism: a bibliographical survey', in Kenneth Lunn and Richard J. Thurlow, eds. *British fascism: essays on the radical right in inter-war Britain*. London: Croom Helm, 1980. pp. 168–204.
2. Stanley G. Payne. *Fascism: comparison and definition*. Madison: U. of Wisconsin P., 1980. pp. 14–21.
3. *ibid.*, p. 23.

ACKNOWLEDGEMENTS

I owe an immense debt of gratitude to all the staff of those numerous libraries which I have used, particularly to the Inter-Library Loans Department of the J.B. Morrell Library, University of York, Magie Lawty, Heather Blackburn, and Debbie Crangle, for their usual efficient and indispensable assistance in acquiring even the most obscure material. I would also like to express especial thanks to Barbara Higginson who produced a beautiful typescript and to my wife, Margaret, for her unfailing help in the time-consuming work of checking and correcting.

ABBREVIATIONS OF PERIODICAL TITLES

ACTA HIST.	Acta Historica
ACTA POL. HIST.	Acta Poloniae Historica
AESTHET. UND KOMMUN.	Aesthetik und Kommunikation
AGRIC. HIST.	Agricultural History
AM. HIST. REV.	American Historical Review
AM. POL. SCI. REV.	American Political Science Review
AM. SOCIOL. REV.	American Sociological Review
ANNALES	Annales: Economies, Sociétés, Civilisations
ANN. DE L'UNIV. DES SCI. SOC. DE TOULOUSE	Annales de l'Université des Sciences Sociales de Toulouse
ANN. DELLA FOND. LUIGI EINAUDI	Annali della Fondazione Luigi Einaudi
ARCH. FÜR SOZIALGESCHICHTE	Archiv für Sozialgeschichte
AUSTRIAN HIST. YEARB.	Austrian History Yearbook
AUST. J. POLIT. HIST.	Australian Journal of Politics and History
BIBLIOTECA DELLA LIBERTÀ	Biblioteca della Libertà (Turin: Centro di Ricerca e Documentazione Luigi Einaudi)
BL. FÜR DTSCH UND INT. POLIT.	Blätter für Deutsche und Internationale Politik
BR. J. OF INT. STUD.	British Journal of International Studies
BULL. CENT. RECH. ETUD. SECONDE GUERRE MOND.	Bulletin du Centre des Recherches et d'Etudes de la Seconde Guerre Mondiale (Belgium)
BULL. INT. INST. SOC. HIST.	Bulletin of the International Institute for Social History
BULL. LEO BAECK INST.	Bulletin of the Leo Baeck Institute
BULL. SOC. HIST. MOD.	Bulletin de la Société d'Histoire Moderne
CAH. D'HIST. (Grenoble)	Cahiers d'Histoire (Grenoble)
CAH. D'HIST. DE LA SECONDE GUERRE MOND.	Cahiers d'Histoire de la Seconde Guerre Mondiale (Belgium)
CAH. INT. DE SOCIOL.	Cahiers Internationaux de Sociologie
CAMBRIDGE HIST. J.	Cambridge Historical Journal
CAMBRIDGE J.	Cambridge Journal

CAN. AMER. REV. OF HUNG. STUD.	Canadian-American Review of Hungarian Studies
CAN. AMER. SLAV. STUD.	Canadian-American Slavic Studies
CAN. HIST. ASS. HIST. PAPERS	Canadian Historical Association Historical Papers
CAN. J. HIST.	Canadian Journal of History
CAN. REV. STUD. NATL.	Canadian Review of Studies of Nationalism
CAN. SLAVIC STUD.	Canadian Slavic Studies
CATHOL. HIST. REV.	Catholic Historical Review
CENT. EUR. HIST.	Central European History
CESK. CAS. HISTORICKY	Československý Časopis Historický
COMP. POLIT.	Comparative Politics
COMP. POLIT. STUD.	Comparative Political Studies
COMP. STUD. IN SOC. AND HIST.	Comparative Studies in Society and History
DTSCH. RUNDSCH.	Deutsche Rundschau
DURHAM UNIV. J.	Durham University Journal
EAST EUR. Q.	East European Quarterly
ECON. HIST. REV.	Economic History Review
ETUD. HIST. HONG.	Etudes Historiques Hongroises
EUR. J. OF SOCIOL.	European Journal of Sociology
EUR. STUD. REV.	European Studies Review
FR. HIST. STUD.	French Historical Studies
G. STOR. LETT. ITAL.	Giornale Storico della Letteratura Italiana
GER. LIFE AND LETT.	German Life and Letters
GER. STUD. REV.	German Studies Review
GES. STAAT ERZIEH.	Gesellschaft, Staat, Erziehung
GESCH. IN WISS. UND UNTERR.	Geschichte in Wissenschaft und Unterricht
GESCH. UND GES.	Geschichte und Gesellschaft
HIST. AIKAK.	Historiallinen Aikakauskirja
HIST. ARKISTO	Historiallinen Arkisto
HIST. CAS.	Historický Časopis
HIST. ET GEOGR.	Historiens et Géographes
HIST. J.	Historical Journal
HIST. OF EDUC. Q.	History of Education Quarterly
HIST. TIDSKR. FOR FINLAND	Historisk Tidskrift för Finland

HIST. TIDSSKR. (Norway)	Historisk Tidsskrift (Norway)
HIST. OF CHILDHOOD Q.	History of Childhood Quarterly
HIST. WORKSHOP	History Workshop Journal
HIST. Z.	Historische Zeitschrift
HISTORICKE STUD.	Historicke Studie
INF. HIST.	Information Historique
INT. AFF.	International Affairs
INT. J. OF COMP. SOCIOL.	International Journal of Comparative Sociology
INT. REV. SOC. HIST.	International Review of Social History
ISTOR. PREGLED	Istoricheski Pregled
ITAL. CONTEMP.	Italia Contemporanea
J. INTER-AMER. STUD.	Journal of Inter-American Studies and World Affairs
J. OF CENT. EUR. AFF.	Journal of Central European Affairs
J. OF CONTEMP. HIST.	Journal of Contemporary History
J. OF ECCLES. HIST.	Journal of Ecclesiastical History
J. OF ECON. HIST.	Journal of Economic History
J. OF EUR. STUD.	Journal of European Studies
J. OF HIST. IDEAS	Journal of the History of Ideas
J. OF INTERDISC. HIST.	Journal of Interdisciplinary History
J. OF ITAL. HIST.	Journal of Italian History
J. OF MOD. HIST.	Journal of Modern History
J. OF PSYCHOHISTORY	Journal of Psychohistory
J. OF SOC. HIST.	Journal of Social History
JAHRB. FÜR GESCH.	Jahrbuch für Geschichte
JAHRB. FÜR GESCH. OSTEUROPAS	Jahrbücher für Geschichte Osteuropas
JAHRB. FÜR GESCH. SOZ. LANDER EUR.	Jahrbuch für Geschichte der Sozialistischen Länder Europas
JAHRB. INST. DTSCH. GES.	Jahrbuch des Instituts für Deutsche Geschichte
JEW. SOC. STUD.	Jewish Social Studies
JUGOSL. IST. CAS.	Jugoslovenski Istorijski Časopis
KWART. HIST.	Kwartalnik Historyczny
LEO BAECK INST. YEARB.	Leo Baeck Institute Yearbook
MIDWEST J. OF POL. SCI.	Midwest Journal of Political Science
MITT. ARCH.	Mitteilungen für die Archivpflege

MITT. DER GES. FÜR SALZBURGER LANDESKUNDE	Mitteilungen der Gesellschaft für Salzburger Landeskunde
MOUVEMENT SOC.	Le Mouvement Social
MOV. DI LIBERAZIONE IN ITALIA	Movimento di Liberazione in Italia
MOV. OPERAIO E SOC.	Movimento Operaio e Socialista
NEUE POLIT. LIT.	Neue Politische Literatur
NEW GER. CRIT.	New German Critique
NUOVA RIV. STOR.	Nuova Rivista Storica
NUOVO OSS.	Il Nuovo Osservatore
OESTERR. MONATSH.	Oesterreichische Monatshefte
OESTERR. Z. FÜR POLITIKWISS.	Oesterreichische Zeitschrift für Politikwissenschaft
PENSIERO POLIT.	Pensiero Politico
POL. WES. AFF.	Polish Western Affairs
POLIT. LIT.	Politische Literatur
POLIT. Q.	Political Quarterly
POLIT. SCI. Q.	Political Science Quarterly
POLIT. STUD.	Politische Studien
POLIT. VIERTELJAHRESSCHR.	Politische Vierteljahresschrift
PSYCHOHIST. REV.	Psychohistory Review
Q. J. OF SPEECH	Quarterly Journal of Speech
QUAD. DI SOCIOL.	Quaderni di Sociologia
QUAD. STOR.	Quaderni Storica
QUELL. UND FORSCHUNG. AUS ITAL. ARCH.	Quellen und Forschungen aus Italienischen Archiven und Bibliotheken
RASS. STOR. RISORGIMENTO	Rassegna Storica del Risorgimento
REV. BELGE DE PHILOLOGIE ET D'HIST.	Revue Belge de Philologie et d'Histoire
REV. BELGE D'HIST. CONTEMP.	Revue Belge d'Histoire Contemporaine
REV. D'ALLEM.	Revue d'Allemagne
REV. DE CIENC. SOC.	Revista de Ciencas Sociales
REV. DE ESTUD. POLITICOS	Revista de Estudios Politicos
REV. DE IST.	Revista de Istorie
REV. DES LANG. VIVANTES (Brussels)	Revue des Langues Vivantes (Brussels)
REV. D'HIST. DEUX. GUERRE MOND.	Revue d'Histoire de la Deuxième Guerre Mondiale
REV. D'HIST. DU FASCISME	Revue d'Histoire du Fascisme

REV. D'HIST. ECCLESIASTIQUE	Revue d'Histoire Ecclesiastique (Belgium)
REV. D'HIST. MOD. ET CONTEMP.	Revue d'Histoire Moderne et Contemporaine
REV. DU NORD	Revue du Nord
REV. ETUD. ITAL.	Revue des Etudes Italiennes
REV. FR. DE SCI. POLIT.	Revue Française de Science Politique
REV. FR. DE SOCIOLOGIE	Revue Française de Sociologie
REV. GEN. BELGE	Revue Générale Belge
REV. HIST. (Paris)	Revue Historique (Paris)
REV. HIST. ARDENNAISE	Revue d'Histoire Ardennaise
REV. OF POLIT.	Review of Politics
REV. ROUM. D'HIST.	Revue Roumaine d'Histoire
RIV. DI STORIA CONTEMPORANEA	Rivista di Storia Contemporanea
RIV. INT. DI SCI. SOC.	Rivista Internazionale di Scienze Sociali
RIV. ITAL. SCI. POLIT.	Rivista Italiana di Scienza Politica
RIV. STOR. DEL. SOC.	Rivista Storica del Socialismo
RIV. STOR. ITAL.	Rivista Storica Italiana
SCAND. J. OF HIST.	Scandinavian Journal of History
SCAND. POLIT. STUD.	Scandinavian Political Studies
SCAND. STUD.	Scandinavian Studies
SCHR. DES BUNDESARCH.	Schriften des Bundesarchivs
SCHWEIZ. MONATSH.	Schweizer Monatshefte
SCHWEIZ. Z. FÜR GESCHICHTE	Schweizerische Zeitschrift für Geschichte
SCI. HIST.	Science Historique
SLAV. AND EAST EUR. REV.	Slavonic and East European Review
SLOVANSKY PREHL.	Slovanský Přehled
SOC. HIST.	Social History (United Kingdom)
SOC. RES.	Social Research
SOC. SCI. (USSR ACAD. OF SCI.)	Social Sciences (USSR Academy of Sciences)
SOC. SCI. INF.	Social Science Information
SOC. SCI. Q.	Social Science Quarterly
SOC. STUD. (USA)	Social Studies (USA)
SOZIALWISS. JAHR. FÜR POLIT.	Sozialwissenschaftliches Jahrbuch für Politik
STANFORD FR. REV.	Stanford French Review

STOR. CONTEMP.	Storia Contemporanea
STOR. E POLIT.	Storia e Politica
STUD. DZIEJ. ZSRR EUR. SRODK.	Studia z Dziejow ZSRR i Europy Srodkowej (Wroclaw)
STUD. POLIT.	Studi Politici
STUD. STOR.	Studi Storici
TIJDSCHR. VOOR GESCHIEDENIS	Tijdschrift voor Geschiedenis
TIMES LIT. SUPPL.	Times Literary Supplement
TORT. SZ.	Történelmi Szemle
VIERTELJAHRSH. FÜR ZEITG.	Vierteljahrshefte für Zeitgeschichte
VIERTELJAHRSCHR. FÜR SOZ. UND WIRTSCHAFTSGESCH.	Vierteljahrschrift für Sozial-und Wirtschaftsgeschichte
WEST. POLIT. Q.	Western Political Quarterly
WEST. SOC. FR. HIST. PROC. ANNU. MEET.	Western Society for French History: Proceedings of the Annual Meeting
WIENER LIB. BULL.	Wiener Library Bulletin
WISS. Z. DER FRIEDRICH-SCHILLER UNIV. JENA THURINGEN GES. UND SPRACHWISS. R.	Wissenschaftliche Zeitschrift der Friedrich-Schiller Universität Jena Thüringen. Gesellschaft und Sprachwissenschaftliche Reihe
WORLD POLIT.	World Politics
YAD VASHEM BULL.	Yad Vashem Bulletin
Z. FÜR BAYERISCHE LANDESG.	Zeitschrift für Bayerische Landesgeschichte
Z. FÜR GESAMTE STAATSWISS.	Zeitschrift für die Gesamte Staatswissenschaft
Z. FÜR GESCH. DER JUDEN	Zeitschrift für die Geschichte der Juden
Z. FÜR GESCH. OBERRHEINS	Zeitschrift für die Geschichte des Oberrheins
Z. FÜR GESCHICHTSWISS.	Zeitschrift für Geschichtswissenschaft
Z. FÜR OSTFORSCHUNG	Zeitschrift für Ostforschung
Z. FÜR POLIT.	Zeitschrift für Politik
Z. FÜR WIRTSCH. UND SOZIALWISS.	Zeitschrift für Wirtschafts-und Sozialwissenschaften

FASCISM: GENERAL

Collections and Anthologies

Gn 1   *Aesthetik und Kommunikation*, **32**, 1978. Issue on fascism with articles by Arno Bammé, Klaus Eschen, Anson G. Rabinbach, Karl-Heinz Roth, Tilla Siegel, Klaus Staeck and Wolf Wagner.

Gn 2   ALFF, Wilhelm, *Der Begriff Faschismus und andere Aufsätze zur Zeitgeschichte*, Frankfurt/M: Suhrkamp, 1971. 182pp.

Gn 3   ALLARDYCE, Gilbert (ed.), *The Place of Fascism in European History*, Englewood Cliffs: Prentice-Hall, 1971. viii, 178pp. Essays.

Gn 4   BARDÈCHE, Maurice, and others, *Études sur le fascisme*, Paris: Les Sept Couleurs, 1974. 350pp.

Gn 5   BOREJSZA, Jerzy W. (ed.), *Faszyzmy Europejskie, 1922–1945 w oczach wspolczesnych i hystoryków* (*European Fascisms in the Eyes of Contemporaries and Historians*), Warsaw: Czytelnik, 1979. 784pp.

Gn 6   *Défense de l'Occident*, **17** (**81**), 1969. Special issue on 'Les fascismes inconnus'. 110pp. Neo-fascist view of some of the lesser known fascisms between the wars.

Gn 7   DELZELL, Charles F. (ed.), *Mediterranean Fascism, 1919–1945: selected documents*, London: Macmillan, 1971. New York: Walker, 1970. xx, 364pp. Italy, Spain and Portugal.

Gn 8   *Fašismus a Evropa: Fascism and Europe: mezinarodni symposium: an International Symposium, v Praze 28–29 srpna 1969, Prague: Vyd. Historicky Ustav ČSAV, 1969–70.* 2 vols. Collection of papers from a symposium organised by the Czechoslovak Academy of Sciences Inst. of History.

Gn 9   *Faszyzm: teoria i praktyka w Europie, 1922–1945: materialy z sympozjum, Wroclaw 26–27 wrzesnia 1974 g*; ed. Kazimierz Dzialocha *et al.* (*Fascism: theory and practice in Europe*), Wroclaw, 1977. 400pp.

Gn 10   GREENE, Nathaniel (ed.), *Fascism: an anthology*. New York: Crowell, 1968. 302pp. Bib. 301–2.

Gn 11   HORSTER, Detlef and NIKOLINAKOS, Marios (eds), *Ist die Epoche des Faschismus beendet?* mit Beiträgen von I. Fetscher et al., Frankfurt/M: Metzler, 1971. 276pp.

Gn 12   *Journal of Contemporary History*, 'International fascism, 1920–1945'; ed. Walter Laqueur and George L. Mosse, London: Weidenfeld & Nicolson. New York: Harper & Row, 1966. x, 197pp. Repr. from *Journal of Contemporary History*, **1** (**1**), 1966.

Gn 13   *Journal of Contemporary History*, 'International fascism: new thoughts and new approaches'; ed. George L. Mosse, London: Sage, 1979. 386pp.

Gn 14   LANDAUER, Karl and HONNEGGER, Hans (eds), *Internationaler Faschismus: Beiträge über Wesen und Stand der faschistischen Bewegung und über den Ursprung ihrer leitenden ideen und triebkräfte*, Karlsruhe: Braun, 1928. 163pp. Includes Bottai on Italy, H. Franke on Germany, Legendre on Spain, P.R. Rohden on France and A. Singer on Hungary.

Gn 15   MOSSE, George Lachmann, *Masses and Man: nationalist and fascist perceptions of reality*, New York: Fertig, 1980. xii, 362pp. A collection of essays on France, Italy and Germany.

Gn 16   *Revue d'Histoire du Fascisme. 1972-*, Paris, ed. François Duprat. Neo-fascist views of fascism.

Gn 17   SCHIEDER, Wolfgang (ed.), *Faschismus als soziale Bewegung: Deutschland und Italien im Vergleich*, Hamburg: Hoffman & Campe, 1976. 211pp. Revised papers from 30th Deutscher Historikertag, Brunswick 1974. 2nd edn, Vandenhoeck & Ruprecht, 1983.

Gn 18   TURNER, Henry Ashby (ed.), *Reappraisals of Fascism*, New York: New Viewpoints, 1975. xiv, 238pp. Bib. 231. Includes articles by K. Epstein, E. Nolte, W.S. Allen, A. Cassels, H.A. Turner, S. Payne, H. Rogger, G.M. Wilson and R. Winegarten.

Gn 19   WEBER, Eugen (ed.), *Varieties of Fascism: doctrines of revolution in the twentieth century*, Princeton: Van Nostrand, 1964. 192pp. Bib. 187-8.

Gn 20   WOOLF, Stuart J. (ed.), *Fascism in Europe*, London: Methuen, 1981. 408pp. Bib. 387-402. Includes contributions by Woolf, H.R. Trevor-Roper, A.J. Nicholls, K.R. Stadler, J. Erös, Zev. Barbu, S. Andreski, A.F. Upton, T.K. Derry, Malene Djursaa, R. Skidelsky, G. Carpinelli, G. Warner, Paul Preston and Christopher Seton-Watson. Rev. version of *European Fascism*, Weidenfeld & Nicolson, 1968.

Gn 21   WOOLF, Stuart J. (ed.), *The Nature of Fascism: proceedings of a conference held by the Reading University Graduate School of Contemporary European Studies*, London: Weidenfeld & Nicolson, 1968, 261pp.

General Surveys and Histories

Gn 22   BURON, Thierry and GAUCHON, Pascal, *Les Fascismes*, Paris: PUF, 1979. 176pp. Bib. 176.

Gn 23   CARSTEN, Frances Ludwig, *The Rise of Fascism*, 2nd edn, Berkeley: University of California Press, 1980. 279pp. Bib. 259–63.

Gn 24   CASSELS, Alan, *Fascism*, New York: Crowell, 1975. xiv, 401pp. Bib. 350–75.

Gn 25   COLLOTTI, Enzo, 'International fascism as a historical phenomenon', *WIENER LIB. BULL.*, **19** (4), 1965. pp. 3–5.

Gn 26   GEARY, Dick, 'The rise of fascism'. *J. OF EUR. STUD.*, **1** (3), 1971. pp. 253–8. Review article.

Gn 27   GRAVELLI, Asvero, *Verso l'Internazionale Fascista*, 2nd edn, Rome: Nuova Europa, 1932. x, 264pp.

Gn 28   HAAS, Werner, *Europa will leben: die nationalen Erneuerungsbewegungen in Wort und Bild*, pref. by Edmund Marhefka, Berlin: Batschari V., 1936. 378pp. Nazi survey of fascist movements in Europe.

Gn 29   HAYES, Paul M., *Fascism*, London: Allen & Unwin. New York: Free Press, 1973. 260pp. Bib. 246–52.

Gn 30   JOES, Anthony James, *Fascism in the Contemporary World: ideology, evolution, resurgence*, foreword by A. James Gregor, Boulder, Col.: Westview Press, 1978. xvi, 238pp. Bib. 225–34.

Gn 31   JOES, Anthony James, 'Fascism: the past and the future'. *COMP. POLIT. STUD.*, **7** (1), 1974. pp. 107–33.

Gn 32   KAMINSKI, Andrzej Jozef, *Faszyzm*, Warsaw: Wiedza Powszechna, 1971. 247pp.

Gn 33   KEDWARD, Harry Roderick, *Fascism in Western Europe, 1900–45*, Glasgow: Blackie, 1969. xi, 260pp. Bib. 243–8.

Gn 34   KITCHEN, Martin, *Fascism*, London: Macmillan, 1976. xii, 106pp. Bib. 93–9.

Gn 35   LAQUEUR, Walter (ed.), *Fascism: a reader's guide: analyses, interpretations, bibliography*, London: Wildwood House. Berkeley: University of California Press, 1976. x, 478pp. Bibs. Penguin edn, 1979.

Gn 36   LARSEN, Stein Ugelvik, and others (eds), *Who Were the Fascists? social roots of European fascism*, ed. Stein Ugelvik Larsen, Bernt Hagtvet and Jan Petter Myklebust, Bergen: Universitetsforlaget, 1980. 816pp. Bibs. Very important on social composition of fascist movements.

Gn 37   LEDEEN, Michael Arthur, *Universal Fascism: the theory and practice of the Fascist International, 1928–1936*, New York: Fertig, 1972. xxi, 200pp. Bib. 187–92. Wisconsin University thesis, 1969.

Gn 38   LEMAÎTRE, Henri, *Les Fascismes dans l'histoire*, Paris: Ed. du Cerf, 1959. 115pp.

Gn 39   LUBASZ, Heinz (ed.), *Fascism: three major regimes*, New York: Wiley, 1973. viii, 188pp. Italy, Germany, Japan.

Gn 40   MICHEL, Henri, *Les Fascismes*, Paris: PUF, 1977. 128pp. Bib. 126.

Gn 41   MICHEL, Henri, 'Introduction sur le fascisme'. *REV. D'HIST. DEUX. GUERRE MOND.*, **17** (**66**), 1967. pp 1–10. Whole issue devoted to 'Sur le fascisme'. See individual entries.

Gn 42   MILZA, Pierre and BENTELI, Marianne, *Le Fascisme au XXe siecle*, Paris: Eds. Richelieu, 1973. 413pp. Bib. 389–97.

Gn 43   MITCHELL, Otis C., *Fascism: an introductory perspective*, Durham, NC: Moore Pub. Co., 1978. 130pp. Bib. 129–30.

Gn 44   NIETHAMMER, Lutz, 'Faschistische Bewegung in der Zwischenkriegzeit in Europa'. In *Faschistische Diktatur in Deutschland: historische Grundlangen*, Mommsen, H. et al, Stuttgart: Klett, 1972. pp. 17–36.

Gn 45   NOCE, Augusto del, *L'Epoca della Secolarizzazione*, Milan: Giuffre, 1970. 256pp. Fascism as a form of revolutionary nationalism in an age of secularisation.

Gn 46   NOLTE, Ernst, *Die Faschismus: von Mussolini zu Hitler: Texte, Bilder und Dokumente*, Munich: Desch, 1968. 403pp.

Gn 47   NOLTE, Ernst, *Die Krise des liberalen Systems und die faschistischen Bewegungen*, Munich: Piper, 1968. 475pp. Bib. 389–431. French version, *Les Mouvements fascistes: l'Europe de 1919 à 1945*, Paris: Calmann-Lévy, 1969.

Gn 48   NOLTE, Ernst, *Three Faces of Fascism: Action Française, Italian Fascism, National Socialism*, London: Weidenfeld & Nicolson, 1965. New York: Holt, Reinhart & Winston, 1966. xi, 561pp. Bib. 547–8. Tr. *Der Faschismus in seiner Epoche*, Munich: Piper, 1963. 4 Aufl. 1971, by Leila Vennewitz.

Gn 49   PAYNE, Stanley G., 'Fascism in Western Europe'. In LAQUEUR, W., Gn 35. pp. 295–311.

Gn 50   PETERSEN, Jens, 'La dimensione europea del fascismo'. *Problemi di Ulisse*, **13** (**82**), 1976. pp. 69–78.

Gn 51   POULSEN, Henning, *Fascisme og Nazisme, 1919–1945*, Copenhagen: Berlingske, 1980. 239pp. Bib. 233–5.

Gn 52   PURCELL, Hugh, *Fascism*, London: Hamilton, 1977. 95pp. Bib. 90–2.

Gn 53 RAMA, Carlos M., *Revolución social y fascismo en el siglo XX*, Buenos Aires: Ed. Palestra, 1962. 346pp.

Gn 54 ROGGER, Hans and WEBER, Eugen (eds), *The European Right: a historical profile*, Berkeley: University of California Press, 1965. vi, 589pp. Bibs.

Gn 55 ROMUALDI, Adriano, *Il Fascismo come fenomeno Europeo*, Rome: Ed. de l'Italiano, 1977. lxxi, 295pp. Bib. 274-87.

Gn 56 ROSNER, Jacob, *Der Faschismus: seine Wurzeln, sein Wesen, seine Ziele: fragmentarische Versuche*, Vienna: Rosner, 1966. 255pp.

Gn 57 RYSZKA, Franciszek, *Le Fascisme européen: diversité et communauté*, Warsaw: Panstw. Wydawn. Nauk., 1977. 19pp.

Gn 58 SCHUEDDEKOPF, Otto-Ernst, *Fascism*, London: Weidenfeld & Nicolson. New York: Praeger, 1973. 224pp. Bib. 217-18. Tr. from the German, *Bis alles in Scherben fällt*, Munich: Bertelsmann, 1973, by Margaret Vallance.

Gn 59 VANDROMME, Pol, *L'Europe en chemise: l'extrême droite dans l'entre-deux-guerres*, Nivelles: Ed. de la Francité, 1971. 165pp.

Gn 60 WEISS, John, *The Fascist Tradition: radical Right-wing extremism in modern Europe*, New York: Harper & Row, 1967. xxxvi, 151pp. Bib. 134-44. Fascism as extreme conservatism.

Historiography, Interpretation and Theory of Fascism

Gn 61 AGNOLI, Johannes, *Zur Faschismusdiskussion: ein Beitrag zur Bestimmung der Verhältnisses von Politik und Ökonomie und der Funktion des heutigen bürgerlichen Staates*, Hamburg: Verlag O., 1973. 63pp.

Gn 62 ALLARDYCE, Gilbert, 'What fascism is not: thoughts on the deflation of a concept'. *AM. HIST. REV.*, **84** (2), 1979. pp. 367-98. With comments by Stanley G. Payne and Ernst Nolte.

Gn 63 BARDÈCHE, Maurice, *Qu'est que le fascisme?* Paris: Les Sept Couleurs, 1961. 195pp.

Gn 64 BESSON, Waldemar, 'Die Interpretation des Faschismus'. *NEUE POLIT. LIT.*, **13** (3), 1968. 306-13. Review of literature.

Gn 65 BOTZ, Gerhard, 'Die historische Erscheinungsform des Faschismus'. *Beitrage zur Historischen Sozialkunde*, **4** (3), 1974. pp. 56-62.

Gn 66 BOURDERON, Roger, *Le Fascisme, idéologie et pratiques: essai d'analyse comparée*, Paris: Eds. Sociales, 1979. 219pp. Bib. 213-14.

Gn 67 BRACHER, Karl Dietrich, 'Kritische Bemerkungen zum Begriff des Faschismus'. In FICHTENAU, Heinrich and ZÖLLNER, Erich (eds), *Beiträge zur neueren Geschichte Österreichs*, Vienna: Bohlau, 1974. pp. 503-10.

Gn 68 BRACHER, Karl Dietrich, *Zeitgeschichtliche Kontroversen: um Faschismus, Totalitarismus, Demokratie*, Munich: Piper, 1976. 158pp. Includes his 'Probleme und Perspektiven der Hitler-Interpretation'.

Gn 69 CARSTEN, Francis Ludwig, 'Interpretations of Fascism'. In LAQUEUR, W. Gn 35, pp. 515-34.

Gn 70 CASSELS, Alan, 'Janus: the two faces of fascism'. *CAN. HIST. ASSOC. HIST. PAPERS*, 1969. pp. 166-84. Also in TURNER, H.A., Gn 18, pp. 69-92.

Gn 71 CASSELS, Alan, 'Fascism as radicalism'. *CAN. J. HIST.*, **15** (**2**), 1980. pp. 259-61.

Gn 72 CLEMENZ, Manfred, '"Alter" und "neuer" Faschismus'. In *Abendroth-Forum: Marburger Gespräche aus Anlass des 70. Geburtstag von Wolfgang Abendroth*, Marburg: VAB, 1977. pp. 384-91.

Gn 73 DITTRICH, Z.R., 'Fascism: a troublesome question'. *Acta Historiae Neerlandica*, **3**, 1968. pp. 26-140.

Gn 74 DÜLFFER, Jost, 'Bonapartism, fascism, and national socialism'. *J. OF CONTEMP. HIST.*, **11** (**4**), 1976. pp. 109-28.

Gn 75 DUSEK, Peter and others (eds), *Faschismus: Theorien, Fallstudien, Unterichtsmodelle*, ed. Peter Dusek, Hubert C. Ehalt, Sylvia Lausecker, Vienna: V. fur Jugend & Volk, 1980. 255pp.

Gn 76 ECKARDT, W., 'The values of fascism'. *J. of Social Issues*, **24**, 1968. pp. 89-104.

Gn 77 ENGEL, Josef, 'Literaturbericht: Zeitgeschichte—Faschismus'. *GESCH. IN WISS. UND UNTERR.*, **20** (**4**), 1969. pp. 239-52.

Gn 78 ERDMANN, Karl Dietrich, 'Nationalsozialismus, Faschismus, Totalitarismus'. *GESCH. IN WISS. UND UNTERR.*, **27** (**8**), 1976. pp. 457-69.

Gn 79 'Fascismes et National Socialisme: une question actuelle'. *ANNALES*, **24** (**1**), 1969. pp. 195-233. Review of literature.

Gn 80 FELICE, Renzo de, *Fascism: an informal introduction to its theory and practice: an interview with Michael A Ledeen*, New Brunswick, NJ: Transaction Books, 1976. 128pp. Bib. 127-8. Tr. of *Intervista sul fascismo*, 4th edn.

Gn 81 FELICE, Renzo de, *Interpretations of Fascism*, Cambridge Mass., Harvard University Press, 1977. xvi, 248pp. Notes and Bib. 193-244. Tr. of *Le interpretazioni del fascismo*, 4th edn, by Brenda Huff Everett.

Gn 82 GREGOR, A. James, 'Professor Renzo de Felice and the fascist phenomenon'. *WORLD POLIT.*, **30** (3), 1978. pp. 433-49.

Gn 83 GALLI, Giorgio, 'Towards a typology of fascism'. *WIENER LIB. BULL.*, **31** (47/48), 1978. pp. 126-30.

Gn 84 GAUCHER, François, *Le Fascisme est-il actuel?* Paris: Librairie Française, 1961. 135pp.

Gn 85 GERSTENBERGER, Peter, Bürgerliche französische Veröffentlichungen über den Faschismus'. *Z. FUR GESCHICHTWISS.*, **21** (4), 1973. pp. 457-65.

Gn 86 GREBING, Helga, *Aktuelle Theorien über Faschismus und Konservatismus: eine Kritik*, Mainz: Kohlhammer, 1974. 117pp. Bib. 111-17. Survey of recent interpretations of fascism particularly in Austria.

Gn 87 GREBING, Helga, *Linksradikalismus gleich Rechtsradikalismus: eine falsche Gleichung*, Stuttgart: Kohlhammer, 1971. 85pp.

Gn 88 GREGOR, A. James, 'Fascism and comparative politics'. (review essay). *COMP. POLIT. STUD.*, **9** (2), 1976. pp. 207-22.

Gn 89 GREGOR, A. James, 'Fascist lexicon', *Transaction*, 8 May 1971. pp. 54-8.

Gn 90 GREGOR, A. James, *The Fascist Persuasion in Radical politics*, Princeton, NJ: Princeton, University Press, 1974. xii, 472pp. Bib. 435-49.

Gn 91 GREGOR, A. James, *Interpretations of Fascism*, Morristown, NJ: General Learning Press, 1974. iv, 281pp. Bib. 263-75.

Gn 92 GREGOR, A. James, 'On understanding fascism: a review of some contemporary literature'. *AM. POLIT. SCI. REV.*, **67** (4), 1973. pp. 1332-47.

Gn 93 HANISCH, Ernst, 'Neure Faschismustheorien'. *Zeitgeschichte*, **1** (1), 1973. pp. 19-23. Review of the literature based on Nolte's six principles for identifying fascist movements.

Gn 94 HAUTSCH, Gert, *Faschismus und Faschismus-Analysen: zur Auseinandersetzung mit einigen Theorien und Pseudo-Theorien*, Frankfurt/M: Röderberg V., 1974. 63pp.

Gn 95 HÜRTEN, Heinz, 'Neuerscheinungen zur Geschichte des

Faschismus'. *HIST. JAHRBUCH*, **89** (**2**), 1969. pp. 420–7. Compares Nolte's theory of fascism with others current 1963–8.

Gn 96   HURST, Michael, 'What is fascism?' *HIST. J.*, **11** (**1**), 1968. pp. 165–85. Review article.

Gn 97   *Italienisch-Deutsche Historiker-Tagung, Faschismus, National-sozialismus: Ergebnisse und Referate*, Brunswick: Limbach, 1964. 196pp. German and Italian texts.

Gn 98   *Journal of Contemporary History*, vol. **11** (**4**), 1976. pp. 1–283. Theories of fascism.

Gn 99   KNÖDLER-BUNTE, Eberhard, 'Fascism as a depoliticized mass movement'. *NEW GER. CRIT.*, **11**, 1977. pp. 39–48.

Gn 100   KOGAN, Norman, 'Fascism as a political system'. In WOOLF, S.J., Gn 21. pp. 11–18.

Gn 101   KORNHAUSER, William, *The Politics of Mass Society*, Glencoe, Ill.: Free Press, 1959. 256pp.

Gn 102   KÜHNL, Reinhard, 'Probleme einer Theorie über den internationalen Faschismus. 1. Die Faschismuskonzeption Ernst Noltes. 2. Empirische Untersuchungen und theoretische Interpretationen'.*POLIT. VIERTELJAHRESSCHR*, **11**, 1970. pp. 318–41; **16** (**1**), 1975. pp. 89–121.

Gn 103   LINZ, Juan José, 'Political space and fascism as a late-comer: conditions conducive to the success or failure of fascism as a mass movement in inter-war Europe'. In LARSEN, S.U., Gn 36. pp. 153–89.

Gn 104   LINZ, Juan José and STEPAN, Alfred (eds), *The Breakdown of Democratic Regimes*, Baltimore: Johns Hopkins University Press, 1978. 742 pp.

Gn 105   LIPSET, Seymour, *Political Man: the social bases of politics*, London: Heinemann. New York: Doubleday, 1960. 432pp. Includes chapter on fascism: left, right and centre.

Gn 106   LOEWENSTEIN, Bedrich, 'K vývoji pojeti fašismu' (The development of the concept of fascism). *Revue Dejin Socialismu* (Czechoslovakia), **9** (**4**), 1969. pp. 559–80.

Gn 107   MACCIOCCHI, Maria Antonietta, *Elements pour une analyse du fascisme: séminaire, Paris III Vincennes, 1974–1975*, Paris: Union Gen. d'Éditions, 1976. 2 vols.

Gn 108   MAIER, Charles S., 'Some recent studies of fascism'. *J. OF MOD. HIST.*, **48** (**3**), 1976. pp. 506–21.

Gn 109   MANGONI, Luisa, 'Cesarismo, Bonapartismo, Fascismo'. *STUD. STOR.*, **17** (3), 1976. pp. 41-61.

Gn 110   MANGONI, Luisa, 'Per una definizione del fascismo: i concetti di Bonapartismo e Cesarismo'. *ITAL. CONTEMP.*, **31** (135), 1979. pp. 17-52.

Gn 111   MARTIN, Bernd., 'Zur Tauglichkeit eines übergreifenden Faschismus-Begriffs: ein Vergleich zwischen Japan, Italien, und Deutschland'. *VIERTELJAHRSH. FÜR ZEITG.*, **29** (1), 1981. pp. 48-73.

Gn 112   MERKL, Peter. 'Comparing fascist movements'. In LARSEN, S.U., Gn 36. pp. 752-83.

Gn 113   MERKL, Peter, 'Democratic development breakdowns and fascism'. *WORLD POLIT.*, **34** (1), 1981. pp. 114-35.

Gn 114   MORAVCOVA, Dagmar, 'Interpretace fašismu v zapadonemečke historiografii v 60 a 70 letech'. (The interpretation of fascism in West German historiography 1960s and 70s). *CESK. CAS. HIST.*, **26** (5), 1978. pp. 657-75.

Gn 115   NEMES, Deszö, *A Fasizmus Kérdéséhez* (*The Problem of Fascism*), Budapest: Magvetö, 1976. 146pp.

Gn 116   NOCE, Augusto del, 'Il problema della definizione storica del fascismo'. *STOR. E POLIT.*, **15** (1), pp. 121-70.

Gn 117   NOLTE, Ernst, 'E il fascismo un fenomeno "epocale"?' *QUELL. UND FORSCHUNG. AUS ITAL. ARCH.*, **57**, 1977. pp. 295-314.

Gn 118   NOLTE, Ernst, 'Kapitalismus, Marxismus, Faschismus'. *Merkur*, **27**, 1973. pp. 111-26.

Gn 119   NOLTE, Ernst, 'Missveständnisse in der Faschismus—Diskussion'. *POLIT. VIERTELJAHRESSCHR.*, **12** (1), 1971. pp. 119-21. On Kühnl's 'Probleme einer Theorie über den internationalen Faschismus', see Gn 102.

Gn 120   NOLTE, Ernst (ed.), *Theorien über den Faschismus*, Cologne: Kiepenheuer & Witsch, 1967. 513pp. Bib. 492-500.

Gn 121   NOLTE, Ernst, 'Zeitgenössische Theorien über den Faschismus'. *VIERTELJAHRSH. FÜR ZEITG.*, **15** (3), 1967. pp. 247-68.

Gn 122   NOLTE, Ernst, 'Zur Phänomenologie des Faschismus'. *VIERTELJAHRSH. FÜR ZEITG.*, **10** (4), 1962 pp. 373-407.

Gn 123   FRIEDRICH, Carl J., 'Fascism versus totalitarianism:

Ernst Nolte's views re-examined'. *CENT. EUR. HIST.*, **4** (**3**), 1971. pp. 271–84.

Gn 124   KITCHEN, Martin, 'Ernst Nolte and the phenomenology of fascism'. *SCIENCE AND SOC.*, **38** (**2**), 1974. pp. 130–49.

Gn 125   NIPPERDEY, Thomas, 'Der Faschismus in seiner Epoche: zu den Werken von Ernst Nolte zum Faschismus'. *HIST. Z.*, **210** (**3**), 1970. pp. 620–38.

Gn 126   ORMOS, Maria and INCZE, Miklos, 'Faschismus und Krise: über einige theoretische Fragen der europäischen faschistischen Erscheinungen'. *ETUD. HIST. HONG., (*2*)*, 1980. pp. 391–410.

Gn 127   PAYNE, Stanley G., *Fascism: comparison and definition*, Madison: University of Wisconsin Press, 1980. 234pp. Bib. 215–17.

Gn 128   PICKL, Norbert, *Die amerikanische Interpretation des faschistischen Totalitarismus*, Munich: Schön, 1965. 217pp. Bib. 173–98. Munich University thesis.

Gn 129   POLL, F.G. van der, 'Nieuwe Literatuur over het fascisme'. (New literature on fascism). *Kleio* (Netherlands), **16** (**11**), 1975. pp. 602–64.

Gn 130   RICHTER, Rolf, 'Zur Faschismusinterpretation in der bürgerlichen Historiographie der USA'. *Z. FÜR GESCHICHTWISS.*, **22** (**8**), 1974. pp. 789–800.

Gn 131   RYSZKA, Franciszek, 'Autoritaryzm i faszyzm' (Authoritarianism and fascism). *KWART. HIST.*, **79** (**2**), 1972. pp. 322–45.

Gn 132   RYSZKA, Franciszek, 'Gondolatok a fasizmusról' (Thoughts on fascism). *TORT. SZ.*, **15** (**1/2**), 1972. pp. 138–52.

Gn 133   SAAGE, Richard, *Faschismustheorien: eine Einführung*, Munich: Beck, 1976. 184pp. Bib. 179–84.

Gn 134   SAAGE, Richard, 'Konservatismus und Faschismus: Anmerkungen zu Ernst Forsthoffs Entwicklung vom "totalen Staat" zum "Staat der Industriegesellschaft" '. *POLIT. VIERTELJAHRES-SCHR* **19** (**2**), 1978. pp. 254–68.

Gn 135   SANTARELLI, Enzo, *Ricerche sul Fascismo*, Urbino: Argalia, 1971. 363pp.

Gn 136   SCHAPIRO, Leonard, 'What is fascism?' *New York Rev. of Books*, **14**, 12 February 1970. pp. 13–15.

Gn 137   SCHIEDER, Wolfgang, 'Faschismus und kein Ende?' *NEUE POLIT. LIT.*, **15** (**2**), 1970. pp. 166–87.

Gn 138   SCHIEDER, Wolfgang, 'Fascismo e nazionalsozialismo: profilo d'un studio strutturale comparativo'. *NUOVA RIV. STOR.*, **54 (1/2)**, 1970. pp. 114-24.

Gn 139   SCHIEDER, Wolfgang, 'Fascism'. In KERNIG, C.D. (ed.), *Marxism, Communism, and Western society: a comparative encyclopedia*, New York: Herder & Herder, 1972. vol. 3. pp. 282-302. Good bibliography.

Gn 140   SCHREWE, E., *Faschismus und Nationalsozialismus*, Hamburg: Hanseatische V., 1934. 58pp.

Gn 141   SCHULZ, Gerhard, *Faschismus-Nationalsozialismus: Versionen und theoretische Kontroversen, 1922-1972*, Berlin: Propylaen V., 1974. 222 pp. Bib. 201-16.

Gn 142   SETON-WATSON, Hugh, 'Fascism, right and left'. *J. OF CONTEMP. HIST.*, **1 (1)**, 1966. pp. 183-97.

Gn 143   SIEGFRIED, Klaus-Jörg, 'Zur Entstehung und sozialen Funktion des Faschismus'. *OESTERR. Z. FÜR POLITIKWISS.*, **7 (4)**, 1978. pp. 477-91.

Gn 144   SOLE-TURA, J., 'The political instrumentality of fascism'. In WOOLF, S.J., Gn 21. pp. 42-50.

Gn 145   STERNHELL, Zeev, 'Fascist ideology'. In LAQUEUR, W., Gn 35. pp. 315-76.

Gn 146   STOLLMANN, Rainer, *Ästhetisierung der Politik: Literaturstudien zum subjektiven Faschismus*, Stuttgart: Metzler, 1978. 221pp. Bib. 210-17.

Gn 147   STRASSER, Otto, *Der Faschismus: Geschichte und Gefahr*, Munich: Olzog, 1965. 109pp. Interprets Hitlerism as fascism.

Gn 148   THAMER, Hans-Ulrich and WIPPERMANN, Wolfgang, *Faschistische und neo-faschistische Bewegungen: Probleme empirischer Faschismusforschung*, Darmstadt: Wissenschaftliche Buchgesellschaft, 1977. xiii, 268pp. Bib. 261-2.

Gn 149   THURLOW, Richard C., 'Fascism and nazism: no Siamese twins'. *Patterns of Prejudice*, **13 (4)**, 1979. pp. 1-8; **14 (1)**, 1980. pp. 5-15; **14 (2)**, 1980. pp. 15-23.

Gn 150   TREVOR-ROPER, Hugh Redwald, 'The phenomenon of fascism'. In WOOLF, W., Gn 20. pp. 19-38.

Gn 151   VALIANI, Leo, 'Osservazioni sul fascismo e sul nazismo'. *RIV. STOR. ITAL.*, **88**, 1976. pp. 509-30.

Gn 152   VIERHAUS, Rudolf, 'Faschistisches Führertum: ein Beitrag zur Phänomenologie des europäischen Faschismus'. *HIST. Z.*, **198**, 1964. pp. 614-39.

Gn 153   WEBER, Eugen, 'Revolution? Counterrevolution? What revolution?" *J. OF CONTEMP. HIST.*, **9 (2)**, 1974. pp. 3-47. Also in LAQUEUR, W., Gn 35. pp. 435-67.

Gn 154   WIPPERMANN, Wolfgang, *Fascismustheorien: zum Stand der gegenwartigen Diskussion*, 2nd edn, Darmstadt: Wissenschaftliche Buchgesellschaft, 1975. x, 183pp.

Origins of Fascism

Gn 155   CAPIZZI, Antonio, *Alle Radici ideologiche dei Fascismi: il mito della liberta individuale da Constant a Hitler*, Rome: Savelli, 1977. 239pp.

Gn 156   MAYER, Arno J., *The Dynamics of Counter-revolution in Europe, 1870-1956: an analytic framework*, New York: Harper & Row, 1971. 173pp. Bib. 151-73.

Gn 157   MOSSE, George Lachmann, 'Caesarism, circuses and monuments'. *J. OF CONTEMP. HIST.*, **6 (2)**, 1971, pp. 167-82. Also in Gn 15.

Gn 158   MOSSE, George Lachmann, 'The genesis of fascism'. *J. OF CONTEMP. HIST.*, **1 (1)**, 1966. pp. 14-26. Also in Gn 12.

Gn 159   ZAPPONI, Niccolo, 'G.L. Mosse e il problema della origini culturali del fascismo: significato di un svolta'. *STOR. CONTEMP.*, **7 (3)**, 1976. pp. 461-80.

Gn 160   PARIS, Robert, *Les Origines du fascisme*, Paris: Flammarion, 1968. 143pp. Bib. 121-9.

Gn 161   TALMON, Jacob L., *The Origins of Totalitarian Democracy*, London: Secker & Warburg, 1955. New York: Praeger, 1960. 366pp.

Intellectual Influences: Sorel, Pareto, Michels, Mosca, Le Bon

Gn 162   ANDREU, Pierre, *Georges Sorel entre le noire et le rouge*, 2nd edn, Paris: Syros, 1982. 312pp. Earlier edn, *Notre maître, M. Sorel*, Paris: Grasset, 1953.

Gn 163   BEETHAM, David, 'From socialism to fascism: the relation between theory and practice in the work of Robert Michels'. *POLIT.*

STUD., **25** (**1**), 1977. pp. 3-24; 2. The fascist ideologue, **25** (**2**), 1977. pp. 161-81.

Gn 164   BENNETT R.J., 'The elite theory as fascist ideology: a reply to Beetham's critique of Robert Michels'. *POLIT. STUD.*, **26** (**4**), 1978. pp. 474-88. With a reply by Beetham pp. 489-90

Gn 165   BOUSQUET, G.H., 'Il Pareto e il fascismo'. *BIBLIOTECA DELLA LIBERTA* (Turin), **4** (**6**), 1967. pp. 30-6.

Gn 166   BUSINO, Giovanni, 'L'opera di Pareto e le sue interpretazioni: a proposito di studi paretiani recenti'. *Giornale degli Economisti e Annali di Economia*, **34** (**5/6**), 1975. pp. 347-75.

Gn 167   CHARZAT, Michel, *Georges Sorel et la révolution au XXe siècle*, Paris: Hachette, 1977. 296pp. Bib. 283-91.

Gn 168   FIOROT, Dino, *Il Realismo politico di Vilfredo Pareto: profilo di una teoria empirica della politica*, Milan: Comunita, 1969. 377pp.

Gn 169   FREUND, Michaël, *Georges Sorel: der revolutionäre Konservatismus*, Frankfurt/M: Klostermann, 1932. 366pp.

Gn 170   FURIOZZI, Gian Biago, *Sorel e l'Italia*, Messina: D'Anna, 1975. 376pp.

Gn 171   GEIGER, Roger L., 'Democracy and the crowd: the social history of an idea in France and Italy, 1890-1914'. *Societas*, **7** (**1**), 1977. pp. 47-71. On ideas of Le Bon, Tarde, Sighele.

Gn 172   GOISIS, Giuseppe Ludovico, 'Sorel e i soreliani italiani'. *Il Mulino*, **22** (**228**), 1973. pp. 615-26.

Gn 173   HOROWITZ, Irving Louis, *Radicalism and the Revolt against Reason: the social theories of Georges Sorel: with a tr. of his essay on the decomposition of Marxism*, London: Routledge & Kegan Paul, 1961. vii, 264pp.

Gn 174   MICHELS, Robert, *First Lectures in Political Sociology*, tr. by Alfred de Grazia, New York: Harper & Row, 1965. 173pp.

Gn 175   MICHELS, Robert, *Sozialismus und Faschismus als politische Strömungen in Italien: historische Studien*, Munich: Meyer & Jessen, 1925. 2 vols.

Gn 176   NYE, Robert A., *The Anti-democratic Sources of élite Theory: Pareto, Mosca, Michels*, Beverley Hills: Sage, 1977. 58pp. Bib. 52-8.

Gn 177   NYE, Robert A., 'Two paths to a psychology of social action: Gustave Le Bon and Georges Sorel'. *J. OF MOD. HIST.*, **45** (**3**), 1973. pp. 411-38.

Gn 178   PARETO, Vilfredo, *Scritti politici*, ed. Giovanni Busino, Turin: UTET, 1974. 2 vols. **1**. *Lo sviluppo di capitalismo, 1872-95.* **2**. *Reazione, liberta, fascismo, 1896-1923.*

Gn 179   PFETSCH, Frank, *Die Entwicklung zum faschistischen Führerstaat in der politischen Philosophie von Robert Michels*, Heidelberg University thesis, 1965. iv, 149pp.

Gn 180   RÖHRICH, Wilfried, 'Georges Sorel and the myth of violence: from syndicalism to fascism'. In MOMMSEN, W.J. and HIRSCHFELD, Gerhard (eds), *Social Protest, Violence and Terror in 19th and 20th Century Europe*, London: Macmillan, 1982. pp. 246-56.

Gn 181   RÖHRICH, Wilfried, *Robert Michels: vom sozialistisch-syndikalistischen zum faschistischen Credo*, Berlin: Duncker & Humblot, 1972. 198pp. Bib. 176-98. Kiel University thesis.

Gn 182   ROTH, Jack J., *The Cult of Violence: Sorel and the Sorelians*, Berkeley: University of California Press, 1980. xi, 359pp. Notes and Bib. 277-350.

Gn 183   ROTH, Jack J., 'The roots of Italian Fascism: Sorel and Sorelismo'. *J. OF MOD. HIST.*, **39** (**1**), 1967. pp. 30-45.

Gn 184   ROTH, Jack J., 'Sorel und die totalitären Systeme'. *VIERTELJAHRSH. FÜR ZEITG.*, **6** (**1**), 1958. pp. 45-59.

Gn 185   SOREL, Georges, *Reflections on Violence*, authorised tr. by T.E. Hulme, New York: AMS Press, 1975. x, 299pp. Repr. of 1914 edn.

Gn 186   TALMON, Jacob Leib, 'The legacy of Georges Sorel: Marxism, violence, fascism'. *Encounter*, **34** (**2**), 1970. pp. 47-60.

Gn 187   TOMMISSEN, Piet, 'Vilfred Pareto und der italienische Faschismus'. In FORSTHOFF, Ernst and HÖRSTEL, Reinhard (eds), *Standorte in Zeistrom*, Munich: Athenäum, 1974.

Marxist and Socialist Theories of Fascism

Gn 188   ABENDROTH, Wolfgang (ed.), *Faschismus und Kapitalismus: Theorien über die sozialen Ursprünge und die Funktion des Faschismus*, by Otto Bauer [*et al.*], Frankfurt/M: Europaische Verlags-Anstalt, 1967. 185pp. Marxist interpretations by Otto Bauer, Herbert Marcuse, Arthur Rosenberg, Angelo Tasca and August Thalheimer.

Gn 189   ABENDROTH, Wolfgang, 'Soziale Funktion und soziale Voraussetzungen des Faschismus'. *Argument*, **12**, 1970. pp. 251-7.

Gn 190   ADAMSON, Walter L., 'Gramsci's interpretation of fascism'. *J. OF HIST. IDEAS*, **41** (**4**), 1980. pp. 615-33.

Gn 191   *Das Argument*, 'Critiques of fascism theory from the West German New Left'. Translation of articles from *Das Argument* in *International Journal of Politics*, **2** (**4**), 1972/3. pp. 3-113. Articles by Kühnl, Blanke, Reiche and Werth, and Abendroth.

Gn 192   *Das Argument*, 'Faschismus und Ideologie', **21** (**117**), 1979. pp. 645-77. Articles by Wolfgang Haug, Ernesto Laclau and Karin Priester.

Gn 193   BLANK, A.S., 'Die deutsche Faschismus in der sowjetischen Historiographie'. *Z. FÜR GESCHICHTWISS.*, **23** (**4**), 1975. pp. 443-52.

Gn 194   BLANKE, Bernhard, 'Thesen zur Faschismus-Diskussion'. *Sozialistische Politik*, **3**, 1969. pp. 52-63.

Gn 195   BOTZ, Gerhard, 'Austro-Marxist interpretations of fascism'. *J. OF CONTEMP. HIST.*, **11** (**4**), 1976. pp. 129-56.

Gn 196   BRAHM, Heinz, 'Die bolschewistische Deutung des deutschen Faschismus in den Jahren 1923 bis 1928'. *JAHRB. FÜR GESCH. OSTEUROPAS*, **12** (**3**), 1964, pp. 350-65. Soviet interpretations of fascism.

Gn 197   BRUCKNER, Peter, 'Perspectives on the fascist public sphere'. *NEW GERM. CRIT.*, **11**, 1977. pp. 94-132.

Gn 198   CAMMETT, John M., 'Communist theories of Fascism, 1920-1935'. *Science and Society*, **31** (**2**), 1967. pp. 149-63.

Gn 199   COLARIZI, Simona, 'Trotsky e il fascismo, di L. Rapone'. *STOR. CONTEMP.*, **10** (**1**), 1979. pp. 174-82. Review of Rapone. Trotsky e il fascismo. See Gn 201.

Gn 200   RAPONE, Leonardo, 'Movimenti fascisti e classi sociali nell'analisi di Lev. D. Trotskij'. *STOR. CONTEMP.*, **7** (**2**), 1976. pp. 267-96.

Gn 201   RAPONE, Leonardo, *Trotskij e il Fascismo*, Rome: Laterza, 1978. xv, 451pp.

Gn 202   WISTRICH, Robert S., 'Leon Trotsky's theory of fascism'. *J. OF CONTEMP. HIST.*, **11** (**4**), 1976. pp. 157-84.

Gn 203   DUTT, Rajani Palme, *Fascism and Social Revolution: a study of the economics and politics of the extreme stages of capitalism*, rev. edn, New York: International Pubs, 1935. 318pp. Comintern version.

Gn 204   *Dzieje Najnowsze* (*Wroclaw*), **10** (**1**), 1978. pp. 1–181. Issue on fascism, ed. Czeslaw Madajczyk.

Gn 205   EAGLETON, Terry, 'What is fascism?' *New Blackfriars*, **57** (**670**), 1976. pp. 100–6.

Gn 206   EICHHOLTZ, Dietrich and GOSSWEILER, Kurt (eds), *Faschismusforschung: Positionen, Probleme, Polemik*, Berlin: Akademie-V., 1980. 459pp. East Germany.

Gn 207   FETSCHER, Iring, 'Faschismus und Nationalsozialismus: zur Kritik des sowjet-marxistischen Faschismusbegriffs'. *POLIT. VIERTELJAHRESSCHR.*, **3** (**1**), 1962. pp. 42–63.

Gn 208   FILATOW, G. 'Fragen der Geschichte des Faschismus und die Gegenwart'. *Sowjetwissenschaft*, **30** (**5**), 1977. pp. 472–84.

Gn 209   GALKIN, Aleksandr A., 'Capitalist society and fascism'. *SOC. SCI. (USSR ACAD. OF SCIENCES)*, **2**, 1970. pp. 128–38.

Gn 210   GALKIN, Aleksandr. A., 'Social'no politicheskaia struktura kapitalisticheskogo obshchestva i fashism' (The socio-political structure of capitalist society and fascism). *Voprosy Filosofii*, **23** (**2**), 1970. pp. 87–97. English summary p. 188.

Gn 211   GOSSWEILER, Kurt, and others (eds), *Faschismus: Entstehung und Verhinderung: Material zur Faschismus—Diskussion*, K. Gossweiler, R. Kühnl and R. Opitz, Frankfurt/M: Röderberg V., 1972. 64pp.

Gn 212   GREBING, Helga, 'Faschismus, Mittelschichten und Arbeiterklasse: Probleme der Faschismusinterpretation in der sozialistischen Linken während der Weltwirtschaftskrise'. *Int. Wissenschaftliche Korrespondenz zur Geschichte der Deutschen Arbeiterbewegung*, **12** (**4**), 1976, pp. 443–60. Socialist left's interpretation of fascism in Germany and Austria.

Gn 213   GRIEPENBURG, Rüdiger and TJADEN, Karl Herman, 'Faschismus und Bonapartismus: zur Kritik der Faschismustheorie August Thalheimers'. *Argument*, **8**, 1966. pp. 461–72.

Gn 214   GUÉRIN, Daniel, 'Fascism and Big Business', 2nd edn, New York: Monad Press, 1973, 318pp. Tr. of *Fascisme et grande capital*, by Frances and Mason Merrill. Trotskyist view.

Gn 215   HAUG, Wolfgang Fritz, 'Faschismus-Theorien in antifaschistischer Perspektive'. *Argument*, **16** (**87**), 1974. pp. 537–42.

Gn 216   HAUG, Wolfgang Fritz and others, 'Ideologische Komponenten in den Theorien über den Faschismus'. *Argument*, **7** (**33**), 1965. pp. 1–34.

16

Gn 217 HENNIG, Eike, 'Einleitung: was heisst und zu welchem Ende studiert man Faschismus?' *Gesellschaft: Beitrage zur Marx. Theorie*, **6**, 1976. pp. 7-18.

Gn 218 HENNIG, Eike, 'Industrie und Faschismus: Anmerkungen zur sowjetmarxistischen interpretation'. *NEUE POLIT. LIT.*, **15** (4), 1970. pp. 432-49.

Gn 219 HORKHEIMER, Max, 'Pourquoi le fascisme?' *Esprit (Paris)*, **5**, 1978. pp. 62-78.

Gn 220 KITCHEN, Martin, 'August Thalheimer's theory of fascism'. *J. OF HIST. OF IDEAS*, **33** (1), 1973. pp. 67-78.

Gn 221 KÜHNL, Reinhard, 'Tendenzen der Faschismusforschung'. *Frankfurter Hefte*, **25**, 1970. pp. 441-7.

Gn 222 KÜHNL, Reinhard, 'Aspekte der Faschismus—Diskussion: historische Aufarbeitung und aktuelle Bedeutung: für Wolfgang Abendroth zum 70. Geburstag'. *BL. FÜR DTSCH. UND INT. POLIT.*, **21** (5), 1976. pp. 531-49.

Gn 223 KÜHNL, Reinhard, 'Diskussion (Fascism)'. In *Abendroth Forum: Marburger Gespräche aus Anlass des 70. Geburstags von Wolfgang Abendroth*, Marburg: VAB, 1977. pp. 392-443.

Gn 224 KÜHNL, Reinhard, 'Faschismus: Versuch einer Begriffs-bestimmung'. *BL. FÜR DTSCH. UND. INT. POLIT.*, **13**, 1968. pp. 1259-67.

Gn 225 KÜHNL, Reinhard, *Faschismustheorien: ein Leitfaden*, Reinbek: Rowohlt, 1979. 333pp.

Gn 226 KÜHNL, Reinhard, *Formen bürgerlicher Herrschaft: Liberalismus, Faschismus*, Reinbek: Rowohlt, 1971. 190pp. Bib. 179-83.

Gn 227 KÜHNL, Reinhard, *Texte zur Faschismus—Diskussion. 1. Positionen und Kontroversen*, Reinbek: Rowohlt, 1974. 279pp. Bib. 265-70.

Gn 228 OPITZ, Reinhard, 'Fragen der Faschismusdiskussion: zu R. Kühnls Bestimmung des Faschismusbegriffs',*Argument*, **12**, 1970. pp. 280-91.

Gn 229 KUHN, Axel, *Das faschistische Herrschaftssystem und die moderne Gesellschaft*, Hamburg: Hoffmann & Campe, 1973. 157pp. Bib. 153-7.

Gn 230 LACLAU, Ernesto, *Politics and Ideology in Marxist theory: capitalism, fascism, populism*, London: NLB, 1977. 203pp.

Gn 231 LEWIN, Erwin, 'Zum Faschismus: Analyse durch die

17

Kommunistische Internationale'. *Beitrage zur Geschichte der Deutschen Arbeiterbewegung (E. Germany)*, **12 (1)**, 1970. pp. 44–59.

Gn 232 LUKÁCS, György, *Die Zerstörung der Vernunft*, Berlin: Aufbau, 1954. 692pp.

Gn 233 MANSILLA, Hugo Celso Felipe, *Faschismus und eindimensionale Gesellschaft*, Nuewied: Luchterhand, 1971. 238pp. Bib. 229–38.

Gn 234 OPITZ, Reinhard, 'Über die Entstehung und Verhinderung von Faschismus'. *Argument*, **16 (87)** 1974. pp. 543–603.

Gn 235 OPITZ, Reinhard, 'Über Faschismus Theorien und ihre Konsequenzen'. *BL. FÜR DTSCH. UND INT. POLIT.*, **15**, 1970. pp. 1267–84.

Gn 236 OPITZ, Reinhard, 'Uber vermeidbare Irrtümer: zum Themenschwerpunkt "Faschismus und Ideologie" in *Argument* 117'. *Argument*, **22 (121)**, 1980. pp. 357–77.

Gn 237 PETZOLD, Joachim, 'Die objective Funktion des Faschismus im subjektiven selbstverständnis der faschisten'. *Z. FÜR GESCHICHTWISS.*, **28 (4)**, 1980. pp. 357–72.

Gn 238 PIRKER, Theo (ed.), *Komintern und Faschismus, 1920–1940: Dokumente zur Geschichte und Theorie des Faschismus*, Stuttgart: Deutsche Verlags-Anstalt, 1965. 203pp.

Gn 239 POULANTZAS, Nicos, *Fascism and Dictatorship: the Third International and the problem of fascism*, London: NLB, 1974. 366pp. Tr. of *Fascisme et dictature*, Paris: Maspero, 1974, by Judith White.

Gn 240 CAPLAN, Jane, 'Theories of Fascism: Nicos Poulantzas as historian'. *HIST. WORKSHOP*, **3**, 1977. pp. 83–100.

Gn 241 RABINBACH, Anson G., 'Marxistische Faschismustheorien: ein Überblick'. *AESTHET. UND KOMMUN.*, **7 (26)**, 1976. pp. 5–19; **8 (27)**, pp. 89–103.

Gn 242 RABINBACH, Anson G., 'Toward a Marxist theory of fascism and national socialism'. *NEW GERM. CRIT.*, **3**, 1974. pp. 127–53.

Gn 243 RABINBACH, Anson G., 'Unclaimed heritage: Ernst Bloch's "heritage of our times", and the theory of fascism'. *NEW GERM. CRIT.*, **11**, 1977. pp. 5–21.

Gn 244 STRACHEY, John, *The Menace of Fascism*, London: Gollancz. New York: Covici, 1933. 272pp.

Gn 245 SZEKELY, Gabor, *A Komintern es a fasizmus 1921–1929 (The Comintern and Fascism)*, Budapest: Kossuth Kiadó, 1980. 271pp.

Gn 246 TOGLIATTI, Palmiro, *Lectures on Fascism*, London: Lawrence & Wishart. New York: Int. Pubs, 1976. xviii, 172pp. Tr. of *Lezioni sul fascismo*. Togliatti (1893-1964), Italian Communist Party leader.

Gn 247 VAJDA, Mihály, 'Crisis and the way out: the rise of fascism in Germany and Italy'. *Telos*, **12**, Summer 1972. pp. 3-26.

Gn 248 VAJDA, Mihály, 'A kispolgári a dekvát osztályszervezete' (The class consciousness of the petit bourgeoisie). *TORT. SZ.*, **15** (**3/4**), 1972. pp. 471-96.

Gn 249 VAJDA, Mihály, *Fascism as a Mass Movement*, London: Allison & Busby. New York: St Martin's Press, 1976. 132pp.

Gn 250 WEISSBECKER, Manfred, 'Die "zeitgeschichtlichen Kontroversen" Karl Dietrich Brachers: ein antikommunistischer Zerrspiegel der Geschichte und Theorie des Faschismus'. *WISS. Z. DER FRIEDRICH-SCHILLER UNIV. JENA THURINGEN. GES. UND SPRACHWISS. R.*, **28** (**2**), 1979. pp. 291-303.

Gn 251 WIPPERMANN, Wolfgang, *Zur Analyse des Faschismus: die sozialistischen und kommunistischen Faschismustheorien, 1921-1945*, Frankfurt/M: Diesterweg, 1981. 152pp.

Gn 252 ZUMPE, Lotte, 'Monopole und Faschismus'. *Geschichtunterricht und Staatsburgekunde*, **20** (**1**), 1978. pp. 17-28.

Sociology and Economics of Fascism

Gn 252 BETIN, Gianfranco and others, *Il Fascismo nell'Analisi Sociologica*; a cura di Luciano Cavalli, Bologna: Il Mulino, 1975. 215pp.

Gn 254 BORKENAU, Franz, 'Zur Sociologie des Faschismus'. In NOLTE, E., Gn 120. pp. 156-81.

Gn 255 BOSSLE, Lothar and others, *Sozialwissenschaftliche Kritik am Begriff und an der Erscheinungsweise des Faschismus*, Wurzburg: Naumann, 1979. 116pp. Bib. 112.

Gn 256 CLEMENZ, Manfred, *Gesellschaftliche Ursprünge des Faschismus*, Frankfurt/M: Suhrkamp, 1972. 314pp. Bib. 309-13.

Gn 257 CUEVA, Agustín, 'La cuestión del fascismo'. *Revista Mexicana de Sociologia*, **39** (**2**), 1977. pp. 469-80.

Gn 258 DAHL, Hans Frederik, *Hva er Fascisme? et essay om fascismens historie og sosiologi*, Oslo: Pax, 1972. 162pp. Bib. 147-57.

Gn 259 GERMANI, Gino, *Authoritarianism, Fascism and National Populism*, New Brunswick, NJ: Transaction Books, 1978. xi, 292pp. Tr. of *Autoritarismo, fascismo e classi sociali*, Bologna: Il Mulino, 1975.

Gn 260 GERMANI, Gino, 'Fascism and class'. In WOOLF, S.J., Gn 21. pp. 65-96.

Gn 261 GERMANI, Gino, 'Political socialisation of youth in fascist regimes: Italy and Spain'. In HUNTINGTON, S.P. and MOORE, C.H., Gn 309. pp. 339-379. First appeared in Italian in *Quaderni di Sociologia*, 1969.

Gn 262 LEDUC, Victor, 'Quelques problèmes d'une sociologie du fascisme'. *CAH. INT. DE SOCIOL.*, **7** (**12**), 1952. pp. 115-30.

Gn 263 LINZ, Juan José, 'Patterns of land tenure, division of labour, and voting behavior in Europe'. *COMP. POLIT.*, **8** (**3**), 1976. pp. 365-430. Much on fascism.

Gn 264 LINZ, Juan José, 'Some notes towards a comparative study of fascism in sociological historical perspective'. In LAQUEUR, W., Gn 35. pp. 3-121.

Gn 265 LUCCHINI, Riccardo, *Sociologie du fascisme*, Fribourg: Ed., Universitaire, 1973. 268pp. Bib. 231-53.

Gn 266 MILWARD, Alan, 'Fascism and the economy'. In LAQUEUR, W., Gn 35. pp. 379-412.

Gn 267 MOORE, Barrington, *Social Origins of Dictatorship and Democracy: lord and peasant in the making of the modern world*, Boston: Beacon Press, 1966. xix, 559pp. Bib. 524-46. Penguin edn, 1969.

Gn 268 MÜLLER, J.B., 'Kommunismus und Nationalsozialismus: ein sozio-ökonomischer Vergleich'. In GREIFFENHAGEN, M., Gn 308. pp. 61-96.

Gn 269 PARSONS, Talcott, 'Some sociological aspects of the fascist movements'. In PARSONS, T., *Essays in Sociological Theory*, Glencoe, Ill.: Free Press, 1954. pp. 124-41.

Gn 270 SACCOMANI, Edda, *Le Interpretazioni Sociologiche del Fascismo*, Turin: Loescher, 1977. 345pp. Bib. 30-4.

Gn 271 TRÉANTON, Jean-René, 'Réflexions sur fascisme et dictature'. *REV. FR. DE SOCIOL.*, **17** (**3**), 1976. pp. 533-40.

Gn 272 TREVES, Renato, 'Interpretazioni sociologiche del fascismo'. In TREVES, R., *Spirito Critico e Spirito Dogmatico*. Milan University, 1954.

Gn 273 WOOLF, Stuart J., 'Did a fascist economic system exist?' In
WOOLF, S.J., Gn 21. pp. 119-51.

Fascism and Modernisation

Gn 274 GARRUCCIO, Ludovico, *L'Industrializzazione tra Nationalismo
e Rivoluzione: le ideologie politiche dei paesi in via di sviluppo*, Bologna: Il
Mulino, 1969. 316pp. Argues for modernising intention of fascism.

Gn 275 GARRUCCIO, Ludovico, 'Le tre eta del fascismo'. *Il
Mulino*, **213**, 1971. pp. 53-73.

Gn 276 GREGOR, A. James, 'Fascism and modernization: some
addenda'. *WORLD POLIT.*, **26** (**3**), 1974. pp. 370-84.

Gn 277 GREIL, Arthur L., 'The modernization of consciousness
and the appeal of fascism'. *COMP. POLIT. STUD.*, **10** (**2**), 1977.
pp. 213-38. Reply by A. James Gregor pp. 239-58.

Gn 278 HUGHES, Arnold and KOLINSKY, Martin, 'Para-
digmatic fascism and modernization: a critique'. *POLIT. STUD.*, **24**
(**4**), 1976. pp. 371-96. Attack on Gregor and Joes' view of fascism.

Gn 279 JOES, Anthony James, 'On the modernity of fascism: notes
from two worlds'. *COMP. POLIT. STUD.*, **10** (**2**), 1977. pp. 259-68.

Gn 280 ORGANSKI, A.F.K., 'Fascism and modernisation'. In
WOOLF, S.J., Gn 21. pp. 19-41.

Gn 281 TURNER, Henry Ashby, 'Fascism and modernization'.
WORLD POLIT., **24** (**4**), 1972. pp. 547-64.

The Psychology of Fascism

Gn 282 ADORNO, Theodor W. and others, *The Authoritarian
Personality*, New York: Harper, 1950. xxxiv, 990pp. Bib. 977-82.

Gn 283 BATAILLE, Georges, 'The psychological structure of
fascism'. *NEW GER. CRIT.*, **16**, 1979. pp. 64-87.

Gn 284 FROMM, Erich, *Escape from Freedom*, New York: Farrar &
Rinehart, 1941. ix, 305pp. British edn, *Fear of Freedom*. Kegan Paul,
1942.

Gn 285 REICH, Wilhelm, *The Mass Psychology of Fascism*, New
York: Farrar, Strauss, 1970. xxxi, 400pp. Tr. of *Die Massenpsychologie
des Faschismus* (first pub. 1933, Copenhagen), by Vincent R. Carfagno.

Gn 286 RYSZKA, Franciszek, 'Les sources psychologiques et sociales du fascisme'. *ACTA POL. HIST.*, **22**, 1970. 252-63.

Gn 287 WESTPHAL, Reinhart, 'Psychologische Theorien über den Faschismus'. *Argument*, **7** (**32**), 1965. pp. 30-9.

Corporativism and the Corporate State

Gn 288 AZPIAZU Y ZULAICA, José Joaquin, *The Corporative State*, St Louis: Herder, 1951. vii, 263pp. Tr. of *El Estado Corporativo*, Madrid, 1951, by William Bresnahan.

Gn 289 BAUDIN, Louis, *Le Corporatisme: Italie, Portugal, Allemagne, Espagne, France*, new edn, Paris: Librairie Générale de Droit et de Jurisprudence, 1942. 221pp.

Gn 290 BOWEN, Ralph, *German Theories of the Corporate State with Special Reference to the Period 1870-1919*, New York: Whittlesey House, 1947. viii, 243pp. Bib. 221-35. Columbia University thesis.

Gn 291 ELBOW, Matthew Heath, *French Corporative Theory, 1789-1948: a chapter in the history of ideas*, New York: Columbia University Press, 1953. 222pp. Bib. 211-17. Columbia University thesis. Ends with Pétain.

Gn 292 MANOILESCU, Mihail, *Le Parti unique: institutions politique des régimes nouveaux*, Paris: Les Oeuvres Françaises, 1936. xv, 254pp.

Gn 293 MANOILESCU, Mihail, *Le Siècle du corporatisme: doctrine du corporatisme intégral et pur*, Paris: Alcan, 1934. 376pp. Bib. 369-72.

Gn 294 MAYER-TASCH, Peter C., *Korporativismus und Autoritarismus: eine Studie zu Theorie und Praxis der berufsständischen Rechts- und Staatsidee*. Frankfurt/M: Athenäum, 1971. viii, 273pp. Bib. 238-62.

Gn 295 NARDI, Vicenzo, *Il Corporativismo Fascista*, Rome, IAT, 1974. 172pp. Bib.

Gn 296 PIROU, G., *Essai sur le corporatisme: corporatisme et libéralisme, corporatisme et étatisme, corporatisme et syndicalisme*, Paris: Librairie du Recueil Sirey, 1938. 172pp.

Gn 297 PRÉ, R., *L'Organisation des rapports économiques et sociaux dans les pays à régime corporatif: (Italie, Autriche, Portugal, Allemagne)*, Paris: Librairie Technique et Economique, 1936. 214pp. Bib. 201-4. Paris University thesis.

Gn 298 SCHMITTER, Philippe C., 'Still the century of corporatism?' *REV. OF POLIT.*, **36** (**1**), 1974. pp. 85-131.

Gn 299   SCHMITTER, Philippe C., 'Reflections on Mihail Manoilescu'. In JOWITT, K. (ed.), *Social Change in Rumania, 1860-1940*, Berkeley: University of California Press, 1978. pp. 117-39.

Gn 300   SPIRITO, Ugo. *Capitalismo e Corporativismo*, Florence: Sansoni, 1933. xx, 157pp.

Gn 301   VALLAURI, Carlo, *Le Radici del Corporativismo*, Rome: Bulzoni, 1971. 234pp. On the differences between Catholic, nationalist and fascist corporatist ideology.

Totalitarianism

Gn 302   ADAM, U.D., 'Anmerkungen zu methodologischen Fragen in den Sozialwissenschaften: das Beispiel Faschismus und Totalitarismus'. *POLIT. VIERTELJAHRESSCHR.*, **16** (**1**), 1975. pp. 55-88.

Gn 303   ARENDT, Hannah, *The Origins of Totalitarianism*; new edn, New York: Harcourt Brace, 1973. xliii, 527pp. Bib. 483-507. British edn, *The Burden of our Time*, 1951.

Gn 304   BUCHHEIM, Hans, *Totalitarian Rule: its nature and characteristics*, Middletown, Conn.: Wesleyan University Press, 1968. 112pp. Bib. 111-12. Tr. of *Totalitäre Herrschaft*, Munich: Kösel, 1962, by Ruth Hein.

Gn 305   FAYE, Jean Pierre, *Langages totalitaires: critique de la raison narrative*, Paris: Hermann, 1972. 771pp.

Gn 306   FLECHTHEIM, Ossip K., 'Faschismus, Nationalsozialismus, Kommunismus, und Stalinismus'. *Vorgänge: Z. für Gesellschaftspolitik (Hamburg)*, **16** (**26**), 1977. pp. 70-8.

Gn 307   FRIEDRICH, Carl J. and BRZEZINSKI, Zbigniew K., *Totalitarian Dictatorship and Autocracy*, Cambridge, Mass.: Harvard University Press, 1956. 346pp.

Gn 308   GRIEFFENHAGEN, Martin and others, *Totalitarismus: zur Problematik eines politischen Begriffs*, by M. Greiffenhagen, Reinhard Kühnl, Johann B. Müller, Munich: List, 1972. 156pp. Bib. 145-52.

Gn 309   HUNTINGTON, Samuel P. and MOORE, Clement Henry (eds), *Authoritarian Politics in Modern Society: the dynamics of one-party systems*, New York: Basic Books, 1970. x, 533pp.

Gn 310   LINZ, Juan José, 'Totalitarian and authoritarian regimes'. In GREENSTEIN, Fred I. and POLSBY, Nelson W., *Handbook of Political Science*, Reading, Mass: Addison-Wesley, 1975. vol. 3. pp. 175-411. Includes good bib.

Gn 311   NEUMANN, Sigmund, *Permanent Revolution: the total state in a world at war*, New York: Harper, 1942. xviii, 388pp. Bib. 311-75.

Gn 312   RADEL, J. Lucien, *Roots of Totalitarianism: the ideological sources of fascism, national socialism, and communism*, New York: Crane, Russak, 1975. ix, 218pp. Bib. 199-211.

Gn 313   SCHLANGEN, Walter, *Die Totalitarismus-These: Entwicklung und Probleme*, Stuttgart: Kohlhammer, 1976. 168pp. Bib. 161-7.

Gn 314   SCHULZ, Gerhard, 'Der Begriff des Totalitarismus und der Nationalsozialismus'. *Soziale Welt*, **12** (2), 1961. pp. 112-28.

Gn 315   SEIDEL, Bruno and JENKNER, Siegfried (eds), *Wege der Totalitarismus Forshung*, 3rd edn, Darmstadt: Wissenschaftliche Buchgesellschaft, 1974. vii, 638pp.

Gn 316   *Totalitarismus und Faschismus: eine wissenschaftliche und politische Begriffskontroverse: Kolloquium im Institut für Zeitgeschichte am Nov. 1978*, Munich: Oldenbourg, 1980. 89pp. Bib. 85-9.

Gn 317   UNGER, Aryeh L., *The Totalitarian Party: party and people in Nazi Germany and Soviet Russia*, Cambridge: Cambridge University Press, 1974. viii, 286pp. Bib. 272-80.

Fascism, Culture and Intellectuals

Gn 318   GRIMM, Reinhold and HERMAND, Jost, *Faschismus und Avantgarde*, Königstein: Athenäum, 1980. vi, 149pp.

Gn 319   HAMILTON, Alastair, *The Appeal of Fascism: a study of intellectuals and fascism, 1919-1945*, foreword by Stephen Spender, London: Blond. New York: Macmillan, 1971. xxiii, 312pp. Bib. 291-5.

Gn 320   WINEGARTEN, R. 'The temptations of cultural fascism'. *WIENER LIB. BULL.*, **23** (1), 1968/69. pp. 34-40.

Fascism, Collaboration and the Second World War

Gn 321   BROCKDORFF, Werner, *Kollaboration oder Widerstand: die Zusammenarbeit mit den Deutschen in den besetzten Ländern während des zweiten Weltkrieges und deren schreckliche Folgen*, Munich: Welsermühl, 1968. 355pp. Bib. 350.

Gn 322   JONG, Louis de, *The German Fifth Column in the Second World*

War, New York: Fertig, 1973. xi, 308pp. Tr. from the Dutch by C.M. Geyl.

Gn 323   LEMBERG, Hans, 'Kollaboration in Europa mit dem Dritten Reich um das Jahr 1941'. In *Das jahr 1941 in der Europäischen Politik*, Munich: Oldenbourg, 1972. pp. 143–62.

Gn 324   LEMKIN, Rafal, *Axis Rule in Occupied Europe: laws of occupation, analysis of government, proposals for redress*, Washington, DC: Carnegie Endowment for International Peace, 1944. xxxviii, 674pp. Bib. 641–51. Repr. Fertig.

Gn 325   LITTLEJOHN, David, *The Patriotic Traitors: a history of collaboration in German-occupied Europe, 1940–1945*, London: Heinemann. Garden City: Doubleday, 1972. xv, 391pp. Bib. 367–75.

Gn 326   NEULEN, Hans Werner, *Eurofaschismus und der zweite Weltkrieg: Europas verratene Söhne*, Munich: Universitas V., 1980. 221pp. Bib. 209–18.

Gn 327   RINGS, Werner, *Life with the Enemy: collaboration and resistance in Hitler's Europe, 1939–1945*, London: Weidenfeld & Nicolson, 1982. 351pp. Bib. 329–42. Tr. of *Leben mit den Feind*, Munich: Kindler, 1979.

The Vatican and Fascism

Gn 328   DESCHNER, Karlheinz, *Mitt Gott und den Faschisten: der Vatikan im Bunde mit Hitler, Mussolini, Franco, und Pavelič*, Stuttgart: Günther, 1965. 301pp.

Gn 329   FALCONI, Carlo. *The Silence of Pius XII*, London: Faber. Boston: Little, Brown, 1970. 430pp. Bib. 419–22. Tr. of *Il Silenzio di Pio XII*, Milan, 1965, by Bernard Wall.

Fascism and Racism

Gn 330   MOSSE, George Lachmann, *Toward the Final Solution: a history of European racism*, London: Dent. New York: Fertig, 1978. xvi, 277pp.

Gn 331   POLIAKOV, Leon, *The Aryan Myth: a history of racist and nationalist ideas in Europe*, London: Chatto & Windus/Heinemann. New York: Basic Books, 1974. xii, 388pp. Tr. of *Le Mythe Aryen*, by Edmund Howard.

NORWAY

The Early Years of the Extreme Right

No 1   ADRIAN, H.C., *Fedrelandslaget i Norsk politikk, 1915-1921 (The Nationalist Party in Norwegian politics)*, Oslo: Inst. of Political Science University of Oslo, 1962.

No 2   FRØLAND, Kaare, *Krise og Kamp: Bygdefolkets Krisehjelp: en kriseorganisasjon i norsk mellomkrigspolitikk (Crisis and Struggle: the Rural People's Emergency Help: an emerging organisation in Norwegian politics between the world wars)*, Oslo: Universitetsforlaget, 1962. 287pp. Bib. 236-41. Organisation which was allied with Nasjonal Samling in 1933 election.

No 3   HØIDAL, Oddvar Karsten, 'Økonomisk Verneplikt and Nordiske Folkereisning: two predecessors of Nasjonal Samling'. *SCAND. STUD.*, **49** (**4**), 1977. pp. 387-411. Quisling's early career, Economic Defence and the Nordic People's Movement, and the role of Frederik Prytz.

No 4   NERBØVIK, Jostein, *Antiparlamentariske straumdrag i Norge, 1905-14 (Anti-Parliamentary forces in Norway, 1905-14)*, Oslo: Universitetsforlaget, 1969. 183pp. Bib. 149-54.

General

No 5   DAHL, Hans Frederik, *Hva er Fascisme? Et essay om fascismens historie og sosiologi*, Oslo: Pax, 1972. 162pp. Bib. 147-57. General, but mainly on Norway.

No 6   DERRY, T.K., 'Norway'. In WOOLF, S.J., Gn 20. pp. 223-36.

No 7   *Kontrast*, **2** (**3**), 1966. Issue on 'Fascismen i Norge'. Includes Hans Frederik Dahl, 'Fascismen i Norge, 1920-1940: et overblikk'. pp. 4-17, Ulf Togersen Våre helter og høvdinger. pp. 29-36 (Our heroes and overlords).

Nasjonal Samling

No 8   AUNE, Arnt Ove., *NS Riksledelse, 1940-1945: organisasjon og rekruttering (The Nasjonal Samling national executive, 1940-1945: organisation and recruitment)*, Bergen University MA thesis, 1975.

No 9   BREVIG, Hans Olaf, *NS: fra parti til sekt, 1933–1937* (*Nasjonal Samling: from party to sect*), Oslo: Pax, 1970. 157pp.

No 10   BRUKNAPP, Dag Olav, *Nasjonal Samling og rasespørsmålet, 1933–1940* (*Nasjonal Samling and race problems*), Bergen University thesis, 1972.

No 11   DANIELSON, Rolf and LARSEN, Stein Ugelvik (eds), *Fra ide til dom: noen trekk fra uitviklingen av Nasjonal Samling* (*From Idea to Judgement: articles on the evolution of Nasjonal Samling*), Bergen: Universitetsforlaget, 1976. 258pp. Indispensable collection of articles mostly from the Bergen University project on the mass membership of NS between 1940 and 1945, by Torgeir Johan Tunshelle and Hans Hendriksen, Hans Hendriksen, Svein Lorentzen, Ida Blom, Dag Olav Bruknapp, Georg Øvsthus, Stein Ugelvik Larsen and Helge Paulsen.

No 12   HAGTVET, Bernt, *Norwegian Fascism: the emergency defense of the bourgeoisie, or utopian anti-modernism?*, New Haven: Yale University Dept of Political Science, 1972.

No 13   HENDRIKSEN, Hans, 'Agrarian fascism in Eastern and Western Norway: a comparison'. In LARSEN, S.U., Gn 36. pp. 651–56.

No 14   HENDRIKSEN, Hans, *Mennesker uten makt: en undersøkelse av Nasjonal Samling i tre Østnorske kommuner* (*People without Power: a local study of Nasjonal Samling in three Eastern Norwegian communities*), Bergen University thesis, 1972.

No 15   HESTVIK, Finn, *Nasjonal Samling i Salten under okkupasjonen* (*The Nasjonal Samling in Salten during the Occupation*), Bergen University thesis, 1972.

No 16   HJORT, Johan Bernhard, *Hvad vi vil: en utredning av Nasjonal Samlings program* (*What we Want: an explanation of the NS programme*), Oslo, 1935–6.

No 17   HØIDAL, Oddvar Karsten, 'Hjort, Quisling and Nasjonal Samling's disintegration'. *SCAND. STUD.*, **47** (**4**), 1975. pp. 467–97.

No 18   JOHNSEN, Bodil Wold, *Nasjonal Samling i Stavanger, 1933–1937* (*The Nasjonal Samling in Stavanger*), Bergen University thesis, 1972.

No 19   LARSEN, Stein Ugelvik, 'The social foundations of Norwegian fascism 1933–1945: an analysis of membership data'. In LARSEN, S.U., Gn 36. pp. 595–620.

No 20   LARSEN, Stein Ugelvik, 'The spread of nazism as a diffusion process: methodological considerations and some results from an analysis of the recruitment to the Nasjonal Samling in Norway, 1933-1945'. In MANN, R., G 484. pp. 186-217.

No 21   LOOCK, Hans-Dietrich, *Quisling, Rosenberg and Terboven: zur Vorgeschichte und Geschichte der nationalsozialistischen Revolution in Norwegen*, Stuttgart: Deutsche Verlags-Anstalt, 1970. 587pp. Bib. 565-79. Relations between Quisling, Joseph Terboven and the Germans in their attempt to set up a NS regime.

No 22   LOOCK, Hans-Dietrich, 'Support for Nasjonal Samling in the thirties'. In LARSEN, S.U., Gn 36. pp. 667-77.

No 23   LUNDE, Gulbrand, *Kampen for Norge: skrifter, foredrag, og avisartikler, 1933-1940 (Struggle for Norway)*, Oslo: Stenersen, 1941-2. 3 vols. Articles by leading NS member.

No 24   MYKLEBUST, Jan Petter, *Hvem var de norske nazistene? Sammenheng mellom sosial, økonomisk og politisk bakgrunn og medlemskap i Nasjonal Samling (Who were the Norwegian Nazis? The relationship between the social, economic and political background related to membership of Nasjonal Samling)*, Bergen University MA thesis, 1974.

No 25   MYKLEBUST, Jan Petter, 'Regional contrasts in the membership base of the Nasjonal Samling: a study of the political ecology of Norwegian fascism, 1933-1945'. In LARSEN, S.U., Gn 36. pp. 621-50.

No 26   NILSON, Sten Sparre, 'Fortolkning av politisk statistikk' (Interpretation of political statistics). *HIST. TIDSSKR. (Norway)*, **54** (**1**), 1975. pp. 56-67. Quisling vote used as example of likely errors in interpreting statistics.

No 27   NILSON, Sten Sparre, 'Wahlsoziologische Probleme des Nationalisozialismus'. *Z. FÜR GESAMTE STAATSWISS.*, **110** (**2**), 1954. pp. 279-311. Compares success of German nazis with failure of NS.

No 28   NILSON, Sten Sparre, 'Who voted for Quisling?' In LARSEN, S.U., Gn 36. pp. 657-66.

No 29   NORDÅS, Hallvard, *Nasjonal Samling og det kommunale styre i Rogaland, 1940-45 (The NS and Local Government Rule in Rogaland)*, Oslo University thesis, 1972.

No 30   NORDBERG, Nina, *Kvinner i Nasjonal Samling: en undersøkelse i Bergen (Women in the Nasjonal Samling: a local study of Bergen)*, Bergen University thesis, 1977.

No 31   [ØSTBYE, Halldis], Irene Sverd (pseud.), *Jødeproblemet og dets losning (The Jewish Problem and its Solution)*, Oslo, 1939. 128pp. Antisemitic solution by NS propaganda chief.

No 32 ØSTBYE, Halldis (ed.), *Nasjonal Samlings historiske kamp, 1933-1940 (Nasjonal Samling's Historic Struggle)*, Oslo, 1943. vol. 1. Official history of Nasjonal Samling sanctioned by the Party.

No 33 ROGNALDSEN, Sven, *NS medlemmene i Bergen, 1940-1945 (The NS Members in Bergen)*, Bergen University thesis, 1972.

No 34 TUNSHELLE, Torgeir Johan, *Nasjonal Samling i Sogn og Fjordane 1933-45 (The Nasjonal Samling in Sogn and Fjordane, 1933-45)*, Bergen University thesis, 1972.

No 35 WYLLER, Thomas Christian, *Fra okkupasjonsårenes maktkamp: Nasjonal Samlings korporative nyordningsforsøk 9 april 1940-1. februar 1942 (From the Struggle for Power in the Years of Occupation: NS's attempt to set up a corporative new order)*, Oslo: Tanum, 1953. 190pp.

No 36 WYLLER, Thomas Christian, 'Hovedtrekk av Nasjonal Samlings ideer om stat og samfunn, 1930-1940' (The main ideas of Nasjonal Samling on state and society). *Statsvetenskaplig Tidskrift for Politik, Statistik, Ekonomi (Lund)*, **56** (**2/3**), 1953. pp. 212-55.

Norwegian Fascism and the Second World War

No 37 ANDENAES, Johannes and others, *Norway and the Second World War*, by J. Andenaes, O. Riste and M. Skodvin, Oslo: Tanum, 1966. 167pp. Bib. 159-63. Includes Andenaes, 'The post-war proceedings against enemy collaborators'.

No 38 BLINDHEIM, Svein, *Nordmenn under Hitlers fane: dei Norske Frontkjemparane (Norwegians under Hitler's Flag)*, Oslo: Noregs Boklag, 1977. 255pp. On the 7000 Norwegians who fought on the Eastern Front for Germany.

No 39 DREVLAND, Ivar, *Lokalstyret i okkupasjonsårene, 1941-1945: et studium av den kommunale nyordning av 1. januar 1941 slik den ble gjennomført Nordland fylke (Local control in the Occupation Years)*, Bergen University thesis, 1970.

No 40 MEYER, Håkon, *Et annet syn (Another view)*, Oslo: Dreyers Forl., 1952. 236pp. Collaborators.

No 41 MILWARD, Alan, *The Fascist Economy in Norway*, Oxford, University Press, 1972. xii, 317pp. Bib. 301-9.

No 42 NOACK, Ulrich, *Norwegen zwischen Friedensvermittlung und Fremdherrschaft*, Krefeld: V. Aufbau der Mitte, 1952. 141pp. Author was historian attached to German legation in Norway.

No 43 OLSTAD, Ivar, *Nyordningen av det kommunale styresettet, 1940-1945: oppland fylke* (*The New Order of the Local Government Administration*), Oslo University thesis, 1969.

No 44 PETRICK, Fritz, *Norwegen und der Zweite Weltkrieg. Z. FÜR GESCHICHTWISS.*, **27** (**6**), 1979. pp. 553-9. Review article.

No 45 SKILBRED, Harold, *The SS and 'Germanic' fascism during World War II: the Norwegian case*, University of California Berkeley thesis, 1974.

No 46 SKODVIN, Magne, 'Litteratur til norske historie, 1939-1945 (Literature on Norwegian history, 1939-1945)'. *HIST. TIDSSKR. (Norway)*, **46**, 1967. pp. 155-68.

No 47 SKODVIN, Magne, *Striden om okkupasjonsstyret i Norge fram til 25. september 1940* (*The Struggle for the Occupation Administration in Norway to 25 September 1940*), Oslo: Petlitz, 1956. 415pp. Oslo University thesis.

No 48 WYLLER, Thomas Christian, *Nyordning og motstand: en framstilling og en analyse av organisasjonenes politiske funksjon under den Tyske okkupasjonen 25.9.1940-25.9.1942* (*New Order and Resistance: an account and analysis of the function of political institutions under German occupation*), Oslo, Universitetsforlaget, 1958. 372pp. Bib. 320-4. Oslo University thesis.

Vidkun Quisling (1887-1945)

No 49 DAHL, Hans Frederik, 'Quisling's statskupp 9. april i forfatnings-historisk perspektiv' (Quisling's coup d'état of 9 April in constitutional historical perspective). *HIST. TIDSSKR. (Norway)*, **55** (**3**), 1976. pp. 267-87.

No 50 FINKE, Heinz, 'Vidkun Quisling'. *Z. FÜR POLIT.*, **32** (**4**), 1942. pp. 266-71.

No 51 HARTMANN, Sverre, *Fører uten folk: Quisling som politisk og psykologisk problem* (*Führer without people: Quisling as a political and psychological problem*), Oslo: Tiden, 1959. 317pp.

No 52 HARTMANN, Sverre, *Fører uten folk: Forsvarsminister Quisling: hans bakgrunn og vei inn i norsk politikk* (*Führer without people: Defence Minister Quisling: his background and route into Norwegian politics*), Oslo: Tiden, 1970. 170pp.

No 53 HAYES, Paul M., 'Bref aperçu de l'histoire de Quisling et du governement de la Norvège de 1940 à 1945'. *REV. D'HIST. DEUX GUERRE MOND.*, **17** (**66**), 1967. pp. 11-30.

No 54   HAYES, Paul M., *Quisling: the career and political ideas of Vidkun Quisling, 1887-1945*, Newton Abbot: David & Charles, 1971. Bloomington: Indiana University Press, 1972. 368pp. Bib. 356-62. Contains list of NS pamphlets and Quisling speeches.

No 55   HAYES, Paul M., 'Quisling's political ideas'. *J. OF CONTEMP. HIST.*, 1 (1), 1966. pp. 145-57.

No 56   HERADSTVEIT, Per Oyvind, *Quisling, hvem var han?* (*Quisling, who was he?*), Oslo: Hjemmet, 1976. 268pp.

No 57   HEWINS, Ralph, *Quisling: prophet without honour*, London: Allen, 1965. New York: Day, 1966. 384pp. Sympathetic biography by British journalist.

No 58   HOBERMAN, John M., 'The psychopathology of an abortive leadership: the case of Vidkun Quisling'. *Tulane Studies in Polit. Science*, 26, 1977. pp. 175-201.

No 59   HOBERMAN, John M., 'Vidkun Quisling's psychological image'. *SCAND. STUD.*, 46 (3), 1974. pp. 242-64.

No 60   HØIDAL, Oddvar Karsten, 'Quisling og Bondepartiet våren 1933' (Quisling and the Farmers' Party in Spring 1933). *HIST. TIDSSKR.* (*Norway*), 57 (3), 1978. pp. 311-16.

No 61   HØIDAL, Oddvar Karsten, 'Quislings stilling ved den norske legasjon i Moskva juni 1927-desember 1929' (Quisling's role at the Norwegian legation in Moscow June 1927-December 1929). *HIST. TIDSSKR.* (*Norway*), 53, 1974. pp. 185-190.

No 62   HØIDAL, Oddvar Karsten, *The Road to Futility: Vidkun Quisling's political career in pre-war Norway*, University of S. California thesis. UM 70-13660. 433pp.

No 63   HØIDAL, Oddvar Karsten, 'Vidkun Quisling's decline as a political figure in pre-war Norway, 1933-1937'. *J. OF MOD. HIST.*, 43 (3), 1971. pp. 440-67.

No 64   KNUDSEN, Harald Franklin, *I was Quisling's Secretary*, London: Britons Pub. Co., 1967. 192pp. Bib. 185-8. Tr. of *Jeg var Quislings sekretaer*, Copenhagen, 1951.

No 65   MOGENS, Viktor, *Tyskerne, Quisling og vi andre* (*The Germans, Quisling and we others*), Oslo: Utenriks Forl., 1945. 297pp. By the leader of the Fatherland League and Quisling's rival on the extreme Right.

No 66   ØSTBYE, Halldis, *Boken om Quisling*, Oslo, 1941. 96pp. Hagiography of Quisling by colleague. Tr. into German as *Ein Buch über Vidkun Quisling*.

No 67   QUISLING, Maria, *Dagbok og andre efterlatte papirer (Diary ana other Posthumous Papers)*, Oslo: Dreyer, 1980. 191pp. Biography by his wife (1900-80).

No 68   QUISLING, Vidkun, 'A Nordic world federation'. *British Union Q.*, 1, 1937. pp. 87-101.

No 69   QUISLING, Vidkun, *Quisling har sagt: citater fra taler og avisartikler*, Oslo: Stenersen, 1940-1. 2 vols. Collection of speeches and articles. Tr. into German as *Quisling ruft Norwegen*, 1942.

No 70   QUISLING, Vidkun, *Russia and Ourselves*, London: Hodder & Stoughton, 1931. 284pp. Tr. of *Russland og vi*. Diary based on his service in the Norwegian legation in Moscow 1927-9.

No 71   QUISLING, Vidkun, defendant, *Straffesak mot Vidkun Abraham Lauritz Jonssøn Quisling i Eidsivating Lagmannsret (The Trial of Quisling in Eidsivating Appeal Court)*, Oslo: Eidsivating Lagstols Landssvikavdeling, 1946. 646pp.

No 72   VOGT, Benjamin, *Mennesket Vidkun og forraederen Quisling (The Man Vidkun and the Traitor Quisling)*, Oslo: Aschehoug, 1965. 182pp. Biography of Quisling.

No 73   WYLLER, Thomas Christian, 'Vidkun Quisling og rettsoppgjøret: en problemskisse' (Quisling and the legal settlement). *Samtiden*, 75 (4), 1966. pp. 204-30.

Fascism and Norwegian literature

No 74   BIRKELAND, Bjorte and LARSEN, Stein Ugelvik (eds), *Nazismen og Norsk litteratur (Nazism and Norwegian literature)*, Oslo: Universitetsforlaget, 1975. 236pp. Bib. 228-33.

No 75   NILSON, Sten Sparre, 'Hamsun, Nietzsche og nazismen'. *Edda*, 52 (5), 1965. pp. 294-314.

No 76   NILSON, Sten Sparre, *Knut Hamsun und die Politik*, Villingen: Ring V., 1964. iv, 240pp. Tr. of *En Ørn i uvaer*, by Fritz Nothardt.

DENMARK

Danmarks National-Socialistiske Arbejder Parti

D 1   BRIX, Knud and HANSEN, Erik, *Dansk nazisme under besaettelsen* (*Danish Nazism during the Occupation*), Copenhagen: Schultz, 1948. 70pp.

D 2   CLAUSEN, Frits, *Hvad vil Danmarks National-Socialistiske Arbejder Parti? otte taler om DNSAP program*, 2nd edn, (*What do the DNSAP want? 8 speeches on the DNSAP programme*), Bovrup: DNSAP Forlag, 1940. 110pp.

D 3   CLAUSEN, Frits, *Med Frits Clausen for Danmarks fremtid: 8 taler om national-socialismen* (*With Frits Clausen for Denmark's future*), Bovrup: DNSAP Forlag, 1939. 125pp. By the leader of Danish nazism.

D 4   DJURSAA, Malene, 'Denmark'. In WOOLF, S.J., Gn 20. pp. 237–56.

D 5   DJURSAA, Malene, *DNSAP: Danske nazister, 1930–1945*, Copenhagen: Gyldendal, 1981. 2 vols. Bib. vol 1. 213–27. English summary. University of Essex thesis, 1979.

D 6   DJURSAA, Malene, 'Who were the Danish Nazis? A methodological report on an ongoing project'. In MANN, R., G 484. pp. 137–54.

D 7   LANGAARD NIELSEN, A., *Frits Clausen i Folketinget* (*Frits Clausen and Parliament*), Bovrup: DNSAP Forlag, 1939. 2 vols.

D 8   POULSEN, Henning, *Besaettelsesmagten og de Danske Nazister: det politiske forhold mellem tyske myndigheder og nazistiske kredse i Danmark, 1940–43* (*The Occupation Forces and the Danish Nazis*), Copenhagen: Gyldendal, 1970. 499pp. Bib. 400–7. Includes a list of DNSAP publications.

D 9   POULSEN, Henning and DJURSAA, Malene, 'Social basis of Nazism in Denmark: the DNSAP'. In LARSEN, S.U., Gn 36. pp. 702–14.

D 10   VAABEN, E., *Hagekorset over Danmark* (*Swastika over Denmark*), Odense: DNSAP Forlag, 1939. 51pp. DNSAP publication.

Denmark under Occupation

D 11   ALKIL, Niels (ed.), *Besaettelsestidens fakta: dokumentarisk handbok med henblik paa lovene af 1945 om landsskadelig virksomhed (Occupation Facts: a documentary handbook with special reference to the laws of 1945 about activities injurious to the state)*, Copenhagen: Schultz, 1945-6. 2 vols. Includes a list of the various nazi organisations during the occupation.

D 12   BINDSLØV-FREDERIKSEN, L., *Pressen under besaettelsen: hovedtraek af den Danske dagspresses vilkaar og virke i perioden, 1940-1945 (The Press during the Occupation: an outline of the conditions and activities of the daily press in the period, 1940-1945)*, Aarhus: Universitetsforlaget, 1960. 551pp. List of periodicals, 519-22. English summary.

D 13   BRØNDSTED, Johannes and GEDDE, Knud, *De fem lange aar: Danmark under besaettelsen, 1940-1945 (Five Long Years: Denmark under occupation)*, Copenhagen: Nordisk Forlag, 1946-7. 3 vols.

D 14   CHRISTIANSEN, Karl O., *Landssviger kriminaliteten i sociologisk belysning (Crimes of Treason in Sociological Perspective)*, Copenhagen: Gad, 1955. 2 vols. Bib. vol. 1, 330-4. Copenhagen University thesis, 1950. English summary.

D 15   KIRCHHOFF, Hans and others, *Besaettelsestidens historie:* [by] Hans Kirchhoff, Henrik S. Nissen, Henning Poulsen, Copenhagen: Fremad, 1964. 238pp. Bib. 235-7.

D 16   LA COUR, Vilhelm (ed.) *Danmark under besaettelsen (Denmark under Occupation)*, Copenhagen: Westermann, 1945-7. 3 vols. Vol. 2 has article by Børge Outze on Danish nazis.

D 17   HAESTRUP, Jørgen and others (eds), *Besaettelsens hvem, hvad, hvor:* Jørgen Haestrup, Henning Poulsen, Hjalmar Petersen (*The occupation, who, what, where*), Copenhagen: Politikens Forlag, 1965. 488pp. Bib. 477-9. Biographical index 385-476.

D 18   POULSEN, Henning, '"Faedrelandet": tysk understøttelse af Danske dagblade, 1939-1945' (Faedrelandet: German support for the Danish daily press). *Historie (Denmark)*, **7**, 1966. pp. 232-72.

D 19   THOMSEN, Erich, *Deutsche Besatzungspolitik in Dänemark, 1940-1945*, Düsseldorf: Bertelsmann, 1971. 277pp. Bib. 267-73.

D 20   VOORHIS, Jerry L., 'A bibliographical note on occupied Denmark, 1940-1943'. *SCAND. STUD.*, **52** (3), 1980. pp. 289-97.

SWEDEN

S 1 CARLSSON, Holger, *Nazismen i Sverige: ett varningsord:* 7th edn. (*Nazism in Sweden: a word of warning*), Stockholm: Trots Allt, 1942. 224pp. Includes a list of nazi publications.

S 2 ELVANDER, Nils, 'Rudolf Kjellén och nationalsocialismen'. *Statsvetenskaplig Tidskrift,* 1, 1966. pp. 15–41. Kjellén (1864–1922) geopolitical conservative theorist who prepared the climate for fascism.

S 3 HAGTVET, Bernt, 'On the fringe: Swedish fascism, 1920–1945'. In LARSEN, S.U., Gn 36. pp. 715–42.

S 4 HOLMGREN, Israel, *Nazishelvetet* (*The Nazi Inferno*), Stockholm: Trots Allt, 1942. 48pp. Bib. 48. Author an anti-nazi professor.

S 5 KUBU, Mert, *Gustav Möllers hemliga polis: en bok om spionaget i Sverige under andra väraldskriget* (*Gustav Möller's Secret Police*), Stockholm: Roben & Sjögren, 1971. 221pp. Bib. 217–18. Includes fifth column activities and fascist activity during World War II.

S 6 LIND, Martin, 'Church and National Socialism in Sweden, 1933–1945'. *Kyrkohistorisk Arsskrift.,* 77, 1977. pp. 303–8. Nazism in Swedish Lutheran Church.

S 7 LUNDBERG, Erik, 'Nils Flygs väg till nazismen' (Nils Flyg's path to Nazism). *Svensk Tidskrift,* 50 (8/9), 1963. pp. 392–402. Nils Flyg (1891–1943) moved from Leninism to nazism after 1938.

S 8 MÖLLER, Artur, *Svensk nazism,* Stockholm: Holmström, 1935. 79pp.

S 9 SASTAMOINEN, Armas Zakarias, *Hitler's svenska förtrupper* (*Hitler's Swedish Avant-garde*), Stockholm: 1947. 228pp.

S 10 SHEPARD, Michael Denison, *Adrian Molin: study of a Swedish right-wing radical,* Northwestern University thesis, 1969. UM 70–00157. 326pp. A representative of the non-nazi extreme right.

S 11 TSCHERNISCHEWA, Olga W., 'Faschistische Strömungen und Organisationen in Schweden bis zum Ende des Zweiten Weltkrieges'. *Nord-Europa Studien (DDR),* 7, 1974. pp. 41–59.

S 12 WÄRENSTAM, Eric, *Sveriges nationella ungdomsförbund och högern, 1928–1934* (*The Swedish National Youth Organisation and the Right*), Stockholm: Svenska Bökforlaget, 1965. xi, 348pp. Radical Right elements in the conservative youth movement.

S 13 WÄRENSTAM, Eric, *Fascismen och nazismen i Sverige,* rev. edn,

Uppsala: Almqvist & Wiksell, 1972. 254pp. 1970 edn omits World War II.

S 14 WIREN, Karl, *Svensk nazism utan mask* (*Swedish Nazism Unmasked*), Stockholm, 1942. 23pp.

FINLAND

General

Fn 1 ALAPURO, Risto, 'Mass support for fascism in Finland'. In LARSEN, S.U., Gn 36. 678–86. Review of support for the Lapua Movement and IKL.

Fn 2 ALAPURO, Risto, 'On the political mobilisation of the agrarian population in Finland: problems and hypotheses'. *SCAND. POLIT. STUD.*, **11**, 1976. pp. 51–76. Includes radical Right movements.

Fn 3 FOL, Jacques, 'La montée du fascisme en Finlande, 1922–1932'. *REV. D'HIST. MOD. ET CONTEMP.*, **18** (1), 1971. 116–23.

Fn 4 HÄMÄLÄINEN, Pekka Kalevi, *Nationalitetskampen och sprakstriden i Finland, 1917–1939* (*The Nationality Struggle and Language Conflict in Finland*), Helsinki: Schildt, 1969. 274pp. Bib. 259–72. Includes activities of extreme Right among Swedish and Finnish speaking groups.

Fn 5 HYVÄMÄKI, Lauri, 'Fasistiset ilmiöt Baltian maissa ja Suomessa 1920-luvun lopussa ja 1930-luvulla' (Manifestations of fascism in the Baltic States and Finland in the late 20s and 30s). *HIST. ARKISTO*, **72**, 1977. pp. 113–37. On the Lapua Movement and IKL in Finland, EVK in Estonia, Ugunkrusts and Perkonkrusts in Latvia.

Fn 6 HYVÄMÄKI, Lauri, *Sinistä ja mustaa: tutkielmia Suomen oikeistoradikalismista* (*Blue and Black: a contribution to Finnish Right-wing radicalism*), Helsinki: Otava, 1971. 282pp. Bib. 271–6.

Fn 7 JUSSILA, Osmo, 'Suomen ja neuvostliiton historiantutkijoiden symposiumi 1975' (Finnish–Soviet historical symposium). *HIST. AIKAK.*, **74** (1), 1976. pp. 59–63. One of the subjects of the Symposium held in Tampere 1975 was fascism in Finland and the Baltic States in the 1920s and 1930s.

Fn 8   KALELA, Jorma, 'Right-wing radicalism in Finland during the inter-war period: perspectives from and an appraisal of recent literature'. *SCAND. J. OF HIST.*, 1 (1/2), 1976. pp. 105-24.

Fn 9   KURJENSAARI, Matti, *Taustelu huomispäivästä: isänmaan opissa, 1918-48 (Tomorrow's Struggle: patriotic doctrine, 1918-48)*, Helsinki: Tammi, 1948. 210pp.

Fn 10   RINTALA, Marvin, 'Äärioikeisto Suomen poliittisessa elämässä, 1917-1939' (The extreme right-wing in Finnish politics). *Politiikka*, 5 (3) 1963. pp. 87-112.

Fn 11   RINTALA, Marvin, 'Extremism in interwar Finland'. *EAST EUR. Q.*, 2 (1), 1968. pp. 45-56.

Fn 12   RINTALA, Marvin, 'Finland'. In ROGGER, H. and WEBER, E., Gn 54. pp. 408-42.

Fn 13   RINTALA, Marvin, *Three Generations: the extreme right wing in Finnish politics*, Bloomington: Indiana University Press, 1962. 281pp. Bib. 258-81. Major study taking in three generations, ie. AKS, Lapua, IKL.

Fn 14   *Suomen Kirjallisuus: aakkosellinen ja aineenmukainen luettelo*, vols. 1921/23-1939/43 (Finish literature: alphabetical and systematic catalogue), Helsinki. For publications of AKS, Lapua and IKL.

Fn 15   UPTON, Anthony F., 'Finland'. In WOOLF, S.J., Gn 20. pp. 191-222.

Fn 16   WAHLBÄCK, Krister, *Från Mannerheim till Kekkonen: huvudlinjer i findlandsk politik, 1917-67 (From Mannerheim to Kekkonen: the mainstream of Finnish politics)*, Stockholm: Aldus/Bonnier, 1967. 250pp. Bib. 246-48. Various interpretations of the Finnish Right radicals pp. 99-116.

Fn 17   WUORINEN, John H., *Nationalism in Modern Finland*, New York: Columbia University Press, 1931. x, 302pp. Bib. 281-94. Columbia University thesis.

The Early Years of the Extreme Right

Fn 18   HYVÄMÄKI, Lauri, 'Fascismin tulo Suomeen, 1922-23' (The coming of fascism to Finland). *HIST. AIKAK.*, 66 (2), 1968. pp. 109-28. English summary.

Fn 19   KLINGE, Matti, *Vihan veljistä valtososialismin: yhteiskunnallisia ja kansallisia näkemyksiä 1910- ja 1920-luvuilta (From Brothers of hate to state socialism: reflections on nation and society in the 1910s and 1920s)*,

Poorvoo: Söderstrom, 1972. 214pp. On early fascistic tendencies including AKS and Lapua Movement.

Fn 20   UOLA, Mikko, 'Lalliliitto: poliittinen mörkö vai Lapuan liikkeen edelläkävijä' (The Lalli League: political ghost or forerunner of the Lapua Movement). *HIST. AIKAK.*, **77** (**3**), 1979. pp. 209-18. A small anti-communist, anti-parliamentary Right-wing movement active briefly in 1929.

Akateeminen Karjala-Seura (Academic Karelia Society) and Student Politics

Fn 21   ALAPURO, Risto, *Akateeminen Karjala-Seura: ylioppilas liike ja kansa 1920- ja 1930-luvulla* (*The Academic Karelia Society: student movement and people in the 1920s and 1930s*), Poorvoo: Söderstrom, 1973. x, 270pp. Bib. 258-70. Standard work on the radical nationalist student group with fascist tendencies.

Fn 22   ALAPURO, Risto, 'Students and national politics: a comparative study of the Finnish student movement in the interwar period'. *SCAND. POLIT. STUD.*, **8**, 1973. pp. 113-40.

Fn 23   KLINGE, Matti, *Ylioppilaskunnan historia* (*History of Student Politics*), Poorvoo: Söderstrom, 1968. 4 vols. Vol. 4 covers 1918-60.

Fn 24   RINTALA, Marvin, 'Finnish students in politics: the Academic Karelia Society'. *EAST EUR. Q.*, **6** (**2**), 1972. pp. 192-205.

The Lapua Movement

Fn 25   ALAPURO, Risto and ALLARDT, Erik, 'The Lapua Movement: the threat of rightist takeover in Finland, 1930-32'. In LINZ, J.J. and STEPAN, A., Gn 104. pp. 122-41.

Fn 26   HAUPTMANN, Hans, *Erneuerung aus Blut und Boden: die Lappobewegung der finnischen Bauernschaft: ein Weg zur Befreiung vom Bolschevismus*, Munich: Lehmann, 1932. 76pp.

Fn 27   HYVÄMÄKI, Lauri, 'Kommunisminvastaisen lainsäädännön synty ja lapuanliike' (The origins of legislative opposition to communism and the Lapua Movement). In TOMMILA, Päiviö, *Kaksi vuosikymmentä suomen sisäpolitiikkaa, 1919-1939*, Poorvoo: Söderstrom, 1964. pp. 145-68.

Fn 28   HYVÄMÄKI, Lauri, 'Mäntsälen kapina Kärkijoukhojen

alkuperäisten asiiakirjojen volossa' (The Mantsala revolt in the light of original Vanguard documents). *HIST. AIKAK.*, **67**, 1969. pp. 89-113. English summary. On the abortive Lapua farmers' revolt in 1932 which led to banning of the Lapua movement.

Fn 29 HYVÄMÄKI, Lauri, 'Ståhlbergs skjutning' (Stahlberg's kidnapping). *HIST. TIDSKR. FOR FINLAND,* **54** (1), 1969. pp. 1-19. A liberal politician kidnapped by Rightist elements pressing for the suppression of Communism.

Fn 30 KARSTEN, Ossian, *Lapporörelsen och dess motståndare (The Lapua Movement and its Opposition)*, Helsinki: Söderstrom, 1930. 39pp.

Fn 31 KOKKO, Arvo, *Lapuan laki: talonpoikaisliike Soumessa v. 1930 (The Lapua Movement: Finnish peasant movement)*, Huopalahti: Tieto Kustannus, 1930. 2 vols. Gives details of membership of the Lapua mass march on Helsinki in 1930.

Fn 32 KORJUS, Jaakko, *Vihtori Kosola legenda jo eläessään (Vihtori Kosola, a legend in his lifetime)*, Poorvoo: Söderstrom [19--?]. 256pp. Covers his career in the civil war 1917-18 and in the Lapua Movement 1930-2.

Fn 33 KOSOLA, Vihtori, *Viimeistä piirtoa myöten: muistelmia elämäni varrelta*, Lapua: Lapuan Kirjapaino, 1935. 263pp. Memoirs of the Lapua Movement leader.

Fn 34 LISTE, Alli, *Lapua laki: 1920-ja-30-luvun suomalaisesta fasismista kertovan lyhytfilmin käsikirjoitus (The Lapua Law)*, Tampere: Sodanja Fasismin Vastainen Työ, 1976. 75pp. Bib. 70-2.

Fn 35 SIHVO, Aarne, *Muistelmani (Memoirs)*, Helsinki: Otava, 1954-6. 2 vols. Memoirs of Major-General Sihvo which includes information on the military's relations with the Lapua Movement.

Fn 36 SOMERSALO, Arne, *Lapuan tie (The Lapua Way)*, Helsinki: Kustannuso-Sakeyhtiö Kirja, 1930. 119pp. By a leader of the Lapua Movement and editor of the journal Ajan Sana.

Fn 37 VUORIMAA, Artturi, *Kolme kuukautta Kosolassa: Lapuan liikkeen pesässä nähtyä kuultua ja kuvitettua*, Mänttä: Tekijä, 1931. 134pp. Memoirs of a Lapuan activist.

Isänmaallinen Kansanliike (The People's Patriotic Movement)

Fn 38 HEINONEN, Reijo E., 'From people's movement to minor party: the People's Patriotic Movement (IKL) in Finland, 1932-1944'. In LARSEN, S.U., Gn 36. pp. 687-701.

Fn 39 HEINONEN, Reijo E., *Papiston osuus Isänmaallisen Kansanliikkeen alkuvaiheissa vuosina, 1932-36 (The Role of the Priests at the Beginning of the Patriotic People's Movement, 1932-36)*, Helsinki University MA, 1965.

Fn 40 KALLIALA, K.J., *Kokoomuspuolue ja IKL (The National Coalition Party and the IKL)*, Helsinki: Kansallinen Kokoomuspuolue, 1936. 18pp.

Fn 41 LAURILA, Juhani, *Suomen Kansan Järjestö: kartoittava tutkimus Suomen Kansan Järjestön aatteista ja suhteesta muihin kansallissosialistisiin suuntauksiin Suomessa lähinnä vuosina, 1932-1934 (The Organisation of the Finnish People: a study of its ideology and its relation to the other National Socialist orientations in Finland, primarily 1932-1934)*, Turku: Turun Yliopiston Valtio-Opin Laitos, 1967. 149pp. Bib. 143-9.

Fn 42 RINTALA, Marvin, 'An image of European politics: the People's Patriotic Movement'. *J. OF CENT. EUR. AFF.*, **22**, 1962. pp. 308-16.

Fn 43 RUUTU, Yrjö, *Ajan vaatimus (The Times Demand)*, Helsinki: Tekijä, 1932. 27pp.

Fn 44 RUUTU, Yrjö, *Uusi suunta: soumalaisen yhteiskuntaohjelman ääriviivoja (A New Direction: an outline of a programme for Finnish Society)*, Jyväskylä: Gummerus, 1920. 183pp. By a leader of the Academic Karelia Society and founder of the National Socialist Society of Helsinki who moved close to fascism but later joined the Social Democrats.

Fn 45 SIMOJOKI, Elias, *Palava pensas: puheita*, 3rd edn, *(The Burning Bush: speeches)* Poorvoo: Söderstrom, 1943. 233pp.

Fn 46 UOLA, Mikko, *Isänmaallisen Kansanliikkeen synty, 1932-1933 (Origins of the People's Patriotic Movement)*, Turku: Turin Yliopiston Suomen Historian Laitos, 1969. 103pp. Bib. 96-9.

Fn 47 [VARRO, Martius], Martti Tertti (pseud.), *Caesar katsoo pohjoiseen: historiallisia kuvitelmia (Caesar looks North: a historical fantasy)*, Jykväskylä: Gummerus, 1938. 135pp. A tract on the necessity of dictatorship by a leading member of IKL who died in the Winter War.

Fn 48 VIRKKUNEN, Sakari, *Elias Simojoki legenda jo eläessään (Elias Simojoki living legend)*, Poorvoo: Söderstrom, 1974. 229pp. Rev. Elias Simojoki leader of IKL's unofficial youth movement and later a member of parliament.

ICELAND

Ic 1   GUDMUNDSSON, Asgeir, 'Nazism in Iceland'. In LARSEN, S.U., Gn 36. pp. 743-50.

Ic 2   ADILS, J., *Markmid Flokks thjódernissinna* (*The Aims of the Nationalist Party*), Reykjavik, 1939.

IRELAND

Ir 1   CULLINGFORD, Elizabeth, *Yeats, Ireland, and Fascism*, London: Macmillan, 1981. viii, 251pp. Bib. 239-44.

Ir 2   HOGAN, James, *Could Ireland become Communist? The facts of the case*, Dublin: Cahill, 1935. xxviii, 138pp.

Ir 3   HOGAN, James, *Modern Democracy*, Cork: University Press. New York: Longmans Green, 1938. 96pp. Professor, advocate of the Corporate State, and Blueshirt.

Ir 4   McLOUGHLIN, Barry, 'Die irischen Blauhemden: faschistischen oder radikale Konservative?'. *Zeitgeschichte*, **8** (**5**), 1981. pp. 169-91.

Ir 5   MANNING, Maurice, *The Blueshirts*, Dublin: Gill and Macmillan, 1970. xi, 276pp. Bib. 251-4.

Ir 6   MANNING, Maurice, 'The Irish experience: the Blueshirts'. In LARSEN, S.U., Gn 36. pp. 557-67.

Ir 7   O'BRIEN, Conor Cruise, 'Yeats and Irish politics'. *Tri-Quarterly*, (**4**), 1964. pp. 91-9.

Ir 8   O'DUFFY, Eoin, *Crusade in Spain*, Dublin: Brown & Nolan, 1938. viii, 256pp. On the Irish Brigade in the Spanish Civil War.

FRANCE

Bibliographies

Fr 1 BLUMENKRANZ, Bernhard, *Bibliographie des Juifs en France*, Paris: Ecole Pratique des Hautes Etudes, Centre d'Etudes Juives, 1961. x, 188p.

Fr 2 BUSI, Frederick, 'A bibliographical overview of the Dreyfus Affair'. *JEW. SOC. STUD.*, **40** (**1**), 1978. pp. 25–40.

Fr 3 Centre de Documentation Juive Contemporaine, *La France de l'Affaire Dreyfus à nos jours*, Paris: CDJC, 1964. xii, 266pp.

Fr 4 DESACHY, Paul, *Bibliographie de l'Affaire Dreyfus*, Paris: Cornély, 1905. vii, 71pp.

Fr 5 MOHLER, Armin, 'Die französische Rechte: Literaturbericht'. *Merkur*, **12** (**1**), 1958. pp. 69–86.

General

Fr 6 ANDERSON, Malcolm, *Conservative Politics in France*, London: Allen & Unwin, 1974. 381pp. Bib. 348–61. Covers all strands of the Right including the reactionary, nationalist and fascist Right.

Fr 7 ARIES, Philippe and WINOCK, Michel, *Un Historien du dimanche*, Paris: Ed. du Seuil, 1980. 218pp. Autobiography of the historian Ariès who supported both Action Française and then Vichy, as told to Winock.

Fr 8 BARRAL, Pierre, 'L'extrème droite'. *Bull. de la Soc. des Professeurs d'Hist. et de Georgraphie de l'Enseignement Public*, **215**, 1969. pp. 317–20.

Fr 9 BRUGMANS, H., 'Pourquoi le fascisme n'a-t-il pas "pris" en France?' *Res Publica*, **7** (**1**), 1965. pp. 77–85.

Fr 10 COSTON, Henry (ed.), *Dictionnaire de la politique française*, Paris: La Librairie Française, 1967–79. 3 vols. Indispensable source for the extreme Right.

Fr 11 COSTON, Henry (ed.), *Partis, journaux, et hommes politiques d'hier et d'aujourd'hui*, Paris: Lectures Françaises, 1960. 620pp. Catalogues fascist and collaborationist organisations.

Fr 12 *Défense de l'Occident: revue mensuelle politique littéraire et artistique*, vol. 1, 1952-. An independent neo-fascist voice often concerned with the past.

Fr 13   DIOUDONNAT, Pierre-Marie, 'Les trois âges du fascisme français', *Contrepoint*, **11**, 1973. pp. 149-69.

Fr 14   DROZ, Jacques, 'Der Nationalismus der Linken und der Nationalismus der Rechten in Frankreich, 1871-1941'. *HIST. Z̧.*, **210** (1), 1970. pp. 1-13.

Fr 15   *Ecrits de Paris: revue des questions actuelles. 1945-*, Paris: Soc. Parisienne d'Édition et de Pub. Right-wing journal with many articles concerning the pre-1945 period.

Fr 16   GIRARDET, Raoul, 'Pour une introduction a l'histoire du nationalisme français'. *REV. FR. DE SCI. POLIT.*, **8** (3), 1958. pp. 505-28.

Fr 17   GRIFFITHS, Richard M., 'Anti-capitalism and the French extra-parliamentary Right, 1870-1940'. *J. OF CONTEMP. HIST.*, **13** (4), 1978. pp. 721-40.

Fr 18   McCLELLAND, J.S. (ed.), *The French Right (from De Maistre to Maurras)*, London: Cape. New York: Harper & Row, 1970. 320pp. Bib. 310-11.

Fr 19   MACHEFER, Philippe (ed.), *Ligues et fascismes en France, 1919-1939*, Paris: PUF, 1974. 95pp. Bib. 94-5. Collection of extracts and documents.

Fr 20   MOHLER, Armin, *Die französische Rechte: vom Kampf um Frankreichs Ideologienpanzer*, Munich: Isar V., 1958. 86pp.

Fr 21   MOHLER, Armin, 'Im Schatten des Jakobinismus die "Konservativen" und die "Rechte" in Frankreich'. In KALTEN-BRUNNER, Gerd-Klaus (ed.), *Rekonstruktion des Konservatismus*, Freiburg: Rombach, 1972. pp. 273-91.

Fr 22   MÜLLER, Klaus-Jürgen, 'French fascism and modernisation'. *J. OF CONTEMP. HIST.*, **11** (4), 1976. pp. 75-107.

Fr 23   PETITFILS, Jean-Christian, *La Droite en France de 1789 à nos jours*, 2nd edn, Paris: PUF, 1976. 126pp. Bib. 125-6.

Fr 24   PLUMYENE, Jean and LASIERRA, Raymond, *Les Fascismes français, 1923-1963*, Paris: Ed. du Seuil, 1963. 318pp.

Fr 25   REMOND, René, *The Right-wing in France: from 1815 to De Gaulle*, Philadelphia: University Press, 1969. 465pp. Bib. 418-48. Tr. of *La Droite en France*, 1963, by James M. Laux.

Fr 26   REMOND, René, 'Y a-t-il un fascisme français?' *Terre*

Humaine, **2** (**7/8**), 1952, pp. 37–47. Minimises rôle of fascism in France.

Fr 27   IRVINE, William D., 'René Rémond's French Right: the interwar years'. *WEST. SOC. FR. HIST. PROC. ANNU. MEET.*, **5**, 1977. pp. 301–9.

Fr 28   RUTKOFF, Peter M., 'Rémond, nationalism and the Right'. *WEST. SOC. FR. HIST. PROC. ANNU. MEET.*, **5**, 1977. pp. 292–301.

Fr 29   SCHNURER, H., 'The intellectual sources of French fascism'. *Antioch Rev.*, **1**, March 1941. pp. 35–49.

Fr 30   SOUCY, Robert L., 'French fascism as class conciliation and moral regeneration'. *Societas*, **1** (**4**), 1971. pp. 287–97.

Fr 31   SOUCY, Robert L., 'The nature of fascism in France'. *J. OF CONTEMP. HIST.*, **1** (**1**), 1966. pp. 27–55.

Fr 23   STERNHELL, Zeev, 'Strands of French fascism'. In LARSEN, S.U., Gn 36. pp. 479–500.

Fr 33   TINT, Herbert, *The Decline of French Patriotism, 1870–1940*, London: Weidenfeld & Nicolson, 1964. 272pp. Includes Barrès, Déroulède, Action Française, fascism.

Fr 34   VALLAT, Xavier, *La Croix, les lys et la peine des hommes*, Paris: Aymon, 1960. 298pp. The Right, 1900 onwards.

Fr 35   WARNER, Geoffrey, 'France'. In WOOLF, S.J., Gn 20. pp. 307–28.

Fr 36   WEBER, Eugen, 'Nationalism, socialism, and national-socialism in France'. *FR. HIST. STUD.*, **2** (**3**), 1962. pp. 273–307.

Fr 37   WEBER, Eugen, 'The Right in France: a working hypothesis'. *AM. HIST. REV.*, **65** (**3**), 1960. pp. 554–68.

Fr 38   WEBER, Eugen, 'France'. In ROGGER, H. and WEBER, E., Gn 54. pp. 71–127.

Fr 39   WINOCK, Michel, 'Le fascisme en France'. *Histoire*, **28**, 1980. pp. 40–9.

The Extreme Right 1890–1918

Fr 40   ANDERSON, Malcolm, 'The Right and the social question in Parliament, 1905–1919'. In SHAPIRO, D., Fr 75. pp. 85–134.

Fr 41   ANDREU, Pierre, 'Bibliographie d'Edouard Berth: vie et

oeuvre'. *BULL. INT. INST. SOC. HIST.*, **7/8**, 1952/3. pp. 196-204.
Berth (1875-1939) close to Maurras and Cercle Proudhon.

Fr 42   BADER, Jeffrey Allen, *The Nationalist Leagues in France after Dreyfus, 1898-1906*, Columbia University thesis, 1975. UM 75-18351. 327pp.

Fr 43   BEAU DE LOMÉNIE, Emmanuel, *Édouard Drumont ou l'anticapitalisme nationale*, Paris: Pauvert, 1968. 487pp.

Fr 44   BERNANOS, Georges, *La Grand peur des bien-pensants: Édouard Drumont*, Paris: Grasset, 1931. 458pp.

Fr 45   BYRNES, Robert Francis, *Anti-semitism in Modern France. 1. The prologue to the Dreyfus Affair*, New Brunswick, NJ: Rutgers University Press, 1950. 348pp. Bib.

Fr 46   DRAULT, Jean (pseud.) [Alfred Gendrot], *Drumont; la France juive et la Libre Parole*, Paris: Malfère, 1935. 344pp.

Fr 47   DRUMONT, Édouard, *La France juive: essai d'histoire contemporaine*, Paris: Marpon & Flammarion, 1886. 2 vols.

Fr 48   DRUMONT, Édouard, *Sur les chemins de la vie: (souvenirs)*, Paris: Crès, 1914. xii, 315pp.

Fr 49   DRUMONT, Édouard, *Le Testament d'un antisémite*, Paris: Dentru, 1894. xxiii, 456pp.

Fr 50   GUERIN, Jules, *Les Trafiquants de l'antisémitisme: la maison Drumont*, Paris: Juven, 1905. ix, 504pp. Guérin of the Ligue Antisémitique.

Fr 51   JENSEN, LaJean Nelson, *Editorials of Édouard Drumont in La Libre Parole 1892-1906: a reflection of the times*, Brigham Young University thesis, 1980. UM 80-27368. 261pp.

Fr 52   WINOCK, Michel, 'Édouard Drumont et l'antisémitisme en France avant l'Affaire Dreyfus'. *Esprit*, **39** (**403**), 1971. pp. 1085-106.

Fr 53   BIETRY, Pierre, *Les Jaunes de France et la question ouvrière*, Paris: Paclot, 1907. vi, 344pp. On the Right-wing 'yellow' unions.

Fr 54   GALLIAN, E., *Les Vérités sociales: ce que sont les Jaunes: resumé de la doctrine des Jaunes*, Paris: Plon-Nourrit, 1907. 22pp.

Fr 55   MOSSE, George Lachmann, 'The French Right and the working classes: les Jaunes'. *J. OF CONTEMP. HIST.*, **7** (**3/4**), 1972. pp. 185-208.

Fr 56   PAWLOWSKI, Auguste, *Les Syndicats jaunes: leur origines, la Fédération Nationale des Jaunes, etc.*, Paris: Alcan, 1911. 188pp.

Fr 57   BYRNES, Robert Francis, 'Morès: the first national socialist'. *REV. OF POLIT.*, **12** (3), 1950. pp. 341–62.

Fr 58   MORES, Antonio Amedeo Maria, Marquis de, *Le Secret des changes*, Marseille: Impr. Marseillaise, 1894. xv, 96pp. Supporter of Drumont.

Fr 59   SCHWARZSCHILD, Steven S., 'The Marquis de Morès: the story of a failure, 1858–1896'. *JEW. SOC. STUD*, **22** (1), 1960. pp. 3–26. Described by Mosse as 'a one-man national socialist movement'.

Fr 60   TWETON, D. Jerome, *The Marquis de Morès: Dakota capitalist, French nationalist*, Fargo, ND: N. Dakota Institute for Regional Studies, 1972. x, 249pp. Bib. 240-4. Reviewed by G.L. Mosse in *North Dakota Quarterly*, Winter 1973.

Fr 61   CHENU, Charles, *La Ligue des Patriotes: son programme, son passé, son avenir*, pref. by Maurice Barrès . . . *et des extraits de discours de Paul Déroulède*, Paris: Tenin, 1916. ix, 136pp.

Fr 62   DEROULEDE, Paul, *Qui vive? France 'quand même': notes et discours 1883–1910*, Paris: Bloud, 1910. viii, 310pp. Paul Déroulède (1846–1914).

Fr 63   DUCRAY, Camille, *Paul Déroulède, 1846–1914: avec documents inédits et planches hors texte*, pref. by Maurice Barrès, Paris: Ambert, 1914. xiii, 274pp.

Fr 64   RUTKOFF, Peter M., 'The Ligue des Patriotes: the nature of the radical Right and the Dreyfus Affair'. *FR. HIST. STUD.*, **8** (4), 1974. pp. 585-603.

Fr 65   RUTKOFF, Peter M., *Revanche and revision: the Ligue des Patriotes and the origins of the radical Right in France, 1882–1900*, Athens: Ohio University Press, 1981. 182pp. Bib. 169-78.

Fr 66   STERNHELL, Zeev, 'Paul Déroulède and the origins of modern French nationalism'. *J. OF CONTEMP. HIST*, **6** (4), 1971. pp. 46-70.

Fr 67   THARAUD, Jérôme and Jean, *La Vie et la mort de Déroulède*, Paris: Emile-Paul, 1914. 257pp.

Fr 68   DOMINIQUE, Pierre, 'Le Fort Chabrol'. *Miroire de l'Histoire*, **7** (74), 1956. pp. 169-77. On the outbreak of anti-semitism in 1899 staged by Jules Guérin.

Fr 69   DOTY, Charles Stewart, 'Parliamentary Boulangism after 1889'. *The Historian*, **32** (2), 1970. pp. 250-69.

Fr 70   FRANK, Walter, *Nationalismus und Demokratie im Frankreich der Dritten Republik, 1871-1918*, Hamburg: Hanseatische Verlagsanstalt, 1933. 652pp. Drumont, Barrès, Maurras, Boulanger, etc.

Fr 71   GIRARDET, Raoul (ed.), *Le Nationalisme français, 1871-1914: textes choisis*, Paris: Colin, 1966. 276pp.

Fr 72   OLIVESI, A., 'La droite à Marseille en 1914'. *Provence Historique*, **7** (**28**), 1957. pp. 175-99.

Fr 73   RIOUX, Jean-Pierre, *Nationalisme et conservatisme: la Ligue de la Patrie Française, 1899-1904*, Paris: Beauchesne, 1977. 117pp.

Fr 74   RYAN, William, *La Croix and the Development of Rightist Nationalism in France*, University of Connecticut thesis, 1970. UM 71-16034. 301pp.

Fr 75   SHAPIRO, David (ed.), *The Right in France, 1890-1918*, Carbondale: S. Illinois University Press, 1962. 144pp. Three essays on the New Right by Shapiro on the Ralliement, D.R. Watson on The Nationalist movement in Paris, 1900-6, Malcolm Anderson on The Right and the social question in Parliament, 1905-19.

Fr 76   SORLIN, Pierre, *La Croix et les juifs, 1880-1899: contribution à l'histoire de l'antisémitisme contemporain*, Paris: Grasset, 1967. 346pp.

Fr 77   SOURY, Jules, *Campagne nationaliste, 1894-1901*, Paris: Maretheux, 1902. 308pp. Sorbonne professor (1842-1915), a Social Darwinist who according to Sternhell 'expressed a vision of the world close enough to nazism'. See Fr 78. p. 159.

Fr 78   STERNHELL, Zeev, *La Droite révolutionnaire, 1885-1914: les origines françaises du fascisme*, Paris: Ed. du Seuil, 1978. 444pp. Bib. 417-34.

Fr 79   SUMLER, David E., 'Domestic influences on the nationalist revival in France, 1909-1914'. *FR. HIST. STUD.*, **6** (**4**), 1970. pp. 517-37.

Fr 80   VIAU, Raphaël, *Vingt ans d'antisémitisme, 1889-1909*, Paris: Charpentier, 1910, 384pp.

Fr 81   WEBER, Eugen, *The Nationalist Revival in France 1905-1914*, Berkeley: University of California Press, 1968. 237pp.

Fr 82   WILSON, Stephen, 'The anti-semitic riots of 1898 in France'. *HIST. J.*, **16** (**4**), 1973. pp. 789-806.

Fr 83   WILSON, Stephen, 'Anti-semitism and Jewish response in France during the Dreyfus Affair'. *EUR. STUD. REV.*, **6** (**2**), 1976. pp. 225-48.

Fr 84   WILSON, Stephen, 'Catholic populism in France at the time of the Dreyfus Affair: the Union Nationale'. *J. OF CONTEMP. HIST.*, **10** (**4**), 1975. pp. 667–705.

Fr 85   WILSON, Stephen, *Ideology and Experience: anti-semitism in France at the time of the Dreyfus Affair*, Rutherford: Fairleigh University Press, 1982. xviii, 812pp. Bib. 747–61.

Fr 86   WILSON, Stephen, 'The Ligue Antisémitique Française'. *WIENER LIB. BULL.*, **25** (**3/4**), 1972. pp. 23–9.

Fr 87   WILSON, Stephen, 'Le monument Henry: la structure de l'antisémitisme en France, 1898–1899'. *ANNALES*, **32** (**2**), 1977. pp. 265–91.

Action Française and Barrès: Bibliographies

Fr 88   GARCIN, Philippe, 'Les deux Barrès'. *Critique*, **17**, 1961. pp. 1011–28. Research review.

Fr 89   JOSEPH, Roger and FORGES, Jean, *Nouvelle bibliographie de Charles Maurras; éd. définitive*, Aix-en-Provence: L'Art de Voir, 1980. 2 vols.

Fr 90   MATTEI, Roberto de, 'Appunti bibliografici su Charles Maurras e l'Action Française'. *CRIT. STOR.*, **10** (**3**), 1973. pp. 133–45 [501–13].

Fr 91   NGUYEN, Victor, 'Situation des études maurrassiennes: contribution à l'étude de la presse et des mentalités'. *REV. D'HIST. MOD. ET CONTEMP.*, **18** (**4**), 1971. pp. 503–38.

Fr 92   OSGOOD, Samuel M., 'Charles Maurras et l'Action Française: note bibliographique: état des travaux americains'. *REV. FR. DE SCI. POLIT.*, **8** (**1**), 1958. pp. 143–7.

F 93   OSGOOD, Samuel M., 'Vues nouvelles sur l'Action Française'. *CAH. D'HIST.*, **14** (**3**), 1969. pp. 289–301.

Fr 94   ZARACH, Alphonse, *Bibliographie barrésienne, 1881–1948*, Paris: PUF, 1951. vii, 358pp.

Action Française: General

Fr 95   ANDREANI, Roland, 'Milieux d'Action Française et

Camelots du Roi dans le Gard avant 1914'. In *Congrès des Savantes de Paris et des Départements*. 96°. Toulouse, 13-17 April 1971, vol. 1. Paris, Bib. Nat., 1976. pp. 255-65.

Fr 96   ARNAL, Oscar Léon, *French Catholics Left and Right: ralliements and the Action Française*, University of Pittsburgh thesis. UM 75-6347. 655pp. Catholic thought 1899-1939.

Fr 97   BALFOUR, R.E., 'The Action Française Movement'. *CAMBRIDGE HIST. J.*, **3** (**2**), 1930. pp. 182-205.

Fr 98   BEAU DE LOMÉNIE, Emmanuel, *Les Responsabilités des dynasties bourgeoises*, Paris: Denoël, 1963. 4 vols. Vol. 4. *Du Cartel à Hitler, 1924-1933*. 557pp. Maurrasian point of view.

Fr 99   BLATT, Joel, 'Relatives and rivals: the responses of the Action Française to Italian Fascism, 1919-26'. *EUR. STUD. REV.*, **11** (**3**), 1981. pp. 263-92.

Fr 100   BORDEAUX, Henry, *Histoire d'un vie*, Paris: Plon, 1955-73. 13 vols. Much on Maurras and Action Française.

Fr 101   BROGAN, Denis Williams, *French Personalities and Problems, 1900-1940*, London: Hamilton, 1946. New York: Knopf, 1947. 228pp. Essays including Maurras, Léon Daudet, Bainville.

Fr 102   BRUGMANS, H., 'Un cas de pathologie politique: l'Action Française'. *Res Publica*, **5**, 1963. pp. 237-44.

Fr 103   CAMPANINI, Giorgio, 'Chiesa, fascismo, e Action Française'. *Civitas*, **28** (**7/8**), 1977. pp. 3-24. On the condemnation of AF in 1926.

Fr 104   CURTIS, Michael, *Three against the Republic: Sorel, Barrès, and Maurras*, Princeton: University Press, 1959. 307pp. Bib. 277-307.

Fr 105   DANSETTE, Adrien, 'L'Église et l'Action Française'. *Esprit*, **19** (**9**), 1951. pp. 275-99; **19** (**10**). pp. 446-58.

Fr 106   DIMIER, Louis, *Vingt ans d'Action Française et autres souvenirs*, Paris: Nouvelle Librairie Nationale, 1926. 362pp.

Fr 107   DIMIER, Louis, *Souvenirs d'action publique et d'université*, Paris: Nouvelle Librairie Française, 1920. 268pp. Author (1865-1943), editor of Action Française.

Fr 108   EPP, René, 'A propos de la condemnation de l'Action Française en 1926'. *Esprit et Vie*, **88** (**19**), 1978. pp. 289-304.

Fr 109   GERIN-RICARD, Lazare de and TRUC, Louis, *Histoire de l'Action Française*, Paris: Fournier-Valdès, 1949. 246pp.

Fr 110   HAVARD DE LA MONTAGNE, Robert, *Chemins de Rome et de France: cinquante ans de souvenirs*, Paris: Nouvelles Eds. Latines, 1956. 220pp.

Fr 111   HAVARD DE LA MONTAGNE, Robert, *Histoire de l'Action Française*, Paris: Amiot-Dumont, 1950. 251pp.

Fr 112   HERBECOURT, Pierre d', 'La condamnation de l'Action Française en Marne-et-Loire'. *Savoir*, **4**, 1978. pp. 20-2.

Fr 113   HUNTINGTON, Frank Charles, *The Ideology of the Action Française*, Yale University thesis, 1953. UM 70-16655. 286pp.

Fr 114   JOSEPH, Roger, *La Crise de l'Action Française, 1926-1939, devant l'historien: examen*, Orleans: Impr. Industrielle, 1964. 40pp.

Fr 115   LATREILLE, André, L'Action Française, les Catholiques de France et le Saint Siège: à propos de quelques ouvrages récents'. *CAH. D'HIST.*, **10** (4), 1965. pp. 389-401.

Fr 116   MARTIN DU GARD, Maurice, *Les Mémorables*, Paris: Flammarion, 1957-60. 2 vols. Includes memories of Maurras and AF.

Fr 117   MARTY, Albert, *L'Action Française racontée par elle-même*, Paris: Nouvelles Eds. Latines, 1968. 489pp.

Fr 118   MASSIS, Henri, *La Guerre de trente ans: destin d'un age, 1909-1939*, Paris: Plon, 1940. xi, 290pp. Rightist intellectual history.

Fr 119   MAZGAJ, Paul, *The Action Française and Revolutionary Syndicalism*, Chapel Hill: University of N. Carolina Press, 1979. ix, 281pp. Bib. 257-67.

Fr 120   MONTESQUIOU-FEZENSAC, Léon, Comte de, *Les Origines et la doctrine de l'Action Française*, Paris: Ligue d'Action Française, 1918. 40pp.

Fr 121   NGUYEN, Victor, 'L'Action Française devant la Réforme'. In *Historiographie de la Réforme: Colloque . . . . Aix-Marseille, 22-24 Sept. 1972*, Paris: Delachaux & Niestlé, 1977. pp. 239-67.

Fr 122   NGUYEN, Victor, 'Notes sur la psycho-sociologie du financement de la presse royaliste au temps de l'Action Française'. In *Presse et Politique: actes du Colloque de Nanterre, 25-26 avril 1975*, Paris: Centre d'Etudes et de Recherches sur la Presse, 1975. pp. 32-50.

Fr 123   NOLTE, Ernst, 'Die Action Française, 1899-1944'. *VIERTEL-JAHRSH. FÜR ZEITG.*, **9** (2), 1961. pp. 124-65.

Fr 124   NORA, Pierre, 'Les deux apogées de l'Action Française'. *ANNALES*, **19** (1), 1964. pp. 127-41.

Fr 125   OSGOOD, Samuel M., *French Royalism since 1870*, The Hague: Nijhoff, 1970. x, 241pp. Bib. 226-36.

Fr 126   PRÉVOTAT, Jacques, 'Remarques sur la notion de civilisation catholique dans la revue l'Action Française, juillet 1892-mars 1908'. *Civilisation Chrétienne*, 1975. pp. 349-65.

Fr 127   PUJO, Maurice, *Les Camelots du Roi*, Paris: Flammarion, 1933. 306pp. On the young stormtroopers of Action Française by their mentor and director (1872-1955).

Fr 128   RENOUVIN, Bertrand, *L'Action Française devant la question sociale, 1899-1944*, Aix-Marseille University thesis. 3ᵉ Cycle 1973. 357pp.

Fr 129   RIVET, Auguste, 'L'Action Française en Haute-Loire, 1906-1945'. *Cah. de la Haute-Loire (Le Puy)*, 1972. pp. 221-40.

Fr 130   ROCHE, Alphonse Victor, *Les Idées traditionalistes en France de Rivarol à Charles Maurras*, Urbana: University of Illinois, 1937. 235pp. Bib. 213-24.

Fr 131   SERANT, Paul, *Les Dissidents de l'Action Française*, Paris: Copernic, 1978. 323pp. On Valois, Dimier, Maritain, Bernanos, Brasillach, Maulnier, C. Roy.

Fr 132   SPADOLINI, Giovanni, 'Il Vaticano e l'Action Française (con documenti inedite del Cardinale Gasparri'. In *Studi in Onere di Giuseppe Chiarelli*, Milan: Giuffre, 1973-4. Vol. 4. pp. 4101-23.

Fr 133   TANNENBAUM, Edward R., *The Action Française: die-hard reactionaries in twentieth-century France*, New York: Wiley, 1962. 316pp. Bib. 291-305.

Fr 134   TANNENBAUM, Edward R., 'The reactionary mentality of the Action Française'. *Historian*, **17** (**1**), 1955. pp. 18-42.

Fr 135   TANNENBAUM, Edward R., 'The social thought of the Action Française'. *INT. REV. SOC. HIST.*, **6**, 1961. pp. 1-18.

Fr 136   TEFAS, Georges, *Les Conceptions Économiques des groupements d'Action Française: étude comparée*, Paris: Impr. des Presses Modernes, 1939. 798pp. Bib. 771-89.

Fr 137   TERRAIL, Gabriel [Mermeix, (pseud.)] *Le Ralliement et l'Action Française*, Paris: Fayard, 1927. 478pp.

Fr 138   THOMAS, Lucien, *L'Action Française devant l'Eglise de Pie X à Pie XII*, Paris: Nouvelles Eds. Latines, 1965. 411pp.

Fr 139   VATON, Bernard, *L'Éclair, journal quotidien du Midi, 1881-*

1944, Montpellier University thesis, 1967. 518pp. Action Française paper pub. in Montpellier.

Fr 140   VIRTANEN, Reino, 'Nietzsche and the Action Française'. Nietzsche's significance for French Rightist thought. *J. OF HIST. IDEAS*, **11** (**2**), 1950. pp. 191-214.

Fr 141   WEBER, Eugen, *Action Française: royalism and reaction in twentieth-century France*, Stanford: University Press, 1962. 594pp. Bib.

Fr 142   WILSON, Stephen, 'The Action Française in French intellectual life'. *HIST. J.*, **12** (**2**), 1969. pp. 328-50.

Fr 143   WILSON, Stephen, 'La France et l'étranger: aspects du nationalisme de l'Action Française'. *REV. D'HIST. MOD. ET CONTEMP.*, **20** (**3**), 1973. pp. 464-79.

Fr 144   WILSON, Stephen, 'Fustel de Coulanges and the Action Française'. *J. OF HIST. IDEAS*, **34** (**1**), 1973. pp. 123-34.

Fr 145   WILSON, Stephen, 'History and traditionalism: Maurras and the Action Française'. *J. OF HIST. IDEAS*, **29** (**3**), 1968. pp. 365-80.

Fr 146   WILSON, Stephen, 'A view of the past: Action Française historiography and its socio-political function'. *HIST. J.*, **19** (**1**), 1976. pp. 135-61.

Fr 147   WINLING, Raymond, 'L'Action Française comme doctrine et idéologie'. *Esprit et Vie*, **88** (**21**), 1978. pp. 323-30.

Charles Maurras (1868-1952)

Fr 147   BARRES, Maurice and MAURRAS, Charles, *La République ou le roi: correspondence inédite, 1888-1923*, ed. Hélène and Nicole Maurras, Paris: Plon, 1970. 709pp.

Fr 148   BEAU DE LOMÉNIE, Emmanuel, *Maurras et son système*, Mont-Secret: Centre d'Études Nationales, 1965. 156pp. First pub. Bourg, 1953.

Fr 149   BROGAN, Denis William, 'The nationalist doctrine of M. Charles Maurras'. *Politica*, February 1935. pp. 286-311.

Fr 150   BUTHMAN, William Curt, *The Rise of Integral Nationalism in France: with special reference to the ideas and activities of Charles Maurras*, New York: Octagon, 1970. 355pp. Bib. 335-50. First pub., Columbia University Press, 1939.

Fr 151   *Cahiers Charles Maurras* (Paris), No. 1—1960-, Paris: SDEDOM. Invaluable source.

Fr 152   CAPITAN-PETER, Colette, *Charles Maurras et l'idéologie d'Action Française: étude sociologique d'une pensée de droite*, Paris: Ed. du Seuil, 1972. 223pp. Bib. 209-21. Paris University thesis.

Fr 153   *Charles Maurras, 1868-1952: chronologie complète de l'oeuvre de Charles Maurras établie par Roger Joseph et Jean Forges*, Paris: Ed. d'Histoire et de l'Art, 1954. 256pp. 21 contributing authors.

Fr 154   DAUDET, Léon, *Charles Maurras et son temps*, Paris: Flammarion, 1930. 169pp.

Fr 155   *Etudes Maurrassiennes (Aix-en-Provence)*, No. 1—1972-, Centre Charles Maurras. See various Colloques Maurras proceedings.

Fr 156   FABREGUES, Jean de, *Charles Maurras et son 'Action Française': un drame spirituel*, Paris: Perrin, 1966. 427pp. Bibs. Author was a journalist of the Action Française persuasion and secretary for a time to Maurras.

Fr 157   GOYARD, Claude, 'La critique de droite: Charles Maurras'. In *Centenaire de la Troisième République: actes du Colloque de Rennes 15-17 mai 1975*, Paris: Delarge, 1975. pp. 243-57.

Fr 158   GOYARD, Claude, 'Maurras, critique de la IIIe République'. In *Histoire des Idées et Idée sur l'Historie: études offerts à Jean-Jacques Chevallier*, Paris: Cujas, 1977. pp. 123-72.

Fr 159   GURIAN, Waldemar, *Der integrale Nationalismus in Frankreich: Charles Maurras und die Action Française*, Frankfurt/M: Klostermann, 1931. viii, 131pp.

Fr 160   *Itineraires*, **122**, April 1968. pp. 5-240. Special issue 'Lorsque Maurras eût les cent ans'.

Fr 161   JOSEPH, Roger, *Les 'faux Maurras': comment on travestit une doctrine faute de pouvoir la refuter*, Paris: La Seule France, 1958, 62pp.

Fr 162   JOSEPH, Roger, *La Vérité sur le procès de Charles Maurras: j'ai vu condamner un juste au bagne: témoignage*, Orléans: Lhermitte, 1966. 138pp.

Fr 163   LECLERC, Gérard, *Un autre Maurras: essai*, Paris: Inst. de Politique Nationale, 1974, 177pp.

Fr 164   MACCEARNEY, James, *Maurras et son temps*, Paris: Michel, 1977. 294pp.

Fr 165   MARITAIN, Jacques, *Une Opinion sur Charles Maurras et le devoir des Catholiques*, Paris: Plon, 1926. 75pp.

53

Fr 166   MASSIS, Henri [Agathon (pseud.)], *Maurras et notre temps: entretiens et souvenirs; éd. définitive augm. de documents inédits*, Paris: Plon, 1961. iv, 454pp.

Fr 167   MAURRAS, Charles, *L'Action Française et la religion catholique*, Paris: Nouvelle Librairie Nationale, 1913. 354pp.

Fr 168   MAURRAS, Charles, *Dictionnaire politique et critique; établi par les soins de Pierre Chardon*, Paris: Cité des Livres, 1931-4. 5 vols.

Fr 169   MAURRAS, Charles, *Enquête sur la monarchie suivie de Une campagne royaliste au Figaro et Si le coup de force est possible, ed. définitive*, Paris: Fayard, 1924. clv, 615pp.

Fr 170   MAURRAS, Charles, *Mes idées politiques; texte établis par Pierre Chardon*, pref. by Pierre Gaxotte, Paris: Fayard, 1968. 317pp.

Fr 171   MAURRAS, Charles, defendant, *Le Procès de Charles Maurras compte rendu sténographique*, Paris: Michel, 1946. 388pp. The transcript of the trials of Maurras and Maurice Pujo, Action Française leaders, before the Cour de Justice, Lyons, January 1945.

Fr 172   MOURRE, Michel, *Charles Maurras*, 2nd edn, Paris: Eds Universitaires, 1958. 145pp. Bib. 9-14.

Fr 173   NAUMANN, Hans, *Charles Maurras und die Weltanschauung der Action Française: mit ein monographischen Bibliographie Charles Maurras*, Leipzig: Hirzel, 1935. xii, 94pp.

Fr 174   NGUYEN, Victor, 'Race et civilisation chez Maurras'. In *Missions et Démarches de la Critique: mélanges offerts au Professor J.A. Vier*, Paris: Klincksieck, 1973. pp. 563-72.

Fr 175   ROUDIEZ, Léon Samuel, *Maurras jusq'à l'Action Française*, Paris: Bonne, 1957. 336pp. Columbia University thesis, 1950.

Fr 176   ROUX, Marie, Marquis de, *Charles Maurras et le nationalisme de l'Action Française*, Paris: Grasset, 1927. 272pp.

Fr 177   SUTTON, Michael, 'Conservatives and conservatism: early Catholic controversy about the politics of Charles Maurras'. *J. OF CONTEMP. HIST.*, **14** (**4**), 1979. pp. 649-76.

Fr 178   SUTTON, Michael, *Nationalism, Positivism and Catholicism: the politics of Charles Maurras and French Catholics, 1890-1914*, Cambridge: University Press, 1983. viii, 334pp. Bib. 263-322.

Fr 179   TORELLI, Maurice, 'Charles Maurras et la théorie du nationalisme intégral'. *Action Nationale (Montreal)*, **64** (**7**), 1975. pp. 581-90; **64** (**9**), 1975. pp. 703-20; **64** (**10**), 1975. pp. 791-800; **65** (**1**), 1975. pp. 16-27.

Fr 180 TUCKER, William Rayburn, 'The legacy of Charles Maurras'. *J. OF POLIT.*, **17** (4), 1955. pp. 570–89.

Fr 181 VALLAT, Xavier, *Charles Maurras: numéro d'écrou 8,321*, Paris: Plon, 1953. 290pp. Interview with Maurras in prison after the war.

Fr 182 VANDROMME, Pol, *Maurras, l'église de l'ordre*, Paris: Eds du Centurion, 1965. 181pp. Bib. 173–8.

Fr 183 VATRE, Eric, *Charles Maurras: un itinéraire spirituel*, Paris: Nouvelles Eds. Latines, 1978. 236pp.

Fr 184 VAULX, Bernard de, *Charles Maurras: (esquisses pour un portrait)*, Moulins: Ed. des Cahiers Bourbonnais, 1968. 158pp.

Fr 185 VIGNE, Octave, *Mes souvenirs sur Charles Maurras, 1868–1952*, Uzès: Peladan, 1978. 120pp.

Maurice Barrès (1862–1923)

Fr 186 BARRES, Maurice, *Barrès par lui-même; image et textes presentés par Jean-Marie Domenach*, Paris: Eds du Seuil, 1954. 191pp. Bib. 188–90.

Fr 187 BARRES, Maurice, *Mes cahiers, 1896–1923; textes choisis par Guy Dupré*, Paris: Plon, 1963. vii, 1131pp.

Fr 188 BARRES, Maurice, *Mes cahiers*, Paris: Plon, 1929–57. 14 vols.

Fr 189 BARRES, Maurice, *L'oeuvre de M. Barrès; annotée par Philippe Barrès*, Paris: Club de l'Honnête Homme, 1965–. 18 vols.

Fr 190 BARRES, Maurice, *Scènes et doctrines du nationalisme; éd. définitive*, Paris: Plon-Nourrit, 1925. 2 vols.

Fr 191 BOISDEFFRE, Pierre de, *Maurice Barrès*, Paris: Eds Universitaires, 1962. 127pp. Bib. 124–7.

Fr 192 *Colloque Maurice Barrès. Actes du Colloque . . . Metz 1973. Mémoires de l'Academie Nationale de Metz*, **Ser. 6. 155**, (2), pp. 201–60.

Fr 193 CURTIUS, Ernst Robert, *Maurice Barrès und die geistigen Grundlagen des französischen Nationalismus*, Bonn: Cohen, 1921. viii, 255pp. Bib. 249–52.

Fr 194 DELBREIL, Jean-Claude, 'Les limites du nationalisme barrésien: Barrès et la Rhénanie, 1919–1923'. *Trav. et Recherches du Centre de Relations Int. Univ. Metz*, 1974. pp. 79–91.

Fr 195   DOTY, Charles Stewart, *From Cultural Rebellion to Counter-revolution: the politics of Maurice Barrès*, Athens: Ohio University Press, 1976. 294pp. Bib. 279-90.

Fr 196   KING, Sylvia M., *Maurice Barrès: la pensée allemande et le problème du Rhine*, Paris: Champion, 1933. x, 296pp. Bib. 271-85.

Fr 197   MADAULE, Jacques, *Le Nationalisme de Maurice Barrès*, Marseilles: Sagittaire, 1943. 269pp.

Fr 198   MASSIS, Henri, *La Pensée de Maurice Barrès*, Paris: Mercure de France, 1909. 84pp. Bib. 73-84.

Fr 199   MIEVILLE, H.L., *La Pensée de Maurice Barrès*, Paris: Nouvelle Rev. Critique, 1934. 249pp.

Fr 200   SOUCY, Robert L., *Fascism in France: the case of Maurice Barrès*, Berkeley: University of California Press, 1972. x, 350pp. Bib. 339-47.

Fr 201   STERNHELL, Zeev, 'Barrès et la gauche: du Boulangisme à la Cocarde, 1889-1895'. *MOUVEMENT SOC.*, **75** (2), 1971. pp. 77-130.

Fr 202   STERNHELL, Zeev, 'Irrationalism and violence in the French radical Right: the case of Maurice Barrès'. In WIENER, Philip Paul and FISCHER, John, *Violence and Aggression in the History of Ideas*, New Brunswick: Rutgers University Press, 1974. pp. 79-98.

Fr 203   STERNHELL, Zeev, *Maurice Barrès et le nationalisme français*, pref. by Raoul Girardet, Paris: Colin, 1972. 395pp. Bib. 374-90. Paris University thesis, 1969.

Fr 204   STERNHELL, Zeev, 'National socialism and anti-semitism: the case of Maurice Barrès'. *J. OF CONTEMP. HIST.*, **8** (4), 1973. pp. 47-66.

Fr 205   THARAUD, Jérôme and Jean, *Mes années chez Bàrres*, Paris: Plon, 1928. 303pp.

Fr 206   THARAUD, Jérôme and Jean, *Pour les fidèles de Barrès*, Paris: Plon, 1944. 231pp.

Fr 207   WEBER, Eugen, 'Inheritance and dilettantism: the politics of Maurice Barrès'. *Historical Reflections*, **2** (1), 1975. pp. 109-31.

Other Prominent Action Française Personalities

Fr 208   ARIES, Philippe, *Le Temps et l'histoire*, Monaco: Ed. du Rocher, 1954. 325pp. Bainville and the AF school of history.

Fr 209 BAINVILLE, Jacques, *Journal, 1901-1935*, Paris: Plon, 1948-9. 3 vols. Bainville (1879-1935), Action Française historian.

Fr 210 JOSEPH, Roger, *Qui est Jacques Bainville? Essai*, Orléans: Lhermitte, 1967. 112pp. Bib. 93-109.

Fr 211 KEYLOR, William R., *Jacques Bainville and the Renaissance of Royalist History in Twentieth-century France*, Baton Rouge: Louisiana State University Press, 1979. xxvi, 349pp. Bib. 329-41.

Fr 212 LINVILLE, Lyle E., 'All along the watchtower: the myth of eternal struggle and World War I in the Nationalist-Royalist writings of Jacques Bainville'. *WEST. SOC. FR. HIST. PROC. ANNU. MEET.*, **2**, 1974. pp. 359-67.

Fr 213 WIEDER, Joachim, *Jacques Bainville, Nationalismus und Klassissismus in Frankreich*, Breslau: Thiel und Hintermeier, 1939. x, 203pp.

Fr 214 BARS, Henry, *Maritain en notre temps*, Paris: Grasset, 1959. 397pp. Bib.

Fr 215 OMACINI, Renato, 'J. Maritain ed i fermenti dell'intellettualità cattolica francese in seno all'Action Française: spunti di reflessione'. *Humanitas (Brescia)*, **NS**, **30** (**12**), 1975. pp. 1090-7.

Fr 216 SCAPINELLI, Giovanna, 'Jacques Maritain e il fascismo'. *Civitas*, **29** (**4**), 1978. pp. 11-28.

Fr 217 SMITH, Brooke W., *Jacques Maritain: anti-modern or ultramodern? an historical analysis of his critics, his thought and his life*, New York: Elsevier, 1976. 194pp. Bib. 163-90.

Fr 218 BOSSAN DE GARAGNOL, E., *Le Colonel La Tour du Pin d'après lui-même*, Paris: Beauchesne, 1934. La Tour du Pin (1834-1924), modern corporatist and early member of Action Française.

Fr 219 BRUCKMANN, Josef, *Hugues Rebell: ein Vorkämpfer des französischen Nationalismus*, Bonn: Röhrscheid, 1937. vi, 118pp. Bib. 111-15. On Hugues Rebell (1867-1905) Action Française activist.

Fr 220 DAUDET, Léon, *Souvenirs des milieux littéraires, politiques, artistiques et médicaux de 1880-1905*, Paris: Nouvelle Librairie Nationale, 1914-21. 6 vols.

Fr 221 DAUDET, Léon, *Souvenirs politiques; réunis par René Wittmann*, Paris: Ed. d'Histoire et d'Art, 1974. x, 307pp. Léon Daudet (1867-1942), AF associate of Maurras.

Fr 222 DOMINIQUE, Pierre (pseud.) [Pierre Lucchini], *Léon Daudet*, Paris: Eds du Vieux Colombier, 1964. 334pp.

Fr 223   JOSEPH, Roger, *Les Combats de Léon Daudet: essai*, Orléans: Auteur, 1962. 184pp.

Fr 224   GLANDY, Anne André, *Maxime Réal del Sarte: sa vie, son oeuvre*, pref. by Henry Bordeaux, Paris: Plon, 1955. 272pp.

Fr 225   RÉAL DEL SARTE, Maxime, *L'Oeuvre de Maxime Réal del Sarte*, intro. Anne André-Glandy, Paris: Plon, 1956. 104pp. Réal del Sarte (1888–1954) one of the leaders of the Action Française Camelots du Roi.

The Second Generation of Fascism in the 1920s and 1930s

Fr 226   ANDREU, Pierre, 'Les idées politiques de la jeunesse intellectuelle de 1927 à la guerre'. *Rev. des Trav. de l'Acad. des Sci. Morales et Polit.*, **ser. 4. 110 (2)**, 1957. pp. 17–35.

Fr 227   ANDREU, Pierre, *Le Rouge et le blanc, 1928–1944*, Paris: La Table Ronde, 1977. 241pp.

Fr 228   *L'Avenir de la République: controverse sur le Parti nouveau, le Syndicat des Partis renovateurs, la Trêve de dix ans . . .; de Charles Albert* [*et al.*], Paris: Librairie Valois, 1927. 438pp. Collection of essays and discussions on new political alignments including the possibility of fascism.

Fr 229   BECK, Yoram, *La Droite nationaliste française: la guerre et la paix, 1933–1938*, Paris University X thesis, 3ᵉ Cycle, 1973. 289pp.

Fr 230   BENDA, Julien, *The Treason of the Intellectuals (La Trahison des clercs)*, tr. by Richard Aldington, New York: Norton, 1969. xii, 244pp. Famous attack on the political passions of Right-wing intellectuals (first pub. 1928).

Fr 231   BLATT, Joel Richard, *French Reaction to Italy, Italian fascism and Mussolini 1919–1925: the views from Paris and the Palazzo Farnese*, University of Rochester thesis, 1977. UM 77-16215. 1182pp.

Fr 232   BONNARD, Abel, *Le Drame du présent. 1. Les modérés*, Paris: Grasset, 1936. 330pp. Minister of Education under Pétain, earlier an associate of Georges Valois and member of Rassemblement National.

Fr 233   MIEVRE, J., 'L'évolution politique d'Abel Bonnard jusq'au printemps 1942'. *REV. D'HIST. DEUX GUERRE MOND.*, **27 (108)**, 1977. pp. 1–26.

Fr 234   BREEN, Catherine Müller-Bapst, *La Droite française et la guerre d'Espagne, 1936–37*, Geneva: Ed. Médécine et Hygiène, 1973. vi, 229pp. Geneva University thesis.

Fr 235   BUSCHKANITZ, Avihu, *L'Influence du fascisme italien sur la droite française dans les années 1922 à 1929*, Paris University Sorbonne thesis, 3ᵉ Cycle, 1976.

Fr 236   *Cahiers de l'Histoire de l'Institut Maurice Thorez*, **11**, **20-1**, 1977. Special issue on the Right between the wars.

Fr 237   CHAMBAZ, Jacques, *Le Front Populaire pour le pain, la liberté, et la paix: quelques aspects du fascisme en France avant le 6 février 1934*, Paris: Eds Sociales, 1961. 223pp. Communist version of history.

Fr 238   DIOUDONNAT, Pierre-Marie, *Je suis partout, 1930–1944: les Maurrassiens devant la tentation fasciste*, Paris: La Table Ronde, 1973. 472pp. On the fascist journal, *Je suis partout*.

Fr 239   GIRARDET, Raoul, 'Notes sur l'esprit d'un fascisme française, 1934–1939'. *REV. FR. DE SCI. POLIT.*, **5** (**3**), 1955. pp. 529–46.

Fr 240   GORDON, Bertram M., 'Radical Right youth in France between the wars'. *WEST. SOC. FR. HIST. PROC. ANNU. MEET.*, **5**, 1977. pp. 313–21.

Fr 241   IRVINE, William D., 'French conservatives and the "New Right" during the 1930s'. *FR. HIST. STUD.*, **8**, 1974. pp. 534–62.

Fr 242   LOUBET DEL BAYLE, Jean-Louis, *Les Non-conformistes des années 30: une tentative de renouvellement de la pensée politique française*, Paris: Ed. du Seuil, 1969. 496pp. Bib. 473–85. See particularly chapter on *Combat* (1934–9). Useful section Biographies pp. 458–71.

Fr 243   MAULNIER, Thierry (pseud.) [Jacques Talagrand], *Au delà du nationalisme*, Paris: Gallimard, 1938. 249pp. AF writer connected with *Je suis partout* and *Combat*.

Fr 244   MAXENCE, Jean-Pierre (pseud.) [Pierre Godmé], *Histoire de dix ans, 1927–1937*, Paris: Gallimard, 1939. 378pp. Important intellectual of the extreme Right (1906–56).

Fr 245   MAZGAJ, Paul, 'The young Sorelians and decadence'. *J. OF CONTEMP. HIST.*, **17** (**1**), 1982. pp. 179–99.

Fr 246   MICAUD, Claude Antoine, *The French Right and Nazi Germany, 1933–1939: a study of public opinion*, New York: Octagon, 1964. 255pp. (First pub. Duke University Press, 1943.)

Fr 247   MÜLLER, Klaus-Jürgen, 'Die französische Rechte und der Faschismus in Frankreich, 1924–1932'. In *Industrielle Gesellschaft und politisches System: Festschrift für Fritz Fischer zum 70. Geburstag*, ed. Dirk Stegmann. [*et al.*], Bonn: V. Neue Gesellschaft, 1978. pp. 413-30.

Fr 248   PIKE, David Wingate, *Les Français et la guerre d'Espagne*, pref. by Pierre Renouvin, Paris: PUF, 1975. 467pp. Bib. 412-19.

Fr 249   *Les Relations Franco-Allemandes, 1933-1939, Strasbourg, 7-10 October 1975*, ed. F.G. Dreyfus, Paris: CNRS, 1976. 424pp. Articles by A. Gisselbrecht, *Quelques interpretations du phenomène nazi en France en 1933 et 1939*, pp. 151-66; and Pierre de Senarclens, *Brasillach, le Fascisme et l'Allemagne: essai d'interpretation*, pp. 179-208.

Fr 250   SOUCY, Robert L., 'French fascist intellectuals in the 1930s: an old New Left?' *FR. HIST. STUD.*, **8** (**3**), 1974. pp. 445-58.

Fr 251   TOUCHARD, Jean, 'L'esprit des années trente'. In GUIRAL, P. and others (eds), *Tendances politiques dans la vie française depuis 1789*, Paris: Hachette, 1960. pp. 90-120.

Georges Valois (1878-1945) and the Faisceau

Fr 252   DOUGLAS, Allen Richard, *Georges Valois and the French Right: a study in the genesis of fascism*, University of California, Los Angeles thesis, 1979. UM 79-21388. 522pp.

Fr 253   GUCHET, Yves, *Georges Valois: l'Action Française, le Faisceau, la république syndicale*, Paris: Eds. Albatros, 1975. 246pp.

Fr 254   GUCHET, Yves, 'Georges Valois ou l'illusion fasciste'. *REV. FR. DE SCI. POLIT.*, **15** (**6**), 1965. pp. 1111-44.

Fr 255   LEVEY, Jules, 'Georges Valois and the Faisceau: the making and breaking of a fascist'. *FR. HIST. STUD.*, **8** (**2**), 1973. pp. 279-304.

Fr 256   LEVEY, Jules, *The Sorelian Syndicalists: Édouard Berth, Georges Valois, and Hubert Lagardelle*, Columbia University thesis, 1967. UM 70-07016. 387pp.

Fr 257   MAZIÈRES, Georges, *L'Oeuvre économique de Georges Valois*, Castelnaudary, 1937. 189pp. Thesis.

Fr 258   STERNHELL, Zeev, 'Anatomie d'un mouvement fasciste en France: le "Faisceau" de Georges Valois'. *REV. FR. SCI. POLIT.*, **26** (**1**), 1976. pp. 5-40.

Fr 259   TINGLEY, Clarence D., 'Georges Valois and the "Faisceau": apocalyptic politics in twentieth-century France'. *WEST. SOC. FR. HIST. PROC. ANNU. MEET.*, **4**, 1976. pp. 382-90.

Fr 260   VALOIS, Georges (pseud.) [Alfred Gressent], *D'un siècle à l'autre: chronique d'une génération; éd. définitive*, Paris: Nouvelle Librairie Nationale, 1924. 299pp. Memoirs.

Fr 261   VALOIS, Georges (pseud.) [Alfred Gressent], *L'Économie nouvelle*, Paris: Nouvelle Librairie Nationale, 1919. 320pp.

Fr 262   VALOIS, Georges (pseud.) [Alfred Gressent], *Le Fascisme*, Paris: Nouvelle Librairie Nationale, 1927. 160pp.

Fr 263   VALOIS, Georges (pseud.) [Alfred Gressent], *L'Homme contre l'argent: souvenirs de dix ans, 1918-1928*, Paris: Valois, 1928. 381pp.

Francisme and Solidarité Française

Fr 264   DENIEL, Alain, *Bucard et le Francisme*, Paris: Jean Picollec, 1979. 334pp. Bib. 320-4.

Fr 265   JACOMET, Arnaud, 'Les chefs du Francisme: Marcel Bucard et Paul Guiraud'. *REV. D'HIST. DEUX GUERRE MOND.*, **25** (**97**), 1975. pp. 45-66.

Fr 266   JACOMET, Arnaud, *Marcel Bucard et le Francisme, 1933-1939*, University of Paris-Nanterre thesis. Maitrîse d'histoire, 1970.

Fr 267   SCHOR, Ralph, 'Xenophobie et extrême-droite: l'exemple de "L'Ami du Peuple" 1928-1937'. *REV. D'HIST. MOD. CONTEMP.*, **23** (**1**), 1976. pp. 116-44.

The Jeunesses Patriotes

Fr 268   SOUCY, Robert L., 'Centrist fascism: the Jeunesses Patriotes'. *J. OF CONTEMP. HIST.*, **16** (**2**), 1981. pp. 349-68.

Fr 269   TAITTINGER, Pierre, *La Rêve rouge*, Paris: Eds. du National, 1930. 366pp. Conservative nationalist (1887-1965), leader of the Les Jeunesses Patriotes and later the Parti National Populaire.

The Events of February 1934

Fr 270   BELOFF, Max, 'The sixth of February'. In JOLL, James (ed.), *The Decline of the Third Republic*, New York: Praeger, 1959, pp. 9-35.

Fr 271   BERSTEIN, Serge, *Le 6 février 1934*, Paris: Gallimard, 1975. 258pp.

Fr 272 BONNEVAY, Laurent Marie Benoit, *Les Journées sanglantes de février 1934: pages d'histoire*, Paris: Flammarion, 1935. 249pp. By the President of the Commission of Inquiry into the events of February 1934.

Fr 273 CHASTENET, Jacques, 'Les journées sanglantes de février 1934'. *Rev. de Paris*, **69** (**3**), 1962. pp. 3–18.

Fr 274 CHAVARDES, Maurice, *Un Campagne de presse: la droite française et le 6 février 1934*, Paris: Flammarion, 1970. 119pp. Bib. 107–13.

Fr 275 CHAVARDES, Maurice, *Le 6 février 1934: la République en danger*, Paris: Calmann-Lévy, 1966. 359pp. Bib. 354.

Fr 276 HENRIOT, Philippe, *Le 6 février*, Paris: Flammarion, 1934. 247pp. Rightist version of events.

Fr 277 KÖLLER, Heinz, *Frankreich zwischen Faschismus und Demokratie, 1932–1934*, Berlin: Akademie V., 1978. iv, 486pp. Bib. 467–78.

Fr 278 LE CLÈRE, Marcel, *Le 6 février*, Paris: Hachette, 1967. 240pp. Bib. 237–8.

Fr 279 RÉMOND, René, 'Explication du 6 février'. *Politique*, **7/8**, 1959. pp. 218–30.

Jacques Doriot (1898–1945) and the Parti Populaire Français

Fr 280 ALLARDYCE, Gilbert D., 'French communism comes of age: Jacques Doriot, Henri Barbé and the disinheritance of the Jeunesses Communistes, 1923–1931'. *DURHAM UNIV. J.*, **46**, 1974. pp. 129–45.

Fr 281 ALLARDYCE, Gilbert D., 'Jacques Doriot et l'esprit fasciste en France'. *REV. D'HIST. DEUX GUERRE MOND.*, **25** (**97**), 1975. pp. 31–44.

Fr 282 ALLARDYCE, Gilbert D., *The Political Transition of Jacques Doriot, 1926–1936*, University of Iowa thesis, 1966. UM 66–11636. 308pp.

Fr 283 ALLARDYCE, Gilbert D., 'The political transition of Jacques Doriot'. *J. OF CONTEMP. HIST.*, **1** (**1**), 1966. pp. 56–74.

Fr 284 ANDREU, Pierre, 'Un point obscur d'histoire: le complot des Acacias'. *SCI. HIST.*, **34** (**5**), 1955. pp. 97–99. Doriot and the founding of PPF.

Fr 285 BARTHELEMY, Victor, *Du Communisme au fascisme: l'histoire d'un engagement politique: Jacques Doriot*, Paris: Michel, 1978. 508pp. Ex-communist who joined Doriot's PPF.

Fr 286 BRUNET, Jean-Paul, 'Doriot: du communisme au fascisme'. *Histoire*, **21**, 1980. pp. 22-9.

Fr 287 BRUNET, Jean-Paul, 'Réflexions sur la scission de Doriot, février–juin 1934'. *MOUVEMENT SOC.*, **70**, 1970. pp. 43-63.

Fr 288 CARRIER, Fred James, *Jacques Doriot: a political biography*, University of Wisconsin thesis, 1968. 360pp.

Fr 289 DORIOT, Jacques, *La France avec nous*, Paris: Flammarion, 1937. 142pp.

Fr 290 DORIOT, Jacques, *Je suis un homme du Maréchal*, Paris: Grasset, 1941. 130pp.

Fr 291 DORIOT, Jacques, *Le Mouvement et les hommes*, Paris: Eds de France, 1942. 59pp. Includes PPF programme.

Fr 292 DORIOT, Jacques, *Refaire la France*, Paris: Grasset, 1938. 120pp.

Fr 293 DRIEU LA ROCHELLE, Pierre, *Avec Doriot*, Paris: Gallimard, 1937. 214pp. Collection of articles from *L'Emancipation Nationale*.

Fr 294 DRIEU LA ROCHELLE, Pierre, *Doriot ou la vie d'un ouvrier français*, Paris: Eds Populaires Françaises, 1936. 31pp.

Fr 295 LEJEUNE, Bernard-Henry, *Historisme de Jacques Doriot et du Parti Populaire Français*, Amiens: Les Nouveaux Cahiers du CERPES, 1977. 1. *Avant le défaite de 1940*. 135pp.

Fr 296 MARION, Paul, *Programme du Parti Populaire Français: Président Jacques Doriot*, Paris: Les Oeuvres Françaises, 1938. 124pp. Bib. 119.

Fr 297 MILLET, Raymond, *Doriot et ses compagnons*, Paris: Plon, 1937. 94pp.

Fr 298 PELLEGRIN, René, *La Vie-éclair de Jacques Doriot*, Villeneuve-les-Avignon: Centre de Synthèse Communautaire, 1970. 153pp. Bib. 151-2. 1. *Jacques Doriot communiste*.

Fr 299 SABIANI, Simon, *Colère du peuple*, pref. by Jacques Doriot, Paris: Les Oeuvres Françaises, 1937. x, 220pp. Parti Populaire Française.

Fr 300 SCOTT, Joanna Vecchiarelli and FOUQUET, Patricia Root, 'The 1934 riots and the emergence of French fascism: the case of

Jacques Doriot'. *WEST. SOC. FR. HIST. PROC. ANNU. MEET.*, **4**, 1976. pp. 391-401.

Fr 301   WOLF, Dieter, *Die Doriot-Bewegung: ein Beitrag zur Geschichte des französischen Faschismus*, Stuttgart: Deutsche Verlags-Anstalt, 1967. 408pp. Bib. 362-90. French tr., *Doriot, du communisme à la collaboration*, Paris: Fayard, 1969.

The Anciens Combattants and Croix de Feu

Fr 302   AUCOUTURIER, Michel, *Au Service des Croix de Feu, octobre 1934-19 juin 1936 et du Parti Social Français, 1936*, Charleville: Impr. des Ardennes, 1936. 288pp.

Fr 303   CHOPINE, Paul, *Six ans chez les Croix de Feu*, Paris: Gallimard, 1935. 191pp.

Fr 304   CLIFFORD-VAUGHAN, Frederick, 'The Croix de Feu: a manifestation of anti-parliamentarism in France'. *AUST. J. POLIT. HIST.*, **12** (1), 1966. pp. 24-31.

Fr 305   CREYSSEL, Paul, *La Rocque contre Tardieu*, pref. by Colonel de la Rocque, Paris: Sorlot, 1938. 127pp. Pro-La Rocque.

Fr 306   FLORIN, Jean-Pierre, 'Des Croix de Feu au Parti Social Française: une mutation réussie? L'exemple de la Féderation du Nord, 1936-1939'. *REV. DU NORD*, **59**, 1977. pp. 233-71.

Fr 307   *La France et l'Allemagne, 1932-1936: Communications présentées au Colloque Franco-Allemand tenu à Paris du 10 au 12 mars 1977*, Paris: CNRS, 1980. 417pp. Articles by Prost on the Ancien Combattants and Machefer on the Croix de Feu.

Fr 308   LACRATELLE, Jacques de, *Qui est La Rocque?* Paris: Flammarion, 1936. 47pp.

Fr 309   LA ROCQUE, Edith de and Gilles de, *La Rocque tel qu'il était*, Paris: Fayard, 1962. 298pp. La Rocque's widow and son defend his policies and ideas.

Fr 310   LA ROCQUE, François, Comte de, *The Fiery Cross: the call to public service in France*, London: Dickson, 1936. 216pp. Tr. of *Service public*, Paris: Grasset, 1934.

Fr 311   LA ROCQUE, François, Comte de, *La Rocque: un chef, des actes, des idées: suivi de documents sur les doctrines de la rénovation nationale*, ed. Henry Malherbe, Paris: Plon, 1936. 137pp.

Fr 312   MACHEFER, Philippe, 'Les Croix de Feu'. *INF. HIST.*, **34** (**1**), 1972. pp. 28-33.

Fr 313   MACHEFER, Philippe, 'Le Parti Social Français'. In RÉMOND, René and BOUDIN, Janine (eds), *La France et les Français en 1938-1939*, Paris: Fond. des Sci. Polit., 1978. pp. 307-26.

Fr 314   MACHEFER, Philippe, 'Le Parti Social Français en 1936-1937'. *INF. HIST.*, **34** (**2**), 1972. pp. 74-80.

Fr 315   MACHEFER, Philippe, 'Sur quelques aspects de l'activité du Colonel de la Rocque et du Progrès Social Français pendant la Second Guerre Mondiale'. *REV. D'HIST. DEUX. GUERRE MOND.*, **15** (**58**), 1965. pp. 35-56.

Fr 316   MACHEFER, Philippe, 'Tardieu et La Rocque'. *BULL. SOC. D'HIST. MOD.*, **72** (**5**), 1973. pp. 11-21.

Fr 317   MACHEFER, Philippe, 'L'Union des Droites, le PSF et le Front de la Liberté, 1936-1937'. *REV. D'HIST. MOD. ET CONTEMP.*, **17** (**1**), 1970. pp. 112-26. Alliance between La Rocque's PSF and Doriot's Freedom Front.

Fr 318   PROST, Antoine, *Les Anciens combattants et la société française. 1914-1939*, Paris: FNSP, 1977. 3 vols. Bib. vol. 1. 207-37. History, sociology and ideology of veterans movements, most of them anti-war and apolitical, a very few extreme Right-wing.

Fr 319   PUJO, Maurice, *Comment La Rocque a trahi*, Paris: Sorlot, 1937. 188pp.

F 320   REMOND, René,'Les anciens combattants et la politique'. *REV. FR. DE SCI. POLIT.*, **5** (**2**), 1955. pp. 267-90.

Fr 321   RUDAUX, Philippe, *Les Croix de Feu et le PSF*, Paris: Eds. France-Empire, 1967. 399pp. Sympathetic account by ex-member.

Fr 322   SOUCY, Robert L., 'France: veterans' politics between the wars'. In WARD, Stephen R. (ed.), *The War Generation*, Port Washington: Kennikat Press, 1975. pp. 59-103.

Fr 323   VEUILLOT, François, *La Rocque et son parti: comme je les ai vus*, Paris: Plon, 1938. 93pp.

Marcel Déat, Neo-Socialism and the Rassemblement National Populaire

Fr 324   ABEL, Jean-Pierre (pseud.) [René Château], *L'Age de Caïn: premier témoinage sur les dessous de la libération de Paris*, Paris: Les Eds. Nouvelles, 1948. 239pp. Material on Déat and RNP.

Fr 325   BAKER, Donald N., 'Two paths to socialism: Marcel Déat and Marceau Pivert'. *J. OF CONTEMP. HIST.*, 11 (1), 1976. pp. 107–28.

Fr 326   BERGOUNIOUX, Alain, 'Le néo-socialisme: Marcel Déat, réformisme traditionnel ou esprit des années trentes'. *REV. HIST.*, 102 (260), 1978. pp. 389–412.

Fr 327   COINTET, Jean-Paul, 'Marcel Déat et le parti unique (été 1940)'.*REV. D'HIST. DEUX. GUERRE MOND.*, 23 (91), 1973. pp. 1–22.

Fr 328   DEAT, Marcel, *Le Parti unique*, Paris: Aux Armes de France, 1942. 180pp. Articles from *L'Oeuvres July–Sept. 1942*.

Fr 329   DEAT, Marcel, *Pensée allemande et pensée française*, Paris: Aux Armes de France, 1944. 160pp.

Fr 330   DEAT, Marcel, *Perspectives socialistes*, Paris: Librairie Valois, 1930. 246pp.

Fr 331   DURAND, Yves and BOHBOT, David, 'La collaboration politique dans les pays de la Loire Moyenne: étude historique et socio-politique du RNP en Indre-et-Loire et dans le Loiret'. *REV. D'HIST. DEUX. GUERRE MOND.*, 23 (91), 1973. pp. 57–76. Rassemblement National Populaire.

Fr 332   GOODMAN, Emily Hartshorne, *The Socialism of Marcel Déat*, Stanford University thesis, 1973. UM 73-30401. 418pp.

Fr 333   GROSSMANN, Stanley, 'L'évolution de Marcel Déat'. *REV. D'HIST. DEUX. GUERRE MOND.*, 25 (97), 1975. pp. 3–29.

Fr 334   GROSSMANN, Stanley, *Neo-socialism: a study in political metamorphosis*, University of Wisconsin thesis, 1969. UM 72-22092. 453pp.

Fr 335   LEFRANC, Georges, 'Marcel Déat à travers quelques-uns de ses écrits'. *INF. HIST.*, 42 (4), 1980. pp. 157–61.

Fr 336   MONTAGNON, Barthélemy, *Neo-socialisme? ordre, autorité, nation*, pref. and commentary by Max Bonnefous, Paris: Grasset, 1933. 140pp.

Fr 337   PROST, Antoine, 'Le rapport de Déat en faveur du parti national unique, juillet 1940: essai d'analyse lexicale'. *REV. FR. DE SCI. POLIT.*, **23** (5), 1973. pp. 933-71.

Fr 338   VARENNES, Claude (pseud.) [Georges Albertini], *Le Destin de Marcel Déat*, Paris: Janmaray, 1948. 254pp.

Henri Dorgères and Dorgèrisme

Fr 339   BARRAL, Pierre, *Les Agrariens française de Méline à Pisani*, Paris: Colin, 1968. 386pp. Bib. 364-72. Includes Dorgères and rural fascism.

Fr 340   DORGERES, Henri (pseud.) [Henri d'Halluin], *Au XXe siècle 10 ans de jacquerie*, Paris: Eds du Scorpion, 1959. 187pp.

Fr 341   DORGERES, Henri (pseud.) [Henri d'Halluin], *Haut les fourches*, Paris: Les Oeuvres Françaises, 1935. 220pp. Leader of the populist, xenophobic, rural fascists.

Fr 342   ORY, Pascal, 'Le Dorgèrisme: institutions et discours d'une colère paysanne, 1929-1939'. *REV. D'HIST. MOD. ET CONTEMP.*, **22** (2), 1975. pp. 168-90.

Fr 343   ORY, Pascal, *Henri Dorgères et la 'Défense Paysanne' des origines à 1939*, Paris University X-Nanterre, Mémoire de Maîtrise, 1970. 259pp.

The Cagoule (Comité Secret d'Action Révolutionnaire) and Mouvement Social Révolutionnaire

Fr 344   BOURDREL, Philippe, *La Cagoule: 30 ans de complots*, Paris: Albin Michel, 1970. 282pp. On the Comité Secret d'Action Révolutionnaire.

Fr 345   DAGORE (pseud.) [Aristide Corre], *Les Carnets secrets de la Cagoule*, pub. by Christian Bernadac, Paris: Ed. France-Empire, 1977. 609pp. Author a collaborator of Deloncle in AF and the Cagoule.

Fr 346   DESERT, Joseph, *Toute la vérité sur l'affaire de la Cagoule, sa trahison, ses crimes, ses hommes*, Paris: Librairie des Sciences et des Arts, 1946. 111pp.

Fr 347   FONTENAY, Fernand, *La Cagoule contre la France: ses crimes, son organisation, ses chefs, ses inspirateurs*, Paris: Eds. Sociales Int., 1938. 188pp.

Fr 348   GORDON, Bertram M., 'Un soldat du fascisme: l'évolution politique de Joseph Darnand'. *REV. D'HIST. DEUX GUERRE MOND.*, **27** (**108**), 1977. pp. 43–70.

Fr 349   GORDON, Bertram M., 'The condottieri of the collaboration: Mouvement Social Révolutionnaire'. *J. OF CONTEMP. HIST.*, **10** (**2**), 1975. pp. 261–82.

Fr 350   GROUSSARD, Georges André, *Chemins secret*, Paris: Bader-Dufour, 1962. Vol. 1. Updated by *Service secret, 1940–45*. Paris, La Table Ronde, 1964. 606pp. Author involved in Cagoule plots and collaboration before joining resistance.

Fr 351   LOUSTAUNAU-LACAU, Georges, *Mémoires d'un français rebelle, 1914–1948*, Paris: Laffont, 1948. 365pp. Author (1894–1955) anti-communist associate of Doriot, member of the Cagoule, and founder of Corvignolles but not a collaborator.

Fr 352   MAHE, Andre and SOULES, Georges, *La Fin du nihilisme*, Paris: Sorlot, 1943. 250pp. MSR tract illustrating a Nietzschean-Sorelian collaborationist ideology.

Fr 353   MONDANEL, Pierre, 'Un point d'histoire: les Cagoulards à Pont-du-Château'. *Ass. des Amis du Vieux Pont-du-Château*, **8**, 1977. pp. 6–13.

Fr 354   TOURNOUX, Jean Raymond, *L'Histoire secrète*, Paris: Plon, 1962. 396pp. Includes Cagoulards.

Fr 355   WARNER, Geoffrey, 'The Cagoulard conspiracy'. *Hist. Today*, **10** (**7**), 1960. pp. 443–50.

Collaborationism and the Second World War

Fr 356   AMOUROUX, Henri, *Le Grande histoire des français sous l'occupation*, Paris: Laffont, 1976–. 8 vols to appear. Bibs. **2**. *Quarante millions de Pétainistes*. **3**. *Les Beaux des Collabos, juin 1941–juin 1942*.

Fr 357   AMOUROUX, Henri, *La Vie des français sous l'occupation*, Paris: Fayard, 1961. 577pp.

Fr 358   ARON, Robert, *Histoire de l'Épuration*, Paris: Fayard, 1967–75. 3 vols.

Fr 359   AZEMA, Jean-Pierre, *La Collaboration, 1940–1944*, Paris: PUF, 1975. 152pp. Bib. 151–2.

Fr 360   AZIZ, Philippe, *Au Service de l'ennemi: Gestapo française en province*, Paris: Fayard, 1972. 186pp.

Fr 361   AZIZ, Philippe, *Tu trahiras sans vergogne: histoire de deux collabos, Bonny et Lafont*, Paris: Le Livre de Poche, 1973. 379pp.

Fr 362   BARDECHE, Maurice, *Lettre à François Mauriac*, Paris: La Pensée Libre, 1947. 195pp. Argues that collaborators served the interests of France.

Fr 363   BILLIG, Joseph, *La Solution finale de la question Juive: essai sur ses principes dans le III*ᵉ *Reich et en France sous l'occupation*, ed. Serge and Beate Klarsfeld, Paris: Klarsfeld, 1977. 207pp. Bib. 187-8.

Fr 364   BOURGET, Pierre, *Histoires secrètes de l'occupation de Paris, 1940-1944*, Paris: Hachette, 1970. Vol. 1. Includes collaboration.

Fr 365   BRINON, Fernand de, *Mémoires*, Paris: LLC, 1949. 261pp. Memoirs of the Vichy ambassador to the occupation authorities.

Fr 366   BRINON, Fernand de, and others, defendants, *Procès de la collaboration: Fernand de Brinon, Joseph Darnand, Jean Luchaire: compte rendu sténographique*, Paris: Albin Michel, 1948. 634pp.

Fr 367   *Bulletin de la Commission de l'Histoire Deuxième Guerre Mondiale*. Series of Enquêtes sur les mouvements de collaboration in various areas. Vol. 219-. 1976-.

Fr 368   BUTLER, Marie-Hélène, 'La collaboration dans la préfecture régionale de Rennes'. *REV. D'HIST. DEUX. GUERRE MOND.*, **30** (**117**), 1980. pp. 3-31.

Fr 369   Centre de Documentation Juive Contemporaine, *Les Juifs sous l'occupation: recueil de textes français et allemands, 1940-44*, Paris: CDJC, 1945. viii, 192pp.

Fr 370   CHANAL, Michel, 'La collaboration dans l'Isère, 1940—1944'. *Cahiers d'Histoire Pub. par les Univ. de Clermont, Lyons, Grenoble*, **22** (**4**), 1977. pp. 377-403.

Fr 371   CHARBONNEAU, Henry, *Les Mémoires de Porthos*, Paris: Desroches, 1967-69. 2 vols. Vol. 2, entitled *Le roman noir de la droite française*, chronicles a journey from Action Française to unambiguous fascism. Information on Cagoule, Mouvement Social Révolutionnaire, Milice.

Fr 372   CHÂTEAUBRIANT, Alphonse de, *Cahiers, 1906-1951*, Paris: Grasset, 1955. 345pp. Châteaubriant (1877-1951) one of the leaders of Front Révolutionnaire National 1943 onwards.

Fr 373   MAUGENDRE, Louis-Alphonse, *Alphonse de Châteaubriant,*

1877-1951, Paris: Bonne, 1977. 443pp. One of the leaders of Front Révolutionnaire National an attempt at rapprochement between the various collaborationist groups.

Fr 374 COTTA, Michèle, *La Collaboration, 1940-1944*, Paris: Colin, 1964. 333pp. Bib. 305-16. List of principal political movements in the occupied zone and the Parisian political press.

Fr 375 DANK, Milton, *The French against the French: collaboration and resistance*, Philadelphia: Lippincott, 1974. London: Cassell, 1978. 365pp. Bib. 342-7.

Fr 376 DAVEY, Owen Anthony, 'The origins of the Légion des Volontaires Française contre le Bolchévisme'. *J. OF CONTEMP. HIST.*, **6** (**4**), 1971. pp. 29-45.

Fr 377 LA MAZIÈRE, Christian de, *Ashes of Honour*, London: Wingate, 1975. 319pp. Tr. of *Le rêveur casqué*, Paris: Laffont, 1972, by Francis Stuart. Author describes experiences in the French Waffen-SS.

Fr 379 LEROY, Jean-Louis, *Histoire d'un marin breton alcoolique engagé volontaire dans la LVF*, Paris: Tema Eds, 1977. 250pp. Memoirs of the LVF.

Fr 380 MABIRE, Jean, *Les S.S. français*, Paris: Fayard, 1973-5. 3 vols.

Fr 381 MERGLEN, Albert, 'Soldats français sous uniformes allemands, 1941-1945: LVF et Waffen-SS Français'. *REV. D'HIST. DEUX GUERRE MOND.*, **27** (**108**), 1977. pp. 71-84.

Fr 382 DELPERRIE DE BAYAC, Jacques, *Histoire de la Milice, 1918-1945*, Paris: Fayard, 1969. 685pp.

Fr 383 LAURENS, André, 'La Milice Française en Ariège, 1943-1944: quelques faits'. *Resistance R4.* (*Toulouse*), **3** (**11**), 1980. pp. 27-39.

Fr 384 LUIRARD, Monique, 'La Milice Française dans la Loire'. *REV. D'HIST. DEUX. GUERRE MOND.*, **23** (**91**), 1973. pp. 77-102.

Fr 385 DIOUDONNAT, Pierre-Marie, 'La pénétration financière allemande dans la presse de la collaboration: l'exemple des éditions Pierre Charron'. *Presse et Politique Colloque: actes du Colloque de Nanterre, mars 1973*, Howlles: CEREP, 1975. pp. 134-46.

Fr 386 DUPRAT, François, 'Les mouvements d'extrême droite en France 1940-41'. *REV. D'HIST. DU FASCISME*, **8**, 1976. pp. 3-11. **9**, 1976. pp. 5-101.

Fr 387 FABRE-LUCE, Alfred, *Journal de la France; éd. définitive*, Paris: Fayard, 1969. 679pp. Pro-Vichy and pro-collaborator view of the events of 1940-5.

Fr 388   GANIER-RAYMOND, Philippe, *Une Certain France: l'antisémitisme 40–44*, Paris: Balland, 1975. 193pp.

Fr 389   GORDON, Bertram M., *Collaborationism in France during the Second World War*, Ithaca: Cornell University Press, 1980. 393pp. Bib. 361–78. List of lesser movements of the collabortion, pp. 357–60.

Fr 390   GORDON, Bertram M., 'Fascists and fissures: the complex history of the Paris collaboration, 1940–44'. *WEST. SOC. FR. HIST. PROC. ANNU. MEET.*, **1**, 1973. pp. 391–410.

Fr 391   GOUNAND, P., 'Les groupements de collaboration dans une ville française occupée: Dijon'. *REV.D'HIST. DEUX. GUERRE MOND.*, **23 (91)**, 1973. pp. 47–56.

Fr 392   GUEHENNO, Jean, *Journal des années noires, 1940–1944*, Paris: Gallimard, 1947. 346pp.

Fr 393   GUILLON, Jean-Marie, 'Les mouvements de collaboration dans le Var: bilan d'une enquête'. *REV. D'HIST. DEUX. GUERRE MOND.*, **29 (113)**, 1979. pp. 91–110.

Fr 394   HOFFMANN, Stanley, 'Collaboration in France during World War II'. *J. OF MOD. HIST.*, **40 (3)**, 1968. pp. 375–95.

Fr 395   JÄCKEL, Eberhard, *Frankreich in Hitlers Europa: die deutsche Frankreich-Politik im 2 Weltkrieg*, Stuttgart: Deutsche Verlags-Anstalt, 1966. 396pp. Bib. 375–87.

Fr 396   LEVY, Claude, *Les Nouveaux Temps et l'idéologie de la collaboration*, Paris: Colin, 1974. x, 260pp. On the journal ed. by Jean Luchaire.

Fr 397   LEVY, Claude, 'La presse de collaboration en France occupée: conditions d'existence'. *REV.D'HIST. DEUX. GUERRE MOND.*, **20 (80)**, 1970. pp. 87–100.

Fr 398   LUCHAIRE, Corinne, *Ma drôle de vie*, Paris: Eds. Sun, 1949. 250pp. Memoirs of the daughter of Jean Luchaire head of the pro-Nazi French press.

Fr 399   MICHEL, Henri, 'Aspects politiques de l'occupation de la France par les allemands, juin 1940–dec. 1944'. *REV. D'HIST. DEUX. GUERRE MOND.*, **14 (54)**, 1964. pp. 1–40.

Fr 400   MILWARD, Alan, *The New Order and the French Economy* Oxford: University Press, 1970. viii. 320pp. Bib. 301–10.

Fr 401   NOVICK, Peter, *The Resistance versus Vichy: the purge of collaborators in liberated France*, London: Chatto & Windus. New York: Columbia University Press, 1968. xv, 245pp. Bib. 225–36.

Fr 402   ORY, Pascal, *Les Collaborateurs, 1940–1945*, Paris: Ed. du Seuil, 1976. 331pp. Bib. 301-9.

Fr 403   ORY, Pascal (ed.), *La France allemande, 1933–1945: paroles du collaborationisme français*, Paris: Gallimard, 1977. 276pp. Collections of writings by fascists and collaborators.

Fr 404   ORY, Pascal, *Le Petit Nazi illustré: une pédagogie hitlérienne en culture française: 'Le Téméraire', 1943–1944*, pref. by Léon Poliakov, Paris: Ed. Albatros, 1979. 122pp.

Fr 405   POLONSKI, Jacques, *La Presse, la propagande, et l'opinion publique sous l'occupation*, Paris: Centre de Doc. Juive Contemp., 1946. 157pp.

Fr 406   REBATET, Lucien, *Les Mémoires d'un fasciste*, pref. by Jean-Jacques Pauvert, Paris: Pauvert, 1976. 1. *Les Décombres, 1938–1940*.

Fr 407   VANDROMME, Pol, *Rebatet*, Paris: Eds. Universitaires, 1968. 127pp. Bib. 123.

Fr 408   ZIMMERMAN, Margarete, 'Ein Bestseller des Okkupationsjahre Lucien Rebatets Pamphlet Les Décombres, 1942'. *Lendemains (Berlin)*, 4 (**14**), 1979. pp. 105-16.

Fr 409   SADOUN, Marc, 'Les facteurs de la conversion au socialisme collaborateur'. *REV. FR. SCI. POLIT.*, **28** (**3**), 1978. pp. 459-87.

Fr 410   SESTER, André, *Résistance et collaboration: aspects vosgiens*, Epinal: Ed. du Sapin D'Or, 1976. 283pp.

Fr 411   SICARD, Maurice Ivan [Saint-Paulien (pseud.)], *Histoire de la collaboration*, Paris: L'Esprit Nouveau, 1964. xi, 610pp. Author was in charge of PPF propaganda in the South.

Fr 412   SUKHOMLIN, Vassilii Karsilievich, *Les Hitlériens à Paris*, tr. by Lily Denis, pref. by Jean-Maurice Hermann, Paris: Editeurs Français Reunis, 1967. 247pp. Diary of Soviet journalist.

Marshal Pétain and the Vichy Government

Fr 413   ARGENSON, Marc Pierre, Marquis d', *Pétain et le pétinisme: essai de psychologie*, Paris: Ed. Créator, 1953. 180pp.

Fr 414   BLOND, Georges, *Pétain, 1856–1951*, Paris: P. de la Cité, 1966. 591pp.

Fr 415   BOURGET, Pierre, *Un certain Philippe Pétain*, Tournai: Casterman, 1966. 319pp.

Fr 416   GRIFFITHS, Richard M., *Marshal Pétain*, London: Constable, 1970. xix, 379pp. Bib. 367-72. US edn, *Pétain: a biography*, New York: Doubleday, 1972.

Fr 417   ISORNI, Jacques, *Pétain a sauvé la France*, Paris: Flammarion, 1964. 140pp.

Fr 418   ISORNI, Jacques, *Philippe Pétain*, Paris: La Table Ronde, 1972/3. 2 vols. Apologia.

Fr 419   JEANTET, Gabriel, *Pétain contre Hitler*, pref. by Jacques Laurent, Paris: La Table Ronde, 1966. xi, 337pp.

Fr 420   NOGUERES, Louis, *La Véritable procès du Maréchal Pétain*, Paris: Fayard, 1955. 659pp. Repr. by Edito-Service, Geneva, 1972.

Fr 421   PELLISSIER, Pierre, *Philippe Pétain*, Paris: Hachette, 1980. 355pp.

Fr 422   PETAIN, Henri Philippe Bénoni Omer, *Actes et écrits; éd. établie . . . par Jacques Isorni*, Paris: Flammarion, 1974. 653pp.

Fr 423   PETAIN, Henri Philippe Bénoni Omer, *Quatre années au pouvoir; avec un avertissement de Jacques Isorni*, 2nd edn, Paris: Couronne Littéraire, 1949. 178pp. Essai de bib. des oeuvres de Pétain 161-75.

Fr 424   PETAIN, Henri Philippe Bénoni Omer, defendant, *Procès du Maréchal Pétain: compte-rendu officiel in extenso des audiences de la Haute Court de Justice, 23 juillet-14 aout 1945*, Paris: Pariente, 1976. 492pp.

Fr 425   PLUMYENE, Jean, *Pétain*, Paris: Eds du Seuil, 1964. 189pp. Bib. 188-9.

Fr 426   TOURNOUX, Jean Raymond, *Pétain et la France: la Seconde Guerre Mondiale*, Paris: Plon, 1980. 574pp.

Fr 427   ARON, Robert, *Les Grandes dossiers de l'histoire contemporaine*, new edn, Paris: Perrin, 1969. 418pp.

Fr 428   ARON, Robert, *Histoire des années 40*, Paris: Tallandier, 1976-. 1. *Histoire de Vichy: la naissance de Vichy*. 522pp.

Fr 429   ARON, Robert and ELGEY, Georgette, *The Vichy regime, 1940-1944*, tr. by Humphrey Hare, London: Putnam. New York: Macmillan, 1958. 536pp. Abridged tr. of *Histoire de Vichy*, Paris: Fayard, 1954. Bib. in US edn 518-20.

Fr 430   AUPHAN, Gabriel Adrien Joseph Paul, *Histoire élémentaire de Vichy*, Paris: Ed. France Empire, 1971. 359pp. Author an Admiral and close friend of Pétain.

73

Fr 431   BECHTEL, Guy, *Laval vingt ans après*, Paris: Laffont, 1963. 373pp. Bib.

Fr 432   COLE, Hubert, *Laval: a biography*, London: Heinemann. New York: Putnam, 1963. vii, 314pp. Bib. 303–4.

Fr 433   JACQUEMIN, Gaston, *La Vie publique de Pierre Laval, 1883–1945*, Paris: Plon, 1972. 350pp.

Fr 434   KUPFERMAN, Fred, *Pierre Laval*, Paris: Masson, 1976. 182pp.

Fr 435   LAVAL, Pierre, defendant, *Procès Laval: compte rendu sténographique*, Paris: Albin Michel, 1946. 311pp.

Fr 436   LAVAL, Pierre, *Laval parle: notes et mémoires rédigés par P. Laval dans sa cellule*, Geneva: Eds. du Cheval Ailé, 1947. 284pp.

Fr 437   MALLET, Alfred, *Pierre Laval*, Paris: Amiot-Dumont, 1955. 2 vols. Bib. Vol. 2, 406–21.

Fr 438   WARNER, Geoffrey, *Pierre Laval and the Eclipse of France*, London: Eyre & Spottiswoode. New York: Macmillan, 1968. xix, 461pp. Bib. 431–45.

Fr 439   BERLIN, René, 'La politique sociale de Vichy, 1940–42'. *Ecrits de Paris*, **359**, 1976. pp. 5–21.

Fr 440   BOURDERON, Roger, 'Le régime de Vichy: était-il fasciste? essai d'approche de la question'. *REV. D'HIST. DEUX. GUERRE MOND.*, **23** (**91**), 1973. pp. 23–45. English tr. in CAIRNS, John (ed.), *Contemporary France*, New York: 1978. pp. 200–27.

Fr 441   BOURDERON, Roger, 'La "Revolution Nationale" dans le Gard: le service de propagande du Maréchal dans les cantons rhodaniens du département, nov. 1940–dec. 1941'. In *Congrès des Savantes de Paris et des Départements, 96ᵉ. Toulouse 13–17 Apr. 1971*. vol. 2, Paris: Bib. Nat., 1976. pp. 379–95.

Fr 442   BOUSSARD, Isabel, *Vichy et la corporation paysanne*, pref. by René Rémond, Paris: FNSP, 1980. 414pp.

Fr 443   BOUTHILLIER, Yves, *Le Drame de Vichy*, Paris: Plon, 1950–1. 2 vols. Memoirs of Vichy Finance Minister.

Fr 444   BRISSAUD, André, *Pétain à Sigmaringen, 1944–45*, Paris: Perrin, 1966. 603pp. Bib. 563–6.

Fr 445   BRISSAUD, André, *La Dernière année de Vichy, 1943–1944*, pref. by Robert Aron, Paris: Perrin, 1965. 587pp. Bib. 535–8.

Fr 446   CARCOPINO, Jérôme, *Souvenirs de sept ans, 1937–1944*, Paris: Flammarion, 1953. 702pp. Memoirs of the Vichy Minister of Education.

Fr 447   COINTET-LABROUSE, Michèle, 'Le gouvernement de Vichy et la jeunesse: sources nouvelles et nouveaux éclairages'. *BULL. SOC. HIST. MOD.*, **75** (**15**), 1976. pp. 13–21.

Fe 448   *Colloque sur le Gouvernement de Vichy et la Révolution National. Le gouvernement de Vichy, 1940–1942: institutions et politiques: Colloque . . . . Paris, 6–7 mars 1970*, Paris: Colin, 1972. 372pp.

Fr 449   DELPECH, François, 'Le persécution nazie et l'attitude de Vichy'. *HIST. ET GEOGR.*, **69** (**273**), 1979. pp. 591–635.

Fr 450   DELPERRIE DE BAYAC, Jacques, *Le Royaume du Maréchal: histoire de la Zone Libre*, Paris: Laffont, 1975. 413pp. Bib. 401–6.

Fr 451   DURAND, Yves, *Vichy, 1940–1944: ouvrage publiée sous la direction de Jacques Buillon*, Paris: Bordas, 1973. 175pp. Bib. 168–9.

Fr 452   FARMER, Paul, *Vichy: political dilemma*, New York: Columbia University Press, 1955. vi, 376pp. Bib. 353–67.

Fr 453   GILLOUIN, René, *J'étais l'ami du Maréchal Pétain: lettre-préface du pasteur Marc Boegner*, Paris: Plon, 1966. 317pp. Concerns the Maurrasians in Vichy.

Fr 454   HALLS, Wilfred Douglas, *The Youth of Vichy France*, Oxford: University Press, 1981. 492pp.

Fr 455   HEROLD-PAQUIS, Jean, *Des illusions . . . désillusions! 15 aout 1944–15 août 1945*, Paris: Bourgoin, 1948. 186pp. Hérold-Paquis (1912–45) executed as a traitor for his broadcasts on Radio Paris.

Fr 466   HOFFMANN, Stanley, 'Aspects du régime de Vichy'. *REV. FR. DE SCI. POLIT.*, **6** (**1**), 1956. pp. 44–69. English version, 'The Vichy circle of conservatives' in HOFFMANN, S., *Decline or Renewal?*, New York: Viking Press, 1974. pp. 3–25.

Fr 457   Hoover Institution, *France during the German occupation, 1940–44: a collection of 292 statements on the government of Marshal Pétain and Pierre Laval*, Stanford: University Press, 1959. 3 vols. Tr. of *La Vie de la France sous l'occupation*, by Philip W. Whitcomb.

Fr 458   KUISEL, Richard F., 'The legend of the Vichy synarchy'. *FR. HIST. STUD.*, **6** (**3**), 1970. pp. 365–98. The synarchy was a supposed secret plot by technocrats to take over Europe.

Fr 459   KUISEL, Richard F. 'Vichy et les origines de la planification économique 1940–1946'. *MOUVEMENT SOC.*, **98**, 1977. pp. 77–101.

Fr 460   KUPFERMAN, Fred, 'Le gouvernement Laval et les tentatives de relance de la collaboration'. *Monde Juif*, **32** (**84**), 1976. pp. 133–52.

Fr 461   KUPFERMAN, Fred, *1944-1945: le procès de Vichy: Pucheu, Pétain, Laval*, Brussels: Ed. Complexe, 1980. 190pp. Bib.

Fr 462   LAUNAY, Jacques de, *Le Dossier de Vichy*, Paris: Juillard, 1967. 319pp. Bib. 311–14.

Fr 463   LAUNAY, Jacques de, *La France de Pétain*, Paris: Hachette, 1972. 199pp. Bib. 194–9.

Fr 464   LEGNANI, Massimo, 'La Francia di Vichy: strutture di governo e centri di potere'. *MOV. DI LIBERAZIONE IN ITALIA*, **25** (**111**), 1973. pp. 107–19. Review article.

Fr 465   LEGNANI, Massimo, 'La Francia di Vichy da la "rivoluzione nazionale" alla "collaborazione"'. *MOV. DI LIBERAZIONE IN ITALIA*, **88**, 1967. pp. 57–69. Review of Michel's *Vichy année 40*.

Fr 466   LEPAGNOT, Christina, *Histoire du Vichy*, Geneva: Vernoy, 1978-9. 2 vols.

Fr 467   MARRUS, Michael Robert and PAXTON, Robert Owen, *Vichy and the Jews*, New York: Basic Books, 1981. xvi, 432pp.

Fr 468   MARTIN DU GARD, Maurice, *La Chronique de Vichy, 1940-1944*, Paris: Flammarion, 1948. 529pp.

Fr 469   MICHEL, Henri, *Pétain et le régime de Vichy*, Paris: PUF, 1978. 126pp.

Fr 470   MICHEL, Henri, *Pétain, Laval, Darlan: trois politiques?* Paris: Flammarion, 1972. 184pp. Bib. 169–76.

Fr 471   MICHEL, Henri, 'Le régime de Vichy et la République de Salò' *STOR. ET POLIT.*, **14** (**1/2**), 1975. pp. 3–20.

Fr 472   MICHEL, Henri, *Vichy année 40*, Paris: Laffont, 1966. 463pp. Bib. 439–51.

Fr 473   NOGUÈRES, Louis, *La Dernière étape: Sigmaringen*. Paris: Fayard, 1956. 251pp. On the government in exile of Pétain in Germany.

Fr 474   PAILLARD, Jean, *1940-1944: la révolution corporative spontanée: solution d'actualité, Annonay:* Éds. du Vivarais, 1979. 350pp.

Fr 475   PAXTON, Robert Owen, *Vichy France*, Morningside edn, New York: Columbia University Press, 1982. xvi, 399pp. Bib. 392–9.

Repr. of *Vichy France: old guard and New Order, 1940–1944*, New York: Knopf. London: Barrie & Jenkins, 1972.

Fr 476   PAXTON, Robert Owen, *Parades and Politics at Vichy: the French officer corps under Marshal Pétain*, Princeton: University Press, 1966. xi, 472pp.

Fr 477   PAXTON, Robert Owen, 'Le régime de Vichy en 1944'. In *La Liberation de la France: actes du Colloque Int. tenu à Paris du 28 au 31 Oct. 1974*, Paris: CNRS, 1976. pp. 324–42.

Fr 478   PUCHEU, Pierre Firmin, *Ma vie: notes écrites a Ksar-es-Souk, à la prison civile de Meknès et à la prison militaire d'Algier*, Paris: Amiot-Dumont, 1948. 380pp. Memoirs of Vichy Minister of the Interior (1899–1944) shot March 1944.

Fr 479   PUCHEU, Pierre Firmin, defendant, *Le Procès Pucheu: avec un avant-propos le procès de General Bethouard par Paul Buttin*, Paris: Amiot-Dumont, 1947. 340pp.

Fr 480   ROUSSO, Henry, *Un Château en Allemagne: la France de Pétain en exil: Sigmaringen, 1944–1945*, Paris: Ed. Ramsey, 1980. 441pp.

Fr 481   SIEGFRIED, André, 'Le Vichy de Pétain, le Vichy de Laval'. *REV. FR. SCI. POLIT.*, **6** (**4**), 1956. pp. 737–49.

Fr 482   United States Office of Strategic Services. *A selected who's who in Vichy France, June 1940–August 1944 . . . 24 Oct. 1944*, Washington, 1944. 358pp. Typescript.

Fr 483   VALLAT, Xavier, defendant, *Le Procès de Xavier Vallat; présenté par ses amis*, Paris: Eds. du Conquistador, 1948. xvi, 591pp.

Fr 484   VALLAT, Xavier, *Souvenirs d'un homme de droite*, Paris: Aymon, 1957–82. 2 vols. **1**. *Le Nez de Cleopatre*, pref. by Charles Maurras. **2**. *Le Grain de sable de Cromwell*.

Fr 485   *Xavier Vallat, 1891–1972*, Paris: Les Amis de Xavier Vallat, 1977. 71pp.

Fr 486   WORMSER, Olivier, *Les Origines doctrinales de la Révolution Nationale Vichy: 10 juillet 1940–31 mars 1941*, Paris: Plon, 1971. 276pp. Bib. 273–4.

Fascism and the Writers

Fr 487   ALBOUY, Serge, *Bernanos et la politique: la société et la droite française de 1900 à 1950*, Toulouse: Privat, 1980. 256pp. Bib. 233–50.

Fr 488 BERNANOS, Georges, *Nous autres français*, Paris: Nouvelle Rev. Française, 1939. 290pp.

Fr 489 *Bulletin de la Société des Amis de Georges Bernanos, 1-60. 1949-69.* cont. as *Courrier Bernanos. 1969-.* See 17-20, 1953 for Bernanos et Maurras.

Fr 490 CLARK, A.R., 'Bernanos: politique et polémiste: a bibliographical essay'. *J. OF EUR. STUD.*, **1** (**1**), 1971. pp. 69-80.

Fr 491 JURT, Joseph, *Les Attitudes politiques de Georges Bernanos jusq'en 1931*, Fribourg: Eds. Universitaires, 1968. 359pp. Bib. 341-55.

Fr 492 MOLNAR, Thomas Steven, *Bernanos: his political thought and prophecy*, New York: Sheed & Ward, 1960. 202pp. Bib.

Fr 493 AMBROISE-COLIN, Charles, *Un Procès de l'Épuration: Robert Brasillach*, Tours: Mâme, 1971. 263pp.

Fr 494 BARDÈCHE, *Maurice (ed.), Hommages à Robert Brasillach*, [by] Raymond Abellio [*et al.*], Lausanne: Amis de Robert Brasillach, 1965. 413pp.

Fr 495 BRASILLACH, Robert, *Oeuvres complètes*, annotated by Maurice Bardèche, Paris: Club de l'Honnête Homme, 1963-6. 12 vols.

Fr 496 *Les Cahiers des Amis de Robert Brasillach*, No. 1-. 1950-. Lausanne: Ass. des Amis de Robert Brasillach.

Fr 497 FOOTITT, Hilary Ann, 'Robert Brasillach and the Spanish Civil War'. *EUR. STUD. REV.*, **6** (**1**), 1976. pp. 123-37.

Fr 498 GEORGE, Bernard, *Robert Brasillach*, Paris: Eds. Universitaires, 1968. 128pp. Bib. 123-5.

Fr 499 ISORNI, Jacques, *Le Procès de Robert Brasillach (19 janvier 1945)*, Paris: Flammarion, 1946. 217pp.

Fr 500 MADIRAN, Jean, *Brasillach*, Paris: Ed. du Club du Luxembourg, 1958. 260pp. Bib. 245-50.

Fr 501 ORY, Pascal, 'La mort de Robert Brasillach'. *Histoire*, **20**, 1980. pp. 82-4.

Fr 502 TUCKER, William Rayburn, 'Politics and aesthetics: the fascism of Robert Brasillach'. *WEST. POLIT. Q.*, **15** (**4**), 1962. pp. 605-17.

Fr 503 TUCKER, William Rayburn, *The Fascist Ego: a political biography of Robert Brasillach*, Berkeley: University of California Press, 1975. 331pp. Bib. 309-18.

Fr 504   VANDROMME, Pol, *Robert Brasillach: l'homme et l'oeuvre*, Paris: Plon, 1956. 254pp. Bib. 253-4.

Fr 505   ANDREU, Pierre, *Drieu, témoin et visionnaire*, pref. by Daniel Halévy, Paris: Grasset, 1952. 219pp.

Fr 506   ANDREU, Pierre and GROVER, Frédéric J., *Drieu la Rochelle*, Paris: Hachette, 1979. 587pp. Bib. 575-9.

Fr 507   *Défense de l'Occident*, No. **50/51**, 1958. Drieu la Rochelle: témoignages et documents par J-M. Aimot.

Fr 508   DESANTI, Dominique, *Drieu la Rochelle: le séducteur mystifié*, Paris: Flammarion, 1978. 476pp. Bib. 447-59.

Fr 509   DRELL-RECK, R., 'French collaborationist literature and its imagery; Drieu la Rochelle and the idea of Germany'. In *Congrès de l'Association Int. de Litterature Comparée, Actes du 6ᵉ Congrès, Bordeaux, 1975*. Stuttgart, 1975. pp. 339-42.

Fr 510   DRIEU LA ROCHELLE, Pierre, *Chroniques politiques, 1934-1942*, 3rd edn, Paris: Gallimard, 1943. 390pp.

Fr 511   DRIEU LA ROCHELLE, Pierre, *Récit secret, suivi de Journal, 1944-45 et l'Exode*, Paris: Gallimard, 1961. 107pp.

Fr 512   DRIEU LA ROCHELLE, Pierre, *Socialisme fasciste*, Paris: Gallimard, 1934. 248pp.

Fr 513   GROVER, Frédéric J., *Drieu la Rochelle and the Fiction of Testimony*, Berkeley: University of California Press, 1958. 275pp. Bib.

Fr 514   GROVER, Frédéric J., *Drieu la Rochelle, 1893-1945: vie, oeuvres, témoignages*, Paris: Gallimard. 1979. 352pp. Bib. 327-41.

Fr 515   HERVIER, Julien, *Deux individus contre l'histoire: Pierre Drieu la Rochelle, Ernst Jünger*, Paris: Klincksieck, 1978. 485pp. Bib. 445-72. Paris IV University thesis, 1974.

Fr 516   LEAL, R.B., 'L'idée de décadence chez Drieu la Rochelle'. *REV. DES LANG. VIVANTES*, **40** (**4**), 1974. pp. 325-40.

Fr 517   LOUBET DEL BAYLE, Jean-Louis, 'Drieu la Rochelle et le fascisme'. *ANN. DE L'UNIV. DES SCI. SOC. DE TOULOUSE*, **21** (**1/2**), 1973. pp. 135-223.

Fr 518   MABIRE, Jean, *Drieu parmi nous*, Paris: La Table Ronde, 1963. 287pp.

Fr 519   MACLEOD, Alexander, *La Pensée politique de Pierre Drieu la Rochelle*, Paris: Ed. Cujas, 1966. 112pp.

Fr 520   PFEIL, Alfred, *Die französische Kriegsgeneration und der*

Faschismus: Pierre Drieu la Rochelle als politischer Schriftsteller, Munich: V. UNI-Druck, 1971. 337pp. Bib. 314–33. Marburg University thesis.

Fr 521 REBOUSSIN, Marcel, *Drieu la Rochelle et le mirage de la politique*, Paris: Nizet, 1980. 168pp.

Fr 522 RICHARD, Lionel, 'Drieu la Rochelle et La Nouvelle Revue Français des années noires'. *REV. D'HIST. DEUX. GUERRE MOND.*, **25** (**97**), 1975. pp. 67–84.

Fr 523 SINGER, Barnett, 'The prison of a fascist personality: Pierre Drieu la Rochelle'. *STANFORD FR. REV.*, **1** (**3**), 1977. pp. 403–14.

Fr 524 SOUCY, Robert L., 'Drieu la Rochelle and the modernist anti-modernism in French fascism'. *MLN: Modern Language Notes*, **95** (**4**), 1980. pp. 922–37.

Fr 525 SOUCY, Robert L., 'Le fascisme de Drieu la Rochelle'. *REV. D'HIST. DEUX. GUERRE MOND.*, **17** (**66**), 1967. pp. 61–84.

Fr 526 SOUCY, Robert L., *Fascist Intellectual: Drieu la Rochelle*, Berkeley: University of California Press, 1979. x, 451pp. Bib. 423–32.

Fr 527 SOUCY, Robert L., 'Psycho-sexual aspects of the fascism of Drieu la Rochelle'. *J. OF PSYCHOHISTORY*, **4** (**1**), 1976. pp. 71–92.

Fr 528 SOUCY, Robert L., 'Romanticism and realism in the fascism of Drieu la Rochelle'. *J. OF HIST. IDEAS*, **31** (**1**), 1970. pp. 69–90.

Fr 529 TUCKER, William Rayburn, 'Fascism and Individualism: the political thought of Pierre Drieu la Rochelle'. *J. OF POLIT.*, **27** (**1**), 1965. pp. 153–77.

Fr 530 VANDROMME, Pol, *Pierre Drieu la Rochelle*, Paris: Eds. Universitaires, 1958. 126pp. Bib. 123–6.

Fr 531 WINOCK, Michel, 'Une parabole fasciste: Gilles de Drieu la Rochelle'. *MOUVEMENT SOC.*, **80**, 1972. pp. 29–47.

Fr 532 CELINE, Louis-Ferdinand (pseud.) [Louis-Ferdinand Destouches], *Louis-Ferdinand Céline: des temoins, correspondence inédits;* [*directeur Dominique de Roux*], Paris: L'Herne, 1963. Essai de bibliographie complète pp. 315–39. New 1972 edn combines L'Herne No. 3 and No. 5 and new 'Essai de bibliographie complète'. pp. 494–512.

Fr 533 CELINE, Louis-Ferdinand (pseud.) [Louis-Ferdinand Destouches], *Oeuvres de Louis-Ferdinand Céline*, pref. by Marcel Aymé, Paris: Ballard, 1966–9. 5 vols.

Fr 534 DAUPHIN, Jean Pierre, *Louis-Ferdinand Céline. 1. Essai de*

*bibliographie des études en langue française consacrées à Louis-Ferdinand Céline
I. 1914-1944*, Paris: Lett. Mod. Minard, 1977. 380pp.

Fr 535   MORAND, Jaqueline, *Les Idées politiques de Louis-Ferdinand Céline*, pref. by Jean-Jacques Chevallier, Paris: Librairie Générale, 1972. 216pp. Bib. 205-11.

Fr 536   OSTROVSKY, Erika, *Céline and his Vision*, New York: University Press, 1967. xiii, 225pp. Bib. 209-20.

Fr 537   COFRANCESCO, Dino, 'Verzo la formazione della coscienza europea: fascismo e bolscevismo dei giudizi degli intellettuali francesi degli anni trenta'. *Crit. Stor. NS*, **12 (2/4)**, 1975. pp. 516-27.

Fr 538   FABRE-LUCE, Alfred, *J'ai vécu plusieurs siècles*, Paris: Fayard, 1974. 402pp. Autobiography of unrepentant man of the extreme Right.

Fr 539   FIELD, Frank, *Three French Writers and the Great War: studies in the rise of communism and fascism*, Cambridge: University Press, 1975. 212pp. Bib. 205-8. Barbusse, Drieu la Rochelle, Bernanos.

Fr 540   JOUVENAL, Bertrand de, *Un Voyageur dans le siècle*, Paris: Laffont, 1979. 1. *1903-1945.* 491pp. Leftist economist who moved to the extreme Right.

Fr 541   KUNNAS, Tarmo, *Drieu la Rochelle, Céline, Brasillach et la tentation fasciste*, Paris: Les Sept Couleurs, 1972. 310pp. Bib. 293-300.

Fr 542   SERANT, Paul, *Le Romantisme fasciste: étude sur l'oeuvre de quelques écrivains français*, Paris: Fasquelle, 1960. 321pp.

The Extreme Right and the Regions

Fr 543   ANDREANI, Pierre, *Le Fascisme et la Corse*, 2nd edn, Marseille: Imp. Marseillaise, 1939. 126pp.

Fr 544   CAERLEON, Ronan, *Complots pour une république bretonne: les dossiers secrets de l'autonomisme breton*, Paris: La Table Ronde 1967. 380pp.

Fr 545   DEJONGHE, Etienne, 'Un mouvement séparatiste dans le Nord et le Pas-de-Calais sous l'occupation, 1940-1944: le Vlaamsch Verbond van Frankrijk'. *REV. D'HIST. MOD. ET CONTEMP.*, **17 (1)**, 1970. pp. 50-78.

Fr 546   *Régions et Régionalisme en France: du XVIIIe siècle à nos jours: actes du Colloque. . . . Strasbourg . . . 1974*, Paris: PUF, 1977. 595pp. Includes Michel Denis on the Mouvement Breton and fascism and Yves Durand on La politique régionale de Vichy.

Fr 547   SIMON, Pierre-Jean, 'Racisme et antisémitisme dans le Mouvement breton des années 30'. *Pluriel*, **18**, 1979. pp. 29–38.

Racism and Anti-Semitism.
See also **The Extreme Right 1890–1918**

Fr 548   DAVIES, Alan T., 'Religion and racism: the case of French anti-semitism'. *J. of Church and State*, **20** (**2**), 1978. pp. 273–86.

Fr 549   *De l'Antijudaisme Antique à l'Antisémitisme Contemporain: Seminaire du Centre Interdisciplinaire d'Études des Religions, et de l'Inst. d'Etudes Hebraïques Univ. de Lille III, 1975-6*, Villeneuve d'Ascq: Presse Univ. de Lille, 1979. 290pp. See article by Jacques Prévotat on AF anti-semitism, pp. 247–75.

Fr 550   *L'Idée de Race dans la Pensée Politique Française Contemporaine; recueil d'articles présenté par Pierre Guiral et Émile Temine:* (Colloque organisé par le Centre d'Etudes de la Penseé Politique Contemporaine, mai 1975), Paris: CNRS, 1977. 281pp. Articles by Victor Nguyen on Maurrasian anti-semitism. pp. 139–55 and Zeev Sternhell on the nationalism of Barrès and Soury. pp. 117–38.

Fr 551   LALOUS, Jean, *La France antisémite de Darquier de Pellepoix*, pref. by Jacques Droz, Paris: Ed. Syros, 1979. vii, 214pp.

Fr 552   PIERRARD, Pierre, *Juifs et Catholiques français de Drumont à Jules Isaac, 1886-1945*, Paris: Fayard, 1970. 336pp.

Fr 553   STERNHELL, Zeev, 'Les origines intellectuelles du racisme en France'. *Histoire*, **17**, 1979. pp. 106–14.

BELGIUM

General

Bl 1   BEAUFAYS, Jean, *Les Partis catholiques en Belgique et aux Pays-Bas, 1918–1958*, pref. by Henri Janne, Brussels: Bruylant, 1973. xvi, 778pp. Bib. 649–724. Includes fascist dissidents from Catholic parties who joined Rex or VNV.

Bl 2   BEAUFAYS, Jean, *Sélection bibliographique de l'histoire de la Belgique 1918–1939: bibliographie introductive à l'histoire de la deuxième guerre mondiale du point de vue belge*, Brussels, 1968. 37pp. Includes Rex and Flemish nationalism.

Bl 3   CARPINELLI, Giovanni, 'Belgium'. in WOOLF, S.J., Gn 20. pp. 283–306.

Bl 4   CHERTOK, Ronald Henry, *Belgian Fascism*, Washington University thesis, 1975. UM 75–21707. 418pp.

Bl 5   SCHEPENS, Luc, 'Fascists and nationalists in Belgium, 1919–1940'. In LARSEN, S.U., Gn 36. pp. 501–23.

Bl 6   STENGERS, Jean, 'Belgium'. In ROGGER, H. and WEBER, E., Gn 54. pp. 128–67.

Bl 7   STENGERS, Jean, 'La droite en Belgique avant 1940'. *Courrier Hebdomadaire du CRISP*, **468/69**, 30 January 1970. 35pp.

Bl 8   VERHOEY, E., 'L'extrême-droite en Belgique'. *Courrier Hebdomadaire du CRISP*, **642/43**, 26 April 1974: **675/76**, 7 March 1975; **715/16**, 1976.

Bl 9   WULLUS-RUDIGER, J. (pseud.) [Armand Wullus], *En marge de la politique belge, 1914–1956*, Brussels: Berger-Lavrault, 1957. xiii, 472pp. Includes material on Rex.

The Early Years of the Extreme Right

Bl 10   BEAUFAYS, Jean, 'Aspects du nationalisme belge au lendemain de la grande guerre'. *Annales de la Faculté de Droit de Liège*, **16 (1/2)**, 1971. pp. 105–74.

Bl 11   DEFOORT, Eric, 'L'Action Française dans le nationalisme belge, 1914–1918'. *REV. BELGE D'HIST. CONTEMP.*, **7 (1/2)**, 1976. pp. 113–52.

Bl 12   DEFOORT, Eric, 'Het Belgische nationalisme voor de eerste wereldoorlog' (Belgian nationalism before the first world war). *Tijdschrift voor Geschiedenis*, **85**, 1972. pp. 524–42.

Bl 13   DEFOORT, Eric, 'Les catholiques belges face à Maurras et à l'Action Française, 1898–1914'. *REV. D'HIST. ECCLESIASTIQUE*, **73 (2)**, 1976. pp. 315–33; **73 (3/4)**, pp. 593–631.

Bl 14   DEFOORT, Eric, *Charles Maurras en de Action Française in België*, Brugge: Orion, 1978. 430pp.

Bl 15   DEFOORT, Eric, 'Le courant réactionnaire dans le catholicisme francophone belge, 1918–1926'. *REV. BELGE D'HIST. CONTEMP.*, **8 (1/2)**, 1977. pp. 81–154.

Bl 16   VAN HAVER, Griet, 'Katholieken in Vlaanderen en de opkomst van het fascisme in Italië' (Catholics in Flanders and the rise of fascism in Italy). *Risorgimento*, **21**, 1979. pp. 259-75.

Rexism

Bl 17   BUTGENBACH, André, *Le Mouvement rexiste et la situation politique de la Belgique*, Brussels: Bruylant, 1937. 68pp. Objective study of Rex. Also in *Revue des Sciences Politique*, Oct./Dec. 1936.

Bl 18   CARPINELLI, Giovanni, 'Per l'interpretazione del fascismo belga: studi recenti sul rexismo'. *MOV. DI LIBERAZIONE IN ITALIA*, **24** (**4**), 1972. pp. 89-105.

Bl 19   DAYE, Pierre, *Études de politique belge*, Louvain: Ed. Lovanis, 1938. 336pp. By a leading Rexist who died in 1960.

Bl 20   DAYE, Pierre, *Guerre et révolution: lettre d'un Belge à un ami français*, Paris: Grasset, 1941. 77pp.

Bl 21   DAYE, Pierre, *Trente-deux mois chez les députés*, Brussels: Ignis, 1942. 221pp. On the Rexist parliamentary group.

Bl 22   DAYE, Pierre, *Petite histoire parlementaire belge*, Paris: La Renaissance du Livres, 1939. 236pp.

Bl 23   DENIS, Jean, *Principes rexistes*, Brussels: Ed. Rex, 1936. 224pp.

Bl 24   DENIS, Jean, *Rex, renaissance de la patrie*, Brussels: Wellens-Godenne [n.d.]. 102pp.

Bl 25   DE SMET, A., 'Les partis politiques belges et la guerre civile espagnole, 1936-1939'. *Res Publica*, **9** (**4**), 1967. pp. 699-713. Includes Rex.

Bl 26   DIMURO, G.F., *Le Mouvement Rexiste, 1935-1940: mémoire dactylographié*, Brussels: Faculté des Sciences Sociales, Politiques et Economiques de l'Université Libre de Bruxelles, 1966.

Bl 27   ETIENNE, Jean-Michel, 'Les origines du rexisme'. *Res Publica*, **9** (**1**), 1967. pp. 87-109.

Bl 28   ÉTIENNE, Jean-Michel, *Le Mouvement rexiste jusqu'en 1940*, pref. by Leo Moulin, Paris: Colin, 1968. xv, 194pp. Bib. 184-90. Rex did not aspire to be a fascist movement but became so after 1938.

Bl 29   GRABINER-KUPPERBERG, R., 'La montée du rexisme: étude de la presse bruxelloise non rexiste, octobre 1935-mai 1936'. *Res Publica*, **11** (**4**), 1969. pp. 717-56. Based on Brussels University thesis, 1966/7.

Bl 30 HOYOIS, Giovanni, 'Au temps de rexisme: Mgr. Picard et Léon Degrelle'. *REV. GEN. BELGE*, Nov. 1959. pp. 83–94. On origins of Rex, by ex-President of the Association Catholique de la Jeunesse Belge.

Bl 31 KRIER, Emile, 'Rex et l'Allemagne, 1933–1940: une documentation'. *CAH. D'HIST. DE LA SECONDE GUERRE MOND.*, **5**, 1978. pp. 173–220.

Bl 32 LAURENT, Pierre-Henri, 'Belgian Rexism and Léon Degrelle'. In *J. of Contemp. Hist.*, International fascism, Gn 13. pp. 295–315.

Bl 33 PFEIFFER, Robert and LADRIÈRE, Jean, *L'Aventure rexiste*, Brussels: Ed. P. de Meyère, 1966. 181pp. Anti-Rex polemic.

Bl 34 SAINT-GERMAIN, Jacques, *La Bataille de Rex*, Paris: Les Oeuvres Françaises, 1937. 218pp. On the origins and history of Rex.

Bl 35 STREEL, José, *Ce qu'il faut penser de Rex*, Brussels: Ed. Rex, 1936. 152pp. Together with Jean Denis the leading ideologist of Rex.

Bl 36 TARCHI, Marco (ed.), *Degrelle e il rexismo*, Rome: Volpe, 1978. 135pp. Bib. 133–5.

Bl 37 VOS, Louis, 'De ideologische orientering van de katholieke studerende jeugd in Vlaanderen, 1936–1940' (The ideological orientation of the Catholic Student Youth in Flanders). *REV. BELGE D'HIST. CONTEMP.*, **8** (**1/2**), 1977. pp. 207–36.

Bl 38 VROYLANDE, Robert, *Quand Rex était petit*, Louvain: Ed. Lovanis, 1936. 191pp. Anti-Rexist tract by ex-Rexist editor.

Bl 39 WALLEF, Danièle, 'The composition of Christus Rex'. In LARSEN, S.U., Gn 36. pp. 517–23.

Bl 40 YDEWALLE, Hubert d', *Le Régime à vau-l'eau*, Brussels: Ed. Rex, 1937. 97pp. Leading Rexist connected with journal *Vlan*. Editor of *Pays Réel*.

The Flemish Variant of Fascism: Verdinaso and the VNV

Bl 41 BAES, Rachel, *Joris van Severen: une âme*, Zulte: Oranje-Uitg., 1965. 286pp. A sympathetic account of the Verdinaso leader.

Bl 42 BRUYNE, Arthur de, *Joris van Severen: droom en daad*, Zulte: Oranje Uitg., 1961. 339pp. Bib. 325–32. Biography of van Severen (1894–1940), leader of Verdinaso, by the leader of Rex-Flanders.

Bl 43   CARPINELLI, Giovanni, 'The Flemish variant in Belgian fascism'. *WIENER LIB. BULL.*, **26** (**3/4**), 1972/3. pp. 20-7.

Bl 44   DELAFORTRIE, Luc, *Joris van Severen en de Nederlanden: een levenebeeld (A biography)*, Zulte: Oranje Uitg., 1963. 270pp.

Bl 45   ELIAS, Hendrik J., *Vijfentwintig jaar Vlaamse beweging, 1914–1939 (Twenty-five years of the Flemish Movement)*, Antwerp: Nederlandsche Boekh., 1969. 4 vols. Bib. vol. 4, 196-240. Includes VNV and Verdinaso.

Bl 46   *Encyclopédie van de Vlaamse Beweging*, comps. Josef Deleu, Gaston Durnez, Reginald de Schryver, Ludo Simons, Tielt: Lanoo, 1973-5. 2 vols. Includes articles on van Severen, Verbond van Dietsche Nationaal-Solidaristen, and VNV.

Bl 47   JONGHE, A.A. de, 'H. J. Elias als leider van het Vlaams Nationaal Verbond: Konttekeningen bij een artikel van Frans van der Elst' (H. J. Elias as leader of the VNV). *REV. BELGE D'HIST. CONTEMP.*, **6** (**3/4**), 1975. pp. 197-238; **7** (**3/4**), 1976. pp. 329-424.

Bl 48   MERMANS, Antoon, *De leider: schets van het leven van Staf de Clercq (The Leader: sketches from the life of Staf de Clercq)*, Antwerp: Uitg. 'Volk en Staat', 1942. 68pp. VNV publication on its leader Gustaaf de Clercq (1884-1942).

Bl 49   MEYERS, Willem C.M., 'Les collaborateurs flamands de France et leurs contacts avec les milieux flamingants belges'. *REV. DU NORD*, **60** (**237**), 1978. pp. 337-46.

Bl 50   SCHEPENS, Luc, 'Joris van Severen: een raadsel' (An enigma). *Ons Erfdeel*, **18**, 1975. pp. 221-39.

Bl 51   VAN BERCKEL, F., *De tragische dood van Joris Van Severen en Jan Rijckoort, Abbeville 20 mei 1940 (The Tragic Death of J. Van Severen and J. Rijckoort)*, Zulte: Oranje-Uitg., 1960. 173pp. Two prominent members of Verdinaso killed by French soldiers in Abbeville.

Bl 52   VAN DER ELST, Frans, 'Dr Elias als leider van het VNV'. *CAH. D'HIST. DE LA SECONDE GUERRE MOND.*, **3**, 1975. pp. 83-105.

Bl 53   WILLEMSEN, Arie Wolter, *Het Vlaams-nationalisme: de geschiedenis van de jaren 1914-1940*, 2nd edn (*Flemish Nationalism: a history of the years 1914-1940*), Utrecht: Uitg. Ambo., 1969. 501pp. Bib. 471-84.

Léon Degrelle

Bl 54   BRASILLACH, Robert, *Léon Degrelle et l'avenir de Rex*, Paris: Plon, 1936. 85pp. Repub. Plon, 1969.

Bl 55   DAYE, Pierre, *Léon Degrelle et le rexisme*, Paris: Fayard, 1937. 251pp. Sympathetic account by leading Rexist.

Bl 56   DEGRELLE, Léon, *Ainsi parla Degrelle: . . . interviews au magnetophone et conversations avec . . . Léon Degrelle . . . recueillés par Wim Dannau de 1965 à 1972, les commentaires de l'auteur, etc.*, Strombeek-Bever: De Schorpioen, 1973–6. 11 vols.

Bl 57   DEGRELLE, Léon, *Les Âmes qui brûlent*, Paris: A la Feuille du Chêne, 1964. 251pp.

Bl 58   DEGRELLE, Léon, *La Cohue de 1940*, Lausanne: Crausaz, 1949. 528pp. Collaboration in Belgium May 1940 to June 1941.

Bl 59   DEGRELLE, Léon, *Degrelle avait raison: recueil de textes écrits par Léon Degrelle entre 1936 et 1940 dans le 'Pays Réel'*, Brussels: Ed. Rex, 1941. 58pp.

Bl 60   DEGRELLE, Léon, 'Un entretien exclusif avec Léon Degrelle'. *Défense de l'Occident*, Nov. 1976. pp. 22–32.

Bl 61   DEGRELLE, Léon, *Face à face avec le rexisme*, Strombeek-Bever: De Schorpioen, 1971. 158pp. Interview by Wim Dannau with Degrelle.

Bl 62   DEGRELLE, Léon, *Le Front de L'Est, 1941–1945*, Paris: La Table Ronde, 1969. 451pp.

Bl 63   DEGRELLE, Léon, *Hitler pour 1000 ans*, Paris: La Table Ronde, 1969. 231pp.

Bl 64   DEGRELLE, Léon, *Révolution des âmes*, Paris: Eds. de France, 1938. 179pp. A collection of articles.

Bl 65   DEGRELLE, Léon, *Die verlorene Legion*, new edn, Oldendorf: Schütz, 1972. 509pp.

Bl 66   LEGROS, Usmard, *Un Homme, un chef: Léon Degrelle*, Brussels: Ed. Rex, 1938. 237pp.

Bl 67   NARVAEZ, Louise, *Degrelle m'a dit* [tr. from Spanish], Paris: Ed. Morel, 1961. 437pp. Complete pro-Rexist history by a latterday supporter.

Bl 68   PAPELEUX, Léon, 'Léon Degrelle ou l'itinéraire d'une trahison'. *La Vie Wallonne*, **53** (**368**), 1979. pp. 220–30.

Bl 69   YDEWALLE, Charles d', *La Cour et la ville, 1934–1940*, Brussels: Les Eds. Libres, 1945. 190pp. Material on Degrelle.

Bl 70   YDEWALLE, Charles d', *Degrelle ou la triple imposture*, Brussels: Ed. Presse de Meyère, 1968. 217pp.

La Légion Nationale

Bl 71   DELMOTTE, M.G., *La Légion Nationale: mémoire dactylographié*, Brussels: Faculté des Sciences Sociales, Politiques, et Economiques de l'Université Libre de Bruxelles, 1964.

Hendrik de Man (1885–1953)

Bl 72   *Bulletin de l'Association pour l'Etude de l'Oeuvre d'Henri de Man, 1974–*, Geneva: Faculté de Droit, Section de Droit Public.

Bl 73   Centre de Recherches et d'Etudes Historiques de la Seconde Guerre Mondiale, *Archief H. de Man*, by Herman Balthazar. Brussels: Studiecentrum, 1971. vii, 55pp.

Bl 74   CLAEYS-VAN HAEGENDOREN, Mieke, *Hendrik de Man: een biografie*, Antwerp: De Nederlandsche Boekh., 1972. 440pp. Most scholarly biography of de Man.

Bl 75   DODGE, Peter, *Beyond Marxism: the faith and works of Hendrik de Man*, The Hague: Nijhoff, 1966. vi, 282pp. Bib. 248–72.

Bl 76   HANSEN, Erik, 'Depression decade: social democracy and planisme in Belgium and the Netherlands, 1929–1939'. *J. OF CONTEMP. HIST.*, **16** (2), 1981. pp. 293–322.

Bl 77   HANSEN, Erik, 'Hendrik de Man and the theoretical foundations of economic planning: the Belgian experience'. *EUR. STUD. REV.*, **8** (2), 1978. pp. 235–57.

Bl 78   MAN, Hendrik de, *A Documentary Study of Hendrik de Man, Socialist Critic of Marxism*, ed. and largely tr. by Peter Dodge, Princeton: University Press, 1979. 362pp. Bib. 355–7.

Bl 79   MAN, Hendrik de, *Gegen den Storm: Memoiren eines europäischen Sozialisten*, Stuttgart: Deutsche Verlags-Anstalt, 1953. 291pp. Latest version of his autobiography.

Bl 80   MAN, J. de and MAN, E. de (eds), *Hendrik de Man: Gesamt-Bibliographie*, Schwarzwald: Ring-V., 1962. 53pp.

Bl 81   *Revue Européenne des Sciences Sociales et Cahiers Vilfredo Pareto*, Vol.

12 (31), 1974. pp. 1-303. Special issue 'Sur l'oeuvre d'Henri de Man'.

Belgium and the Second World War

Bl 82   Centre de Recherches et d'Études Historiques de la Seconde Guerre Mondiale, *Archief de Vlag*, by W. Steenhaut en M. Van de Steen, Brussels, 1977. viii, 152pp. Inventory of the archives of the collaborationist Deutsch-Vlaemische Arbeits-gemeinschaft.

Bl 83   GILLINGHAM, John Bennett, *Belgian Business in the Nazi New Order*, Ghent: Jan Dhondt Foundation, 1977. 237pp. Bib. 197-216.

Bl 84   GOTOVICH, José, 'Problèmes de l'historiographie de la Belgique pendant la second guerre mondiale'. *Septentrion (Rekkem)*, **5** (**3**), 1976. pp. 5-13.

Bl 85   GOTOVICH, José, 'La seconde guerre mondiale en Belgique: questions archivistiques'. *REV. BELGE DE PHILOLOGIE ET D'HIST.*, **47**, 1969. pp. 510-22.

Bl 86   JANSSENS, G., 'De "Auslandsorganisation" der NSDAP in België'. *Spiegel Historiael (Haarlem)*, **12** (**7/8**), 1977. pp. 424-9.

Bl 87   MARTIN, Dirk, 'De duitse "vijfde kolonne" in België, 1936-1940'. *REV. BELGE D'HIST. CONTEMP.*, **11** (**1/2**), 1980. pp. 85-117.

Bl 88   MEYERS, Willem C.M., 'Bibliographie: la Belgique dans la seconde guerre mondiale'. *BULL. CENT. RECH. ETUD. SECONDE GUERRE MOND.*, **6**. November 1975. pp. 5-24.

Bl 89   PAPELEUX, Léon, 'Milieux collaborateurs et presse censurée en régions francophones, 1940-1944'. *La Vie Wallonne*, **50**, 1976. pp. 227-37.

Bl 90   SAINT-LOUP (pseud.), *Les S.S. de la Torson d'Or: Flamands et Wallons au combat, 1941-1945*, Paris: Presses de la Cité, 1975. 379pp.

Bl 91   VADON, Jacques, 'Les mouvements de collaboration dans les Ardennes, 1942-1944'. *Rev. Hist. Ardennaise*, **9**, 1974. pp. 193-206.

Bl 92   *Vlamingen aan het Oostfront*, Deel 1. *Het Vlaams Legion*, Antwerp: Etnika, 1973. 245pp. The Flemish Legion on the Eastern Front.

Bl 93   WILLEQUET, Jacques, 'Les fascismes belges et la seconde guerre mondiale'. *REV. D'HIST. DEUX. GUERRE MOND.*, **17** (**66**), 1967. pp. 85-109.

NETHERLANDS

General

Ne 1   DUNK, H.W. van der, 'Konservatismus und faschismus in den Niederlanden'. *Mededelingen van het Nederlandse Historisch Instituut te Rome*, **38**, 1976. pp. 157-66.

Ne 2   HANSEN, Erik, 'Fascism and nazism in the Netherlands, 1929-39'. *EUR. STUD. REV.*, **11** (3), 1981. pp. 355-85.

Ne 3   HAZEU, Wim and others (comps), *Vrolijk klimaat* (*Cheerful Climate*), by Wim Hazeu, Jaap Meijer, Harry Scholten, The Hague: Nijgh & Van Ditmar, 1968. 96pp. On Dutch fascism.

Ne 4   JONGE, A.A. de, *Crisis en critiek der democratie: anti-democratische stromingen en de daarin levende denkbeelden over de staat in Nederland tussen de wereld-oorlog* (*Crisis and Criticism of Democracy: anti-democratic currents and contemporary ideas on the state between the world wars*), Assen: Van Gorcum, 1968. 436pp. Bib. 388-98. Broad survey of authoritarian movements, clubs and groups from 1920-39.

Ne 5   JONGE, A.A. de, 'Nederland en het fascisme in de jaren dertig' (The Netherlands and fascism in the 1930s). *Spiegel Historiael*, **15** (1), 1980. pp. 621-6.

Ne 6   JOOSTEN, Leonardus Martinus Henricus, *Katholieken en fascisme in Nederland, 1920-1940*, Hilversum: Uitg. Brand, 1964. 457pp. Nijmegen University thesis.

Ne 7   SCHÖFFER, Ivo, 'Fascisme en nationaal-socialisme in Nederland'. *TIJDSCHR. VOOR GESCHIEDENIS*, **78** (1), 1965. pp. 59-67. Review of JOOSTEN, L., Ne 6, and KOOY, G.A., Ne 17.

Nationaal Socialistische Beweging (NSB)

Ne 8   AARSE, J.A.A. and MARINUS, B. (comps), *'Houzee Kameraad': een documentaire over de NSB*, Amsterdam: De Arbeiderspers, 1967. 304pp.

Ne 9   BLOKZIJL, Max, *Max Blokzijl spreekt tot de jeugd: een boek voor de oude en de jonge generation* (*Max Blokzijl Speaks to the Young*), Utrecht: Nenasu, 1944. 191pp. Max Blokzijl (1884-1944), leading NSB propagandist.

Ne 10   BLOKZIJL, Max, defendant, *Processen . . . Max Blokzijl: zijn berechting veroordeling en executie (Max Blokzijl: his trial, condemnation and execution)*, Amsterdam: Uitg. Buyten en Schipperheyn, 1947. (Rijksinstituut voor Oorlogsdocumentatie.) 96pp.

Ne 11   BUNING, L., 'De radicale Boerenbeweging en de NSB in Drenthe' (The radical farmers' movement and the NSB in Drenthe). *Spiegel Historiael*, **12** (**5**), 1977. pp. 302–11.

Ne 12   GEELKERKEN, Cornelis yan, *Voor volk en vaderland, tien jaren strijd van de Nationaal-Socialistische Beweging der Nederlanden 1931–14 Dec. 1941*, 2nd edn, Utrecht: Nenasu, 1941. 544pp. By a leading member of the NSB.

Ne 13   GENECHTEN, Robert van, defendant, *Van Genechten: zijn berechting en voorordeling* Amsterdam: Rijksinstituut voor Oorlogsdocumentatie, 1948. 80pp. Report of his trial.

Ne 14   GENECHTEN, Robert van, *De zelfmoord van het kapitalisme (The Suicide of Capitalism)*, Utrecht: Nenasu, 1937. 237pp. Robert van Genechten (1895–1945), Flemish nationalist and legal expert of NSB.

Ne 15   HAGTINGIUS, D.J., *Groei en afval van de NSB in Alkemaar en het Geestmerambacht (The Growth in Disaffection from the NSB in Alkemaar)*, Amsterdam University, Dept. of Political Science thesis, 1976.

Ne 16   JONGE, A.A. de, *Het nationaal-socialisme in Nederland: voorgeschiedenis, ontstaan en ontwikkeling*, 2nd edn (*National Socialism in the Netherlands: prehistory, origins and evolution*), The Hague: Kruseman, 1979. 199pp. Bib. 194–5. First edn, 1968. Standard history of the NSB by a historian in the Nolte tradition.

Ne 17   KOOY, G.A., *Het echec van een 'volkse' beweging: nazificatie en denazificatie en Nederland, 1931–1945 (The Failure of a 'Volkische' Movement)*, Assen: Van Gorcum, 1964. 359pp. Thesis in sociology. Examines the nazification process in Winterswijk in Gelderland.

Ne 18   KWIET, Konrad, 'Zur Geschichte der Mussert-Bewegung'. *VIERTELJAHRSH. FÜR ZEITG.*, **18** (**2**), 1970. pp. 164–95.

Ne 19   LINDEMANN, L., *Het socialisme van het NSB: een documentatie voor het tijdvak einde 1931 tot somer 1940 (The Socialism of the NSB: a documentation from the end of 1931 to summer 1940)*, Leiden: Nenasu, 1941. 331pp. NSB view of its ideology.

Ne 20   LOOGMAN, P., *De NSB in Drente*, Amsterdam University thesis, Dept. of Geography, 1976.

Ne 21   MARCHANT, Hendrik Pieter, *Een staatkundige epidemie: het ziektebeeld van het Dietse nationaal-socialisme in Nederland (A Political*

Epidemic: the syndrome of German nazism in the Netherlands), 's-Hertogenbosch, 1936. 234pp.

Ne 22   MEYERS, J., 'Mussert in opmars: de beste jaren van de NSB, 1932-1935' (Mussert in advance: the best years of the NSB). *Maatstaf*, **29 (8/9)**, 1981. pp. 150-63.

Ne 23   PAAPE, A.H., 'Le mouvement national-socialiste en Hollande: aspects politiques et historiques'. *REV. D'HIST. DEUX GUERRE MOND.*, **17 (66)**, 1967. pp. 31-60.

Ne 24   ROST VAN TONNINGEN, M.M., *Correspondentie,* comp. and ed. E. Fraenkel-Verkade, A.J. Van der Leeiuw, The Hague: Nijhoff, 1967. 244pp. 1. *1921-Mei 1942*. Correspondence of Rost van Tonningen (1894-1945) one of the leading members of the NSB.

Ne 25   SCHMIDT, Otto, 'A quantitative analysis of support for the National-Socialist Movement (NSB) from 1935 to 1940 in the city of Amsterdam'. *Acta Politica*, **14 (4)**, 1979. pp. 479-508.

Ne 26   SCHÖFFER, Ivo, *Het Nationaal-socialistische beeld van de geschiedenis der Nederlanden: een historiografische en bibliografische studie (The National-socialist Picture of Netherlands history)*, Arnhem: Van Loghum Slaterus, 1956. 359pp. List of periodicals 263-73. List of sources 280-319. Bib. 335-42.

Ne 27   SMIT, R.E., *Kring 5 en kring 32: de Nationaal-Socialistische Beweging in Den Haag en omgeving, van december 1931 tot april 1935 (Circle 5 and Circle 32: the NSB in The Hague and environs)*, Amsterdam University thesis, Dept. of Geography, 1975.

Ne 28   VAN OSSENBRUGGEN, M.O., *De ontwikkeling van de Nationaal-Socialistische Beweging in Rotterdam van december 1931 tot april 1935 (The Development of the NSB in Rotterdam)*, Amsterdam University thesis, Dept. of Geography, 1975.

Ne 29   VAN ROON, G., *Protestants Nederland en Duitsland, 1933-1941*, Utrecht: Het Spectrum, 1973. 413pp. The Dutch Protestant churches and relations with the NSB and the occupying Germans.

Ne 30   VELLENGA, S.Y.A., *Katholiek Zuid Limburg en het fascisme: een onderzoek naar het kiesgedrag van de Limburger in de jaren dertig (Catholic South Limburg and Fascism; an inquiry into the electoral behaviour of Limburgers in the 1930s)*, Assen: Van Gorcum, 1975. xvi, 173pp. Bib. xii-xvi.

Ne 31   VOS, J.F., *Het ledenverloop van de Nationaal-Socialistische Beweging in Nederland (The Decline in Membership of the NSB)*, Rotterdam Erasmus University thesis, Dept. of History, 1971.

Ne 32   WAL, S.L. van der, 'De Nationaal-Socialistische Beweging in Nederlands-Indië' (The NSB in the Dutch East Indies). *Bijdragen en Mededelingen van het Historisch Genootschap*, **82**, 1968. pp. 35-6.

Ne 33   WUSTEN, Herman van der, and SMIT, Ronald, 'Dynamics of the Dutch National Socialist Movement (the NSB), 1931-1935'. In LARSEN, S.U., Gn 36. pp. 524-41.

Anton Adriaan Mussert (1894-1946)

Ne 34   BOER, Piet, *Mussert: Entstehung und Kampf des niederländische Nationalsozialismus*, Herrsching b. Munich: Deutscher Hort V., 1939. 42pp.

Ne 35   HAVENAAR, R., *Verrader voor het vaderland: een biografische schets van Anton Adriaan Mussert (Betrayer of the Fatherland: a biographical sketch of A.A. Mussert)*, The Hague: Krusemann, 1978. 126pp.

Ne 36   MEYERS, J., 'Musserts grote vergissing (1937)' (Mussert's great error). *Maatstaf*, **29** (**10**), 1981. pp. 94-106.

Ne 37   MUSSERT, Anton Adriaan, *De bronnen van het Nederlandse nationaal-socialisme (The Sources of Dutch National-socialism)*, Utrecht: Hoofdkwartier NSB, 1937. 31pp.

Ne 38   MUSSERT, Anton Adriaan, defendant, *Het proces Mussert (The Mussert Trial)*, The Hague: Nijhoff, 1948. (Rijksinstituut voor Oorlogsdocumentatie.) xii, 344pp.

Ne 39   MUSSERT, Anton Adriaan, *Vijf notas van Mussert aan Hitler over de samenwerking van Duitschland en Nederland in een bond van Germaansche volkeren, 1940-1944 (Five Notes from Mussert to Hitler on the cooperation of Germany and Holland in a Confederation of Germanic Peoples)*, The Hague: Nijhoff, 1947. (Rijksinstituut voor Oorlogsdocumentatie.) 140pp.

Ne 40   ROGIER, L.J., 'Mussert bij Mussolini en Pacelli' (Mussert's visits to Mussolini and Pacelli). *Annalen van het Thijmgenootschap*, **43** (**2**), 1955. pp. 97-108.

Ne 41   STOKES, Lawrence D., 'Anton Mussert and the Nationaal-Socialistische Beweging der Nederlanden, 1931-1945'. *History*, **56** (**188**), 1971. pp. 387-407.

Other Fascist Tendencies

Ne 42   BOHM, R.P.S.M., and LINDE, H.M. van der, 'Het italiaans

Fascisme in de Nederlandse pers' (Italian fascism in the Dutch press).
Spiegel Historiael, **15** (**7/8**), 1980. pp. 403–9.

Ne 43   JONGE, A.A. de, 'Conservatieve en revolutionnaire anti-democraten' (Conservative and revolutionary anti-democrats). *Spiegel Historiael*, **4** (**7/8**), 1969. pp. 417–24. On the anti-democratic circles of the 1920s as forerunners of fascism.

Ne 44   WICHMAN, Erich and EIKEBOOM, Henk, *Het fascisme in Nederland: zie pro en contra*, Baarn: Hollandiadrukkerij, 1925. Pro Wichman, contra Eikeboom.

Ne 45   WIGERSMA, Baltus, *G.J.P.J. Bolland: een schets*, Haarlem: Boissevain, 1922. Bolland (1854–1922), leader of Hegelian fascist group.

Ne 46   WIGERSMA, Baltus, *Het wezen het fascisme* (*The Nature of Fascism*), Bussum: Van Dishoeck, 1934. 176pp.

Ne 47   ZAAL, Wim, *De herstellers: lotgevallen van de Nederlandse fascisten en van Wouter Lutkie's tijdsschrift Aristo.* (*The Restorers: adventures of the Dutch fascists in Wouter Lutkie's journal Aristo*), Utrecht: Ambo, 1966. 264pp. Concerned with the fascist group led by Father Lutkie and its journal Aristo, of the reconstructed version of which, Zaal was editor (1957–65). Also discusses Zwart Front.

Ne 48   ZAAL, Wim, *De Nederlandse fascisten*, Amsterdam: Wetenschappelijke Uitg., 1973. 228pp. Fascists rather than nazis.

Netherlands and the Second World War

Ne 49   AMSTERDAM. Rijksinstituut voor Oorlogsdocumentatie. *Studies over Nederland in Oorlogstijd*, ed. A.H. Paape, The Hague: Nijhoff, 1972. Vol. 1.

Ne 50   BOLHUIS, J.J. van and others (eds), *Onderdrukking en verzet: Nederland in oorlogstijd*, ed. J.J. van Bolhuis, C.D.J. Brandt, H.M. van Randwijk, B.C. Slotemaker (*Oppression and Resistance*), Arnhem: Van Loghum Slaterus, 1947–55. 4 vols. Contains an article on NSB by Bolhuis and one on the Netherlands Union amongst others.

Ne 51   HIRSCHFELD, Gerhard, 'Collaboration and attentism in the Netherlands, 1940–41'. *J. OF CONTEMP. HIST.*, **16** (**3**), 1981. pp. 467–86.

Ne 52   HOFFMANN, Gabriele, *NS-Propaganda in den Niederlanden: Organisationen und Lenkung der Publizistik unter deutscher Besatzung, 1940–1945*, Berlin: Verlag Dokumentation, 1972. 296pp. Bib. 270–90.

Ne 53   JONG, Louis de, *Het Koninkrijk der Niederlanden in de Tweede Wereldoorlog, 1939–1945*, ed. Rijksinstituut voor Oorlogs-documentatie, The Hague: Staatsdrukkerij, 1969-80. 10 vols. Official history of the Netherlands during World War II. Vol 1 includes one of the best summaries of nazi and fascist activity.

Ne 54   KWIET, Konrad, *Reichskommissariat Niederlande: Versuch und Scheitern nationalsozialistische Neuordnung*, Stuttgart: Deutsche Verlags-Anstalt, 1968. 172pp. Bib. 157-65. Free University of Berlin thesis.

Ne 55   MASON, Henry Lloyd, *The Purge of Dutch Quislings: emergency justice in the Netherlands*, The Hague: Nijhoff, 1952. xii, 199pp. Bib. 164-93. Columbia University thesis.

Ne 56   Nationalsozialistische Deutsche Arbeiter Partei. Schutzstaffel, *De S.S. in Nederland: documenten uit SS-archieven, 1933–1945*, ed. *N.K.C.A. in't Veld*, The Hague: Nijhoff, 1976. 2 vols. Bib. 1647-52.

Ne 57   PRESSER, Jacob, *Ashes in the Wind: the destruction of Dutch Jewry*, London: Souvenir Press, 1968. xv, 556pp. Tr. of *Ondergang*, The Hague, 1965, by Arnold Pomerans. US edn, *The Destruction of Dutch Jewry*, Dutton, 1969.

Ne 58   SCHUURSMA, R., 'Dutch fascists' share in crime'. *WIENER LIB. BULL.*, **20** (**2**), 1966. pp. 34-7.

Ne 59   VELD, N.K.C.A. in't, 'The SS in relation to the Netherlands'. *Netherlands J. of Sociology*, **13** (**2**), 1977. pp. 125-39.

Ne 60   WARMBRUNN, Werner, *The Dutch under German Occupation, 1940–1945*, Stanford: University Press, 1963. xiii, 338pp. Bib. 316-31. Chapter 4: the National Socialist Movement of the Netherlands.

Ne 61   ZEE, Sytze van der, *Voor Führer, volk en vaderland sneuvelde. . . .: de SS in Nederland, Nederland in der SS* (*Killed for Führer, people and Fatherland*), The Hague: Krusemann, 1975. 248pp. Bib. 236-9. Collaboration.

LUXEMBURG

L 1   KOCH-KENT, Henri, *Hitlertum in Luxemburg, 1933–1944*, by H. Koch-Kent, Jean Hames, Francis Steffen, Luxembourg: Impr. Hermann, 1972. 47pp.

L 2   KOCH-KENT, Henri, *Luxemburg im SD-Spiegel: ein Bericht vom 12 Juli 1940*, Luxembourg: Impr. Hermann, 1973. 48pp.

L 3   KRIER, Emile, *Deutsche Kultur- und Volkstumspolitik von 1933 bis 1940 in Luxemburg*, Bonn: 1979. 808pp. Bonn University thesis, 1975.

L 4   MERSCH, Carole, *Le National-socialisme et la presse luxembourgeoise de 1933-1940*, Luxembourg: St Paul, 1979. 185pp.

PORTUGAL

General

P 1   GRAHAM, Lawrence and MAKLER, Harry M. (eds), *Contemporary Portugal: the revolution and its antecedents*, Austin: University of Texas Press, 1979. xliii, 357pp. Includes articles by Schmitter, Lucena, Wiarda, Makler.

P 2   MARTINS, Hermínio, 'Portugal'. In WOOLF, S.J., Gn 20. pp. 302–36. Sees Salazar as fascist.

P 3   OLIVEIRA MARQUES, A.H. de, *History of Portugal*, New York: Columbia University Press, 1972. 2 vols. Vol. 2. *From Empire to Corporate State*. 303pp. Portuguese fascism pp. 177–94.

P 4   ROBINSON, Richard Alan Hodgson, *Contemporary Portugal: a history*, London: Allen & Unwin, 1979. 279pp. Bib. 276–81.

Integralism, The Military Dictatorship, and Pre-Fascism

P 5   CAMPINOS, Jorge, *A ditadura militar, 1926-1933*, Lisbon: Dom Quixote, 1975. 264pp.

P 6   CARVALHO, José Fernando Rivera Martins de, *O pensamento integralista perante o Estado Novo*, Lisbon: Pensamento Politico, 1971. 77pp. Influence of Integralist thought on Salazarist state.

P 7   FERRÃO, Carlos, *O Integralismo e a República: autópsia de um mito*, Lisbon: Inquerito, 1964-6. 3 vols. Vol. 3 pub. by O Século.

P 8   GALLAGHER, Thomas G., 'The mystery train: Portugal's

military dictatorship, 1926-32'. *EUR. STUD. REV.*, **11** (**3**), 1981. 325-53.

P 9   *Integralismo Lusitano: a questão iberica*, Lisbon: Almeida, Miranda, 1916. 352pp. Bib. Essays by leading Integralists.

P 10   OLIVEIRA MARQUES, A.H. de, 'Revolution and Counter-revolution in Portugal: problems of Portuguese history, 1900-1930'. In KOSSOK, M. (ed.), *Studien über die Revolution*, Berlin: Akademie V., 1969. pp. 403-18. Claims Integralism as foundation of fascist ideology.

P 11   PROENÇA, Raul, *Acerca do Integralismo Lusitano*, Lisbon: Seara Novo, 1964. xiv, 104pp. Articles from *Seara Novo*.

P 12   PROENÇA, Raul, *Paginas de politica*, Lisbon: Seara Novo, 1938-9. 2 vols. Integralism.

Estado Novo and the Salazarist Dictatorship

P 13   ALMEIDA, João de, *O Estado Novo*, Lisbon: Parceira, A.M. Pereira, 1932. 371pp.

P 14   AMEAL, João de, *Construção do Novo Estado*, Oporto: Liv. Tavares Martins, 1938. 64pp.

P 15   ASSAC, Jacques Ploncard d', *Doctrine du nationalisme*, Paris: La Librairie Française, 1958. 350pp. Defence of corporatism by ex-associate of Doriot.

P 16   ASSAC, Jacques Ploncard d', *L'État corporatif: l'expérience portugaise: doctrine et législation*, Paris: La Librairie Française, 1960. 223pp.

P 16   BRONGERSMA, Edward, *De opbouw von een corporatieven staat: het nieuwe Portugal*, 2nd edn (*The Construction of a Corporate State*), Utrecht: Spectrum, 1941. xi, 589pp. Bib. 573-83.

P 17   CAETANO, Marcello, *Lições de direito corporativo*, Lisbon: Oficina Gráfica, 1935. 168pp. Portuguese corporatist theory.

P 18   CAETANO, Marcello, *Problemas da revolução corporativa*, Lisbon: Ed. Acção, 1941. 156pp. Essays.

P 19   CAMPINOS, Jorge, *Ideologia politica do estado Salazarista*, tr. from the French by Arthur Mauricio, Lisbon: Portugalia, 1965. 65pp.

P 20   CAMPOS, Fernando, *Paginas corporativas, com algumas palavras, etc.*, Lisbon: Oficinas Gráficas 1941. 209pp. Collected articles of a leading corporatist theorist.

P 21   CLAUSS, Max Walter, 'Salazars autoritäres Regime in Portugal'. *VIERTELJAHRSH. FÜR ZEITG.*, 5 (4), 1957. pp. 379-85.

P 22   COTTA, Freppel, *Economic Planning in Corporative Portugal*, pref. by Dr Marcello Caetano, London: King, 1937. xiv, 188pp. Bib. 187-8

P 23   DERRICK, Michael, *The Portugal of Salazar*, London: Paladin, 1938. New York: Campion Books, 1939. 168pp. Pro-Salazar.

P 24   FERRAZ DE SOUSA, Abel, *Ressurgimento em Portugal*, São Paulo: Ed. Lep S.A., 1962. 221pp.

P 25   FIGUEIREDO, Antonio de, *Portugal: fifty years of dictatorship*. Harmondsworth: Penguin, 1975. New York: Holmes & Meier, 1976. 261pp. Bib. 259-61.

P 26   GEORGEL, Jacques, *Le Salazarisme: histoire et bilan, 1926-1974*, pref. by Mario Soares, Paris: Ed. Cujas, 1981. 310pp. Bib. 305-8.

P 27   GALLAGHER, Thomas G., *The Theory and Practice of Portuguese Authoritarianism: Salazar, the Right and the Portuguese military. 1926-1968*, Manchester University thesis, 1978.

P 28   LUCENA, Manuel, *L'Évolution du système corporatif portugais à travers les lois, 1933-1971*, Paris: Inst. des Sciences Sociales du Travail, 1971. 2 vols. Thesis.

P 29   MAYER, Anton, *Portugal und sein Weg zum autoritären Staat*, Leipzig: Goldmann, 1939. 101pp. Nazi pro-Salazar view.

P 30   PONCINS, Léon de, *Le Portugal renaït*, Paris: Beauchesne, 1936. 276pp.

P 31   SCHMITTER, Philippe C., *Corporatism and Public Policy in Authoritarian Portugal*, London: Sage, 1975. 72pp. Bib. 69-72. Influences on Salazar were Integralism, social Christianity, Italian fascism, French solidarism.

P 32   SCHMITTER, Philippe C., 'The social origins, economic bases and political imperatives of authoritarian rule in Portugal'. In LARSEN, S.U., Gn 36. pp. 435-66.

P 33   SILVA, Josue da, *Legião portuguesa: forca repressiva do fascismo*, Lisbon: Diabril, 1975. 107pp. On the paramilitary Portuguese Legion. Includes Preto's National Syndicalists.

P 34   WIARDA, Howard J., *Corporation and Development: the Portuguese experience, 1933-1974*. Amherst: University of Massachusetts Press, 1977. xiii, 447pp. Bib. 407-33. Salazar was not a fascist but the Blueshirts (National Syndicalists) were.

Antonio de Oliveira Salazar (1889-1970)

P 35   ASSAC, Jacques Ploncard d', *Salazar*, Paris: La Table Ronde, 1967. 350pp. Includes National Syndicalists.

P 36   EGERTON, F.C.C., *Salazar: rebuilder of Portugal*, London: Hodder & Stoughton, 1943. 336pp. A eulogy.

P 37   FERRO, Antonio, *Salazar, Portugal and her leader*, tr. by H. de Barros Gomes and John Gibbons, London: Faber & Faber, 1939. 364pp. By a follower of Salazar.

P 38   GONÇALVES, Assis, *Intimidades de Salazar: o homem e a sua epoca: memorias do seu Secretario nos primeiros sete e dificeis anos da su vida publica*, 2nd edn, Lisbon: Bertrand, 1972. 235pp.

P 39   KAY, Hugh, *Salazar and Modern Portugal*, London: Eyre & Spottiswoode. New York: Hawthorn, 1970. xxiii, 478pp. Bib. 465-6.

P 40   LICHTERVELDE, Louis, Comte de, 'Pensées politiques du Dr. Salazar'. *Bull. Acad. Royale de Belgique. Classe des Lettres et des Sciences Morales et Politiques*, **43** (**5**), 1957. pp. 30-43.

P 41   MASSIS, Henri, *Salazar face à face; trois dialogues politiques*, Paris: La Palatine, 1961. 167pp. Conversations with Salazar 1938-60 by a French Maurrasian.

P 42   MEDINA, João, *Salazar em Franco*, Lisbon: Atica, 1977. 146pp.

P 43   NOGUEIRA, Alberto Franco, *Salazar*, Coimbra: Atlantida, 1977. 1. *A mocidade e os principios, 1889-1928: estudio biografico*. xii, 339pp.

P 44   RUDEL, Christian, *Le Portugal et Salazar*, Paris: Éds. Ouvrières, 1968. 160pp.

P 45   RUDEL, Christian, *Salazar*, Paris: Mercure de France, 1969. 276pp. Bib. 275-6.

P 46   OLIVEIRA SALAZAR, Antonio de, *Dictionnaire politique de Salazar; établi par Jacques Ploncard D'Assac*, Lisbon: SNI, 1964. 261pp.

P 47   OLIVEIRA SALAZAR, Antonio de, *Discursos e notas politicas*, Coimbra: Coimbra Editora, 1935-68. 5 vols.

P 48   SARAIVA, J. Silva, *O pensamento politico de Salazar*, Coimbra: Coimbra Editora, 1953. 279pp. Bib.

P 49   SÉRANT, Paul, *Salazar et son temps*, Paris: Les Septs Couleurs, 1961. 211pp. Defence of Salazar by French neo-fascist.

Nacional Sindicalismo

P 50   MEDINA, João, *Salazar e os fascistas: Salazarismo e Nacional-sindicalismo: a historia dum conflito, 1932–1935*, Lisbon: Bertrand, 1979. 249pp.

P 51   NEVÉS DA COSTA, A., *Para alem da ditadura*. **1**, *Solucões corporativas*, Lisbon: Nacional Sindicalismo, 1933. A tract of the National Syndicalists the extreme Rightist opponents of Salazar's moderation.

SPAIN

Bibliographies

Sp 1   AMADOR GARRANDI, Florencio, *Ensayo bibliográfico de las obras y folletos publicados con motivo del Movimiento Nacional de 600 titulos y 250 notas bibliograficos*, Bermeo: Diputación Provincial de Vizcaya, 1940. 163pp.

Sp 2   BARDI, Ubaldo, *La guerra civile di Spagna: saggio per una bibliografia italiana*, Urbino: Argalia, 1974. 134pp.

Sp 3   CIERVA Y DE HOCES, Ricardo de la, *Bibliografia general sobre la Guerra de España, 1936–1939 y sus antecedentes históricos: fuentes para la historia contemporanea de España*, Madrid: Ed. Ariel, 1968. 729pp. Essential bibliography including much ephemera relevant to the Falange.

Sp 4   CORTADA, James W., 'A select bibliography of materials published outside of Spain on the Franco period of Spanish history, 1939–1971'. *Cuadernos de Historia Economica de Cataluña*, **6**, 1971. Suppl. pp. 1–114.

Sp 5   GARCÍA DURÁN, Juan, *Bibliography of the Spanish Civil War, 1936–1939*, Montivideo: El Siglo Illustrado, 1964. 559pp.

Sp 6   GIRALT I RAVENTOS, Emili, *El franquisme i l'oposicio: una bibliografia critica, 1939–1975*, Barcelona: Enciclopedia Catalana, 1981. 885pp.

Sp 7   Madrid University. Cátedra de Historia Contemporánea de España. *Cuadernos bibliograficos de la Guerra de España, 1936–1939*,

Madrid: Universidad, 1966-. Anejos. 1970 - Ser. 2 includes list of periodicals pub. during Civil War.

General

Sp 8   COVERDALE, John F., *Italian Intervention in the Spanish Civil War*, Princeton: University Press, 1975. xxi, 455pp. Bib. 421–37.

Sp 9   LINZ, Juan José, 'The party systems of Spain: past and future'. In LIPSET, S.M. and ROKKAN, S., *Party Systems and Voter Alignments*, New York: Free Press, 1967. pp. 197–282.

Sp 10   PAYNE, Stanley G., 'La derecha in Italia y España'. *Boletin de Ciencia Politica*, **13/14**, 1974. pp. 65–82.

Sp 11   PAYNE, Stanley G., 'Spanish nationalism in the twentieth century'. *REV. OF POLIT.*, **26**, 1964. pp. 403–22.

Sp 12   PAYNE, Stanley G., *Politics and the Military in Spain*, Stanford: University Press. Oxford: University Press, 1967. xiii. 574pp. Bib. 537–61

Sp 13   PAYNE, Stanley G., 'Spain'. In ROGGER, H. and WEBER, E., Gn 54. pp. 168–207.

Sp 14   PAYNE, Stanley G., 'Spanish fascism in comparative perspective'. *Iberian Studies*, **2** (1), 1973. pp. 3–12.

Sp 15   PRESTON, Paul, 'Spain'. In WOOLF, S.J. Gn 20. pp. 329–51.

Sp 16   RAMA, Carlos M., *Fascismo y anarquismo en la España contemporanea*, Barcelona: Bruguera, 1979. 284pp.

Sp 17   VIÑAS, Angel, *La Alemania nazi y el 18 de julio: antecedentes de la intervencion alemana en la Guerra Civil Española*, Madrid: Alianza, 1974. 558pp. 521–56.

The Origins of the Extreme Right in Spain

Sp 18   BEN-AMI, Shlomo, *Fascism from Above: the dictatorship of Primo de Rivera in Spain, 1923-1930*, Oxford: University Press, 1983. xiv, 454pp. Bib. 403–28.

Sp 19   BEN-AMI, Shlomo, 'The dictatorship of Primo de Rivera: a political reassessment'. *J. OF CONTEMP. HIST.*, **12** (1), 1977. pp. 65–84.

Sp 20 BEN-AMI, Shlomo, 'The forerunners of Spanish fascism: Unión Patriótica and Unión Monárquica'. *EUR. STUD. REV.*, **9 (1)**, 1979. pp. 49–79.

Sp 21 CANNISTRARO, Philip V. and CORTADA, James W., 'Francisco Cambó and the modernisation of Spain: the technocratic possibilities of fascism'. *REV. OF POLIT.*, **3 (1)**, 1975. pp. 66–82. A rich Catalan fascist of 1920s.

Sp 22 CIERVA Y DE HOCES, Ricardo de la, *Historia de la Guerra Civil española: anticedentes, monarquía y república, 1898–1936*, Madrid: San Martin, 1969. 826pp. Chapter 12 pp. 507–75 on fascism.

Sp 23 JIMÉNEZ CAMPO, Javier 'Aproximación a un modelo de partido fascista: el caso del Partido Nacionalista Español'. *Sistema*, **22**, 1978. pp. 75–92. A small fascist group founded in 1930 by a neurologist José Maria Albiñana.

Sp 24 PASTOR, Manuel, 'Un ensayo del fascismo en España, 1930–1933: J. M. Albinaña y el PNE'. *Tiempo de Historia*, **8**, July 1975. pp. 26–39.

Sp 25 PASTOR, Manuel, *Los origines del fascismo en España*, Madrid: Tucar, 1975. 134pp. Covers 1923–30 including the Partido Nacionalista Español.

Sp 26 RATCLIFF, Dillwyn Fritschel, *Prelude to Franco: political aspects of the dictatorship of General Miguel Primo de Rivera*, pref. by Saul K. Padover, New York: Las Americas Pub. Co., 1957. 113pp.

The Second Republic and the Extreme Right

Sp 27 JIMÉNEZ CAMPO, Javier, *El fascismo en la crisis de la Segunda Republica Española*, Madrid: Centro de Investigaciones Sociologicos, 1979. 349pp. Bib. 343–9. Madrid University thesis.

Sp 28 PORTUONDO, Ernesto, *La Segunda Republica; reforma, fascismo y revolución*, Madrid: Ed. Revolución, 1981. 274pp.

Sp 29 PRESTON, Paul, *The Coming of the Spanish Civil War: reform, reaction, and revolution in the Second Republic, 1931–1936*, London: Macmillan, 1978. xiv, 264pp. Bib. 233–47.

Sp 30 PRESTON, Paul, *The Spanish Right under the Second Republic: an analysis*, Reading: University Graduate School of Contemporary European Studies, 1971. 39pp.

Sp 31   ROBINSON, Richard Alan Hodgson, *The Origins of Franco's Spain: the Right, the Republic and revolution, 1931-1936*, Newton Abbott: David & Charles, 1970. Pittsburgh: University of Pennsylvania Press, 1971. 475pp. Bib. 428-54. Survey of the Right including the Falange.

Sp 32   ROBINSON, Richard Alan Hodgson, 'The parties of the Right and the Republic'. In CARR, Raymond (ed.), *The Republic and the Civil War in Spain*, London: Macmillan, 1971. pp. 46-78.

Acción Española, Calvo Sotelo and the Monarchist Right

Sp 33   ANSON, Luis Maria, *Acción Española*, Zaragoza: Editorial Circulo, 1960. 248pp. On the authoritarian monarchist party.

Sp 34   AUNÓS Y PÉREZ, Eduardo, *La reforma corporativa del estado*, Madrid: Aguilar, 1935. xviii, 271pp. Bib. 269-71. Author associated with Acción Española. Earlier sent by Miguel Primo de Rivera to study the Corporate State in Italy.

Sp 35   FOARD, Douglas W., 'Ramiro de Maeztu y el fascismo'. *Historia, 16*, **4**, 1979. pp. 106-15.

Sp 36   MAEZTU Y WHITNEY, Ramiro, Conde de, *Obra*, Madrid: Editora Nacional, 1974. 1309pp. Clerical reactionary of the extreme Right (1875-1936).

Sp 37   MORODO LEONCIO, Raúl, 'La formalización de Acción Española'. *REV. DE ESTUD. POLIT.*, Nueva Epoca. **1**, 1978. pp. 29-47. Acción Española represented the traditionalist sector of the Spanish Right. Members became the political class under Franco.

Sp 38   PAYNE, Stanley G., '1936: Calvo Sotelo y la Gran Derecha'. *Nueva Historia*, **2** (**20**), 1978. pp. 88-95.

Sp 39   PRESTON, Paul, 'Alfonsist monarchism and the coming of the Spanish Civil War'. *J. OF CONTEMP. HIST.*, **7** (**3/4**), 1972. pp. 89-114.

Sp 40   SORIANO FLORES DE LEMUS, Julian, *Calvo Sotelo ante la Segunda República*, Madrid: Editora Nacional, 1975. 174pp.

Unión Militar Española

Sp 41   CACHO ZABALZA, Antonio, *La Unión Militar Española*, Alicante: Egasa, 1940. 67pp.

The Carlists

Sp 42   BLINKHORN, Martin, *Carlism and Crisis in Spain, 1931–1939*, Cambridge: University Press, 1975. xii, 394pp. Bib. 362–86.

Sp 43   BURGO, Jaime del, *Requetés en Navarra antes del alzamiento*, San Sebastian: Ed. Española, 1939. 188pp. On the Carlist militia which amalgamated with the Falangists in 1937.

Sp 44   REDONDO, Luis and ZAVALA, Juan de, *El Requeté; la tradición no muere*, Barcelona: AHR, 1957. 556pp. Bib. 539–43.

Sp 45   RESA, José Maria, *Memorias de un Requeté*, pref. by Tomas García Rebull, Barcelona: Ed. Bayer, 1968. 159pp.

Sp 46   WINSTON, Colin M., 'The proletarian Carlist road to fascism: Sindicalismo Libre'. *J. OF CONTEMP. HIST.*, **17** (**4**), 1982. pp. 557–85.

Juntas de Ofensiva Nacional Sindicalista

Sp 47   GUILLÉN SALAYA, Francisco, *Anecdotario de la JONS: (historia y anecdota de la Juntas de Ofensiva Nacional Sindicalista)*, San Sebastian: Ed. Yugos y Flechas, 1938. 146pp. Falangist activist.

Sp 48   *JONS; antologia y prologo de Juan Aparicio*, Barcelona: Editora Nacional, 1939. 335pp. Anthology from the journal of the Juntas de Ofensiva Nacional Sindicalista edited by the one-time secretary of one of its founders, Ramiro Ledesma Ramos.

Falange Española and National Syndicalism

Sp 49   ALCÁZAR DE VELASCO, Angel, *Serrano Súñer en la Falange*, Barcelona: Eds Patria, 1941. 196pp. Ramón Serrano Súñer, leader of Juventudes de Acción Popular, a clericalist youth movement. Franco's brother-in-law. Minister of the Interior in 1938.

Sp 50   ALCÁZAR DE VELASCO, Angel, *Los 7 dias de Salamanca*, Madrid: G. del Toro, 1976. 308pp.

Sp 51   ALVAREZ PUGA, Eduardo, *Diccionario de la Falange*, Barcelona: DOPESA, 1977. 92pp.

Sp 52   ALVAREZ PUGA, Eduardo, *Historia de la Falange*, pref by

Manuel Hedilla, Barcelona: DOPESA, 1969. 216pp. Repr. of series of articles from *Mundo*.

Sp 53   AVILA S. PASCUAL, Justo de, *Metodologia de nacional-sindicalismo*, Valencia: Domenech, 1942. 48pp.

Sp 54   BRAVO MARTÍNEZ, Francisco, *Historia de la Falange Española de las JONS*, Madrid: Editora Nacional, 1943. 214pp. Author was JONS leader in Salamanca.

Sp 55   CIERVA Y DE HOCES, Ricardo de la, 'Un aspecto de la evolución politica de la zona nacional en guerra: la trajectoria de la Falange hasta la unificación de 1937'. In *Aproximación Historica a la Guerra Española, 1936-1939*, Madrid: Universidad, 1970. pp. 205-40. On events of April 1937 when Franco absorbed Falange into a wider state party.

Sp 56   DÁVILA, Sancho and PEMARTÍN, Julián, *Hacia la historia de la Falange*. Vol. 1, Jerez de la Frontera: Jerez Industrial, 1938. *1. Primera contribución de Sevilla.*

Sp 57   DÍAZ DOIN, Guillermo, *Cómo llegó Falange al poder*, Buenos Aires: Aniceto Lopez, 1940. 158pp. Analysis of Falangism.

Sp 58   FOUQUET, Patricia Root, *The Falange in pre-Civil War Spain: leadership, ideology and origins*, University of California, San Diego thesis, 1972. UM 72-22466. 264pp.

Sp 59   GARCÍA VENERO, Maximiano, *Historia de la unificación (Falange y Requeté en 1937)*, Madrid, 1970. 260pp. Rev. version of *Falange en la guerra España: la unificación y Hedilla*, Paris: Ruedo Iberico, 1967. Written by a Falangist journalist hired by Manuel Hedilla Larrey, last leader of the independent Falange, ousted by Franco in 1937.

Sp 60   GUILLÉN SALAYA, Francisco, *Historia del sindicalismo español*, 2nd edn, Madrid: Ed. Nacional, 1943. 198pp.

Sp 61   GUTIÉRREZ PALMA, Emilio, *1931-1936: sindicatos y agitadores revolucionarios nacional-sindicalistas*, Valladolid: Eds Libertad [1937?]. 64pp.

Sp 62   HEDILLA LARREY, Manuel, *Testimonio de Manuel Hedilla; (escrita por Maximiano García Venero bajo la direccion de Manuel Hedilla)*, 2nd edn, Barcelona: Acervo, 1976. 629pp. Hedilla's supporters' version of material in García Venero's *Falange en el guerra de España*.

Sp 63   HOEHL, Egbert, 'Glorreiche Tradition und national Erneuerung: Spanien und der Falangismus'. *BL. FÜR DTSCH. UND INT. POLIT.*, 11, 1966. pp. 686-95, 920-31.

Sp 64   JEREZ RIESCO, José Luis, *La Falange, partido fascista*, Barcelona: BAU, 1977. 128pp.

Sp 65   JATO, David, *La rebelión de los estudiantes: apuntes para una historia del alegre SEU*, Madrid: CIES, 1953. 358pp. History of the Sindicato Español Universitario, the Falange's student syndicate.

Sp 66   KLUGE, Franz Hermann, *National spanische Kampfzeitungen*, Hamburg: Evert, 1937. 51pp. Contains a useful list of Falangist periodicals.

Sp 67   LUCHINI, Alberto (ed.), *I Falangisti spagnoli, cosa vogliono, perché si battono*, Florence: Beltrami Ed., 1936. 41pp.

Sp 68   MARTIN, Raúl, *La contrarevolución falangista*, Paris: Ruedo Iberico, 1971. iv, 235pp.

Sp 69   MARTINEZ VAL, José Maria, *Por que no fue posible la Falange?* Barcelona: Dopesa, 1975. 211pp.

Sp 70   NELLESSEN, Bernd, *Die verbotene Revolution: Aufstieg und Niedergang der Falange*, Hamburg: Leibniz V., 1963. 216pp. Bib. 204–13. Hamburg University thesis.

Sp 71   PAYNE, Stanley G., 'Social composition and regional strength of the Spanish Falange'. In LARSEN, S.U. Gn 36. pp. 423–34.

Sp 72   PAYNE, Stanley G., *Falange: a history of Spanish fascism*, Stanford: Stanford University Press. Oxford: University Press, 1961. ix, 316pp. Bib. 298–307.

Sp 73   POZHARSKAIA, S.P., 'Fashistskaia Falanga v Ispanii' (The fascist Falange in Spain). *Novaia i Noveishaia Istoriia*, (**5**), 1972. pp. 103–15; (**1**), 1973. pp. 120–35.

Sp 74   RODRIGUEZ DE VALCARCEL, Alejandro, *El Movimiento y el pueblo español*, Madrid: Eds del Movimiento, 1968. 220pp. The Falange in 1939.

Sp 75   RUDEL, Christian, *La Phalange: histoire du fascisme en Espagne*, Paris: Éds et Pubs Premières, 1972. 315pp. Bib. 307–9.

Sp 76   SOUTHWORTH, Herbert Rutledge, *Antifalange: estudio crítica de 'Falange en la guerra de España: la unificación y Hedilla' de Maximiano García Venero*, Paris: Ruedo Iberico, 1967. xxiii, 286pp. Bib. 269–78. List of Falangist journals 166–7. Tr. by José Martinez. Detailed page-by-page critique of García Venero's Hedillista apologia.

Sp 77   SOUTHWORTH, Herbert Rutledge, 'The Falange: an analysis of Spain's fascist heritage'. In PRESTON, Paul (ed.), *Spain in*

Crisis: the evolution and decline of the Franco regime, Hassocks, Harvester Press, 1976. pp. 1-22.

Sp 78 SOUTHWORTH, Herbert Rutledge, 'Permanencia del fascismo español? Que es el fascismo?' *REV. DE CIENC. SOC. (Puerto Rico)*, **15** (**1**), 1971. pp. 119-34.

Sp 79 VELARDE FUERTES, Juan, *El nacionalsindicalismo, cuarenta años después: analisis critico*, Madrid: Editora Nacional, 1972. 314pp.

Falangist Ideology

Sp 80 ARRESE, José Luis de, *La revolución social del nacionalsindicalismo*, Madrid: Editora Nacional, 1940. 229pp. Reissued 1959. Most complete publication of the Falange programme.

Sp 81 ARRESE, José Luis de, *Obras seleccionadas. 1. Treinta años de política*, Madrid: Aguado, 1966. 487pp. Collection of political writings by one of Falange's camisa vieja (old guard). Falange leader after Serrano years.

Sp 82 CANTARERO DEL CASTILLO, Manuel, *Falange y socialismo*, Barcelona: DOPESA, 1973. 368pp.

Sp 83 ELISEDA, Francisco Moreno y Herrera, Marqués de la, *Autoridad y libertad*, Madrid: Gonzalez, 1945. 226pp. Bib. 223-6. Wealthy corporatist supporter of fascism. One of Falangist deputies in Cortez in 1934.

Sp 84 ELISEDA, Francisco Moreno y Herrera, Marqués de la, *Fascismo, catolicismo, monarquía*, Madrid: Eds Fax, 1935. 207pp. Author broke with Falange but remained supporter of Italian fascism.

Sp 85 LAIN ENTRALGO, Pedro, *Los valores morales del nacional-sindicalismo*, Madrid: Editora Nacional, 1941. 157pp. Justification of Falange violence.

Sp 86 MARTINEZ CARRASCO, Alfonso, *Fascismo en España*, Madrid: Ed. Jupiter [1934?]. Essays by various authors including José Antonio.

Sp 87 MUNOZ ALONSO, Adolfo, *Persona, sindicalismo y sociedad*, Madrid: Cabal, 1973. 344pp. Bib. 330. Falange as a mainly syndicalist organisation.

Sp 88 PEMARTÍN, Julián, *Teoría de la Falange*, 2nd edn, Madrid: Editora Nacional, 1942. 66pp.

Sp 89 PEMARTÍN, José, *Que es 'lo nuevo': consideraciones sobre el momento Español presente*, 3rd edn, Madrid: Espasa-Calpe, 1940. 379pp. Bib. 373-6.

Sp 90   PEREZ DE CABO, Juan Bautista, *Arriba España*, pref. by José Antonio Primo de Rivera, 2nd edn, Orense: Impr. La Region, 1939. 124pp. One of the first Falangist theoretical national syndicalist works. Author executed 1941 by Franco for conspiracy.

Sp 91   SÁNCHEZ MAZAS, Rafael, *Fundación, hermandad y destino*, Madrid: Eds del Movimiento, 1957. xv, 291pp. Essays by a Falangist writer.

The Falange, Literature and Culture

Sp 92   CASTELLÁ GASSOL, Juan, 'Ortega y la Falange'. *Casa de las Americas (Cuba)*, **3** (**19**), 1963. pp. 45-9. Ortega y Gasset unconsciously attracted to the fascist mentality?

Sp 93   GAROSCI, Aldo, *Gli intellettuali e la guerra di Spagna*, Turin: Einaudi, 1959. xiii, 482pp. Bib. 457-70.

Sp 94   MAINER, José-Carlos (ed.), *Falange y literatura*, Barcelona: Ed. Labor, 1971. 300pp. Bib. 67-9. Anthology of Falangist literature.

Sp 95   SCHWARTZ, Kessel, 'Culture and the Spanish Civil War: a fascist view, 1936-1939'. *J. OF INTER-AMER. STUDIES*, **7** (**4**), 1965. pp. 557-77.

Falange Española: Local Studies

Sp 96   BERNANOS, Georges, *A Diary of my Times*, London/New York: Macmillan, 1938. 269pp. Tr. of *Les Grands cimitières sous la lune*, Paris: Plon, 1938, by Pamela Morris. Describes Falangist activity on Majorca.

Sp 97   MELEIRO, Fernando, *Anecdotario de la Falange de Orense*, Madrid: Eds del Movimiento, 1957. 179pp. Author was a Falangist candidate for the Cortez.

Sp 98   MORA VILLAR, Manuel Felipe de la, *Los sangrientas cinco rosas*, pref. by M. García Venero: *la historia de la Falange de Santander*, Santander: Aldus Velarde, 1971. 179pp.

Sp 99   MOURE-MARIÑO, Luis, *Galicia en la guerra*, Madrid: Eds Españoles, 1939. 298pp. Author a leading Galacian national syndicalist.

Sp 100   SUAREZ CORTINA, M., *El fascismo en Asturias, 1931-1937*, Gijon: Canada Silverio, 1981. 312pp.

Sp 101   TAMARON, José de Mora-Figueroa, Marqués de, *Datos para la historia de la Falange gaditana, 1934-1939*, Jerez de la Frontera: Graf. del Exportador, 1974. 215pp. On the Falange in Cadiz.

Sp 102   ZAYAS, Alfonso de, Marqués de, *Historia de la vieja guardia de Baleares*, Madrid: Eds del Movimiento, 1955. 218pp.

Falangist Memoirs

Sp 103   ANDES, Conde de los, 'Un episodio en la historia de la Falange Española'. *Historia y Vida*, 3 (**25**), 1970. pp. 39-41. Ex-member of Falange explains his departure.

Sp 104   ANSALDO, Juan Antonio, *Para que?* (*de Alfonso XIII a Juan III*), Buenos Aires: Vasca Ekin, 1951. 563pp. By monarchist who joined Falange but was expelled in 1934.

Sp 105   GUILLÉN SALAYA, Francisco, *Los que nacimos con el siglo: biografía de una juventud*, Madrid: Editorial Colenda, 1953. 218pp.

Sp 106   MONTES AGUADO, Gumersindo, *Vieja Guardia*, pref. by E. Giménez Caballero, Madrid: Aguilar, 1939. 330pp.

Sp 107   VINIELLES TREPAT, Magín, *La sexta columna: diario de un combatiente leridano*, pref. by Rafael García Serrano, Barcelona: Acervo, 1971. 309pp.

Falangist Personalities: José Antonio Primo de Rivera (1903-36)

Sp 108   ÁLVAREZ GUTIÉRREZ, L., 'Ensayo bibliográfico sobre José Antonio Primo de Rivera'. In *Estudios de Historia Contemporanea*, ed. Vicente Palacio Atard, Madrid: Instituto Jeronimo Zurita del CSIC, 1976. Vol. 1. pp. 441-95.

Sp 109   ARRESE, José Luis de, *El estado totalitario en el pensamiento de José Antonio*, pref. by Raimundo Fernández Cuesta, Madrid: Vicesecretaria de Educación Popular, 1945. 81pp. Repr. 1959.

Sp 110   BARILLI, Manlio, *José Antonio Primo de Rivera precursore ed eroe*, pref. by Giorgio Pini, Rome: Ed. S. Michele, 1940. 91pp.

Sp 111   BRAVO MARTÍNEZ, Francisco, *José Antonio: ante la justicia roja*, Madrid: Vicesecretaria de Educación Popular, 1941. 142pp.

Sp 112   BRAVO MARTÍNEZ, Francisco, *José Antonio: el hombre, el jefe, el camarada*, Madrid: Eds Españolas, 1939. 248pp.

Sp 113   CIERVA Y DE HOCES, Ricardo de la, 'El interrogatorio de José Antonio'. *Historia y Vida*, **88**, July 1975. pp. 50–63.

Sp 114   DÁVILA, Sancho, *José Antonio, Salamanca y otras cosas*, Madrid: Aguado, 1967. 144pp.

Sp 115   *Dolor y Memoria de España en el Segundo Aniversario de la Muerte de José Antonio*, Barcelona: Ed. Jerarquia, 1939. 328pp.

Sp 116   FUENTES IRUROZQUI, Manuel, *El pensamiento económico de José Antonio Primo de Rivera*, Madrid: Capel, 1957. 189pp.

Sp 117   GIBELLO, Antonio, *José Antonio: apuntes para una biografia polémica*, Madrid: Doncel, 1974. 485pp. Doc. 403–85.

Sp 118   GIBSON, Ian, *En busca de José Antonio*, Barcelona: Planeta, 1980. 334pp. Bib. 327–9. Anti-José Antonio polemic in the Southworth tradition.

Sp 119   IMATZ, Arnaud, *José Antonio et la Phalange espagnol*, Paris: Eds Albatros, 1981. 615pp. Bib. 599–615.

Sp 120   LOPEZ MEDEL, Jesus, *Continuidad politica y convivencia: estudios de téoria e interpretación política joseantoniana*, 2nd edn, Madrid: Ed. y Pub. Populares, 1967. 359pp.

Sp 121   MAUGER, Gilles, *José Antonio: chef et martyr*, Paris: Nouvelles Eds Latines, 1955. 185pp.

Sp 122   MIGUEL MEDINA, Cecilia de, *La personalidad religiosa de José Antonio*, Madrid: Almena, 1975. 179pp. Bib. 161–70. Catholic aspects of his ideology stressed.

Sp 123   MUÑOZ ALONSO, Adolfo, *Un pensador para un pueblo*, 3rd edn, Madrid: Almena, 1969. 525pp. Bib. 413–41. Definitive pro-Falangist biography of José Antonio, stressing the Catholic humanistic elements in his ideas.

Sp 124   NIN DE CARDONA, José Maria, 'Evocación filosofica y politica del pensamiento de José Antonio Primo de Rivera en el XL aniversario de su muerte'. *REV. DE ESTUD. POLIT.*, **212**, 1977. pp. 281–300.

Sp 125   NIN DE CARDONA, José Maria, *José Antonio: la posibilidad politica truncada*, Madrid: Org. Sala Ed., 1973. xx, 251pp.

Sp 126   PEMARTÍN, Julián, *José Antonio*, 3rd edn, Madrid: Pubs. Españolas, 1974. 55pp.

Sp 127 PRIMO DE RIVERA, José Antonio, *Discursos y escritos, 1922-1936; José Antonio Primo de Rivera; (recopilación prol. de Agustin del Rio Cisneros)*, Madrid: Instituto de Estudios Politicos, 1976. 2 vols. Collected works.

Sp 128 PRIMO DE RIVERA, José Antonio, defendant, *Frente a frente: (José Antonio Primo de Rivera frente al Tribunal Popular)*; *texto taquigrafico*, Madrid: S. Martin, 1963. 364pp. Transcript of the trial.

Sp 129 PRIMO DE RIVERA, José Antonio, *José Antonio Primo de Rivera: der Troubadour der spanischen Falange; Auswahl und Kommentar seiner Reden und Schriften von Bernd Nellessen*, Stuttgart: Deutsche Verlags-Anstalt, 1965. 116pp. Extracts from the writings including articles from the journals *ABC*, *El Fascio*, *Falange Español*, and *Haz*.

Sp 130 PRIMO DE RIVERA, José Antonio, *José Antonio y la revolución nacional; textos seleccionados y ordenados por Agustin del Rio Cisneros*, 6th edn, Madrid: Eds del Movimiento, 1972. xxxii, 421pp. Bib. 417-21.

Sp 131 PRIMO DE RIVERA, José Antonio, *El mensaje de José Antonio*, 5th edn, Madrid: Eds del Movimiento, 1974. 106pp. Bib. 99-106.

Sp 132 PRIMO DE RIVERA, José Antonio, *Obras; edición cronológica; recopilación de Agustin del Rio Cisneros*, 8th edn, Madrid: Del Nac. de la Sección Femenina del Movimiento, 1974. xxvii, 1153pp.

Sp 133 PRIMO DE RIVERA, José Antonio, *El pensiamento de José Antonio; introducción y sistematización de textos por Agustin del Rio Cisneros*, 3rd edn, Madrid: Eds del Movimiento, 1971. 241pp.

Sp 134 PRIMO DE RIVERA, José Antonio, *Selected writings*, ed. and introduced by Hugh Thomas; tr. by Gudie Lawaetz, London: Cape, 1972. New York: Harper & Row, 1975. 271pp. Bib. 271.

Sp 135 PRIMO DE RIVERA, José Antonio, *The Spanish Answer: passages from the spoken and written message of José Antonio . . . 1903-1936*, selected and tr. by Juan MacNab Calder, Madrid, 1964. 293pp.

Sp 136 PRIMO DE RIVERA, José Antonio, *Textos biográficos y espistolario José Antonio intimo; recopilación de Agustin del Rio Cisneros y Enrique Pavon Pereyra*, 3rd edn, Madrid: Eds del Movimiento, 1968. xiii, 759pp. Bib. 757-9.

Sp 137 RIO CISNEROS, Agustin del. *José Antonio y la nueva sociedad.* Madrid, Eds del Movimiento, 1973. 64p.

Sp 138 RIO CISNEROS, Agustin del, *José Antonio y la conquista del tiempo nuevo: (conferencia pronunciada en Alicante el dia 20 de Nov. de 1961)*, Madrid: Eds del Movimiento, 1962. 60pp. Bib. 59-60.

Sp 139   ROJAS VILA, Carlos, *Prieto y José Antonio: socialismo y Falange ante la tragedia civil*, Barcelona: Dirosa, 1977, 267pp. On relations between José Antonio and Indalecio Prieto (1883-1962), Socialist leader who showed an interest in national syndicalism but refused to join the Falange.

Sp 140   ROJAS VILA, Carlos, *Memorias ineditas de José Antonio Primc de Rivera*, Barcelona: Planeta, 1977. 309pp.

Sp 141   SANTA MARINA, Luys, *Hacia José Antonio*, Barcelona: AHR, 1958. 233pp.

Sp 142   SERRANO SÚÑER, Ramón, *Semblenza de José Antonio, joven* Barcelona: Pareja y Borras, 1958. 61pp.

Sp 143   THOMAS, Hugh, 'The hero in the empty room, José Antonio and Spanish fascism'. *J. OF CONTEMP. HIST.*, **1** (1), 1966. pp. 174-82.

Sp 144   XIMENEZ DE SANDOVAL, Felipe, *José Antonio: biografia apasionada*, 4th edn, Madrid: Ed. Bullón, 1963. 535pp. First edn, 1941.

Falangist Personalities: Ramiro Ledesma Ramos (1905-36)

Sp 145   AGUADO, Emiliano, *Ramiro Ledesma en la crisis de España*, Madrid: Editora Nacional, 1942. 122pp.

Sp 146   APARICIO, Juan, *Ramiro Ledesma, fundador de las JONS*, 2nd edn, Madrid: Ed. de la Vicesecretaria de Educación Popular, 1942. 116pp.

Sp 147   BORRÁS Y BERMEJO, Tomás, *Ramiro Ledesma Ramos*, Madrid: Editora Nacional, 1971. 791pp. Hagiography.

Sp 148   LEDESMA RAMOS, Ramiro, *Los escritos filosóficos de Ramiro Ledesma Ramos*, Madrid: M. Minuesa de los Rios, 1941. xiv, 180pp.

Sp 149   LEDESMA RAMOS, Ramiro, *Fascismo en España? Discurso a las juventudes de España*, Barcelona: Ariel, 1968. 334pp. Reissue of two works, the first pub. in 1935 under the name of Roberto Lanzas the second also pub. in 1935 by 'La Conquista del Estado'.

Sp 150   LEDESMA RAMOS, Ramiro, *Ramiro Ledesma Ramos*, selected and pref. by Antonio Macipe Lopez, 2nd edn, Barcelona: Ed. F.E., 1942. 287pp.

Sp 151   MONTERO DÍAZ, Santiago, *Ramiro Ledesma Ramos*,

Madrid: Circulo Cultural Ramiro Ledesma Ramos, 1962. 75pp.
Ledesma's writings pp. 47-72.

Sp 152   MORENO HERNANDEZ, Miguel, *El nacional sindicalismo de Ramiro Ledesma Ramos*, Madrid: Deleg. Nac. de Org. del Movimiento, 1963. 143pp.

Sp 153   PAYNE, Stanley G., 'Ledesma Ramos and the origins of Spanish fascism'. *Mid-America*, **43** (4), 1961. pp. 226-41. Based on Aguado's work of 1942.

Sp 154   SANCHEZ DIANA, José Maria, *Ramiro Ledesma Ramos: biografía política*, Madrid: Editora Nacional, 1975. 352pp. Bib. 340-4. Works of Ledesma pp. 345-8.

Falangist Personalities: Ernesto Giménez Caballero (1899-   )

Sp 155   FOARD, Douglas W., *Ernesto Giménez Caballero and the Revolt of the Aesthetes*, Washington University thesis, 1972. UM 72-24220. 265pp.

Sp 156   FOARD, Douglas W., *Ernesto Giménez Caballero: o la revolución del poeta: estudio sobre el nacionalismo cultural hispánico en el siglo XX*, Madrid: Instituto de Estudios Politicos, 1975. 241pp. Bibs. Bowdlerised version of Foard's thesis, tr. by Giménez Caballero himself.

Sp 157   FOARD, Douglas W., 'The forgotten Falangist: Ernesto Giménez Caballero'. *J. OF CONTEMP. HIST.*, **10** (1), 1975. pp. 3-18.

Sp 158   GIMÉNEZ CABALLERO, Ernesto, *Genio de España: exaltaciones a una resurrección nacional y del mundo*, Madrid: La Gaceta Literaria, 1932. 341pp. 5th edn, Barcelona, 1939.

Sp 159   GIMÉNEZ CABALLERO, Ernesto, *Memorias de un dictador*, Barcelona: Planeta, 1979. 330pp.

Sp 160   GIMÉNEZ CABALLERO, Ernesto, *La Nueva catolicidad: teória general sobre el fascismo en Europa, en España*, 2nd edn, Madrid: La Gaceta Literaria, 1933. 220pp.

Sp 161   GIMÉNEZ CABALLERO, Ernesto, *Roma madre*, Madrid: Jerarquia, 1939. xxxii, 236pp. First pub. 1938, Milan: Hoepli, *Roma: risorta nel mundo*.

Sp 162   PLANA, Manuel, 'Alle origini del fascismo espagnolo: Giménez Caballero e l'esempio italiano'. *MOV. DI LIBERAZIONE IN ITALIA*, **25** (111), 1973. pp. 65-88.

Sp 163   TANDY, Lucy and SFERRAZZA, Maria, *Ernesto Giménez Caballero y La Gaceta Literaria o la generacion del 27*, Madrid: Turner, 1977. 170pp.

Falangist Personalities: Onésimo Redondo y Ortega (1905-36)

Sp 164   *Onésimo Redondo: Caudillo de Castilla*, Valladolid: Ed. Libertad, 1937. 225pp.

Sp 165   REDONDO Y ORTEGA, Onésimo, *Onésimo Redondo: textos politicos*, Madrid: Doncel, 1975. 326pp. Onésimo Redondo, one of founders of Juntas de Ofensiva Nacional-Sindicalistas.

Sp 166   REDONDO Y ORTEGA, Onésimo, *Obras completas: ed. cronologica*, Madrid: Pubs. Españolas, 1955. 2 vols.

Other Falangist Personalities

Sp 167   CALLEJA Y LOPEZ, Juan José, *Yägue: un corazon al rojo*, Barcelona: Ed. Juventud, 1963. 239pp. Juan de Yägue Blanco (1891-1952), military supporter of Franco and member of Falange.

Sp 168   MONTES AGUADO, Gumersindo, *Pepe Sainz: una vida en la Falange*, [n.p.]: Eds Pallas de Horta, 1939. 156pp. José Sainz, jefe provincial of Toledo.

Sp 169   RIDRUEJO, Dionisio, *Escrito en España*, pref. by Ramon Serrano Súñer. Madrid: G. del Toro, 1976. 460pp. Falange jefe provincial of Valladolid.

Sp 170   *Dionisio Ridruejo: de la Falange a la oposición* (Juan Benet *et al.*), Madrid: Taurus, 1976. 516pp. Bib. of works by Ridruejo 431-98. Festschrift for Dionisio Ridruejo (1912-75), poet and prose writer known as Spain's Goebbels, later jailed by Franco. 'Dionisio y la Falange' by N. Perales pp. 23-42.

Sp 171   RUIZ DE ALDA Y MIQUÉLEIZ, Julio, *Obra completa*, Barcelona: Eds. F.E., 1939. 345pp. Aviator and one of founders of the Falange.

Franco and Franquismo to 1945

Sp 172   ARRARÁS IRIBARREN, Joaquin, *Francisco Franco*, London: Bless, 1938. 223pp. Bib. 223.

Sp 173 BEYME, Klaus von, *Vom Faschismus zur Entwicklungsdiktatur: Machtelite und Opposition in Spanien*, Munich: Piper, 1971. 208pp. Bib. 191-203.

Sp 174 BLAYE, Edouard de, *Franco and the politics of Spain*. . . ; tr. by Brian Pearce, postscript to Part II by Richard Gott, Harmondsworth: Penguin, 1976. 576pp. Bib. 554-9.

Sp 175 CARR, Raymond and FUSI AIZPURUA, Juan Pablo, *Spain: dictatorship to democracy*, London: Allen & Unwin, 1979. xxi, 282pp. Chapters on Francoism and the institutions of Francoism.

Sp 176 CIERVA Y DE HOCES, Ricardo de la, *Historia del Franquismo: origines y configuración, 1939-1945*, Barcelona: Planeta, 1975, 437pp.

Sp 177 CIERVA Y DE HOCES, Ricardo de la, *Francisco Franco: un siglo de España*, Madrid: Editora Nacional, 1972/3. 3 vols. Bibs. Pro-Franco, but scholarly.

Sp 178 COLES, S.F.A., *Franco of Spain: a full-length biography*, London: Spearman, 1955. Westminster, MD: Newman Press, 1956. 264pp. Bib. 245-8.

Sp 179 CROZIER, Brian, *Franco: a biographical history*, London: Eyre & Spottiswoode, 1967. xxii, 589pp. Bib. 526-37. Sympathetic to Franco.

Sp 180 FRANCO BAHAMONDE, Francisco, *Pensamiento politico de Franco: antologia . . . sistematización de textos y preambulo de Agustin del Rio Cisneros*, Madrid: Eds del Movimiento, 1975. 2 vols.

Sp 181 FRANCO BAHAMONDE, Francisco, *Palabras del Caudillo, 19 de abril de 1937-7 de diciembre de 1942*, 3rd edn, Madrid: Editora Nacional, 1943. 548pp. Speeches, etc.

Sp 182 GALLO, Max, *Spain under Franco: a history*, London: Allen & Unwin, 1973. 390pp. Bib. 374-81. Tr. of *Histoire de l'Espagne franquiste*, Paris: Laffont, 1969, by Jean Stewart.

Sp 183 GEORGEL, Jacques, *Le Franquisme: histoire et bilan, 1939-1969*, Paris: Ed. du Seuil, 1970. 398pp. Bib. 387-94.

Sp 184 GONZALEZ GONZALEZ, Manuel-Jesus, *La económia politica del franquismo 1940-1970: dirigismo, mercado y planificación*, Madrid: Tecnos, 1979. 460pp.

Sp 185 HILLS, George, *Franco: the man and his nation*, London: Hale, 1967. New York: Macmillan, 1968. 464pp. Bib. 449-56.

Sp 186 JIMÉNEZ CAMPO, Javier, 'Integración simbolica en el

primer franquismo, 1939-1945'. *REV. DE ESTUD. POLIT.*, **14**, 1980. pp. 125-43.

Sp 187   JIMÉNEZ CAMPO, Javier, 'Rasgos basicos de la ideológia dominante entre 1939 y 1945'. *REV. DE ESTUD. POLIT.*, **15**, 1980. pp. 79-117.

Sp 188   LLOYD, Alan, *Franco*, Garden City, NY: Doubleday, 1969. London: Longmans, 1970. 256pp. Bib. 243-7.

Sp 189   MARTIN, Claude, *Franco: soldat et chef d'état*, Paris: Aymon, 1959. 470pp.

Sp 190   PAYNE, Stanley G., *Franco's Spain*, New York: Crowell, 1967. London: Routledge & Kegan Paul, 1968. xvii, 142pp. Bib. 127-32.

Sp 191   PAYNE, Stanley G., 'Intrigas falangistas contra Franco'. *Historia 16*, **1**, 1976. pp. 35-41.

Sp 192   ROMERO CUESTA, Armando, *Objective: matar a Franco: la Falange contra el Caudillo*, Madrid: Eds. 99, 1976. 124pp. On Falangist manoeuvrings against Franco in 1940-1.

Sp 193   SERRANO SÚÑER, Ramón, *Entre Hendaya y Gibraltar*, 9th edn, Madrid: Eds y Pubs Espanolas, 1947. 405pp. Franco's brother-in-law, Minister of the Interior in the Nationalist zone and later Foreign Minister. Covers 1937-42.

Sp 194   SOUTHWORTH, Herbert Rutledge, *Le Mythe de la croisade de Franco*, Paris: Ruedo Iberico, 1964. viii, 327pp. Bib. 295-317. After a review of the literature of the Civil War concludes that Franco's struggle was a fascist one.

Sp 195   TRYTHALL, J. William D., *Franco: a biography*, foreword by Raymond Carr, London: Hart-Davis, 1970. 304pp. Bib. 281-7. US edn, *El Caudillo*, New York: McGraw-Hill, 1971.

Sp 196   VILAR, Sergio, *Dictature militaire et fascisme en Espagne: origines, reproduction, luttes*, Paris: Anthropos, 1977. 258pp.

116

SWITZERLAND

General

Sw 1   BÜTLER, Heinz, '*Wach auf, Schweizervolk*': *die Schweiz zwischen Frontismus, Verrat und Selbsthauptung, 1914-1940*, Gümlinge: Zytglogge, 1980. 253pp. Bib. 245-57.

Sw 2   GILG, Peter and GRUNER, Erich, 'Nationale Erneuerungsbewegungen in der Schweiz, 1925-1940'. *VIERTELJAHRSH. FÜR ZEITG.*, **14** (1), 1966. pp. 1-25.

Sw 3   GRUBER, Christian, *Die politischen Parteien der Schweiz im Zweiten Weltkrieg*, Frankfurt/M: Europa V., 1966. 267pp. Bib. 257-67. Zürich University thesis, 1966.

Sw 4   MAIER, Karl-Hans, *Die antiliberalen Erneuerungsbewegung in der Schweiz und das Entstehen des liberal-sozialen 'Landesring der Unabhängigen'*, Tubingen University thesis, 1955.

Sw 5   *Schalom! wir werden euch töten: Texte und Dokumente zum Antisemitismus in der Schweiz, 1930-1980*, Zürich: Econ. V., 1979. 317pp.

The Nazi Influence

Sw 6   BOURGEOIS, Daniel, *Le Troisième Reich et la Suisse, 1933-1941*, Neuchâtel: La Baconnière, 1974. xx, 464pp. Bib. 419-42.

Sw 7   DREIFUSS, Eric, *Die Schweiz und das Dritte Reich: vier deutschschweize Zeitungen im Zeitalter des Faschismus, 1933-1939*, foreword by Willy Bretscher, Frauenfeld: Huber, 1971. ii, 251pp. Bib. 237-49.

Sw 8   LACHMANN, Günter, *Der Nationalsozialismus in der Schweiz, 1931-1945: ein Beitrag zur Geschichte der Auslandsorganisation der NSDAP*, Berlin: Ernst Reuter Gesellschaft, 1962. 114pp. Bib. 7-13.

Sw 9   MEYER, Alice, *Anpassung oder Widerstand: die Schweiz zur Zeit des deutschen Nationalsozialismus*, Frauenfeld: Huber, 1966. 227pp. Bib. 217-18. Swiss reactions to Hitler, pro and anti.

Sw 10   PADEL, Gerd Hellmut, *Die politische Presse der deutschen Schweiz und der Aufstieg des Dritten Reiches, 1933-1939: ein Beitrag zur Geschichte geistigen Landesverteidigung*, Zürich: Gut, 1951. 185pp. Bib. 183-5. Zürich University thesis.

Sw 11 RÜTHEMANN, Walter, *Volksbund und SGAD: National-sozialistische Schweizerlische Arbeiter Partei, Schweizerische Gesellschaft der Freunde einer Autoritären Demokratie: ein Beitrag zur Geschichte der politischen Erneuerungsbewegungen in der Schweiz, 1933-1944*, Zürich: Juris, 1979. x, 333pp. Bib. 313-27.

The Suisse Romande and Fascism

Sw 12 JOSEPH, Roger, 'Le fascisme en Valois, 1933-1941'. *Annales Valaisannes (Sion)*, **52**, 1977. pp. 137-59.

Sw 13 JOSEPH, Roger, *L'Union Nationale, 1932-1939: un fascisme en Suisse Romande*, Neuchâtel: Ed. de la Baconnière, 1975. xxiii, 438pp. Bib. 418-26. Fusion of L'Union de Défense Economique with more extreme Ordre Politique National to become L'Union Nationale.

Sw 14 OLTRAMARE, Georges, *Les souvenirs nous vengent*, Geneva: L'Autre Son de Cloche, 1956. 259pp. Memoirs. Oltramare (1896-1960) leader of L'Union Nationale.

Sw 15 OLTRAMARE, Georges, 'L'Union Nationale'. *Neue Schweizer Rundschau*. **NS, 1**, 1933. pp. 94-7.

Sw 16 *Georges Oltramare, l'Homme qui Demain* . . . Geneva: Ed. de l'Arbalète, 1937. iv, 159pp.

The Italian Fascist Influence

Sw 17 CANTINI, Claude, *Le Fascisme italien à Lausanne, 1920-1943*, Lausanne: Ed. Cedips, 1976. 71pp.

Sw 18 JOSEPH, Roger, 'The Martignoni Affair: how a Swiss politican deceived Mussolini'. *J. OF CONTEMP. HIST.*, **9 (1)**, 1974. pp. 77-90. Angiolo Martignoni (1890-1952).

The National Front

Sw 19 GLAUS, Beat, 'The National Front in Switzerland'. In LARSEN, S.U., Gn 36, pp. 467-78.

Sw 20 GLAUS, Beat, *Die Nationale Front: eine Schweizer faschistische Bewegung, 1930-1940*, Zürich: Benziger V., 1969. 504pp. Bib. 479-86. Basle University thesis.

Sw 21   GRIMM, Bruno, *Das Ende der Nationalen Front*, Zürich: Der Aufbruch, 1940. 99pp.

Sw 22   HENNE, Rolf, *Die Rolle der Schweiz im kommenden Europa: Rede, gehalten am 3 Kongress der Int. Arbeitsgemeinschaft der Nationalisten im Nobel-Inst. zu Oslo am 27 Juni 1936*, Zürich: Nationale Front V., 1936. 12pp. Speech by Rolf Henne (1901-66) a leading member of the National Front.

Sw 23   HENNE, Rolf, *Kampfruh*, Zürich: Front V., 1935. 32pp.

Sw 24   JÖHR, Walter Adolf, *Die ständische Ordnung: Geschichte, Idee und Neuaufbau*, Berne: Haupt, 1937. xii, 361pp.

Sw 25   LANG, Paul, *Tote oder lebendige Schweiz? Versuch eines Systems politischer Morphologie entwickelt an der Dynamik des Eidgenossischen Staates*, Zürich: Raschner, 1932. iv, 163pp. Ideologist of the New and National Fronts.

Sw 26   LARESE, Dino, *Julius Schmidhauser*, Amriswil: Amrisweiler Bücherei, 1965. 30pp. Student-councillor at the Federal Inst. of Technology in Zürich involved in foundation of the Neue Front.

Sw 27   SCHAFFNER, Jakob, *Der Schicksalsweg des deutschen Volkes*, Berlin: Eher, 1943. 75pp. Jakob Schaffner (1875-1944) leading National Front member.

Sw 28   TOBLER, Rober, *Wesen und Ziele der Nationalen Bewegung*, Zürich: Front V., 1933. 38pp. One of leaders of the National Front.

Sw 29   WEILENMAN, Hermann (ed.), *Staat und Parteien: Liberalismus, Erneuerung, Demokratie in der schweizerischen Politik der Gegenwart*, Zürich: Volkshochschul, 1935. 169pp. Includes Paul Lang on *Die Erneuerungsbewegung in Fronten*.

Sw 30   WOLF, Walter, *Faschismus in der Schweiz: die Geschichte der Frontenbewegungen in der deutschen Schweiz, 1930-1945*, Zürich: Flamberg, 1969, 530pp. Bib. 485-503. Full list of publications of various Front organisations; also useful biographical index pp. 505-17.

Sw 31   ZÖBERLEIN, Klaus-Dieter, *Die Anfänge der deutsch-schweizerischen Frontismus: die Entwicklung der politischen Vereinigungen Neue Front und Nationale Front bis zu ihrem Zusammenschluss im Frühjahr 1933*, Meisenheim: Hain, 1970. 275pp. Bib. 265-75.

Sw 32   ZOPFI, Hans, *Anekdoten und Erinnerungen*, Affoltern: Aehren V., 1952. 265pp. Memoirs of a journalist on the Schauffhauser Bauer.

AUSTRIA

General

Au 1   BERG, Friedrich, *Die weisse Pest: Beitrage zur völkischen Bewegung in Österreich*, Vienna: Munster V., 1926. 70pp.

Au 2   BOTZ, Gerhard, 'Genesis und Inhalt der Faschismus Theorien Otto Bauers'. *INT. REV. SOC. HIST.*, **19** (1), 1974. pp. 28–53.

Au 3   CARSTEN, Francis Ludwig, *Fascist Movements in Austria: from Schönerer to Hitler*, London: Sage, 1977. 356pp. Bib. 337–44.

Au 4   COLLOTTI, Enzo, 'Considerazioni sull' "austrofascismo"'. *STUD. STOR.*, **18** (4), 1963. pp. 703–28.

Au 5   DUSEK, Peter, *Alltagsfaschismus in Österreich*, St Pölten: Niederösterr. Pressehaus, 1979. 109pp.

Au 6   FELLNER, Fritz, 'The background of Austrian fascism'. In SUGAR, P.F., E 23. pp. 15–23.

Au 7   HOLTMANN, Everhard, 'Austrofaschismus als fixierte Idee: eine Erwiderung auf Manfred Hahn'. *Zeitgeschichte*, **6**, 1978/9. pp. 427–31.

Au 8   HOLZER, Willibald, 'Erscheinungsformen des Faschismus in Österreich, 1918–1938: zu einigen Aspekten über Forschungsgeschichte, Genese und Deutungsproblematik'. In KREISSLER, F., 'Deux fois l'Autriche: . . . actes du Colloque de Rouen 8–12 Nov. 1977', Rouen: Centre d'Etudes et de Recherches Autrichiennes, 1978. pp. 69–155. Special No. of *Austriaca*, 1 (4), 1978. pp. 69–170.

Au 9   JAGSCHITZ, Gerhard, 'Faschismus und Nationalsozialismus in Österreich bis 1945'. In *Fašismus a Evropa*, Gn 8. pp. 66–83.

Au 10   JEDLICKA, Ludwig, *Vom alten zum neuen Osterreich: Fallstudien zur österreichischen Zeitgeschichte, 1900–1975*, St Pölten: Niederösterr. Pressehaus, 1975. 496pp. A collection of previously pub. articles.

Au 11   KITCHEN, Martin, *The Coming of Austrian Fascism*, London: Croom Helm. Montreal: McGill-Queen's University Press, 1980. 299pp. Bib. 285–94. Mostly on Austro-marxists and socialists, but has chapter on the extreme Right and Austro-fascism.

Au 12   KLEMPERER, Klemens von, 'On Austro-fascism'. *CENT. EUR. HIST.*, **11** (3), 1978. pp. 313–17. Review article.

120

Au 13 KLINGENSTEIN, Grete, 'Bemerkungen zum Problem des Faschismus in Österreich'. *Oesterr. in Gesch. und Lit.*, **14** (1), 1970. pp. 1-12.

Au 14 NEUGEBAUER, Wolfgang, 'Aktuelle faschistische Strömungen in Österreich'. *Zeitgeschichte*, **4**, 1976/7. pp. 280-91.

Au 15 *Österreich 1927 bis 1938: Protokoll des Symposiums in Wien 23 bis 28 Oct. 1972*, ed. Ludwig Jedlicka und Rudolf Neck, Munich: Oldenbourg. Vienna: V. für Gesch. und Politik, 1973. 276pp. Includes Adam Wandruszka's article 'Die Erbschaft von Krieg und Nachkrieg'.

Au 16 PAULEY, Bruce F., 'Fascism and the Führerprinzip: the Austrian example'. *CENT. EUR. HIST.*, **12** (3), 1979. pp. 272-96.

Au 17 PAULEY, Bruce F., 'Nazis and Heimwehr fascists: the struggle for supremacy in Austria, 1918-1938'. In LARSEN, S.U., Gn 36, pp. 226-38.

Au 18 RATH, R. John, 'Authoritarian Austria'. In SUGAR, P.F., E 23. pp. 24-43.

Au 19 RITTER, Harry R., 'Recent writings on inter-war Austria'. *CENT. EUR. HIST.*, **12**, 1979. pp. 297-311. Rev. of literature.

Au 20 SIMON, Walter B., *The Political Parties of Austria*, Columbia University thesis, 1957. UM 00-21828. 381pp. Useful for the Nazi vote in elections of early 1930s.

Au 21 STADLER, Karl R., 'Austria'. In WOOLF, S.J., Gn 20. pp. 93-115.

Au 22 WHITESIDE, Andrew G., 'Austria'. In ROGGER, H. and WEBER, E., Gn 54. pp. 308-63.

Au 23 WISTRICH, Robert S., 'Fascist movements in Austria'. *WIENER LIB. BULL.*, **30** (43/44), 1977. pp. 60-4.

The Extreme Right 1890-1918

Au 24 BIBL, Viktor, *Georg von Schönerer: ein Vorkämpfer des Grossdeutschen Reiches*, Leipzig: Brandstaetter, 1942. 23pp. Bib. l.

Au 25 FERBER, Walter, 'Georg Ritter von Schönerer: zur Vorgeschichte des Nationalsozialismus'. *Hochland*, **63**, 1971. pp. 326-32.

Au 26 GAWRECKI, Dan, 'Počatky extrémního nemeckého nacionalismu: Schönerer a rakouské sleszko' (The beginnings of extreme

121

German nationalism: Schönerer and Austrian Silesia). *Slezsky Sbornik*, **68** (**2**), 1970. pp. 133-41.

Au 27   PICHL, Eduard (ed.), *Georg Schönerer*, Oldenburg: Stalling, 1938. 6 vols. [in 3]. Repr. of vols. pub. 1912-23. Schönerer (1842-1921), Pan-German leader.

Au 28   SCHORSKE, Carl E., 'Politics in a new key: Schönerer'. *J. OF MOD. HIST.*, **39** (**4**), 1967. pp. 343-86.

Au 29   WARREN, John Christopher Peter, *The Political Career and Influence of Georg Ritter von Schönerer*, London University thesis, 1963.

Au 30   WHITESIDE, Andrew G., *The Socialism of Fools: Georg Ritter von Schönerer and Austrian Pan-Germanism*, Berkeley: University of California Press, 1975. 404pp. Bib. 371-96.

Au 31   WISTRICH, Robert S., 'George von Schönerer and the genesis of modern Austrian antisemitism'. *WIENER LIB. BULL.*, **29** (**39/40**), 1976/7. pp. 20-9.

Au 32   CILLER, Alois, *Die Vorläufer des Nationalsozialismus: Geschichte und Entwicklung der nationalen Arbeiterbewegung im deutschen Grenzland*, Vienna: Ertl V., 1932. 159pp. On the nationalist trade unions particularly in Bohemia as the forerunners of national socialism before 1914.

Au 33   CILLER, Alois, *Deutscher Sozialismus in den Sudetenländer und der Ostmark*, Hamburg: Hanseatische Verlagsanstalt, 1939. 191pp.

Au 34   CROWLEY, Christopher Julian, *Libertatem delendam est: Franz Haiser, austro-völkische elitist, 1871-1945*, City University of New York thesis, 1979. UM 79-08456. 510pp. A radical Right figure active 1907-32.

Au 35   FERBER, Walter, *Die Vorgeschichte der NSDAP in Österreich: ein Beitrag zur Geschichtsrevision*, Constanz: Merk, 1954. 40pp.

Au 36   HANISCH, Ernst, 'Zur Frühgeschichte des Nationalsozialismus in Salzburg, 1913-1925'. *MITT. DER GES. FÜR SALZBURGER LANDESKUNDE*, **117**, 1977. pp. 371-410.

Au 37   HEIDRICH, Anne, *Die völkische Kampf im steirischen Unterland vor dem Weltkrieg*, Brunn: Rohrer-Callwey, 1944. 113pp.

Au 38   JUNG, Rudolf, *Der National Sozialismus: seine Grundlagen, seine Werdegang, und seine Ziele*, 3rd edn, Munich: Boepple, 1922. 160pp. Bib. 159. One of the Bohemian leaders of the German National-Socialist Workers party.

Au 39   KÜHNELT-LEDDIHN, Erik, 'The Bohemian background of national socialism'. *J. OF HIST. IDEAS*, **9** (3), 1948. pp. 339-71.

Au 40   KUPPE, Rudolf, *Dr Karl Lueger: Persönlichkeit und Wirken*, Vienna: Brüder Hollinek, 1947. 195pp. Bib. 191-3. Dr Karl Lueger (1844-1910), Christian Socialist mayor of Vienna, militant Catholic and anti-semite.

Au 41   SCHNEE, Heinrich, *Karl Lueger: Leben und Wirken ein grossen sozial- und kommunalpolitikers: umrisse eine politische Biographie*, Berlin: Duncker & Humblot, 1960. 123pp. Bib. 117-23.

Au 42   SKALNIK, Kurt, *Dr Karl Lueger: der Mann zwischen den Zeiten*, Munich: Herold, 1954. 192pp. Bib. 181-2.

Au 43   McGRATH, William J., *Dionysian Art and Populist Politics in Austria*, New Haven: Yale University Press, 1974. 269pp. Bib. 253-8. University of California thesis, *Wagnerism in Austria*, 1965.

Au 44   MOLISCH, Paul, *Geschichte der Deutschnationalen Bewegung in Österreich von ihren Anfangen bis zum der Monarchie Zerfall*, Jena: Fischer, 1926. x, 278pp.

Au 45   RIEHL, Walter, *Unser Endziel: eine Flugschrift für deutschen Nationalsozialismus*, 5th edn, Vienna: Deutsche, 1918. 15pp. The programme of the DNSAP (DAP before May 1918).

Au 46   WHITESIDE, Andrew G., *Austrian National-Socialism before 1918*, The Hague: Nijhoff, 1962. 143pp. Bib. 123-33. The DNAP to 1918. Contains list of workers' nationalist organisation journals, pp. 80-1.

Au 47   WHITESIDE, Andrew G., 'The Deutsche Arbeiterpartei, 1904-1918: a contribution to the origins of fascism'. *Austrian Hist. Newsletter*, **4**, 1963. pp. 3-14. With comments by Robert A. Kann.

Au 48   WHITESIDE, Andrew G., 'Nationaler Sozialismus in Österreich vor 1918'. *VIERTELJAHRSH. FÜR ZEITG.*, **9** (4), 1961. pp. 333-59.

The Extreme Right in the First Republic

Au 49   ARDELT, Rudolf Gustav, *Zwischen Demokratie und Faschismus: deutschnationales Gedankengut in Österreich, 1919-1930*, Vienna: Geyer, 1972. 212, xvi, pp. Bib. i-xvi. Salzburg University thesis. Pangermanism and nationalism.

Au 50   BOTZ, Gerhard, 'Bewaffnete Zusammenstösse und Strategie des früfaschistischen Terrors in Österreich: an Beispielen aus dem

Jahre 1923'. *Archiv. Mitteilungsblatt des Vereins der Geschichte für Arbeiterbewegung*, **13**, 1973. pp. 41-50, 58-68.

Au 51 BOTZ, Gerhard, 'Faschismus und Lohnabhängige in der Ersten Republik: zur "sozialen Basis" und propagandistischen Orientierung von Heimwehr und Nationalsozialismus'. *Oesterr. in Gesch. und Lit.*, **21** (**2**), 1977. pp. 102-28.

Au 52 BOTZ, Gerhard, *Gewalt in der Politik: Attentate, Zusammenstösse Putschversuche, Unruhen in Österreich, 1918 bis 1934*, Munich: Fink, 1976. 358pp. Bib. 281-91. Vienna University thesis, 1966.

Au 53 BOTZ, Gerhard, 'Gewalt und politisch-gesellschaftlicher Konflict in der Ersten Republik, 1918 bis 1933'. *OESTERR. Z. FÜR POLITIKWISS.*, **4** (**4**), 1975. pp. 511-34.

Au 54 BOTZ, Gerhard, 'Political violence, its forms and strategies in the First Austrian Republic'. In MOMMSEN, Wolfgang J. and HIRSCHFELD, Gerhard (eds), *Social Protest, Violence, and Terror in Nineteenth and Twentieth-century Europe*, London: Macmillan, 1982. pp. 300-29.

Au 55 HAAG, John G. 'Blood on the Ringstrasse: Vienna's students, 1918-1933'. *WIENER LIB. BULL.*, **29** (**39/40**), 1976. pp. 29-34.

Au 56 JEDLICKA, Ludwig, 'Die Anfänge des Rechtsradikalismus in Österreich, 1919-1925'. *Wiss. und Weltbild*, **24** (**2**), 1971. pp. 96-110.

Au 57 NUSSER, Horst. G.W., *Konservative Wehrbände in Bayern, Preussen, und Österreich, 1918-1933; mit einer Biographie von Forstrat Georg Escherich, 1870-1941*, Munich: Neisser, 1973. 363pp.

Au 58 OBERKOFLER, Gerhard, 'Einige Dokumente über die Funktion der Beamtenschaft beim Aufbau des "Austrofaschismus"'. *Zeitgeschichte*, **2** (**9/10**), 1975. pp. 216-26. Fascist influences among civil servants in the 1920s.

Au 59 WACHE, Karl (ed.), *Deutscher Geist in Österreich: ein Handbuch des völkischen Lebens der Ostmark*, Dornbirn: Bruton, 1933. 411pp. Bib. 69. Includes Heinz Cohrs, 'Das innere Gefüge der NSDAP Osterreichs', pp. 287-306; A Frauenfeld 'Der Aufstieg des Gaues Wien der NSDAP', pp. 281-86; Herbert Muller, 'Heimatschutzbewegung, Heimatwehr, Heimwehr, Heimatbund, Heimatblock-Partei', pp. 241-49; R. Hainz, 'Die NSDAP', pp. 251-80; Karl Jung, 'Die völkische Presse in Osterreich', pp. 345-52.

Au 60 WANDRUSZKA, Adam, 'Österreichs politische Struktur'. In BENEDIKT, Heinrich (ed.), *Geschichte der Republik Osterreich*, Vienna: V. für Gesch. und Politik, 1954. pp. 289-485. Includes material on the Heimwehr.

Heimwehr Fascism

Au 61 EDMONDSON, Clifton Earl, 'Earl Heimwehr aims and activities'. *AUSTRIAN HIST. YEARB.*, **8**, 1972. pp. 105-47.

Au 62 EDMONDSON, Clifton Earl, *The Heimwehr and Austrian politics, 1918-1936*, Athens: University of Georgia Press, 1978. x, 352pp. Bib. 325-42. Duke University thesis, 1966.

Au 63 HILTL, Hermann, Ritter von, *Ein Gedenkbuch*, Vienna: Bernhardt, 1931. 211pp. By the founder of the Frontkämpfervereinigung.

Au 64 HOFMANN, Josef, *Der Pfrimer-Putsch: der steirische Heimwehrprozess des Jahres 1931*, Vienna: Stiasny, 1965. 200pp. Dr Walter Pfrimer, leader of the Heimwehr in Upper Styria led an abortive *coup* in 1931.

Au 65 JEDLICKA, Ludwig, 'The Austrian Heimwehr'. *J. OF CONTEMP. HIST.*, **1** (**1**), 1966. pp. 127-44.

Au 66 JEDLICKA, Ludwig, 'Ernst Rüdiger Fürst Starhemberg und die politische Entwicklung in Österreich im Frühjahr 1938'. In *Österreich und Europa: Festgarbe für Hugo Hantsch zum 70. Geburstag.* Graz: V. Styria, 1965. pp. 547-64.

Au 67 JEDLICKA, Ludwig, 'Zur Vorgeschichte des Korneuburger Eides, 18 Mai 1930'. *Oesterr. in Gesch. und Lit.*, **7** (**4**), 1963. pp. 146-53.

Au 68 KEREKES, Lajos, *Abenddämmerung einer Demokratie: Mussolini, Gömbös und die Heimwehr*, Vienna: Europa V., 1966. 235pp. Bib. 223-9.

Au 69 KEREKES, Lajos, 'Akten zu den geheimen Verbindungen zwischen der Bethlen-Regierung und der österreichischen Heimwehrbewegung, 1928-1931'. *ACTA HIST.*, **11** (**1-4**), 1965. pp. 299-339.

Au 70 KEREKES, Lajos, 'Italien, Ungarn und die österreichischen Heimwehrbewegung'. *Oesterr. in Gesch. und Lit.*, **9** (**1**), 1965. pp. 1-13.

Au 71 KONDERT, Reinhart Ditmar, 'Schober und die Heimwehr: der Niedergang des Austrofaschismus, 1929-1930'. *Zeitgeschichte*, **3** (**6**), 1976. pp. 163-75. Johannes Schober (1874-1932), Federal Chancellor in 1929, had close relations with the Heimwehr.

Au 72 KONDERT, Reinhart Ditmar, *The Rise and Early History of the Austrian Heimwehr Movement*, Rice University thesis. UM 72-26441. 210pp.

Au 73 Österreichischen Heimatschutzes amt des Bundesführers. Propagandastelle, *Heimatschutz in Österreich*, Vienna: Zoller V., 1934. 341pp.

Au 74 RAPE, Ludger, *Die österreichische Heimwehr und ihre Beziehungen*

125

zur bayerischen Rechten zwischen 1920 und 1923, Vienna University thesis, 1968. v, 649pp. Bib. 641-8.

Au 75   RINTELEN, Anton, *Erinnerungen an Österreichs Weg: Versailles, Berchtesgarden, Grossdeutschland*, 2nd edn, Munich: Bruckmann, 1941. 345pp. Memoirs of the Landeshauptmann of Styria in the early Heimwehr.

Au 76   SCHUMY, Vinzenz, *Kampf um Kärntens Einheit und Freiheit*, Vienna: Goschl, 1950. 381pp. Bib. 379-81. Carinthia 1914-18.

Au 77   BENEDIKT, Ursula, *Vinzenz Schumy, 1878-1962: eine politische Biographie*, Vienna University thesis, 1966. Schumy a prominent Heimwehr member.

Au 78   SCHWEIGER, L., *Geschichte der neiderösterreichischen Heimwehr von 1928-1930 mit besonderer Berücksichtigung der sogenannten 'Korneuburger Eides'*, Vienna University thesis, 1954. 2 vols.

Au 79   STARHEMBERG, Ernst Rüdiger, Fürst von, *Between Hitler and Mussolini: memoirs*, London: Hodder & Stoughton. New York: Harper, 1942. xi, 290pp. German edn *Memoiren; mit einer Einleitung von Heinrich Drimmel*, Vienna: Amalthea V., 1971.

Au 80   STEINACHER, Hans, *Zu Kärntens Freiheitskampf: meine Erinnerungen an Kärntens Ringen um Freiheit und Einheit in den Abwehrkampfen 1918/19 um die Volksabstimmung 1920*, Klagenfurt: Heyn, 1970. 452pp.

Au 81   STEINBÖCK, Erwin, *Die Volkswehr in Kärnten: unter Berücksichtigung des Einsatzes der Freiwilligenverbände*, Vienna: Stiasny, 1963. 93pp.

Catholic Right-Wing Ideology and the Spann Circle

Au 82   BREUNING, Klaus, *Die Vision des Reiches: deutscher Katholizismus zwischen Demokratie und Diktatur, 1929-1934*, Munich: Hüber, 1969. 403pp. Bib. 351-91. Münster University thesis. Study of Catholic Reich ideology.

Au 83   DIAMANT, Alfred, *Austrian Catholics and the First Republic: democracy, capitalism, and the social order, 1918-1934*, Princeton: University Press, 1960. xii, 325pp. Bib. 293-311. Othmar Spann, corporative ideology and the Vogelsang School amongst others.

Au 84   HAAG, John G., 'Marginal men and the dream of the Reich: eight Austrian National-Catholic intellectuals, 1918-1938'. In

LARSEN, S.U., Gn 36. pp. 239-48. Spann, Eibl, Gleispach, Hugelmann, Menghin, Ritter von Srbik, Hudal and Father Schmidt.

Au 85   HAAG, John G., *Othmar Spann and the Politics of 'Totality': corporatism in theory and practice*, Rice University thesis, 1969. UM 69-19293. 209pp. Spann (1878-1950), corporatist theoretician.

Au 86   HAAG, John G., 'Othmar Spann and the quest for a true state'. *AUSTRIAN HIST. YEARB.*, **12/13**, 1976/7. pp. 227-50.

Au 87   HAAG, John G., 'The Spann circle and the Jewish question'. *LEO BAECK INST. YEARB.*, **18**, 1973. pp. 93-126.

Au 88   HUDAL, Alois, *Die Grundlagen des Nationalsozialismus: eine ideengeschichtliche Untersuchung von katholischer Warte*, Leipzig: Gunther, 1937. 294pp. Bib. 294. Bishop Alois Hudal (1878-1951) suggests a certain compatability between Catholicism and nazism.

Au 89   SCHNELLER, Martin, *Zwischen Romantik und Faschismus: der Beitrag Othmar Spanns zum Konservatismus der Weimarer Republik*, Stuttgart: Klett, 1970. 225pp. Bib. 210-20.

Au 90   SIEGFRIED, Klaus-Jörg, *Unversalismus und Faschismus: das Gesellschaftsbild Othmar Spanns: zur politischen Funktion seiner Gesellschaftslehre und Ständestaatskonzeption*, Vienna: Europa V., 1974. 289pp. Bib. 263-84. Spann's theory of society.

Au 91   SPANN, Othmar, *Gesamtausgabe*, ed. Walter Heinrich [*et al.*], under the ed. direction of Oskar Müllern, Graz: Akad. Druck- und Verlagsanstalt, 1963-79. 22 vols. Bib.

Au 92   WEINZIERL-FISCHER, Erika, 'Osterreichs Katholiken und der Nationalsozialismus'. *Wort und Wahrheit*, **18**, 1963. pp. 417-39, 493-526; **20**, 1965. pp. 777-804.

The Anschluss Movement

Au 93   EICHSTÄDT, Ulrich, *Von Dollfuss zu Hitler: Geschichte des Anschlusses Österreichs, 1933-38*, Wiesbaden: Steiner, 1955. x, 558pp. Bib. 536-8.

Au 94   LOW, Alfred, 'The Anschluss movement, 1918-1938 in recent historical writing: German nationalism and Austrian patriotism'. *CAN. REV. STUD. NATL.*, **3** (2), 1976. pp. 212-25.

Au 95   RITTER, Harry R., 'Hermann Neubacher and the Austrian Anschluss movement, 1918-40'. *CENT. EUR. HIST.*, **8** (4), 1975.

pp. 348-69. The Landesleiter of the Austrian NSDAP, founder of Pan-German clubs in 1925.

Au 96   ROSAR, Wolfgang, *Deutsche Gemeinschaft: Seyss-Inquart und der Anschluss*, Vienna: Europa V., 1971. 441pp. Bib. 411-16. Vienna University thesis, 1969.

Austrian National Socialism

Au 97   ACKERL, Isabella, 'Das Kampbündnis der NSDAP mit der Grossdeutschen Volkspartei vom 15 Mai 1933'. In *Das Jahr 1934: 25 Juli; Protokoll des Symposiums in Wien am 8 Oct. 1974*, Vienna: V. für Gesch. und Politik, 1975. pp. 21-35.

Au 98   AUERBACH, Hellmuth, 'Eine nationalsozialistische Stimme zum Wiener Putsch, vom 25. Juli 1934: dokumentation'. *VIERTELJAHRSH. FÜR ZEITG.*, **12** (2), 1964. pp. 201-18.

Au 99   BOTZ, Gerhard, 'The changing patterns of social support for Austrian national socialism, 1918-1945'. In LARSEN, S.U., Gn 36. pp. 202-25.

Au 100   BOTZ, Gerhard, 'Die österreichischen NSDAP-Mitglieder: Probleme einer quantitativen Analyse aufgrund der NSDAP-Zentralkartei im Berlin Document Center'. In MANN, R., G484. pp. 98-136. Membership of the Austrian Nazi Party based on documents at the Berlin Document Centre.

Au 101   BRÜGEL, Johann Wolfgang, 'Dollfuss und die Austronazi'. *Zukunft.*, **8**, 1959. pp. 222-7.

Au 102   BUKEY, Evans B., 'The Nazi Party in Linz, Austria, 1919-1939: a sociological perspective'. *GER. STUD. REV.*, **1** (3), 1978. pp. 302-26.

Au 103   DANNEBERG, Robert, *Die Wiener Wahlen 1930 und 1932: statistisches Betrachtungen*, Vienna, 1932. 68pp. Useful for the NSDAP performance in the two elections.

Au 104   EBNER, Anton, 'Der 25 Juli 1934 und Dr. Anton Rintelen'. *Österr. in Gesch. und Lit.*, **6** (10), 1962. pp. 461-4. Rintelen's own account of his attempted Nazi *coup* against Dollfuss.

Au 105   EDLINGER, Günther, *Friedrich Funder und die 'Reichspost' in ihrer Stellungnahme zur Politik des Nationalsozialismus gegenüber Österreich von 1930 biz zum Anschluss 1938*, Vienna University thesis, 1964.

Au 106   EPPEL, Peter, *Zwischen Kreuz und Hakenkreuz: die Haltung der*

Zeitschrift 'Schönerer Zukunft' zum Nationalsozialismus in Deutschland, 1934–38, Vienna: Bohlau, 1980. 407pp. Bib. 377–90.

Au 107 *Die Erhebung der Österreichischen Nationalsozialisten im Juli 1934: (Akten der Historischen Kommission des Reichführers)*, Vienna: Europa V., 1965. 300pp. Repr. of a report by the SS Reichführer in 1938 on the Nazi attempt at a *coup* on July 25 1934.

Au 108 FELDMAN, Angela, *Landbund für Österreich: Ideologie, Organisation, Politik*, Vienna University thesis, 1967.

Au 109 HOUSTON, Wendell Robert, *Ernst Kaltenbrunner: a study of an Austrian SS and police leader*, Rice University thesis, 1972. UM 72-26421. 243pp.

Au 110 JAGSCHITZ, Gerhard, 'Die Anhaltelager in Österreich, 1933–1938'. In *Vom Justizpalast zum Heldenplatz: Studien und Dokumentation 1927 bis 1938*, ed. Ludwig Jedlicka und Rudolf Neck, Vienna: Osterr. Staatsdruckerei, 1975. pp. 128–51. Survey of the social composition of the NSDAP based on the prisoners in Wöllersdorf prison in May 1934.

Au 111 JAGSCHITZ, Gerhard, *Der Putsch: die nationalsozialististen 1934 in Österreich; unter mitarb. von Alfred Baubin*, Graz: V. Styria., 1976. 260pp. Bib. 235–43.

Au 112 JAGSCHITZ, Gerhard, 'Zur Struktur der NSDAP in Österreich vor dem Juliputsch'. In *Das Jahr 1934: 25 Juli: Protokoll des Symposiums in Wien am 8 Oct. 1974*, Vienna: V. für Gesch. und Politik, 1975. pp. 9–20.

Au 113 JAGSCHITZ, Gerhard, 'Zwischen Befriedung und Konfrontation: zur Lage der NSDAP in Österreich 1934 bis 1936'. In *Juliabkommen von 1936*, Vienna: V. für Gesch. und Politik, 1977. pp. 156–87.

Au 114 JEDLICKA, Ludwig, 'Gauleiter Josef Leopold, 1889–1941'. In *Geschichte und Gesellschaft: Festschrift für Karl R. Stadler zum 60. Geburstag*, ed. Gerhard Botz [*et al.*], Vienna: Europa V., 1974. pp. 143–61.

Au 115 KITCHEN, Martin, 'Militarism and the development of fascist ideology: the political ideas of Colonel Max Bauer'. *CENT. EUR. HIST.*, **8** (**3**), 1976. pp. 199–220. An associate of Ludendorff who was active in assisting the early National Socialist Party in Austria.

Au 116 LANGOTH, Franz, *Kampf um Österreich: Erinnerungen eines Politikers*, Wels: V. Welsermuhl, 1951. 396pp. Bib. 391–6. Memoirs of the leader of Hilfswerk set up to assist nazis after their banning in 1933.

Au 117 LUDWIG, Eduard, 'Das Fanal, das keiner sah: Ballhausplatz 25 Juli 1934' *OESTERR. MONATSH.*, **20** (7/8), 1964. pp. 37-40. On the abortive Nazi *coup* of 1934.

Au 118 MAASS, Walter B., *Assassination in Vienna*, New York: Scribner, 1972. x, 180pp. Bib. 173-4. The assassination of Dollfuss.

Au 119 MEIXNER, A., *Die Anfänge der NSDAP in Österreich bis 1929*, Vienna: Inst. für Zeitgeschichte, 1969. Seminararbeit.

Au 120 PAULEY, Bruce F., 'A case study in fascism: the Styrian Heimatschutz and Austrian national socialism'. *AUST. HIST. YEARB.*, **12/13** (1), 1976/7. pp. 251-73. Comments by Botz and reply by Pauley. pp. 274-81.

Au 121 PAULEY, Bruce F., 'From splinter party to mass movement: the Austrian Nazi breakthrough'. *GER. STUD. REV.*, **2** (1), 1979. pp. 7-29.

Au 122 PAULEY, Bruce F., *Hitler and the forgotten Nazis: a history of Austrian national socialism*, Chapel Hill: University of N. Carolina Press, 1981. xxi, 292pp. Bib. 268-82. University of Rochester thesis, 1967: *Hahnenschwanz and Swastika: the Styrian Heimatschutz and Austrian national socialism, 1918-1934*.

Au 123 SAGEDER, Josef, *Soziale Grundlagen des Nationalsozialismus in Oberösterreich*, Linz: Inst. für Neue Geschichte und Zeitgeschichte, 1971. Hausarbeit.

Au 124 SCHILLING-SCHLETTER, Alexander, Dr. *Walter Riehl und die Geschichte des Nationalsozialismus; mit einem Anhang: Hitler in Österreich*, Leipzig: Forum V., 1933. 380pp.

Au 125 SCHOPPER, Hans, *Presse im Kampf: Geschichte der Presse während der Kampfjahre der NSDAP, 1933-1938, in Österreich*, Brno: Rohrer, 1942. 404pp.

Au 126 SCHWARZ, Robert, 'Die nationalsozialistische Propagandapresse und ihr Werben um die österreichische Arbeiterschaft'. In *Wien 1938*, Au 179. pp. 105-15.

Au 127 SCHWARZ, Robert, *'Sozialismus' der Propaganda: das Werben des Völkischen Beobachters um die österreichische Arbeiterschaft 1938/39; mit ein Einleitung von Gerhard Botz Ideologie und soziale Wirklichkeit des Sozialismus in die Ostmark*, Vienna: Europa V., 1975. 159pp. Bib. 137-41. On the Nazi's socialist propaganda to woo the workers.

Au 128 SCHWARZ, Robert, 'The Nazi press propaganda in Austria, 1933-1938'. *Duquesne Rev.*, **7** (1), 1961. pp. 29-38.

Au 129 SPANN, Gustav, 'Die illegale Flugschriftpropaganda der österreichischen NSDAP vom Juliputsch 1934 bis Juliabkommen 1936'. In *Das Juliabkommen von 1936: Vorgeschichte, Hintergrunde und Folgen: Protokoll des Symposium in Wien am 10 und 11 Juni 1976*, Munich: Oldenbourg, 1977. pp. 188–97.

Au 130   WAGNER, Gottfried, 'Juli 1934 in Lamprechtshausen'. *Zeitgeschichte*, 1 (9/10), 1974. pp. 209–15. On the Nazi uprising in Lamprechtschausen.

Au 131   WALSER, Harald, 'Wer stand hinter der NSDAP? Ein Beitrag zur Geschichte Vorarlbergs 1933 und 1934'. *Zeitgeschichte*, 7 (8), 1980. pp. 288–97.

Au 132   WILLIAMS, Maurice, 'Delusions of grandeur: the Austrian National Socialists'. *CAN. J. HIST.*, 14 (3), 1979. pp. 417–36.

The Fatherland Front and the Dollfuss Regime

Au 133   ASPETSBERGER, Friedbert, *Literarisches Leben im Austrofaschismus: der Staatspreis*, Königstein: Hain, 1980. vi, 222pp. Bib. 205–14.

Au 134   BÄRNTHALER, Irmgard, *Die Vaterländische Front: Geschichte und Organisation*, Vienna: Europa V., 1971. 238pp. Bib. 229–33. Vienna University thesis.

Au 135   BUSSHOFF, Heinrich, *Das Dollfuss-Regime in Österreich: in geistesgeschichtlicher Perspektive unter besonderer Berücksichtigung der 'Schönerer Zukunft' und 'Reichspost'*, Berlin: Duncker & Humblot, 1968. 322pp. Bib. 314–22. Wurzburg University thesis, 1964.

Au 136   HAHN, Manfred, 'Der "Ständesstaat" als unverwüstliches Ideologen: eine Erwiderung auf Everhard Holtmanns Entgegnung'. *Zeitgeschichte*, 6, 1978/9. pp. 432–8. Reply to Holtmann, Au 7.

Au 137   *International Tagung der Historiker der Arbeiterbewegung. Arbeiterbewegung und Faschismus: der Februar 1934 in Österreich*, ed. Gerhard Botz, Vienna: 1976. 464pp. Held in Linz 1974. Includes Botz's article, *Faschistische Bewegungen und Lohnabhängige in Österreich*, pp. 329–45.

Au 138   JEDLICKA, Ludwig, 'Neue Forschungsergebnisse zum 12. Februar 1934'. *Oesterr. in Gesch. und Lit.*, 8 (2), 1964. pp. 69–87.

Au 139   JEDLICKA, Ludwig, 'Das autoritäre System in Österreich: ein Beitrag zur Geschichte der europäischen Rechtsbewegungen'. *Aus Polit. und Zeitgesch.*, **B30/70**, 25 July 1970. pp. 3–15. On Dollfuss and the Ständestaat.

131

Au 140   JEDLICKA, Ludwig, 'Die Jahr 1933-1935 in der öster-reichischen Innenpolitik'. *Veröffentlichungen des Verbandes Osterr. Geschichtsvereine*, **15**, 1963. pp. 257-77.

Au 141   KEREKES, Lajos, *Az osztrák tragédia, 1933-1938 (The Austrian Tragedy)*, Budapest: Kossuth Kiadó, 1973. 221pp. Bib. 219-22.

Au 142   LESER, Norbert, 'Neue Literatur zum 12. Februar 1934'. *Zeitgeschichte*, **2**, 1975. pp. 156-9.

Au 143   MATTHES, Reinar, *Das Ende der Ersten Republik Österreich: Studien zur Krise ihres politischen Systems*, Berlin: Monath, 1979. 544pp. Free University of Berlin thesis, 1979.

Au 144   RATH, R. John and SCHUM, Carolyn W., 'The Dollfuss-Schuschnigg regime: fascist or authoritarian?' In LARSEN, S.U., Gn 36, pp. 249-57.

Au 145   RAUCHENSTEINER, Manfried, 'Das Jahr 1934 in der österreichischen Geschichte: Thesen zur Ausstellung des Öster-reichischen Staatsarchivs'. *Mitteilungen des Oesterreichischen Staatsarchivs*, **28**, 1975. pp. 435-42.

Au 146   ROSSBACHER, Karlheinz, 'Literatur und Ständestaat'. *Zeitgeschichte*, **2** (**9/10**), 1975. pp. 203-12. Rev. article.

Au 147   SCHUSCHNIGG, Kurt von, *The brutal takeover: the Austrian ex-Chancellor's account of the Anschluss with Austria by Hitler*, London: Weidenfeld & Nicolson. New York: Atheneum, 1971. viii, 383pp. Tr. of *Im Kampf gegen Hitler*, by Richard Berry.

Au 148   SIEGFRIED, Klaus-Jörg, *Klerikalfaschismus: zur Entstehung und sozialen Funktion der Dollfuss-Regime in Österreich: ein Beitrag zur Faschismusdiskussion*, Frankfurt/M: Lang, 1979. 132pp. Bib. 121-32.

Au 149   SIEGFRIED, Klaus-Jörg, 'Zur Entstehung und sozialen Funktion des Faschismus: ein Beitrag zur Faschismusdiskussion am Beispiel des österreichischen Dollfuss-Regimes'. *Oesterr. in Gesch. und Lit.*, **7**, 1978. pp. 477-91.

Au 150   STAUDINGER, Anton, 'Zur "Österreich" Ideologie des Ständestaates'. In *Das Juliabkommen von 1936; Vorgeschichte, Hintergrunde und Folgen: Protokoll des Symposium in Wien am 10 und 11 Juni 1976*, Munich: Oldenbourg, 1977. pp. 198-240.

Anti-Semitism in Austria

Au 151   ARKEL, D. van, *Anti-semitism in Austria*, Leiden: Universitaire Pers Leiden, 1966. xix, 213pp. Bib. 197-209. Leiden University thesis.

Au 152 AUER, Johann, 'Antisemitische Strömungen in Wien, 1921-1923'. *Oesterr. in Gesch. und Lit.*, **10**, 1966. pp. 23-7.

Au 153 BOTZ, Gerhard, ' "Arisierungen" und nationalsozialistische Mittelstandspolitik in Wien, 1938 bis 1940'. *Wiener Geschichtsblätter*, **29** (**1**), 1974. pp. 122-36. Nazi anti-semitism in Vienna.

Au 154 BOTZ, Gerhard, 'National socialist Vienna: anti-semitism as a housing policy'. *WIENER LIB. BULL.*, **29** (**39/40**), 1976. pp. 47-55.

Au 155 BOTZ, Gerhard, *Wohnungspolitik und Judendeportation in Wien 1938 bis 1945: zur Funktion des Antisemitismus als ersatz national-sozialistischer Sozialpolitik*, Vienna: Geyer, 1975. 200pp. Bib. 125-35.

Au 156 FELLNER, Günter, *Antisemitismus in Salzburg, 1918-1938*, Vienna: Geyer, 1979. vi, 266pp. Bib. 249-61.

Au 157 FRAENKEL, Josef (ed.), *The Jews of Austria: essays on their life, history and destruction*, London: Vallentine Mitchell, 1967. xv, 584pp. Bib. 547-66. Includes Pulzer's article on the development of political anti-semitism in Austria. pp. 429-43.

Au 158 KARBACH, Oskar, 'Die politische Grundlagen des deutsch-österreichischen Antisemitismus'. *Z. FÜR GESCH. DER JUDEN*, **1**, 1964. pp. 1-8; **2**, pp. 103-16; **4**, pp. 169-78.

Au 159 PULZER, Peter George Julius, *The Rise of Political Anti-semitism in Germany and Austria*, New York: Wiley, 1964. xiv, 364pp. Cambridge University thesis, 1960.

Au 160 ROSENKRANTZ, Herbert, 'Bemerkungen zu neueren Arbeiten über das Problem der Judenverfolgung und das Anti-semitismus in Österreich'. *Oesterr. in Gesch. und Lit.*, **22** (**2**), 1978. pp. 90-100.

Au 161 ROSENKRANTZ, Herbert, *Reichskristallnacht 9. November 1938 in Österreich*, Vienna: Europa V., 1968. 72pp. Bib. 61-8.

Au 162 ROSENSAFT, Menachem Z., 'Jews and anti-semites in Austria at the end of the nineteenth century'. *LEO BAECK INST. YEARB.*, **20**, 1976. pp. 57-86. Schönerer, Lueger, von Vogelsang.

Au 163 WEINZIERL-FISCHER, Erika, *Zu wenig Gerechte: Österreicher und Judenfolgung, 1938-1945*, Graz: Styria, 1969. 208pp. Bib. 205-8.

The Anschluss and After

Au 164 *Anschluss, 1938: Protokoll des Symposiums in Wien am 14 und 15, März 1978*, Munich: V. für Geschichte und Politik, 1981. 464pp.

Au 165 BERNBAUM, John A., 'The new elite: nazi leadership in Austria, 1938-1945'. *AUSTRIAN HIST. YEARB.*, **14**, 1978. pp. 145-58.

Au 166 BERNBAUM, John A., *Nazi Control in Austria: the creation of the Ostmark, 1938-1940*, University of Maryland thesis, 1972. UM 72-29423. 300pp.

Au 167 BOTZ, Gerhard, *Die Eingliederung Österreichs in das Deutsch Reich: Planung und Verwirklichung des politisch-administrativen Anschlusses, 1938-1940*, Vienna: Europa V., 1972. 192pp. Bib. 179—86.

Au 168 BOTZ, Gerhard, 'Gross-Wien: the nationalsozialistische Stadterweiterung im Jahre 1938'. *Österr. in Gesch. und Lit.*, **17** (**1**), 1973. pp. 3-14.

Au 169 BOTZ, Gerhard, *Wien vom 'Anschluss' zum Krieg: nationalsozialistische Machtübernahme und politisch-soziale Umgestaltung am Beispiel der Stadt Wien, 1938-39*, 2nd edn with an intro. by Karl R. Stadler, Vienna: Jugend & Volk, 1980. 646pp. Bib. 567-83.

Au 170 HANISCH, Ernst, '1938 in Salzburg'. *MITT. DER GES. FÜR SALZBURGER LANDESKUNDE*, **118**, 1978. pp. 257-309.

Au 171 HANISCH, Ernst, 'Vierzig Jahr nach dem "Anschluss": neue wissenschafliche Literatur'. *Zeitgeschichte*, **6**, 1978/9. pp. 117-27.

Au 172 JEDLICKA, Ludwig, 'Der 13 März 1938 in der Sicht der historischen Forschung'. *Donauraum*, **13**, 1968. pp. 141-55.

Au 173 KLUSACEK, Christine and others (comps), *Dokumentation zur österreichischen Zeitgeschichte, 1938-1945*, ed. Christine Klusacek, Herbert Steiner, Kurt Stimmer, Vienna: V. für Jugend und Volk, 1971. 595pp. Bib. 589-93. Extracts from journals, illegal pamphlets, official documents etc.

Au 174 LUŽA, Radomir V., 'Nazi control of the Austrian Catholic Church, 1939—1941'. *CATHOL. HIST. REV.*, **63** (**4**), 1977. pp. 537-72.

Au 175 MAASS, Walter B., *Country without a name: Austria under nazi rule 1938-1945*, New York: Ungar, 1979. x, 178pp. Bib. 165-7.

Au 176 RINGLER, Ralf Roland, *Illusion einer Jugend: Lieder, Fahnen und das bittere Ende: Hitler-Jugend in Österreich: ein Erlebnisbericht*, St Pölten: V. Niederösterreich Pressehaus, 1977. 223pp.

Au 177 SLAPNICKA, Harry, *Oberösterreich als es 'Oberdonnau' hiess, 1938-1945*, Linz: Oberösterreichischer Landesverlag, 1978. 515pp. Bibs.

Au 178   STADLER, Karl R., *Österreich, 1938–1945 im Spiegel der NS-Akten*, Vienna: Herold, 1966. 427pp. Bib. 409–11.

Au 179   *Wien 1938*, Vienna: Verein für Geschichte der Stadt Wien, 1978. 326pp. Bib. 312–21. Includes Isabella Ackerl, 'Die Propaganda der Vaterländischen Front für die geplante Volksbefragung vom 13 März', pp. 18–24; Jagschitz, 'NSDAP und Anschluss in Wien 1938', pp. 147–57; Wolfgang Neugebauer, pp. 126–35; Wolfgang Meyer, pp. 77–87; Pieter Csendes, pp. 70–6; Felix Czeihe, pp. 60–9.

GREECE

Gr 1   ANDRICOPOULOS, Yannis, 'The power base of Greek authoritarianism'. In LARSEN, S.U., Gn 36, pp. 568–84.

Gr 2   CLIADAKIS, Harry C., *Greece, 1935–1941: The Metaxas regime and the diplomatic background to World War II*, New York University thesis, 1970. UM 72-09776. 334pp.

Gr 3   CLIADAKIS, Harry C., 'The political and diplomatic background to the Metaxas dictatorship, 1935–36'. *J. OF CONTEMP. HIST.*, **14** (**1**), 1979. pp. 117–38.

Gr 4   CLIADAKIS, Harry C., 'Le régime de Metaxas et la deuxième guerre mondiale'. *REV. D'HIST. DEUX GUERRE MOND.*, **27** (**107**), 1977. pp. 19–38.

Gr 5   FLEISHER, Hagen, 'Greece under Axis occupation, 1941–1944: a bibliographical survey'. 2 parts. *Modern Greek Society*, **5** (**1**), 1977. pp. 4–47; **6** (**1**), 1978. pp. 13–50.

Gr 6   GATOPOULOS, Demetrios, *Historia tes katochēs meta sullogēs istorikōn kai laografikon anekhdotōn tōn etōn, 1940–44*, Athens: Dmitrakis, 1946-7. 4 vols. Comprehensive work on the occupation.

Gr 7   HONDROS, John L., *The German Occupation of Greece*, Vanderbilt University thesis, 1969. UM 70-05453. 372pp.

Gr 8   METAXAS, Ioannēs, *Logoi kai skepseis, 1936–1941*, Athens: Ikaros, 1969. 2 vols. Writings of the dictator.

Gr 9   METAXAS, Ioannēs, *To prosōpiko tou Hēmerologio*, Athens: Kentrikē Pōlēsis Bibliōpleion tēs Estias, 1951-64. 4 vols. Letters, documents and speeches. Vol. 4. 1933-41.

Gr 10   RICHTER, Heinz, *Griechenland zwischen Revolution und Konter-revolution, 1936-1946*, Frankfurt/M: Europäische Verlagsanstalt, 1973. 623pp. Bib. 605-13.

Gr 11   XYDIS, Stephen G., 'Modern Greek nationalism'. In SUGAR, P.F. and LEDERER, I.J., E 21. pp. 207-58.

EASTERN EUROPE

E 1   AMBRI, Mariano, *I falsi fascism: Ungheria, Jugoslavia, Romania, 1919-1945*, Rome: Jouvence, 1980. 293pp.

E 2   *Anale de Istorie (Romania)*, **25** (**5**) and **25** (**6**), 1979. Issues on Fascism in Eastern Europe.

E 3   ARMSTRONG, John Alexander, 'Collaborationism in World War II: the integral nationalist variant in Eastern Europe'. *J. OF MOD. HIST.*, **40** (**3**), 1968. pp. 396-410.

E 4   BOIADZHIEVA, Elena and VELICHKOV, Alexandur, 'Nauchna srechta mezhdu istoritsite ot Bulgariia i Ungariia po vuposite na fashizma' (Scholarly meeting between the historians of Bulgaria and Hungary on the problems of fascism). *ISTOR. PREGLED*, **35** (**1**), 1979. pp. 144-47. Describes papers presented at a conference in Sofia 16-17 October 1978 on Hungarian and Bulgarian fascism, 1919-39.

E 5   BOREJSZA, Jerzy W., 'East European perceptions of Italian fascism'. In LARSEN, S.U., Gn 36. pp. 354-66.

E 6   BOREJSZA, Jerzy, W., *Fascismo e l'Europa orientale: dalla propaganda all'aggressione*, Rome: Laterza, 1981. 305pp. Tr. of *Rzym i wspolnota faszystowska*, Warsaw, 1980.

E 7   BOREJSZA, Jerzy W., 'Italian fascism and East Central Europe, 1922-1943'. In *Poland at the 14th Int. Congress of the Historical Sciences in San Francisco*, Wroclaw: Zaklad Narodowy Im. Ossolinskich Wydawn. Polskiej. Akad. Nauk., 1975. pp. 257-85.

E 8   BOREJSZA, Jerzy W., 'Die Rivilität zwischen Faschismus und Nationalsozialismus in Ostmitteleuropa'. *VIERTELJAHRSH. FÜR ZEITG.*, **29** (**4**), 1981. pp. 579-614.

E 9   BROSZAT, Martin, 'Faschismus und Kollaboration in Ostmitteleuropa zwischen den Weltkriegen'. *VIERTELJAHRSH. FÜR ZEITG.*,
14 (3), 1966. pp. 225–51.

E 10   BROWN, MacAlister, 'The Third Reich's mobilization of the
German Fifth Column in Eastern Europe'. *J. OF CENT. EUR. AFF.*,
19 (2), 1959. pp. 128–48. On ethnic German minorities in Eastern
Europe 1937–9, particularly the Volksdeutsche Mittelstelle.

E 11   *Dyktatury w Europie Srodkowo-Wschodniej, 1918–1939: Konferencja
naukowa w Instytucie Historii Polskiej Akad. Nauk 2–3 XII 1971 (Dictatorial
Regimes in East Central Europe)*, Wroclaw: Zaklad Narodowy im.
Ossolinskich, 1973. 233pp. Articles by Lossowski on Baltic states and
the ideology of authoritarian regimes; Ryszka on authoritarian state
and connections with the fascist state; and Zarnowski on the fascist
nature of various dictatorial regimes.

E 12   HILLGRUBER, Andreas, *Südost-Europa im Zweiten Weltkreig:
Literaturbericht und Bibliographie*, Frankfurt/M: Bernard & Graefe,
1962. 150pp.

E 13   JANOS, Andrew C., 'The one-party state and social mobilisation: East Europe between the wars'. In HUNTINGTON, S.P. and
MOORE, C.H., Gn 309. pp. 204–36.

E 14   LACKÓ, Miklós, 'Ostmitteleuropäischer Faschismus: ein
Beitrag zur allgemeinen Faschismus-Definition'. *VIERTELJAHRSH.
FÜR ZEITG.*, **21 (1)**, 1973. pp. 39–51.

E 15   LACKÓ, Miklós, 'Zur Frage der Besonderheiten des südosteuro-
päischen Faschismus'. In *Fašismus a Evropa*, Gn 8, Vol. **2**. pp. 2–22.

E 16   ORLOW, Dietrich, *The Nazis in the Balkans: a case study of
totalitarian politics*, Pittsburgh: University of Pittsburgh Press, 1968.
viii, 235pp. Bib. 190–225.

E 17   PAIKERT, G.C., *The Danubian Swabians: German populations in
Hungary, Rumania and Yugoslavia and Hitler's impact on their patterns*, The
Hague: Nijhoff, 1967. xvi, 324pp. Bib. 306–14.

E 18   PECH, Stanley Z., 'Political parties in Eastern Europe,
1848–1939: comparisons and continuities'. *East Cent. Eur.*, **5 (1)**, 1978.
pp. 1–38. Long bibliographical essay covering Czechoslovakia,
Slovenia, and Croatia.

E 19   POLONSKY, Antony, *The Little Dictators: the history of Eastern
Europe since 1918*, London: Routledge & Kegan Paul, 1975. xii,
212pp.

E 20   ROTHSCHILD, Joseph, *East Central Europe between the Two*

World Wars, Seattle: University of Washington Press, 1974. xvii, 420pp. Bib. 397-407.

E 21 SUGAR, Peter F. and LEDERER, Ivo J. (eds), *Nationalism in Eastern Europe*, Seattle: University of Washington Press, 1969. ix, 465pp.

E 22 SUGAR, Peter F., 'Fascism in inter-war Eastern Europe: the dichotomy of power and influence'. In SINANIAN, S. and others (eds), *Eastern Europe in the 1970's*, New York: Praeger, 1972. pp. 13-32.

E 23 SUGAR, Peter F. (ed.), *Native Fascism in the Successor States, 1918-1945*, Santa Barbara: Clio Press, 1971. 166pp.

E 24 VAGO, Bela and MOSSE, G.L. (eds), *Jews and non-Jews in Eastern Europe*, New York: Wiley, 1974. xviii, 334pp. Int. Symposium held in Haifa University, May 1972.

E 25 VAGO, Bela, *The Shadow of the Swastika: the rise of fascism and antisemitism in the Danube basin, 1936-1939*, Farnborough: Saxon House, 1975. 431pp.

E 26 VAGO, Bela, 'Fascism in Eastern Europe'. In LAQUEUR, W., Gn 35. pp. 229-53.

E 27 VOLKMANN, Hans-Erich (ed.), *Die Krise des Parlamentarismus in Ostmitteleuropa zwischen den beiden Weltkriegen*, Marburg: Herder Inst., 1967. 184pp. Covers Baltic States, Czechoslovakia, Poland.

ALBANIA

Al 1 AMERY, Julian, *Sons of the Eagle: a study in guerrilla war*, London: Macmillan, 1948. xii, 354pp.

Al 2 COSTA, Nicholas J., 'Invasion: action and reaction: Albania, a case study'. *EAST EUR. Q.*, **10**, 1976. pp. 53-63.

Al 3 JACOMONI DI SAN SAVINO, Francesco, *La politica dell'Italia in Albania*, Bologna: Cappelli, 1965. 380pp. Covers 1926-43.

Al 4 SERRA, Alessandro, *Albania, 8 settembre 1943-9 marzo 1944*, Milan: Longanesi, 1974. 320pp.

Al 5 ZAVALANI, T., 'Albanian nationalism'. In SUGAR, P.F. and LEDERER, I.J., E 21. pp. 55-92.

BULGARIA

B 1   BUSCH-ZANTNER, Richard, *Bulgarien*, 2nd edn, Leipzig: Goldmann, 1943. 238pp.

B 2   CHARY, Frederick B., *The Bulgarian Jews and the Final Solution, 1940-1944*, Pittsburgh: University of Pittsburgh Press, 1972. xiv, 246pp.

B 3   Deutsches Auslandswissenschaftliches Institut, Berlin, *Bulgarien*, Leipzig: Harrassowitz, 1942. Vol. 1. Bibliography covering 1939-42 ed. Henrica Maria Lindemaier.

B 4   DIMITROV, Ilcho, *Bulgaro-italianski politicheski otnosheniia, 1922-1943 (Bulgarian-Italian Political Relations)*, Sofia: Izd. Nauka i Izkustvo, 1976. 471pp.

B 5   DIMITROV, Ilcho, *Bulgarskata demokratichna obshestvenost, fashizmut i voinata 1934-39 (Bulgarian Democratic Circles, Fascism and War, 1934-39)*, Sofia: Izd. Otech. Front, 1976. 331pp.

B 6   DIMITROV, Ilcho, 'Ewolucja dyktatury faszystowskiej v Bulgarii 1934-1939' (The evolution of the fascist dictatorship in Bulgaria). *STUD. DZIEJ. ZSRR EUR. SRODK.*, **10**, 1974. pp. 75-94.

B 7   DIMITROV, Mihail, *Poiava, razvitie i ideologiia na fashizma v Bulgariia (Appearance, Development, and Ideology of Fascism in Bulgaria)*, Sofia: BRP, 1947. 110pp. Covers 1923-44.

B 8   DOLAPTCHIEVA, J., 'Bibliographie sur la guerre et la résistance'. *REV. D'HIST. DEUX GUERRE MOND.*, **18** (**72**), 1968. pp. 83-93.

B 9   GENCHEV, Nikolai, 'Nuzhni sa seriozni izsledvaniia za fashizma v Bulgaria' (Serious studies of fascism in Bulgaria are necessary). *ISTOR. PREGLED*, **24** (**4**), 1968. pp. 88-91.

B 10   GORNENSKI, Nikifor, 'La politique intérieure [of Bulgaria 1940-5]'. *REV. D'HIST. DEUX GUERRE MOND.*, **18** (**72**), 1968. pp. 23-42.

B 11   IOTSOV, Iaroslav, 'Po niakoi vuprosi na Bulgarskiia fashizum' (On some problems of Bulgarian fascism). *ISTOR. PREGLED*, **23** (**1**), 1967. pp. 82-97.

B 12   KAZASOV, Dimo, *Burni godini, 1918-1944 (Stormy Years)*, Sofia: Naroden Pechat, 1949. 783pp. Memoirs of Zveno member who moved to the Left.

B 13   KAZASOV, Dimo, 'Fashizmut i Bulgarskite partii' (Fascism and the Bulgarian parties). *ISTOR. PREGLED*, **24** (**5**), 1968. pp. 94-100.

B 14   KECHALES, Haim, *Korot Yehude Bulgaryah (The History of the Bulgarian Jews)*, Tel Aviv: Davar, 1969-72. 4 vols. Bib.

B 15   KHADZHINIKOLOV, Veselin, 'Oshte za fashizma i negoviti osobenosti v Bulgariia' (More on fascism and its peculiarities in Bulgaria). *ISTOR. PREGLED*, **24** (**6**), 1968. pp. 50-63.

B 16   KOLEV, Zheliazko, *Suiuz na Bulgarskite Natsionalni Legioni (The Union of Bulgarian National Legions)*, Sofia: Nauka i Iskustvo, 1976. 163pp.

B 17   KOSTOV, Pavel, 'Ustanoviavane, kharakter, etapi i neprekusnatost na fashistkata diktatura v Bulgariia' (Establishment, character, stages and continuity of the fascist dictatorship in Bulgaria). *ISTOR. PREGLED*, **23** (**3**), 1967. pp. 96-102.

B 18   KRALEV, Krali, 'Vasil Kolarov za kharaktera na fashizma i fashistkata ideologiia v Bulgariia' (Vasil Kolarov on the character of fascism and fascist ideology in Bulgaria). *Godishnik na Katedrite po Nauchen Komunizum Iistorii na BKP*, **11**, 1977. pp. 33-117.

B 19   MIGEV, Vladimir, 'Istoriia fashizma v zapadnoi Evrope' (The history of fascism in Western Europe). *ISTOR. PREGLED*, **35** (**2**), 1979. pp. 112-20. Compares Bulgarian fascism with that in Western Europe.

B 20   MIGEV, Vladimir, *Utvurzhdavane na monarcho-fashistkata diktatura v Bulgariia, 1934-1936 (Consolidation of the Monarcho-fascist Dictatorship in Bulgaria)*, Sofia: Akad. na Bulgarska Naukite Inst. za Istoriia, 1977. 188pp. English summary 184-6.

B 21   MIGEV, Vladimir, 'Za periodite na fashistkata diktatura ot 1934 do 1944' (On the period of the fascist dictatorship from 1934 to 1944). *ISTOR. PREGLED*, **23** (**2**), 1967. pp. 98-101.

B 22   MILLER, Marshall Lee, *Bulgaria during the Second World War*, Stanford: Stanford University Press, 1975. xii, 290pp. Bib. 256-78.

B 23   NATAN, Zhak, 'Kharakter, sushtnost i glavni etapi v razvitieto na Bulgarskiia fashizum' (Nature and essence of Bulgarian fascism and the main stages of its development). *ISTOR. PREGLED*, **22** (**6**), 1966. pp. 84-96.

B 24   NATAN, Zhak, 'Zakluicheniia i izvodi po osnovnite vuprosi na diskusiiata za fashizma v Bulgariia' (Conclusions about basic problems from the discussion of fascism in Bulgaria). *ISTOR. PREGLED*, **25** (**1**), 1969. pp. 109-18. Review article.

B 25   PUNDEFF, Marin V., 'Bulgarian nationalism'. In SUGAR, P.F. and LEDERER, I.J., E 21. pp. 93–165.

B 26   RADULOV, Stefan, 'Narodniiat sgovor i genezisut na Bulgarskiia fashizum, 1921–1923' (The democratic entente and the genesis of fascism in Bulgaria). *Izvestiia na Instituta po Istoriia na BKP*, **33**, 1975. pp. 373–408. Dr Aleksandr Tsankov and his circle.

B 27   RADULOV, Stefan, 'Za ideologiiata na Bulgarskiia fashizum' (On the ideology of Bulgarian fascism). *ISTOR. PREGLED*, **24** (**5**), 1968. pp. 88–93.

B 28   SHOPOV, Iordan, 'Pronikvane na fashizma v srednoto obrazovanie 1934–1939' (The penetration of fascism into secondary education). *ISTOR. PREGLED*, **31** (**5**), 1975. pp. 45–56.

B 29   TOSHKOVA, Vitka, *Bulgariia i Tretiiat Raikh, 1941–1944: politicheski otnosheniia*, Sofia: Izd. Nauka i Izkustvo, 1975. 256pp. Bib. 245–55.

B 30   TSANKOV, Aleksandr, *Trite stopanski sistemi: kapitaliz'm, komuniz'm, i natsional-sotsialis'm* (*The Three Economic Systems*), Sofia, 1942. 179pp.

YUGOSLAVIA

General

Y 1   AVAKUMOVIC, Ivan, 'Yugoslavia's fascist movements'. In SUGAR, P.F., E 23. pp. 135–43.

Y 2   DJORDJEVIĆ, Dimitrije, 'Fascism in Yugoslavia, 1918–1941'. In SUGAR, P.F., E 23. pp. 125–34.

Y 3   LEDERER, Ivo J., 'Nationalism and the Yugoslavs'. In SUGAR, P.F. and LEDERER, I.J., E 21. pp. 396–438.

The Ustasha Movement and Independent Croatia

Y 4   BALEN, Sime, *Pavelić*, Zagreb: Biblioteka Društva Novinara

Hrvatske, 1952. 144pp. Ante Pavelić (1869-1959) leader of the Ustasha Revolutionary Organisation.

Y 5 CRLJEN, Danijel, *Naš poglavnik* (*Our Leader*), Zagreb: Velebit, 1943. 237pp. On Ante Pavelić.

Y 6 KRIZMAN, Bogdan, 'A. Pavelić i sl. Kvaternik kod A. Hitlera u ljeto 1941' (The visit of Pavelić and Kvaternik to Hitler, Summer 1941). *Historijski Zbornik*, **23/24**, 1970/1. pp. 307-32.

Y 7 PAVELIĆ, Ante, *Die Kroatische Frage*, Berlin: Privat druck des Instituts für Grenz- und Auslandstudien, 1941. 39pp.

Y 8 BASTA, Milan, *Agonija i slom Nezavisne Države Hrvatske* (*The Collapse of the Independent Croatian State*), Belgrade: Rad, 1971. 412pp. Bib. 405-6. First pub. 1963 as *Rat posle rata*, Stvarnost. A Communist version of events in Croatia.

Y 9 BIBER, Dušan, 'Ustaše i Treči Rajk: prilog problematici jugoslovenskonemačkih odnosa, 1933-39' (Ustashi and the Third Reich: a contribution to the problems of Yugoslav-German relations). *JUGOSL. IST. CAS.*, **3**, 1964. pp. 37-56. Discusses Ustashi activities in the Third Reich.

Y 10 CRLJEN, Danijel, *Nacela Hrvatskog Ustaskog pokreta* (*The Principles of the Croatian Ustasha Movement*), Zagreb: Tiskra Matice Hrvatskih Akademičara, 1942. 117pp.

Y 11 Croatia, *Laws and Statutes. Zbornik zakona i naredaba Nezavisne Države Hrvatske* (*Collection of Laws and Decrees of the Independent State of Croatia*), Zagreb, 1941-5. 5 vols [in 4].

Y 12 DIEDERICH, Clemens (ed.), *Die Kroaten*, Zagreb: Velebit, 1942. 260pp. Includes useful article by Ivo Bogdan on the early Croatian nationalist journals.

Y 13 DRAGOUN, Théodore, *Le Dossier de Cardinal Stepinac*, Paris: Nouvelles Eds Latines, 1958. 286pp. Doc. 77-264. Alois Stepinac Archbishop of Zagreb.

Y 14 FRICKE, Gert, *Kroatien, 1941-1944: der 'Unabhängige Staat', in der Sicht des deutschen Bevollmächtigten Generals in Agram, Glaise von Horstenau*, Freiburg: Rombach, 1972. 206pp. Bib. 203-4.

Y 15 HORY, Ladislaus and BROSZAT, Martin, *Der kroatische Ustascha-Staat, 1941-1945*, Stuttgart: Deutsche Verlags-Anstalt, 1964. 183pp.

Y 16 JAREB, Jere, *Pola stoljeća Hrvatske politike: povodom Mačekove autobiografije* (*A Half-century of Croatian Politics*), Buenos Aires: Knjižnica Hrvatske Revije, 1960. 180pp. Bib. 143-73. Repr. of articles from *Hrvatska Revija*.

Y 17   JELIĆ-BUTIĆ, Fikreta, *Ustaše i Nezavisna Država Hrvatska, 1941-1945* (*Ustasha and the Independent Croatian State*), Zagreb: Liber, 1977. 331pp.

Y 18   JELIĆ-BUTIĆ, Fikreta, 'Ustaski pokret i hrvatsko nacionalno pitanje' (The Ustasha Movement and the Croatian struggle). *JUGOSL. IST. CAS.*, **4**, 1969. pp. 185-90.

Y 19   JELINEK, Yeshayahu, 'The authoritarian parliament: the Croatian state Sabor of 1942'. *CAN. SLAVIC. STUD.*, **22** (**2**), 1980. pp. 260-73.

Y 20   JELINEK, Yeshayahu, 'Nationalities and minorities in the Independent State of Croatia'. *Nationalities Papers*, **8** (**2**), 1980. pp. 195-210.

Y 21   KOVAČIĆ, Matija, *Od Radića do Pavelića: Hrvatska u borbi za svoju samostalnost* (*From Radić to Pavelić: Croatia in the struggle for its independence*), Munich, 1970. 302pp. Exile Ustasha version of events in the Independent Croatian State.

Y 22   KRIZMAN, Bogdan, 'Razgran ičenje Ustaške države' (Fixing the boundaries of the Ustashi state). *JUGOSL. IST. CAS.*, **10** (**1/2**), 1971, pp. 107-45.

Y 23   KRIZMAN, Bogdan, 'Pitanje priznanja Ustaške države 1941 godine' (The struggle for the recognition of the Ustasha State). *JUGOSL. IST. CAS.*, **9** (**1/2**), 1970. pp. 90-121.

Y 24   *Kroatien Baut Auf*, Zagreb: Europa V., 1943. 171pp. Includes 'Das Lebensweg des Poglavnik' (Life of the Leader Pavelić).

Y 25   LAURIÈRE, Hervé, *Assassins au nom de Dieu*, pref. by Jean Perrigault, Paris: La Vignie, 1951. 176pp.

Y 26   LISAK, Erih, and others, defendants, *Sudjenje Lisaku, Stepincu, Šaliću, i družini Ustaško-Križarskim zločincima i njihovim pomagačima* (*The Proceedings against the Ustashi-crusader Traitors Lisak, Stepinac, Salić, and their Collaborators*), Zagreb: Stanič, 1946. 494pp. Trial held Sept.-Oct. 1946.

Y 27   MACEK, Vladko, *In the Struggle for Freedom*, New York: Speller, 1957. 280pp. Non-Ustasha version of events in Croatia 1941-4.

Y 28   MAKANEC, Julije, *Entwicklung der kroatischen Nationalismus*, Zagreb, 1944. 102pp. Ustashi theoretician.

Y 29   MENEGHELLO-DINČIĆ, Kruno, 'L'État Oustacha de Croatie, 1941-1945'. *REV. D'HIST. DEUX GUERRE MOND.*, **19** (**74**), 1969. pp. 43-65.

Y 30 MEŠTROVIĆ, Ivan, *Uspomene na političke ljude i dogadjaje* (*Memoirs of Politicians and Events*), Buenos Aires: Knjižnica Hrvatske Revije, 1961. 417pp. Sympathetic account of Croatian state by sculptor (1883–1962).

Y 31 NOVAK, Victor, *Velika optužba: pola vijeka klerikalizma u Hrvatskoj*, 2nd edn (*Magnum Crimen: a century of clericalism in Croatia*), Sarajevo: Svjetlost, 1960. 3 vols. First pub. 1948.

Y 32 PATEE, Richard, *The Case of Aloysius Stepinac*, Milwaukee: Bruce, 1953. xvi, 499pp. Bib. 498–9.

Y 33 PARIS, Edmund, *Genocide in Satellite Croatia, 1941–1945: a record of racial and religious persecutions and massacres*, Chicago: American Institute for Balkan Affairs, 1961. 306pp. Bib. 291–6. 2nd edn 1962.

Y 34 SCOTTI, Giacomo, *Ustascia tra il fascio e la svastica: storia e crimini del movimento Ustascia*, Udine: Ed. Incontri, 1976. 211pp. Bib. 205–11.

Y 35 SINOVČIĆ, Marko, *NDH u svietlu dokumenata* (*The Independent Croatian State in the Light of Documents*), Buenos Aires: Hrvatska Misao, 1950. 284pp. Ustasha view of events written in exile.

Y 36 SPERBER, Manes, 'Mort d'un contemporain'. *Preuves*, March 1960. pp. 60–5. The death of Pavelić who died in a German hospital in Madrid in 1959.

Y 37 *Tajni Dokumenti Odnosima Vatikana i Ustaške NDH* (*Secret Documents on the relations between the Vatican and the Independent Croatian State*), Zagreb, 1952. 143pp. Appendix of photographs and facsimiles.

German Nazis in Yugoslavia

Y 38 BAGNELL, Prisca von Dorotka, *The Influence of National-socialism on the German Minority in Yugoslavia: a Study of the Relationships of Social, Economic and Political Organisations between the German Minority of the Vojvodina and the Third Reich, 1933–1941*, Syracuse University thesis, 1977. UM 77-30708. 226pp.

Y 39 BIBER, Dušan, *Nacizem in Nemci v Jugoslaviji, 1933–1941* (*National Socialism and Germans in Yugoslavia*), Ljubljana: Cankarjeva Založba 1966. 480pp.

Dimitrije Ljotić, Zbor, and Serbian Nationalists

Y 40 GLIGORIJEVIĆ, Bronislav, 'Napad ljotićevaca na studente Tehnickog Fakulteta u Beogradu u Oktobru 1940 i rasturanje Ljotićevog Zbora' (Disturbances among the students of the technical faculty in Belgrade in October 1940 and the spread of Ljotić's Zbor movement). *Istorijski Glasnik*, **20** (**2**), 1963. pp. 52–82.

Y 41 GLIGORIJEVIĆ, Bronislav, 'Organizacija jugoslovenskikh nacionalista (ORJUNA)' (The Organisation of Yugoslav Nationalists). *Istoriya XX Veka. Zbornik Radova (Belgrade)*, **5**, 1963. pp. 315–99.

Y 42 GLIGORIJEVIĆ, Bronislav, 'Politicki pokreti i grupe s nacionalsocijaličkom ideologijom i njihova fuzija u Ljotićevom Zboru' (Political movements and groups with a national socialist ideology and their fusion with Ljotić's Zbor). *Istorijski Glasnik*, **4**, 1965. pp. 35–83.

Y 43 KOSTIĆ, Bosko, *Za istoriju našik dana: odlomci iz zapisa za vreme okupacije (The History of our Days)*, Lille: Lausier, 1949. 273pp. Zbor version of the occupation.

Y 44 KRAKOV, Stanislav, *General Milan Nedić*, Munich: Iskra, 1963. Vol. 1. Milan Nedić (1877–1946), Zbor activist.

Y 45 LJOTIĆ, Dimitrije V., *Iz moga života (From my Life)*, Munich: Iskra, 1952. 229pp. Collection of essays by the leader of the Zbor Movement, Maurrasian in inspiration.

Y 46 LJOTIĆ, Dimitrije V., *Dimitrije Ljotić u revoluciji i ratu (Dimitrije Ljotić in Revolution and War)*. Munich: Iskra, 1961. 430pp. Ljotić (1891–1945).

Y 47 MARTIĆ, Milos, 'Dimitrije Ljotić and the Yugoslav national movement Zbor, 1935–1945'. *EAST EUR. Q.*, **14** (**2**), 1980. pp. 219–39.

Y 48 PAREZANIN, Ratko, *Drugi svetski rat i Dimitrije V. Ljotić (World War II and D. V. Ljotić)*, Munich: Iskra, 1971. 530pp.

Y 49 RAŠEVIĆ, Veljko, *Ogled o švatanjima Dimitrija Ljotića (An Essay on Understanding Dimitrije Ljotić)*, Paris: Izd. Naše Reči, 1953. 47pp.

Yugoslavia and the Second World War

Y 50 BRAJOVIĆ, Petar, *Yugoslavia in the Second World War*, Belgrade: Borba, 1977. 239pp. Bib. 239. Tr. of *Jugoslavija u drugom svetskom ratu*.

Y 51 CULINOVIĆ, Ferdo, *Okupatorska podjela Jugoslavije* (*The Occupation Administration in Yugoslavia*), Belgrade: Vojnoizdavački Zavod, 1970. 688pp.

Y 52 HARRIMAN, Helga H., *Slovenia under Nazi occupation, 1941-1945*, New York: Studia Slovenia, 1977. 94pp. Bib. 66-70.

Y 53 *International Conference on the History of the Resistance Movement, Les systèmes d'occupation en Yougloslavie: rapports* (ed. Petar Brajović, Jovan Marjanović, and Franjo Tudjman), Belgrade: Inst. pour l'Etude du Mouvement Ouvrier, 1963. 564pp. F. Tudjman on the Independent Croatian State, pp. 135-262.

Y 54 KARAPANDZIC, Borivoje M., *Gradjanski rat u Srbiji, 1941-1945* (*Civil War in Serbia*), Munich: Iskra, 1958. 488pp. Anti-communist version of events.

Y 55 LEVENTAL, Zdenko (ed.), *The Crimes of the Fascist Occupants and their Collaborators against Jews in Yugoslavia*, Belgrade: Federation of Jewish Communities of the Federative Republic of Yugoslavia, 1957. xix, 245pp. Text in Serbo-Croat; English summary.

Y 56 MLAKAR, Boris, 'Domobranstvo na Tolminskem' (Collaboration in the Tolmin area). *Goriski Letnik*, **6**, 1979. pp. 217-40. On the Slovenian White Guard collaborators.

Y 57 TIMOTIJEVIĆ, Slavica, 'Organi kvislinške uprave u Srbiji za vreme II svetskog rata' (The organ of the quisling government in Serbia during the war). *Arhivski Pregled* (*Belgrade*), 1967. pp. 177-88.

Y 58 Vojnoistorijski Institut, Belgrade, *Bibliografija izdanja o narodnooslobodilačkom ratu, 1941-45*, Vinko Branica [*et al.*] (comps) (*Bibliography of Publications on the National Liberation war*), Belgrade, 1964. 815pp.

ROMANIA

General

Rm 1 BARBU, Zevedei, 'Rumania'. In WOOLF, S.J., Gn 20. pp. 151-70.

Rm 2   COPIOU, Nicolae, 'Sur la pénétration de l'idéologie nazie en Roumanie et l'attitude protestataire de l'intellectualité roumaine'. *REV. ROUM. D'HIST.*, **3** (**2**), 1964. pp. 243-53.

Rm 3   FISCHER-GALATI, Stephen, 'Fascism in Romania'. In SUGAR, P.F., E 23. pp. 112-21.

Rm 4   FISCHER-GALATI, Stephen, 'Romanian nationalism'. In SUGAR, P.F. and LEDERER, I.J., E 21. pp. 373-95.

Rm 5   GEORGESCU, Titu, 'Sur la cinquième colonne Hitlérienne en Roumanie'. *REV. D'HIST. DEUX GUERRE MOND.*, **18** (**70**), 1968. pp. 19-38. Iron Guard, National Christian League, Crusade for Romanianism led by Stelescu and Radescu, German Nazi organisations in Romania.

Rm 6   *Împotrivă Fascismului: sesiunea stiintifica privind analiza critică si demascarea fascismului în Romania, Bucaresti 4-5 martie 1971 (Against Fascism: scientific session concerning the critical analysis and the unmasking of fascism in Romania)*, Bucharest, 1971. 318pp. 22 papers covering the socio-economic foundations of fascism, the Legion and literature, the regime of September 1940, the Legion in parliament and other topics.

Rm 7   NEDELCU, Florea, 'Etude concernant le rôle de l'Allemagne hitlérienne dans l'évolution des organisations fascistes de Roumanie dans la période, 1933-1937'. *REV. ROUM. D'HIST.*, **10** (**6**), 1971. pp. 991-1011.

Rm 8   PĂTRĂȘCANU, Lucrețiu D., *Problemele de baza ale României*, 3rd edn, (*Basic Problems of Romania*), Bucharest: Ed. de Stat, 1946. 337pp. Iron Guard discussed.

Rm 9   PĂTRĂȘCANU, Lucrețiu D., *Sous trois dictatures*, Paris: Vitiano, 1946. 326pp. Tr. of *Sub trei dictaturi*, Bucharest: Forum, 1945. Marxist.

Rm 10   IONIȚĂ, Gh. I., 'Demascarea fascismului in scrierile social-politice ale lui Lucrețiu Pătrășcanu' (The exposure of fascism in the social-political writings of Lucrețiu Pătrășcanu). *Anale de Istorie*, **16** (**6**), 1970. pp. 145-63.

Rm 11   PROST, Henri, *Destin de la Roumanie, 1918-1954*, pref. by Albert Mousset, Paris: Ed. Berger Levrault, 1954. xiv, 279pp.

Rm 12   ROBERTS, Henry L., *Rumania: political problems of an agrarian state*, New Haven: Yale University Press, 1951. 414pp. Bib. 381-99. Oxford University thesis, 1948. Good analysis of fascism.

Rm 13   TURCZYNSKI, Emanuel, 'The background of Romanian fascism'. In SUGAR, P.F., E 23. pp. 101-11.

Rm 14   WEBER, Eugen, 'Romania'. In ROGGER, H. and WEBER, E., Gn 54. pp. 501–74.

Early Manifestations of the Extreme Right

Rm 15   BALAN, Ion Dodu, *Octavian Goga: monografie*, Bucharest: Minerva, 1975. 468pp. Bib. 350–98. 'Transylvanian poet (1881–1938) and lyrical fascist', Roberts, H.L., Rm 12. p. 192.

Rm 16   CUZA, Alexander C., *Nationalitatea in arta: introducere la doctrina nationalista-crestina* (*Nationality in Art: introducing the National Christian doctrine*), Bucharest, 1927. xii, 305pp. A.C. Cuza anti-semite, admirer of Edouart Drumont and founder of the League of Christian National Defence.

Rm 17   DURANDIN, Catherine, 'Les intellectuels et la paysannerie roumaine de la fin du XIXe siècle aux années 1930'. *REV. D'HIST. MOD. ET CONTEMP.*, **26** (**1**), 1979. pp. 144–55. Peasant–intellectual relations including Goga, Cuza and Codreanu.

Rm 18   GOURINARD, Pierre, 'La Roumanie et la pensée maurrassienne'. *Cahiers du Cercle Fustel de Coulanges* (*Paris*), **NS 1**, 1970. pp. 24–7.

Rm 19   OLDSON, William, *The Historical and Nationalist Thought of Nicolae Iorga*, New York: Columbia University Press, 1973 (East European monographs). 135pp. Bib. 119–32. Iorga (1871–1940) was one of the foremost of the political anti-semites and a key influence on the Legionary Movement.

The Legion of the Archangel Michael (Iron Guard)

Rm 20   AGRIGOROAIEI, I., 'Noi rezultate în analiza critică a fascismului din România' (New results of the critical analysis of Romanian fascism). *Anuarul Institutului de Istorie si Arheologie A.D. Xenopol* (*Iasi*), **9**, 1972. pp. 511–22.

Rm 21   ARMON, Theodor I., 'Fascismo italiano e Guardia di Ferro'. *STOR. CONTEMP.*, **3** (**3**), 1972. pp. 505–48.

Rm 22   ARMON, Theodor I., 'La Guardia di Ferro'. *STOR. CONTEMP.*, **7** (**3**), 1976. pp. 507–44.

Rm 23   BARBU, Zevedei, 'Psycho-historical and sociological perspectives on the Iron Guard: the fascist movement of Romania'. In LARSEN, S.U., Gn 36. pp. 379–94.

Rm 24   BELEMACE, Doru, *Revoluţia fascista*, 2nd edn, Bucharest: Bucovina, 1940. 182pp. Fascism as seen by the Legionary Movement.

Rm 25   BRADESCO, Faust, *Antimachiavélisme Legionnaire*, Rio de Janeiro: Dacia, 1963. 70pp.

Rm 26   BROSZAT, Martin, 'Die Eiserne Garde und das Dritte Reich: zum Problem des Faschismus in Ostmitteleuropa'. *POLIT. STUD.*, **9**, 1958. 628–36.

Rm 27   CHARLÉ, Klaus, *Die Eiserne Garde: eine Darstellung der völkischen Erneuerungsbewegung in Rumänien*, Berlin: Deutscher Rechtsverlag, 1939. 112pp. Bib. 112.

Rm 28   FĂTU, Mihai and SPĂLĂŢELU, Ion, *Gărda de Fier: organizaţie teroristă de tip fascist (The Iron Guard: a fascist type terrorist organisation)*, Bucharest: Politica, 1971. 431pp. One of first studies to use Romanian state archives and Communist Party material. German edn, *Die Eiserne Garde*, by same publisher, 1975.

Rm 29   'Garda de Fier: o bandă dusmană pusă să jefuiască şi să stoarcă tara' (The Iron Guard: an enemy band set to pillage and crush the country). *Magazin Istoric*, **13** (**6**), 1979. pp. 41–5.

Rm 30   GUIRAUD, Paul, *Codreanu et la Garde de Fer*, Rio de Janeiro: Dacia, 1967; Champs-sur-Marne, 1974. (First pub. 1940.) 78pp. Author was a Franciste leader.

Rm 31   HERNAN-BASTIDA (pseud.), *Rumania, de la Guardia de Hierro a la Guardia Roja*, pref. by Rafael García Serrano, Barcelona: L. de Caralt, 1945. 255pp.

Rm 32   HERSENI, Traian, *Mişcărea legionara muncitorimea si taranimea*, 2nd edn (*The Legionary Movement for Workers and Peasants*), Bucharest: Ed. Mişcării Legionare, 1940. 36pp.

Rm 33   IONESCU, Nae, *Fenomenul legionar (The Legionary Phenomenon)*, intro. by Constantin Papanace, Rome: Ed. Armatolii, 1963. 37pp.

Rm 34   LONGCHAMP, Jean Paul de, *La Garde de Fer: ou l'histoire d'une bande d'assassins*, Paris: SEFA, 1975. 133pp.

Rm 35   MARIN, Vasile, *Crez de generatie (Creed of a Generation)*, cu un cuvânt inainte de Corneliu Zelea Codreanu, pref. by Nae Ionescu, 2nd edn, Karlsfeld: Ion Mării, 1977. xvi, 235pp. Repr. of 2nd edn pub. Tip Bucovina, 1937. Vasile Marin (1904–37), leading Legionary killed in Spanish Civil War.

Rm 36   MOȚA, Ion, *Correspondenta cu 'Serviciul mondial' 1934–1936* (*Correspondent for World Service*), intro. by Constantin Papanace, Rome: Ed. Armatolii, 1954. 55pp.

Rm 37   MOȚA, Ion, *L'uomo nuovo*, Padua: Ed. di Ar, 1978. 288pp. Tr. of *Cranii de lemn* (*Wooden Skulls*), Sibu, 1936. Ion Moța (1902–37), founder of Actiunea Romaneâscă, anti-semite and romantic nationalist, second most important Legionary leader after Codreanu, died on the Madrid Front in 1937.

Rm 38   MUȘAT, Ștefan, 'Coloana v-a Hitleristă in România' (Hitler's fifth column in Romania). *Anale de Istorie*, **16** (**6**), 1970. pp. 128–44. Codreanu and the Iron Guard.

Rm 39   NEDELCU, Florea, 'Date noi privînd legăturile Gărzii de Fier cu nazismului' (New information on the Iron Guard's connection with nazism). *REV. DE IST.*, **32** (**7**), 1979. pp. 1351–4.

Rm 40   PANINI-FINOTTI, Alfonso, *Da Codreanu a Antonescu: Romania di ieri e di oggi*, 11th edn, Verona: Ed. L'Albero, 1941. 271pp. Bib. 269. Pro-Iron Guard.

Rm 41   PAPANACE, Constantin, *Evocări* (*Evocations*), Madrid, 1965. 191pp. History of the Iron Guard.

Rm 42   PAPANACE, Constantin, *Orientări pentru legionari*, Rome: Ed. Armatolii, 1952. 35pp.

Rm 43   PAPANACE, Constantin, *Orientări politice în primul exil, 1939–1940*, Rome: Ed. Armatolii, 1953. 43pp. Author a Macedonian and close adviser of Codreanu.

Rm 44   PAPANACE, Constantin and SIMA, Horia, *Evolutia Mișcării Legionare dupa arestarea si asasinarea capitanului* (*Evolution of the Legionary Movement after the Imprisonment and Assassination of the Captain*), Rome: Ed. Armatolii, 1977. 46pp.

Rm 45   PETRASCU, Nicola, *Din viața legionara* (*From Legionary Days*), Munich: Omul Nou, 1952. 243pp.

Rm 46   RONNETT, Alexander E., *Romanian Nationalism: the Legionary Movement*, tr. from Romanian by Vasile C. Barsan, Chicago: Loyola University Press, 1974. 81pp. Bib. 70. Pro-Legion.

Rm 47   SIMA, Horia, *Histoire du Mouvement Légionnaire*, Rio de Janeiro: Ed. Dacia, 1972. Vol. 1. 1919–37.

Rm 48   SPĂLĂTELU, Ion and FĂTU, Mihai, 'Legionarismul: o pagină intunecată din istoria contemporană a României' (The Legionary current; a sombre page of contemporary history in Romania). *Lupta de Clasa*, **50** (**9**), 1970. pp. 56–66.

Rm 49   STOEDTNER, Gerhard, 'Weltanschauung und Kampf der "Eisernen Garde" Rumäniens'. *Z̆. FÜR POLIT.*, **27** (**6**), 1937. pp. 334-42.

Rm 50   THARAUD, Jérôme and Jean, *L'Envoyé de l'Archange*, Paris: Plon, 1939. 242pp. Sympathetic account by associates of Barrès.

Rm 51   VAGO, Bela, 'Romanian fascist emigrés'. *WIENER LIB. BULL.*, **18**, (**3**), 1964. p. 41.

Rm 52   WEBER, Eugen, 'The men of the Archangel'. *J. OF CONTEMP. HIST.*, **1** (**1**), 1966. pp. 101-26.

Corneliu Zelea Codreanu (1899-1938)

Rm 53   CODREANU, Corneliu Zelea, *Circulările căpitanului, 1934-1937* (*The Circular Letters of the Captain*), [n.p.]: Delatopoloveni, 1937. 137pp.

Rm 54   BANEA, Ion, *Căpitanul* (*The Captain*), 2nd edn, Sibiu: Ed. Totul pentru Tara, 1937. 143pp. Laudatory but useful biography of Codreanu.

Rm 55   CODREANU, Corneliu Zelea, *Circulări şi manifeste, 1927-1938*, 2nd edn, Bucharest: Ed. Mişcării Legionare, 1942. 284pp. Reissued by Omul Nou, Munich, 1951. A collection of statements by the Iron Guard leader.

Rm 56   CODREANU, Corneliu Zelea, *Corneliu Z. Codreanu in perspectiva a douazeci de ani* (*Codreanu in Perspective over 20 Years*), Madrid: Ed. Libertatea, 1959. 72pp.

Rm 57   CODREANU, Corneliu Zelea, *For my Legionaries: the Iron Guard*, Madrid: Ed. Libertatea, 1976. xvi, 353pp. Tr. of *Pentru legionari*, first pub. Sibiu: Ed. Totul Pentru Tara, 1936. German edn, *Eiserne Garde*, 3rd edn, Brunnen V., 1942. Also French, Spanish and Italian edns.

Rm 58   CODREANU, Corneliu Zelea, *Însemnări dela Jilava*, Munich: Omul Nou, 1951. 66pp. Prison notes.

Rm 59   ESCOLAR, Thomas and NIETO, Jesus, *Vida y doctrina de Cornelio Codreanu*, Barcelona, 1941. 123pp.

Rm 60   ROSSI DELL'ARNO, Giulio de, *Cornelio Codreanu: pensieri e massime di vita*, Rome: Maglione, 1940. 77pp.

Rm 61   SBURLATI, Carlo, *Codreanu il capitano*, Rome: Volpe, 1970.

230pp. 'Naive eulogy of Codreanu and the Legionary Movement', E 26.

Rm 62   SIMA, Horia, *Dos movimientos nacionalos: José Antonio Primo de Rivera y Corneliu Zelea Codreanu*, Madrid: Eds Europas, 1960. 132pp. By the successor to Codreanu as leader of the Romanian Iron Guard.

Royal Dictatorship, Legionary Régime and the Second World War

Rm 63   BOLITHO, Hector, *Roumania under King Carol*, New York: Longmans Green, 1940. 175pp.

Rm 64   BROSZAT, Martin, 'Das Dritte Reich und die rumänische Judenpolitik'. *Gutachten des Inst. für Zeitgeschichte*, 1958. pp. 102-83.

Rm 65   CHIRNOAGA, Platon, General, *Un Chapître d'histoire roumain, 1940-1945*, Rio de Janeiro: Dacia, 1962. 74pp. Legionary version of events.

Rm 66   ERESHCHENKO, Margarita Dmitrievna, *Korolevskaia diktatura v Rumynii, 1938-1940 (The Royal Dictatorship in Romania)*, Moscow: Nauka, 1979. 171pp. Bib. 156-68.

Rm 67   HILLGRUBER, Andreas, *Hitler, König Carol und Marschall Antonescu: die deutsch-rumänischen Beziehungen, 1938-1944*, 2nd edn, Wiesbaden: Steiner, 1965. xvii, 382pp. Bib. 357-66.

Rm 68   LEBEDEV, Nikolai Ivanovich, *Krakh fashizma v Rumynii (The Collapse of Fascism in Romania)*, Moscow: Nauka, 1976. 632pp. Bib.

Rm 69   LEBEDEV, Nikolai Ivanovich, *Zheleznaia Gvardiia, Karol'II, i Gitler: iz istorii rumynskogo fashizma, monarkhii ee vneshnepoliticheskoi 'igry na dvukh stolakh' (The Iron Guard, King Carol and Hitler)*, Moscow: Mezhdunarodnye Otnosheniia, 1968. 327pp. Bib. 318-26.

Rm 70   NEDELCU, Florea, 'Carol al II-lea şi Gărda di Fier: de la relaţii amicale la criză, 1930-1937' (Carol II and the Iron Guard: from friendly relations to crisis). *Studii*, **24** (5), 1971. pp. 1009-28.

Rm 71   NEDELCU, Florea, 'De la relaţii cordiale la exterminare reciprocă: Carol II şi Gărda de Fier' (From cordial relations to mutual extermination: Carol II and the Iron Guard). *Magazin Istoric*, **7** (5), 1973. pp. 77-85.

Rm 72   NEDELCU, Florea, *De la restauratie la dictadura regala din viaţa politică a României, 1930-1938 (From the Restoration to the Royal Dictatorship in Romanian Political Life)*, Cluj-Napoca: Ed. Dacia, 1981. 446pp. First edn, *Viaţa politică din Romania*, 1973.

152

Rm 73   *Pe Marginea Prapăstiei, 21-23 ianuarie 1941 (On the Brink of the Abyss, 21-23 January 1941)*, Bucharest, 1942. 2 vols. Polemic against the Iron Guard and their attempted *coup* of January 1941 issued by Antonescu regime.

Rm 74   POPESCU-PUŢURI, Ion and others (eds), *La Roumanie pendant la deuxième guerre mondiale*, Bucharest: Ed. Acad. Republ. Popul. Romane, 1964. 143pp. Contains essays on the penetration of nazi ideology and on the military dictatorship.

Rm 75   SAVU, Alexandru Gh., *Dictatura regale, 1938-1940 (Royal Dictatorship)*, Bucharest: Politica, 1970. 482pp.

Rm 76   SAVU, Alexandru Gh., 'Rebeliunea legionara in versiunea Generalului Hansen' (General Hansen's version of the Legionary rebellion). *Magazin Istoric*, **9** (2), 1975. pp. 58-61. Erik Hansen, Wehrmacht officer, on the 1941 *coup* attempt.

Rm 77   SHAPIRO, Paul A., 'Prelude to dictatorship in Romania: the National Christian Party in power, Dec. 1937-Feb. 1938'. *CAN.-AMER. SLAV. STUD.*, **8** (1), 1974. pp. 45-88.

Rm 78   SIMION, Aurică, *Regimul politic din România în perioada septembrie 1940-ianuarie 1941 (The Political Regime in Romania Sept. 1940-Jan. 1941)*, Cluj-Napoca: Ed. Dacia, 1976. 326pp. On the Legionary-Antonescu dictatorship, the Legionary rebellion, and hostilities between Antonescu and the Legion.

Rm 79   SOCOR, Vladimir and JELINEK, Yeshayahu, 'Polish diplomatic reports on the political crisis in Romania, September 1940'. *Southeastern Europe*, **6** (1), 1979. pp. 94-112.

Rm 80   VAGO, Bela, 'Romania during the war: a survey of literature'. *WIENER LIB. BULL.*, **17** (2), 1963. p. 26.

Rm 81   ZAHARIA, Gh., 'Quelque données concernant la terreur fasciste en Roumanie, 1940-1944'. *REV. ROUM. D'HIST.*, **3** (1), 1964. pp. 115-33.

HUNGARY

General

H 1   BÁRÁNY, George, 'The dragon's teeth: the roots of Hungarian fascism'. In SUGAR, P.F., E 23. pp. 73-82.

H 2   BÁRÁNY, George, 'Hungary: from aristocratic to proletarian nationalism'. In SUGAR, P.F. and LEDERER, I.J., E 21. pp. 259-309.

H 3   DEÁK, István, 'Hungary'. In ROGGER, H. and WEBER, E., Gn 54. pp. 364-407.

H 4   ERÖS, János, 'Hungary'. In WOOLF, S.J., Gn 20. pp. 117-150.

H 5   MACARTNEY, Carlyle Aylmer, *October Fifteenth: a history of modern Hungary*, 2nd edn, Edinburgh: University Press, 1961. 2 vols. Very significant general history which has been accused of excessive sympathy for Szálasi.

H 6   MAJOR, Robert, *25 év ellenforradalmi sajtó, 1919-1944 (25 years of the Counterrevolutionary Press)*, Budapest: Cserépfalvi, 1945. 108pp. Quotes extensively from the nazi press.

H 7   NAGY-TALAVERA, Nicholas M., *The Green Shirts and Others: a history of fascism in Hungary and Rumania*, Stanford: Hoover Inst. Press, 1970. xi, 427pp. Bib. 401-7. University of California thesis. Comparative study.

H 8   RÁNKI, György, 'The problem of fascism in Hungary'. In SUGAR, P.F., E 23. pp. 65-72.

H 9   RÁNKI, György, 'Orientamenti per una valutazione del fascismo in Ungheria e nei paesi dell'Europa orientale'. *RIV. STOR. DEL SOC.*, 7 (21), 1964. pp. 143-61.

H 10   SULYOK, Deszö, *A magyar tragédia (The Hungarian Tragedy)*, New Brunswick, NJ: Author, 1954. Bib. 609-14. Polemical work on interwar period.

The Beginnings of the Extreme Right

H 11   KESSLER, Joseph A., *Turanism and Pan-Turanism in Hungary, 1890-1945*, University of California, Berkeley thesis, 1967. UM 67-11638. 655pp. Neo-nationalism.

154

H 12   SZABÓ, Miklós, 'Az 1901-es egyetemi "kereszt-mozgalom"': adalék a magyarországi szélsojobboldal elötörténetehez' (The Cross Movement in 1901: a contribution to the prehistory of the far Right in Hungary). *TORT. SZ.*, **13** (**4**), 1970. pp. 483-516.

The Horthy-Gömbös Right

H 13   BALAZS, Bela, 'A Horthy-fasizmus társadalmának és ideológiájának néhány jellemzö vonása' (Some characteristic features of the fascist regime of Horthy). *A Magyar Tudomanyos Akademia Tarsadalmi es Torteneti, Tudomanyok Osztalyanak Közlemenyei*, **9** (**1**), 1959. pp. 97-116.

H 14   BIGLER, Robert M., 'Heil Hitler and Heil Horthy! The nature of Hungarian racial nationalism and its impact on German-Hungarian relations, 1919-1945'. *EAST EUR. Q.*, **8** (**3**), 1974. pp. 252-72.

H 15   HORTHY, Miklós, *Confidential Papers*, ed. Miklós Szinai and László Szücs, Budapest: Corvina P., 1965. xxi, 439pp. Tr. of *Horthy Miklós titkos iratai*, Budapest, 1963.

H 16   ORMOS, Maria, 'Horthyisme et fascisme'. *REV. HIST. (Paris)*, **251** (**1**), 1974. pp. 117-22.

H 17   VAS, Zoltán, *Horthy*, 2nd edn, Budapest: Szépirodalmi Könyvkiadó, 1977. 714pp.

H 18   CSEPANYI, Deszö, *A Gömbös-kormany szocialpolitikaja, 1935-36* (*The Social Politics of the Gömbös Government*), Szeged: Attila Jozsef University Szeged, 1966. 63pp.

H 19   GLATZ, Ferenc and STIER, M., 'Megyei küzdelmek a Gömbösi reformtörekvések körül' (The struggles in committee over the Gömbös attempts at reform). *TORT. SZ.*, **14**, 1971. pp. 157-87.

H 20   KONYA, Sándor, *Gömbös kisérlete totális fasiszta diktatúra megteremtésére* (*Gömbös' Attempt to Create a Totalitarian Fascist Dictatorship*), Budapest: Akad. Kiado, 1968. 201pp. Gyula Gömbös (1886-1936) and the radical Right.

H 21   KONYA, Sándor, 'Az elsö Gömbös-kormány megalakulása és programja' (The establishment and programme of Gömbös' first Ministry). *Szazadok*, **97** (**2**), 1963. pp. 332-68.

H 22   SZOKOLY, Endre, 'És Gömbös Gyula a kapitány' (Gömbös the Captain), Budapest: Gondolat, 1960. 424pp.

H 23   KLEIN, Bernard, *Hungarian Politics from Bethlen to Gömbös: the decline of liberal conservatism and the rise of Right-radicalism*, Columbia University thesis, 1962. UM 65-07505. 269pp.

H 24   NEMES, Deszö, *A fasizmus kérdéséhez (The Question of Fascism)*, Budapest: Magvetö Kiadó, 1976. Bethlen, Horthy, and Gömbös rather than the national socialists.

H 25   ROMPORTLOVA, Marta, 'Charakteristika a kořeny fašistických rysu meziválečného režimu v Madarsku' (The characteristics and roots of the fascist elements of the interwar regime in Hungary). *Sbornik Praci Filosoficke Fakulty Brnenske. Rada Hist.*, **29 (27)**, 1980. pp. 225-34.

Ferenc Szálasi and the Arrow Cross Movement

H 26   ABRAHAM, Ferenc and KUSSINSZKY, Endre (eds), *A Szálasi per: Szálasi, Szöllösi, Csia, Gera, Vajna, Béregfy, Kemeny bünügyének fötárgyalása és az itelet (The Szálasi Trial: the main trial and the verdict in the case against Szálasi . . .)*, Budapest: Hirado Könyvtar, 1946. 192pp.

H 27   FRANK, László, *Zöld ár*, 2nd edn, Budapest: Zrínyi Katonai Kiadó, 1977, 206pp. On Száiasi and his Arrow Cross Movement.

H 28   KARSAI, Elek (ed.), *'Szálasi naplója': a nyilasmozgalom a II Világháború idején (The Szálasi Diary: The Arrow Cross in the Second World War)*, Budapest: Kossuth, 1978. 490pp. For various changes of name of Szálasi's party see pp. 16-17.

H 29   ROZSNYÓI, Ágnes, 'October Fifteenth: (history of Szálasi's putsch)'. *ACTA HIST.*, **8 (1/2)**, 1961. pp. 57-105.

H 30   ROZSNYÓI, Ágnes, *A Szálasi puccs (Szálasi's Coup d'état)*, 2nd edn, Budapest: Kossuth, 1977. 104pp. Bib. 104.

H 31   TÖRÖK, Andras, *Szálasi álarc nelkül: öt év a Szálasi-mozgalomban (Szálasi Unmasked)*, Budapest, 1941. 117pp. Arrow Cross activist earlier in the Böszörményi movement who became disillusioned by what he saw as Szálasi's abandonment of the social programme.

H 32   VOZÁRY ALADÁR, R., *Igy történt 1944: marcius 19-1945 január 18 (History of 1944)*, Budapest: Halász, 1945. 160pp.

H 33   DEGRÉ, Alajos, 'Kisérlet jobboldali pártegység megteremtésére Zala megyében 1944 nyarán' (An attempt to create unity among the parties of the Right in the Zala committee in summer 1944). *Szazadok*, **98 (5/6)**, 1964. pp. 1188-95.

H 34   ENDRE, László, *A zsidókról a berni per tanulságai* (*On the Jews; the lessons of the Bern trial*), Budapest: Kossuth, 1942. 71pp. László Endre (1895-1946) leading national socialist and rabid anti-semite, executed in 1946.

H 35   FENYO, Mario D., *Hitler, Horthy and Hungary: German-Hungarian relations, 1941-1944*, New Haven: Yale University Press, 1972. 279pp. Bib. 251-66. Material on Szálasi's *coup* of October 1944.

H 36   FIALA, Ferenc, *Zavaros évek: a Horthy-korszaktol-Kadar-Janosig* (*Troubled Years*), 2nd edn, Munich, 1966. 173pp. Memoirs of Szálasi's press chief and notorious anti-semite.

H 37   FIALA, Ferenc and MARSCHALKO, Lajos, *Vádló bitofák: a magyar nemzet igazi sirasoi* (*Accusing Gallows*), London: Sueli, 1958. 285pp. A view of Hungary from two ex-Arrow Cross exiles and anti-semites.

H 38   GAZSI, Józef, 'A honvedelmi minisztérium a nyilas puccs után' (The Ministry of National Defence following the Arrow Cross putsch). *Leveltari Szemle*, **14** (**4**), 1964. pp. 119-52.

H 39   GAZSI, József and GELLÉRT, Tibor, 'A fasiszták kisérletei Magyarország népességének elhurcolására 1944-1945-ben' (The attempts of the fascists to deport the population of Hungary). *Hadtortenelmi Kozlemenyek*, **11** (**2**, 1964. pp. 297-333.

H 40   GLATZ, Ferenc, 'Hóman Bálint és a nemzetiszocialistak összeütközéso Székesfehérvárott, 1944-ben' (Bálint Hóman and the impact of national socialism in Székesfehérvár). *Fejer Megyei Torteneti Evkonyv* (*Székesfehérvár*), 1970. pp. 187-202.

H 41   GOSZTONYI, Peter, *Endkampf an der Donau, 1944/45*, Vienna: Molden, 1969. 356pp. Bib. 334-43. The last days of the Szálasi regime.

H 42   GOSZTONYI, Peter, 'Német katonai okmányok október 15 elotörténetéhez' (German military documents regarding the history of the events leading to 15 Oct. 1944). *Uj Latohatar*, **12**, 1969. pp. 515-23.

H 43   *Harc Budapestért, 1944-1947: bibliográfia hazánk felszabadulásának 30. évforduójára; szerk . . . . Mitru Ibolya* (*The Struggle for Budapest: bibliography of the liberation of our homeland on the 30th anniversary*), Budapest: Fs Z EK, 1975. 294pp. Bibliography of the history of Budapest, 1944-7 including the Szálasi regime and the siege.

H 44   *Hazánk Felszabadulása 1944-1945: Bibliográfia és dokumentum gyüjtemény* (*Liberation of our Country, 1944-45: bibliography and collection of documents*), Budapest: Fóvarosi Szabó Ervin Könyvtar, 1955. 192pp. See pp. 112-27 for Arrow Cross Movement regime, its removal and fate. Includes contemporary pamphlets.

H 45 HIMLER, Martin, *Igy neztek ki a magyar nemzet sirásói (This is what the Gravediggers of the Hungarian Nation Looked Like)*, New York: St Mark's Printing, 1958. 196pp. By the Hungarian-American whose team first interrogated the Hungarian war criminals.

H 46 KARSAI, Elek, *Itél a nép (The People Judge)*, Budapest: Kossuth, 1977. 291pp. On war crimes trials.

H 47 KONKOLY, Kálmán, 'Waren Ungarns Pfeil-Kreuzler Nazis?'. *POLIT. STUD.*, **17** (**167**), 1966. pp. 304-16.

H 48 KUN, Andor (comp.), *Berlinböl jelentik (Berlin Reports)*, Budapest: Keresztes Kiadó, 1945. 251pp. On Arrow Cross Movement and the Germans.

H 49 LACKÓ, Miklós, *Arrow Cross Men, National Socialists, 1935-1944*, Budapest: Akad. Kiadó, 1969. 112pp. Abridged version of *Nyilasok nemzetiszocialisták*, Budapest: Kossuth, 1966. 350pp. Bib. 334-47.

H 50 LACKÓ, Miklós, 'Les Croix-Flèchées, 1935-1944'. *REV. D'HIST. DEUX GUERRE MOND.*, **16** (**62**), 1966. pp. 53-68.

H 51 LACKÓ, Miklós, 'A magyarorszagi nyilas mozgalom, 1935-1944' (The Hungarian Arrow Cross Movement). *Elet es Tudomany*, **20** (**38**), 1965. pp. 1805-8; **20** (**39**), 1965. pp. 1852-5.

H 52 LACKÓ, Miklós, 'The social roots of Hungarian fascism: the Arrow Cross'. In LARSEN, S.U., Gn 36. pp. 395-400.

H 53 LÉVAI, Jenö, *A pesti gettó: csodálatos megmenekülesenek hiteles törtenete (The Ghetto of Pest: the true story of a wonderful escape)*, Budapest: Oficina, 1946. 174pp. On the nazi and Arrow Cross reign of terror 1944-5.

H 54 LÉVAI, Jenö, *Endre László: a magyar háborús bünosök listavezetöje (László Endre the Leader on the List of Hungarian War Criminals)*, Budapest: Müller, 1945. 112pp. A leading Arrow Cross member.

H 55 LÉVAI, Jenö, *Horogkereszt, kaszáskereszt, nyilaskereszt (The Swastika, Scythe Cross and Arrow Cross)*, Budapest: Müller, 1945. 124pp. On the various national socialist movements.

H 56 LÉVAI, Jenö, 'The war crimes trials relating to Hungary: a follow-up'. *Hungarian Jewish Stud.*, **3**, 1973. pp. 251-90.

H 57 MALNASI, Ödön, *A magyar nemzet öszinte története (A Sincere History of the Hungarian Nation)*, 2nd edn, Munich: Mikes Kelemen Kör, 1959. 300pp. First pub. 1937, when author was convicted in the courts. Chief ideologist of the Arrow Cross Movement.

H 58   PINTÉR, István and SZABÓ, László (eds), *Criminals at Large: documents*, Budapest: Pannonia, 1961. 330pp. Hungarian war criminals in the West.

H 59   PRONÁI, Pál, *A határban a Halál kaszál: fejezetek Pronái Pál feljegyzéseiből; szerkeztette és bevezeto tanulmannyol ellata Szabó Ágnes es Pamlényi Ervin* (*Death Scything Nearby: chapters from the notes of Pál Pronái*), Budapest: Kossuth, 1963. 384pp. Notes of a military man involved with the Whites in the Civil War, then Arrow Cross leader in 1944.

H 60   RÁNKI, György, 'Az 1939-es Budapesti választások' (The 1939 elections in Budapest). *TORT. SZ.*, **19** (**4**), 1976. pp. 613-30.

H 61   RÁNKI, György, 'The fascist vote in Budapest in 1939'. In LARSEN, S.U., Gn 36. pp. 401-16.

H 62   SOLYOM, József and SZABÓ, László, 'A zuglói nyilas per' (*The Trial of the Zugló Nyilas*), Budapest: Kossuth, 1967. 382pp. Arrow Cross murderers of Jews in Zugló, a district of Budapest, tried in June 1967.

H 63   TELEKI, Eva, *Nyilas uralom Magyarorszagón, 1944 október 16-1945 április 4* (*The Arrow Cross Regime in Hungary*), Budapest: Kossuth, 1974. 387pp. Bib. 297-387.

H 64   TELEKI, Eva, 'A nyilas uralmi rendszer berendezkedése 1944 október-novemberjeben' (The establishment of the Arrow Cross regime in Oct.-Nov. 1944). *TORT. SZ.*, **15** (**1/2**), 1972. pp. 154-97.

H 65   TILKOVSZKY, Lóránt, 'A nyilasok törvényjavaslata a nemzetiségi kérdés rendezéséröl' (Arrow Cross legislation to settle the nationalities question). *Szazadok*, **99** (**6**), 1965. pp. 1247-58.

Other Extreme Right-Wing Movements

H 66   DÓSA (Mrs), Rudolf, *A MOVE: egy jellegzetes magyar fasiszta szervezet, 1918-1944* (*MOVE: a typical Hungarian fascist organisation*), Budapest: Akad. Kiadó, 1972. 228pp. A history of the most important Rightist secret society under Horthy, Magyar Orszagos Vederö Egyesület (Ass. of Hungarian National Defence).

H 67   SIPOS, Péter, 'Az Imrédy-kormány megala-kulásánk történetéröl' (On the history of the establishment of the Imrédy Cabinet). *Szazadok*, **100** (**1**), 1966. pp. 62-97.

H 68   SIPOS, Péter, 'Az Imrédy-kormány válsága és bukása' (Crisis and fall of the Imrédy Cabinet). *TORT.SZ.*, **9** (**1**), 1966. pp. 42-84.

H 69   SIPOS, Péter, *Imrédy Béla és a Magyar Megujulás Pártja* (*Bela Imrédy and the Hungarian Renaissance Party*), Budapest: Akad. Kiadó, 1970. 261pp. Bib. 256–61. Upper-class fascism led by former Governor of National Bank, Prime Minister in 1938.

H 70   SZAKÁCS, Kálmán, *Kaszáskeresztesek* (*The Scythe Cross Men*), Budapest: Kossuth, 1963. 126pp.

H 71   SZAKÁCS, Kálmán, 'Kraishee pravie dvizheniia v Vengerskoi derevnie v tridsatie godi' (Movements of the extreme Right in the Hungarian villages in the 1930s). *ACTA HIST.*, 12 (3/4), 1966. pp. 347–71. Covers Böszormenyi, Mesko and Festetich.

H 72   TILKOVSZKY, Lóránt, 'A Volksbund szerepe Magyarország második világháborús történetében' (The role of the Volksbund in Hungarian history between the two wars). *TORT. SZ.*, 11, 1968. pp. 294–312.

H 73   TILKOVSZKY, Lóránt, 'Volksdeutsche Bewegung und ungarische Nationalitätenpolitik, 1938–1941'. *ACTA HIST.*, 12 (1/2), 1966. pp. 59–112; 12 (3/4), 1966. pp. 319–46. On the Volksdeutsche Kameradschaft and the Volksbund der Deutsche in Ungarn.

Hungary and the Second World War

H 74   DEÁK, István, 'Collaborationism in Europe, 1940–1945: the case of Hungary'. *AUSTRIAN HIST. YEARB.*, 15/16, 1979/80. pp. 157–76. With comments by Tamas Bogyay.

H 75   BRAHAM, Randolph L., *The Hungarian Jewish catastrophe: a selected and annotated bibliography*, New York: Yivo Inst. for Jewish Research, 1962. 86pp.

H 76   BRAHAM, Randolph L., *The Politics of Genocide: the Holocaust in Hungary*, New York: Columbia University Press, 1981. 2 vols. Definitive and superb history which includes much on ultra-Right especially the Arrow Cross and Szálasi's period of rule.

H 77   GEYER, Arthúr, *A Magyarorzági fasizmus zsidóüldözésének bibliográfiája, 1945–1958* (*Bibliography of the Fascist Persecutions of the Jews in Hungary*), Budapest: Magy. Izraeliták Országos Képviseletének Kiad., 1958. 167pp. 250 entries.

H 78   NAGY-TALAVERA, Nicholas M., 'The second world war as mirrored in the Hungarian fascist press'. *EAST EUR. Q.*, 4 (2), 1970. pp. 179–208.

H 79   ÖLVEDI, Ignác, *A Budai Vár es a debreceni csata: Horthyék katasztrófapolitikája 1944 öszén*, 2nd edn, Budapest: Zrinyi Katonai Kiadó, 1974. 242pp. Bib. 239-43.

H 80 PINTÉR, István, 'Az egységes fasiszta munkásszervezetek étrehozására irányuló kísérletek crödje, 1944 március 19-1944 október' (The failure of the attempt to create unified fascist working class organisations). *Parttorteneti Kozlemenyek,*, **15** (3), 1969. pp. 3-31.

H 81 RÁNKI, György, *1944 március 19. magyarország nemét megszállása* (*The German Occupation of Hungary on 19 March, 1944*), 2nd edn, Budapest: Kossuth, 1978. 324pp. Bib. 319-24.

H 82 TILKOVSZKY, Lóránt, *SS-toborzás Magyarországon* (*SS Recruitment in Hungary*), Budapest: Kossuth, 1974. 192pp. Bib. 186-92. German summary in *ACTA HIST.*, **20**, 1974. pp. 127-81.

POLAND

General

P1 1 ANDRESKI, S., 'Poland'. In WOOLF, S.J., Gn 20. pp. 171-89. Mostly on Dmowski and National Democracy and the Camp of National Unity.

P1. 2 BROCK, Peter, 'Polish nationalism'. In SUGAR, P.F. and LEDERER, I.J., E 21. pp. 310-72.

P1 3 WANDYCZ, Piotr S., 'Fascism in Poland, 1918-1939'. In SUGAR, P.F., E 23. pp. 92-7.

P1 4 WERESZYCKI, Henryk, 'Fascism in Poland'. In SUGAR, P.F., E 23. pp. 85-91.

Narodowa Demokracja (National Democracy) and Roman Dmowski (1864-1939)

P1 5 BIELECKI, Tadeusz, *W szkole szkice i wspomnienia Dmowskiego* (*In the School of Dmowski*), London: Polska Fundacija Kulturalna, 1968. 318pp. Memoirs of Roman Dmowski by one of his more extreme supporters. Chronicles the move towards fascism after 1934.

Pl 6   DMOWSKI, Roman, *Pisma (Writings)*, Czestochowa: Gmachowski, 1937–8. Vols. 2–10.

Pl 7   FOUNTAIN, Alvin Marcus, *Roman Dmowski: party, tactics, ideology 1895–1907.* Boulder: Columbia University Press, 1980. xiii, 240pp. Bib. 217–31. (East European monographs).

Pl 8   MICEWSKI, Andrzej, *Roman Dmowski*, Warsaw: Verum, 1971. 423pp. Bib. 406–15.

Pl 9   WAPIŃSKI, Roman, *Roman Dmowski*, Warsaw: Iskry, 1979. 102pp. Bib. 102.

Pl 10   KALABINSKI, Stanislaw, *Antynarodowa polityka Endecji w rewolucji, 1905–1907* (Anti-national politics of Endecja in the revolution), Warsaw: Panstw. Wydawn. Nauk., 1955. 479pp. Bib.

Pl 11   RUDNICKI, Szymon, 'Narodowa Demokracja po przewrocie majowym: zmiony organizacyjne i ideologiczne, 1926–1930' (National Democracy after the May 1926 *coup d'état*: organisational and ideological transformations). In *Najnowsze-Dzieje Polski, 1914–1939*, vol. 11, 1967. pp. 27–56.

Pl 12   TEREJ, Jerzy Janusz, *Idee, mity, realia: szkice do dziejów Narodowej Demokracji (Ideas, Myths, Realities: essays towards a history of National Democracy)*, Warsaw: Wiedza Powszechna, 1971. 245pp. Bib. 245.

Pl 13   TEREJ, Jerzy Janusz, *Rzeczywistość i polityka: ze studiów nad dziejami najnowszymi Narodowej Demokracji (Reality and Politics: concerning studies on the later period of National Democracy's history)*, Warsaw: Ksiazka i Wiedza, 1971. 455pp. Bib. 433–42. Describes the secession of the more fascist elements in 1934.

Pl 14   WAPIŃSKI, K., *Endecja na Pomorzu, 1920–1939 (National Democracy in Pomerania, 1920–1939)*, Gdansk: Gdanskie Tow. Nauk., 1966. 163pp. Bib. 153–6.

Pl 15   WAPIŃSKI, Roman, 'Miejsce Narodowej Demokracji w zyciu politycznym II Rzeczypospolitej' (The place of National Democracy in the political life of the Second Republic). *Dzieje Najnowsze*, (1), 1969. pp. 47–62.

Pl 16   WAPIŃSKI, Roman, *Narodowa Demokracja, 1893–1939: ze studiów nad dziejami myśli nacjonalistycznej (National Democracy, 1893–1939: studies in the history of nationalist thought)*, Wroclaw: Ossolineum, 1980. 337pp.

Pl 17   WAPIŃSKI, Roman, 'Z dziejów tendencji nacjonalistycznych: o stanowisku Narodowej Demokracji wobec kwestii narodowej w latach, 1893–1939' (From the history of nationalist tendencies: on the position of National Democracy on the national question). *KWART. HIST.*, **80** (4), 1973. pp. 817–44.

The Extreme Right in the Second Republic

Pl 18   AJNENKIEL, Andrzej, *Polska po przewrocie majowym: zarys dziejów politycznych Polski, 1926–1939 (Poland after the May Revolution)*. Warsaw: Wiedza Powszechna, 1980. 724pp. Bib. 710.

Pl 19   *Bibliografia Historii Polski*, vol. III. 1918–1945. Warsaw: Panstw. Wydawn. Nauk., 1974. See pp. 263–4 for list of more obscure references on the ONR (National Radical Camp).

Pl 20   HOLZER, Jerzy, 'The political Right in Poland, 1918–1939'. *J. OF CONTEMP. HIST.*, **12** (3), 1977. pp. 395–412.

Pl 21   JEDRUSZCZAK, Tadeusz, *Polsudczycy bez Pilsudskiego: powstanie Obozu Zjednoczenia Narodowego w 1937 roku (The Pilsudski followers without Pilsudski: the rise of the Camp of National Unity in 1937)*, Warsaw: Panstw. Wydawn. Nauk., 1963. 227pp. Bib. 217–23. Transformations within Sanacja coalition including agreement with Union of Young Nationalists. Some active fascist groups within the coalition.

Pl 22   MAJCHROWSKI, Jacek M., *Czynniki jednoczace narod w myśli politycznej Obozu Zjednoczenia Narodowego (Factors unifying the Nation in the Political Thought of the Camp of National Unity)*, Cracow: Jagiellonian University, 1978. 118pp.

Pl 23   MAJCHROWSKI, Jacek M., 'The origin and early activities of the Pax movement in Poland'. *EAST. EUR. Q.*, **12** (4), 1979. pp. 385–97. Semi-fascist in the 1930s, its head under the communists was Boleslaw Piasecki, earlier ONR-Falanga leader.

Pl 24   MICEWSKI, Andrzej, 'Polish youth in the thirties'. *J. OF CONTEMP. HIST.*, **4** (3), 1969. pp. 155–67.

Pl 25   MICEWSKI, Andrzej, *Z geografii politycznej II Rzeczypospolitej: szkice (The Political Geography of the Second Republic)*, 2nd edn, Cracow: Znak, 1966. 406pp. A study of interwar politics especially of the Right. See pp. 262–89 for extreme rightist tendencies in the OWP, Endecja, ONR, and the Podbipieta group.

Pl 26   POBÓG-MALINOWSKI, Wladyslaw, *Najnowsza historia polityczna Polski* (Recent Political History of Poland), 2nd edn, vol. 2, London: Swiderski, 1967. 900pp.

Pl 27   POLONSKY, Antony, *Politics in Independent Poland: the crisis of constitutional government*. Oxford: University Press, 1972. xvi, 572pp. Bib. 524-60.

Pl 28   WYNOT, Edward D., *Polish Politics in Transition: the Camp of National Unity and the struggle for power, 1935-1939*, Athens: University of Georgia Press, 1974. xvi, 294pp. Bib. 269-85. Indiana University thesis, 1970.

Obóz Narodowo-Radykalny (ONR) (The National Radicals)

Pl 29   BLIT, Lucjan, *The Eastern Pretender: Boleslaw Piasecki, his life and times*, London: Hutchinson, 1965, 223p. Biography of leader of the ONR-Falanga movement, the only completely unambiguous Polish fascist movement. He later headed the Catholic Pax organisation under the Communist regime.

Pl 30   PIASECKI, Boleslaw, *Duch czasów nowych a Ruch Mlodych* (*The New Spirit of the Times and the Youth Movement*), Warsaw, 1935. 64pp. Piasecki (1914-79), leader of ONR-Falanga.

Pl 31   PIASECKI, Boleslaw, *Przelom narodowy: zasady programu Narodowo-Radykalnego* (*National Crisis: basic programme of the National Radicals*), Warsaw, 1938. 15pp.

Pl 32   HOWORKA, Michal, *Walka o Wielka Polske* (*The Struggle for Greater Poland*), Poznan, 1934. 123pp. ONR tract.

Pl 33   KACZMAREK, Zygmunt, 'Secesje mlodych w Obozie Narodowym w Wielkoposce w latach 1933-34'. (Secession of the youth in the National Camp of Greater Poland in the years 1933-34). *KWART. HIST.*, **84** (**3**), 1977. pp. 607-29. On the foundation of ONR.

Pl 34   MALATYNSKI, Antoni, *Nowy ruch narodowy* (*New National Movement*), Warsaw: Redunta, 1936. 160pp. On the ONR.

Pl 35   RUDNICKI, Szymon, 'Program spoleczny Obozu Narodowo-Radykalnego (ONR): stosunek do kwestii robotniczej' (The social programme of the ONR: its relation to the worker question). *Z Pola Walki*, **3** (**31**), 1965. pp. 25-46 [633-54].

Pl 36   RUDZINSKI, Eugeniusz, 'Bojowki ONR na ulicach Warszawy w 1934 roku' (ONR street gangs in Warsaw in 1934). *Pokolenia Biuletyn Komisja Historyczny KCZMS*, **4/5**. 1962. pp. 103-9.

Pl 37   SZECHTER, S., 'Próby faszystowskiego przewrotu (pazdziernik 1937 r.)'. (Attempts at a fascist *coup* in Oct. 1937). *Wies Wspolczesna*,

10, 1960. pp. 129-34. On Koc's plan for a *coup* with Falanga supporters.

Pl 38   ZALESKI, Wojciech, *Polska bez proletariatu* (*Poland without a Proletariat*), Warsaw: *ABC*, 1937. ONR-ABC publication by the editor of their journal *ABC*.

Nazi Tendencies in the German Minority

Pl 39   GRUNBERG, Karol, *Nazi-Front Schlesien: niemieckie organizacje polityczne w województwie śląskim w latach 1933-1939* (*German Organisations in the Silesian region in the years 1933-1939*), Kotowice: Slask, 1963. 231pp. Bib. 208-13.

Pl 40   POTOCKI, Stanislaw, *Polozenie mniejszości niemieckiej w Polsce, 1918-1938* (*The Situation of the German Minority in Poland, 1918-1938*), Gdansk: Wydawn. Morskie, 1969. 502pp.

Pl 41   POTOCKI, Stanislaw, 'Tendencje polityczne mniejszości niemieckiej w województwie pomorskim w latach 1920-1939' (Political tendencies of the German minority in Pomerania 1920-1939). *Gdanskie Zeszyty Humanistyczne. Ser. Histoire*, **12** (**18**), 1969. pp. 7-52.

Pl 42   SZEFER, Andrzej, 'O próbie zespolenia mniejszości niemieckiej w województwie śląskim w latach, 1933-1939' (Efforts toward unity by the German minority in the Silesian provinces). *Slaski Kwartalnik Historyczny Sobotka*, **20** (**2**), 1965. pp. 187-203. On the Volksbund and Jungdeutsche Partei.

Anti-Semitism

Pl 43   GOLCZEWSKI, Frank, *Polnische-jüdische Beziehungen, 1881-1922: eine Studie zur Geschichte des Antisemitismus in Osteuropa*, Wiesbaden: Steiner, 1981. x. 391pp.

Pl 44   GUNZENHAUSER, Max (ed.), *Bibliographie zur Nationalitätenfrage und zur Judenfrage der Republik Polen, 1919-1939*, 2nd edn, Stuttgart: Weltkriegsbucherei, 1943. 76pp. Including works on anti-semitism.

Pl 45   HELLER, Celia Stopnicka, *On the Edge of Destruction: Jews of Poland between the two world wars*, New York: Columbia University Press, 1977. xi, 369pp. Chapter on organised terror and abuse includes ONR-Falanga, ONR-ABC, OWP, ZMN.

Pl 46   WYNOT, Edward D., '"A necessary cruelty": the emergence of official anti-semitism in Poland, 1936–1939'. *AM. HIST. REV.*, **76** (**4**), 1971. pp. 1035–58.

The Ukranian Nationalists

Pl 47   CIESLAK, Tadeusz, 'Hitlerowski sojuz z nacjonalizmem ukrainskim w Polsce' (The Hitlerite alliance with the Ukranian nationalists in Poland). *Z Dziejow Stosunkow Polsko-Radzieckich (Warsaw)*, **5**, 1969. pp. 93–107.

Pl 48   KUBIIOVYCH, Volodymyr, *Ukraintsi v Heneral'nii Hubernii, 1939–1941. (The Ukrainians in the Generalgovernment, 1939–1941)*, Chicago; Denysiuk, 1975. 664pp. Author prominent in the Generalgovernment.

Poland and the Second World War

Pl 49   BROSZAT, Martin, *Nationalsozialistische Polenpolitik, 1939–1945*, Frankfurt/M: Fisher, 1965. 228pp. Bib. 173–221.

Pl 50   KOSICKI, Jerzy and KOZLOWSKI, Waclaw, *Bibliografiá piśmiennictwa polskiego za lata, 1944–1953 o hitlerowskich zbrodniach wojennych (Bibliography of Polish Writings for the Years 1944–53 on Hitler's War Crimes)*, Warsaw: Wyd. Prawnicze, 1955. 177pp.

Pl 51   MADAJCZYK, Czeslaw, *Polityke III Rzeszy w okupowanej Polsce: okupacja Polski, 1939–1945 (The politics of the Third Reich in Poland)*, Warsaw: Panstw. Wydawn. Nauk., 1970. 2 vols. Bib. Vol. 2, 423–42.

CZECHOSLOVAKIA

General

C 1   HAJEK, Milos, 'Le caratteristiche del fascismo in Cecoslovacchia'. *RIV. STOR. DEL SOC.*, **8** (**24**), 1965. pp. 105–20.

C 2   HAVRÁNEK, Jan, 'Fascism in Czechoslovakia'. In SUGAR, P.F., E 23. pp. 47–55.

C 3   *Přispěvky k Dějinám Fašismu v Československu a Madarsku: autorní studii* (*Contributions towards a History of Fascism in Czechoslovakia and Hungary*), Bratislava: SAV, 1969. 322pp. Pref. by L'udovit Holotnik. Essays.

C 4   WEISS, John, 'Fascism in Czechoslovakia, 1919–1939'. *East Cent. Eur.*, **4** (**1**), 1977. pp. 35–43.

C 5   ZACEK, Joseph F., 'Czechoslovak fascisms'. In SUGAR, P.F., E 23. pp. 56–62.

C 6   ZACEK, Joseph F., 'Nationalism in Czechoslovakia'. In SUGAR, P.F. and LEDERER, I.J., E 21. pp. 166–206.

The Czech Extreme Right

C 7   CAMPBELL, F. Gregory, *Confrontation in Central Europe: Weimar Germany and Czechoslovakia*, Chicago: University Press, 1975. xvi, 383pp. Bib. 345–74. Some discussion of Czech fascists, Jiri Stříbrný and General Gajda.

C 8   FIC, Vladimir, 'Česká krajní nacionalistická pravice na Moravě a pokus o vytvoření Národního Sjednoceni, 1932–1935' (The Czech extreme nationalist Right in Moravia and the attempt to set up a National Front, 1932–1935). *Časopis Matice Moravske*, **96** (**3/4**), 1977. pp. 295–312. Covers the National Fascist Community of Radola Gajda, National League of Jiri Stříbrný, and radical group of National Democratic Party.

C 9   FIRSOV, E.F., 'Chekhoslovatskaia natsional'no-demokraticheskaia partiia v period politicheskogo krizisa, 1925–1926' (The Czech National Democratic Party in a period of political crisis). *Vestnik Moskovskogo Univ.*, **ser. 8.** *Istoriia*, (**3**), 1979. pp. 30–42. National Democratic Party move towards fascism with 'Young Generation' and 'Movement of Rebirth'.

C 10   GAJANOVÁ, Alena, *Dvojí tvář: z historie předmnichovského fašismu* (*Two-face: history of fascism before Munich*), Prague: Nase Vojsko, 1962. 209pp.

C 11   KAMENEC, Ivan, 'Prenikanie fašistickej ideologie a organizacii Narodnej Obce Fašistickej do slovenskeho politickeho života v medzivojnovom obdobi' (Penetration of fascist ideology and of organisations of the National Fascist Community into Slovak national life between the wars). *HISTORICKE STUD.*, **24**, 1980. pp. 43–76.

C 12   KUČERA, Bohumil, 'Brněnský fašistický puč v roce 1933 před státním soudem' (The fascist *putsch* in Brno before the State Court). *Pravnehistoricke Studie*, **21**, 1978. pp. 85–111.

C 13   LOEWENSTEIN, Bedrich, 'Il radicalismo di destra ir Cecoslovacchia e la prima guerra mondiale'. *STOR. CONTEMP.*, **I** (**3**), 1970. pp. 503–28. World War I and the pre-fascist radical Right

C 14   PASÁK, Tomáš, 'K problematice NOF v letech hospodársk krize na počátku třicátých let' (On the problem of the National Fascis Community in the years of the economic crisis and at the beginning o the 30s). *Sbornik Historicky*, **13**, 1965. pp. 93–132. On Gajda's Národn Obce Fašistická.

The Slovak Extreme Right and the Independent Slovak State

C 15   ANDERLE, Josef, 'The establishment of Slovak autonomy ir 1938'. In RECHCIGL, Miloslav (ed.), *Czechoslovakia: past and present* The Hague: Mouton, 1968. Vol. 1. pp. 76–97.

C 16   BARTLOVA, Alena, 'Programova linia klerikalizmu na Slovensku, 1905–1938' (The programme of Slovakian clericalism 1905–1938). *HISTORICKE STUD.*, **22**, 1977. pp. 69–102.

C 17   CONWAY, John, 'The churches, the Slovak state, and the Jews, 1939–1945'. *SLAV. AND EAST EUR. REV.*, **52** (**126**), 1974. pp 85–112.

C 18   ČULEN, Konštantín, *Po Svätoplukovi druhá naša hlava: živo Dr. Jozefa Tisu (After Svatopluk our second head of state: the life of Dr. Jozef Tiso)*, Cleveland: Prva Katolićka Slovenska Jednota, 1947. Vol. 1 Laudatory biography of Tiso (1887–1947), head of the German-supported Slovak state.

C 19   ĎURICA, Milan Stanislao, 'Dr. Joseph Tiso and the Jewish problem in Slovakia'. *Slovakia*, **7**, 1957. pp. 1–22.

C 20   GRÉBERT, Arvéd, 'Dr. Jozef Tiso in the light of Nazi documents'. *Slovakia*, **25** (**48**), 1975. 5–17. Exculpates Tiso in treatment of Jews.

C 21   GUARDA-NARDINI, Lisa, *Tiso: una terza proposta*, Padua: CESEO Liviana Ed., 1978. 87pp. Bib. 84–7.

C 22   JELINEK, Yeshayahu, 'Dr. Jozef Tiso and his biographers'. *East Cent. Eur.*, **6** (**1**), 1979. pp. 76–84. Review article.

C 23   POLAKOVIČ, Štefan, *Tisova nauka (Tiso's Teaching)*, Bratislava: Naklad. HSLS, 1941. 386pp.

C 24   SCHNEIDER, Franz M., 'Josef Tiso, Katholischer Priester und Staatspräsident in Slowakei'. *Slovak Studies*, **10**, 1970. pp. 7–146.

C 25 SUTHERLAND, Anthony X., *Dr. Josef Tiso and Modern Slovakia*, Cleveland: First Catholic Slovak Union, 1978. 141pp. Sympathetic to Tiso.

C 26 SUTHERLAND, Anthony X., 'Tiso's formative years and the early political career'. *Slovakia*, **24** (**47**), 1974. pp. 24–35. Covers years 1894–1930.

C 27 TISO, Josef, and others, defendants, *Pred súdom národa: process Dr. J. Tisom, Dr. F. Ďurčanskym, A. Machom v Bratislave v dnoch 2 dec. 1946–15. apr. 1947 (Facing the Court of the People: the trial of Dr. J. Tiso, etc.*), Bratislava: Povereníctvo Informacii, 1947. 5 vols.

C 28 TISO, Josef, *Ideológia slovenskej ľudovej strany (Ideology of the Slovak People's Party)*, Prague: Tiskovy Odbor USCS, 1930. 16pp.

C 29 DANÁŠ, Jozef, *Ľudácky separatizmus a hitlerovské Nemecko (People's Party separatism and Hitler's Germany)*, Bratislava: Vyd. Politickej Literatury, 1963. 181pp. Bib. 149–52. Communist version covering 1938–40.

C 30 DANÁŠ, Jozef, 'O vzťahoch HSLSs hitlerovským Nemeckom v predvečer vzniku tzv. slovenskeho statu' (Data on the relations of Hlinka's Slovak People's Party with Hitler's Germany on the eve of the foundation of the so-called Slovak state). *HIST. CAS.*, **7** (**1**), 1959. pp. 53–73.

C 31 DAXNER, Igor, *Ľudáctvo pred národným súdom, 1945–1947 (The People's Party before the Court of the Nation)*, Bratislava: Vyd. Slovenskej Akad. Vied., 1961. 209pp.

C 32 DÉRER, Ivan, *Slovenský vývoj a ľudácká zrada (Slovak Development and the People's Party Betrayed)*, Prague: Kvasnička a Hampl, 1946. 346pp. Social democratic view of the development of the People's Party before 1939.

C 33 DRESS, Hans, *Slowakei und faschistische Neuordnung Europas, 1939–1941*, Berlin: Akademie V., 1972. 199pp. Bib. 179–96. E. German account.

C 34 DURČANSKÝ, Ferdinand, 'Mit Tiso bei Hitler: die Slowakischen Republik'. *POLIT. STUD.*, **7** (**80**), 1956. pp. 1–10.

C 35 DURČANSKÝ, Ferdinand (ed.), *Právo Slovákov na samostatnost vo svetle documentov (The Slovaks' Right to Independence in the Light of Documents)*, Buenos Aires: Slovenský Oslobodzovací Výbor, 1954. 96pp.

C 36 ĎURICA, Milan Stanislao, 'The republic of Slovakia: its origin and existence'. *Slovak Stud.*, **1**, 1961. pp. 105–21.

C 37   ĎURICA, Milan Stanislao, *La Slovacchia e le sue relazioni politich* *con la Germania, 1938-1945*, Padua: Marsilio, 1964. Vol. 1. Covers Oc 1938-Sept. 1939. 274pp.

C 38   ĎURICA, Milan Stanislao, *Die slowakische Politik, 1938/39 ir Lichte der Staatslehre Tisos*, Bonn: Semmel, 1967. 48pp. Denies fascis character of Tiso's regime.

C 39   EL MALLAKH, Dorothea H., *The Slovak Autonomy Movemen 1935-1939: a study in unrelenting nationalism*, New York: Columbi University Press, 1979 (East European monographs). xvi, 260pp.

C 40   HEJL, Frantisek, 'K otazce ideologie a praxe klerofašismu n Slovensku' (The question of the ideology and practice of clerica fascism in Slovakia). *SLOVANSKY PREHL.*, **61** (**1**), 1975. pp. 49-57

C 41   *Die Hlinka-Partei: Geschichte, Ideologie, Organisation, Kultur Wirtschaft, Sozialpolitik*, Bratislava: Hlinka-Partei, 1943. 77pp. Officia Slovakian publication.

C 42   HOENSCH, Jörg Konrad, *Die Slowakei und Hitlers Ostpolitik Hlinkas Slowakische Volkspartei zwischen Autonomie und Separation, 1938-39* Cologne: Bohlau, 1965. xii, 390pp. Bib. 357-79.

C 43   HYSKO, Miroslav, *O protinárodnej politike l'udáckeho fašizmu (O the Anti-popular Politics of People's Party Fascism*), Bratislava: Slovensk Vyd. Politickej Lit., 1954. 54pp.

C 44   JELINEK, Yeshayahu, 'Between nationalism and communism the "Slovak question"'. *CAN. REV. STUD. NATL.*, **2**, 1975. pp 334-41. Review article.

C 45   JELINEK, Yeshayahu, 'Clergy and fascism: the Hlinka Party ir Slovakia and Croatian Ustasha Movement'. In LARSEN, S.U. Gn 36. pp. 367-78.

C 46   JELINEK, Yeshayahu, 'The final solution: the Slovak version' *EAST EUR. Q.*, **4** (**4**), 1971. pp. 431-41.

C 47   JELINEK, Yeshayahu, *The Parish Republic: Hlinka's Slovak People's Party, 1939-1945*, New York: Columbia University Press 1976 (East European monographs). viii, 206pp. Bib. 173-92. Indiana University thesis, 1966.

C 48   JELINEK, Yeshayahu, 'The Slovak Right: conservative o radical? a reappraisal'. *East. Cent. Eur.*, **4** (**1**), 1977. pp. 20-34.

C 49   JELINEK, Yeshayahu, 'The Slovak state in post-war histori ography: (an annotated bibliography)'. *Slovakia*, **28** (**51/52**), 1978/9 pp. 17-24.

C 50   JELINEK, Yeshayahu, 'Slovakia's internal policy and the Third Reich, Aug. 1940-Feb. 1941.' *CENT. EUR. HIST.*, **4** (**3**), 1971. pp. 242-70.

C 51   JELINEK, Yeshayahu, 'Storm-troopers in Slovakia: the Radobrana and the Hlinka Guard'. *J. OF CONTEMP. HIST.*, **6** (**3**), 1971. pp. 97-119.

C 52   JELINEK, Yeshayahu, 'The Vatican, the Catholic Church, the Catholics, and the persecution of the Jews during World War II: the case of Slovakia'. In MOSSE, George L. and VAGO, B. (eds), *Jews and non-Jews in Eastern Europe, 1918-1945*, Jerusalem, 1974. pp. 167-208.

C 53   KAMENEC, Ivan, 'Snem Slovenskej Republiký a jeho postoj k problému židovskehó obyvateľ'stva na Slovensku v rokoch, 1939-1945' (The Parliament of the Slovak Republic and its attitude toward the problem of the Jewish population in Slovakia). *HIST. CAS.*, **17** (**3**), 1969. pp. 329-62.

C 54   KIRSCHBAUM, Joseph M., 'The politics of Hlinka's Slovak People's Party in the Slovak Republic'. *Slovakia*, **1**, 1951. pp. 43-49.

C 55   KIRSCHBAUM, Joseph M., *Slovakia: nation at the cross-roads of Central Europe*, New York: Speller, 1960. 371pp. Bib.

C 56   KIRSCHBAUM, Joseph M. (ed.), *Slovakia in the 19th and 20th centuries: proceedings of the Conference on Slovakia . . . . June 17-18 1971 in Toronto*, Toronto: Slovak World Congress, 1973. 358pp. Bib. 351-68.

C 57   KRAMER, Juraj, *Iredenta a separatizmus v Slovenskej politike: studia o ich vztahu, 1919-1938 (Irredentism and Separatism in Slovakian Politics)*, Bratislava: Slovenske Vyd. Politickej Lit., 1957. 248pp.

C 58   KRAMER, Juraj, *Slovenské autonomistické hnutie v rokoch, 1918-1929 (The Slovakian Separatist Movement in the Years 1918-1929)*, Bratislava: Vyd, Slovenskej Akad. Vied., 1962. 483pp. Bib.

C 59   KUBÁT, J. (ed.), *O luďáckem fašismu (On People's Party Fascism)*, Prague: Naše Vojsko, 1956. 153pp. Collection of essays.

C 60   LETTRICH, Jozef, *History of Modern Slovakia*, New York: Praeger, 1956. 329pp. Bib. 319-23. Considers Tiso a fascist.

C 61   LIPSCHER, Ladislav, *L'udácka autonomia: ilúzie a skutočnost (The People's Party Autonomy: illusions and reality)*, Bratislava: Slovenské Vyd. Politickej Lit., 1957. 319pp.

C 62   LIPSCHER, Ladislav, *Die Juden in Slowakischen Staat, 1939-1945*, Munich: Oldenbourg, 1980. 210pp.

C 63   LIPSCHER, Ladislav, 'Vývin a charakteristické črty fašismu na Slovensku' (Slovak fascism its character and evolution). In *Prispevky k Dejinam Fasismu*, C 3. pp. 9–60.

C 64   MIKUŠ, Joseph A., *Slovakia: a political history, 1918–1950*, rev. edn, tr. from the French by Kathryn Day Wyatt and Joseph A. Mikuš, Milwaukee: Marquette University Press, 1963. xxxiii, 392pp. Bib. 365–84.

C 65   ODDO, Gilbert Lawrence, *Slovakia and its People*, New York: Speller, 1960. 370pp. Apologia for Tiso.

C 66   ORCIVAL, Francois d', *Le Danube était noire: la cause de la Slovaquie indépendente*, Paris: Eds de la Table, 1968. 309pp. Bib. 303–4.

C 67   PAUČO, Jozef, *Tak sme sa poznali: predstavitelia Slovenskej republiky v spomienkach (And so We become Acquainted)*, Middletown, Pa.: Jednota Press, 1967. 281pp. Memoirs.

C 68   POLAKOVIČ, Štefan, *K základom slovenského štátu: filosoficke eseje (About the Foundations of the Slovak state: philosophical essay)*, Turčiansky Svätý Martin: Matica Slovenska, 1939. 176pp. Bratislava University professor and ideologist of the Slovakian People's Party.

C 69   PREČAN, Vilém, 'Nacistická politika a Tisův režim v předvečer povstání' (Nazi policy and the Tiso regime on the eve of the uprising). *Historie a Vojenstvi*, 6, 1969. pp. 1082–146.

C 70   PREČAN, Vilém, *Slovenské narodné povstánie: Nemci a Slovensko 1944: dokumenty (The Slovak National Uprising: Germans and Slovaks: documents)*, Bratislava: Epocha, 1971. 701pp.

C 71   SIDOR, Karol, 'O takzvanom slovenskam narodnam socializme' (About the so-called Slovak national socialism). *Kalendar Jednoty*, 1964. pp. 143–53. By the Slovak Independent State Minister to the Holy See.

C 72   ŠIRÁCKY, Andrej, *Klerofašistická ideológia ľudáctva (Clerico-fascist Ideology of the People's Party)*, Bratislava: Vyd. Slovenskej Akad. Vied., 1955. 143pp. Anti-HSLS polemic.

C 73   ŠPRINC, Mikulaš (ed.), *Slovenská Republika, 1939–1945*, Scranton: Lach, 1949. x, 253pp. Collective work by supporters of the autonomous state.

C 74   STANEK, Imrich, *Zrada a pád: Hlinkovští separatisté a tak zvaný Slovenský štát (Betrayal and Downfall: the Hlinka separatists and the so-called Slovak state)*, Prague: Statní Naklad. Politické Lit., 1958. 411pp.

C 75   SUŠKO, Ladislav, 'Hlinková Garda od svojho vzniku az po salzburské rokovania, 1938–1940' (The Hlinka Guard from its creation to the Salzburg talks). *Zbornik Muzea Slovenskeho Narodneho Povstania*, **2**, 1968. pp. 167-258.

C 76 VIETOR, Martin, 'Príspevok k objasneniu fašistického charakteru tzv. slovenského štátu' (A contribution to the understanding of the fascist nature of the so-called Slovak state). *HIST. CAS.*, **8** (**4**), 1960. pp. 482-508.

C 77 VNUK, František, 'Die slowakische Haltung zum Nationalsozialismus'. *Slowakei*, **4**, 1966. pp. 3-9.

C 78 WOLFF, Richard J., 'The Catholic Church and the dictatorships in Slovakia and Croatia, 1939-1945'. *Records of the Amer. Cath. Hist. Soc. of Philadelphia*, **88** (**1/4**), 1977. pp. 3-30.

Extreme Rightist Tendencies amongst the German Minority

C 79 ARNDT, Veronika, 'Ständische ideologie im Henleinfaschismus: das Problem Franz Künzels'. *JAHRB. FÜR GESCH. SOZ. LÄNDER EUR.*, **18** (**2**), 1974. pp. 199-211.

C 80 BACHSTEIN, Martin K., 'Der Volkssozialismus in Böhmen: nationaler Sozialismus gegen Hitler'. *Bohemia*, **14**, 1973. pp. 340-71. Popular national socialism of O. Strasser and W. Jaksch (1896-1966).

C 81 BROSZAT, Martin, 'Das Sudetendeutsche Freikorps'. *VIERTELJAHRSH. FÜR ZEITG.*, **9** (**1**), 1961. pp. 30-49.

C 82 BRÜGEL, Johann Wolfgang, 'Nazis without Hitler? Nazis before Hitler: the story of the DNSAP'. *East Cent. Eur.*, **6** (**1**), 1979. pp. 40-6.

C 83 BRÜGEL, Johann Wolfgang, *Tschechen und Deutsche, 1918-1938*, Munich: Nymphenburger V., 1967. 662pp. Bib. 636-54.

C 84 BURIAN, Peter, 'Chancen und Grenzen des sudetendeutschen Aktivismus'. In BOSL, Karl and others (eds), *Aktuelle Forschungsprobleme um die Erste Tschechoslowakische Republik*, Munich: Oldenbourg, 1969. pp. 133-49.

C 85 ČERNÝ, Bohumil, 'Schwarze Front v Československu, 1933-1938' (The Black Front in Czechoslovakia). *CESK. CAS. HIST.*, **14** (**3**), 1966. pp. 328-57. Otto Strasser's Prague group.

C 86 CÉSAR, Jaroslav and ČERNÝ, Bohumil, 'The Nazi fifth column in Czechoslovakia'. *Historica*, **4**, 1962. pp. 191-255.

C 87 CÉSAR, Jaroslav and ČERNÝ, Bohumil, 'Nemecka iredenta

a Henleinovci v ČSR v letech, 1930–1938' (German irredentism and Henlein's Party in Czeechoslovakia, 1930–1938). *CESK. CAS. HIST.*, **10** (**1**), 1962. pp. 1–17.

C 88 CÉSAR, Jaroslav and ČERNÝ, Bohumil, *Od sudeteněmeckého separatismu k plánům odvety: iredentitický puč německych nacionalistu v ČSR v letech 1918–1919* (*From Sudeten German Separatism to Plans for Revanche: the irredentist putsch of German nationalists in the Czech Republic*), Liberec: Severočeske Krajské Naklad, 1960. 231pp.

C 89 CÉSAR, Jaroslav and ČERNÝ, Bohumil, 'The policy of German Activist parties in Czechoslovakia in 1918–1938'. *Historica*, **6**, 1963. pp. 239–81.

C 90 HAAG, John, '"Knights of the Spirit": the Kameradschaftsbund'. *J. OF CONTEMP. HIST.*, **8** (**3**), 1973. pp. 133–53. Sudeten German organisation of 1920s which became fascist but non-nazi.

C 91 HÖLLER, Franz (ed.), *Von der SdP zur NSDAP: ein dokumentarischer Bildbericht von der Befreiung des Sudetenländes*, Karlsbad: Kraft, 1939. 112pp.

C 92 KRÁL, Václav (ed.), *Die Deutschen in der Tschechoslowakei, 1933–1947: Dokumentensammlung*, Prague: Naklad. Československé Akad. Věd, 1964. 663pp. Collection of mostly German documents on Nazi policies towards Czechoslovakia including material on the Henlein Party.

C 93 KVAČEK, Robert, 'K historii Henleinovy Sudeteněmecké Strany' (Concerning the history of Henlein's Sudeten German Party). *Dejepis v Skole*, **5**, 1957. pp. 193–200; **6**, 1957. pp. 241–9.

C 94 NITTNER, Ernst (ed.), *Dokumente zur Sudetendeutschen Frage 1916 bis 1967*, new edn, Munich: Ackermann-Gemeinde, 1967. 583pp. Bib. 559–81.

C 95 SMELSER, Ronald M., 'Hitler and the DNSAP: between democracy and Gleichschaltung'. *Bohemia*, **20**, 1979. pp. 137–50.

C 96 SMELSER, Ronald D., 'Nazis without Hitler: the DNSAP and the first Czechoslovak Republic'. *East Cent. Eur.*, **4** (**1**), 1977. pp. 1–19.

C 97 SMELSER, Ronald M., 'Reich National Socialist and Sudeten German Party élites: a collective biographical approach'. *Z. FÜR OSTFORSCHUNG*, **23** (**4**), 1974. pp. 639–60.

Czechoslovakia and the Second World War

C 98   AMORT, Čestimír (ed.), *Heydrichiáda*, Prague: Naše Vojsko, 1965. 320pp. Bib. 318–20. Nazi documents from the Heydrich period.

C 99   BRANDES, Detlef, *Die Tschechen unter deutschem Protektorat*, Munich: Oldenbourg, 1969–75. 2 vols. Bib. vol. 1, 271–6. 1. *Besatzungspolitik, Kollaboration, und Widerstand im Protektorat Böhmen und Mähren bis Heydrichs Tod, 1939–1942*. 2. *Besatzungspolitik, Kollaboration, und Widerstand im Protektorat Böhmen und Mähren von Heydrichs Tod bis zum Prager Aufstand, 1942–1945*.

C 100   BRÜGEL, Johann Wolfgang, *Tschechen und Deutsche, 1939–46*, Munich: Nymphenburger V., 1974. 326pp. Bib. 311–20.

C 101   KRÁL, Váçlav, 'Kolaborace nebo rezistence?' (Collaboration or resistance?). *Dejiny a Soucasnost*, **7** (**7**), 1965. pp. 1–7.

C 102   MASTNY, Vojtech, *The Czechs under Nazi Rule: the failure of national resistance, 1939–1942*, New York: Columbia University Press, 1971. xiii, 274pp. Bib. 239–61. Material on collaboration.

C 103   MIKULA, Karel and SCHUBERT, Erich (eds), *Zeitungen und Zeitschriften im Protektorat Böhmen und Mähren*, Prague: Orbis, 1941. 261pp.

C 104   OTAHÁLOVÁ, Libuše and ČERVINKOVÁ, Milada (eds), *Dokumenty z historie československé politiky, 1939–1943* (*Documents from the History of Czechoslovakian Politics, 1939–1943*), Prague: Akademia, 1966. 2 vols. Some documents on collaboration.

C 105   PASÁK, Tomáš, 'K činnosti Českého národního výboru na počatku okupace' (On the function of the Czech National Committee at the beginning of the occupation). In FIALA, Z. and NOVY, R. (eds), *Z českých dějin*, Prague: Universita Karlova, 1966. pp. 289–315.

C 106   PASÁK, Tomáš, 'Vývoj Vlajky v obdobi okupace' (Vlajka's development in the occupation period). *Historie a Vojenstvi*, **5**, 1966. pp. 846–95. On the pro-nazi group Vlajka (Banner).

C 107   PASÁK, Tomáš, 'Problematika moravského extrémně-pravicového hnutí v roce 1939' (Problems of the extreme Right-wing movement in the year 1939 in Moravia). *Slezky Sbornik*, **66** (**1**), 1968. pp. 16–27.

C 108   PFAFF, Ivan, 'Kollaboration: am tschechischen Beispiel'. *Neue Deutsche Hefte*, **23** (**4**), 1976. pp. 769–81.

175

C 109   TESAŘ, Jan, '"Zachrana národa" a kolaborace' (The 'Saving of the Nation' and collaboration). *Dejiny a Soucasnost*, **10** (5), 1968. pp. 5–10.

Subcarpathian Rus and Vološin

C 110   MAGOSSI, Robert, *The Shaping of a National Identity: Subcarpathian Rus, 1848–1948*, Cambridge, Mass.: Harvard University Press, 1978. xiii, 640pp. Bib. 465–585. Includes Stefan Fentsik and the Russian National Blackshirt Guard.

C 111   PROCHAZKA, Theodore, 'Some aspects of the Carpatho-Ukrainian history in post-Munich Czechoslovakia'. In RECHCIGL, Miloslav (ed.), *Czechoslovakia: past and present*, The Hague: Mouton, 1968. Vol. 1. pp. 107–14. Vološin's Ukrainian National Union.

C 112   STERCHO, Peter, *Diplomacy of Double Morality: Europe's crossroads in Carpatho-Ukraine, 1919–1939*, New York: Carpathia Research Center, 1971. xxii, 495pp. Bib.

C 113   WINCH, Michael, *Republic for a Day: an eye-witness account of the Carpatho-Ukraine incident*, London: Hale, 1939. 286pp. On the short-lived Carpatho-Ukrainian state under Vološin created under nazi protection.

RUSSIA AND THE UKRAINE

General

R 1   ROGGER, Hans, 'Russia'. In ROGGER, H. and WEBER, E., Gn 54. pp. 443–500.

The Extreme Right before 1918

R 2   BROCK, John Joseph, *The Theory and Practice of the Union of the Russian People, 1905–1907: a case study of 'Black Hundred' politics*, University of Michigan thesis, 1972. UM 73–11052. 342pp.

R 3   EDELMAN, Robert, *Russian Nationalism and Class Consciousness:*

the rise of the All-Russian Nationalist Party, 1907–1912, Columbia University thesis, 1974. 455pp.

R 4   JABLONOWSKI, Horst, 'Die russischen Rechtsparteien, 1905–1917'. *In Russland Studien: gedenkschriften für Otto Hötzsch*, Stuttgart: Deutsche Verlags-Anstalt, 1957. pp. 43–55.

R 5   LÖWE, Heinz-Dietrich, *Antisemitismus und reationäre Utopie: russischer Konservatismus im Kampf gegen den Wandel von Staat und Gesellschaft, 1890–1917*, Hamburg: Hoffmann & Campe, 1978. 303pp. Bib. 281–92. Freiburg University thesis. Summary in English.

R 6   LYUBOSH, S.B., *Russkii fashist Vladimir Purishkevich (Russian fascist V. Purishkevich)*, Leningrad: Byloe, 1925. 56pp. Claims that V.M. Purishkevich, pre-1918 politician, was a fascist.

R 7   POPIELOVSKY, Dimitrii V., 'Russian national thought and the Jewish question'. *Soviet Jewish Affairs*, **6** (1), 1976. pp. 3–17.

R 8   RAWSON, Don, *The Union of the Russian People, 1905–1907: a study of the radical Right*, University of Washington thesis, 1971. UM 71–28463. 251pp.

R 9   ROGGER, Hans, 'The formation of the Russian Right, 1900–6'. *California Slavic Studies*, **3**, 1964. pp. 66–94.

R 10   ROGGER, Hans, 'Was there a Russian fascism? The Union of the Russian People'. *J. OF MOD. HIST.*, **36** (4), 1964. pp. 398–415.

Fascism in Exile

R 11   DORFMAN, Ben, 'White Russians in the Far East'. *Asia*, March 1935. pp. 166–72.

R 12   GINS, Georgii Konstantinovich, *Na putiakh k gosudarstvu budshchevo: ot liberalizma k solidarizmu (On the Road to the State of the Future: from liberalism to solidarism)*, Harbin: Chisareva, 1930. 210pp. A pro-Mussolini solidarist and fascist, anti-communist and nationalist.

R 13   GROZIN, N.N., *Zashchitniia rubashki (Protective Shirts)*, Shanghai: Vseobshchii Russkii Kalendar, 1939. 325pp. A biography of A.A. Vonsiatsky (1898–1965) founder of the VNRP (All-Russian National Revolutionary Party).

R 14   OBERLÄNDER, Erwin, 'The All-Russian Fascist Party'. *J. OF CONTEMP. HIST.*, **1** (1), 1966. pp. 158–73.

R 15   RODZAEVSKY, Konstantin Vladimirovich, *Kritika Sovetskogo gosudarstva (Criticism of the Soviet State)* Shanghai: Vserossiiskaia

Fashistkaia Partiia, 1935-7. 2 vols. Rodzaevsky (1907-45), leader of VFP (All-Russian Fascist Party).

R 16   SEMENOV, Grigorii Mikhailovich, *O sebe: vospominaniia, mysli i vyvody* (*About Myself: memories, ideas and conclusions*), Harbin: Zaria, 1938. 228pp. Memoirs of Semenov (1890-1945), who came close in exile in Manchuria to Rodzaevsky's Russian Fascist Party without joining it.

R 17   STEPHAN, John J., *The Russian Fascists: tragedy and farce in exile, 1925-1945*, London: Hamilton. New York: Harper & Row, 1978. xxii, 450pp. Bib. 423-31. Russian fascist movements in exile were to be found in Tientsin, Berlin, Buenos Aires, Tokyo, Cairo, Chicago, Valparaiso, Paris, and Putnam (Conn.). Mostly on Rodzaevsky and Vonsiatsky.

R 18   TARADANOV, Genadii V. and KIBARDIN, Vladimir, *Azbuka fashizma* (*ABC of Fascism*), ed. K.V. Rodzaevsky, 2nd edn, Harbin: Nash Put', 1935. 110pp. Bible of Russian fascism commissioned by RFP leader Rodzaevsky.

Ukrainian Nationalism

R 19   ARMSTRONG, John Alexander, *Ukrainian Nationalism, 1939-45*, 2nd edn, New York: Columbia University Press, 1963. xvi, 361pp. Bib. 327-47.

R 20   ILNYTZKYI, Roman, *Deutschland und die Ukraine, 1934-1945: Tatsachen europäischer Ostpolitik: ein Vorbericht*, 2nd edn, Munich: Ost Europa Inst., 1958. 2 vols. Bib. Vol. 1, pp. 358-70. Vol. 2, pp. 414-22.

R 21   MOTYL, Alexander J., *The Turn to the Right: the ideological origins and development of Ukrainian nationalism, 1919-1929*, New York: Columbia University Press, 1980. (East European monographs). 212pp. Bib. pp. 192-202. Mainly on Dontsov's nationalist ideology.

R 22   SHEVTSOV, V.D., *Ukraïns'kyi burzhuaznyi natsionalizm u korychnevii uniformi* (*Ukrainian Bourgeois Nationalism in Uniforms*), Kiev: Naukova Dumka, 1981. 148pp.

R 23   SPECTOR, S., 'The destruction of Ukrainian Jewry as seen by Ukrainian nationalist historians'. *YAD VASHEM BULL.*, **6/7**, 1960. pp. 35-6.

R 24   SZOTA, W., 'Zarys rozwoju OUN i UPA' (Outline of the development of OUN and UPA). *Wojskowy Przeglad Historyczny*, **8 (1)**, 1963. pp. 163-218. OUN—Organisation of Ukrainian Nationalists. UPA—Ukrainian Insurrectionary Army.

The Second World War

R 25   DALLIN, Alexander, 'Portrait of a collaborator'. *Survey*, **35**, 1961. pp. 114-19. Mikhail Oktan, League for Struggle against Bolshevism demagogue in the Orel area.

R 26   DALLIN, Alexander, 'The Kaminsky Brigade: a case study of Soviet disaffection'. In RABINOWITCH, Alexander and Janet, *Revolution and politics in Russia*, Bloomington: Indiana University Press, 1972. pp. 243-80, 386-96. Bronislaw Vladislavovich Kaminsky, renegade Russian who fought with Germans.

R 27   DALLIN, Alexander, *German Rule in Russia, 1941-1945: a study of occupation policies*, 2nd edn, London: Macmillan, 1981. xx, 707pp. Includes collaboration of Russians and Ukrainians.

R 28   DALLIN, Alexander, *The German Occupation of the USSR in World War II: a bibliography*, Washington: External Research Office of Intelligence Research, 1955. 76pp.

R 29   SHATOV, Mikhail (comp.), *Bibliografiia osvoboditel'nogo dvizheniia narodov Rossii v god Vtoroi Mirovoi Voiny, 1941-1945 (Bibliography of the Liberation Movement of the Russian People in the Years of the Second World War)*, New York: All-Slavic Publishing House, 1961. 208pp. Bibliography of the Vlasov dissident collaborationist movement led by Andrei Andreevich Vlassov (1900-46).

BALTIC STATES

General

Bs 1   BOREJSZA, Jerzy W., 'L'Italia e le tendenze fasciste nei paesi Baltici, 1922-1940'. *ANN. DELLA FOND. LUIGI EINAUDI*, **8**, 1974. pp. 279-316. Italian fascist influence quite strong in Lithuania and Latvia but not in Estonia. More influence in all three states than nazism.

Bs 2   CZOLLEK, Roswitha, *Faschismus und Okkupation: Wirtschaftspolitische Zielsetzung und Praxis des faschistischen deutschen Besatzungsregimes in den baltischen Sowjetrepubliken während des Zweiten Weltkrieges*, Berlin: Akademie V., 1974. 224pp. Bib. 205-19.

Bs 3   CZOLLEK, Roswitha and ŠTEIMANIS, Jozef, 'Der Faschismus im Baltikum in der sowjetischen Historiographie'. *JAHRB. FÜR GESCH. SOZ. LANDER EUR.*, **24** (**1**), 1980. pp. 85-102.

Bs 4   LOSSOWSKI, Piotr, *Kraje baltyckie na drodze od democracji parlamentarnej do diktatury, 1918-1934 (The Baltic Countries between Parliamentary Democracy and Dictatorship)*, Wroclaw: Wyd. Polskiej Akad. Nauk, 1972. 304pp. Useful on Vabadussõjalaste Liit (Vaps).

Bs 5   MAAMÄGI, V.A. and ARUMAË, H.T., 'Fasismi Baltiassa' (Fascism in the Baltic States). *HIST. ARKISTO*, **72**, 1977. pp. 93-112

Bs 6   MYLLYNIEMI, Seppo, *Die baltische Krise, 1938-1941*, Stuttgart: Deutsche Verlags-Anstalt, 1979. 167pp. Bib. 160-4. Tr. of *Baltian kriisii, 1938-1941*, Helsinki, 1977, by Dietrich Assmann.

Bs 7   MYLLYNIEMI, Seppo, *Die Neuordnung der Baltischen Länder, 1941-1944: nationalsozialistischen Inhalt der deutschen Besatzungspolitik*, tr. Dietrich Assmann, Helsinki, 1973. 308pp. Bib. 298-304.

Bs 8   RAUCH, Georg von, 'Zur Krise des Parlamentarismus in Estland und Lettland'. In VOLKMANN, H.-E., E 27. pp. 135-55. On Vabs and Ugunkrust Movements.

Bs 9   RAUCH, Georg von, *The Baltic States: the years of independence: Estonia, Latvia, Lithuania, 1917-1940*, Berkeley: University of California Press, 1974. xv, 265pp. Bib. 242-55. Tr. of *Geschichte der baltischen Staaten*. Useful on extreme Right in Estonia and Latvia.

Bs 10   SLAVENAS, Julius Paulius, 'Nazi ideology and policy in the Baltic States'. *Lituanus*, **11** (**1**), 1965. pp. 34-47.

Bs 11   TAAGAPERA, Rein, 'Civic culture and authoritarianism in the Baltic States, 1930-1940'. *EAST EUR. Q.*, **7** (**4**), 1973. pp. 407-12.

ESTONIA

Bs 12   *Eesti Rahvas Nõukogude Liidu Suures Isamaasõjas, 1941-45 (The Estonian People in the Great Patriotic War)*, Tallinn: Eesti Raamat, 1971-7. 2 vols.

Bs 13   *Eesti Riik ja Rahvas Teises Maailmasõjas*, [ed. by] Richard Maasing [*et al.*] (*The Estonian Republic and its People during World War II*), Stockholm: Karjastus Eesti, 1954-62. 10 vols. Collection of essays including native Estonian collaboration with the Germans and local fascist activity. Vols. 11-15 pub. Tallinn: Ajaleke 'Kodumaa' Valjaanne.

Bs 14   HEHN, Jürgen von, 'Zur Geschichte der deutschbaltischen nationalsozialistischen Bewegung in Estland'. *Z. FÜR OSTFOR-SCHUNG*, **26** (4), 1977. pp. 597-650.

Bs 15   KNORRING, Gustav von, 'Krisenjahre in Estland'. *Baltische Hefte*, **8** (2), 1962. pp. 86-95. On the depression in Estonia 1931-33 and the growth of the Vaps Movement.

Bs 16   KUULI, Olaf, *Six Years of Fascist Dictatorship in Estonia*, tr. by G. Liiv, Tallinn: Perioodika, 1975. 102pp. On Päts' dictatorship.

Bs 17   KUULI, Olaf, *Vapsidest isamaaliiduni: fašismi ja fašismivastase võitluse ajaloost kodanlikus Eestis* (*From Vaps to Patriotic Movement: concerning the history of fascism and the anti-fascist struggle in bourgeois Estonia*), Tallinn: Eesti Raamat, 1976. 236pp. Sections 2-4 concerned with the Päts' dictatorship and the Vabadussõjalaste Liit (Vaps) movement.

Bs 18   LAAMAN, Eduard, *Konstantin Päts: poliitika ja riigimees* (*K. Päts: politician and statesman*), Stockholm: Vaba-Eesti, 1949. 338pp. Sympathetic account by socialist author.

Bs 19   LIPPING, Imre, 'The emergence of Estonian authoritarianism'. In ZIEDONIS, Arvids and others, *Baltic History*, Columbus: Ass. for the Advancement of Baltic Studies, 1974. pp. 209-16. Much on Vaps movement whose threat led to the Päts *coup d'état*.

Bs 20   ÖPIK, Oskar [Oskar Mamers (pseud.)], *Häda võidetuile* (*Anguish of the Defeated*), Stockholm: EMP, 1958. 311pp. Mamers a member of the collaborationist government in Estonia.

Bs 21   ÖPIK, Oskar [Oskar Mamers (pseud.)], *Kahe sõja vahel* (*Between Two Wars*), Stockholm: EMP, 1957. 287pp.

Bs 22   PARMING, Tönu, *The Collapse of Liberal Democracy and the Rise of Authoritarianism in Estonia*, Beverly Hills: Sage, 1975. 73pp. Bib. 68-73. Useful material on Vaps Movement.

Bs 23   PUSTA, Kaarel R., *Saadiku paevik I* (*Diplomatic Diary*), Geislingen: Kultuur, 1964. Vol. 1. 314pp. Further memoirs which speculate on death of Artur Sirk leader of Vaps Movement. Was he killed in Luxemburg by Päts' police?

Bs 24   SIILIVASK, Karl, 'Die bürgerlich-nationalistische Diktatur in Estland, 1920-1940'. *Z. FÜR GESCHICHTWISS.*, **22** (8), 1974. 801-7.

Bs 25   TOMINGAS, William, *Vaikiv ajastu Eestis* (*The Silent Era in*

181

Estonia), New York: Eesti Ajaloo Instituut, 1961. 554pp. Critical account of Päts' *coup* written by a member of the extreme Right Vaps Movement.

Bs 26 UUSTALU, Evold, *Eesti vabariik, 1918-1940: ajalooline ülevaade sõnas ja pildis* (The Estonian Republic, 1918—1940: a historical review in words and pictures), Lund: Eesti Kirjanike Kooperativ, 1968. 267pp. Bib. 265-6. General work on Estonian Republic which includes information on Vaps Movement.

Bs 27 VIHALEM, Paul, *Eesti kodanluse üleminek saksa fašismi teenistusse* (*Transition of the Estonian Bourgeoisie in the Service of German fascism*), Tallinn: Eesti Raamat, 1971. 148pp. Claims Vaps/nazi connections.

Bs 28 WIESELGREN, Per, *Från hammaren till hakkorset: Estland, 1939-1941* (*From Hammer to Swastika: Estonia 1939-1941*), Stockholm: Ide och Form Förlag, 1942. 294pp.

LATVIA

Bs 29 CELMIŅŠ, Gustavs, *Eiropas krustcelos* (*Europe's Crossroads*), Heidenheim: Dzintarzeme, 1947. 199pp. Memoirs of the leader of the Latvian Ugunkrust Movement.

Bs 30 HEHN, Jürgen von, *Lettland zwischen Demokratie und Diktatur: zur Geschichte des Lettischen Staatsreichs vom 15.5.1934*, Munich: Isar V., 1957. 76pp. Describes Perkonkrust Movement as only genuine fascist movement in Latvia.

Bs 31 KROEGER, Erhard, *Des Auszug aus der alten Heimat: die Umsiedlung der Baltendeutschen*, Tübingen: V. des Deuschen Hoch-schullehre-Zeitung, 1967. 198pp. Unrepentant memoirs of former leader of German nazis in Latvia.

Bs 32 RIMSCHA, Hans von, 'Zur Gleichschaltung der deutschen Volksgruppen durch das Dritte Reich: am Beispiel der deutsch-baltischen Volksgruppe in Lettland'. *HIST. Z.*, **192** (**1**), 1956. pp. 29-63.

Bs 33 RUDEVICS, Ansis, *Fašistiskā diktatūra Latvija, 1934-1940*, Riga: Latvijas Valsts Izd, 1961. 184pp.

Bs 34 RÜDIGER, Wilhelm von, *Aus dem letzten Kapitel: deutsch-baltischer Geschichte in Lettland, 1919-1945*, Meine: Kluge, 1954-5. 2 vols. Author a leader of the German minority in Latvia.

Bs 35 SILGAILIS, Arturs, *Latviešu légions: dibināšana formēšana un kauju gaitas otrā pasaules karā* (*The Latvian Legion: establishment, formation* and the course of its struggle during the Second World War), 2nd edn, Copenhagen: Imanta, 1964. 399pp.

LITHUANIA

Bs 36   BROSZAT, Martin, 'Die Memeldeutschen Organisationen und der Nationalsozialismus'. *Gutachten des Inst. für Zeitg.*, **1**. 1958. pp. 395-400.

Bs 37   BULUVAS, Juozas, *Vokiškuju fašistu okupacinis Lietuvos valdymas, 1941-1944 m (The German Fascist Occupation of Lithuania)*, Vilnius: Lietuvos TSR Mokslu Akad. Ekonomikos Inst., 1969. 294pp. Bib. 284-8.

Bs 38   DOBROVOLSKAS, J., 'Lietuviškuju buržuaziniu nacionalistu antiliaudinis veikimas okupaciniame Hitlerininku valdžios aparate 1941-1944' (The Lithuanian bourgeoisie's anti-popular activities in the occupation administration of the Hitlerite government). *Lietuvos TSR Mokslu Akademijos Darbai*, **serija A, 2** (**13**), 1962. pp. 155-72.

Bs 39   *Gitlerovskaia Okkupatsiia v Litve: sbornik statei (Hitlerite Occupation of Lithuania)*, Vilnius: Mintis, 1966. 354pp. Collection of articles including one by Yu. Butenas on nationalist collaborators.

Bs 40   *Lietuviu Enciklopedija (Lithuanian Encyclopedia)*, Boston: Lietuviu Enciklopedijos Leidykla, 1953-1966. 35 vols. Contains articles on the Iron Wolf movement and Tautininkai (Nationalist Party). Vol. 30. pp. 440-9.

Bs 41   Lietuvos TSR, Vilnius, Mokslu Akademija, *Faktai kaltina: Geležinis Vilkas (The Facts accuse: the Iron Wolf)*, Vilnius: Mintis, 1965. 140pp. Ed. B. Baranauskas. Collection of documents on the extreme Rightist secret society, the Iron Wolf.

Bs 42   Lietuvos TSR, Vilnius. Mokslu Akademija, *Hitlerininku penktoji kolona Lietuvoje (Hitler's Fifth Column in Lithuania)*, Vilnius: VPMLL, 1961. 227pp. Ed. B. Baranauskas.

Bs 43   MISIUNAS, Romuald, 'Fascist tendencies in Lithuania'. *SLAV. AND EAST EUR. REV.*, **48** (**110**), 1970. pp. 88-109. Discusses Smetona regime, the Nationalists and Iron Wolf.

Bs 44   PLIEG, Ernst Albrecht, *Das Memelland, 1920-1939: deutsche Autonomiebestrebungen in litauischen Gesamtstaat*, Wurzburg: Halzner V., 1962. xii, 268pp. Bib. 249-55.

Bs 45   SABALIŪNAS, Leonas, *Lithuania in Crisis: nationalism to communism, 1939-1940*, Bloomington: Indiana University Press, 1972.

xxi, 293pp. Comments on the 'fascist coloration' that integral nationalism in Lithuania acquired.

Bs 46 SHOHAT, Azriel, 'The beginnings of anti-semitism in independent Lithuania'. *Yad Vashem Studies*, **2**, 1958. pp. 7–48.

Bs 47 ŠLIOGERIS, Vaclovas, *Antanas Smetona: zmogus ir valstybininkas* (*Antanas Smetona: man and statesman*), Sodus, Mich.: Bachunas, 1966. 181pp. Author was Smetona's military aide.

ITALY

Bibliographies and Reference Works

It 1 ARRIGO, Giuseppe d', *Eroi della guerra e della rivoluzione: 39 monografie*, 2nd edn, Rome: Ed. della Lupa, 1937. 230pp. Biographies of fascists.

It 2 *Bibliografia Fascista: rassegna mensile del movimento culturale fascista il Italia a all'estero*, ed. Giorgio Berlutti e Cornelio di Marzio et al., Rome: Berlutti, 1926–42. Monthly and semi-monthly.

It 3 CARUCCI, P. and others, *Uomini e volti del fascismo*, ed. Ferdinando Cordova, Rome: Bulzoni, 1980. 579pp.

It 4 *Dizionario di Politica*, ed. Partito Nazionale Fascista, pref. by F. Mezzasoma, Rome: Ist della Enciclopedia Italiana, 1940. 4 vols.

It 5 EVOLA, Niccolo Domenico, *Origini e dottrina del fascismo*, Florence: Sansoni, 1935. xiii, 166pp. Repr. AMS P., 1975. Bibliography.

It 6 GAZZETTI, Fernando (ed.), *Lo stato fascista, 1921–1935*, Rome: AGIL, 1935. 89pp. Bibliography.

It 7 Istituto Nazionale per le Relazioni Culturali con l'Estero. *La bibliografia italiana*, ed. Gianneto Avanzi, 2nd edn, Rome, 1946 xxiv, 579pp.

It 8 Istituto Nazionale per le Relazioni Culturali con l'Estero. *Mussolini e il fascismo*, Rome, 1941. xxxii, 81pp. (*Bibliografia del Ventennio*, **ser. 1**).

It 9 *ITALY*. Camera dei Deputati, Biblioteca. *Opere sul fascismo possedute dalla Biblioteca . . . al 28 ottobre 1934–anno. XII*, 3rd edn, Rome: Seg. Gen. della Camera Fascista, 1935. xv, 550pp. Discorsi e scritti di Benito Mussolini. pp. 384–96.

It 10   *ITALY*. Confederazione Fascista dei Professionisti e degli Artisti. *Bibliografia del fascismo i libri coloniali: guida bibliografica commentata sull opere pubblicate in Italia nel 10 decennio del regime*, ed. Angelo Vittori Pellegrineschi, Rome, 1934. 150pp.

It 11   *ITALY*. Confederazione Fascista dei Professionisti e degli Artisti. *Bibliografia generale del fascismo. Rome, 1932–33*. 2 vols. *Opere di Mussolini* Vol. **2**, 1–24. **1**. ed. Vincenzo Fago. **2**. ed. Giani Calderone.

It 12   MÀDARO, Luigi, *Bibliografia fascista*, Milan: Mondadori, 1935. 181pp.

It 13   MELOGRANI, Piero, 'Bibliografia orientativa sul fascismo'. *NUOVO OSS.*, **50**, May 1966. pp. 421–38; **56/57**, Nov.–Dec. 1966. pp. 962–82.

It 14   PARENTI, Marino (ed.), *Bibliografia Mussoliniana. 1. Serie cronologica delle edizioni a stampa degli scritti e discorsi di Benito Mussolini*, Florence: Sansoni, 1940. xv, 287pp.

It 15   POMBA, Giuseppe Luigi (ed.), *La civilta fascista illustrata nella dottrina e nelle operè*, intro. by Benito Mussolini, Turin: UTET, 1928. viii, 688pp.

It 16   SANTANGELO, Giulio and BRACALE, Carlo (eds), *Guida bibliografica del fascismo*, Rome: Libreria del Littorio, 1928. xi, 320pp.

Historiography, Interpretation, Review Articles

It 17   ADDIS SABA, Marina, *Il dibattito sul fascismo: le interpretazioni degli storici e dei militanti politici*, Milan: Longanesi, 1976. 149pp.

It 18   ALATRI, Paolo, 'Recenti studi sul fascismo'. *STUD. STOR.*, **3** (**4**), 1962. pp. 757–836.

It 19   AMBRI, Mariano, '"Fascismi" e fascismo'. *Affari Estera*, **9** (**34**) 1977. pp. 351–69. Historiography of Italian fascism and precedents in Europe.

It 20   BAUM, Hans-Rainer, 'Zur italienischen bürgerlichen Historiographie über den Faschismus'. *Z. FÜR GESCHICHTWISS*, **29** (**7**), 1981. pp. 604–10.

It 21   BIBES, Geneviève, 'Le fascisme italien: état des travaux depuis 1945'. *REV. FR. DÉ SCI. POLIT.*, **19** (**6**), 1968. pp. 1191–244.

It 22   BOSWORTH, Richard J.B., 'The British press, the Conservatives, and Mussolini, 1920-1934'. *J. OF CONTEMP. HIST.*, **5** (**2**), 1970. pp. 163-82.

It 23   BOSWORTH, Richard, J.B., 'The historiography of modern Italy: recent developments'. *AUST. J. OF POLIT. AND HIST.*, **23** (**1**), 1977. pp. 41-53.

It 24   CANNISTRARO, Philip V., 'Il fascismo italiano visto dagli Stati Uniti: cinquant' anni di studi e di interpretazioni'. *STOR. CONTEMP.*, **2** (**3**), 1971. pp. 599-633.

It 25   CARACCIOLO, Alberto, 'Dalle interpretazioni del fascismo all'analisi del sistema mondiale dopo gli anni trenta'. *QUAD. STOR.*, **10** (**1**), 1975. pp. 227-42.

It 26   COLOMBO, Arturo, 'Fascismo, antifascismo e resistenza: lineamenti per un bilancio storiografico del trentennale'. *Risorgimento*, **27** (**3**), 1975. pp. 123-60.

It 27   DELZELL, Charles F., 'The Italian anti-fascist resistance in retrospect: three decades of historiography'. *J. OF MOD. HIST.*, **47** (**1**), 1975. pp. 66-96.

It 28   DELZELL, Charles F., 'Italian historical scholarship: a decade of recovery and development, 1945-1955'. *J. OF MOD. HIST.*, **28** (**4**), 1956. pp. 374-88.

It 29   DELZELL, Charles F., 'Mussolini's Italy twenty years after'. *J. OF MOD. HIST.*, **38** (**1**), 1966. pp. 53-8.

It 30   DIGGINS, John P., 'American Catholics and Italian fascism'. *J. OF CONTEMP. HIST.*, **2** (**4**), 1967. pp. 51-68.

It 31   DIGGINS, John P., *Mussolini and Fascism: the view from America*, Princeton: University Press, 1972. xx, 524pp. Bib. 497-506.

It 32   FELICE, Renzo de, 'Il fenomeno fascista'. *STOR. CONTEMP.*, **10** (**4/5**), 1979. pp. 619-32.

It 33   FELICE, Renzo de and LEDEEN, Michael, 'Fascism and the Italian malaise'. *Society*, **13** (**3**), 1976. pp. 53-9.

It 34   GIOVANNINI, Claudio, 'Alle origini del fascismo: il retorno dell' interpretazione radicale'. *Il Mulino*, **21** (**223**), 1972. pp. 890-920.

It 35   GRAMSCI, Antonio, *Socialismo e fascismo: l'ordine nuovo, 1921-1922*, 2nd edn, Turin: Einaudi, 1967. xviii, 544pp.

It 36   GRAMSCI, Antonio, *Sul fascismo*, ed. Enzo Santarelli, Rome: Ed. Riuniti, 1973. 451pp.

It 37   GUARANI FASANO, Elena, 'Travaux récents sur le fascisme italien'. *ANNALES*, **19** (**1**), 1964. pp. 83-102.

It 38   KESERICH, Charles, 'The British Labour press and Italian fascism'. *J. OF CONTEMP. HIST.*, **10** (4), 1975. pp. 579-90.

It 39   LEDEEN, Michael A., Renzo de Felice and the controversy over Italian fascism'. *J. OF CONTEMP. HIST.*, **11** (4), 1976. pp. 269-83.

It 40   LEGNANI, Massimo, 'Guerra, dopoguerra, e fascismo nella interpretazione di Giorgio Candeloro'. *ITAL. CONTEMP.*, **30** (**132**), 1978. pp. 99-102. Review of Candeloro's *Storia dell'Italia moderna.* **8**, 1914-1922.

It 41   LI PERA, Lucia, *Il fascismo dalla polemica alla storiografia: un saggio introduttivo con i confronti antoligici da A. Gramsci*, Messina: D'Anna, 1975. 190pp. Bib. 189-90.

It 42   LODA, Natale, 'Interpretazioni del fascismo'. *STUD. POLIT.*, **3**, 1954. pp. 555-72.

It 43   LOPUKHOV, Boris Removich, 'Il problema del fascismo italiano negli scritti di autori sovietici'. *STUD. STOR.*, **6** (2), 1965. pp. 239-57.

It 44   LYTTLETON, Adrian, 'Italian fascism'. In LAQUEUR, W. Gn 35 pp. 125-51.

It 45   MACK SMITH, Dennis and LEDEEN, Michael A., *Un monumento al Duce? contributo al dibattito sul fascismo,* intro. and bib. by Piero Meldini, Florence: Guaraldi, 1976. 88pp.

It 46   MAIER, Charles S., 'Some recent studies of fascism'. *J. OF MOD. HIST.*, **48** (3), 1976. pp. 506-21.

It 47   MILZA, Pierre, *L'Italie fasciste devant l'opinion française, 1920–1940*, Paris: Colin, 1967. 264pp. Bib. 251-3.

It 48   NOCE, Augusto del, 'Idee per l'interpretazione del fascismo.' In CASUCCI, F., It 124. pp. 370-83.

It 49   NOCE, Augusto del, 'Per una definizione del fascismo'. In PAVETTO, R., It 131. pp. 11-46.

It 50   NOETHER, Emiliana Pasca, 'Italy reviews its fascist past'. *AM. HIST REV.*, **61** (4), 1956. pp. 877-99.

It 51   PAVONE, Claudio, 'Italy: trends and problems'. *J. OF CONTEMP. HIST.*, **2** (1), 1967. pp. 48-76.

It 52   PETERSEN, Jens, 'Il fascismo italiano visto dalla repubblica Weimar'. *STOR. CONTEMP.*, **9** (3), 1978. pp. 497-529.

It 53   PETERSEN, Jens, 'Der italienische Faschismus aus der Sicht der Weimarer Republik: einige deutsche Interpretationen'. *QUELL. UND FORSCHUNG. AUS. ITAL. ARCH.*, **55/56**, 1976. pp. 315-60. Weimar views of fascism including Michels, von Beckerath, Leibholz, and the Social Democrats.

It 54   PETERSEN, Jens, 'Der italienische Faschismus zwischen politischer Polemik und historischer Analyse'. *GESCH. IN WISS. UND UNTERR.*, **27** (**5**), 1976. pp. 257-72.

It 55   PRIESTER, Karin, 'Anmerkungen zum Thema italienischer Faschismus'. *BL. FÜR DTSCH. UND INT. POLIT.*, **19**, 1974. pp. 797-819. Marxist.

It 56   PRIESTER, Karin, *Der italienische Faschismus: ökonomische und ideologische Grundlagen*, Cologne: Pahl-Rugenstein, 1972. 336pp. Bib. 324-36.

It 57   RÉMOND, René, 'Il fascismo visto dalla cultura cattolica francese'. *STOR. CONTEMP.*, **2** (**4**), 1971. pp. 685-96.

It 58   ROSA, Gabriele de, 'Considerazioni storiografiche sulla crisi dello stato prefascista e sull'antifascismo'. *MOV. DI LIBERAZIONE IN ITALIA*, **57** (**5**), 1959. pp. 17-79.

It 59   SANTARELLI, Enzo, *Fascismo e neofascismo: studi e problemi di ricerca*, Rome: Ed. Riuniti, 1974. xiii, 323pp. Bib. xxiii.

It 60   SPADOLINI, Giovanni, 'La polemica sul fascismo'. *Nuova Antologia*, **110**, Aug. 1975. pp. 443-8.

It 61   *Storia Contemporanea.*, **10** (**4/5**), 1979. Special issue on 'Il fascismo: interpretazioni e ricerche'. Includes articles by de Felice, It 32; Conti, It 684. Gentile, It 257.

It 62   THAMER, Hans-Ulrich, 'Ansichten des Faschismus: der italienische Faschismus in der politischen und wissenschaftlichen Diskussion'. *NEUE POLIT. LIT.*, **22** (1), 1977. pp. 19-35. On de Felice's theories.

It 63   TOGLIATTI, Palmiro, *Lezioni sul fascismo*, pref. by Ernesto Ragioneri, Rome: Ed. Riuniti, 1970. xxvii, 200pp. By the Italian Communist Party leader.

It 64   TRANFAGLIA, Nicola, *Dallo stato liberale al regime fascista: problemi e ricerche*, Milan: Feltrinelli, 1973. 297pp.

It 65   VALIANI, Leo, 'Salvatorelli storico dell'unita d'Italia a del fascismo'. *RIV. STOR. ITAL.*, **86** (**4**), 1974. pp. 723-49.

It 66   VALIANI, Leo, 'La storia del fascismo nella problematica della storia contemporanea a nella biografia di Mussolini'. *RIV. STOR. ITAL.* **79** (**2**), 1967. pp. 459-81.

It 67   VALIANI, Leo, 'Lo storico dei propri tempi'. *RIV. STOR. ITAL.*, **72** (4), 1960. pp. 774–92. Comment on Chabod as a historian of fascism.

It 68   VIVARELLI, Roberto, 'Italia liberale e fascismo: considerazioni su di una recente storia d'Italia'. *RIV. STOR. ITAL.* **82** (3), 1970. pp. 669–703.

It 69   VIVARELLI, Roberto, 'Italian fascism'. *HIST. J.*, **17** (3), 1974. pp. 644–51.

It 70   WOOLF, Stuart J., 'Risorgimento e fascismo: il senso della continuità nella storiografica italiana'. *Belfagor*, **20** (1), 1965. pp. 71–91.

It 71   WUNDERER, Otto, *Der italienische Faschismus in der analyse der österreichischen sozialdemokratischen Partei, 1922–1933*, Vienna University thesis, 1974.

Fascism and the Extreme Right: General

It 72   ACERBO, Giacomo, *Fra due platoni di esecuzione: avvenimenti e problemi dell'epoca fascista*, Bologna: Cappelli, 1968. 775pp.

It 73   ARTIERI, Giovanni, *Quattro momenti di storia fascista*, Naples: Berisio, 1968. 337pp. Notes and bib. 308–19.

It 74   BASSO, Lelio, *Due totalitarismi: fascismo e democrazia cristiana*, Milan: Garzanti, 1951. 291pp.

It 75   BOCCA, Giorgio, *L'Italia fascista*, Milan: Mondadori, 1973. 141pp. Bib. 135–6.

It 76   CANZIO, Stefano, *La dittatura debole: storia dell'Italia fascista e dell'antifascismo militante dal 1926 al 1945*, Milan: La Pietra, 1980. 762pp. First pub. as Vol. 4, *Compendio di storia d'Italia*.

It 77   CARADONNA, Giulio, *Validità del fascismo*, Cassino: IPEM, 1963. 183pp.

It 78   CAROCCI, Giampiero, *Storia del fascismo*, 2nd edn, Milan: Garzanti, 1961. 105pp. Bib. 103–4.

It 79   CASSELS, Alan, *Fascist Italy*, New York: Crowell, 1968. London: Routledge & Kegan Paul, 1969. vii. 136pp. Bib. 117–27.

It 80   CATALANO, Franco, *L'Italia dalla dittatura alla democrazia, 1919–1948*, 2nd Edn, Milan: Lerici, 1965. 871pp. Bib. 807–46.

It 81   CHABOD, Federico, *A History of Italian Fascism*, London:

Weidenfeld & Nicolson, 1963. 192pp. Bib. 163-83. Tr. of *L'Italia contemporanea, 1918-1949*, Turin: Einaudi, 1961, by Muriel Grindrod.

It 82 CUSIN, Fabio, *Antistoria d'Italia, 1922-1943*, Turin: Einaudi, 1948. 539pp.

It 83 DELZELL, Charles F., *Mussolini's Enemies: the Italian anti-fascist resistance*, New York: Fertig, 1974. xxxix, 620pp. Bib. 579-83. First pub. Princeton University Press., 1961.

It 84 FINER, Herman, *Mussolini's Italy*, Hamden: Archon. London: Gollancz, 1964. 564pp.

It 85 GALLO, Max, *Mussolini's Italy: twenty years of the fascist era*, New York: Macmillan, 1973. London: Abelard-Schuman, 1974. xv, 452pp. Tr. of *L'Italie de Mussolini*, Paris: Perrin, 1964, by Charles Lam Markmann.

It 86 GAMBETTI, Fidia, *1919-1945: inchiesta sul fascismo*, Milan: Mastellone, 1953. 350pp. Communist version of events.

It 87 GREGOR, A. James, *Italian Fascism and Developmental Dictatorship*, Princeton: University Press, 1980. xv, 427pp. Bib. 387-412.

It 88 KING, Bolton, *Il fascismo in Italia*, pref. by Aldo Berselli, Bologna: Patron, 1973. 163pp.

It 89 MACGREGOR-HASTIE, Roy, *The Day of the Lion: the life and death of fascist Italy, 1922-1945*, London: MacDonald, 1963. New York: Coward-McCann, 1964. 395pp. Bib. 374-80.

It 90 MACK SMITH, Dennis, *Italy: a modern history*, new edn, Ann Arbor: University of Michigan Press, 1969. xi, 542pp. Bib. 527-42.

It 91 MACK SMITH, Dennis, *Mussolini's Roman Empire*, London: Longmans, 1976. xiii, 322pp. Bib. 289-310. Penguin edn, 1979.

It 92 MANTICA, Paulo, 'Il fascismo in Italia'. *Historica*, **23** (**2**), 1970. pp. 66-84. Author an anti-parliamentary syndicalist before the first world war.

It 93 MILZA, Pierre and BERSTEIN, Serge, *Le Fascisme italien, 1919-1945*, Paris: Ed. du Seuil, 1980. 441pp. Bib. 417-23. First pub. as *L'Italie fasciste*, 1970.

It 94 NENNI, Pietro, *Vent'anni di fascismo*, ed. Gioietta Dallo, 2nd edn, Milan: Ed. Avanti, 1965. 485pp. French edn pub. Maspero, 1960 Democratic anti-fascist view.

It 95 PARIS, Robert, *Histoire du fascisme en Italie*, Paris: Maspero, 1962. 1. *Des origines à la prise du pouvoir*. 367pp.

It 96   PELLIZZI, Camillo, *Una rivoluzione mancata*, Milan: Longanesi, 1949. 275pp.

It 97   PERTICONE, Giacomo, *La politica italiana nell'ultimo trentennio*, Rome: Leonardo, 1945. 3 vols. Debate about the place of fascism in Italian history.

It 98   PREZZOLINI, Giuseppe, *Diario*, Milan: Rusconi, 1978-80. 2 vols. Covers 1900-68. Ex-nationalist who became a fascist.

It 99   PREZZOLINI, Giuseppe, *L'italiano inutile*, 2nd edn, Florence: Vallecchi, 1964. 460pp. Correspondence and reminiscence.

It 100   PREZZOLINI, Giuseppe, *Sul fascismo, 1915-1975*, Milan: Pan, 1976. 191pp.

It101   PIASENTI, Paride, *1918-1948: da Vittorio Venete alla Repubblica*, Milan: Santi, 1960. iii, 159pp. Bib. 132.

It 102   REPACI, Antonino, *Fascismo vecchio e nuovo, e altri saggi*, pref. by D. Riccardo Peretti Griva, Turin: Bottegna d'Erasmo, 1954. 201pp.

It 103   SAITTA, Armando, 'Dal fascismo alla Resistenza: profilo storico documenti, 4th edn, Florence: La Nuova Italia, 1967. 294pp. Dizionario bio-bibliografico pp. 271-88.

It 104   SALADINO, Salvatore, 'Italy'. In ROGGER, H. and WEBER, E., Gn 54 pp. 208-58.

It 105   SALVATORELLI. Luigi and MIRA, Giovanni, *Storia d'Italia nel periodo fascista*, 6th edn, Milan: Mondadori, 1969. 2 vols. Rev. edn of *Storia del fascismo*.

It 106   SALVEMINI, Gaetano, *Under the Ax of Fascism*, New York: Fertig, 1969. xiv, 402pp. Bib. 393-402. Repr. of 1946 edn. First pub. 1936.

It 107   SANTARELLI, Enzo, *Storia del fascismo*, 2nd edn, Rome: Ed. Riuniti, 1973. 3 vols. Bib. Vol. 1 xxi-xxvii. First pub. as *Storia del movimento e del regime fascista*.

It 108   SARTI, Roland (ed.) *The Ax Within: Italian fascism in action*, New York: New Viewpoints, 1974. xiv, 278pp. Bib. 257-65.

It 109   SCHMIDT, Carl Theodore, *The Corporate State in Action: Italy under fascism*: New York: Oxford University Press, 1939. 173pp. Bib. 166-8.

It 110   SCHNEIDER, Herbert Wallace, *The Fascist Government of Italy*, New York: Van Nostrand, 1936. xii, 173pp. Bib. 155-63.

It 111   SETON-WATSON, Christopher, *Italy from Liberalism to*

Fascism, 1870-1925, London: Methuen. New York: Barnes & Noble, 1967. x, 772pp. Bib. 714-25.

It 112   SETTEMBRINI, Domenico, *Fascismo: controrivoluzione imperfetta*, Florence: Sansoni, 1978. 358pp. Bib. 349-53. Compares fascism and communism.

It 113   STEINER, H. Arthur, *Government in Fascist Italy*, New York: McGraw-Hill, 1938. xii, 158pp. Bib. 145-51.

It 114   TAMARO, Attilio, *Venti anni di storia, 1922-1943*, Rome: Ed. Tiber, 1953. 491pp. Bib. 489-91. Written from Nationalist point of view.

It 115   TANNENBAUM, Edward R., *The Fascist Experience: Italian society and culture, 1922-1945*, New York: Basic Books, 1972, vi, 357pp. British edn, *Fascism in Italy: society and culture, 1922-1945*, London: Allen Lane, 1973.

It 116   TANNENBAUM, Edward R., 'The goals of Italian fascism'. *AM. HIST. REV.*, **74** (4), 1969. pp. 1183-204.

It 117   VALERI, Nino (ed.), *Storia d'Italia.* **5**. *Dalla crisi del primo dopoguerra alla fondazione della Repubblica*, ed. Franco Catalano, Turin: UTET, 1960. xi, 710pp. Bib.

It 118   VINCIGUERRA, Mario, *Il fascismo visto da un solitario ed altri saggi sull'Italia dal 28 ottobre ad oggi*, Florence: Le Monnier, 1963. 179pp.

It 119   WISKEMANN, Elizabeth, *Fascism in Italy: its development and influence*, 2nd edn, London: Macmillan. New York: St Martin's Press, 1970. 141pp. Bib. 130-2.

It 120   WOOLF, Stuart J., 'Italy'. In WOOLF, S.J., Gn 20. pp. 39-63.

It 121   ZANGRANDI, Ruggero, *Il lungo viaggio attraverso il fascismo: contributo alla storia di una generazione*, Milan: Garzanti, 1971. 2 vols.

Anthologies and Collections

It 122   ANTONICELLI, Franco (ed.), *Trent' anni di storia italiana, 1915-1945: lezioni con testimonianze*, Turin: Einaudi, 1961. xxix, 387pp.

It 123   AQUARONE, Alberto and VERNASSA, Maurizio (eds), *Il regime fascista*, Bologna: Il Mulino, 1974. 527pp. Bib. 505-22.

It 124   CASUCCI, Costanzo (ed.), *Il fascismo: antologia di scritti critici*, Bologna: Il Mulino, 1961. 464pp.

It 125   CATALANO, Franco, *Dall'unita al fascismo*, Milan: Cisalpino, 1961. 346pp. Collected articles and essays 1958-60.

It 126   *Cesare Barbieri Courier*, 1980. Special issue on fascism. Articles by Cassels, Delzell, Deakin, Noether, Segrè.

It 127   CHICCO, Francesco and LIVIO, Gigi (comps), *1922-1945: sintesi storica e documenti del fascismo e dell'antifascismo italiani*, Turin: Paravia, 1970. vii, 375pp.

It 128   *Fascismo e Antifascismo: lezioni e testimonianze*, 3rd edn, Milan: Feltrinelli, 1971. 2 vols.

It 129   FELICE, Renzo de (ed.), *Autobiografia del fascismo: antologia di esti fascisti, 1919-1945*, Bergamo: Minerva Italica, 1978. 640pp.

It 130   FELICE, Renzo de (ed.), *Il fascismo e i partiti italiani: testimonianze del 1921-1923*, Bologna: Cappelli, 1966. 555pp. Bib. 551. Repr. of essays written before 1923.

It 131   PAVETTO, Renato (ed.), *Il problema storico del fascismo*, Florence: Vallecchi, 1970. 107pp. Articles by del Noce, de Felice, Ungari, Abrate.

It 132   *I Probleme di Ulisse*, **30** (**82**), 1976. Issue on 'Fascismo e neo-fascismo'. Articles by Lelio Basso, Silvio Bertoldi, Gianpasquale Santomassimo, Camillo Brezzi, Paolo Alatri, Umberto Cerroni, Enzo Santarelli, Valerio Castronovo, Jens Petersen, Enzo Collotti.

It 133   *Rev. D'Hist. Deux. Guerre Mond.*, **7** (**26**), 1957. Special issue 'Sur l' Italie mussolinienne'.

It 134   SALVEMINI, Gaetano, *Scritti sul fascismo*, Milan: Feltrinelli, 1961-74. 3 vols.

It 135   SALVEMINI, Gaetano, *Scritti vari, 1900-1957*, ed. Giorgio Agosti e Allesandro Galante Garrone, Milan: Feltrinelli, 1978. 990pp.

It 136   VOLPE, Gioacchino, *Scritti sul fascismo, 1919-1938*, pref. by Piero Buscaroli, Rome: Volpe, 1976. Vol. 1. 1919-1938. 261pp.

Pre-fascism: Antecedents on the Extreme Right

It 137   BIANCHI, Gianfranco, *Aspetti del 'protofascismo' in Italia*, Milan: CELUC, 1967. xiv, 204pp. Bib. 132-49.

It 138   CERBONE, Carlo (ed.), *L'antiparlamentarismo italiano, 1870-1919*, Rome: Volpe, 1972. 109pp. Bib. 105-9.

It 139   MACK SMITH, Dennis, 'The prehistory of fascism'. *Occidente*, **10 (6)**, 1954. pp. 509-21.

It 140   PATRUCCO, Armand Italo, *The Critics of the Italian Parliamentary System*. 1860-1915, Columbia University thesis, 1969. UM 72-19084. 434pp.

It 141   ROSEN, Edgar Robert, 'Italiens Kriegseintritt im Jahre 1915 als innenpolitisches Problem der Giolitti-Aera: ein Beitrag zur Vorgeschichte des Faschismus'. *HIST. Z.*, **187 (2)**, 1959. pp. 289-363.

It 142   SANTARELLI, Enzo, 'Le socialisme nationale en italie: précédents et origines'. *MOUVEMENT SOC.*, **50**, 1965. pp. 41-70.

It 143   VAUSSARD, Maurice, *De Pétrarque a Mussolini: évolution du sentiment nationaliste italien*, Paris: Colin, 1961. 303pp.

It 144   VINCI, Antonio *Prefigurazioni del fascismo*, Milan: Celuc, 1974. 268pp. Bib. 249-57. Concerns the ideological antecedents of fascism.

It 145   WEBSTER, R.A., *Industrial Imperialism in Italy, 1908-1915*, Berkeley: University of California Press, 1975. vii, 392pp. Italian tr. has subtitle *studio sul prefascismo*.

The Italian Nationalists

It 146   ALFF, Wilhelm, 'Die Associazione Nazionalista Italiana von 1910.' *VIERTELJAHRSH. FÜR ZEITG.*, **13 (1)**, 1965. pp. 32-63.

It 147   ALFF, Wilhelm, 'Il nazionalismo prescursore del fascismo'. *Veltro*, **8**, 1964. pp. 981-1007.

It 148   BERTELLI, Sergio, 'Incunaboli del nazionalismo'. *Nord e Sud*, **8 (1)**, 1961. pp. 75-94.

It 149   CANNISTRARO, Philip, 'Italy, modern'. *CAN. REV. STUD. NATL.*, **2**, 1975. pp. 92-108. Bibliographical article on Italian nationalism.

It 150   CORRADINI, Enrico, *Discorsi politici, 1902-1923*, Florence: Vallecchi, 1923. 506pp.

It 151   CORRADINI, Enrico, *Il nazionalismo italiano*, Milan: Treves, 1914. vii, 264pp.

It 152   CUNSOLO, Ronald S., *Enrico Corradini and Italian Nationalism, 1896-1923*, New York University thesis, 1962. UM 66-09674. 480pp.

It 153   CUNSOLO, Ronald S., 'Enrico Corradini e la teoria del nazionalismo proletario'. *RASS. STOR. RISORGIMENTO*, **65 (3)**, 1978. pp. 341-55.

It 154   DRAKE, Richard, *Byzantium for Rome: the politics of nostalgia in Umbertian Italy, 1878-1900*, Chapel Hill: University of N. Carolina Press, 1980. xxviii, 308pp. Bib. 269-94. Chapter 9. The politics of nostalgia and the genesis of nationalism: Enrico Corradini, 1865-1931.

It 155   OCCHINI, Pier Ludovico, *Enrico Corradini*, Florence: Rinascimento del Libro, 1933. xlvii, 324pp. Contains excellent bibliography of Corradini's works.

It 156   TAEYE-HENEN, Monique de, *Le Nationalisme d'Enrico Corradini et les origines du fascisme dans la revue florentine 'Il Regno'. 1903-1906*, Paris: Didier, 1973. 127pp. Bib. 116-23.

It 157   *La Cultura Italiana Del' 900 attraverso le riviste*, Turin: Einaudi, 1960-2. 5 vols. **1**. *Leonardo, Hermes, Il Regno*, ed. Delia Frigessi. **3**. *La Voce, 1908-14*, ed. Angelo Romano. **4**. *Lacerba, La Voce, 1914-1916*, ed. Gianni Scaglia. **5**. *L'Unita, La Voce Politica*, ed. Francesco Golzio and Augusto Guerra.

It 158   CUNSOLO, Ronald S., 'The fusion between Italian nationalism and fascism'. *CAN. REV. STUD. NATL.*, **3** (**2**), 1976. pp. 192-211.

It 159   CUNSOLO, Ronald S., 'Modern Italian nationalism to 1945'. *CAN. REV. STUD. NATL.*, **6**, 1979. pp. 139-47.

It 160   DE GRAND, Alexander J., *The Italian Nationalist Association and the Rise of Fascism in Italy*, Lincoln: University of Nebraska Press, 1978. x, 238. Bib. 229-31. University of Chicago thesis.

It 161   DRAKE, Richard, 'Theory and practice of Italian nationalism, 1900-1906'. *J. OF MOD. HIST.*, **53** (**2**), 1981. pp. 213-41.

It 162   FEDERZONI, Luigi, *Italia di ieri per la storia di domani*, Milan: Mondadori, 1967. 317pp. Memoirs of leading Nationalist.

It 163   GAETA, Franco, *Nazionalismo italiano*, Naples: Ed. Scientifiche Italiane, 1965. 247pp.

It 164   GAETA, Franco (ed.), *La stampa nazionalista*, Bologna: Cappelli 1965. xc, 593pp. Extracts from Nationalist journals *Il Regno, La Voce, Idea Nazionale*, etc.

It 165   GENTILE, Emilio, *La Voce e l'eta giolittiana*, Milan: Pan, 1972. 215pp.

It 166   LEONI, Francesco, *Origini del nazionalismo italiano*, Naples: Morano, 1970. 123pp. Bib. 115-17.

It 167   MOLINELLI, Raffaele, *I nazionalisti italiani e l'intervento*, Urbino: Argalia, 1973. 152pp. Bib. 147-8.

It 168   MOLINELLI, Raffaele, *Per una storia del nazionalismo italiano*, Urbino: Argalia, 1966. 207pp.

It 169   PERFETTI, Francesco (ed.), *Il nazionalismo italiano*, intro. by Mario Tedeschi, Milan: Ed. del Borghese, 1969. 332pp. Anthology.

It 170   PERFETTI, Francesco (ed.), *Il nazionalismo italiano dalle origini alla fusione col fascismo.* Bologna: Cappelli, 1977. 292pp. Anthology.

It 171   PREZZOLINI, Giuseppe, *La Voce, 1908-1913: cronaca, antalogia e fortuna di una rivista: con la collaborazione di Emilio Gentile e di Vanni Scheiwiller*, Milan: Rusconi, 1974. 1032pp.

It 172   PREZZOLINI, Giuseppe and PAPINI, Giovanni, *Vecchio e nuovo nazionalismo*, Milan: Lombardo, 1914. 131pp. Repr. Rome: Volpe, 1967. On the breach with Corradini and the Nationalists.

It 173   RONZIO, Romolo, *La fusione del nazionalismo con il fascismo*, Rome: Edizione Italiane, 1943. xviii, 254pp.

It 174   SALVADORI, M., 'Nationalism in modern Italy: 1915 and after'. *Orbis*, **10**, 1976. pp. 1157-75.

It 175   VALLAURI, Carlo, 'Dal nazionalismo al fascismo'. *STOR. E POLIT.*, **5** (**3**), 1966. pp. 465-79.

It 176   VALLAURI, Carlo, 'Il programma economico nazionalista e la genesi del corporativismo fascista'. *STOR. E POLIT.*, **7** (**4**), 1968. pp. 612-36.

It 177   VANNONI, Gianni, 'Maffeo Pantaleoni di fronte al fascismo'. *STOR. E POLIT.*, **13** (**4**), 1974. pp. 598-620. Pantaleoni (1857-1924) Nationalist economist.

It 178   VOLPE, Gioacchino, *L'Italia in cammino: l'ultimo cinquantennio*, 3rd edn, Milan: Fratelli, 1931. xxviii, 278pp. History of Italian Nationalism by a fascist historian. Repr. Rome: Volpe, 1973.

It 179   VOLPE, Gioacchino, 'Il nazionalismo tra le due guerre'. *Veltro*, **8**, 1964, pp. 481-504.

Gabriele D'Annunzio (1863-1938)

It 180   ALATRI, Paolo, *Nitti, D'Annunzio e la questione adriatica*, Milan: Feltrinelli, 1976. 544pp. First pub. 1959.

It 181   ANNUNZIO, Gabriele d', *Carteggio D'Annunzio-Mussolini, 1919-1938*, ed. Renzo de Felice e Emilio Mariano, Milan: Mondadori,

1971. cxxii, 511pp. Bib. 497-501. Correspondence between D'Annunzio and Mussolini.

It 182   ANNUNZIO, Gabriele d', *La penultima ventura: scritti e discorsi fiumani*, ed. Renzo de Felice, Milan: Mondadori, 1974. lxxxvi, 580pp. Bib. 569-72.

It 183   ANNUNZIO, Gabriele d', *Scritti politici*, intro. and ed. by Paolo Alatri, Milan: Feltrinelli, 1980. 308pp. Bib. 51-3.

It 184   BONDY, François, 'D'Annunzio and Mussolini'. *Encounter*, **38** (**4**), 1972. pp. 61-6.

It 185   BRAGANTI, Allesandra, 'Letteratura e fascismo nel carteggio D'Annunzio-Mussolini'. *MOV. DI LIBERAZIONE IN ITALIA*, **25** (**110**), 1973. pp. 79-104.

It 186   FELICE, Renzo de, *La Carta del Carnaro: nei testi di Alceste De Ambris e di Gabriele d'Annunzio*, Bologna: Il Mulino. 1974. 141pp. Doc. 77-141. On the neosyndicalist constitution drawn up for Fiume by D'Annunzio and De Ambris.

It 187   FELICE, Renzo de, *D'Annunzio politico, 1918-1938*, Rome: Laterza, 1978. xv, 284pp.

It 188   FELICE, Renzo de, *Sindicalismo rivoluzionario e fiumanesimo nel carteggio De Ambris-D'Annunzio, 1919-1922*, Brescia: Morcelliana, 1966. 364pp. Carteggio 157-260. Appendix 261-352 contains writings of De Ambris.

It 189   LEDEEN, Michael A., *The First Duce: D'Annunzio at Fiume*, Baltimore: Johns Hopkins University Press, 1977. xi, 225pp. Tr. of *D'Annunzio a Fiume*.

It 190   RIZZO, Giovanni, *D'Annunzio e Mussolini: le verità sui loro rapporti*, Bologna: Cappelli, 1960. 317pp.

It 191   SALINARI, Carlo, 'Le origini del nazionalismo e l'ideologia di Pascoli e D'Annunzio'. *Societa*, **14** (**3**), 1958. pp. 459-86.

It 192   VALERI, Nino, *D'Annunzio davanti al fascismo: con documenti inediti*, Florence: Le Monnier, 1963. 179pp.

Filippo Tommaso Marinetti and Futurism

It 193   GENTILE, Emilio, 'La politica di Marinetti'. *STOR. CONTEMP.*, **7** (**3**), 1976. pp. 415-38.

It 194   JOLL, James, *Intellectuals in politics: three biographical essays*, London: Weidenfeld & Nicolson, 1960. xiv, 203pp. Leon Blum, Walter Rathenau, F. T. Marinetti.

It 195   MARINETTI, Filippo Tommaso, *Opere*, Milan: Mondadori, 1968. 4 vols. [in 3].

It 196   OESTEREICHER, Emil, 'Fascism and the intellectuals: the case of Italian futurism'. *SOC. RES.*, **41** (**3**), 1974. pp. 515-33.

It 197   SHARKEY, Stephen R. and DOMBROWSKI, Robert S., 'Revolution, myth and mythical politics: the futurist solution'. *J. OF EUR. STUD.*, **6** (**4**), 1976. pp. 231-47.

The Syndicalists and Fascism

It 198   ASSENATO, Mario, 'Germi di fascismo negli intellettuali secondari in Puglia, 1913-1914'. *Il Ponte*, **29** (**1**), 1973. pp. 63-82; **29** (**2/3**). pp. 316-36. Syndicalists in Apulia.

It 199   BARBADORO, Idomeneo, *Storia del sindicalismo italiano dalla nascito al fascismo*, Florence: La Nuova Italia, 1973. 2 vols.

It 200   BEGNAC, Ivon de, *L'arcangelo sindicalista (Filippo Corridoni): con un'appendice documentaria*, Verona: Mondadori, 1943. 926pp. Filippo Corridoni (1888-1915) leading syndicalist who became a cult figure in fascist Italy.

It 201   BERTRAND, Charles Lloyd, *Revolutionary Syndicalism in Italy, 1912-1922*, University of Wisconsin thesis, 1969. UM 69-22347. 399pp.

It 202   DEANGELIS, Susanna, 'Sergio Panunzio: rivoluzione e o stato dei sindicati'. *STOR. CONTEMP.*, **11** (**6**), 1980. pp. 969-87.

It 203   GREGOR, A. James, *Sergio Panunzio: il sindicalismo ed il fondamento razionalo del fascismo*, Rome: Volpe, 1978. xi, 326pp.

It 204   PALOSCIA, Leonardo, *La concezione sindicalista di Sergio Panunzio*, pref. by Francesco Carnelutti, Rome: Gismondi, 1949. 53pp. Bib. 49-53.

It 205   MALUSARDI, Edoardo, *Elementi di storia del sindicalismo fascista*, pref. by G. Bottai, 3rd edn, Lanciano: Carabba, 1938. xi, 198pp.

It 206   MELIS, Renato, *Sindicalisti italiani; in una scelta di scritti di Art. Labriola, E. Leone, A. O. Olivetti, S. Panunzio*. Rome: Volpe, 1964. 377pp. Bib. 42.

It 207   ROBERTS, David D., *The Syndicalist Tradition and Italian Fascism*, Manchester: University Press. Chapel Hill; University of N. Carolina Press, 1979. x, 410pp. Bib. 390-400.

It 208   ROVERI, Allessandro, *Dal sindicalismo rivoluzionario al fascismo:*

capitalismo agrario e socialismo nel Ferrarese, 1870-1920, Florence: La Nuova Italia, 1972. xiii, 397pp.

It 209   SCHWARZENBACH, Claudio, *Il sindicalismo fascista*, Milan: Mursia, 1972. 142pp.

It 210   VALIANI, Leo, 'Il movimento sindicale sotto il fascismo, 1929-1939'. In VALIANI, Leo (ed.), *Dall'antifascismo alla Resistenza*, Milan: Feltrinelli, 1959. pp. 39-70.

The Origins of Fascism, 1915-22

It 211   ALATRI, Paolo, *Le origini del fascismo*, 5th edn, Rome: Ed. Riuniti, 1971. xxvii, 381pp. Bib. 280-310.

It 212   BAGLIERI, Joseph, 'Italian fascism and the crisis of liberal hegemony. 1901-1922'. In LARSEN, S.U. Gn 36. pp. 318-36.

It 213   BARTOLOTTI, Mirella (ed.), *Le origini del fascismo*, Bologna: Zanichelli, 1969. 204pp. Bib. 199-204.

It 214   BONOMI, Ivanoe, *From Socialism to Fascism: a study of contemporary Italy*, London, Hopkinson, 1924. xiii, 147pp. Tr. of *Dal socialismo al fascismo*, Rome, Formiggini, 1924, by John Murray.

It 215   BONOMI, Ivanoe, *La politica italiana dopo Vittorio Veneto*, Turin: Einaudi, 1953. 173pp. Memoirs of the veteran socialist leader (1873-1951) covering the period from the end of the war to July 1922.

It 216   CATALANO, Franco, *Potere economico e fascismo: la crisi del dopoguerra, 1919-1921*, Milan: Lerici, 1964. 340pp. Bib. 327-40.

It 217   FARNETI, Paolo, 'La crisi della democrazia italiana e l'avvento del fascismo, 1919-1922' *RIV. ITAL. SCI POLIT.*, **5** (**1**), 1975. pp. 45-82.

It 218   FEDELI, Ugo, *Un decennio di storia italiana, 1914-1924: la nascita del fascismo: conversazione tenute in Ivrea al Centro Culturale Olivetti gennaio-marzo 1959*, Ivrea: Centro Culturale Olivetti, 1959. 82pp.

It 219   FELICE, Renzo de, 'Le origini del fascismo'. In *Nuove Questione di Storia Contemporanea*, Milan: Marzorati, 1968. Vol. 1. pp. 719-98.

It 220   GIOVANNINI, Claudio, *L'Italia da Vittorio Veneto all'Aventino: storia politica delle origini del fascismo, 1918-1925*, Bologna: Patron, 1972. x, 429pp.

It 221   GRANATA, Ivano, 'Storia nazionale e storia locale: alcune considerazioni sulla problematica del fascismo delle origini, 1919-1922'. *STOR. CONTEMP.*, **11** (**3**), 1980. pp. 503-44.

It 222   GRANDI, Dino, *Giovani*, Bologna: Zanichelli, 1941. vii, 238pp. Essays 1913-20 by war veteran who became a leading fascist.

It 223   GRANDI, Dino, *Le origini e la missione del fascismo*, Bologna: Campitelli, 1922. 106pp.

It 224   KOGAN, Norman, 'The origins of Italian fascism'. *Polity*, 2 (1), 1969. pp. 100-5. Review article.

It 225   LANZILLO, Agostino, *Le rivoluzioni del dopoguerra: critiche e diagnosi*, Citta di Castello: Il Solco, 1922. xx, 258pp. Author a radical syndicalist who became a fascist.

It 226   MACK SMITH, Dennis, 'Origini del fascismo: riesame di alcuni aspetti e di alcune personalità della moderna storia d'Italia'. *Occidente*, 9 (1), 1953. pp. 40-7.

It 227   PAPA, Emilio Raffaele, *Fascismo e cultura: il prefascismo*, 3rd edn, Venice: Marsilio, 1978. 317pp.

It 228   PASSERIN D'ENTREVES, Ettore (ed.), *Dal nazionalismo al primo fascismo*, Turin: Giappichelli, 1967. viii. 148pp.

It 229   PETRACCHI, Giorgio, 'L'avvento del fascismo in un inedito per l'Italia di Giacento Menotti Serrati'. *STOR. CONTEMP.* 11 (4), 1980. pp. 635-56.

It 230   PROCACCI, Giuliano, 'Appunti in tema di crisi dello stato liberale e di origini del fascismo'. *STUD. STOR.*, 6 (2), 1965. pp. 221-37.

It 231   PROCACCI, Giovanna, 'Italy: from interventionism to fascism, 1917-1919'. *J. OF CONTEMP. HIST.*, 3 (4), 1968. pp. 153-76.

It 232   ROCCA, Massimo, *Come il fascismo divenne una dittatura: storia interna del fascismo dal 1914-1925*, Milan: Ed. Librarie Italiane, 1952. 370pp. Author was one of the fascist moderates who was expelled from the Party and exiled.

It 233   ROCCA, Massimo, *Il primo fascismo*, Rome: Volpe, 1964. 245pp.

It 234   SALVEMINI, Gaetano, *The Origins of Fascism in Italy*, intro. by R. Vivarelli, New York: Harper & Row, 1973. xx, 445pp. Bib. xiv-xx. Tr. of *Origini del fascismo*, Feltrinelli, 1966, by R. Vivarelli.

It 235   TRANFAGLIA, Nicola, 'Dalla neutralita italiana alle origini del fascismo'. *STUD. STOR.*, 10 (2), 1969. pp. 334-86.

It 236   TASCA, Angelo [Angelo Rossi (pseud.)], *The Rise of Italian Fascism*, pref. by Herman Finer, New York: Fertig, 1966. xvi, 376pp. Tr. of *La naissance du fascisme*, 1938, by Peter and Dorothy Wait.

Longer Italian edn, *Nascita e avvento del fascismo: l'Italia dal 1918 al 1922*, Florence, 1950.

t 237   VALERI, Nino, *Da Giolitti a Mussolini: momenti della crisi del liberalismo*, Milan: Il Saggiatore, 1967. 255pp.

t 238   VALERI, Nino, 'Sulle origini del fascismo'. In ROTA, Ettore, (ed.), *Questioni di storia contemporanea*, Milan: Marzorati, 1953. Vol. **3**. pp. 733–58. Bibliographical article.

t 239   VAUSSARD, Maurice, *Avènement d'une dictature: l'Italie entre la guerre et le fascisme, 1915-1925*, Paris: Hachette, 1971. 204pp.

t 240   VIVARELLI, Roberto, *Il dopoguerra in Italia e l'avvento del fascismo, 1918-1922*, Naples: Ist. Italiano per gli Studi Storici, 1967. Vol. 1. 620pp.

t 241   VIVARELLI, Roberto, *Il fallimento del liberalismo: studi sulle origini del fascismo*, Bologna: Il Mulino, 1981. 353pp.

t 242   VOLPE, Gioacchino, *Guerra, dopoguerra, fascismo*, Venice: La Nuovo Italia, 1928. viii, 470pp. Collection of essays on the origins of fascism.

The Origins of Fascism: Local Studies

t 243   ARBIZZANI, Luigi, 'L'avvento del fascismo nel Bolognese, 1920-1922'. *MOV. OPERAIO E SOC.*, **10** (2), 1964. pp. 83–102; **10** (3/4), 1964. pp. 253–76.

t 244   BENVENUTI, Sergio, *Il fascismo nelle Venezia Tridentina, 1919-1924*, Trento: Soc. di Studi Trentini di Scienze Storiche, 1976. viii, 299pp.

t 245   BERMANI, Cesare, *Novara 1922: battaglia al fascismo*, Rome: Nuove Edizioni Operaie, 1978. 346pp. Bib. 311–19.

t 246   CANTAGALLI, Roberto, *Storia del fascismo fiorentino, 1919-1925*, Florence: Vallecchi, 1972. x, 448pp.

t 247   CARDOZA, Anthony L., *Agrarian Élites and Italian Fascism: the province of Bologna, 1901-1926*. Princeton: University Press, 1982. xvi, 477pp. Bib. 455–62. Princeton University thesis, 1975.

t 248   CASALI, Luciano, 'Fascisti, repubblicani e socialisti in Romagna nel 1922: la "conquista" di Ravenna'. *MOV. DI LIBERAZIONE IN ITALIA*, **20** (93), 1968. pp. 12–36.

t 249   CASALI, Luciano and others, *Movimento operaio e fascismo nell' Emilia Romagna, 1919-1923*, Rome: Ed, Riuniti, 1973. 363pp.

It 250   CAVANDOLI, Rolando, *Le origini del fascismo a Reggio Emilia, 1919-1923*, Rome: Ed. Riuniti, 1973. 271pp. Bib. 265-71.

It 251   COLAPIETRA, Raffaele, 'Alcuni documenti sui primi anni del fascismo a Napoli, 1923-1924.' *STOR. E POLIT.*, **8** (**2**), 1969. pp. 253-62.

It 252   COLAPIETRA, Raffaele, *Napoli tra dopoguerra e fascismo*, Milan: Feltrinelli, 1962. 323pp.

It 253   COLARIZI, Simona, *Dopoguerra e fascismo in Puglia, 1919-1926*, pref. by Renzo de Felice, Bari: Laterza, 1971. vii, 453pp.

It 254   CORNER, Paul, *Fascism in Ferrara, 1915-1925*, Oxford: University Press, 1975. xii, 300pp. Bib. 289-95. Oxford University thesis, 1971.

It 255   DEMERS, Francis Joseph, 'Caporetto e il sorgere del fascismo a Cremona'. *STOR. CONTEMP.*, **8** (**3**), 1977. pp. 533-48.

It 256   DEMERS, Francis Joseph, *Le origini del fascismo a Cremona*, tr. L. de Felice, Bari; Laterza, 1979. 350pp. Columbia University thesis, 1972. UM 75-09327.

It 257   GENTILE, Emilio, 'La crisi del socialismo e la nascita del fascismo nel mantovano'. *STOR. CONTEMP.*, **10** (**4/5**), 1979. pp. 733-96.

It 258   GRANATA, Ivano, *La nascita del sindicato fascista: l'esperienza di Milano*, Bari: De Donato, 1981. 278pp.

It 259   GRANATA, Ivano, 'Il sindicalismo fascista alla conquista di Milano "rossa" gennaio-luglio 1922'. *Risorgimento*, **29** (**1/2**), 1977. pp. 58-84.

It 260   KELIKIAN, A., *Brescia, 1915-1926: from liberalism to corporatism*, Oxford University thesis, 1978.

It 261   MICCICHE, Giuseppe, *Dopoguerra e fascismo in Sicilia, 1919-1927*, Rome: Ed. Riuniti, 1976. 232pp.

It 262   MILLOZZI, Michele, *Le origini del fascismo nell'Anconetano*, Urbino: Argalia, 1974. 163pp. Bib. 117-54.

It 263   NIEDDU, Luigi, *Dal combattentismo al fascismo in Sardegna*, intro. by Franco Catalano, Milan: Vangelista, 1979. 344pp.

It 264   ONOFRI, Nazario Sauro, *La straga di pallazo d'accursio: origine e nascita del fascismo bolognese, 1919-1920*, Milan: Feltrinelli, 1980. 326pp.

It 265   PIVA, Francesco, *Lotte contadine e origini del fascismo: Padova Venezia, 1919-1922*, Venice: Marsilio, 1977. 300pp.

It 266   PRETI, Luigi, *Le lotte agrarie nella Valle Padana*, Turin: Einaudi, 1955. 481pp.

It 267   PREZIOSI, Anna Maria, *Borghesia e fascismo in Friuli negli anni 1920-1922*, Rome: Bonacci, 1980. 221pp.

It 268   RAMELLA, Secondo, *L'azione sindacale nell'agro novarese dal 1918 al 1925: socialisti e fascisti a confronto*, Novara: Riva, 1962. 151pp.

It 269   ROVERI, Alessandro, 'Il fascismo ferrarese nel 1919-1920', *Annali dell'Istituto Giangiacome Feltrinelli*, 1972. pp. 106-54.

It 270   ROVERI, Alessandro, *Le origini del fascismo a Ferrara, 1918-1921*, Milan: Feltrinelli, 1974. 232pp. Doc. 215-23.

It 271   SECHI, Salvatore, *Dopoguerra e fascismo in Sardegna: il movimento autonomistico nella crisi dello stato liberale, 1918-1926*, Turin: Einaudi, 1970. 504pp. On the Partito Sardo d'Azione.

It 272   SILVESTRI, Carlo, *Dalla redenzione al fascismo: Trieste, 1918-1922*, Udine: Del Bianco, 1959. xv, 159pp. Bib.

It 273   SNOWDEN, Frank M., 'From Sharecropper to proletarian: the background to fascism in rural Tuscany, 1880-1920'. In DAVIS John A. (ed.), *Gramsci and Italy's Passive Revolution*, London: Croom Helm. New York: Barnes & Noble, 1979. pp. 136-71.

It 274   SQUERI, Lawrence Louis, *Politics in Parma, 1900-1925: the rise of fascism*, University of Pennsylvania thesis, 1976. UM 77-10225. 301pp.

It 275   VAINI, Mario, *Le origini del fascismo a Mantova, 1914-1922*, pref. by Gastone Manacorda, Rome: Ed. Riuniti, 1961. 266pp. Bib. 180-3.

It 276   VECCHIA, Pier A., *Storia del fascismo bresciano, 1919-1922*, pref. by A. Turati, Brescia: Vannini, 1929. 287pp.

Paramilitary Groups, Squadrismo and Violence

It 277   AQUARONE, Alberto, 'Violenza e consenso nel fascismo italiano'. *STOR. CONTEMP.*, **10** (**1**), 1978. pp. 145-55.

It 278   CORDOVA, Ferdinando, *Arditi e Legionari d'annunziani: crisi ed evoluzione del combattentismo nella politica del dopoguerra, 1918-1926*, Padua: Marsilio, 1969. xi, 245pp. Bib. 186-204.

It 279   CANCOGNI, Manlio, *Storia dello squadrismo*, Milan: Longanesi, 1959. 206pp.

It 280   LEDEEN, Michael A., 'Italy: war as a style of life'. In WARD, Stephen, R. (ed.), *The War Generation*, Port Washington: Kennikat Press, 1975. pp. 104–34.

It 281   LYTTLETON, Adrian, 'Fascism and violence in post-war Italy: political strategy and social conflict'. In MOMMSEN, W.J. and HIRSCHFELD, Gerhard (eds), *Social Protest, Violence and Terror in Nineteenth- and Twentieth-century Europe*, London: Macmillan, 1982. pp. 257–74.

It 282   PETERSEN, Jens, 'Violence in Italian fascism, 1919–1925'. In MOMMSEN, W.J., and HIRSCHFELD, Gerhard, It 281, pp. 275–99.

It 283   ROVERI, Alessandro, *L'affermazione dello squadrismo fascista nelle campagne ferraresi, 1921–1922*, Ferrara: Italo Bovolenta Ed., 1979. ix, 120pp. Doc. 71–113.

It 284   SABBATUCCI, Giovanni, *I combattenti nel primo dopoguerra*, Bari: Laterza, 1974. vi, 423pp. On the pre-war paramilitary organisations including Associazione Nazionale Combattenti e Reduci.

It 285   TUNINETTI, Dante Maria, *Squadrismo, squadristi piemontesi*, Rome: Pinciana di U. Zuccucci, 1942. 309pp.

It 286   VICENTINI, Raffaele, *Il movimento fascista veneto attraverso il diario di uno squadrista*, pref. by Luigi Zambon, Venice: Zanetti, 1935. x, 278pp.

Fascism, 1922–39

It 287   BARNES, John Strachey, *The Universal Aspects of Fascism*, London: Williams & Norgate, 1928. xxi, 247pp. Bib. 243–7.

It 288   BALBO, Italo, *Diario 1922*, Milan: Mondadori, 1932. 214pp.

It 289   BONO, Emilio de, defendant, *Il delitto Matteotti tra il Viminale e l'Aventino: dagli atti del processo De Bono davanti all' Alta Corte di Giustizia*, ed. Giuseppe Rossini, Bologna: Il Mulino, 1966. 1037pp.

It 290   ROSSI, Cesare, *Il delitto Matteotti nei procedimenti giudiziari e nelle polemiche giornalistiche*, Milan: Ceschina, 1965. 591pp.

It 291   SILVESTRI, Carlo, *Matteotti, Mussolini e il dramma italiano*, Rome: Ruffolo, 1947. xliii, 386pp.

It 292   BORGESE, Giuseppe Antonio, *Goliath: the march of fascism*, New York: Viking Press, 1937. ix, 483pp. Classic of anti-fascism.

It 293   CHIURCO, Giorgio Alberto, *Storia della rivoluzione fascista*, Florence: Vallecchi, 1929. 5 vols. Bib. vol. 5. 437-68.

It 294   COLAPIETRA, Raffaele, 'La marcia su Roma'. *STOR. E POLIT.*, **3** (**2**), 1964. pp. 242-57. Review of Repaci. See It 297.

It 295   FERRARIS, Efrem, *Le marcia su Roma: veduta di Viminale*, Rome: Ed. Leonardo, 1946. 148pp.

It 296   SAITTA, Armando, 'La marche sur Rome (1922) et la classe politique italienne'. *INF. HIST.*, **29** (**4**), 1967. pp. 156-61.

It 297   REPACI, Antonino, *La marcia su Roma: mito e realtà*, Rome; Canesi, 1963. 2 vols. Bib. vol. 2, 463-70.

It 298   VALERI, Nino, 'La marcia su Roma'. In *Fascismo e Antifascismo*. See It 128, vol. 1.

It 299   COSTAMAGNA, Carlo, *Storia e dottrina del fascismo*, Turin: UTET, 1938. xv, 454pp.

It 300   EBENSTEIN, William, *Fascist Italy*, New York; American Book Co., 1939. x, 310pp. Bib. 301-5.

It 301   FARINACCI, Roberto, *Storia del fascismo*, Cremona: Cremona Nuova, 1940. 419pp.

It 302   FARINACCI, Roberto, *Storia della rivoluzione fascista*, Cremona; Cremona Nuova, 1937-9. 3 vols. [in 1]. Written largely by Giorgio Masi.

It 303   FERRARI, Francesco Luigi, *Le Régime fasciste italien*, Paris; Spes, 1928. 374pp. By an anti-fascist exile.

It 304   FERRERO, Guglielmo, *Four Years of Fascism*, London: King, 1924. 133pp. Tr. of *Da Fiume a Roma*, by E. W. Dickes.

It 305   GOAD, Harold Elsdale, *The Making of the Corporative State: a study of fascist development*, rev. edn. London: Christophers, 1934. 149pp. Bib. 141-5.

It 306   GORGOLINI, Pietro, *The Fascist Movement in Italian Life*, pref. by Benito Mussolini, ed. and intro. by M.D. Petre, London: Unwin, 1923. 216pp. Tr. of *Il fascismo nella vita italiana*, Turin, 1923, by M.D. Petre.

It 307   LYTTLETON, Adrian, 'Fascism in Italy: the second wave'. *J. OF CONTEMP. HIST.*, **1** (**1**), 1966. pp. 75-100.

It 308   LYTTLETON, Adrian, *The Seizure of Power: fascism in Italy 1919-1929*, London: Weidenfeld & Nicolson, 1973. 544pp. Bib. 515-26.

It 309   MAIER, Charles S., *Recasting Bourgeois Europe: stabilisation in France, Germany and Italy in the decade after World War 1*, Princeton: University Press, 1975. xiv, 650pp. Bib. 596–607.

It 310   MISSIROLI, Mario, *Il fascismo e il colpo di stato dell'ottobre 1922*, Bologna: Cappelli, 1966. 244pp. Repr. of essays first pub. 1922–4.

It 311   NITTI, Francesco Saverio, *Bolshevism, Fascism and Democracy*, London: Allen & Unwin. New York: Macmillan, 1927. 223pp. Tr. of *Bolscevismo, fascismo e democrazia*, 1927, by Margaret M. Green.

It 312   PREZZOLINI, Giuseppe, *Fascism*, tr. Kathleen Macmillan, London; Methuen, 1926. New York: Dutton, 1927. xiii, 201pp.

It 313   PITIGLIAMI, Fausto, *The Italian Corporative State*, London: King. New York: Macmillan, 1933. xxv, 293pp. Bib. 285–6.

It 314   ROCCA, Massimo, *Idee sul fascismo*, Florence: La Voce, 1924. 357pp.

It 315   SALVATORELLI, Luigi, *Nazionalfascismo*, pref. by Giorgio Amendola, Turin: Einaudi, 1977. xxv, 124pp. First pub. 1923.

It 316   SALVEMINI, Gaetano, *The Fascist Dictatorship in Italy*, Vol. 1, New York: Holt, 1927. London: Cape, 1929. 328pp.

It 317   SCHNEIDER, Herbert Wallace, *Making the Fascist State*, New York: Fertig, 1968. xi, 392pp. Bib. 365–85. First pub. New York: Oxford University Press, 1928.

It 318   SILLANI, Tomaso (ed.), *L'état mussolinien et les réalisations du fascisme en études et documents*, Paris: Plon, 1931. 379pp. Tr. of *Lo stato mussoliniano e le realizzazione del fascismo nella nazione*, 1930.

It 319   STURZO, Luigi, *Italy and Fascism*; tr. Barbara Barclay Carter, pref. by Gilbert Murray, New York: Fertig, 1967. This tr. first pub. by Faber & Gwyer, 1926. Author (1871–1959) was founder of the Partito Popolare Italiano; exiled in 1924.

It 320   TRENTIN, Silvio, *Dieci anni di fascismo totalitario in Italia: dall'istituzione de Tribunale Speciale alla proclamazione dell'Impero, 1926–1936*, pref. by Enzo Santarelli, Rome: Ed. Riuniti, 1975. 267pp. Bib. 267. Tr. of *Dix ans de fascisme en Italie*.

It 321   VILLARI, Luigi, *The Awakening of Italy: the fascist regeneration*, London: Methuen, 1924. v, 292pp. Another edn, *The Fascist Experiment*, London: Faber & Gwyer, 1926.

It 322   VOLPE, Gioacchino, *History of the Fascist Movement*, Rome: Ed. di Novissima, 1936. 152pp. Tr of article in *Enciclopedia Italiana*, 1932, vol. 10, pp. 851–78. Author a leading fascist historian.

It 323   VOLPE, Gioacchino, *Storia del movimento fascista*, Milan: Ist per gli Studi di Politica Nazionale e Internazionale, 1939. 246pp.

Fascist Ideology

It 324   BERTELE, Aldo, *Aspetti ideologici del fascismo*, Turin: Druetto, 1930. 237pp.

It 325   CARLI, Mario and FANELLI, Giuseppe Attilio (eds), *Antologia degli scrittori fascisti*, Florence; Bemporad, 1931. ix, 673pp.

It 326   CANEPA, Antonio, *Sistema di dottrina del fascismo*, Rome: Formiggini, 1937. 3 vols.

It 327   EVOLA, Julius Cesare Andrea, *Il fascismo: saggio di una analisi dal punto di vista della destra*, 2nd edn, Rome: Volpe, 1970. 219pp. By the anti-semite and leading racial theorist under Mussolini.

It 328   GENTILE, Emilio, 'Alcune considerazioni sull'ideologia del fascismo'. *STOR. CONTEMP.*, **5** (**1**), 1974. pp. 115–25.

It 329   GENTILE, Emilio, *Le origini dell'ideologia fascista, 1918–1925*, Bari: Laterza, 1975. x, 475pp.

It 330   GERMINO, Dante, 'Italian fascism in the history of political thought'. *MIDWEST. J. OF POLIT. SCI.*, **8** (**2**), 1964. pp. 109–26.

It 331   GREGOR, A. James, *The Ideology of fascism: the rationale of totalitarianism*, New York: Free Press, 1969. xv, 493pp. Bib. 455–67.

It 332   NOCE, Augusto del, 'Les origines intellectuelles du fascisme'. *Contrepoint*, **26**, 1978. pp. 9–28. Based on de Felice's work.

It 333   LYTTLETON, Adrian (ed.), *Italian Fascisms from Pareto to Gentile*, tr. Douglas Parmée, London: Cape. New York: Harper, 1973. 318pp.

It 334   PANUNZIO, Sergio, *Che cos'è fascismo*, Milan; Alpes, 1924. 85pp.

It 335   PANUNZIO, Sergio, *Teoria generale dello stato fascista*, 2nd edn, Padua: Cedam, 1939. xix, 597pp.

It 336   PETERSEN, Jens, 'Die Entstehung des Totalitarismusbegriffs in Italien'. In FUNKE, Manfred (ed.), *Totalitarismus*, Düsseldorf: Droste, 1978.

The Fascist Party

It 337   CANEPA, Antonio, *L'organizzazione del PNF*, Palermo: Ciuni, 1939. 277pp.

It 338   GAMBINO, Antonio, *Storia del PNF*, Milan: Sugar, 1962. 199pp.

It 339   GERMINO, Dante, *The Italian Fascist Party in Power: a study in totalitarian rule*, Minneapolis: University Press, 1959. xii, 181pp. Harvard University thesis, 1956.

It 340   FELICE, Renzo de, 'Primi elementi sul finanziamento del fascismo dalle origini al 1924'. *RIV. STOR DEL SOC.*, **7** (**22**), 1964. pp. 223-51.

It 341   RAPPA, Sebastian B., *Achille Starace and the Italian Fascist Party, 1931-1939: the creation of the totalitarian myth*, New York University thesis, 1977. UM 78-03130. 308pp.

It 342   SAITTA, Armando, 'Les différent groups qui coexistèrent à l'intérieur du fascisme'. *Crit. Stor.*, **12**, 1975. pp. 389-416.

It 343   SIVINI, Giordano, 'Sul finanziamento del fascismo dalle origini al 1924'. *RIV. STOR. DEL SOC.*, **7** (**23**), 1964. pp. 627-30.

Agriculture and Agrarian Affairs

It 344   CALICE, Nino, 'La politica agraria fascista in Basilicata'. *STUD. STOR.*, **19** (**2**), 1978. pp. 397-423.

It 345   COHEN, Jon S., 'Fascism and agriculture in Italy: policies and consequences'. *ECON. HIST. REV.*, **32** (**1**), 1979. pp. 70-87.

It 346   CORNER, Paul, 'Considerazioni sull'agricoltura capitalistica durante il fascismo'. *QUAD. STOR.*, **29/30**, 1975. pp. 519-29.

It 347   CORNER, Paul, 'Fascist agrarian policy and the Italian economy in the inter-war years'. In DAVIS, John A. (ed.), *Gramsci and Italy's Passive Revolution*, London: Croom Helm. New York: Barnes & Noble, 1979. pp. 239-74.

It 348   MARUCCO, Dora, 'Note sulla mezzadria al'avvento del fascismo'. *RIV. DI STOR. CONTEMP.*, **3** (**3**), 1974. pp. 377-88. On the share-cropping system.

It 349   PRETI, Domenico, 'La politica agraria del fascismo: note introduttive'. *STUD. STOR.*, **14** (**4**, 1973. pp. 802-69.

It 350   SCHMIDT, Carl Theodore, *The Plough and the Sword: labour*

and property in fascist Italy, New York: Columbia University Press, 1938.
vii, 197pp. Bib. 177–89.

It 351   SERENI, Emilio, *La questione agraria della rinascita nazionale italiana*, Rome: Einaudi, 1946. 461pp.

The Organisation of the State

It 352   AQUARONE, Alberto, *L'organizzazione dello stato totalitario*, Turin: Einaudi, 1965. ix, 620pp.

It 353   CASSESE, Sabino, *La formazione dello stato amministrativo*, Milan: Giuffre, 1974. 400pp. Collected articles on economic planning and administration.

It 354   JOCTEAU, Gian Carlo, *La magistratura e i conflitti di lavoro durante il fascismo, 1926–1934*, pref. by Nicola Tranfaglia, Milan: Feltrinelli, 1978. xii, 455pp.

It 355   LETO, Guido, *OVRA fascismo, anti-fascismo*, 2nd edn, Bologna: Cappelli, 1952. 262pp. By the political police chief under Mussolini.

It 356   LETO, Guido, *Polizia segreta in Italia*, Rome: Bianco, 1961. x, 249pp.

It 357   MARTINELLI, Franco, *L'OVRA: fatti e retroscena della polizia politica fascista*, Milan: De Vecchi, 1967. 610pp.

It 358   MELOGRANI, Piero, *Rapporti segreti della polizia fascista, 1938–1940*, Rome: Laterza, 1979. 135pp. Police in Milan.

It 359   MORGAN, Philip, 'I primi podestà fascisti, 1926–32'. *STOR. CONTEMP.*, **9**, 1978. pp. 407–23.

It 360   *Il Ponte*, **8** (**10**), 1952. 'Trent'anni dopo'. Special issue on life under the fascist regime.

It 361   PRELOT, Marcel, *L'Empire fasciste: les origines, les tendances, et les institutions de la dictature et du corporatisme italien*, Paris: Librairie du Recueil, 1936. xii, 258pp.

It 362   QUAZZA, Guido, (ed.), *Fascismo e società italiana*, Turin: Einaudi, 1973. 253pp. Essays on the economy by Castronovo, the army by Rochat, the magistrature by Guida Neppi Modona, the Church by Giovanni Miccoli, culture by Norberto Bobbio.

It 363   ROSSI, Cesare, *Il tribunale speciale: storia documentata*, Milan: Ceschina, 1952. 395pp.

It 364   SABBATUCCI, Giovanni, 'Fascist institutions: recent problems and interpretations'. *J. OF ITAL. HIST.*, **2** (**1**), 1979. pp. 75–92.

It 365 SCORZA, Carlo, *La notte del Gran Consiglio*, intro. by Gianfranco Bianchi, Milan: Palazzi, 1968. 222pp. Memoirs of the Fascist Party Secretary on the Grand Council.

It 366 VAUSSARD, Maurice, *La Conjuration du Grand Conseil fasciste contre Mussolini*, Paris: Del Duca, 1965. 252pp.

Youth and Education

It 367 GIUNTELLA, M. Christina, 'I gruppi universitari fascisti nel primo decennio del regime'. *MOV. DI LIBERAZIONE IN ITALIA*, **24** (**107**), 1972. pp. 3–38.

It 368 ISNENGHI, Mario, *L'educazione dell'italiano: il fascismo e l'organizazzione della cultura*, Bologna: Cappelli, 1979. 471pp.

It 369 KOON, Tracy, *Believe, Obey, Fight: political socialization of youth in fascist Italy, 1922-43*, Stanford University thesis, 1977. UM 78-02186. 507pp.

It 370 LEDEEN, Michael A., 'Italian fascism and youth'. *J. OF CONTEMP. HIST.*, **4** (**3**), 1969. pp. 137–54.

It 371 MAZZATOSTA, Teresa Maria, *Il regime fascista tra educazione e propaganda, 1935-1943*. Bologna: Cappelli, 1978. xii, 243pp.

It 372 NELLO, Paolo, *L'avanguardismo giovanile alle origini del fascismo*, Rome: Laterza, 1978. 209pp.

It 373 NELLO, Paolo, 'Mussolini e Bottai: due modi diversi di concepire l'educazione fascista della gioventù'. *STOR. CONTEMP*, **8** (**2**), 1977. pp. 335–68.

It 374 OSTENC, Michel, *L'éducation en Italie pendant le fascisme*. Paris, Inst. d'Hist. des Relations Int. Contemp. Univ. de Paris I, 1980. 422pp. Bib. 387–418.

It 375 OSTENC, Michel, 'Les étudiants fascistes italiens des années 1930'. *MOUVEMENT SOC.*, **120**, 1982. pp. 95–130.

It 376 OSTENC, Michel, 'Una tappa della fascistizzazione: la scuola e la politica dal 1925 al 1928'. *STOR. CONTEMP.*, **4** (**3**), 1973. pp. 481–505.

It 377 TOMASI, Tina, *Idealismo e fascismo nella scuola italiana*, Florence: La Nuova Italia, 1969. vi, 195pp.

It 378 WOLFF, Richard J., 'Catholicism, fascism and Italian education from the riforma Gentile to the Carta della Scuola, 1922-1939'. *HIST. OF EDUC. Q.*, **20** (**1**), 1980. pp. 3–26.

Intellectuals, Culture and Fascism

It 379   AGAZZI, Emilio, 'Benedetto Croce e l'avvento del fascismo'. *RIV. STOR. DEL SOC.*, **9 (27)**, 1966. pp. 76–103.

It 380   BENEDETTI, Ulisse, *Benedetto Croce e il fascismo*, Rome: Volpe, 1967. 239pp. Bib. 227–36.

It 381   CAPANNA, F., 'Croce di fronte al fascismo'. *NUOVA RIV. STOR.*, **48 (5/6)**, 1964. pp. 579–605.

It 382   CEVA, Bianca, 'Croce e le vicende politiche italiane fra il 1914 e il 1935 attraverso l'epistolario'. *MOV. DI LIBERAZIONE IN ITALIA*, **20 (91)**, 1968. pp. 103–15.

It 383   CROCE, Benedetto, *Scritti e discorsi politici, 1943–1947*, Bari: Laterza, 1963. 2 vols.

It 384   DI LALLA, Manlio, 'Croce, tra fascismo e antifascismo'. *Nord e Sud*, **19 (148)**, 1972. pp. 69–115.

It 385   MACK SMITH, Dennis, 'Croce and fascism'. *CAMBRIDGE J.*, **2 (6)**, 1949. pp. 343–56.

It 386   CANCOGNI, Manlio, and MANACORDA, Giuliano, *Libro e moschetto: dialogo sulla cultura italiana durante il fascismo*, Turin: ERI, 1979. 210pp. Bib. 203–10.

It 387   CANNISTRARO, Philip V., 'Burocrazia e politica culturale nello stato fascista: il Ministero della Cultura Popolare'. *STOR. CONTEMP.*, **1 (2)**, 1970. pp. 273–98.

It 388   CANNISTRARO, Philip V., *La fabbrica del consenso: fascismo e mass media*, Bari: Laterza, 1975. xvi, 498pp. New York University thesis, 1971.

It 389   CANNISTRARO, Philip V., 'Mussolini's cultural revolution: fascist or nationalist?' *J. OF CONTEMP. HIST.*, **7 (3/4)**, 1972. pp. 115–39.

It 390   DE GRAND, Alexander J., 'Curzio Malaparte: the illusion of the fascist revolution'. *J. OF CONTEMP. HIST.*, **7 (1/2)**, 1972. pp. 73–89.

It 391   GRANA, Gianni, *Malaparte*. Florence: La Nuova Italia, 1968. 165pp. Curzio Malaparte Suckert (1898–1957).

It 392   DE GRAZIA, Victoria, *The culture of consent: mass organisation of leisure in fascist Italy*, Cambridge: University Press, 1981. x, 310pp. Bib. 291–300.

It 393   CILIBERTO, Michele, 'Intellettuali e fascismo: note su Delio

Cantimori'. *STUD. STOR.*, **17** (**1**), 1976. pp. 57-93. Rennaissance historian who moved from Marxism to fascism.

It 394   DE MICHELI, Mario, *Consenso, fronda, opposizione: intellettuali nel ventennio fascista*, Milan: Clup, 1977. 159pp. Bib. 134-42.

It 395   DOMBROWSKI, Robert S., 'Le fascisme et la création littéraire en Italie'. *REV. ETUD. ITAL.*, **22** (**1/2**), 1976. pp. 32-59.

It 396   FERRAROTTO, Marinella, *L'accademia d'Italia: intellettuali e potere durante il fascismo*, Naples: Liguori, 1977. 163pp.

It 397   GENTILE, Giovanni, *Che cosa è il fascismo: discorsi e polemiche*, Florence: Vallecchi, 1925. 262pp.

It 398   GENTILE, Giovanni, *Origini e dottrini del fascismo*, 3rd edn, Rome: Ist. Nazionale Fascista di Cultura, 1934. 103pp.

It 399   GOETZ, Helmut, 'Giovanni Gentile und der Faschismus'. *GESCH. IN WISS. UND UNTERR.*, **27** (**2**), 1976. pp. 100-5.

It 400   HARRIS, Henry Silton, *The Social Philosophy of Giovanni Gentile*. Urbana: University of Illinois Press, 1960. 387pp.

It 401   ISNENGHI, Mario, *Intellettuali militanti e intellettuali funzionari: appunti sulla cultura fascista*, Turin: Einaudi, 1979. 290pp.

It 402   ISNENGHI, Mario, *Il mito della grande guerra da Marinetti a Malaparte*, Bari: Laterza, 1970. 383pp. On the psychological effects of war on intellectuals like Malaparte, Marinetti and Corradini.

It 403   LAZZARI, Giovanni, *I littoriali della cultura e dell'arte: intellettuali e potere durante il fascismo*, Naples: Liguori, 1979. 175pp.

It 404   LEONE DE CASTRIS, Arcangelo, *Egemonia e fascismo: il problema degli intellettuali negli anni trenta*, Bologna: Il Mulino, 1981. 195pp. Interpretation of Gramsci's ideas on fascism.

It 405   LUTI, Giorgino, *Cronache letterarie tra le due guerre, 1920-1940*, Bari: Laterza, 1966. 276pp.

It 406   MANGONI, Luisa, *L'interventismo della cultura: intellettuali e riviste del fascismo*, Bari: Laterza, 1974. 386pp.

It 407   MONTICONE, Alberto, 'La radio quale strumento della politica fascista: problemi di interpretazione e di metodo'. *STOR. E. POLIT.*, **17** (**4**), 1978. pp. 707-28.

It 408   NOETHER, Emiliana Pasca, 'Italian intellectuals under fascism'. *J. OF MOD. HIST.*, **43** (**4**), 1971. pp. 630-48.

It 409   RICHERI, G., 'Italian broadcasting and fascism, 1924-1937'. *Media Culture and Society*, **2** (**1**), 1980. pp. 49-56.

It 410   TURI, Gabriele, *Il fascismo e il consenso degli intellettuali*, Bologna: Il Mulino, 1980. 394pp.

It 411   VITA-FINZI, Paolo, 'Italian fascism and the intellectuals'. In WOOLF, S.J., Gn 21. pp. 226-44.

It 412   ZAGGARIO, Vito, 'Fascismo e intellettuali'. *STUD. STOR.*, **22** (2), 1981. pp. 289-304.

It 413   ZEPPI, Stelio, *Il pensiero politico dell'idealismo italiano e il nazionalfascismo*, Florence: La Nuova Italia, 1973. 303pp.

Italian Racism and Anti-Semitism

It 414   BERNARDINI, Gene, 'The origins and development of racial anti-semitism in fascist Italy'. *J. OF MOD. HIST.*, **49** (3), 1977. pp. 431-53.

It 415   CAFFAZ, Ugo, *L'antisemito italiano sotto il fascismo*, Florence: La Nuova Italia, 1975. 131pp. Bib. 124-31.

It 416   CANEPA, Andrew M., 'Half-hearted cynicism: Mussolini's racial policies'. *Patterns of Prejudice*, **13** (6), 1979. pp. 18-27.

It 417   FELICE, Renzo de, *Storia degli ebrei italiani sotto il fascismo*, pref. by Delio Cantimori, 3rd edn, Turin: Einaudi, 1972. xxxvi, 628pp. Doc. 473-616.

It 418   LEDEEN, Michael A., 'The evolution of Italian fascist anti-semitism'. *JEW. SOC. STUD.*, **37** (1), 1975. pp. 3-17.

It 419   MAYDA, Giuseppe, *Ebrei sotto Salò: la persecuzione antisemita, 1943-1945*, Milan: Feltrinelli, 1978. 274pp.

It 420   MICHAELIS, Meir, 'The Duce and the Jews: an assessment of the literature on Italian Jewry under fascism, 1922-1945'. *Yad Vashem Studies*, **11**, 1976. pp. 7-32.

It 421   MICHAELIS, Meir, *Mussolini and the Jews: German-Italian relations and the Jewish question in Italy, 1922-1945*. Oxford: University Press, 1978. xii, 472pp. Bib. 432-62.

It 422   MICHAELIS, Meir and LEDEEN, Michael A., 'Communications on the article "The evolution of Italian fascist anti-semitism", by M.A. Ledeen', *JEW. SOC. STUD.*, **39** (3), 1977. pp. 259-62.

It 423   PISANO, Giorgio, *Mussolini e gli ebrei*, Milan: FPE, 1967. 211pp.

It 424   PRETI, Luigi, *Impero fascista: africani ed ebrei*, Milan: Mursia,

1968. 375pp. Doc. 165-368. First pub. as *I mito dell'Impero e della razza nell'Italia degli anni '30.*

It 425   VALABREGA, Guido, 'Il fascismo e gli ebrei: appunti per un consuntivo storiografico'. In FONTANA, S. It 458. pp. 401-26.

Support for the Regime: Class, Sex, Generation

It 426   BERNABEI, Marco, 'La base di massa del fascismo agrario'. STOR. CONTEMP., **6** (**1**), 1975. pp. 123-53. Fascist farm-workers in the Po Valley.

It 427   BARNES, Samuel H., 'The legacy of fascism: generational difference in Italian political attitudes and behaviour'. *COMP. POLIT. STUD.*, **5** (**1**), 1972. pp. 41-57.

It 428   CORNER, Paul, 'La base di massa del fascismo: il casso di Ferrara'. *ITAL. CONTEMP.*, **26** (**114**), 1974. pp. 5-31.

It 429   CATALANO, Franco, *Fascismo e piccola borghesia: crisi economica, cultura e dittatura in Italia, 1923-1925*, Milan: Feltrinelli, 1979. 402pp. Bib. 383-94.

It 430   DE GRAND, Alexander J., 'Women under Italian fascism'. *HIST. J.*, **19** (**4**), 1976. pp. 947-68.

It 431   FELICE, Renzo de, 'Italian fascism and the middle classes'. In LARSEN, S.U., Gn 36. pp. 312-17.

It 432   LANARO, Silvio, *Nazione e laboro: saggio sulla cultura borghese in Italia 1870-1925*, Venice: Marsilio, 1979. 296pp. Includes the middle-class roots of fascism.

It 433   LEDEEN, Michael A., 'Fascism and the generation gap'. *EUR. STUD. REV.*, **1** (**3**), 1971. pp. 275-83.

It 434   MACCIOCCHI, Maria-Antoinietta, *La donna nera: consenso femminile e fascismo*, Milan: Feltrinelli, 1976. 162pp. Bib. 157-9.

It 435   MORI, Renato, 'Considerazioni e ricordi sul "consenso" al regime'. *STOR. E POLIT.*, **16** (**1**), 1977. pp. 135-42.

It 436   PETERSEN, Jens, 'Elettorato e base sociale del fascismo negli anni venti'. *STUD. STOR.*, **16** (**3**), 1975. pp. 627-69.

It 437   ROBERTS, David D., 'Petty bourgeois fascism in Italy: form and content'. In LARSEN, S.U., Gn 36. pp. 337-47.

It 438   SNOWDEN, Frank M., 'On the social origins of agrarian fascism in Italy'. *EUR. J. OF SOCIOL.*, **13** (**2**), 1972. pp. 268-95.

It 439   TREVES, Renato, 'Il fascismo e il problema delle generazioni'. *QUAD. DI SOCIOL.*, **13** (**2**), 1964. pp. 119-46.

It 440   ZANGARINI, Maurizio, 'La composizione sociale della classe dirigente nel regime fascista: il caso di Verona'. *ITAL. CONTEMP.*, **30** (**132**), 1978. pp. 27-47.

Fascism and the Press

It 441   BUONO, Oreste del (comp.), *Eia, Eia, Eia, Alala! la stampa italiana sotto il fascismo, 1919-1943: antologia . . .*, pref by Nicola Tranfaglia, Milan: Feltrinelli, 1971. xxiv, 474pp.

It 442   MELOGRANI, Piero (ed.), *Corriere della Sera, 1919-1943*, Bologna: Cappelli, 1965. xciii, 624pp. Anthology.

It 443   SIGNORETTI, Alfredo, *La Stampa in camicia nera, 1932-1943*, Rome: Volpe, 1968. 269pp. *La Stampa*, Turin.

It 444   SOLINAS, Stenio (ed.), *Alla conquista dello stato: antologia della stampa fascista dal 1919 al 1925*, Rome: Volpe, 1978. 590pp. Bib. 581-90.

It 445   VIGEZZI, Brunello, *1919-1925: dopoguerra e fascismo: politica e stampa in Italia*, saggi di E. Decleva [*et al*], Bari: Laterza, 1965. xxi, 805pp. On the editorial policies of leading Italian newspapers.

It 446   VITTORIA, Albertina, 'Le reviste di regime: Gerarchia, Civilta Fascista, Critica Fascista'. *Studi Romani*, **28** (**3**), 1980. pp. 312-34.

Local Studies of Fascism

It 447   APIH, Elio, 'Fascism in North-Eastern Italy'. In BOSWORTH, Richard, J.B. and CRESCIANI, Gianfranco (eds), *Altro Polo; a volume of Italian studies.* Sydney University, 1979. pp. 105-23.

It 448   APIH, Elio, *Italia: fascismo e anti-fascismo nella Venezia Giulia, 1918-1943: ricerche storiche*, Bari: Laterza, 1966. x, 480pp. Sociological study of the climate in which fascism developed in Venezia Giulia.

It 449   BERTI, Giuseppe, 'Note sul fascismo piacentino negli anni 1925-40'. *MOV. DI LIBERAZIONE IN ITALIA*, **21** (**95**), 1969. pp. 77-106.

It 450   BIANCHI, Bruna, 'Il fascismo nelle campagne Veneziane, 1929-40'. *ITAL. CONTEMP.*, **28** (**123**), 1976. pp. 33-68.

It 451   CANTAGALLI, Roberto, *Cronache fiorentine del ventennio fascista*, Rome: Cadmo, 1981. 390pp.

It 452   *Convegno I Fasci Siciliani e la Societa Nazionale. I fasci siciliani*, Giuseppe Giarrizzo [*et al*], Bari: De Donato, 1975-6. 2 vols.

It 453   *Convegno Nazionale di Studi Promosso Dalla Regione Campania. Mezzogiorno e fascismo: atti del Convegno . . . Salerno-Monte S. Giacomo 11-14 dicembre 1975*, ed. Pietro Laveglia, Naples: Ed. Scientifiche Italiane, 1978. 2 vols.

It 454   CURCIO, Carlo, 'Sindicalisti e nazionalisti a Perugia fra il 1928 e il 1933'. *PAGINE LIBERE*, NS.1 (**16**), 1956. pp. 16-26.

It 455   DEANTONELLIS, Giacomo, *La fine del fascismo a Napoli*, Milan: Ares, 1967. 223pp. Bib. 213-14.

It 456   DORSO, Guido, *La rivoluzione meridionale: saggio storico-politico sulla lotta politica in Italia*, 2nd edn, Turin: Gobetti, 1950, lvii, 280pp.

It 457   FATICA, Michele, 'Appunti per una storia di Napoli nell'eta del fascismo'. *RIV. DI STOR. CONTEMP.*, **5**, 1976. pp. 386-420. Also in It. 453.

It 458   FONTANA, Sandro (ed.), *Il fascismo e le autonomie locali*, Bologna: Il Mulino, 1973. 435pp. Proceedings of a meeting held St Vincent, 1972.

It 459   GRUBER, Alfons, *Südtirol unter dem Faschismus*, 2nd edn, Bolzano: Athesia, 1979. 253pp.

It 460   GUERRINI, Libertario and BERTOLO, Gianfranco, 'Le campagne toscane e marchigiane durante il fascismo: note sulle situazioni economica e sociale dei ceti contadini'. *MOV. DI LIBERAZIONE IN ITALIA*, **22** (**101**), 1970. pp. 111-60.

It 461   MASELLA, Luigi, 'Mezzogiorno e fascismo'. *STUD. STOR.*, **20** (**4**), 1979. pp. 779-98. Survey of studies of fascism in southern Italy in 1920s.

It 462   MILLOZZI, Michele (ed.), *Il fascismo marchigiano nei fondi dell'ACS, 1922-1925: fonti e documenti*, Urbino: Argalia, 1977. 286pp.

It 463   MUZZIOLI, Giuliano, 'Le campagne modernesi durante il fascismo: sette anni di crisi, 1927-33'. *STUD. STOR.*, **15** (**4**), 1974. pp. 908-50.

It 464   NENCI, Giacomina (ed.), *Politica e società in Italia dal fascismo alla Resistenza: problemi di storia nazionale e storia umbra: (atti del Convegno su L'Italia e L'Umbria del Fascismo al Resistenza)*, Bologna: Il Mulino, 1978. 479pp.

It 465   PALLA, Marco, *Firenze nel regime fascista, 1929-1934*, Florence: Olschki, 1978. vii, 416pp.

It 466   PORTO, Salvo, *Mafia e fascismo: l'azione del prefetto Mori in Sicilia, 1925-1929*, Palermo: Flaccovio, 1977. 159pp. Bib. 159.

It 467   REECE, Jack E., 'Fascism, the Mafia and the emergence of Sicilian separatism, 1919-43'. *J. OF MOD. HIST.*, **45** (**2**), 1973. pp. 261-76.

It 468   RICCARAND, Elio, *Fascismo e antifascismo in Valle d'Aosta, 1919-1936*, Aosta: Ist. Stor. della Resistenza, 1978. 207pp.

It 469   SOLDANI, Simonietta, 'La Toscana nel regime fascista, 1922-1939'. *STUD. STOR.*, **10** (**3**), 1969. pp. 644-52.

It 470   TOGNARINI, Ivan, *Fascismo, antifascismo, resistenza in una citta'operaia*, Florence: CLUSF, 1980. **1**. *Piombino dalla guerra al crollo del fascismo, 1918-1943*. 337pp.

It 471   *La Toscana nel Regime Fascista, 1922-1939: convegno di studi promosso dall' Unione Regionale Toscane . . .*, ed. A. Binazzi e I. Cuasti, Florence: Olschki, 1971. 2 vols.

It 472   VANNI, Renzo, *Fascismo e antifascismo in provincia di Pisa dal 1920 al 1944*, Pisa: Giardini, 1967. 318pp. Bib. 299-301.

It 473   VIVARELLI, Roberto, 'La Toscana nel regime fascista'. *RIV. STOR. ITAL.*, **85** (**3**), 1973. pp. 689-97.

It 474   ZACCARIA, Giuseppe, 'Conflitti interni al fascismo reggiano dal 1927 alla metà degli anni trenta'. *Richerche Storiche* (Reggio Emilia), **14**, 1980. pp. 7-24.

Fascism and the German Extreme Right

It 475   CASSELS, Alan, 'Mussolini and German Nationalism, 1922-1925'. *J. OF MOD. HIST.*, **35** (**2**), 1963. pp. 137-57.

It 476   CIARLANTINI, Franco, *Hitler e il fascismo*, 2nd edn, Florence: Bemporad, 1933. 70pp.

It 477   DEAKIN, Frederick William, *The Brutal Friendship: Mussolini, Hitler and the fall of Italian fascism*, London: Weidenfeld & Nicolson. New York: Harper & Row, 1962. xiv, 896pp. Rev. Penguin edn, 1966. 575pp. Bib. 533-7.

It 478   DOMARUS, Max, *Mussolini und Hitler: zwei Wege, gleiches Ende*, Würzburg: Selbstverl. 1977. 512pp.

It 479   FELICE, Renzo de, *Mussolini e Hitler: i rapporti segreti, 1922-1933 con ducumenti inediti*, Florence: Le Monnier, 1975. 315pp.

It 480   FELICE, Renzo de, *I rapporti tra fascismo e nazionalsocialismo fino all'andata al potere de Hitler, 1922–1933: appunti e documenti*, Naples: Ed. Scientifiche, 1971. 208pp.

It 481   HITLER, Adolf and MUSSOLINI, Benito, *Hitler e Mussolini: lettere e documenti*, ed. Vittorio Zincone, Milan: Rizzoli, 1946. 218pp.

It 482   MICHAELIS, Meir, 'I rapporti tra fascismo e nazismo prima dell' avvento di Hitler al potere, 1922–1933'. *RIV. STOR. ITAL.*, **85** (3), 1973. pp. 544–600.

It 483   ROSEN, Edgar Robert, 'Mussolini und Deutschland, 1922–1923'. *VIERTELJAHRSH. FÜR ZEITG.*, **5** (1), 1957. pp. 17–41.

Fascism, Catholics and the Church

It 484   BAGET BOZZO, Gianni, 'Il fascismo e l'evoluzione del pensiero politico cattolico'. *STOR. CONTEMP.*, **5** (**4**), 1974. pp. 671–97.

It 485   BELCI, Franco, 'Storia nazionale e storia locale in alcuni studi recenti su Chiesa Cattolica e fascismo'. *ITAL. CONTEMP.*, **3** (2), 1979. pp. 99–106.

It 486   BINCHY, Daniel A., *Church and state in fascist Italy*, 2nd edn, Oxford: University Press, 1970. xiv, 774pp. Bib. 754–62.

It 487   BREZZI, Camillo, 'Appunti sulla recente storiografia relativa ai rapporti tra fascismo e Chiesa Cattolica'. *Cultura e Scuola (Rome)*, **15** (**57**), 1976. pp. 89–99.

It 488   CANDELORO, Giorgio, *Il movimento cattolico in Italia*, 3rd edn, Rome: Ed. Riuniti, 1972. xii. 555pp.

It 489   CASTELLI, Giulio, *La chiesa e il fascismo*, Rome: L'Arnia, 1951. viii, 572pp.

It 490   DALLA TORRE, Giuseppe, *Azione Cattolica e fascismo*, new edn, Rome: AVE, 1964. 144pp.

It 491   GUASACO, Maurilio, *Fascisti e cattolici in una citta rossa: i cattolici alessandrini di fronte al fascismo, 1919*–1939, Milan: Angeli, 1978. 129pp.

It 492   JEMOLO, Arturo Carlo, *Church and State in Italy, 1850–1960*, Oxford: Blackwell. Philadelphia: Dufour, 1960. 344pp. Abridged tr of *Chiesa e stato negli ultimi cento anni*, by David Moore.

It 493   MONTICONE, Alberto (ed.), *Cattolici e fascisti in Umbria, 1922–1945*, Bologna: Il Mulino, 1978. 483pp. *Convegno su Laicato*

Cattolico e Chiesa Locale in Umbria dal Fascismo alla Resistenza, Foligno, 1975.

It 494   PELLICANI, Antonio, *Il papa di tutti: la Chiesa Cattolica, il fascismo e il razzismo, 1929-1945*, pref. by Carlo Falconi, Milan: Sugar, 1964. xiv, 145pp.

It 495   REINERI, Mariangiola, *Cattolici e fascismo a Torino, 1925-1943*, Milan: Feltrinelli, 1978. 266pp.

It 496   SCOPPOLA, Pietro (comp.) *La chiesa e il fascismo: documenti e interpretazioni*, Bari: Laterza, 1971. xliii, 414pp. Pub. 1967 as *Chiesa e stato nella storia d'Italia*.

It 497   SCOPPOLA, Pietro, and TRANIELLO, Francesco (eds), *I Cattolici tra fascismo e democrazia*, Bologna: Il Mulino, 1975. 461pp.

It 498   SOAVE, Sergio and ZUNINO, Giorgio, 'La chiesa e i Cattolici nell'autunno del regime fascista'. *STUD. STOR.*, **18** (**3**), 1977. pp. 69-95. Review article.

It 499   TRAMONTIN, Silvio, 'Il conflitto tra Azione Cattolica e fascismo: i fatti del 1931 nel Veneto'. *Civitas*, **25** (**5/6**), 1974. pp. 3-34.

It 500   TRAMONTIN, Silvio, 'Le violenze fasciste contro i Cattolici Veneti nel 1926'. *Civitas*, **25** (**1**), 1974. pp. 3-30.

It 501   WEBSTER, Richard A., *The cross and the Fasces: Christian Democracy and fascism in Italy*, Stanford: University Press, 1960. xiv. 229pp. Bib. 215-24.

Economic Conditions, Industry and Technology

It 502   ABRATE, Mario, *La lotta sindacale nella industrializzazione in Italia, 1906-1926*, 2nd edn, Milan: Angeli, 1968. xvi, 502pp.

It 503   ALATRI, Paolo and others, *Fascismo e capitalismo*, ed. Nicola Tranfaglia, Milan: Feltrinelli, 1976. 224pp. Essays.

It 504   AQUARONE, Alberto, 'Aspirazioni tecnocratiche del primo fascismo'. *Nord e Sud*, **11** (**52**), 1964. pp. 109-28.

It 505   CASTRONOVO, Valerio, 'Potere economico e fascismo'. *RIV. DI STOR. CONTEMP.*, **2** (**3**), 1972. pp. 273-313.

It 506   CASTRONOVO, Valerio, 'La politica economica del fascismo e il mezzogiorno'. *STUD. STOR.*, **17** (**3**), 1976. pp. 25-39.

It 507   CATALANO, Franco, *L'economia italiana di guerra: la politica economico-finanziaria del fascismo dalla guerra d'Etiopia alla caduta del regime,*

1935-1943, Milan: Ist. Nazionale per la Storia del Movimento di Lib, 1969. 143pp. Bib. 135-40. Suppl. to *Mov. di Liberazione in Italia*, **97**, 1969.

It 508   CIOCCA, Pierluigi and TONIOLO, Gianni (eds.) *L'economia italiana nel periodo fascista*, Bologna: Il Mulino, 1976. 448pp. Bib. 409-44. Special issue of *Quaderni Storici*, **29/30**, 1975.

It 509   DAMASCELLI, Ester Fano, 'La "restaurazione antifascista liberista": ristagno e sviluppo economico durante il fascismo'. *MOV. DI LIBERAZIONE IN ITALIA*, **23 (104)**, 1971. pp. 47-99.

It 510   D'ANGELO, Luigi, 'Tre recenti contributi sulla storia economica e sociale del fascismo'. *STOR. E POLIT.*, **13 (4)**, 1974. pp. 621-39.

It 511   DELMONTE, Alfredo, 'Profiti e sviluppo economico nelli anni 1881-1961 con particolare riferimento a periodo fascista'. *RIV. INT. DI SCI. SOC.*, **85 (3/4)**, 1977. pp. 241-66.

It 512   DONATI, Edgardo, 'Fascismo e crisi economica'. *STUD. STOR.*, **17 (3)**, 1976. pp. 223-45.

It 513   EINZIG, Paul, *The economic foundations of fascism*, 2nd edn, London: Macmillan, 1934. xii, 160pp.

It 514   GALLO, Giampaolo, 'Politica industriale e politica fascista'. *PENSIERO POLIT.*, **6 (1)**, 1973. pp. 86-91. Review article.

It 515   GUALERNI, Gualberto, *La politica industriale fascista, 1922-1935*, Milan: Inst. Sociale Ambrosiano, 1956. x, 157pp. Bib. 141-51.

It 516   GUARNERI, Felice, *Battaglia economiche tra le due grandi guerre*, Milan: Garzanti, 1953. 2 vols. By the economic director of Confindustria.

It 517   HAIDER, Carmen, *Capital and Labour under Fascism*, London: King. New York: Columbia University Press, 1930. 296pp. Bib. 286-9. Columbia University thesis.

It 518   LA FRANCESCA, Salvatore, *La politica economica del fascismo*, Bari: Laterza, 1972. vii, 108pp.

It 519   LOMBARDINI, S., 'Italian fascism and the economy'. In WOOLF, S.J., Gn 21. pp. 152-64.

It 520   MELOGRANI, Piero, 'Confindustria e fascismo tra il 1919 e il 1925'. *NUOVO OSS.*, **6 (44/45)**, 1965. pp. 835-73.

It 521   MELOGRANI, Piero, *Gli industriali e Mussolini: rapporti tra Confindustria e fascismo dal 1919 al 1929*, Milan: Longanesi, 1972. 325pp.

It 522   MERLIN, Gianni, *Com'erano pagati i lavoratori durante il fascismo*, Rome: Cinque Lune, 1970. 150pp. Bib. 149-50.

It 523   MORI, Giorgio, *Industrie und Wirtschaftspolitik in Italien zur Zeit des Faschismus, 1922 bis 1939*, Cologne: Forschungsinstitut für Sozial und Wirtschaftgeschichte an de Univ. zu Köln, 1979. 35pp.

It 524   MORI, Giorgio, 'Métamorphose ou réincarnation? industrie, banque et régime fasciste en Italie, 1923-1933'. *REV. D'HIST. MOD. ET CONTEMP.*, **25** (2), 1978. pp. 235-74.

It 525   MORI, Giorgio, 'Per una storia dell'industria italiana durante il fascismo'. *STUD. STOR.*, **12** (1), 1971. pp. 3-35.

It 526   PEDROCCO, G., *Fascismo e nuove tecnologie: l'organizzazione industriale da Giolitti a Mussolini*, Bologna: Clueb, 1980. 122pp.

It 527   PIRELLI, Alberto, *Dopoguerra, 1919-1932: note ed esperienze*, Milan: Tip. Ghezzi, 1961. 195pp. Memoirs of a leader of industry.

It 528   PRETI, Domenico, *Economia e istituzioni nello stato fascista*, Rome: Ed. Riuniti, 1980. 391pp.

It 529   ROMANO, Sergio, *Giuseppe Volpi: industria e finanza tra Giolitti e Mussolini*, Milan: Bompiani, 1979. 266pp. Giuseppe Volpi di Misurata (1877-1947), Cabinet minister and financier.

It 530   ROSENSTOCK-FRANCK, Louis, *L'Economie corporative fasciste en doctrine et en fait: ses origines historiques et son évolution*, pref. by Bernard Lavergne, Paris: Librairie Universitaire, 1934. xv. 433pp. Bib. 1-4.

It 531   ROSSI, Ernesto, *I padroni del vapore e fascismo*, new edn, Bari: Laterza, 1966. 355pp.

It 532   ROTELLI, Carlo, 'Un problema storiografico aperto: agricoltura e industria in Toscana sotto il fascismo'. *ITAL. CONTEMP.*, **29** (**129**), 1977. pp. 27-53.

It 533   SAPELLI, Giulio, 'La classe operaia durante il fascismo: problemi e indicazioni di ricerca'. *Annali Dell'Istituto Giangiacomo Feltrinelli*, **20**, 1979/80. pp. vii-xcviii.

It 534   SAPELLI, Giulio, 'Organizzazione scientifica del lavoro e innovazione tecnologica durante il fascismo'. *ITAL. CONTEMP.*, **28** (**125**), 1976. pp. 2-28.

It 535   SARTI, Roland, *Fascism and Industrial Leadership in Italy, 1919-1940: a study in the expansion of private power under fascism*. Berkeley: University of California Press, 1971. xii, 154pp. On relations between Confindustria, organised industrial interests and the fascist regime.

It 536   SARTI, Roland, 'Fascist modernization: traditional or revolutionary?' *AM. HIST. REV.*, **75** (**4**), 1970. pp. 1029-45.

It 537   SARTI, Roland, 'Mussolini and the industrial leadership in the battle of the lira, 1925-1927'. *Past and Present*, **47**, May 1970. pp. 97-112.

It 538   SYLOS LABINI, Paolo, 'La politica economica del fascismo e la crisi del'29'. *Nord e Sud*, **12** (**70**), 1965. pp. 59-66.

It 539   SZYMANSKI, Albert, 'Fascism, industrialism and socialism: the case of Italy'. *COMP. STUD. IN SOC. AND HIST.*, **15** (**4**), 1973. pp. 395-404.

It 540   TONIOLO, Gianni, *L'economia dell'Italia fascista*, Rome: Laterza, 1980. xx, 354pp.

It 541   VAUDAGNA, Maurizio, 'Structural change in fascist Italy'. *J. OF ECON HIST.*, **38** (**1**), 1978. pp. 181-204. With comments by D.E. Moggridge.

It 542   WELK, William George, *Fascist Economic Policy: an analysis of Italy's economic experiment*. Cambridge, Mass.: Harvard University Press, 1938. xx, 365pp. Bib. 335-44.

Corporativism and the Syndicates

It 543   AMBRIS, Alceste de, *Dopo un ventennio di rivoluzione: il corporativismo*, Bordeaux: Mione, 1935. 135pp. Critique of fascist corporativism by a collaborator of D'Annunzio.

It 544   AQUARONE, Alberto, 'La politica sindicale del fascismo'. *NUOVO OSS.*, **6** (**44/45**), 1965. pp. 874-88.

It 545   BRAVO, Gian Mario, 'Sindicalismo fascista e corporativismo, 1922-1945'. In *Il Movimento Sindicale in Italia: rassegna di studi, 1945-1969*, Turin: Einaudi, 1970. pp. 63-82. Review article.

It 546   CAPOFERRI, Pietro, *Venti anni col fascismo e con i sindicati*, Milan: Gastaldi, 1957. 314pp.

It 547   CATALANO, Franco, 'Le corporazioni fasciste e la classe lavoratrice dal 1925 al 1929'. *NUOVA RIV. STOR.*, **43** (**1**), 1959. pp. 31-66.

It 548   CORDOVA, Ferdinando, *Le origini dei sindicati fascisti, 1918-1926*, Bari: Laterza, 1974. v, 481pp.

It 549   FIELD, George Lowell, *The syndical and corporative institutions of Italian fascism*, New York: Columbia University Press, 1938. 209pp.

It 550   GIBELLI, Camillo, 'I sindicati fascisti a Genova negli anni della grande crisi, 1929-1933'. *MOV. OPERAIO E SOC.*, **19** (**4**), 1973. pp. 309-55.

It 551   GRADILONE, Alfredo, *Bibliografia sindicale corporativa, 1923-1940*, Rome: Ist. Nazionale di Cultura Fascista, 1942. viii, 1101pp.

It 552   MERLI, Stefano, 'Corporativismo fascista e illusioni riformistiche nei primi anni del regime'. *RIV. STOR. DEL SOC.*, **2** (**5**), 1959. pp. 121-37.

It 553   ROSSONI, Edmondo, *Le idee della riconstruzione: discorsi sul sindicalismo fascista*, Florence: Bemporad, 1923. vii, 108pp. By a syndicalist (1885-1965) and head of the fascist trade union confederation.

It 554   TINGHINO, John J., *Edmondo Rossoni: fascist champion of labor*, New York University thesis, 1982. UM 82-14849. 310pp.

It 555   SANTOMASSIMO, Gianpasquale, 'Aspetti della politica culturale del fascismo: il dibattito sul corporativismo e l'economia politica'. *ITAL. CONTEMP.*, **26** (**121**), 1975. pp. 2-26.

It 556   SANTOMASSIMO, Gianpasquale, 'Ugo Spirito e il corporativismo'. *STUD. STOR.*, **14** (**1**), 1973. pp. 61-113.

It 557   SAPELLI, Giulio, 'Sindicati fascista, grande industria e classe operaia a Torino, 1929-1934'. *RIV. DI STOR. CONTEMP.*, **2** (**1**), 1973. pp. 40-64.

It 558   UVA, Bruno, 'Le idee corporative in Italia dalla Restaurazione al 1922'. *STOR. E POLIT.*, **4** (**4**), 1965. pp. 603-68.

It 559   UVA, Bruno, *La nascita dello stato corporativo e sindicale fascista*, Rome: Carucci, 1974. 302pp.

It 560   VALLAURI, Carlo, *Le radici del corporativismo*, Rome: Bulzoni, 1971. 234pp.

Benito Mussolini (1883-1945)

It 561   AMICUCCI, Ermanno, *I 600 giorni di Mussolini: dal Gran Sasso a Dongo*, Rome; Faro, 1949. iv, 313pp. On Mussolini's later adventures including his rescue by the nazis. By the editor of *Corriere della Sera* under the Salò Republic.

It 562   AROMA, Nino d', *Mussolini segreto*, Bologna: Cappelli, 1958. vi, 469pp.

It 563   BALABANOVA, Anzhelika, *Il Traditore* [*The Traitor*]: *Benito Mussolini and his 'conquest of power'*, New York: Popolizio, 1942. 320pp.

It 564   BANDINI, Franco, *Vita e morte segreta di Mussolini*, Milan: Mondadori, 1978. 463pp. Bib. 439–43.

It 565   BEGNAC, Ivon de, *Palazzo Venezia: storia di un regime*, Rome: La Rocca, 1950. 766pp. Bib. 681–8. Pro-Mussolini biography.

It 566   BEGNAC, Ivon de, *Trent'anni di Mussolini, 1883–1915*, pref. by F.T. Marinetti, Rome: Menaglia, 1934. xv, 280pp. Bib. xiv–xv.

It 567   BEGNAC, Ivon de, *Vita di Benito Mussolini: (dalle origini al 24 maggio 1915)*, Milan: Mondadori, 1936–40. 3 vols. Includes material from *Trent'anni*. See It 566.

It 568   BERNERI, Camillo, *Mussolini: psicologia di un dittatore*, ed. Pier-Carlo Masini, Milan: Ed. Azione Comune, 1966. 116pp.

It 569   BERTOLDI, Silvio, *Mussolini tale e quale*, 2nd edn, Milan: Longanesi, 1965. 277pp.

It 570   BIANCINI, Bruno, *Dizionario Mussoliniano: 1500 affermazioni e definizioni del Duce su 1000 argomenti*, 2nd edn, Milan: Hoepli, 1940. viii, 239pp.

It 571   BIONDI, Dino, *La fabbrica del Duce*, Florence: Vallecchi, 1967. vii, 362pp.

It 572   BITELLI, Giovanni, *Benito Mussolini*, 2nd edn, Turin: Paravia, 1938. 152pp. Bib. of Mussolini's writings pp. 136–51.

It 573   BOREJSZA, Jerzy, W., *Mussolini byl pierwszy (Mussolini was the First)*, Warsaw: Czytelnik, 1979. 491pp.

It 574   BORGHI, Armando, *Mussolini, Red and Black; with an epilogue Hitler, Mussolini's disciple*, New York: Haskell House, 1974. 207pp. Tr. of *Mussolini in camicia*, Naples: Ed. Scientifiche Italiane, 1961, by Dorothy Daudley.

It 575   BOZZETTI, Gherardo, *Mussolini dirretore dell'Avanti*, pref. by Ugoberto Alfassio Grimaldi, Milan: Feltrinelli, 1979. 258pp.

It 576   BOZZI, Carlo, *Lenin e Mussolini: protagonisti del secolo*, Rome: Volpe, 1978. 409pp.

It 577   BRISSAUD, André, *Mussolini*, Paris: Perrin, 1975–83. 2 vols. **1**. *Le Révolutionnaire*. **2**. *La Folie du pouvoir*.

It 578   COLLIER, Richard, *Duce: a biography of Benito Mussolini*, London: Collins. New York: Viking Press, 1971. 447pp. Bib. 395–419.

It 579   CORTESI, Luigi, *Mussolini e il fascismo alla vigilia del crollo*, Rome: Ed. Cooperativa, 1975. 40pp.

It 580   DABROWSKI, Roman, *Mussolini: twilight and fall*, pref. by H.C. Stevens. London: Heinemann. New York: Roy, 1956. xii, 248pp. Tr. of *Sto dni Mussoliniego*, by H.C. Stevens.

It 581   DALLA TANA, Luciano, *Mussolini massimalista*, Parma; Guanda, 1963. 173pp. Mussolini's early socialism.

It 582   DELZELL, Charles F., 'Benito Mussolini: a guide to the biographical literature'. *J. OF MOD HIST.*, **35** (**4**), 1963. pp. 339-53.

It 583   DOLFIN, Giovanni, *Con Mussolini nella tragedia: diario del capo della segreteria particolare del Duce, 1943-1944*, Milan: Garzanti, 1949. viii, 295pp. On the last years of Mussolini by his secretary.

It 584   DORSO, Guido, *Mussolini alla conquista del potere*, foreword by Guido Muscetta, Milan: Mondadori, 1961. 361pp. First pub. Turin: Einaudi, 1949.

It 585   FELICE, Renzo de, *Benito Mussolini: quattro testimonianze*, Alcestis de Ambris [*et al*], Florence: La Nuova Italia, 1976. xviii, 203pp. By de Ambris, L. Campolonghi, M. Girardon, M. Rygier.

It 586   FELICE, Renzo de, *Mussolini*, Turin: Einaudi, 1965-. 1. *Mussolini il rivoluzionario 1883-1920*. 2. *Mussolini il fascista* (1). La conquista del potere, 1921-1925. (2). L'organizazzione dello stato fascista, 1925-1929. 3. *Mussolini il Duce* (1). Gli anni del consenso, 1929-1936. (2). Lo stato totalitario, 1936-1940. Monumental fundamental biography of Mussolini.

It 587   FERMI, Laura, *Mussolini*, Chicago: University Press, 1961. vii, 477pp. Bib. 461-7.

It 588   FESTA, Elio, 'I biografi di Mussolini'. *NUOVA RIV. STOR.*, **45** (**3**), 1961. pp. 467-513.

It 589   FESTA, Elio, 'La vita di Benito Mussolini della nascita alla prima giovinezza'. *NUOVA RIV. STOR.*, **47** (**3/4**), 1963. pp. 241-81.

It 590   FREDA, Italo, 'Mussolini dal socialismo al fascismo'. *RIV. STOR. DEL SOC.*, **9** (**27**), 1966. pp. 221-30. Review of Renzo de Felice's *Mussolini*. See It 586.

It 591   FUSTI CAROFIGLIO, Mario, *Vita di Mussolini e storia del fascismo: predappio, Piazza Venezia, Piazzale Loreto*, Turin: Soc. Ed. Torinese, 1950. vii, 472pp.

It 592   GENTIZON, PAUL, *Souvenirs sur Mussolini*, intro. by Junio Valerio Borghese, Palermo: Lo Monaco, 1958. 454pp.

It 593   GHIDETTI, Enrico (ed.), *Mussolini: nascita di un dittatore*, Firenze: Vallecchi, 1978. xii, 246pp.

It 594   GIUDICE, Gaspare, *Benito Mussolini*, Turin: UTET, 1969. xi, 708pp. Bib. 689–93.

It 595   GREGOR, A. James, *Young Mussolini and the intellectual origins of fascism*, Berkeley: University of California Press, 1979. xii, 271pp. Bib. 253–60.

It 596   GUICHONNET, Paul, *Mussolini et le fascisme*, Paris: PUF, 1966. 128pp. Bib. 123–5.

It 597   HALPERIN, Samuel William, *Mussolini and Italian fascism*, Princeton: Van Nostrand, 1964. 191pp. Bib. 183–5. Doc. 89–182.

It 598   HIBBERT, Christopher, *Benito Mussolini: the rise and fall of Il Duce*, rev. edn, Harmondsworth: Penguin, 1975. 416pp. Bib. 387–96. First pub. Longmans, 1961. US. edn, *Mussolini*, Ballantine, 1972.

It 599   JOES, Anthony James, *Mussolini*, New York: Watts, 1982. 405pp. Bib. 397–9.

It 600   KIRKPATRICK, Sir Ivone, *Mussolini: a study in power*. Westport: Greenwood Press, 1976. 726pp. Bib. 697–707. First pub. Hawthorn Books, 1964.

It 601   KNOX, MacGregor, *Mussolini Unleashed, 1939–1941: politics and strategy in Italy's last war*, Cambridge: University Press, 1982. x, 385pp. Bib. 368–73.

It 602   LUDWIG, Emil, *Colloqui con Mussolini*, tr. Tomaso Gnoli, intro. by Brunello Vigezzi, Milan: Mondadori, 1970. 218pp. First pub. 1935.

It 603   LUNA, Giovanni de, *Benito Mussolini: soggettività e practica di una dittatura*, Milan: Feltrinelli, 1978. 161pp.

It 604   MACK SMITH, Dennis, *Mussolini*, London: Weidenfeld & Nicolson, 1981. xiv, 429pp. Bib. 389–416.

It 605   MEGARO, Gaudens, *Mussolini in the Making*, New York: Fertig, 1967. 347pp Repr. of Houghton Mifflin edn, 1938.

It 606   MELOGRANI, Piero, 'The cult of the Duce in Mussolini's Italy'. *J. OF CONTEMP. HIST.*, **11** (**4**), 1976. pp. 221–37.

It 607   MONELLI Paolo, *Mussolini: the intimate life of a demagogue*, New York: Vanguard, 1954. 304pp. Tr. of *Mussolini piccolo borghese*, 4th edn, Milan: Garzanti, 1954, by Brigid Maxwell.

It 608   *Mussolini: (raccolta di testimonianze)*, 2nd edn, Rome: Centro Ed. Nazionale, 1958. 643pp.

It 609   MUSSOLINI, Benito, *My Autobiography*; tr. and foreword by Richard Washington Child, Westport: Greenwood Press, 1970. xix. 318pp. Repr. of Hutchinson edn, 1928.

It 610   MUSSOLINI, Benito, *Fascism: doctrine and institutions*, New York: Fertig, 1968. 313pp. Repr. of 1935 edn.

It 611   MUSSOLINI, Benito, *Memoirs, 1942-43; with documents relating to the period*, New York: Fertig, 1975. xxviii, 320pp. Bib. 286-95. Tr. of *Il tempo de bastone e della carota*, by Frances Lobb. Repr. of Weidenfeld & Nicolson edn, 1947. Greenwood Press edn, tr. by Frances Frenaye, *The Fall of Mussolini*, 1975.

It 612   MUSSOLINI. Benito, *Mussolini as Revealed in his Political Speeches, Nov. 1914-Aug. 1923*, selected, tr. and ed. Barone Bero Quaranta di San Severino, New York: Fertig, 1976. xxviii, 375pp. Repr. of Dent edn, 1923.

It 613   MUSSOLINI, Benito, *Mussolini e la Voce*, ed. Emilio Gentile, Florence; Sansoni, 1976. xi, 239pp. Selected letters.

It 614   MUSSOLINI, Benito, *Opere omnia*, ed. Edoardo e Diulio Susmel, Florence; Volpe, 1952-78. 38 vols.

It 615   MUSSOLINI, Benito, *Scritti politici*, intro. and ed. by Enzo Santarelli, Milan: Feltrinelli, 1979. 357pp. Bib. 65-8.

It 616   MUSSOLINI, Edvige Mancini, *Mio fratello Benito: memorie raccolta e trascritte da Roscetta Ricci Crisolini*, Florence; La Fenice, 1957. 243pp.

It 617   MUSSOLINI, Rachele Guidi, *Mussolini: an intimate biography by his widow . . . as told to Albert Zarca*, New York: Morrow, 1974. vi, 291pp. Tr. of *Mussolini sans masque*.

It 618   MUSSOLINI, Vittorio, *Vita con mio padre*, Milan: Mondadori, 1957. 231pp.

It 619   NOLTE, Ernst, 'Marx und Nietzsche im Socialismus des jungen Mussolini'. *HIST. Z.*, **191**, 1960. pp. 249-335.

It 620   PETACCO, Arrigo, *Riservato per il Duce: i segreti del regime conservati nell'archivio personale di Mussolini*, Milan: Mondadori, 1979. 147pp.

It 621   PINI, Giorgio, *Filo diretto con Palazzo Venezia*, Bologna: Cappelli 1950. 257pp. Memories of Mussolini by the editor of *Popolo d'Italia*.

It 622   PINI, Giorgio and SUSMEL, Diulio, *Mussolini: l'uomo e l'opera*, Florence: La Fenice, 1953-8. **1**. *Dal socialismo al fascismo, 1883-1919*. **2**. *Dal fascismo alla dittatura, 1919-1925*. **3**. *Dalla dittatura* *all'Impero, 1925-1938.* **4.** *Dall'Impero alla Repubblica, 1938-1945.* 3rd edn, 1963.

It 623   POLL, Ferdinand van der, *Benito Mussolini portret contra zelfportret,* Groningen: Wolters, 1964. iii, 309pp. Amsterdam University thesis.

It 624   ROCHAT, Giorgio, 'Mussolini: chef de guerre, 1940-1943'. *REV. D'HIST DEUX GUERRE MOND.,* **24** (**100**), 1975. pp. 43-66.

It 625   ROSSI, Cesare, *Trentatre vicende mussoliniane,* Milan: Ceschina, 1958. 645pp.

It 626   ROUX, Georges, *La chute de Mussolini, 1936-1945; texte de présentation de Raymond Cartier,* Paris: Club des Amis du Livre, 1961. 287pp.

It 627   ROUX, Georges, *Mussolini,* Paris: Fayard, 1960. 505pp.

It 628   RUMI, Giorgio, 'Mussolini, Il Popolo d'Italia, e l'Ungheria, 1918-1922'. *STOR. CONTEMP.,* **6**, 1975. pp. 675-96.

It 629   SANTOMASSIMO, Gianpasquale, 'Il fascismo degli anni trenti'. *STUD. STOR.,* **16** (**1**), 1975. pp. 102-25. Criticism of de Felice in *Mussolini Il Duce.* See It 586.

It 630   SARFATTI, Margherita Grassini, *The Life of Benito Mussolini,* pref. by Benito Mussolini, tr. Frederic Whyte, London: Butterworth, New York: Stokes, 1925. 352pp.

It 631   SETTEMBRINI, Domenico, 'Mussolini and the legacy of revolutionary socialism'. *J. OF CONTEMP. HIST.,* **11** (**4**), 1976. pp. 239-68.

It 632   SETTIMELLI, Emilio, *Edda contra Benito: indagine sulla personalità del Duce attraverso un memoriale autografo di Edda Ciano Mussolini qui riprodotto,* Rome: Corso, 1952. 147pp. Edda Ciano Mussolini, Benito's daughter.

It 633   SIMONINI, Augusto, *Miti vecchi e nuovi in Benito Mussolini,* Messina: D'Anna, 1978. 142pp.

It 634   SIMONINI, Augusto, *Il linguaggio di Mussolini,* Milan: Bompiani, 1978. 227pp.

It 635   SPAMPANATO, Bruno, *Contromemoriale . . . ; con un'appendice storica e con una documentazione fotografica inedita,* Rome: Illustrato, 1952. 3 vols. Vol 1, 3rd edn. Vol. 2, 2nd edn. A defence of Mussolini and fascism based mainly on his last years.

It 636   SPERCO, Willy, *Tel fut Mussolini,* Paris: Fasquelle, 1955. 243pp.

It 637   SUSMEL, Diulio, *Mussolini e il suo tempo*, Milan: Garzanti, 1950. 338pp.

It 638   SUSMEL, Diulio, *Nenni e Mussolini: mezzo secolo di fronte*, Milan: Rizzoli, 1969. 356pp. Bib. 353-7. Pietro Nenni, leader of the Socialist Party.

It 639   TITONE, Virgilio, 'Mussolini e un quarantennio di storia italiana'. *Nuova Antologia*, **110**, Nov. 1975. pp. 318-48.

It 640   TRIPODI, Nino, *Il fascismo secondo Mussolini*, Rome: Ciarrapico, 1978. 174pp.

It 641   VACCARINO, Giorgio, 'Mussolini devant ses biographes: apropos de quelques récentes biographies de Benito Mussolini'. *REV. D'HIST. DEUX GUERRE MOND.*, **4 (26)**, 1957. pp. 67-82.

It 642   VALERA, Paolo, *Mussolini*, ed. Enrico Ghidetti, Milan: Longanesi, 1975. xxxix, 202pp. Bib. xxxvi-xxxix.

It 643   VIVARELLI, Roberto, 'Benito Mussolini: dal socialismo al fascismo'. *RIV. STOR. ITAL.*, **79 (2)**, 1967. pp. 438-58. On de Felice's *Mussolini il rivoluzionario*. See It 586.

It 644   WOOLF, Stuart J., 'Mussolini as revolutionary'. *J. OF CONTEMP. HIST.*, **1 (2)**, 1966. pp. 187-96. Discussion of de Felice's *Mussolini il rivoluzionario*. See It 586.

Other Fascist Personalities

It 645   ALFASSIO GRIMALDI, Ugoberto and BOZZETTI, Gherardo, *Farinacci, il più fascista*, Milan: Bompiani, 1972. 254pp. Roberto Farinacci (1892-1945).

It 646   FORNARI, Harry, *Mussolini's Gadfly, Roberto Farinacci*. Nashville: Vanderbilt University Press, 1971. xiv, 237pp. Bib. 217-20. City University of New York thesis, 1969.

It 647   AQUARONE, Alberto, 'Badoglio militare e politico'. *Affari Estera*, **6 (22)**, 1974. pp. 167-73.

It 648   PIERI, Piero and ROCHAT, Giorgio, *Pietro Badoglio*, Turin: UTET, 1974. viii, 914pp. Bib. 867-99. Pietro Badoglio (1871-1956).

It 649   BOTTAI, Giuseppe, *Scritti*, ed. Roberto Bartolozzi e Riccardo del Giudice, Bologna: Cappelli, 1965. 423pp. Bib. 410-11. Bottai (1895-1959) major contributor to fascist ideology later declared to be a traitor to the movement.

It 650   BOTTAI, Giuseppe, *Vent'anni e un giorno, 24 luglio 1943*,

Milan: Garzanti, 1949. 326pp. Apologetics from the former editor of *Critica Fascista.*

It 651   DE GRAND, Alexander J., *Bottai e la cultura fascista*, tr. Pietro Negri, Rome: Laterza, 1978, vii, 301pp.

It 652   DE GRAND, Alexander J., 'Giuseppe Bottai e il fallimento del fascismo revisionista'. *STOR. CONTEMP.*, **6** (**4**), 1975. pp. 697-731.

It 653   D'ORSI, Angelo, 'Il fascismo di Bottai'. *PENSIERO POLIT.*, **12** (**1**), 1979. pp. 87-101. Review article.

It 654   GENTILE, Emilio, 'Bottai e il fascismo: osservazioni per biografia'. *STOR. CONTEMP.*, **10** (**3**), 1979. pp. 551-70.

It 655   GENTILI, Rino, *Giuseppe Bottai e la riforma fascista nella scuola*, Florence: La Nuova Italia, 1979. vi, 218pp.

It 656   GOLDBRUNNER, Hermann, 'Aus der Bibliothek eines intellektuellen Faschisten: Giuseppe Bottai'. *QUELL. UND FORSCH. AUS. ITAL. ARCH.*, **60**, 1980. pp. 535-78.

It 657   GUERRI, Giordano Bruno, *Giuseppe Bottai, un fascista critico; ideologia e azione del gerarca che avrebbe voluto portare l'intelligenza nel fascismo e il fascismo alla liberalizzazione*, Milan: Feltrinelli, 1976. 275pp. Bib. 259-65.

It 658   PANICALI, Anna (ed.), *Bottai: il fascismo come rivoluzione del capitale*, Bologna: Cappelli, 1978. 200pp. Includes list of Bottai's writings.

It 659   ZAGARRIO, Vito, 'Bottai: un fascista critico?' *STUD. STOR.*, **17** (**4**), 1976. pp. 267-71.

It 660   CIANO, Galeazzo, Conte, *Ciano's Hidden Diary, 1937-1938*; tr. and notes by Andreas Mayor, intro. by Malcolm Muggeridge, New York: Dutton, 1953. 220pp.

It 661   GUERRI, Giordano Bruno, *Galeazzo Ciano: una vita, 1903-1944*, Milan: Bompiani, 1979. 718pp. Bib. 695-703.

It 662   SUSMEL, Diulio, *Vita sbagliata di Galeazzo Ciano*, Milan: Palazzi, 1962. 395pp. Bib.

It 663   VERGANI, Orio, *Ciano una lunga confessione . . . in appendice una biografia fotografica curata de Valerio E Marino e da Guido Vergani*, Milan: Longanesi, 1974. 253pp.

It 664   FELICE, Renzo de, 'Giovanni Preziosi e le origine del fascismo, 1917-1931'. *RIV. STOR. DEL SOC.*, **5** (**17**), 1962. pp. 493-555. 'The dean of Italian Jew-baiters'. Michaelis. See It 421.

It 665   ISNENGHI, Mario, *Papini*. Florence, La Nuova Italia, 1972. 219pp. Bib. 206–13. Giovanni Papini (1881–1956) pragmatist, then Nationalist, then futurist, eventually fascist.

It 666   PAPINI, Giovanni, *Tutte le opere*, Milan: Mondadori, 1958–66. 10 vols.

It 667   PAPINI, Giovanni, *Un uomo finito*, Florence; Vallecchi, 1974. xi, 229pp. Bib. xi. Autobiography.

It 668   SIMA, Vintila, *Giovanni Papini*, tr O. Nemi, Rome: Volpe, 1972, 172pp.

It 669   ROCCO, Alfredo, *Scritti e discorsi*. Milan, Giuffre, 1938. 3 vols. Author (1875–1935) was a Nationalist ideologist who later became Minister of Justice.

It 670   UNGARI, Paolo, *Alfredo Rocco e l'ideologia giuridica del fascismo*, Brescia: Morcelliana, 1963. 136pp.

The Second World War and the Salò Republic

It 671   ALFASSIO GRIMALDI, Ugoberto, *La stampa di Salò*, Milan: Bompiani, 1979. 116pp.

It 672   ARALDI, Vinicio, *La crisi italiana del '43*, Milan: Silva, 1964. 251pp.

It 673   BELLOTTI, Felice, *La Repubblica di Mussolini 26 luglio 1943–23 aprile 1945*, Milan: Zagara, 1947. 228pp.

It 674   BENINI, Zenone, *Vigilia a Verona*, pref. by Piero Operti, Milan: Garzanti, 1949. xlvii, 171pp. On the Verona trial of Ciano and others.

It 675   BRISSAUD, André, *La Tragédie de Vérone: Grandi et Ciano contre Mussolini, 1943–1944*, Paris: Perrin, 1971. 396pp. Bib. 391–4.

It 676   MAYER, Domenico, *La verità sul processo di Verona*, ed. Casa Editrice Avanti, Verona: Mondadori, 1945. 164pp.

It 677   MONTAGNA, Renzo, *Mussolini e il processo di Verona*, Milan: Omnia, 1949. 234pp. By the Chief of Police in the Salò Republic.

It 678   VENÈ, Gian Franco, *La Fin du fascisme: il processo di Verona*, tr. M. de Wasmer, Paris: Buchet-Chastel, 1965. 235pp.

It 679   BERTOLDI, Silvio, *Salò: vita e morte della Repubblica Sociale Italiano*, Milan: Rizzoli, 1976. 431pp. Bib. 409–11.

It 680   BIANCHI, Gianfranco, *Perché e come cadde il fascismo: 25 luglio crollo di un regime*, Milan: Mursia, 1970. xiii, 908pp. Bib. 811-77. The end of fascism, 1943-7.

It 681   BOCCA, Giorgio, *La Repubblica di Mussolini*, 2nd edn, Bari: Laterza, 1977. 391pp.

It 682   CIONE, Edmondo, *Storia della Reppublica Sociale Italiana*, 2nd edn, Rome: Latinata, 1951. viii, 539pp. Pro-Mussolini.

It 683   COLLOTTI, Enzo, *L'amministrazzione tedesca dell'Italia occupata, 1943-1945: studio e documenti*, Milan: Lerici, 1963. 607pp. Doc. 220-591.

It 684   CONTI, Giuseppe, 'La RSI e l'attivita del fascismo clandestino nell'Italia liberata dal settembre 1943 all' aprile 1945'. *STOR. CONTEMP.*, **10** (**4/5**), 1979. pp. 941-1018.

It 685   DEFEO, Italo, *L'ultima Italia*, Turin: ERI, 1967. 201pp. Bib. 191.

It 686   GALANTI, Francesco, *Socializzazione e sindacalismo della RSI: 23 documenti*, Rome: Magi-Spinetti, 1949. xii, 175pp.

It 687   GALBIATI, Enzo, *Il 25 luglio e la MVSN*, 2nd edn, Milan: Bernabo, 1950. 336pp. By the chief of the Milizia Voluntaria per la Sicurezza Nazionale on the fall of Mussolini in 1943.

It 688   GENCARELLI, E., 'Les sources d'archives italiennes sur la seconde guerre mondiale'. *REV. D'HIST. DEUX GUERRE MOND.*, **23** (**92**), 1973. pp. 69-85.

It 689   LANFRANCHI, Ferruccio, *L'Inquisizione nera (banditismo fascista)*, Milan: Nibbio, 1945. 297pp. Repression in the Salò Republic.

It 690   MANUNTA, Ugo, *La caduta degli angeli: storia interna della Repubblica Sociale Italiana*, Rome: Azienda Ed. Italiana, 1947. 241pp.

It 691   MONELLI, Paolo, *Roma 1943*, 4th edn, Rome: Migliaresi, 1946. 465pp.

It 692   MOURIN, Maxime, *Ciano contre Mussolini*, Paris: Hachette, 1960. 190pp.

It 693   PANSA, Giampaolo, 'Nascita della RSI in una città di provincia:Casale Monferrato'. *MOV. DI LIBERAZIONE IN ITALIA*, **18** (**84**), 1966. pp. 36-70.

It 694   PAOLUCCI, Vittorio, *La Repubblica Sociale Italiana e il Partito Fascista Repubblicano, settembre 1943-marzo '44*, Urbino: Argalia, 1949. 246pp.

It 695   PINI, Giorgio, *Itinerario tragico, 1943-1945*, Milan: Omnia, 1950. 319pp. On the Salò Republic by the Under-Secretary of the Interior.

It 696   PISENTI, Piero, *Una repubblica necessaria: (RSI)*, Rome: Volpe, 1977. 259pp.

It 697   RAVA, Franco and SPINI, Giorgio, 'Fonti documentarie e memorialistiche per la storia della crisi dello stato italiano, 1940-1945'. *RIV. STOR. ITAL.*, **61** (3), 1949. pp. 404-31; **61** (4). pp. 574-602.

It 698   SCHRÖDER, Josef, *Italien im Zweiten Weltkrieg: eine Bibliographie. . .*, intro. by Renzo de Felice, Munich: Bernard & Graefe, 1978. 1127pp.

It 699   SETTO, Sandro, 'Potere economico e Repubblica Sociale Italiana'. *STOR. CONTEMP.*, **8** (2), 1977. pp. 257-87.

It 700   SILVESTRI, Carlo, *Mussolini, Graziani e l'antifascismo, 1943-1945*, Milan: Longanesi, 1949. 585pp. Rodolfo Graziani (1882-1955), Field-Marshall and Defence Minister in the Salò Republic.

It 701   TAMARO, Attilio, *Due anni di storia, 1943-1945*, Rome: Tosi, 1948-50. 3 vols.

It 702   ZANGRANDI, Ruggero, *1943: 25 luglio-8 settembre*, 2nd edn, Milan: Feltrinelli 1964. 1184pp.

GERMANY

The Extreme Right, 1890-1918

G 1   DÜDING, Dieter, *Der nationalsoziale Verein, 1896-1903: der gescheiterte Versuch einer parteipolitischen Synthese von Nationalismus, Sozialismus und Liberalismus*, Munich: Oldenbourg, 1972. 211pp. Bib. 205-8.

G 2   ELEY, Geoffrey, *Reshaping the German Right: radical nationalism and political change after Bismark*. New Haven: Yale University Press, 1980. xii, 387pp. Bib. 371-3. Pan-German League, Navy League, Colonial Society, Defence League, etc.

G 3   ETUE, George Edward, *The German Fatherland Party, 1917-1918*,

University of California, Berkeley thesis, 1959. 99pp. Party led by von Tirpitz and W. Kapp.

G 4 GASMAN, Daniel, *The Scientific Origins of National Socialism: Social Darwinism in Ernst Häckel and the German Monist League*. New York: Elsevier. London: MacDonald, 1971. xxxii, 208pp. Bib. 183-202. Chicago University thesis, 1969.

G 5 HAMEL, Iris, *Völkischer Verband und nationale Gewerkschaft: der Deutschnationale Handlungsgehilfen-Verband, 1893-1933*. Frankfurt/M: Europäische Verlagsanstalt, 1967. 289pp. Bib. 270-82. Hamburg University thesis.

G 6 JARAUSCH, Konrad Hugo, *Students, society and politics in Imperial Germany: the rise of academic illiberalism*. Princeton: University Press, 1982. xvi, 448pp.

G 7 KENNEDY, Paul and NICHOLLS, Anthony James (eds), *Nationalist and Racialist Movements in Britain and Germany before 1914*, London: Macmillan, 1981. xi, 210pp. Conference papers.

G 8 KRUCK, Alfred, *Geschichte des Alldeutschen Verbändes, 1890-1939*, Wiesbaden: Steiner, 1954. vi, 258pp. Bib. 241-50.

G 9 KUPISCH, Karl, *Adolf Stoecker: Hofprediger und Volkstribun: ein historische Porträt*, Berlin: Haude & Spener, 1970. 94pp. Adolf Stoecker (1835-1904) anti-semitic leader of the Christian Social Party.

G 10 LEVY, Richard S., *The Downfall of the Anti-Semitic Political Parties in Imperial Germany*, New Haven: Yale University Press, 1975. ix, 335pp. Bib. 309-23.

G 11 MASSING, Paul W., *Rehearsal for Destruction: a study of political anti-semitism in Imperial Germany*, New York: Harper, 1949. xviii, 341pp.

G 12 MATTHEIER, Klaus, *Die Gelben: nationale Arbeiter zwischen Wirtschaftsfrieden und Streik*, Düsseldorf: Schwann, 1973. 408pp. Bib. 366-405. Bochum University thesis. On the nationalist trade unions.

G 13 PECK, Abraham J., *Radicals and Reactionaries: the crisis of conservatism in Wilhelmine Germany*, Washington DC: University Press of America, 1978. xiii. 376pp. Bib. 344-63.

G 14 PHELPS Reginald H., 'Theodor Fritsch und der Anti-semitismus. *DTSCH. RUNDSCH.*, **87** (5), 1961. pp. 442-9. Virulent antisemite and editor of the journal *Hammer*.

G 15 PUHLE, Hans-Jürgen, *Agrarische Interessenpolitik und preussischer Konservatismus im Wilhelminische Reich, 1893-1914: ein Beitrag zur Analyse des Nationalismus in Deutschland am Beispiel des Bundes der Landwirte und der*

234

Deutsch-Konservativen Partei, 2nd edn, Bonn: V. Neue Gesellschaft, 1975. 392pp. Bib. 339-77. Free University of Berlin thesis.

G 16 PUHLE, Hans-Jürgen, 'Conservatism in modern German history'. *J. OF CONTEMP. HIST.*, **13** (4), 1978. pp. 689-720.

G 17 PUHLE, Hans-Jürgen, 'Radikalisierung und Wandel des deutschen Konservatismus vor dem Ersten Weltkrieg'. In RITTER, G.A. (ed.), *Deutsche Parteien vor 1918*, Cologne: Kiepenheuer & Witsch, 1973. pp. 165-86.

G 18 PUHLE, Hans-Jürgen, *Von der Agrarkrise zum Präfaschismus: Thesen zum Stellenwert der agrarischen Interessenverbände in der deutschen Politik am Ende des 19 Jahrhunderts*, Wiesbaden: Steiner, 1972 60pp.

G 19 PUHLE, Hans-Jürgen, 'Some social and political roots of prefascism in Germany, 1890-1914'. In IGGERS, George G. (ed), *Two Lectures in Modern German History*, Amherst: Council on Int. Studies, 1978. 62pp.

G 20 RIQUARTS, Kurt-Gerhard, *Der Antisemitismus als politische Partei in Schleswig-Holstein und Hamburg, 1871-1914*, Kiel University thesis, 1975. 442pp.

G 21 SCHILLING, Konrad, *Beiträge zu einer Geschichte des radikale Nationalismus in der Wilhelminischen Ära, 1890-1909: die Entstehung des radikalen Nationalismus, etc.*, Cologne University thesis, 1968. 707pp. Bib. 697-707.

G 22 STEGMANN, Dirk, *Die Erben Bismarcks: Parteien und Verbände in der Spätphase des Wilhelminischen Deutschlands Sammlungspolitik, 1897-1918*, Cologne: Kiepenheuer & Witsch, 1970. 584pp. Bib. 526-60.

G 23 STEGMANN, Dick, 'Zwischen Repression und Manipulation: konservative Machteliten und Arbeiter-und Angestelltenbewegung, 1910-1918; ein Beitrag zur Vorgeschichte der DAP/NSDAP'. *ARCH. FÜR SOZIALGESCH.*, **12**, 1972. pp. 351-432.

G 24 VOLKOV, Shulamit, 'The social and political function of late 19th century anti-semitism: the case of the small handicraft masters'. In WEHLER, H.U. (ed.), *Sozialgeschichte heute: Festschrift für Hans Rosenberg*, Göttingen: Vandenhoeck & Ruprecht, 1974. pp. 416-31.

G 25 VOLKOV, Shulamit, *The Rise of Popular Antimodernism in Germany: the urban master artisans, 1873-1896*, Princeton: University Press, 1978. ix, 399pp. Bib. 355-86.

G 26 WEHLER, Hans-Ulrich, *Das deutsche Kaiserreich, 1871-1918*, 2nd edn, Göttingen: Vandenhoeck & Ruprecht, 1975. 275pp. Bib. 257-69.

G 27   WEIDENFELD, Gerhard, *VDA: Verein für das Deutschtum im Ausland: Allgemeiner Deutscher Schulverein, 1881–1918: ein Beitrag zur Geschichte des deutschen Nationalismus und Imperialismus im Kaiserreich,* Frankfurt/M: Lang, 1976. 507pp.

G 28   WHITE, A.D., 'Kolbenheyer's use of the term 'Volk', 1910–1933: a study in nationalist ideology'. *GER. LIFE AND LETT.*, **23** (4), 1969/70. pp. 355–62.

G 29   WINKLER, Heinrich August, 'From social protectionism to national socialism: the German small-business movement in comparative perspective'. *J. OF MOD. HIST.*, **48** (1), 1976. pp. 1–18. Review article.

Forerunners and Roots of National Socialism: Economic, Racial, Ideological, Cultural

G 30   BRONDER, Dietrich, *Bevor Hitler kam: eine historische Studie,* Hanover: Pfeiffer, 1964. 446pp.

G 31   BUTLER, Rohan D'Olier, *The Roots of National Socialism, 1783–1933,* New York: Fertig, 1968. 314pp. Bib. 300–14. Repr. of Faber edn, 1942.

G 32   CARSTEN, Francis Ludwig, 'The historical roots of national socialism'. In FEUCHTWANGER, E.J. (ed.), *Upheaval and Continuity: a century of German history,* London: Wolff, 1973. pp. 116–33.

G 33   CHAMBERLAIN, Houston Stewart, *Foundations of the nineteenth century,* intro. by George Mosse, New York: Fertig, 1968. 2 vols. Tr. of *Die Grundlagen des neunzehnten Jahrhunderts,* 1910, by John Lees.

G 34   FIELD, Geoffrey G., *Evangelist of Race: the Germanic vision of Houston Stewart Chamberlain,* New York: Columbia University Press, 1981. 565pp. Bib. 519–43.

G 35   VANSELOW, Albert, *Das Werk Houston Stewart Chamberlains: eine Bibliographie,* Munich: Bruckmann, 1927, 37pp.

G 36   COHN, Norman Rufus Colin, *Warrant for Genocide: the myth of the Jewish world-conspiracy and the Protocols of the Elders of Zion,* New York: Harper & Row, 1966. London, Eyre & Spottiswoode, 1967. 303pp. Penguin edn, 1970. Bib. 320–7.

G 37   DAHRENDORF, Ralf, *Society and Democracy in Germany,* Garden City: Doubleday, 1967. xvi, 482pp. Bib. 451–64. Tr. of *Gesellschaft und Demokratie in Deutschland,* Munich, 1965.

G 38   FIELD, Geoffrey G., 'Nordic racism'. *J. OF HIST. IDEAS.*, **38**(3), 1977. pp. 523–40.

G 39   GELLATELY, Robert, *The Politics of Economic Despair: shopkeepers and German politics, 1890–1914*, London: Sage, 1974. xvi, 317pp. Bib. 253–99.

G 40   GLASER, Hermann, *The Cultural Roots of National Socialism*, Austin: University of Texas Press. London: Croom Helm, 1978. 289pp. Bib. 258–81. Tr. of *Spiesser-Ideologie*, Freiburg: Rombach, 1964, by Ernest A. Menze.

G 41   LAGARDE, Paul de (pseud.) [Paul Anton Bötticher], *Schriften für das deutsche Volk*, Munich: Lehmanns V., 1934. 2 vols. Author (1827–1891) advocate of conservative national regeneration.

G 42   LOUGEE, Robert W., *Paul de Lagarde, 1827–1891: a study of radical conservatism in Germany*, Cambridge, Mass: Harvard University Press, 1962. viii, 357pp. Bib. 321–6.

G 43   LEBOVICS, Herman, *Social Conservatism and the Middle Classes in Germany, 1914–1933*. Princeton: University Press, 1969. xi, 248pp. Bib. 221–43.

G 44   LENK, Kurt, *'Volk und Staat': Strukturwandel politischer Idelogien im 19. und 20 Jahrhunderten*, Stuttgart: Kohlhammer, 1971. 196pp. Bib. 177–84.

G 45   MEYER, Henry Cord, *Mitteleuropa in German thought and action, 1815–1945*, The Hague; Nijhoff, 1955. xv, 378pp. Bib. 346–85.

G 46   MOELLER VAN DEN BRUCK, Arthur, *Germany's Third Empire*, intro. by Mary Agnes Hamilton, London: Allen & Unwin, 1934. 268pp. Abridged trs. of of *Das Dritte Reich*, pub. in Hamburg, 1934. Author (1871–1950) conservative thinker.

G 47   PETZOLD, Joachim, 'Zur Funktion des Nationalismus: Moeller van den Brucks Beiträge zur faschistische Ideologie'. *Z. FÜR GESCHICHTWISS.*, **21** (**11**), 1973. pp. 1285–300.

G 48   SCHWIERSKOTT, Hans-Joachim, *Arthur Moeller van den Bruck und der revolutionäre Nationalismus in der Weimarer Republik*, Göttingen: Musterschmidt, 1962. 202pp. Works of Moeller 181–9. Bib. 190–5. Erlangen University thesis.

G 49   SILFEN, Paul Harrison, *The Völkische Ideology and the Roots of Nazism: the early writings of Moeller van den Bruck*, Jericho: Exposition Press, 1973. 85pp. Bib. 81–4.

G 50   MOSSE, George Lachmann, *The Crisis of German Ideology: intellectual origins of the Third Reich*. New York, Grosset & Dunlap, 1964. London, Weidenfeld & Nicolson, 1966. vii, 373pp. Notes 321–57.

G 51 MOSSE, George Lachmann, *Germans and Jews: the Right, the Left and the search for a 'third force' in pre-nazi Germany*, New York: Fertig, 1970. 260pp.

G 52 MOSSE, George Lachmann, *The Nationalization of the Masses: political symbolism and mass movements in Germany from the Napoleonic wars through the Third Reich*, New York: Fertig, 1975. xiv, 252pp.

G 53 PELINKA, Anton, 'Die Wurzeln der nationalsozialistischen Ideologie'. *Aus. Polit. Und Zeitg.*, **22**, 2 June 1979. pp. 25-31.

G 54 PLESSNER, Helmuth, *Die verspätete Nation: über die politische Verführbarkeit bürgerlichen Geistes*, 2nd edn Stuttgart: Kohlhammer, 1959. 174pp. First pub. as *Das Schicksal deutschen Geistes*, 1935.

G 55 SCHIEDER, Theodor, 'Zum Problem der historische Wurzeln des Nationalsozialismus'. *Aus. Polit. Und Zeitg.*, **13**, 30 January 1963. pp. 19-27.

G 56 SCHWEDHELM, Karl (ed.), *Propheten des Nationalismus*, Munich: List, 1969. 319pp. Bib. 269-81. Covers Dühring, Chamberlain, von Treitschke, Eckart, Lagarde, etc.

G 57 STACKELBERG, Roderick, *Idealism Debased: from völkisch ideology to national socialism*, Kent: Kent State University Press, 1981. xiii, 202pp. Bib. 180-94.

G 58 STERN, Fritz Richard, *The Failure of Illiberalism: essays on the political culture of modern Germany*, London: Allen & Unwin. New York: Knopf, 1972. xliv. 233pp.

G 59 STERN, Fritz Richard, *The Politics of Cultural Despair: a study in the rise of the Germanic ideology*, Berkeley: University of California Press, 1961. 367pp. Bib. Columbia University thesis, 1954. On Lagarde, Langbehn, Moeller van den Bruck.

G 60 STRUVE, Walter, *Elites against Democracy: leadership ideals in bourgeois political thought in Germany, 1890-1933*, Princeton: University Press, 1973. xii, 486pp. Bib. 465-75.

G 61 SZAZ, Zoltan Michael, 'The ideological precursors of national socialism'. *WEST. POLIT. Q.*, **16** (4), 1963. pp. 924-45.

G 62 VERMEIL, Edmond, 'Quelques aperçus sur les origines du nazisme hitlérien'. In *On The Track Of Tyrrany*, ed. Max Beloff, London: Vallentine Mitchell, 1959. pp. 201-10.

G 63 VIERECK, Peter, *Metapolitics: from the Romantics to Hitler*, New York: Capricorn, 1965. 371pp. First pub. Knopf, 1941.

G 64 WERESZYCKI, Henryk, 'From Bismarck to Hitler: the

problem of continuity from the Second to the Third Reich'. *POL. WEST. AFF.*, **14** (1), 1973. pp. 19-32.

G 65   ZMARZLIK, Hans-Günter, 'Das Sozialdarwinismus in Deutschland als geschistliches Problem'. *VIERTELJAHRSH. FÜR. ZEITG.*, **11**, 1963. pp. 246-73.

The Extreme Right and National Socialism: General

G 66   BARIÉTY, Jacques and DROZ, Jacques, *Republique de Weimar et régime hitlérien, 1918-1945: histoire de l'Allemagne*, Vol. 3, Paris: Hatier, 1973. 223pp.

G 67   BRACHER, Karl Dietrich, *Deutschland zwischen Demokratie und Diktatur: Beiträge zur neueren Politik und Geschichte*, Bern: Scherz, 1964. 415pp. Bib. 408-11.

G 68   BRACHER, Karl Dietrich, *The German Dictatorship: the origins, structure and consequences of national socialism*, intro. by Peter Gay, London: Weidenfeld & Nicolson. New York: Praeger, 1970. xv. 553pp. Bib. 503-33. Tr. of *Die deutsche Diktatur*, Cologne, 1969, 5th edn, 1976, by Jean Steinberg.

G 69   BRADY, Robert Alexander, *The Spirit and Structure of German fascism*, foreword by Harold J. Laski, New York: Fertig, 1969. xix, 420pp. Repr. of 1937 edn.

G 70   BROSZAT, Martin, *German National Socialism, 1919-1945*, Santa Barbara: Clio Press, 1966. viii, 154pp. Bib. 91-5. Tr. of *Der Nationalsozialisus*, Stuttgart, 1960, by Kurt Rosenbaum and Inge Boehm.

G 71   BROSZAT, Martin, 'National socialism: its social basis and psychological impact'. In FEUCHTWANGER, E.J. (ed.), *Upheaval and Continuity: a century of German history*, London: Wolff, 1973. pp. 134-51.

G 72   CRAIG, Gordon, *Germany, 1865-1945*. Oxford: University Press, 1978. xv, 825pp. Bib. 774-809.

G 73   FRAENKEL, Ernst, *The Dual State: a contribution to the theory of dictatorship*, tr. by E.A. Shils, Oxford: University Press, 1941. xvi, 248pp. Bib. 211-40.

G 74   GLUM, Friedrich, *Der Nationalsozialismus: Werden und Vergehen*, Munich: Beck, 1962. xiv, 474pp. Bib. 457-65.

G 75   GREBING, Helga, *Der Nationalsozialismus: Ursprung und Wesen*, 17th edn, Munich: Olzog, 1967. 160pp. Bib. 151-60.

G 76 GRIMM, Gerhard, *Der Nationalsozialismus: Programm und Verwirklichung*, Munich: Olzog, 1981. 333pp. Bib. 281-305.

G 77 GROSSER, Alfred (ed.), *Dix leçons sur le nazisme: ouvrage collectif*, Paris: Fayard, 1976. 250pp.

G 78 HEIDEN, Konrad, *A history of national socialism*, London: Methuen, 1934. New York, Knopf, 1935. 430pp. Tr. of *Geschichte des Nationalsozialismus*, Berlin: Rowohlt, 1932.

G 79 HERZSTEIN, Robert Edwin, *Adolf Hitler and the German trauma, 1913-1945: an interpretation of the nazi phenomenon*, New York: Putnam, 1974. xiv, 294pp. Bib. 271-83.

G 80 HIRSCH, Kurt (ed.), *Signale von Rechts: 100 Jahre Programme rechtsradikaler Parteien und Organisationen, 1867-1967*, Munich: Goldmann, 1967. 167pp.

G 81 HOLBORN, Hajo, (ed.), *Republic to Reich: the making of the nazi revolution*, tr. by Ralph Manheim, New York: Random House, 1972. xx, 491pp. Essays.

G 82 KETELSEN, Uwe Karsten, *Völkische-nationale und nationalsozialistische Literatur in Deutschland, 1890-1945*, Stuttgart: Metzler, 1976, ix, 116pp.

G 83 KLEMPERER, Klemens von, *Germany's New Conservatives: its history and dilemma in the twentieth century*, foreword by Sigmund Neumann, Princeton: University Press, 1957. xxvi, 250pp. Bib. 227-42.

G 84 KOHN, Hans, *The Mind of Germany: the education of a nation*, London: Macmillan. New York: Scribner, 1960. xiv. 370pp.

G 85 LINDENBERG, Christoph, *Die Technik des Bösen: zür Vorgeschichte und Geschichte des Nationalsozialismus*, 2nd edn, Stuttgart: V. Freies Geistesleben, 1978. 110pp.

G 86 McRANDLE, James Harrington, *The Track of the Wolf: essays on national socialism and its leader, Adolf Hitler*, Evanston: Northwestern University Press, 1965. ix, 261pp. Bib. 249-61.

G 87 MEINECKE, Friedrich, *The German Catastrophe: reflections and recollections*, Cambridge, Mass: Harvard University Press, 1950. xiii, 121pp. Tr. of *Die deutsche Katastrophe*, Wiesbaden, 1946, by Sidney B. Fay.

G 88 NICHOLLS, Anthony James, 'Germany'. In WOOLF, S.J., Gn 20. pp. 65-91.

G 89 NOLTE, Ernst, *Der Nationalsozialismus*, Frankfurt/M: Ullstein, 1970. 250pp.

G 90   RHODES, James Michael, *The Hitler Movement: a modern millenarian revolution*, Stanford: Hoover Inst. Press, 1980. 253pp. Bib. 239-48.

G 91   RITTER, Gerhard, *The German Problem: basic questions of German political life past and present*, tr. by Sigurd Burckhardt, Columbus: Ohio State University Press, 1965. ix. 233pp. Bib. 211-23.

G 92   SNYDER, Louis Leo, *Roots of German Nationalism*. Bloomington: Indiana University Press, 1978. x, 309pp. Bib. 295-300.

G 93   TURNER, Henry Ashby (ed.), *Nazism and the Third Reich*, New York: Quadrangle Books, 1972. 262pp. Bib. 249-56. Nine journal articles.

G 94   WAITE, Robert G.L. (ed.), *Hitler and Nazi Germany*, New York: Holt, Rinehart & Winston, 1965. 122pp. Bib. 116-22. Essays.

G 95   WEINSTEIN, Fred, *The Dynamics of Nazism: leadership, ideology and the Holocaust*, New York: Academic Press, 1980. xviii, 168pp.

Non-Nazi Extreme Rightist Currents in the Weimar Republic

G 96   ALBERTIN, Lothar, 'Stahlhelm und Reichsbanner: Bedrohung und Verteidigung der Weimarer Demokratie durch politische Kampfverbände'. *NEUE POLIT. LIT.*, **13**, 1968. pp. 456-65.

G 97   BERGHAHN, Volker R., *Der Stahlhelm: Bund der Frontsoldaten, 1918-1935*, Düsseldorf: Droste, 1966. 304pp. Bib. 289-94. London University thesis.

G 98   DUESTERBERG, Theodor, *Der Stahlhelm und Hitler*, pref. by Wolfgang Müller, Wolfenbüttel: Wolfenbüttel Verlags-Anstalt, 1949. 157pp. Bib. 154-7.

G 99   KLOTZBÜCHER, Alois, *Der politische Weg des Stahlhelm, Bund des Frontsoldaten in der Weimarer Republik; ein Beitrag zur Geschichte der 'Nationalen Opposition' 1918-1933*, University of Erlangen-Nürnberg thesis, 1964. xxv, 349pp. Bib. 326-49.

G 100   ASCHER, Abraham and LEWY, Günter, 'National bolshevism in Weimar Germany: alliance of political extremes against democracy'. *SOC. RES.*, **23** (4), 1956. pp. 450-80.

G 101   CAREY, Ann Terese, *Ernst Niekisch and National Bolshevism in Weimar Germany*. Rochester University thesis, 1972. UM 72-28730. 494pp.

G 102   DUPEUX, Louis, 'Le "national-bolchévisme": nationalisme absolu et révolution prolétarienne en Allemagne sous la République de Weimar'. *BULL. SOC. HIST. MOD.*, **71** (**2**), 1972. pp. 2-10.

G 103   DUPEUX, Louis, *Strategie communiste et dynamique conservatrice: essai sur les différents sens de l'expression 'national-bolchévisme' en Allemagne sous la République de Weimar, 1919-1933*, Paris: Champion, 1976, vii, 627pp. Bib. 589-608. Paris University thesis, 1974.

G 104   KLEMPERER, Klemens von, 'Towards a Fourth Reich? The history of national bolshevism in Germany'. *REV. OF POLIT.*, **13** (**2**), 1951. pp. 191-210.

G 105   PAETEL, Karl Otto, *Versuchung oder Chance? Zür Geschichte des deutschen Nationalbolschewismus, 1918-1932*, Göttingen: Musterschmidt, 1965. 343pp. Bib. 310-32.

G 106   SAUERMANN, Uwe, *Ernst Niekisch: zwischen allen Fronten . . . mit einem bio-bibliographischen Anhang von Armin Mohler*, Munich: Herbig, 1980. 236pp. Bib. 219-36.

G 107   SCHÜDDEKOPF, Otto-Ernst, *Nationalbolschewismus in Deutschland, 1918-1933*, 2nd edn, Frankfurt/M: Ullstein, 1973. 576pp. Bib. 550-70. First edn, *Linke Leute von Rechts*.

G 108   SONTHEIMER, Kurt, 'Der Tatkreis'. *VIERTELJAHRSH. FÜR ZEITG.*, **7** (**3**), 1959. pp. 229-60. Hans Zehrer and national bolshevism.

G 109   WARD, James Joseph, *Between Left and Right: Ernst Niekisch and national bolshevism in Weimar Germany*, State University of New York thesis, 1973. UM 73-19982. 406pp.

G 110   STRUVE, Walter, 'Hans Zehrer as a neoconservative élite theorist'. *AM. HIST. REV.*, **70** (**4**), 1965. pp. 1035-57.

G 111   BORST, Gert, *Die Ludendorff-Bewegung, 1919-1961: eine Analyse monologer Kommunikationsformen in der sozialen Zeitkommunikation*, Augsburg: Blasaditsch V., 1969. xi, 357pp. Munich University thesis. Erich Ludendorff (1865-1937).

G 112   FRENTZ, Hans, *Der unbekannte Ludendorff: der Feldherr in seiner Umwelt und Epoche*, Wiesbaden: Limes V., 1972. 318pp.

G 113   PIAZZA, Richard, *Ludendorff: the totalitarian and völkische politics of a military specialist*, Northwestern University thesis, 1969. UM 70-00140. 203pp.

G 114   THOSS, Bruno, *Der Ludendorff-Kreis, 1919-1923: München als Zentrum der Mitteleuropäischen Gegenrevolution zwischen Revolution und Hitler-Putsch*, Munich: Wölfle, 1978. v, 537pp. Bib. 495-523.

G 115   BRAATZ, Werner, 'Two neo-conservative myths in Germany, 1919-1932: the "Third Reich" and the "New State"'. *J. HIST. IDEAS.*, **32** (**4**), 1971. pp. 569-84.

G 116   CHAMBERLAIN, Brewster Searing, *The Enemy on the Right: the Alldeutsche Verband in the Weimar Republic, 1918-1926.* University of Maryland thesis, 1973. UM 73-18236. 461pp.

G 117   CHANADY, Attila, 'The disintegration of the German National People's Party, 1924-1930'. *J. OF MOD. HIST.*, **39** (**1**), 1967. pp. 65-91.

G 118   HERTZMAN, Lewis, *DNVP: Right-Wing Opposition in the Weimar Republic, 1918-1924*, Lincoln, Neb.: University of Nebraska Press, 1963. 263pp. Bib. 247-55.

G 119   HERTZMAN, Lewis, 'The founding of the German National People's Party (DNVP) November 1918-January 1919'. *J. OF MOD. HIST.*, **30** (**1**), 1958. pp. 24-36.

G 120   LEOPOLD, John A., *Alfred Hugenberg: the radical nationalist campaign against the Weimar Republic*, New Haven: Yale University Press, 1978. xvi, 298pp. Bib. 266-89.

G 121   LIEBE, Werner, *Die Deutschnationale Volkspartei, 1918-1924.* Düsseldorf: Droste, 1956. 190pp. Bib. 183-6.

G 122   STRIESOW, Jan, *Die Deutschnationale Volkspartei und die Völkische-Radikalen, 1918-1922.* Frankfurt/M: Haag & Herchen, 1981. 2 vols. Bib. vol. 2. 739-75.

G 123   DIEHL, James M., 'Germany: veterans' politics under three flags'. In WARD, Stephen R., (ed.), *The War Generation*, Port Washington: Kennikat Press, 1975. pp. 135-86.

G 124   DIEHL, James M., *Paramilitary Politics in Weimar Germany.* Bloomington: Indiana University Press, 1977. x, 406pp. Bib. 379-98. University of California, Berkeley thesis, 1972.

G 125   ERGER, Johannes, *Der Kapp-Lüttwitz-Putsch: ein Beitrag zur deutschen Innenpolitik, 1919-20.* Düsseldorf: Droste, 1967. 365pp. Bib. 353-61. Heidelberg University thesis, 1963.

G 126   FELDMAN, Gerald, 'Big business and the Kapp *Putsch*'. *CENT. EUR. HIST.*, **4** (**2**), 1971. pp. 99-130.

G 127   ORLOW, Dietrich, 'Preussen und Kapp-Putsch'. *VIERTELJAHRSH. FÜR ZEITG.*, **26** (**2**), 1978. pp. 191-236.

G 128   FENSKE, Hans, *Konservatismus und Rechtsradikalismus in Bayern nach 1918*, Bad Homberg: Gehlen, 1969. 340pp. Bib. 323-34. Freiburg University thesis, 1965.

G 129   FREKSA, Friedrich (ed.), *Kapitan Ehrhardt: Abenteuer und Schicksale*, Berlin: Scherl, 1924. 346pp. Leader of the extreme Rightist gang which murdered Rathenau.

G 130   KRÜGER, Gabriele, *Die Brigade Ehrhardts*, Hamburg: Leibniz-V., 1971. 176pp. Bib. 166–72.

G 131   HOEPKE, Klaus-Peter, *Die deutsche Rechte und der italienische Faschismus: ein Beitrag zum Selbstverständnis und zur Politik von Gruppen und Verbänden der deutschen Rechten*, Düsseldorf: Droste, 1968. 348pp. Bib. 331–40.

G 132   KOCH, Hannsjoachim, *Der deutsche Bürgerkrieg: eine Geschichte der deutschen und österreichischen Freikorps, 1918–1923*, Berlin: Ullstein, 1978. 487pp. Bib. 432–81.

G 133   OERTZEN. Friedrich Wilhelm von, *Die deutschen Freikorps, 1918–1923; mit einem Anhang Das Sudetendeutsche Freikorps 1938 von Willi Körbel*, Munich: Bruckmann, 1939. xiv, 525pp. Bib. 513–19.

G 134   POSSE, Ernst Hans, *Die politischen Kampfbünde Deutschlands*, 2nd edn, Berlin: Junker & Dünnhaupt, 1931. 103pp. On the Freikorps.

G 135   SCHULTZE, Hagen, *Freikorps und Republik, 1918–1920*, Boppard: Boldt, 1969. xi, 363pp. Bib. 335–49.

G 136   WAITE, Robert G.L., *Vanguard of Nazism: the Free Corps movement in postwar Germany 1918–23*, Cambridge, Mass: Harvard University Press, 1952. xii, 344pp. Bib. 297–332. Harvard University thesis, 1949.

G 137   LARGE, David Clay, *The Politics of Law and Order: a history of the Bavarian Einwohnerwehr, 1918–1921*, Philadelphia: American Philosophical Soc., 1980. 87pp. Bib. 79–84.

G 138   LOHALM, Uwe, *Völkischer Radikalismus: die Geschichte des Deutsch-Völkischen Schutz und Trutz-Bundes, 1919–1923*, Hamburg: Leibniz, 1970. 492pp. Bib. 335–481.

G 139   MOHLER, Armin, *Die konservative Revolution in Deutschland, 1918–1933: ein Handbuch*, Darmstadt: Wiss. Buchgesellschaft, 1972. xxx, 554pp. Bib. 173–483.

G 140   NEUROHR, Jean Frederic, *Der Mythos vom Dritten Reich: zur Geistesgeschichte des Nationalsozialismus*, Stuttgart: Cotta, 1957. 286pp. Bib. 274–6.

G 141   NEVILLE, Joseph B., 'Ernst Reventlow and the Weimar Republic: a völkisch radical confronts Germany's social question'. *Societas*, **7** (**3**), 1977. pp. 229–51.

G 142   SONTHEIMER, Kurt, *Antidemokratisches Denken in den Weimarer Republik: die politischen Ideen des deutschen Nationalismus zwischen 1918 und 1933*, Munich: Nymphenburger V., 1962. 413pp. Bib. 401–9.

G 143   SOUTHERN, David B., 'Anti-democratic terror in the Weimar Republic: the Black Reichswehr and the Feme-murders'. In MOMMSEN W.J. and HIRSCHFELD, Gerhard (eds), *Social Protest, Violence and Terror in Nineteenth- and Twentieth-century Europe*, London: Macmillan, 1982. pp. 330–41.

G 144   WULFF, Reimer, *Die Deutschvölkische Freiheitspartei, 1922– 1928*, Marburg University thesis, 1968. 311pp.

The Third Reich: General

G 145   ALEFF, Eberhard (ed.), *Das Dritte Reich; mit Beiträgen von Walter Tormin, Eberhard Aleff und Friedrich Zipfel*, Hanover: V. für Lit. und Zeitg., 1970. 301pp. Bib. 241–5.

G 146   BROSZAT, Martin, *The Hitler State: the foundation and development of the internal structure of the Third Reich*, London: Longman, 1981. xvii, 378pp. Bib. 362–9. Tr. of *Der Staat Hitlers*, Munich, 1969, by John W. Hiden.

G 147   BUCHHEIM, Hans, *The Third Reich: its beginnings, its development, its end*, London: Wolff, 1961, 98pp. Tr. of *Die Dritte Reich*, Munich, 1958, by Allan and Lieselotte Yahraes.

G 148   DOUCET, Friedrich W., *Im Banne des Mythos: die Psychologie des Dritten Reiches*, Esslingen am Neckar: Bechtle, 1979. 295pp. Bib. 280–7.

G 149   EBENSTEIN, William, *The Nazi State*, New York: Farrar & Rinehart, 1943. xi, 355pp.

G 150   GISEVIUS, Hans-Bernd, *To the Bitter End*, Westport: Greenwood Press, 1975. 632pp. Tr. of *Bis zum bitteren Ende*, Hamburg: Rutten & Loening, 1960.

G 151   GLASER, Hermann, *Das Dritte Reich: Anspruch und Wirklichkeit*, 4th edn, Freiburg: Herder, 1963. 191pp. Bib. 178–87.

G 152   GÖHRING, Martin, *Alles oder Nichts: zwölf Jahre totalitärer Herrschaft in Deutschland*. 1. *1933–1939*, Tübingen: Mohr, 1966. 354pp. Bib. 341–50.

G 153   HEGNER, H.S., *Die Reichskanzlei, 1933–1945: Anfang und*

Ende des Dritten Reiches, 3rd edn, Frankfurt/M: V. Frankfurter Bücher, 1960. 448pp. Bib. 440-3.

G 154 HILDEBRAND, Klaus, *Das Dritte Reich*, 2nd edn, Munich: Oldenbourg, 1980. 244pp. Bib. 195-224.

G 155 HIRSCHFELD, Gerhard and KETTENACKER, Lothar (eds), *Der 'Führerstaat': Mythos und Realität: Studien und Politik des Dritten Reiches*, intro. by Wolfgang J. Mommsen, Stuttgart: Klett-Cotta, 1981. 465pp. Papers in English and German by Mason, Hans Mommsen, Hildebrand, Kettenacker, Kershaw, Caplan, Noakes, Matzerath, Fröhlich, Gies, Hauner, Jamin, Boehnert, Milward, Wendt and Hüttenberger.

G 156 HOFER, Walther, *Die Diktatur Hitlers bis zum Beginn des Zweiten Weltkrieges, 1933-1939*, 3rd edn, Konstanz: Athenaion, 1971. 266pp. Bib. 226-60.

G 157 HUBER, Heinz and MÜLLER, Artur (eds), *Das Dritte Reich: seine Geschichte in Texten, Bilden und Dokumentation*, Munich: Desch, 1964. 2 vols.

G 158 International Council for Philosophy and Humanistic Studies, *The Third Reich*, ed. Maurice Baumont, John H.E. Fried and Edmond Vermeil, New York: Praeger. London: Weidenfeld & Nicolson, 1955. xv, 910pp.

G 159 MAU, Hermann and KRAUSNICK, Helmut, *German History, 1933-1945: an assessment by German historians*, London: Wolff, 1959. New York: Ungar, 1963. 157pp. Tr. of *Deutsche Geschichte der jüngsten Vergangenheit*, Tübingen: Wunderlich, 1956.

G 160 NEUMANN, Franz, *Behemoth: the structure and practice of national socialism, 1933-1944*, 2nd edn, London: Cass, 1967. 649pp. First pub. 1944.

G 161 SALOMON, Ernst von, *Fragebogen: the questionnaire*, pref. by Goronwy Rees, Garden City: Doubleday, 1955. 525pp. Tr. of *Der Fragebogen*, Hamburg, 1951, by Constantine Fitzgibbon. Attack on denazification and apologia for the Third Reich from a nihilistic, revolutionary conservative.

G 162 SHIRER, William L., *The Rise and Fall of the Third Reich: a history of nazi Germany*, London: Secker & Warburg. New York: Simon & Schuster 1960. 1245pp. Bib. 1181-91. Pan edn, 1964.

G 163 STACHURA, Peter D. (ed.), *The Shaping of the Nazi State*. London: Croom Helm. New York: Barnes & Noble, 1978. 304pp. Includes articles by A. Tyrell, C. Fischer, Stachura, J. Stephenson, G. Giles, J. Noakes, M.S. Phillips, J. Caplan, G. Stoakes.

G 164   STEINER, John M., *Power, Politics, and Social Change in National Socialist Germany: a process of escalation into mass destruction*, The Hague: Mouton, 1976. xx, 466pp. Bib. 427–43.

G 165   VOGELSANG, Thilo, *Die nationalsozialistische Zeit: Deutschland 1933 bis 1939*, Frankfurt/M: Ullstein, 1968. 178pp. Bib. 171–2.

The Third Reich: Documents

G 166   ANGER, Walter (ed.), *Das Dritte Reich in Dokumenten*, Frankfurt/M: Europaïsche Verlagsanstalt, 1957. 216pp. Bib. 207–8.

G 167   HOFER, Walther (ed.), *Der Nationalsozialismus: Dokumente, 1933–1945*, Frankfurt/M: Fischer, 1957. 397pp. Bib. 373–85.

G 168   International Military Tribunal, *The Trial of the Major War Criminals*, Nuremburg: IMT, 1949. 42 vols. Documents in evidence, vols. 25–42.

G 169   JACOBSEN, Hans-Adolf and JOCHMANN, Werner, (eds), *Ausgewählte Dokumente zur Geschichte des Nationalsozialismus, 1933–1945*, Bielefeld: V. Neue Gesellschaft, 1961–6. 3 vols.

G 170   KÜHNL, Reinhard, *Der deutsche Faschismus in Quellen und Dokumenten*, 3rd edn, Cologne: Pahl-Rugenstein, 1977. 530pp. Bib. 503–12.

G 171   NOAKES, Jeremy and PRIDHAM, Geoffrey (eds), *Documents on Nazism, 1919–1945*, London: Cape, 1974. 704pp.

G 172   PINNOW, Hermann, *Der Staat der Gewalt: Quellentexte und Berichte über die nationalsozialistische Diktatur*, Stuttgart: Klett, 1960. 79pp. Bib. 78–9.

G 173   POLIAKOV, Leonard and WULF, Josef (eds), *Das Dritte Reich und seine Denker: Dokumente*, Berlin-Grunewald: Arani, 1959. 560pp.

G 174   RÜHLE, Gerd, *Das Dritte Reich: dokumentarische Darstellung des Aufbaus der Nation*, Berlin: Hummel, 1934–40. 8 vols.

G 175   SNYDER, Louis Leo. (ed.), *Hitler's Third Reich: a documentary history*, Chicago: Nelson-Hall, 1981. xviii, 619pp.

Bibliographies, Archives, Reference Works

G 176   American Historical Association, *Guides to German records microfilmed at Alexandria, Va.* Washington, DC, National Archives, 1958– Over 70 vols. of catalogues to nazi records.

G 177 BAYNES, Norman H., *A Short List of Books on National Socialism*, London, Kay & Staples, 1943. 15pp.

G 178 BENZE, Rudolf, *Wegweiser ins Dritte Reich: Einführung in das völkische Schrifttum*, 3rd edn, Brunswick: Appelhans, 1934. 44pp.

G 179 BERNBAUM, John A., 'The captured German records: a bibliographical survey'. *Historian.*, **32** (**4**), 1970. pp. 564–75.

G 180 Birmingham Public Libraries, *National socialist literature in Birmingham Reference Library:* a bibliography, intro. by Lord Dacre of Glanton, Birmingham: Social Sciences Dept., 1980. x, 74pp.

G 181 BOBERACH, Heinz, 'Das Schriftgut der staatlichen Verwaltung, der Wehrmacht und der NSDAP aus der Zeit von 1933–1945: Versuch einer Bilanz'. *Der Archivar.*, **22** (**2**), 1969. pp. 137–51.

G 182 BROSZAT, Martin, 'Bibliographie zur Geschichte der nationalsozialistischen Zeit'. *POLIT. STUD.*, **9** (**96**), 1958. pp. 280–4.

G 183 BROWDER, George Clark, 'Potentials of the Berlin Document Centre'. *CENT. EUR. HIST.*, **5** (**4**), 1972. pp. 362–80.

G 184 BRÜDIGAM, Heinz, *Wahrheit und Fälschung: das Dritte Reich und seine Gegner in der Literatur seit 1945: Versuch eines kritischen Überblicks.* Frankfurt/M: Roderberg, 1959. 93pp.

G 185 *Das Deutsche Führerlexicon, 1934/35*, Berlin: Stollberg, 1934. 2 vols.

G 186 FEST, Joachim C., *The Face of the Third Reich: portraits of the nazi leadership*, tr. Michael Bullock, London: Weidenfeld & Nicolson. New York: Pantheon, 1970. xiii, 402pp. Bib. 386–91.

G 187 FRÖHLICH, Elke, 'Akten aus der NS-Zeit in bayerischen Stadtarchiven'. *MITT. ARCH. IN BAYERN,* **23**, 1977. pp. 55–60.

G 188 GOGUEL, Rudi, *Antifaschistischer Widerstand und Klassenkampf: die faschistische Diktatur 1933 bis 1945 und ihrer Gegner: Bibliographie deutschsprachiger Literatur, etc.*, Berlin: Militärv. der DDR, 1976. 567pp.

G 189 GOLDBACH, Marie-Louise and others (eds), *Bibliographie zur Deutschlandpolitik, 1941–1974*, Frankfurt/M: Metzner, 1975. 248pp.

G 190 HEINZ, Grete and PETERSON, Agnes F. (comps.), *NSDAP Hauptarchiv: guide to the Hoover Institution microfilm collection*, Stanford: Hoover Inst., 1964. 175pp.

G 191 HELD, Walter, *Verbände und Truppen der deutschen Wehrmacht und Waffen-SS im Zweiten Weltkreig: eine Bibliographie deutschsprachigen Nachkriegsliteratur*, Osnabrück: Biblio-V., 1978. xxiii, 649pp. Suppl. to

G. Tessin, *Verbände und Truppen der deutschen Wehrmacht und Waffen-SS im Zweiten Weltkrieg*, 1972.

G 192   HÜTTENBERGER, Peter, *Bibliographie zum Nationalsozialismus*, Göttingen: Vandenhoeck & Ruprecht, 1980. 214pp.

G 193   KEHR, Helen and LANGMAID, Janet (comps), *The Nazi Era, 1919–1945: a select bibliography of published works from the early roots to 1980*, London: Mansell, 1982. xvi, 621pp.

G 194   KEMPNER, Robert M.W., *Das Dritte Reich im Kreuzverhör*, Königstein: Athenäum, 1980. 300pp. First pub. 1969. Biographical sketches of nazi war criminals.

G 195   KEMPNER, Robert M.W., 'Nuremberg trials as sources of recent German political and historical materials'. *AM. POLIT. SCI. REV.*, **44** (2), 1950. pp. 447–59.

G 196   KENT, George O., 'Research opportunities in West and East German archives in the Weimar period and the Third Reich'. *CENT. EUR. HIST.*, **12** (1), 1979. pp. 38–67.

G 197   Michigan University Library, *German archival material in the Rare Book Room, the University of Michigan Library*, prep. by Gerhard L. Weinberg, Ann Arbor, 1960. 8pp.

G 198   Nationalsozialistische Deutsche Arbeiter-Partei, *Deutsche Volkskunde im Schrifftum: ein Leitfaden für die Schulungs- und Erziehungsarbeit der NSDAP*, Berlin: Eher, 1938. 152pp.

G 199   Nationalsozialistische Deutsche Arbeiter-Partei, *Nationalsozialistische Bibliographie: Monatshefte der parteiamtlichen Prüfungskommission zum Schutze der NS Schrifftums*, ed. Philipp Bouhler, Berlin: Eher, 1936–44. 9 vols.

G 200   Nationalsozialistische Deutsche Arbeiter-Partei, *Nationalsozialistische Bibliographie*. Beihefte, 1–4, Berlin: Eher, 1939–42. 4 vols. See also G 941.

G 201   Nationalsozialistische Deutsche Arbeiter-Partei, Reichsorganisationsamt. *Partei Statistik*, Munich: Eher, 1935. 3 vols.

G 202   PAECHTER, Heinz, *Nazi-Deutsch: a glossary of contemporary German usage. . .* , 2nd edn, New York: Ungar, 1944. 128pp.

G 203   PHILLIPS, Leona Rasmussen, *Adolf Hitler and the Third Reich: an annotated bibliography*, New York: Gordon Press, 1977. 251pp.

G 204   ROTHFEDER, Herbert P., (comp.), *Checklist of selected German pamphlets and booklets of the Weimar and nazi period in the Univ. of Michigan Library*, Ann Arbor: University of Michigan Library, 1961. 214pp.

G 205 SAGITZ, W., *Bibliographie des Nationalsozialismus*, Cottbus: Heine, 1937. 168pp.

G 206 SNYDER, Louis Leo, *Encyclopaedia of the Third Reich*, London: Hale. New York: McGraw Hill, 1976. 410pp. Bib. 389–410.

G 207 STACHURA, Peter D., *The Weimar Era and Hitler, 1918–1933: a critical bibliography*, Oxford: Clio Press, 1977. 275pp.

G 208 Städtische Volksbücherei, *Nuremberg, Nationalsozialismus: ein Buchenverzeichnis*, Nuremberg: Städtische Bücherei, 1965. 160pp.

G 209 STOCKHORST, Erich, *Fünftausend Köpfe: wer war was im Dritten Reich*, Velbert: Blick & Bild, V., 1967. 461pp.

G 210 ULLMANN, Hans-Peter, *Bibliographie zur Geschichte der deutschen Parteien und Interessenverbände*, Göttingen: Vandenhoeck & Ruprecht, 1978. 263pp.

G 211 United States, Department of State, *A catalog of files and microfilms of the German Foreign Ministry Archives, 1920–1945*, comp. and ed. by George O. Kent, Stanford: Hoover Inst., 1962–72. 4 vols.

G 212 United States, National Archives and Records Service. *Records of the United States Nuremberg War Crimes Trials interrogations, 1946–1949*, Washington DC: National Archives Trust Fund Board, 1977. 99pp.

G 213 United States, Senate. Subcommittee on War Mobilization. *Nazi Party Membership Records*. Washington, DC: USGPO, 1946. 4 vols.

G 214 VOLZ, Hans, *Daten der Geschichte der NSDAP*, 14th edn, Berlin: Ploetz, 1943. viii. 160pp.

G 215 WEINBERG, Gerhard L. and others (comps), *Guide to Captured German Documents*, Montgomery: Human Resources Research Inst., 1952. 90pp. Suppl. Washington, DC: National Archives, 1959.

G 216 Wiener Library, *From Weimar to Hitler: Germany, 1918–1933*, 2nd edn, London: Vallentine Mitchell, 1964. x, 268pp. Bibliography.

G 217 Wiener Library, *Persecution and Resistance under the Nazis*, London: Inst. of Contemp. Hist., 1978. 500pp. Bibliography.

G 218 WISTRICH, Robert S., *Who's Who in Nazi Germany*, London: Weidenfeld & Nicolson, 1982. 359pp. Bib. 353–9.

G 219 WOLFE, Robert (ed.), *Captured German and Related Records: a national archives conference*, Athens: Ohio University Press, 1974. 279pp.

Historiography and Interpretation

G 220   ARON, Raymond, 'Is there a Nazi mystery?' *Encounter,* **54** (**6**), 1980. pp. 29–41.

G 221   ARONSFELD, C.C., 'Whitewashing Hitler: "revisionist" history distorters at work'. *Patterns of Prejudice,* **14** (**1**), 1980. pp. 16–23.

G 222   AY, Karl-Ludwig, 'Die Deutsche Revolution, 1914–1948: Bemerkungen über gesellschaftlichen Wandel und Epochenbegriff'. *Z. FÜR BAYERISCHE LANDESG.*, **36** (**3**), 1973. pp. 877–96.

G 223   AYÇOBERRY, Pierre, *The Nazi Question: an essay on the interpretations of national socialism, 1922–1975,* New York: Pantheon, 1981. xiv, 257pp. Bib. 242–7. Tr. of *La Question nazie,* by Robert Hurley.

G 224   BARRACLOUGH, Geoffrey, 'New nazi history'. *New York Rev. of Books,* 19 Oct., 2 Nov. 16 Nov. 1972. pp. 37–43, 32–8, 25–31.

G 225   BESSON, Waldemar, 'Neuere Literatur zur Geschichte des Nationalsozialismus'. *VIERTELJAHRSH. FÜR ZEITG.*, **9** (**3**), 1961. pp. 314–30.

G 226   BINDER, Gerhart, 'Revisionsliteratur in der Bundesrepublik: Literaturbericht' *GESCH. IN WISS. UND UNTERR.*, **17**, 1966. pp. 179–200.

G 227   BODENSIECK, Heinrich, 'Nationalsozialismus in revisionistischer Sicht.' *Aus Polit. Und Zeitg.*, **11**, 20 March 1961. pp. 175–80.

G 228   BODENSIECK, Heinrich, *Das nationalsozialistische Reich in der Literatur des gespaltenen Deutschland von 1945 bis 1959,* Schleswig: Evangelischen Akad, 1960. 79pp.

G 229   BOESCH, Joseph, 'Neue Literatur zur Geschichte des Nationalsozialismus'. *SCHWEIZ. Z. FÜR GESCH.*, **5**, 1955. pp. 206–14.

G 230   BREDOW, Wilfried von, 'Das Deutsche Reich und der Zweite Weltkrieg'. *ARCH. FÜR SOZIALG.*, **20**, 1980. pp. 560–5. Review article.

G 231   BROSZAT, Martin, 'William Shirer und die Geschichte des Dritten Reiches'. *HIST. Z.*, **196**, 1963. pp. 112–23.

G 232   CARSTEN, Francis Ludwig, 'What German historians say about the nazis'. *Listener,* **53** (**1358**), 10 March 1955. pp. 415–17.

G 233   CONWAY, John S., 'Hermann Rauschning as historian and opponent of nazism'. *CAN. J. OF HIST.*, **8** (**1**), 1973. pp. 67–78.

G 234   DORPALEN Andreas, 'Weimar Republic and nazi era in West German perspective'. *CENT. EUR. HIST.*, **11** (**3**), 1978. pp. 211–30.

G 235   DROZ, Jacques, 'Les historiens français devant l'histoire allemande'. In *Europa: Erbe und Aufgabe*, ed. Martin Göhring, Wiesbaden: Steiner, 1956.

G 236   DUPEUX, Louis, 'Historiographie récente du Troisième Reich'. *REV. D'ALLEM.*, **10** (**2**), 1978. pp. 275–92.

G 237   DUPEUX, René, 'René Capitant et l'analyse idéologique du nazisme, 1934–1939'. *Francia*, **5**, 1979. pp. 627–37.

G 238   DUPEUX, René, 'La République de Weimar et le IIIe Reich: essai de bibliographie et d'historiographie récente, 1972–1977'. *REV. D'ALLEM.*, **10** (**1**), 1978. pp. 24–48

G 239   EPSTEIN, Klaus P., 'Der Nationalsozialismus in amerikanischer und englischer Sicht'. *Aus Polit. Und Zeitg.*, **13**, 30 January 1963. pp. 32–40.

G 240   FAULENBACH, Bernd, *Ideologie des deutschen Weges: die deutsche Geschichte in der Historiographie zwischen Kaiserreich und National-sozialismus*, Munich: Beck 1980. xiii, 517pp. Bib. 445–510. Bochum University thesis.

G 241   GOETZ, Helmut, 'Nationalsozialismus und Bolschewismus: ein Vergleich'. *SCHWEIZ. MONATSH.*, **39**, 1959/60. pp. 849–58.

G 242   GROSSHUT, Friedrich, 'Nationalsozialismus und Boulangismus'. *DTSCH. RUNDSCH.*, **88**, 1962. pp. 111–120.

G 243   HAMMEN, Oscar J., 'German historians and the advent of the national socialist state'. *J. OF MOD HIST.*, **13** (**2**), 1941. pp. 161–88.

G 244   HEFFTER, Heinrich, 'Forschungsprobleme des Geschichte des Nationalsozialismus'. *GESCH. IN WISS. UND UNTERR.*, **3** (**4**), 1952. pp. 197–215.

G 245   HIDEN, John and FARQUHARSON, John E., *Explaining the Third Reich: historians and Hitler's Germany*, London: Batsford, 1983. 176pp.

G 246   HILDEBRAND, Klaus, 'Nationalsozialismus ohne Hitler? das Dritte Reich als Forschungsgegenstand der Geschichtwissenschaft'. *GESCH. IN WISS. UND UNTERR.*, **31** (**5**), 1980. pp. 289–304.

G 247   HILDEBRAND, Klaus, 'Noch einmal: zur Interpretation des Nationalsozialismus'. *GESCH. IN WISS. UND UNTERR.*, **32** (**4**), 1981. pp. 199–204.

G 248 HILDEBRAND, Klaus and MOMMSEN, Hans, 'National-sozialismus oder Hitlerismus?' In BUSCH, M. (ed.), *Personalichkeit und Struktur in der Geschichte*, Düsseldorf: Droste, 1977.

G 249 HILLGRUBER, Andreas, *Endlich genug über Nationalsozial-ismus und Zweiten Weltkrieg? Forschungsstand und Literatur*, Düsseldorf: Droste, 1982. 104pp.

G 250 HILLGRUBER, Andreas, 'Innen-und Aussenpolitik Deutsch-lands von 1933-1945: Literaturbericht'. *GESCH. IN WISS UND UNTERR.*, **26** (**9**), 1975. pp. 578-94; **25**(**4**), 1974. pp. 239-56; **27**(**8**), 1976. pp. 509-20.

G 251 KOHN, Hans, 'National socialism and Germany'. *Yale Review*, **48** (**2**), 1958. pp. 191-203.

G 252 KREN, George M., 'Psychohistorical interpretations of national socialism'. *GER. STUD. REV.*, **1** (**2**), 1978. pp. 150-72.

G 253 KREN, George M., 'Psychohistorians contra the Third Reich'. *PSYCHOHIST. REV.*, **5** (**2**), 1976. pp. 34-40.

G 254 KRIEGER, Leonard, 'Nazism: highway or byway?' *CENT. EUR. HIST.*, **11** (**1**), 1978. pp. 3-22.

G 255 KÜHNL, Reinhard, 'Der deutsche Faschismus: National-sozialismus und Dritte Reich in Einzeluntersuchungen und Gesamt-darstellungen'. *NEUE POLIT. LIT.*, **15**, 1970. pp. 13-43.

G 256 KÜHNL, Reinhard, 'Der deutsche Faschismus in der neueren Forschung'. *Argument*, **15** (**3**), 1973. pp. 152-82.

G 257 KÜHNL, Reinhard, *Deutschland zwischen Demokratie und Faschismus: zur Problematik der bürgerlichen Gesellschaft seit 1918*, Munich: Hanser, 1969. 187pp.

G 258 KÜHNL, Reinhard, *Das Dritte Reich in der Presse der Bundes-republik: Kritik eines Geschichtsbildes*, Frankfurt/M: Europaïsche Ver-lagsanstalt, 1966. 217pp.

G 259 LOEWENBERG, Peter, 'Psychohistorical perspectives in modern German history'. *J. OF MOD. HIST.*, **47** (**2**), 1975. pp. 229-79.

G 260 LOZEK, Gerhard and RICHTER, Rolf, *Legende oder Recht-fertigung? Zur Kritik der Faschismustheorien in der bürgerlichen Geschichts-schreibung*, Frankfurt/M: V. Marxistische Blätter, 1980. 100pp.

G 261 LOZEK, Gerhard, and WALTER, Georg, 'Vom Dritten Reich zur Bundesrepublik: zur positiven Umwertung des faschistischen Staates in der westdeutschen Historiographie'. *Z. FUR GESCHICHT-WISS.*, **16** (**10**), 1968. pp. 1253-64.

G 262 MASON, Timothy W., 'The coming of the nazis'. *TIMES LIT. SUPPL.*, 1 February, 1974. pp. 93-6. Review article.

G 263 MASON, Timothy W., 'Intention and explanation: a current controversy about the interpretation of national socialism'. 'In HIRSCHFELD, G. and KETTENACKER, L., G 155. pp. 23-42.

G 264 MATZERATH, Horst and VOLKMANN, Heinrich, 'Modernisierungstheorie und Nationalsozialismus'. In KOCKA, Jurgen (ed.), *Theorien in der Praxis des Historikers: Forschungsbeispiele und Diskussion*, Göttingen: Vandenhoeck & Ruprecht, 1977. pp. 86-116.

G 265 MEINECKE, Friedrich, 'Militarismus und Hitlerismus'. In BERGHAHN, Volker R., (ed.), *Militarismus*, Cologne: Kiepenheuer & Witsch, 1975. pp. 188-95.

G 266 MEYERS, Peter and RIESENBERGER, Dieter (eds), *Der Nationalsozialismus in der historisch-politischen Bildung*, Göttingen: Vandenhoeck & Ruprecht, 1979. 218pp. Bib. 215-18.

G 267 MOMMSEN, Hans, 'National socialism: continuity and change'. In LAQUEUR, W., Gn 35. pp. 179-210.

G 268 MOSSE, George Lachmann, *Nazism: a history and comparative analysis of national socialism; an interview with Michael A. Ledeen*, New Brunswick, NJ: Transaction. Oxford: Blackwell, 1978. 134pp.

G 269 PERZ, Bertrand and SAFRIAN, Hans, 'Wege und Irrwege der Faschismusforschung'. *Zeitgeschichte.*, **7**, 1980. pp. 437-59. Review article.

G 270 PETZOLD, Joachim, 'War Hitler ein Revolutionär? Zum Thema Modernismus und Antimodernismus in der Faschismus-Diskussion'. *BL. FÜR DTSCH. UND INT. POLIT.*, **23** (2), 1978. pp. 186-205.

G 271 *Recherches Internationales à la Lumière du Marxisme*, No. **69/70**, 1971/72. Issue on 'Le fascisme Hitlérien: études actuelles'. 212pp. Includes articles by André Gisselbrecht, Gert Schäfer, Reinhard Opitz, Eberhard Czichon, Dietrich Eichholtz, Günter Hartung, Victor Klemperer.

G 272 REIN, Gustav, *Bonapartismus und Faschismus in der deutschen Geschichte*, Göttingen: Musterschmidt, 1960. 34pp.

G 273 SAUER, Wolfgang, 'National socialism: totalitarianism or fascism?' *AM. HIST. REV.*, **73** (5), 1967. pp. 404-24. Also in LAQUEUR, W., Gn 35.

G 274 SNELL, John L. (ed.), *The Nazi Revolution: Germany's guilt or fate?*, Boston: Heath, 1959. 97pp.

254

G 275 VERMEIL, Edmond, *Doctrinaires de la révolution allemande, 1918-1938*, Paris: Sorlot, 1938. 392pp.

G 276 WALDMAN, Loren K., 'Mass-society theory and religion: the case of the nazis'. *Am. J. of Polit. Sci.*, **20** (2), 1976. pp. 319-26.

G 277 WALDMAN, Loren K., *Models of Mass Movements: the case of the nazis*, Chicago University thesis, 1973. 358pp.

G 278 WEISSBECKER, Manfred, *Entteufelung der braunen Barbarei: zu einigen neueren Tendenzen in der Geschichtschreibung der BRD über Faschismus und faschistische Führer*, Frankfurt/M: V. Marxistische Blätter, 1975. 122pp.

G 279 WHITESIDE, Andrew G., 'The nature and origin of national socialism'. *J. OF CENT. EUR. AFF.*, **17** (1), 1957. pp. 48-73. Survey of literature.

Nazi Ideology

G 280 BERNING, Cornelia, *Vom 'Abstammungsnachweis' zum 'Zuchtwort': Vokabular des Nationalsozialismus*, foreword by Werner Betz, Berlin: De Gruyter, 1964. vi, 225pp. Bib. 219-25.

G 281 BREITLING, Rupert, *Die nationalsozialistische Rassenlehre: Entstehung, Austreitung, Nutzen, und Schaden einer politischen Ideologie*, Meisenheim: Hain, 1971. 77pp. Bib. 77.

G 282 BROSZAT, Martin, 'Soziale Motivation und Führer-Bindung des Nationalsozialismus'. *VIERTELJAHRSH. FÜR ZEIT-GESCH.*, **18** (4), 1970. pp. 392-409.

G 283 BROSZAT, Martin, 'Die völkische Ideologie und der Nationalsozialismus'. *DTSCH. RUNDSCH.*, **84** (1), 1958. pp. 53-68.

G 284 FEDER, Gottfried, *The Programme of the NSDAP and its General Conceptions*, Munich: Eher, 1932. 51pp. Tr. of *Das Program der NSDAP*, Munich: Eher, 1932, by E.T.S. Dugdale. Feder (1883-1941), one of the earliest members of the NSDAP.

G 285 FETSCHER, Iring, 'Die industrielle Gesellschaft und die Ideologie der Nationalsozialisten'. *GES. STAAT ERZIEH.*, **7**, 1962. pp. 6-23.

G 286 GAMM, Hans Jochen, *Der braune Kult: das Dritte Reich und seine Ersatzreligion: ein Beitrag zur politischen Bildung*, Hamburg: Rütten & Loening, 1962. 222pp. Bib. 221-2.

G 287 GREGOR, A. James, 'Nordicism revisited'. *Phylon.*, **22**, 1961.

pp. 351-61. On Hans Günther (1891-1968), leading nazi ideologist of racialism.

G 288   GRUCHMANN, Lothar, *Nationalsozialistische Grossraumordnung: die Konstruktion einer 'deutschen Monroe-Doktrin'*, Stuttgart: Deutsche Verlags-Anstalt, 1962. 196pp.

G 289   HÄRTLE, Heinrich, *Nietzsche und der Nationalsozialismus*, Munich: Eher, 1937. 171pp. Bib. 165-7.

G 290   HOLBORN, Hajo, 'Origins and political character of nazi ideology'. *POLIT. SCI. Q.*, **79** (**4**), 1964. pp. 542-54.

G 291   JACOBSEN, Hans-Adolf, 'Kampf um Lebensraum: zur Rolle des Geopolitikers Karl Haushofer im Dritten Reich'. *GER. STUD. REV.*, **4**, 1981. pp. 79-104.

G 292   KLUKE, Paul, 'Nationalsozialistische Europa-Ideologie'. *VIERTELJAHRSH. FÜR ZEITG.*, 3 (**3**), 1955. pp. 240-75. English tr. in HOLBORN, H., G 81.

G 293   KOEHL, Robert, 'Feudal aspects of national socialism'. *AM. POLIT. SCI. REV.* **54** (**4**), 1960. pp. 921-33.

G 294   KUHN, Axel, 'Herrschaftsstruktur und Ideologie des Nationalsozialismus'. *NEUE POLIT. LIT.*, **16**, 1971. pp. 395-406.

G 295   LANE, Barbara Miller and RUPP, Leila J., (eds), *Nazi Ideology before 1933: a documentation*, Manchester: University Press; Austin: University of Texas Press, 1978. xxviii, 180pp.

G 296   LOOCK, Hans-Dietrich, 'Zur "Grossgermanischen Politik" des Dritten Reiches'. *VIERTELJAHRSH. FÜR ZEITG.*, **8** (**1**), 1960. pp. 37-63.

G 297   LUTZHÖFT, Hans-Jürgen, *Der nordische Gedanke in Deutschland, 1920-1940*, Stuttgart: Klett, 1971. 439pp. Bib. 409-32. Kiel University thesis.

G 298   RAUSCHNING, Hermann, *Germany's Revolution of Destruction*, London: Heinemann. New York: Alliance Book Co., 1939. xvii, 317pp. US edn *The Revolution of Nihilism*. Tr. of *Die Revolution des Nihilism*, by E.W. Dickes.

G 299   RYSZKA, Franciszek, 'The principles of leadership in the legislation of the nazi Third Reich'. *POL. WES. AFF.*, **3**, 1962. pp. 261-93.

G 300   SALLER, Karl, *Die Rassenlehre des Nationalsozialismus in Wissenschaft und Propaganda*, Darmstadt: Progress-V., 1961. 179pp. Bib. 173-5.

G 301   VERMEIL, Edmond, 'L'antisémitisme dans l'idéologie nazie (sources-expression)'. *Bull. D'Hist. Deux Guerre Mond.*, **6** (**24**), 1956. pp. 2–22.

G 302 WERNER, Karl Friedrich, *Das NS-Geschichtsbild und die deutsche Geschichtswissenschaft*, Stuttgart: Kohlhammer, 1967. 123pp. Bib. 109–23.

G 303 WERNER, Karl Ferdinand, 'On some examples of the national socialist view of history'. *J. OF CONTEMP. HIST.*, **3** (**2**), 1968. pp. 193–206.

G 304 WINDELL, George G., 'Hitler, national socialism, and Richard Wagner'. *J. OF CENT. EUR. HIST.*, **22**, 1962/3. pp. 479–97.

The Origins and Early Years of the NSDAP

G 305 DREXLER, Anton, *Mein politisches Erwachen: aus dem Tagebuch ein deutsch sozialistische Arbeiters*, 4th edn, Munich: Deutsche Volksverlag, 1937. 70pp. First pub. 1919. Anton Drexler (1884–1942), one of the founders of the Deutsche Arbeiterpartei, forerunner of the NSDAP.

G 306 FRANZ-WILLING, Georg, 'Munich: birthplace and centre of the National Socialist Workers' Party'. *J. OF MOD. HIST.*, **29** (**4**), 1957. pp. 319–34.

G 307 FRANZ-WILLING, Georg, *Ursprung der Hitlerbewegung, 1919–1922*, 2nd edn, Preussisch Oldendorf: Schutz, 1974. 391pp. Bib. 373–8.

G 308 MASER, Werner, *Der Sturm auf die Republik: Frühgeschichte der NSDAP*, Stuttgart: Deutsche Verlags-Anstalt, 1973. 524pp. Bib. 491–501. Rev. edn of *Die Frühgeschichte der NSDAP*.

G 309 NICHOLLS, Anthony James, 'Hitler and the Bavarian background to national socialism'. In NICHOLLS, A.J. and MATTHIAS, E., G 345. pp. 99–128.

G 310 ORLOW, Dietrich, 'The organizational history and structure of the NSDAP, 1919–1923'. *J. OF MOD. HIST.*, **37** (**2**), 1965. pp. 208–26.

G 311 PHELPS, Reginald H., 'Anton Drexler: der Gründer der NSDAP'. *DTSCH. RUNDSCH.*, **87**, 1961. pp. 1134–43.

G 312 PHELPS, Reginald H., 'Before Hitler came: Thule Society and Germanen Orden'. *J. OF MOD. HIST.*, **35** (**3**), 1963. pp. 245–61.

G 313 PHELPS, Reginald H., 'Hitler als Parteiredner im Jahre

1920'. *VIERTELJAHRSH. FÜR. ZEITG.*, **11** (**3**), 1963. pp. 274-330.

G 314   PHELPS, Reginald H., 'Hitler and the Deutsche Arbeiter-partei'. *AM. HIST. REV.*, **68** (**3**), 1963. pp. 974-86.

G 315   PHELPS, Reginald H., 'Hitlers "Grundlegende": Rede über den Antisemitismus'. *VIERTELJAHRSH. FÜR ZEITG.*, **16** (**4**), 1976. pp. 390-420.

G 316   SIDMAN, Charles F., 'Die Auflagenkurve des "Völkischen Beobachters" und die Entwicklung des Nationalsozialismus Dezember 1920 bis November 1923'. *VIERTELJAHRSH. FÜR ZEITG.*, **13** (**1**), 1965. pp. 112-18.

G 317   TYRELL, Albrecht, *Vom 'Trommler' zum 'Führer': der Wandel von Hitlers Selbstverständnis zwischen 1919 und 1924 und die Entwicklung der NSDAP*, Munich: Fink, 1975. 296pp. Bib. 281-92. Bonn University thesis.

The NSDAP before 1933

G 318   BECKARS, Peter, 'Die Entwicklung der Krefelder NSDAP bis 1933'. *Heimat (Krefeld)*, **50**, 1979. pp. 92-8.

G 319   BÖHNKE, Wilfried, *Die NSDAP in Ruhrgebiet, 1920-1933*, Bonn: V. Neue Gesellschaft, 1974. 239pp. Bib. 227-39.

G 320   BRÄUNSCHE, Ernst Otto, 'Die Entwicklung der NSDAP in Baden bis 1932/33'. *Z. FÜR GESCH. OBERRHEINS.*, **125**, 1977. pp. 331-75.

G 321   BROSZAT, Martin, 'Die Anfänge der Berliner NSDAP, 1926/27'. *VIERTELJAHRSH. FÜR ZEITG.*, **8** (**1**), 1960. pp. 85-118.

G 322   CONZE, Werner, *Der Nationalsozialismus: Hitlers Kampf gegen den demokratischen Staat, 1919-1934*, Stuttgart: Klett, 1959. 80pp.

G 323   DEUERLEIN, Ernst (ed.), *Der Aufstieg der NSDAP, 1919-1933 in Augenzeugenberichten*, 2nd edn, Düsseldorf: Rauch, 1968. 462pp. Bib. 431-47. Extracts from speeches, newspapers, etc.

G 324   FARQUHARSON, John E., 'The NSDAP in Hannover and Lower Saxony, 1921-1926'. *J. OF CONTEMP. HIST.*, **8** (**4**), 1973. pp. 103-20.

G 325   FIGGE, Reinhard, *Die Opposition der NSDAP im Reichstag*, Cologne University thesis, 1963. xx, 199pp. Bib. i-xx.

G 326   FRANK, Robert Henry, *Hitler and the National Socialist*

Coalition, 1924–1932. Johns Hopkins University thesis, 1969. UM 72-16845. 583pp.

G 327   FRANZ-WILLING, Georg, *Putsch und Verbotszeit des Hitler-bewegung, November 1923–Februar 1925*, Preussisch Oldendorf: Schütz, 1977. 464pp. Bib. 447–53.

G 328   FRICK, Wilhelm, *Die Nationalsozialisten im Reichstag, 1924–1931*, new edn, Munich: Eher, 1932. 160pp.

G 329   GENUNEIT, Jürgen, 'Die Anfänge der NSDAP in Vilsbiburg'. *Storchenturm (Dingolfing)*, **12** (**23**), 1977. pp. 47–62.

G 330   HAMBRECHT, Rainer, *Der Aufstieg der NSDAP in Mittel-und Oberfranken, 1925–1933*, Nuremberg: Stadtarchiv, 1976. xi, 612pp. Bib. 576–94. Würzberg University thesis, 1975.

G 331   HOLZER, Jerzy, *Parteien und Massen: die politische Krise in Deutschland, 1928–1930*, Wiesbaden: Steiner, 1975. 106pp. Abridged tr. of *Kryzys polityczny w Niemczech*, Warsaw, 1970.

G 332   HORN, Wolfgang, *Führerideologie und Parteiorganisation in der NSDAP, 1919–1933*, Düsseldorf: Droste, 1972. 451pp. Bib. 436–48. Mannheim University thesis, 1970.

G 333   HÜTTENBERG, Peter, 'Die Anfänge die NSDAP im Westen'. In FÖRST, Walter (ed.), *Zwischen Ruhrkampf und Wiederaufbau*, Cologne: Grote, 1972. pp. 53–82.

G 334   JABLONSKY, David, *The Verbotszeit: a study of the Nazi Party leadership in dissolution, 9 Nov. 1923–16 Feb. 1925*, University of Kansas thesis, 1979. UM 79-25824. 291pp.

G 335   JOCHMANN, Werner (ed), *Nationalsozialismus und Revolution: Ursprung und Geschichte der NSDAP in Hamburg, 1922–1933: Dokumente.* Frankfurt/M: Europäische Verlagsanstalt, 1963. xi, 444pp.

G 336   KREBS, Albert, *The Infancy of Nazism: the memoirs of Ex-Gauleiter Albert Krebs; 1923–1933*, ed. William Sheridan Allen, New York: New Viewpoints, 1976. xiii, 328pp. Bib. 316–20. Tr. of *Tendenzen und Gestalten der NSDAP*, Stuttgart, Deutsche Verlags-Anstalt, 1959, by W.S. Allen.

G 337   KÜHNL, Reinhard, 'Zur Funktionswandel der NSDAP von ihrer Gründing bis zur Machtergreifung'. *BL. FÜR. DTSCH. UND INT. POLIT.*, **12** (**8**), 1967. pp. 802–11.

G 338   LÖNNE, Karl Egon, 'Der "Völkische Beobachter" und der italienischen Faschismus'. *QUELL. UND FORSCHUNG. AUS. ITAL. ARCH.*, **51**, 1971. pp. 539–84.

G 339   MANN, Rosemarie, 'Entstehung und Entwicklung der

NSDAP in Marburg bis 1933'. *Hessisches Jahrb. Für Landesg.*, **22**, 1972. pp. 254-342.

G 340   MASON, Timothy W., 'The legacy of 1918 for national socialism'. In NICHOLLS, A.J., and MATTHIAS, E., G 345. pp. 215-39.

G 341   MATZERATH, Horst and TURNER, Henry Ashby, 'Die Selbstfinanzierung der NSDAP, 1930-1932'. *GESCH. UND GES.*, **3**, 1977, pp. 59-92.

G 342   MAURER, Ilse and WENGST, Udo (eds), *Politik und Wirstchaft in der Krise, 1930-1932: Quellen zur Ära Brüning*, Düsseldorf: Droste, 1980. 2 vols.

G 343   MÜHLBERGER, Detlef, *The Rise of National Socialism in Westphalia*, 1920-33, London University thesis, 1975.

G 344   NICHOLLS, Anthony James, *Weimar and the Rise of Hitler*, 2nd edn, London: Macmillan. New York: St Martin's Press, 1979. xiii, 151pp. Bib. 130-44.

G 345   NICHOLLS, Anthony James and Matthias, Erich (eds), - *German Democracy and the Triumph of Hitler: essays on recent German history*, London: Allen & Unwin, 1971. 271pp.

G 346   NOAKES, Jeremy, 'Conflict and development in the NSDAP, 1924-1927'. *J. OF CONTEMP. HIST.*, **1** (**4**), 1966. pp. 3-36.

G 347   NOAKES, Jeremy, *The Nazi Party in Lower Saxony, 1921-1933*. Oxford: University Press, 1971. xvi, 276pp. Bib. 252-63.

G 348   NYORMARKAY, Joseph, *Charisma and Factionalism in the Nazi Party*. Minneapolis: University of Minnesota Press, 1967. 161pp. Bib. 153-8. University of Minnesota thesis, 1963.

G 349   NYORMARKAY, Joseph, 'Factionalism in the National Socialist Workers' Party, 1925-26: the myth and the reality of the "Northern Opposition"' In TURNER, H.A., G 93. pp. 21-44.

G 350   ORLOW, Dietrich, 'The conversion of myth into political power: the case of the Nazi Party, 1925-26'. *AM. HIST. REV.*, **72** (**3**), 1967. pp. 906-24.

G 351   *The Path to Dictatorship, 1918-1933: 10 essays*, by Theodor Eschenburg [*et al*], intro. by Fritz Stern, Garden City: Doubleday, 1966. xxii, 217pp. British edn *The Road to Dictatorship*, 1964.

G 352   POOL, James and Suzanne, *Who financed Hitler? the secret funding of Hitler's rise to power, 1919-1933*, New York: Dial Books. London: Raven Books, 1978. 535pp. Bib. 521-8.

G 353   PRIDHAM, Geoffrey, *Hitler's Rise to Power: the nazi movement in Bavaria, 1923-1933*. London: Hart-Davis MacGibbon. New York: Harper & Row, 1973. xvi, 380pp. Bib. 353-66.

G 354   RIETZLER, Rudolf, *Kampf in der Nordmark: das Aufkommen das Nationalsozialismus in Schleswig-Holstein, 1919-1928*, Neumünster: Wachholtz, V. 1982. 560pp.

G 355   ROESKE, Ulrich, 'Zum Verhältnis zwischen DNVP und NSDAP'. *WISS Z. DER HUMBOLDT-U. ZU BERLIN. GES. UND SPRACHWISS. R.*, **22** (**1/2**), 1973. pp. 27-38.

G 356   SCHILDT, Gerhard, *Die Arbeitsgemeinschaft Nord-West: Untersuchungen zur Geschichte der NSDAP 1925/26*, Freiburg University thesis, 1964. xlvi, 194pp. Bib. xxvii-xlvi.

G 357   SCHULZ, Gerhard, *Aufstieg des Nationalsozialismus: Krise und Revolution in Deutschland*, Frankfurt/M: Propylaen V., 1975. 92pp.

G 358   SCHÖN, Eberhard, *Die Entstehung des Nationalsozialismus in Hessen*, Meisenheim: Hain, 1972. xix, 227pp. Bib. 215-27.

G 359   STACHURA, Peter D., 'The political strategy of the Nazi Party, 1919-1933'. *GERM. STUD. REV.*, **3** (**2**), 1980. pp. 261-88.

G 360   STOLTENBERG, Gerhard, *Politische Stromungen im Schleswig-Holsteinischen Landvolk, 1918-1933: ein Beitrag zur politischen Meinungsbildung in der Weimarer Republik*, Düsseldorf: Droste, 1962. 218pp.

G 361   TRACEY, Donald R., 'The development of the National Socialist Party in Thuringia, 1924-30', *CENT. EUR. HIST.*, **8** (**1**), 1975. pp. 23-50.

G 362   TYRELL, Albrecht (ed.), *Führer befiehl: Selbstzeugnisse aus der Kampfzeit der NSDAP: Dokumentation und Analyse*, Düsseldorf: Droste, 1969. 403pp. Bib. 389-95.

G 363   TYRELL, Albrecht, 'Führergedanke und Gauleiterwechsel: die Teilung des Gaues Rhineland der NSDAP 1931'. *VIERTEL-JAHRSH. FÜR. ZEITG.*, **23** (**4**), 1975. pp. 341-74.

G 364   VOGT, Martin, 'Zur Finanzierung der NSDAP zwischen 1924 und 1928'. *GESCH. IN WISS. UND UNTERR.*, **21** (**4**), 1970. pp. 234-43.

The Munich Putsch 1923

G 365   CAHILL, John James, *The NSDAP and May Day 1923: confrontation and aftermath, 1923-1927*, Cincinnati University thesis, 1973. UM 74-01683. 279pp.

G 366   DEUERLEIN, Ernst (ed), *Der Hitler-Putsch: bayerische Dokumente zum 8. und 9. November 1923*. Stuttgart: Deutsche Verlags-Anstalt, 1962. 759pp. Documentary collection.

G 367   FAVEZ, Jean-Claude, 'Hitler et la Rechswehr en 1923'. *REV. D'HIST. MOD. ET CONTEMP.*, **17** (**1**), 1970. pp. 22-49.

G 368   FRANZ-WILLING, Georg, *Krisenjahr der Hitlerbewegung: 1923*, Preussisch Oldendorf: Schutz, 1975. 408pp. Bib. 393-9.

G 369   GORDON, Harold J., *Hitler and the Beer Hall Putsch*. Princeton: University Press, 1972. xii, 666p. Bib. 633-47.

G 370   HOFMANN, Hanns Hubert, *Der Hitler-Putsch: Krisenjahre deutscher Geschichte 1920-1924*, Munich: Nymphenburger V., 1961. 335pp. Bib. 295-327.

G 371   PHELPS, Reginald H., 'Dokumente aus der "Kampfzeit" der NSDAP, 1923'. *DTSCH. RUNDSCH.*, **84**, 1958. pp. 459-68, 1034-44.

G 372   STEGER, Bernd, 'Der Hitlerprozess und Bayerns Verhältnis zum Reich, 1923/24'. *VIERTELJAHRSH. FÜR ZEITG.*, **25** (**4**), 1977. pp. 441-66.

G 373   VOGELSANG, Thilo, 'Die Reichswehr in Bayern und der Münchener Putsch, 1923'. *VIERTELJAHRSH. FÜR ZEITG.*, **5** (**1**), 1957. pp. 91-101.

The Strassers and 'Left' Nazism

G 374   BANKIER, David, 'Otto Strasser und die Judenfrage'. *BULL. LEO BAECK INST.*, **60**, 1981. pp. 3-20.

G 375   BRÄCKEL, Thomas, 'Antikapitalismus und Antimarxismus der "Linke" Flügel der NSDAP auf dem Weg in das faschistische Herrschaftssystem'. *Argument*, **22** (**121**), 1980. pp. 389-94.

G 376   DIXON, Joseph Murdoch, *Gregor Strasser and the Organization of the Nazi Party, 1925-1932*, Stanford University thesis, 1966. UM 66-14650. 256pp.

G 377   HOVDKINN, Øystein, 'Goebbels, Hitler og det nasjonal-sosialistiske venstre'. *HIST. TIDSSKR.*, **55** (**3**), 1976. pp. 288-316. On the nazi 'Left'.

G 378   KISSENKOETTER, Udo, *Gregor Strasser und die NSDAP*, Stuttgart: Deutsche Verlags-Anstalt, 1978. 219pp. Bib. 211-15. Cologne University thesis.

G 379   KÜHNL, Reinhard, *Die nationalsozialistische Linke, 1925–1930: eine Untersuchung über Geschichte, Struktur, und Ideologie der Strasser-Gruppe*, Meisenheim: Hain, 1966. 378pp. Bib. 262–9. Marburg University thesis.

G 380   KÜHNL, Reinhard, 'Zur Programmatik der nationalsozialistischen Linken: das Strasser-Programm von 1925/26'. *VIERTEL-JAHRSH. FÜR ZEITG.*, **14** (**3**), 1966. pp. 317–33.

G 381   PAETEL, Karl Otto, 'Otto Strasser und die "Schwarze Front" des "Wahren Nationalsozialismus"'. *POLIT. STUD.*, **8** (**92**), 1957. pp. 269–81.

G 382   REED, Douglas, *The Prisoner of Ottawa: Otto Strasser*, London: Cape, 1953. 272pp.

G 383   SCHMIDT, Klaus F., 'Die "nationalsozialistischen Briefe"', 1925–30: Programm, Anschauungen, Tendenzen, Anmerkungen zu innerparteilichen Diskussionen und Richtungskampfen der NSDAP'. In *Paul Kluke zum 60 Geburstag*, Frankfurt/M: Europäische V., 1968. pp. 111–26.

G 384   STACHURA, Peter D., 'Der Fall Strasser: Gregor Strasser, Hitler and national socialism, 1930–1932'. See G 163. pp. 88–130.

G 385   STACHURA, Peter D., *Gregor Strasser and the Rise of Nazism*, London: Allen & Unwin, 1983. 192pp.

G 386   STRASSER, Otto, *Hitler and I*, London: Cape. Boston: Houghton Mifflin, 1940. 248pp.

G 387   STRASSER, Otto, *Mein Kampf: eine politische Autobiographie*, Frankfurt/M: H. Heine V., 1969. 234pp.

G 388   WÖRTZ, Ulrich, *Programmatik und Führerprinzip: das Problem des Strasser-Kreises in der NSDAP: eine historisch-politische Studie, etc.* Erlangen-Nuremberg University thesis, 1966. v, 249, 124app. Bib. 118a–124a.

G 389   WOLFFSOHN, Michael, 'Linker und rechter National-sozialismus', *Z. FÜR POLIT.*, **24** (**1**), 1977. pp. 56–80.

The Nazi Seizure and Consolidation of Power

G 390   ABRAHAM, David, *The Collapse of the Weimar Republic: political economy and crisis*, Princeton: University Press, 1981. 366pp. Bib. 328–49.

G 391   ALLEN, William Sheridan, *The Nazi Seizure of Power: the experience of a single German town, 1930–1935*, Chicago: Quadrangle, 1965. London: Eyre & Spottiswoode, 1966. xi, 345pp. Bib. 305–36.

G 392   BECKER, Josef, 'Brüning, Prälat Kaas und das Problem einer Regierungsbeteiligung der NSDAP, 1930–1932'. *HIST. Z.*, **196**, 1963. pp. 74–111.

G 393   BRACHER, Karl Dietrich, *Der Auflösung der Weimarer Republik: eine Studie zum Problem des Machtverfalls in der Demokratie*, pref. by Hans Herzfeld and Otto Stammer, 5th edn, Villingen: Neckar V., 1971. xvii, 710pp. Bib. 650–94. 1978 edn by Athenäum.

G 394   BRACHER, Karl Dietrich and others, *Die nationalsozialistische Machtergreifung: Studien zur Errichtung des totalitären Herrschaftssystems in Deutschland 1933/34*, by K.D. Bracher, Wolfgang Sauer and Gerhard Schulz, 2nd edn, Cologne: Westdeutscher V., 1962. xx, 1034pp. Bib. 973–1009. Also 3 vols. ed. Ullstein, 1973.

G 395   BRÜDIGAM, Heinz, *Das Jahr 1933: Terrorismus an der Macht: eine Dokumentation über die Errichtung der faschistischen Diktatur*, Frankfurt /M: Roderberg, 1978. 136pp. Bib. 127–32.

G 396   BUCHLOH, Ingrid, *Die nationalsozialistische Machtergreifung in Duisburg: eine Fallstudie*, Duisberg: Braun, 1980. xvii, 216pp. Bib. 197–209. Düsseldorf University thesis, 1978.

G 397   BURCKHARDT, Bernd, *Eine Stadt wird braun: die national-sozialistische Machtergreifung in der schwäbische Provinz*, intro. by H.A. Winkler, Hamburg: Hoffmann & Campe, 1980. 160pp. Bib. 159–60.

G 398   CONWAY, John S., 'Machtergreifung or due process of history: the historiography of Hitler's rise to power'. *HIST. J.*, **7** (3), 1965. pp. 399–413.

G 399   DOBROWSKI, Michael N. and WALLIMANN, Isidore (eds), *Towards the Holocaust: the social and economic collapse of the Weimar Republic*, Westport: Greenwood Press, 1983, 440pp.

G 400   DOMRÖSE, Ortwin, *Der NS-Staat in Bayern von der Machtergreifung bis zum Röhm-Putsch*, Munich: Wölfle, 1974. 398pp. Bib. 393–6.

G 401   GIES, Horst, 'NSDAP und Landwirtschaftliche Organisa-tionen in der Endphase der Weimarer Republik'. *VIERTELJAHRSH. FÜR ZEITG.*, **15** (4), 1967. pp. 341–76.

G 402   GROSSER, Alfred (ed.), *Hitler, la presse et la naissance d'une dictature*, Paris: Colin, 1959. 262pp. Extracts from western newspapers on Hitler's seizure of power.

G 403   HARDACH, Gerd and KÜHNL, Reinhard (eds), *Die Zerstörung der Weimarer Republik*, 2nd edn, Cologne: Pahl-Rugenstein, 1979. 290pp.

G 404   HENTSCHEL, Volker, *Weimars letzte Monate und der Untergang der Republik*, Düsseldorf: Droste, 1978. 180pp. Bib. 171-7.

G 405   HOEGNER, Wilhelm, *Flucht vor Hitler: Erinnerungen an die Kapitulation der ersten deutschen Republik 1933*, foreword by Wolfgang Jean Stock, Munich: Nymphenburger V., 1977. 295pp.

G 406   JASPER, Gotthard (ed.), *Von Weimar zu Hitler, 1930-1933*, Cologne: Kiepenheuer & Witsch, 1968. 527pp. Bib. 507-16. Collection of journal articles.

G 407   KAISER, Klaus, *Braunschweiger Presse und Nationalsozialismus: der Aufstieg der NSDAP im Lande Braunschweig im Spiegel der Braunschweiger Tageszeitungen, 1930 bis 1933*, Brunswick: Waisenhaus Druck. & V., 1970. 196pp. Bib. 187-90. Free University of Berlin thesis.

G 408   KATER, Michael H., 'Sozialer Wandel in der NSDAP im Zuge der nationalsozialistischen Machtergreifung'. In SCHIEDER, W., Gn 17. pp. 25-67.

G 409   LEPSIUS, M. Rainer, 'The collapse of an intermediary power structure, 1933-34'. *INT. J. OF COMP. SOCIOL.*, **9** (**3/4**), 1968. pp. 289-301.

G 410   LEPSIUS, M. Rainer, *Extremer Nationalismus: Strukturbedingungen vor der nationalsozialistischer Machtergreifung*, Stuttgart: Kohlhammer, 1966. 40pp.

G 411   MANVELL, Roger and FRAENKEL, Heinrich, *The Hundred Days to Hitler*, London: Dent. New York: St Martin's Press, 1974. 245pp. Bib. 233-5.

G 412   MATTHIAS, Erich and MORSEY, Rudolf (eds), *Das Ende der Parteien, 1933*, Düsseldorf: Droste, 1960. xv, 816pp.

G 413   MEINCK, Jürgen, *Weimarer Staatslehre und Nationalsozialismus: eine Studie zum Problem der Kontinuität im staatsrechtlichen Denken in Deutschland 1928 bis 1936*, Frankfurt/M: Campus V., 1978. 367pp. Bib. 323-67. Marburg University thesis, 1976.

G 414   MEISSNER, Hans Otto, *30 Januar, 33: Hitlers Machtergreifung*, Esslingen: Bechtle, 1976. 453pp.

G 415   MÖLLER, Horst, 'Die nationalsozialistische Machtergreifung: Konterrevolution oder Revolution?' *VIERTELJAHRSH. FÜR ZEITG.*, **31** (**1**), 1981. pp. 25-51.

G 416 NIPPERDEY, Thomas, '1933 und Kontinuität der deutschen Geschichte'. *HIST. Z.*, **227** (1), 1978. pp. 86–111.

G 417 PINGEL, Henner, *Das Jahr 1933: NSDAP-Machtergreifung in Darmstadt und im Volkstaat Hessen*, 2nd edn, *mit zahlreichen Dokumenten und einer austgewählten Gesetzsammlung*, Darmstadt: Author, 1978. 245pp. Bib. 195–210. First pub. as *Darmstadt, 1933*, 1977.

G 418 PLESSE, Sigurd, *Die nationalsozialistische Machtergreifung im Oberharz: Clausthal-Zellerfeld, 1929–1933*, Clausthal-Zellerfeld: Pieper, 1970. 94pp.

G 419 POPPLOW, Ulrich, 'Die Machtergreifung in Augenzeugenbericht: Göttingen, 1932–1935'. *Göttinger Jahrbuch.*, **25**, 1977. pp. 157–86.

G 420 REHBERGER, Horst, *Die Gleichschaltung des Landes Baden 1932/33*, Heidelberg: Winter, 1966. 162pp. Bib. 159–62. Heidelberg University thesis.

G 421 REICHE, E.G., 'From spontaneous to legal terror: SA, police and the judiciary, 1933–34'. *EUR. STUD. REV.*, **9**, 1979. pp. 237–64.

G 422 ROLOFF, Ernst-August, *Bürgertum und Nationalsozialismus, 1930–33: Braunschweigs Weg ins Dritte Reich*, Hanover: V. für Lit & Zeitgeschehen, 1961. 174pp.

G 423 SCHAAP, Klaus, *Die Endphase der Weimarer Republik in Freistaat Oldenburg, 1928–1932*. Düsseldorf: Droste, 1978. 313pp.

G 424 SCHNABEL, Thomas, (ed.), *Die Machtergreifung in Südwestdeutschland: das Ende der Weimarer Republik in Baden und Württemburg, 1928–1933*, Stuttgart: Kohlhammer, 1982. 300pp.

G 425 SCHWARZWÄLDER, Herbert, *Die Machtergreifung der NSDAP in Bremen 1933*, Bremen: Schünemann, 1966. 158pp. Bib. 146.

G 426 STACHURA, Peter D. (ed.), *The Nazi Machtergreifung*, London, Allen & Unwin, 1983. xiv, 192pp.

G 427 STOKES, Lawrence D., 'Der Fall Stoffregen: die Absetzung des Eutner Bürgermeisters im Zuge der NS-Machtergreifung'. *Z. für Ges. Schleswig-Holstein Gesch.*, **104**, 1979. pp. 253–86.

G 428 TAYLOR, Alan John Percivale, 'Hitler's seizure of power'. In TAYLOR, *Europe: grandeur and decline*. Harmondsworth: Penguin, 1967. pp. 204–19.

G 429 TIMPKE, Henning (ed.), *Dokumente zur Gleichschaltung des Landes Hamburg, 1933*, Frankfurt/M: Europäische Verlagsanstalt, 1964. 327pp.

G 430 TORMIN, Walter, *Die Jahre 1933–1934: die Gleichschaltung*, 4th edn, Hanover: V. für Lit. & Zeitgeschehen, 1963. 63pp. Bib. 61–2.

G 431 WHEATON, Eliot Barculo, *Prelude to Calamity: the nazi revolution, 1933–1935: with a background survey of the Weimer era*, London: Gollancz. Garden City: Doubleday, 1969. xix, 523pp. Bibs. Review of literature; chronologies, statistics; excellent bibliography.

G 432 WIESEMANN, Falk, *Die Vorgeschichte der nationalsozialistische Machtübernahme in Bayern, 1932–1933*, Berlin: Duncker & Humblot, 1975. 328pp. Bib. 316–23. Munich University thesis.

G 433 WINKLER, Heinrich August, 'German society, Hitler and the illusion of restoration, 1930–1933'. *J. OF CONTEMP. HIST.*, **11** (**4**), 1976. pp. 1–16.

The Reichstag Fire

G 434 BIERNAT, Karl Heinz, *Der Reichstag brennt: Hintergrunde und Auswirkungen der faschistischen Reichstagsbrandprovokation*, Berlin: Dietz, 1960. 98pp.

G 435 BROSZAT, Martin, 'Zum Streit um den Reichstagsbrand: eine grundsatzliche Erörterung'. *VIERTELJAHRSH. FÜR ZEITG.*, **8** (**3**), 1960. pp. 275–9.

G 436 HOFER, Walther and GRAF, Christoph, 'Neue Quellen zum Reichstagsbrand'. *GESCH. IN WISS UND UNTERR.*, **27** (**2**), 1976. pp. 65–88.

G 437 HOFER, Walther and others (eds), *Der Reichstagsbrand: eine wissenschaftliche Dokumentation*, Berlin: Arani, 1972. 2 vols. Bib.

G 438 TOBIAS, Fritz, *The Reichstag Fire*, intro. by A.J.P. Taylor, London, Secker & Warburg, 1963. New York: Putnam, 1974. 348pp. Bib. 323–30. Tr. of *Die Reichstagsbrand*. Rastatt, Grote, 1962, by Arnold Pomerans.

Electoral Support for the Nazis

G 439 BRACHER, Karl Dietrich, 'Plebiszit und Machtergreifung: eine kritische Analyse der nationalsozialistischen Wahlpolitik, 1933–34'. In *On The Track of Tyrrany*, ed. Max Beloff, London: Vallentine Mitchell, 1959. pp. 1–43.

G 440 BURNHAM, Walter Dean, 'Political immunization and political confessionalism: the United States and Weimar Germany'. *J. OF INTERDISC. HIST.*, **3** (1), 1972. pp. 1-30. Nazism not an extremism of the centre.

G 441 CHILDERS, Thomas, 'The social bases of the national socialist vote'. *J. OF CONTEMP. HIST.*, **11** (4), 1976. pp. 17-42.

G 442 CIOLEK-KÜMPER, Jutta, *Wahlkampf in Lippe: die Wahlkampfpropaganda der NSDAP zur Landtagswahl am 15 Januar 1933*, Munich: V. Dokumentation, 1976. 406pp. Bib. 383-400.

G 443 DIEDERICH, Nils and others (eds), *Wahlstatistik in Deutschland: Bibliographie der deutschen Wahlstatistik, 1848-1975*, Munich: V. Dokumentation, 1976. ix, 206pp.

G 444 ESCHENBURG, Theodor, 'Streiflichter zur Geschichte der Wahlen im Dritten Reich'. *VIERTELJAHRSH. FÜR ZEITG.*, **3** (3), 1955. pp. 311-16. On the industrial elections of 1935.

G 445 FALTER, Jürgen W., 'Radicalisation of the middle classes or mobilisation of the unpolitical: the theories of Seymour M. Lipset and Reinhard Bendix on the electoral support of the NSDAP in the light of recent research'. *SOC. SCI. INF.*, **20** (2), 1981. pp. 389-430.

G 446 FALTER, Jürgen W., 'Wählerbewegungen zur NSDAP, 1924-1933'. In BUSCH, Otto (ed.), *Wählerbewegung in der europäischen Geschichte*, Berlin: Colloquium V., 1980. pp. 159-202.

G 447 FALTER, Jürgen W., 'Wer verhalf der NSDAP zum Sieg?' *Aus Polit. und Zeitg.*, **28/29**, 14 July 1979. pp. 3-21.

G 448 FARIS, Ellsworth, 'Takeoff point for the National Socialist Party: the Landtag election in Baden 1929'. *CENT. EUR. HIST.*, **8** (2), 1975. pp. 140-71.

G 449 HACKETT, David Andrew, *The Nazi Party in the Reichstag Elections of 1930*. University of Wisconsin thesis, 1971. UM 71-16871. 881pp.

G 450 HAMILTON, Richard F., *Who Voted for Hitler?* Princeton: University Press, 1982. xv, 664pp.

G 451 LOOMIS, Charles P. and BEEGLE, J. Allen, 'The spread of German nazism in rural areas'. *AM. SOCIOL. REV.*, **11** (6), 1946. pp. 724-34.

G 452 McKIBBIN, R.I., 'The myth of the unemployed: who did vote for the nazis?' *AUS. J. POLIT. HIST.*, **15** (2), 1969. pp. 25-40.

G 453 MILATZ, Alfred, *Wähler und Wahlen in der Weimarer Republik*, Bonn: Bundeszentrale für Politische Bildung, 1965. 152pp. Bib. 152.

G 454   O'LESSKER, Karl, 'Who voted for Hitler? A new look at the class basis of naziism'. *Am. J. of Sociol.*, **74** (**1**), 1968. pp. 63-9.

G 455   PASSCHIER, Nico, 'The electoral geography of the nazi landslide'. In LARSEN, S.U., Gn 36. pp. 283-300.

G 456   SCHNAIBERG, Allan, 'A critique of Karl O'Lessker's "Who voted for Hitler?"' *Am. J. of Sociol*, **74** (**6**), 1969. pp. 732-35. See G 454.

G 457   SCHUMACHER, Martin, *Wahlen und Abstimmungen, 1918–1933: eine Bibliographie zur Statistik und Analyse der politischen Wahlen in der Weimarer Republik*, Düsseldorf: Droste, 1976. 155pp.

G 458   STACHURA, Peter D., 'Der kritische Wendepunkt? Die NSDAP und die Reichstagswahlen vom 20 Mai 1928'. *VIERTEL-JAHRSH. FÜR ZEITG.*, **26** (**1**), 1978. pp. 66-99.

G 459   WEBER, Alexander, *Soziale Merkmale der NSDAP-Wähler: eine Zusammenfassung bisheriger impirischer Untersuchungen und eine Analyse in den Gemeinden der Länder Baden und Hessen*, Freiburg University thesis, 1969. 281pp.

G 460   WERNETTE, Dee Richard, *Political Violence and German Elections: 1930 and July 1932*, University of Michigan thesis, 1974. UM 75-10334. 213pp.

The Social Composition of the NSDAP

G 461   ABEL, Theodore F., *The Nazi Movement: why Hitler came to power*, new edn, New York: Prentice-Hall, 1965. 322pp. First pub. as *Why Hitler Came to Power*, 1938.

G 462   ABRAHAM, David, 'Nazism and the working class'. *Radical Hist. Rev.*, **18**, 1978. pp. 161-5. Review.

G 463   ASTEL, Karl and WEBER, Erna, *Die Kinderzahl der 29000 politischen Leiter des Gaues Thüringen der NSDAP und die Ursachen der ermittelten Fortplanzungshäufigkeit*, Berlin: Metzner, 1943. 187pp. Nazi data on occupational backgrounds, etc.

G 464   BESSEL, Richard J. and JAMIN, Mathilde, 'Nazis, workers and the uses of quantitative evidence'. *SOC. HIST.*, **4** (**1**), 1979. pp. 111-16. Comment on Conan Fischer's work.

G 465   BROSZAT, Martin, 'Zur Struktur der NS-Massenbewegung'. *VIERTELJAHRSH. FÜR ZEITG.*, **31** (**1**), 1983. pp. 52-76.

G 466   CHILDERS, Thomas, 'National socialism and the new middle class'. In MANN, R., G 484. pp. 19-33.

G 467   DOUGLAS, Donald M., 'The parent cell: some computer

notes on the composition of the first Nazi Party group in Munich, 1919-1921'. *CENT. EUR. HIST.*, **10** (1), 1977. pp. 55-72.

G 468   GEIGER, Theodore Julius, *Die soziale Schichtung des deutschen Volkes: soziographischer Versuch auf statistischer Grundlage*, Stuttgart: Enke, 1967. iv, 142p. Bib. 139-42. Repr. of 1932 edn.

G 469   GENUNEIT, Jurgen, 'Methodische Probleme der quantitativen Analyse früher NSDAP-Mitgliederlisten'. In MANN, R., G 484. pp. 34-66.

G 470   GERTH, Hans H., 'The Nazi Party: its leadership and composition'. *Am. J. of Sociol.*, **45**, 1940. pp. 517-41.

G 471   HEBERLE, Rudolf, *From Democracy to Nazism: a regional case study on political parties in Germany*, New York: Fertig, 1970. 130pp. Bib. 128-30. First pub. by Louisiana State University Press, 1945. Abridged tr. of *Landbevölkerung und Nationalsozialismus: eine soziologische Untersuchung der politischen Willensbildung in Schleswig-Holstein 1918 bis 1932*, Stuttgart: Deutsche Verlags-Anstalt, 1963.

G 472   HEBERLE, Rudolf, 'Zur Soziologie der nationalsozialistischen Revolution: Notizen aus dem Jahre 1934', *VIERTELJAHRSH. FÜR ZEITG.*, **13** (4), 1965. pp. 438-45.

G 473   HENNIG, Eike, *Bürgerliche Gesellschaft und Faschismus in Deutschland: ein Forschungsbericht*, Frankfurt/M: Suhrkampf, 1977. 423pp.

G 474   HENNIG, Eike, 'Regionale Unterschiede bei der Entstehung des deutschen Faschismus: ein Plädoyer für mikroanalystische Studien zur Erforschung der NSDAP', *POLIT. VIERTELJAHRESSCHR.*, **21** (2), 1980. pp. 152-73.

G 475   HOLMES, Kim R., 'The forsaken past: agrarian conservatism and national socialism in Germany'. *J. OF CONTEMP. HIST.*, **17** (4), 1982. pp. 671-88.

G 476   JANNER, William, 'National socialists and social mobility'. *J. OF SOC. HIST.*, **9** (3), 1976. pp. 339-68.

G 477   KATER, Michael H., 'Methologische Überlegungen über Möglichkeiten und Grenzen einer Analyse der sozialen Zusammensetzung der NSDAP von 1925 bis 1945'. In MANN, R., G 484. pp. 155-85.

G 478   KATER, Michael H., *The Nazi Party: a social profile of members and leaders, 1919-1945*, Oxford: Blackwell, 1983. xiv, 415pp.

G 479   KATER, Michael H., 'Zur Soziographie der frühen NSDAP'. *VIERTELJAHRSH. FÜR ZEITG.*, **19** (2), 1971. pp. 124-59.

G 480   KELE, Max H., *Nazis and Workers: national socialist appeals to German labor, 1919-1933*. Chapel Hill: University of N. Carolina Press, 1972. 243pp. Bib. 219-37.

G 481   KOSHAR, Rudy, 'Two "nazisms": the social context of nazi mobilization in Marburg and Tübingen'. SOC. HIST., 7 (1), 1982. pp. 27-42.

G 482   KROHN, Claus-Dieter and STEGMANN, Dirk, 'Kleingewerbe und Nationalsozialismus in einer agrarisch-mittelständischen Region: Beispiel Lüneburg, 1930-1939'. *ARCHIV. FÜR SOZIAL-GESCH.*, 17, 1977. pp. 41-98.

G 483   MADDEN, James Paul, *The Social Composition of the Nazi Party*, University of Oklahoma thesis, 1976. UM 77-12749. 330pp.

G 484   MANN, Reinhard (ed.), *Die Nationalsozialisten: Analysen faschistischer Bewegungen*, Stuttgart: Klett-Cotta, 1980. 224pp.

G 485   MASON, Timothy W., 'Arbeiter-nazis'. *AESTHET. UND KOMMUN.*, 7 (26), 1976. pp. 52-5.

G 486   MERKL. Peter H., 'The nazis of the Abel collection: why they joined the NSDAP'. In LARSEN, S.U., Gn 36. pp. 268-82.

G 487   MÜHLBERGER, Detlef, 'The sociology of the NSDAP: the question of the working-class membership'. *J. OF CONTEMP. HIST.*, 15 (3), 1980. pp. 493-511.

G 488   PETZOLD, Joachim, 'Class and Hitler'. *JAHRB. FÜR GESCH.*, 21, 1980. pp. 247-88.

G 489   PRATT, Samuel Alexander, *The Social Basis of Nazism and Communism in Urban Germany: a correlation study of the July 31 1932 Reichstag elections in Germany*, Michigan State College MA thesis, 1948.

G 490   ROGOWSKI, Ronald, 'The Gauleiter and the social origin of fascism'. *COMP. STUD. IN SOC. AND HIST.*, 19 (4), 1977. pp. 399-430.

G 491   ROLOFF, Ernst-August, 'Wer wählte Hitler? Thesen zur Sozial-und Wirtschaftsgeschichte der Weimarer Republik'. *POLIT. STUD.*, 15, 1964. pp. 293-300.

G 492   SALDERN, Adelheid von, *Mittelstand im Dritten Reich: Handwerker, Einzelhändler, Bauern*, Frankfurt/M: Campus V., 1979. 401pp. Bib. 359-87.

G 493   SCHUON-WIEHL, Annaliese K., *Faschismus und Gesell-*

271

schaftsstruktur: am Beispiel des Aufstiegs des Nationalsozialismus, Frankfurt/
M: Europäische Verlagsanstalt, 1970. 102pp. Bib. 101-2.

G 494   STACHURA, Peter D., 'Who were the nazis? A socio-
political analysis of the national socialist Machtübernahme'. *EUR.
STUD. REV.*, **11** (3), 1981. pp. 293-324.

G 495   STOKES, Lawrence D., 'The social composition of the Nazi
Party in Eutin, 1925-32'. *INT. REV. OF SOC. HIST.*, **23** (1), 1978. pp.
1-32.

G 496   TILTON, Timothy Alan, *Nazism, Neo-nazism and the Peasantry*.
Bloomington: Indiana University Press, 1975. xvi, 186pp. Bib. 171-82.

G 497   TIPTON, Frank B., 'Small business and the rise of Hitler'.
Bus. Hist. Rev., **53** (2), 1979. pp. 235-46. Review article.

G 498   WERNETTE, Dee Richard, 'Quantitative methods in
studying political mobilization in late Weimar Germany'. *Hist.
Methods Newsl.*, **10** (3), 1977. pp. 97-101. Review article.

G 499   WINKLER, Heinrich August, 'Der Entbehrliche Stand zur
Mittelstandpolitik im Dritten Reich'. *ARCH. FÜR SOZIALGESCH.*,
17, 1977. pp. 1-40.

G 500   WINKLER, Heinrich August, 'Extremismus der Mitte?
Sozialgeschichtlicher Aspekte der nationalsozialistischen Machtergreifung'. *VIERTELJAHRSH. FÜR ZEITG.*, **20** (2), 1972. pp.
175-91. Review article.

G 501   WINKLER, Heinrich August, *Mittelstand, Demokratie und
Nationalsozialismus: die politische Entwicklung von Handwerk und Kleinhandel
in der Weimarer Republic*, Cologne: Kiepenheuer & Witsch, 1972.
307pp. Bib. 269-86. Free University of Berlin thesis, 1970.

G 502   WINKLER, Heinrich August, 'Mittelstandsbewegung oder
Volkspartei? zur sozialen Basis der NSDAP'. In SCHIEDER, W.,
Gn 17. pp. 97-118.

G 503   WULF, Peter, *Die politische Haltung schleswig-holsteinischen
Handwerks, 1928-1932*, Cologne: Westdeutscher V., 1969, 160pp.

G 504   ZOFKA, Zdenek, *Die Ausbreitung des Nationalsozialismus auf
dem Lande: eine regionale Fallstudie zur politischen Einstellung der
'Landbevölkerung' in der Zeit des Aufstiegs und der Machtergreifung der
NSDAP, 1928-1936*, Munich: Wölfle, 1979. vii, 380p. Bib. 361-80.
Munich University thesis.

272

Government, Administration and Bureaucracy in the Third Reich

G 505   BORCH, Herbert von, *Obrigkeit und Widerstand: zur politischen Soziologie des Beamtentums*, Tübingen: Mohr, 1954. 243pp.

G 506   CAPLAN, Jane, 'Bureaucracy, politics and the national socialist state'. In STACHURA, P.D., G 163 pp. 234-56.

G 507   CAPLAN, Jane, 'The politics of administration: the Reich Interior Ministry and the German civil service, 1933-1943'. *HIST. J.*, **20** (**3**), 1977. pp. 707-36.

G 508   DÜLFFER, Jost, 'Der Beginn des Krieges, 1939: Hitler, die innere Krise und das Mächtesystem'. *GESCH. UND GES.*, **2** (**4**), 1976. pp. 443-70.

G 509   FRÖHLICH, Elke and BROSZAT, Martin, 'Politische und soziale Macht auf dem Lande; die Durchsetzung der NSDAP im Kreis Memmingen'. *VIERTELJAHRSH. FÜR ZEITG.*, **25** (**4**), 1977. pp. 546-72.

G 510   GRUCHMANN, Lothar, 'Die "Reichsregierung" im Führerstaat: Stellung und Funktion des Kabinetts im nationalsozialistischen Herrschaftssystem'. In *Klassenjustiz und Pluralismus: Festschrift für Ernst Fraenkel*, Hamburg: Hoffmann & Campe, 1973. pp. 187-223.

G 511   HÜTTENBERGER, Peter, 'Nationalsozialistische Polykratie'. *GESCH. UND GES.*, **2** (**4**), 1976. pp. 417-42.

G 512   MARX, Fritz Morstein, *Government in the Third Reich*, 2nd edn, New York: McGraw Hill, 1937. xiii, 199pp.

G 513   MATZERATH, Horst, *Nationalsozialismus und kommunale Selbstverwaltung*, Stuttgart: Kohlhammer, 1970. 503pp. Bib. 456-79.

G 514   NOAKES, Jeremy (ed.), *Government, Party and People in nazi Germany*, Exeter: University of Exeter, 1980. 103pp. Bib. 98-102.

G 515   MOMMSEN, Hans, *Beamtentum im Dritten Reich; mit ausgewählten Quellen zur nationalsozialistischen Beamtenpolitik*, Stuttgart: Deutsche Verlags-Anstalt, 1966. 246pp.

G 516   PETERSON, Edward Norman, 'The bureaucracy and the Nazi Party'. *REV. OF POLIT.*, **28** (**2**), 1966. pp. 172-92.

G 517   PETERSON, Edward Norman, *The Limits of Hitler's Power*. Princeton: University Press, 1969. xxiii, 472pp. Bib. 452-63.

G 518   SCHMEER, Karlheinz, *Die Regie des öffentlichen Lebens im Dritten Reich*, Munich: Pohl, 1956. 164pp. Bib. 153-64.

G 519   TEPPE, Karl, *Provinz, Partei, Staat: zur provinziellen Selbstverwaltung im Dritten Reich, untersucht am Beispiel Westfallens*, Munster i W.: Aschendorff, 1977. xii, 300pp. Bib. 257-88.

Law, Justice and the Courts

G 520   BLANKE, Thomas and others, *Der Unrechts-Staat: Recht und Justiz im Nationalsozialismus; red. Kritische Justiz*, with contributions by Bernhard Blanke, Frankfurt/M: Europäische Verlagsanstalt, 1979. 211pp.

G 521   *Die Deutsche Justiz und der Nationalsozialismus*, Stuttgart: Deutsche Verlags-Anstalt, 1968-. Series of works on nazi justice.

G 522   HATTENHAUER, Hans, 'Justiz, Nationalsozialismus und Zeitgeschichte: zugleich eine Rezension'. *GESCH. IN WISS. UND UNTERR.*, **27** (**11**), 1976. pp. 690-4.

G 523   JOHE, Werner, *Die gleichgeschaltete Justiz: Organisation des Rechtswesens und Politisierung der Rechtsprechung, 1933-1945*, Frankfurt/M: Europäische Verlagsanstalt, 1967. 258pp. Bib. 245-54. Hamburg University thesis, 1964.

G 524   SCHORN, Hubert, *Der Richter im Dritten Reich: Geschichte und Dokumente*, Frankfurt/M: Klostermann, 1959. 742pp.

G 525   STAFF, Ilse (ed.), *Justiz im Dritten Reich: eine Dokumentation*, 2nd edn, Frankfurt/M: Fischer, 1978. 234pp. Bib. 228-31.

G 526   WAGNER, Walter, *Der Volksgerichtshof im nationalsozialistischen Staat*, Stuttgart: Deutsche Verlags-Anstalt, 1974. 991pp.

The SA, SS, and Gestapo

G 527   ARTZT, Heinz, *Mörder in Uniform: Organisationen die zu Vollstreckern nationalsozialistische Verbrechen wurden*, Munich: Kindler, 1979. 206pp.

G 528   BAYLE, François, *Psychologie et éthique du national-socialisme: étude anthropologique des dirigeants SS*, Paris; PUF, 1953. xx, 546pp. Bib. 539-46. Paris University thesis, 1952.

G 529   BENNECKE, Heinrich, *Hitler und die SA*, Munich: Olzog, 1962. 264pp. Bib. 262-4.

G 530   BESSEL, Richard J., 'Militarismus im innenpolitischen Leben der Weimarer Republik: von den Freikorps zur SA'. In

MÜLLER, K.J. and OPITZ, E. (eds), *Militär und Militarismus in der Weimarer Republic*, Düsseldorf; Droste, 1978. pp. 193–222.

G 531   BESSEL, Richard J., *The SA in the Eastern regions of Germany, 1925–1937*, Oxford University thesis, 1980.

G 532   BLOCH, Charles, *Die SA und die Krise des NS-Regimes 1934*, Frankfurt/M: Suhrkampf, 1970. 176pp. On SA purge of 1934.

G 533   BOEHNERT, Gunnar Charles, *A Sociography of the SS Officer Corps, 1925–1939*, London University thesis, 1978. iv, 262pp.

G 534   BROWDER, George Clark, 'Die Anfänge des SD'. *VIERTELJAHRSH. FÜR ZEITG.*, **27** (**2**), 1979. pp. 299–324. Documents.

G 535   BROWDER, George Clark, *SIPO and SD, 1931–1940: formation of an instrument of power*, University of Wisconsin thesis, 1969. UM 69–00881. 502pp.

G 536   BUCHHEIM, Hans, *SS und Polizei im NS-Staat*, Duisdorf b. Bonn: Studiengesellschaft für Zeitprobleme, 1964. 224pp.

G 537   BUCHHEIM, Hans, 'Die SS in der Verfassung des Dritten Reiches'. *VIERTELJAHRSH. FÜR ZEITG.*, **3** (**2**), 1955. pp. 127–57.

G 538   DELARUE, Jacques, *The Gestapo: a history of horror*, New York: Morrow, 1964. xxviii, 384pp. Bib. 365–8. Tr. of *Histoire de la Gestapo*, Paris: Fayard, 1962, by Mervyn Savill.

G 539   DICKS, Henry Victor, *Licensed Mass Murder: a sociopsychological study of some SS killers*, London: Heinemann, 1972. New York: Basic Books, 1973. xiii, 283pp. Bib. 270–4.

G 540   DIELS, Rudolf, *Lucifer ante Portas: zwischen Severing und Heydrich*, Zürich: Interverlag, 1949. 326pp.

G 541   FISCHER, Conan, *Stormtroopers: a social, economic and ideological analysis, 1929–35*, London, Allen & Unwin, 1983. xiv, 239pp. Bib. 226–32. Sussex University thesis, 1980.

G 542   FISCHER, Conan, 'The SA of the NSDAP: social background and ideology of the rank and file in the early 1930's'. *J. OF CONTEMP. HIST.*, **17** (**4**), 1982. pp. 651–70.

G 543   FISCHER, Conan and HICKS, Carolyn, 'Statistics and the historian: the occupational profile of the SA of the NSDAP'. *SOC. HIST.*, **5** (**1**), 1980. pp. 131–40. Includes rejoinder by R. Bessel and M. Jamin.

G 544   GEORG, Enno, *Die wirtschaftlichen Unternehmungen der SS*, Stuttgart: Deutsche Verlags-Anstalt, 1963. 154pp. Göttingen University thesis.

275

G 545 HÖHNE, Heinz, *The Order of the Death's Head: the story of Hitler's SS*; London, Secker & Warburg, 1969. xii, 690pp. Bib. 659–72. Tr. of *Der Orden unter dem Totenkopf*, Gütersloh: Mohn, 1967, by Richard Barry.

G 546 Institut für Zeitgeschichte, Munich, *Anatomy of the SS state*; [by] Helmut Krausnick [*et al*], London: Collins. New York: Walker, 1968. xv, 614pp. Bib. 601–4. Tr. of *Anatomie des SS-Staates*, 2nd edn, pub. by Deutscher Taschenbuch-V., 1979, by Richard Barry [*et al*]. Other authors Hans Buchheim, Martin Broszat, Hans-Adolf Jacobsen.

G 547 JAMIN, Mathilde, 'Methodische Konzeption einer quantitativen Analyse zur sozialen Zussamensetzung der SA'. In MANN, R., G 484. pp. 84–97.

G 548 KATER, Michael H., *Das Ahnenerbe der SS, 1935–1945: ein Beitrag zur Kulturpolitik des Dritten Reiches*, Stuttgart: Deutsche Verlags-Anstalt, 1974. 522pp. Bib. 468–88. Heidelberg University thesis, 1966.

G 549 KATER, Michael, H., 'Ansätze zu einer Soziologie der SA bis zum Röhm-Krise'. In ENGELHARDT, Ulrich and others (eds). *Sozial Bewegung und politische Verfassung*, Stuttgart, Klett: 1976. pp. 798–831.

G 550 KATER, Michael H., 'Zum gegenseitigen Verhältnis von SA und SS in der Sozialgeschichte der Nationalsozialismus vom 1925 bis 1939'. *VIERTELJAHRSCHR. FÜR SOZ. UND WIRTSCHAFTS-GESCH.*, **62** (**3**), 1975. pp. 339–79.

G 551 KOEHL, Robert, 'The character of the nazi SS'. *J. OF MOD HIST.*, **34** (**3**), 1962. pp. 275–83.

G 552 MERKL, Peter H., 'Die alten Kämpfer der NSDAP: Auswertung von 35 Jahre alten Daten'. *SOZIALWISS. JAHRB. FÜR POLITIK.*, **2**, 1971. pp. 495–518.

G 553 MERKL, Peter H., 'Approaches to political violence: the stormtroopers, 1925–33'. In MOMMSEN W.J. and HIRSCHFELD, Gerhard (eds), *Social Protest, Violence and Terror in Nineteenth- and Twentieth-century Europe*, London: Macmillan, 1982. pp. 367–83.

G 554 MERKL, Peter H., *The Making of a Stormtrooper*. Princeton: University Press, 1980. xix, 328pp. Bib. 309–23.

G 555 MERKL, Peter H., *Political Violence under the Swastika: 581 early nazis*. Princeton: University Press, 1975. xiv, 735pp. Bib. 725–9.

G 556 MERKL, Peter H., 'Zur quantitativen Analyse von Lebensläufen "Alter Kämpfer"'. In MANN, R., G 484. pp. 67–83.

G 557 Nationalsozialistische Deutsche Arbeiter-Partei. Hauptamt Schrifttumspflege, *Das Schrifttum der SA*, Munich: Eher, 1942. 23pp.

G 558 PAETEL, Karl Otto, 'The Black Order: a survey of the literature on the SS'. *WIENER LIB. BULL.*, **13** (**3/4**), 1959. pp. 34–5.

G 559 PAETEL, Karl Otto, 'Die SS: ein Beitrag zur Soziologie des Nationalsozialismus'. *VIERTELJAHRSH. FÜR ZEITG.*, **2** (**1**), 1954. pp. 1–33.

G 560 REICHE, Eric G., *The Development of the SA in Nuremberg, 1922 to 1934*, University of Delaware thesis, 1972. UM 72-32014. 304pp.

G 561 REITLINGER, Gerald, *The SS: alibi of a nation, 1922–1945*, new foreword by Martin Gilbert, London: Arms & Armour, 1981. xi, 502pp. Bib. 455-60. First pub. by Heinemann, 1956.

G 562 WERNER, Andreas, *SA und NSDAP: SA 'Wehrband', 'Parteitruppe' oder 'Revolutionsarmee': Studien zur Geschichte der SA und der NSDAP, 1920-1933*, Erlangen University thesis, 1965. xxxvii, 599pp. Bib. i–xiv.

G 563 ZIPFEL, Friedrich, 'Gestapo and the SD: a sociographic profile of the organisers of terror'. In LARSEN, S.U., Gn 36. pp. 301-11.

The NSDAP and the Army

G 564 BERGHAHN, Volker R., 'NSDAP und "Geistige Führung" der Wehrmacht, 1939-1943'. *VIERTELJAHRSH. FÜR ZEITG.*, **17** (**1**), 1969. pp. 17-71.

G 565 CARSTEN, Francis Ludwig, *The Reichswehr and Politics, 1918-1933*, Oxford: University Press, 1966. viii, 427pp. Bib. 406-11. First pub. as *Reichswehr und Politik*, Cologne, 1964.

G 566 CRAIG, Gordon, 'Reichswehr and national socialism: the policy of Wilhelm Groener, 1928-1932'. *POLIT. SCI. Q.*, **63** (**2**), 1948. pp. 194-229.

G 567 DEUERLEIN, Ernst, 'Hitlers Eintritt in der Politik und die Reichswehr'. *VIERTELJAHRSH. FÜR ZEITG.*, **7** (**2**), 1959. pp. 177-227.

G 568 GOSSWEILER, Kurt, *Kapital, Reichswehr und NSDAP, 1919-1924*, Berlin: Akademie V., 1982. 616pp.

G 569 HALLGARTEN, George Wolfgang, *Hitler, Reichswehr und Industrie: zur Geschichte der Jahre, 1918-1933*, 2nd edn, Frankfurt/M: Europäische Verlagsanstalt, 1955. 139pp.

G 570 MÜLLER, Klaus-Jürgen, *Das Heer und Hitler: Armee und nationalsozialistisches Regime, 1933–1940*, Stuttgart: Deutsche Verlags-Anstalt, 1969, 711pp. Bib. 589–696.

G 571 MÜLLER, Klaus-Jürgen, 'The army in the Third Reich: a historical interpretation'. *J. of Strategic Stud.*, **2** (2), 1979. pp. 123–52.

G 572 O'NEILL, Robert John, *The German Army and the Nazi Party, 1933–1939*, London: Cassell, 1966. 286pp. Bib. 247–56.

G 573 QUINETT, Robert L., 'The German army confronts the NSFO'. *J. OF CONTEMP. HIST.*, **13** (1), 1978. pp. 53–64. The National Sozialistischer Führungs-Offiziere existed to make committed nazis out of apolitical German soldiers.

G 574 VOGELSANG, Thilo, 'Hitlers Brief an Reichenau vom 4 Dezember 1932: Dokumentation'. *VIRTELJAHRSH. FÜR ZEITG.*, **7** (4), 1959. pp. 429–37.

G 575 VOGELSANG, Thilo, 'Reichswehr und Hitler'. *Oesterr. in Gesch. und Lit.*, **5** (7), 1961. pp. 339–53.

G 576 VOGELSANG, Thilo, *Reichswehr, Staat und NSDAP: Beiträge zur deutschen Geschichte 1930–1932*, Stuttgart: Deutsche Verlags-Anstalt, 1962. 506pp. Bib. 493–500.

G 577 WHEELER-BENNETT, John W., *The Nemesis of Power: the German army in politics, 1918–1945*, London: Macmillan, 1953. New York: St Martin's Press, 1954. xvi, 829pp. Bib. 767–79.

The NSDAP and Industry

G 578 CZICHON, Eberhard, *Wer verhalf Hitler zur Macht? zum Anteil der deutschen Industrie an der Zerstörung der Weimarer Republik*, 5th edn, Cologne: Pahl-Rugenstein, 1979. 165p. Bib. Hitler as a tool of big business.

G 579 GOSSWEILER, Kurt, 'Hitler und das Kapital, 1925–1928'. *BL. FÜR DTSCH. UND INT. POLIT.*, **23**, 1978. pp. 842–60, 993–1009.

G 580 HÖRSTER-PHILIPPS, Ulrike, *Grosskapital und Faschismus, 1918–1945: Dokumente*, 2nd edn, Cologne: Pahl-Rugenstein, 1981. 388pp. Bib. 374–81. First edn, *Wer war Hitler wirklich?*

G 581 KUHN, Axel, 'Die Unterredung zwischen Hitler und Papen im Hause des Barons von Schröder'. *GESCH. IN WISS UND UNTERR.*, **24**, 1973. pp. 709–22.

G 582 NEEBE, Reinhard, *Grossindustrie, Staat und NSDAP, 1930–1933: Paul Silverberg und der Reichsverband der Deutschen Industrie in der*

Krise der Weimarer Republik, Göttingen: Vandenhoeck & Ruprecht, 1981. 314pp. Bib. 285-305.

G 583 PETZINA, Dieter, 'Hitler und die deutsche Industrie'. *GESCH. IN WISS. UND UNTERR.*, **17** (**8**), 1966. pp. 482-91.

G 584 SCHWEITZER, Arthur, *Big Business in the Third Reich*. Bloomington: Indiana University Press, 1964. xii, 739pp. Bib. 617-40.

G 585 SAAGE, Richard, 'Zum Verhältnis von Nationalsozialismus und Industrie'. *Aus Polit. und Zeitg.*, **25**, 1 March 1975. pp. 17-39.

G 586 STEGMANN, Dirk, 'Antiquierte personalisierung oder sozialökonomische Faschismusanalyse? eine Antwort auf H.A. Turners Kritik'. *ARCH. FÜR SOZIALGESCH.*, **17**, 1977. pp. 275-96.

G 587 STEGMANN, Dirk, 'Kapitalismus und Faschismus in Deutschland, 1929-1934'. *Gesellschaft: Beiträge zur Marxschen Theorie*, **6**, 1976. pp. 19-91.

G 588 STEGMANN, Dirk, 'Zum Verhältnis von Grossindustrie und Nationalsozialismus, 1930-1933: ein Beitrag zur Geschichte der sogenannten Machtergreifung'. *ARCH. FÜR SOZIALGESCH.*, **13**, 1973. pp. 399-482.

G 589 THYSSEN, Fritz, *I paid Hitler*, London: Hodder & Stoughton. New York, Farrar & Rinehart, 1941. xxix, 281pp.

G 590 TRUMPP, Thomas, 'Zur Finanzierung der NSDAP durch die deutsche Grossindustrie: Versuch einer Bilanz'. *GESCH. IN WISS. UND UNTERR.*, **32** (**4**), 1981. pp. 223-41.

G 591 TURNER, Henry Ashby, 'Big business and the rise of Hitler'. *AM. HIST. REV.*, **75** (**1**), 1969. pp. 56-70.

G 592 TURNER, Henry Ashby, 'Emil Kirdorf and the Nazi Party'. *CENT. EUR. HIST.*, **1** (**4**), 1968. pp. 324-44. Emil Kirdorf (1847-1938), coal magnate from the Ruhr who supported the nazis.

G 593 TURNER, Henry Ashby, *Faschismus und Kapitalismus in Deutschland: Studien zum Verhältnis zwischen Nationalsozialismus und Wirstchaft*, 2nd edn, Göttingen: Vandenhoeck & Ruprecht, 1980. 185pp. Six essays from journals.

G 594 TURNER, Henry Ashby, 'Fritz Thyssen und *I paid Hitler*'. *VIERTELJAHRSH. FÜR ZEITG.*, **19** (**3**), 1971. pp. 225-44.

G 595 TURNER, Henry Ashby, 'Grossunternehmertum und Nationalsozialismus, 1930-1933: kritisches und ergänzendes zu zwei neuen Forschungsbeiträgen'. *HIST. Z.*, **221** (**1**), 1975. pp. 18-68. Review article.

G 596 VOGELSANG, Reinhard, *Der Freundeskreis Himmler*, Göttingen: Musterschmidt, 1972. 182pp. Bib. 171-6.

G 597 WEISBROD, Bernd 'Economic power and political stability reconsidered: heavy industry in Weimar Germany'. *SOC. HIST.*, 4 (2), 1979. pp. 241-63. Heavy industry did not uniformly support the nazis.

G 598 WINKLER, Heinrich August, 'Unternehmerverbände zwischen Ständideologie und Nationalsozialismus'. *VIERTELJAHRSH. FÜR ZEITG.* 17 (4), 1969. pp. 341-71. Employers' Associations and the NSDAP.

The Economy

G 599 BARKAI, Avraham, 'Wirtschaftliche Grundanschauungen und Ziele der NSDAP'. *JAHRB. INST. DTSCH. GESCH.*, 7, 1978. pp. 355-85. Documents on economic policy.

G 600 BARKAI, Avraham, *Die Wirstchaftssystem des Nationalsozialismus: der historische und ideologische Hintergrund, 1933-1936*, Cologne: V. Wissenschaft & Politik, 1977. 214pp. Bib.

G 601 BECKENBACH, Ralf, *Der Staat im Faschismus: Ökonomie und Politik im Deutschen Reich, 1920 bis 1945*, Berlin: V. für das Studium der Arbeiterbewegung, 1974. 134pp. Bib. 127-34. Free University of Berlin thesis.

G 602 BIRKENFELD, Wolfgang, *Der synthetische Treibstoff, 1933-1945: ein Beitrag zur nationalsozialistischen Wirtschafts- und Rüstungspolitik*, Göttingen: Musterschmidt, 1964. 279pp. Bib. 267-73.

G 603 DUBAIL, René, *Une expérience d'économie dirigée: l'Allemagne national-socialiste*, Paris: Dupont, 1962. 171pp.

G 604 EICHHOLTZ, Dietrich, 'Alte und "neue" konzeptionen: bürgerliche Literatur zur Wirtschaftsgeschichte des Faschismus in Deutschland'. *Jahrb. für Wirtschaftsgesch.*, 3, 1971. pp. 231-55. Review article.

G 605 EICHHOLTZ, Dietrich, *Geschichte der deutschen Kriegswirtschaft, 1939-1945*, 2nd edn, Berlin: Akademie V., 1971. 1. 1939-41. 408pp. Bib. 387-98.

G 606 ERBE, René, *Die nationalsozialistische Wirtschaftspolitik, 1933-1939 im Lichte der modernen Theorie*, Zürich: Polygraphischer V., 1958. 197pp. Bib. 194-5.

G 607 FORSTMEIER, Friedrich and VOLKMANN, Hans-Erich

(eds), *Wirtschaft und Rüstung am Vorabend des Zweiten Weltkrieges*, Düsseldorf: Droste, 1975. 415pp.

G 608   HENNIG, Eike, *Thesen zur deutschen Sozial- und Wirtschaftsgeschichte, 1933-1938*, Frankfurt/M: Suhrkampf, 1973. 263pp. Bib. 254–64. Marxist.

G 609   HENNING, Friedrich-Wilhelm (ed.), *Probleme der nationalsozialistischen Wirtschaftspolitik*, by Fritz Blaich [*et al.*], Berlin: Duncker & Humblot, 1976. 174pp.

G 610   KADRITZKE, Niels, *Faschismus und Krise: zum Verhältnis von Politik und Ökonomie im Nationalsozialismus*, Frankfurt/M: Campus V., 1976. 216pp. Bib. 204–16.

G 611   KLEIN, Burton H., *Germany's Economic Preparations for War*, Cambridge Mass.: Harvard University Press, 1959. xi, 272pp. Bib. 259–64.

G 612   MASON, Timothy W., 'The primacy of politics: politics and economics in national socialist Germany'. In WOOLF, S.J., Gn 21. pp. 165–195. Rev. version of article which first appeared in *Argument*, **41**, 1966.

G 613   MEINCK, Gerhard, *Hitler und die deutsche Aufrüstung, 1933–1937*, Wiesbaden: Steiner, 1959. vii, 246pp. Bib. 240–6.

G 614   MILWARD, Alan S., *The German Economy at War*, London: Athlone Press, 1965. vi, 214pp. Bib. 195–208.

G 615   PETZINA, Dieter, *Autarkiepolitik im Dritten Reich: der nationalsozialistische Vierjahresplan*, Stuttgart: Deutsche Verlags-Anstalt, 1968. 204pp. Mannheim Wirtschaftshochschule thesis, 1964.

G 616   PETZINA, Dieter, *Die deutsche Wirtschaft in der zwischenkreigzeit*, Wiesbaden: Steiner, 1977. 205pp. Bib. 191–205.

G 617   SOHN-RETHEL, Alfred, *Economy and Class Structure of German Fascism*, London: CSE Books, 1979. 159pp. Tr. of *Ökonomie und Klassenstruktur des deutschen Faschismus*, by Martin Sohn-Rethel.

G 618   TURNER, Henry Ashby, 'Hitlers Einstellung zu Wirtschaft und Gesellschaft vor 1933'. *GESCH. UND GES.*, **2**, 1976. pp. 89–117.

G 619   UHLIG, Heinrich, *Die Warenhäuser im Dritten Reich*, Cologne; Westdeutscher V., 1956. viii, 230pp. Bib. 228–30. Department stores in nazi Germany.

G 620   VOLKMANN, Hans-Erich, *Wirtschaft im Dritten Reich: eine Bibliographie*, Munich: Bernard & Graefe, 1980. 139p.

Agriculture

G 621 DARRÉ, Richard Walther, *Neuadel aus Blut und Boden*, Munich: J.F. Lehmann, 1939. 239pp. First pub. 1934. Author (1895-1953), Minister of Agriculture in the Third Reich.

G 622 GIES, Horst., *R. Walther Darré und die nationalsozialistische Bauernpolitik in den Jahren bis 1933*, Frankfurt University thesis, 1966. 177pp. Bib. 167-76.

G 623 FARQUHARSON, John E., *The Plough and the Swastika: the NSDAP and agriculture in Germany, 1928-1945*, London: Sage, 1976. vii, 312pp. Bib. 272-9.

G 624 GRUNDMANN, Friedrich, *Agrarpolitik im Dritten Reich: Anspruch und Wirklichkeit des Reichserbhofgesetzes*, Hamburg: Hoffmann & Campe, 1979. 233pp. Bib. 214-27. Marburg University thesis, 1978.

G 625 KRÜDENER, Jürgen von, 'Zielkonflikte in der national-sozialistische Agrarpolitik'. *Z. FÜR WIRTSCH. UND SOZIALWISS.*, **94**, 1974. pp. 335-61.

G 626 LOVIN, Clifford R., 'Reorganisation in the Third Reich: the Reich Food Corporation, 1933-1936'. *AGRIC. HIST.*, **43** (**4**), 1969. 447-61.

G 627 TORNOW, Werner (ed.), *Chronik der Agrarspolitik und Agrarwirtschaft des Deutschen Reiches von 1933-1945*, Hamburg: Parey, 1972. 193pp. Bib. 191-3.

Labour and Social Policy in the Third Reich

G 628 DE WITT, Thomas E.J., 'The economics and politics of welfare in the Third Reich'. *CENT. EUR. HIST.*, **11** (**3**), 1978. pp. 256-78.

G 629 DE WITT, Thomas E.J., 'The nazification of welfare: organisation and policy, 1930-1939'. *Societas*, **7** (**4**), 1977. pp. 303-27.

G 630 MASON, Timothy W., *Arbeiterklasse und Volksgemeinschaft: Dokumente und Materialien zur deutschen Arbeiterpolitik, 1936-1939*, Opladen: Westdeutscher V., 1975. lxiii, 1299pp. Bib. xliii-lxiii.

G 631 HERBST, Ludolf, 'Die Krise des nationalsozialistischen Regimes am Vorabend des Zweiten Weltkrieges und die forcierte Aufrüstung'. *VIERTELJAHRSH. FÜR ZEITG.*, **26** (**3**), 1978. pp. 347-92. Comment on Mason's *Arbeiterklasse*, see G 630.

G 632 MASON, Timothy W., 'Labour in the Third Reich, 1933-1939'. *Past and Present*, **33**, 1966. pp. 112-41.

G 633 MASON, Timothy W., *Sozialpolitik im Dritten Reich: Arbeiterklasse und Volksgemeinschaft*, Opladen: Westdeutscher V., 1977. 374pp. Bib. 335-66. Revision of the intro. to *Arbeiterklasse*, see G 630.

G 634 MÜLLER, Markus, 'Die Stellung der Arbeiters im nationalsozialistischen Staat: Quellenmässige Erschliessung'. *GESCH. IN WISS. UND UNTERR.*, **26** (1), 1975. pp. 1-21.

G 635 SCHUMANN, Hans-Gerd, *Nationalsozialismus und Gewerkschaftsbewegung: die Vernichtung der deutschen Gewerkschaften und der Aufbau der 'Deutschen Arbeitsfront'*, Hanover: Goedel, 1958. 219pp. Bib. 187-219.

G 636 TEPPE, Karl, 'Zur sozialpolitik des Dritten Reiches am Beispiel der Sozialversicherung'. *ARCH. FÜR SOZIALGESCH.*, **17**, 1977. pp. 195-250.

Social Life and Public Opinion

G 637 BLEUEL, Hans Peter, *Strength Through Joy: sex and society in Nazi Germany*, ed. and with a pref. by Heinrich Fraenkel, London: Secker & Warburg. Philadelphia: Lippincott, 1973. xi, 272pp. US edn, *Sex and Society in Nazi Germany*. Tr. of *Das saubere Reich*. Bern, 1972, by J. Maxwell Brownjohn.

G 638 FOCKE, Harald and REIMER, Uwe, *Alltag unterm Hakenkreuz: wie die Nazis das Leben der deutschen veränderten: ein aufklärendes Lesebuch*, Reinbek bei Hamburg: Rowohlt, 1979. 191pp.

G 639 GERMANY. Reichssicherheitshauptamt, *Meldung aus dem Reich: Auswahl aus den geheimen Lageberichten des Sicherheitsdienstes der SS, 1939-1944*, ed. Heinz Boberach, Neuwied: Luchterhand, 1965. xxxii, 551pp. Selection of public opinion surveys collected by the SD.

G 640 GRUNBERGER, Richard, *A Social History of the Third Reich*, Harmondsworth: Penguin, 1974. 663pp. Bib. 593-4. First pub. Weidenfeld & Nicholson, 1971. US edn, *The 12-year Reich*, New York: Holt Rinehart, 1971.

G 641 GRUNFELD, Frederick V., *The Hitler File: a social history of Germany and the nazis, 1918-1945*, intro. by H.R. Trevor-Roper, London: Weidenfeld & Nicolson. New York: Random House, 1974. 374pp.

G 642 KERSHAW, Ian, *Der Hitler-Mythos: Volksmeinung und*

Propaganda im Dritten Reich, intro. by Martin Broszat, Stuttgart: Deutsche Verlags-Anstalt, 1980. 215pp. Bib. 198–209.

G 643   KERSHAW, Ian, *Popular Opinion and Political Dissent in the Third Reich: 1933–1945*, Oxford: University Press, 1983. xvi, 426pp. Bib. 394–411.

G 644   RABINBACH, Anson G., 'The aesthetics of production in the Third Reich'. *J. OF CONTEMP. HIST.*, 11 (3), 1976. pp. 43–74.

G 645   SCHOENBAUM, David, *Hitler's Social Revolution: class and status in nazi Germany, 1933–1939*, Garden City: Doubleday, 1966. London: Weidenfeld & Nicolson, 1967. xxiii, 336pp. Bib. 309–24.

Propaganda and Mass Media

C 646   BAIRD, Jay W., *The Mythical World of Nazi War Propaganda, 1939–1945*. Minneapolis: University of Minnesota Press, 1974. xii, 329pp. Bib. 309–22.

G 647   BESSEL, Richard J., 'The rise of the NSDAP and the myth of nazi propaganda'. *WIENER LIB. BULL.*, 33 (51/52), 1980. pp. 20–9.

G 648   GRIESWELLE, Detlef, *Propaganda der Friedlosigkeit: eine Studie zu Hitlers Rhetorik, 1920–1933*, Stuttgart: Enke V., 1972. 233pp. Bib. 196–210.

G 649   HAGEMANN, Walter, *Publizistik im Dritten Reich: ein Beitrag zur Methodik der Massenführung*, Hamburg: Hansischer Gildenverlag, 1948. 575pp. Bib. 507–14.

G 650   HERZSTEIN, Robert Edwin, *The War that Hitler Won: the most infamous propaganda campaign in history*, New York: Putnam, 1978. 491pp. Bib. 467–75.

G 651   POHLE, Heinz, *Der Rundfunk als Instrument der Politik: zur Geschichte des deutschen Rundfunks von 1923–1938*, Hamburg: Hans Bredow Inst, V., 1955. 480pp. Bib. 462–75.

G 652   ZEMAN, Z.A.B., *Nazi Propaganda*, 2nd edn, Oxford: University Press, 1973. xvii, 260pp. Bib. 236–46.

The Press

G 653   ABEL, Karl-Dietrich, *Presselenkung im NS-Staat: eine Studie zur Geschichte der Publizistik in der nationalsozialistischen Zeit*, foreword by Hans Herzfeld, Berlin: Colloquium V., 1968. 172pp.

G 654   BOVERI, Margaret, *Wir lügen alle: eine Hauptstadtzeitung unter Hitler*, Olten: Walter, 1965. 744pp. Bib. 715-24. *Berliner Tageblatt's* attempt to compromise with Goebbels.

G 655   FREI, Norbert, *Nationalsozialistische Eroberung der Provinzpresse: Gleichschaltung, Selbstanpassung und Resistenz in Bayern*, Stuttgart: Deutsche Verlags-Anstalt, 1980. 360pp. Bib. 340-54. Munich University thesis, 1979.

G 656   GÜNSCHE, Karl-Ludwig, *Phasen der Gleichschaltung: Stichtags-Analysen deutscher Zeitungen, 1933-1938*, Osnabrück: Fromm, 1970. 95pp. Bib. 91.

G 657   HAGEMANN, Jurgen, *Die Presselenkung im Dritten Reich*, Bonn: Bouvier, 1970. 398pp. Bib. 323-73.

G 658   HALE, Oron J., *The Captive Press in the Third Reich*, Princeton: University Press, 1964. xii, 353pp. Bib. 341-6.

G 659   MARTENS, Erika, *Zum Beispiel-Das Reich: zur Phänomenologie der Presse im totalitären Regime*, Cologne: V. Wissenschaft & Politik, 1972. 294pp. Bib. 285-9.

G 660   STOREK, Henning, *Dirigierte Öffentlichkeit: die Zeitung als Herrschaftsmittel in den Anfangsjahren der nationalsozialistischen Regierung*, Opladen: Westdeutscher V., 1972. 156pp. Bib. 146-56.

Women in the Third Reich

G 661   KESSLER, Hannelore, *Die deutsche Frau: nationalsozialistische Frauenpropaganda im Völkischen Beobachter*, Cologne: Pahl-Rugenstein, 1981. 127pp. Bib. 123-7.

G 662   KLAUS, Martin, *Mädchen in der Hitlerjugend: die Erziehung zur deutsche Frau*, Cologne: Pahl-Rugenstein, 1980. 260pp. Bib. 155-63.

G 663   KLINKSIEK, Dorothee, *Die Frau im NS-Staat*, Stuttgart: Deutsche Verlags-Anstalt, 1982. 220pp.

G 664   KOONZ, Claudia, 'Nazi women before 1933: rebels against emancipation'. *SOC. SCI. Q.*, **56** (4), 1976. pp. 553-63.

G 665   MASON, Timothy W., 'Der Frauenarbeit im NS-Staat'. *ARCH. FÜR SOZIALGESCH.*, **19**, 1979. pp. 579-84.

G 666   MASON, Timothy W., 'Women in Germany, 1925-1940: family, welfare and work'. *HIST. WORKSHOP.*, **1**, 1976. pp. 74-113; **2**, 1976. pp. 5-32.

G 667   SCHOLTZ-KLINK, Gertrud, *Die Frau im Dritten Reich: eine Dokumentation*, Tübingen: Grabert, 1978. 546pp.

G 668   STEPHENSON, Jill, *The Nazi Organisation of Women*, London: Croom Helm, 1981. 246pp. Bib. 231-7.

G 669   STEPHENSON, Jill, *Women in Nazi Society*, London: Croom Helm. New York: Barnes & Noble, 1975. vii, 223pp.

G 670   WINKLER, Dorte, *Frauenarbeit im Dritten Reich*. Hamburg: Hoffmann & Campe, 1977. 253pp. Bibs.

The Nazis, Religion and the Churches

G 671   BAUMGÄRTNER, Raimund, *Weltanschauungskampf im Dritten Reich: die Auseinandersetzung der Kirchen mit Alfred Rosenberg*, Mainz: Matthias-Grünewald V., 1977. xxxii, 275pp. Rosenberg *v.* the Church.

G 672   BUCHHEIM, Hans, *Glaubenkrise im Dritten Reich: drei Kapitel nationalsozialistischer Religionspolitik*, Stuttgart: Deutsche Verlags-Anstalt, 1953. 223pp. Bib. 205-7.

G 673   CHADWICK, Owen, 'The present stage of the Kirchen-kampf enquiry'. *J. OF ECCLES. HIST.*, **24** (1), 1973. pp. 33-50.

G 674   CONWAY, John S., 'Der deutsche Kirchenkampf: Tendenzen und Probleme seiner Erforschung an Hand neuerer Literatur'. *VIERTELJAHRSH. FÜR ZEITG.*, **17** (4), 1969. pp. 423-49.

G 675   CONWAY, John S., *The Nazi Persecution of the Churches, 1933-1945*, London: Weidenfeld & Nicolson. New York: Basic Books, 1968. xxxi, 474pp. Bib. 455-64.

G 676   CONZEMIUS, Victor, *Églises chrétiennes et totalitarisme national-socialisme: un bilan historique*, Louvain: Pubs. Universitaire, 1969. 161pp.

G 677   DAHM, Karl-Wilhelm, 'German Protestantism and politics, 1918-1939'. *J. OF CONTEMP. HIST.*, **3** (1), 1968. pp. 29-49.

G 678   DIEHN, Otto, *Bibliographie zur Geschichte des Kirschenkampfes, 1933-1945*, Göttingen: Vandenhoeck & Ruprecht, 1958. 249pp.

G 679   ERICKSEN, Robert P., 'Theologian of the Third Reich: the case of Gerhard Kittel'. *J. OF CONTEMP. HIST.*, **17** (3), 1977. pp. 595-622.

G 680   FRIEDLANDER, Saul, *Pius Twelfth and the Third Reich: a documentation*, London: Chatto & Windus. New York: Knopf, 1966.

xxv, 238pp. Tr. of *Pius XII et le IIIe Reich*, Paris, 1964, by Charles Fullman.

G 681 *Zur Geschichte des Kirchenkampfes: gesammelte Aufsätze*, Göttingen: Vandenhoeck & Ruprecht, 1965-71. 2 vols.

G 682 HELMREICH, Ernst Christian, *The German Churches under Hitler: background, struggle and epilogue*. Detroit: Wayne State University Press, 1979. 616pp. Bib. 577-600.

G 683 HEHL, Ulrich von, *Katholische Kirche und Nationalsozialismus in Erzbistum Köln, 1933-1945*, Mainz: Matthias-Grünewald V., 1977. xxx, 269pp. Bib. x-xxviii.

G 684 JUNKER, Detlef, *Die deutsche Zentrumspartei und Hitler 1932/33: ein Beitrag zur Problematik des politischen Katholizismus in Deutschland*, Stuttgart: Klett, 1969. 247pp. Bib. 236-45. Kiel University thesis, 1967.

G 685 KRETSCHMAR, Georg (ed.), *Dokumente zur Kirchenpolitik des Dritten Reiches*, Munich: Kaiser, 1971-5. 2 vols.

G 686 LEWY, Günter, *The Catholic Church and Nazi Germany*, New York: McGraw Hill, 1964. xv, 416pp. Bib. 345-404.

G 687 MÜLLER, Hans, (ed.), *Katholische Kirche und Nationalsozialismus: Dokumente, 1930-1935*, intro. by Kurt Sontheimer, Munich: Nymphenburger V., 1965. 373pp. Bib. 353-66.

G 688 PIERARD, Richard, 'Why did German Protestants welcome Hitler?' *Fides et Historia*, **10** (**2**), 1978. pp. 8-29.

G 689 REPGEN, Konrad, *Hitlers Machtergreifung und der deutsche Katholizismus: Versuch einer Bilanz*, Saarbrücken: Vereinigung der Freunde der V. Univ. des Saarlandes, 1967. 35pp.

G 690 SCHOLDER, Klaus, *Die Kirchen und das Dritten Reich*. Frankfurt/M: Propyläen-V., 1977-. **1**. *Vorgeschichte und Zeit der Illusionen, 1918-1934*.

G 691 WRIGHT, Jonathon R., 'The German Protestant Church and the Nazi Party in the period of the seizure of power, 1932-33'. *Stud. in Church Hist.*, **14**, 1977. pp. 393-418.

G 692 ZIPFEL, Friedrich, *Kirchenkampf in Deutschland, 1933-1945: Religionsverfolgung und Selbstbehauptung der Kirchen in der nationalsozialistischer Zeit*, Berlin: De Gruyter, 1965. xiv, 517pp. Bib. 543-50.

Nazism and the Intellectuals

G 693   ALTER, Reinhard, *Gottfried Benn: the artist and politics, 1910–1934*. Frankfurt/M: Lang, 1976. 149pp. Bib. 145–9. The poet (1886–1956) and the extreme Right.

G 694   BENDERSKY, Joseph William, *Carl Schmitt: theorist for the Reich*, Princeton: University Press, 1983. xiv, 320pp. Bib. 289–312. Michigan State University thesis, 1975.

G 695   MAUS, Ingeborg, *Bürgerliche Rechtstheorie und Faschismus: zur sozialen Funktion und actuellen Wirkung der Theorie Carl Schmitts*, Munich: Fink, 1976. 194pp. Bib. 168–88. Frankfurt/M University thesis.

G 696   TOMMISSEN, Piet, 'Carl-Schmitt Bibliographie'. In *Festschrift für Carl Schmitt zum 70. Geburstag*, ed. H. Barion [*et al.*], Berlin, 1959. pp. 273–330.

G 697   TOMMISSEN, Piet, 'Zweite Forsetzungsliste der C.S.-Bibliographie vom Jahre 1959'. *Rev. Eur. Sci. Soc.*, **16** (**44**), 1978. pp. 187–238. Carl Schmitt bibliography.

G 698   CARSTEN, Francis Ludwig, '"Volk ohne Raum": a note on Hans Grimm'. *J. OF CONTEMP. HIST.*, **2** (**2**), 1967. pp. 221–7. Hans Grimm (1875–1959), German author.

G 699   KAISER, Helmut, *Mythos, Rausch und Reaktion: der Weg Gottfried Benns und Ernst Jüngers*, Berlin: Aufbau-V., 1962. 371pp.

G 700   PATRI, Aimé, 'Un exemple d'engagement: Martin Heidegger et le nazisme'. *Contract Social.*, **6** (**1**), 1962. pp. 37–42.

G 701   SCHROERS, Rolf, 'Der kontemplative Aktivist: Versuch über Ernst Jünger'. *Merkur*, **19**, 1965. pp. 211–25.

G 702   SCHWARZ, Hans-Peter, *Der konservative Anarchist: Politik und Zeitkritik Ernst Jüngers*, Freiburg: Rombach, 1962. 320pp. Bib. 267–315.

G 703   SIMS, Amy R., 'Intellectuals in crisis: historians under Hitler'. *Virginia Q. Rev.*, **54** (**2**), 1978. pp. 246–62.

G 704   SIMS, Amy R., *Those Who Stayed Behind: German historians and the Third Reich*, Cornell University thesis, 1979. UM 79-10835. 429pp.

G 705   PRÜMM, Karl, *Die Literatur des soldatischen Nationalismus der 20er Jahre, 1918–1933: Gruppenideologie und Epochenproblematik*, Kronberg: Scriptor V., 1974. 2 vols. Bib. vol. 2. 102–26, Saarbrücken University thesis, 1963.

G 706   STUTZ, Ernst, *Oswald Spengler als politische Denker*, Berne: Francke, 1958. 279pp. Bib. 247–79.

Nazism and Culture

G 707 ALBRECHT, Gerd, *Nationalsozialistische Filmpolitik: eine soziologische Untersuchung uber die Spielfilme des Dritten Reiches*, Stuttgart: Enke, 1969. xii, 562pp. Bib. 533–41.

G 708 FLITNER, Andreas (ed.), *Deutsches Geistesleben und Nationalsozialismus: eine Vortragsreihe der Universität Tübingen*, Tübingen: Wunderlich, 1965. 243pp.

G 709 GEISSLER, Rolf, *Dekadenz und Heroismus: Zeitroman und völkisch-nationalsozialistische Literaturkritik*, Stuttgart: Deutsche Verlags-Anstalt. 1964. 168pp.

G 710 HINKEL, Hermann, *Zur Funktion des Bildes im deutschen Faschismus: Bildbeispiele, Analysen, didaktische Vorschläge*, Steinbach: Anabas-V., 1975. 144pp. Bib. 141–4.

G 711 MOSSE, George Lachmann (ed.), *Nazi Culture: intellectual, cultural and social life in the Third Reich*, New York: Grosset & Dunlap, 1968. London: Allen, 1969, 386pp.

G 712 PHILIPS, M.S., 'The nazi control of the German film industry'. *J. OF EUR. STUD.*, 1 (1), 1971. pp. 37–68.

G 713 RICHARD, Lionel, *Le Nazisme et la culture*, Paris: Maspero, 1978. 393pp. Bib. 379–81.

G 714 RICHARD, Lionel, *Nazisme et littérature*, Paris: Maspero, 1971. 202pp. Bib. 191–3.

G 715 RISCHER, Walter, *Die nationalsozialistische Kulturpolitik in Düsseldorf, 1933–1945*, Düsseldorf: Triltsch, 1972. ix, 219pp. Bib. 212–18. Cologne University thesis.

G 716 STROTHMANN, Dietrich, *Nationalsozialistische Literaturpolitik: ein Beitrag zur Publizistik im Dritten Reich*, 2nd edn, Bonn: Bouvier, 507pp. Bib. 459–83.

G 717 VONDUNG, Klaus, *Völkisch-nationale und nationalsozialistische Literatur-Theorie*, Munich: List, 1973. 247pp. Bib. 226–41.

G 718 WELCH, David Albert, *Propaganda and the German Cinema, 1933–1945*. London University thesis, 1979. 534pp.

G 719 WULF, Josef (ed.), *Kunst und Kultur im Dritten Reich*, Gütersloh: Mohn, 1963–4. 5 vols. Separately pub. vols. on art, literature, film, press, theatre.

Education

G 720 BERNETT, Hajo, *Nationalsozialistische Leibeserziehung: eine Dokumentation über Theorie und Organisation*, Schorndorf: Hofmann, 1966. 232pp.

G 721 DEMICHELE, M.D., 'The nazi pattern of education in Third Reich Germany'. *SOC. STUD. (USA).*, **62** (**1**), 1971. pp. 3–7.

G 722 EILERS, Rolf, *Die nationalsozialistische Schulpolitik: eine Studie zur Funktion er Erziehung im totalitären Staat*, Cologne: Westdeutscher V., 1963. xii, 152pp. Bib. 141–9. Bonn University thesis.

G 723 GAMM, Hans-Jochen, *Führung und Verführung: Pädagogik der Nationalsozialismus*, Munich: List, 1964. 494pp. Bib. 484–8.

G 724 LINGELBACH, Karl Christoph, *Erziehung und Erziehungstheorien im nationalsozialistischen Deutschland: Ursprünge und Wandlungen der 1933–1945 in Deutschland vorherrschenden erziehungstheoretischen Strömungen*, Weinheim: Beltz, 1970. 341pp. Bib. 255–338.

G 725 ORLOW, Dietrich, 'Die Adolf-Hitler-Schulen'. *VIERTEL-JAHRSH. FÜR ZEITG.*, **13** (**3**), 1965. pp. 272–84.

G 726 PETERS, Elke, *Nationalistische-völkische Bildungspolitik in der Weimar Republik: Deutschkunde und Höhere Schule in Preussen*, Weinheim: Beltz, 1972. 224pp. Bib. 155–92. Free University of Berlin thesis.

G 727 SCHOLTZ, Harald, 'Die "NS-Ordensburgen"'. *VIERTEL-JAHRSH. FÜR ZEITG.*, **15** (**3**), 1967. 269–98.

G 728 SCHOLTZ, Harald, *NS-Ausleseschulen: Internatsschulen als Herrschaftsmittel des Führerstaates*, Göttingen: Vandenhoeck & Ruprecht, 1973. 427pp.

G 729 ÜBERHORST, Horst (ed.), *Elite für die Diktatur: die national-politischen Erziehungsanstalten 1933–1945: ein Dokumentarbericht*, Düsseldorf: Droste, 1969. 441pp.

Higher Education and Research

G 730 ABENDROTH, Wolfgang and others, *Nationalsozialismus und die deutsche Universität: Universitätstage 1966*, Berlin: De Gruyter, 1966. 223pp.

G 731 ADAM, Uwe Dietrich, *Hochschule und Nationalsozialismus: die Universität Tübingen im Dritten Reich*, Tübingen: Mohr, 1977. x, 240pp. Bib. 229–34.

G 732 BEYERSCHEN, Alan D., *Scientists under Hitler: politics and the physics community in the Third Reich*, New Haven: Yale University Press, 1977. xii, 287pp. Bib. 263–76.

G 733   CARMON, Arye, 'Die Einführung des Führerprinzips in die deutsch Universität: das Ende der akademischen Freiheit'. *Neue Sammlung*, **17**, 1977. pp. 553–74.

G 734   CARMON, Arye. *The University of Heidelberg and National Socialism, 1930–1935*, University of Wisconsin thesis, 1974. UM 74–16199. 438pp.

G 735   GÖTZ VON OLENHUSEN, Albrecht, 'Die "nichtarischen" Studenten an den deutschen Hochschulen: zur nationalsozialistischen Rassenpolitik, 1933–1945'. *VIERTELJAHRSH. FÜR ZEITG.*, **14** (**2**), 1966. pp. 175–206.

G 736   HARTSHORNE, Edward Yarnell, *The German Universities and National Socialism*. London, Allen & Unwin, 1937. 184p.

G 737   HEIBER, Helmut, *Walter Frank und sein Reichsinstitut für Geschichte des Neuen Deutschlands*, Stuttgart: Deutsche Verlags-Anstalt, 1966. 1273pp.

G 738   KUHN, Helmut and others, *Die deutsche Universität im Dritten Reich: acht Beiträge*, Munich: Piper, 1966. 282pp.

G 739   RINGER, Fritz K., *The Decline of the German Mandarins: the German academic community, 1890–1933*, Cambridge, Mass: Harvard University Press, 1969. 528pp. Bib. 453–75.

G 740   WEINREICH, Max, *Hitler's Professors: the part of scholarship in Germany's crimes against the Jewish people*, New York: Yiddish Scientific Inst., 1946. 291pp.

G 741   ZNEIMER, Richard, 'The nazis and the professors: social origin, professional mobility and political involvement of the Frankfurt University Faculty, 1933–1939'. *J. OF SOC. HIST.*, **12** (**1**), 1978. pp. 147–58.

The Nazis and Students

G 742   BLEUEL, Hans Peter and KLINNERT, Ernst, *Deutsche Studenten auf dem Weg ins Dritte Reich: Ideologien, Programme, Aktionen, 1918–1935*, Gütersloh: Mohn, 1967. 294pp. Bib. 262–71.

G 743   FAUST, Anselm, *Der Nationalsozialistische Deutsche Studentenbund: Studenten und Nationalsozialismus in der Weimarer Republik*, Düsseldorf: Schwann, 1973. 2 vols. Bib. vol. 2. pp. 164–79. Munich University thesis, 1971.

G 744   GILES, Geoffrey J., 'The rise of the National Socialist Students' Association and the failure of political education in the Third Reich'. In STACHURA, P.D., G 163. pp. 160–85.

G 745   KATER, Michael H., 'Der NS-Studentenbund von 1926 bis 1928: Randgruppe zwischen Hitler und Strasser'. *VIERTELJAHRSH. FÜR ZEITG.*, **22** (**2**), 1974. pp. 148–90.

G 746   KATER, Michael H., *Studentenschaft und Rechtsradikalismus in Deutschland 1918–1933: eine sozialgeschichtliche Studie zum Bildungskrise in der Weimarer Republik*, Hamburg: Hoffmann & Campe, 1975. 361pp. Bib. 309–44.

G 747   STEINBERG, Michael Stephen, *Sabres and Brown Shirts: the German students' path to national socialism. 1918–1935*, Chicago: University Press, 1978. vi, 237pp. Bib. 225–32.

The Hitler Youth

G 748   BRANDENBURG, Hans-Christian, *Die Geschichte der HJ: Wege und Generation*, Cologne: Wissenschaft & Politik, 1968. 347pp. Bib. 333–41.

G 749   GRIESMAYR, Gottfried and WÜRSCHINGER, Otto, *Idee und Gestalt der Hitler-Jugend*, 3rd edn, Leoni am Starnberger See: Druffel V., 1980. 324pp. Doc. 317–18.

G 750   HORN, Daniel, 'Coercion and compulsion in the Hitler youth, 1933–1945'. *Historian*, **4** (**4**), 1979. pp. 639–63.

G 751   HORN, Daniel, 'The Hitler Youth and educational decline in the Third Reich'. *HIST. OF EDUC. Q.*, **16** (**4**), 1976. pp. 425–47.

G 752   HORN, Daniel, 'The National Socialist Schülerbund and the Hitler Youth, 1929–1933'. *CENT. EUR. HIST.*, **11** (**4**), 1978. pp. 355–75.

G 753   KATER, Michael H., 'Die Artamanen: völkische Jugend in der Weimarer Republik'. *HIST. Z.*, **213**, 1971. pp. 577–638.

G 754   KATER, Michael H., 'Bürgerliche Jugendbewegung und Hitlerjugend in Deutschland von 1926 bis 1939'. *ARCH. FÜR SOZIALGESCH.*, **17**, 1966. pp. 127–74.

G 755   KATER, Michael H., 'Hitlerjugend und Schule im Dritten Reich'. *HIST. Z.*, **228**, 1979. pp. 572–623.

G 756   KLÖNNE, Arno, *Hitlerjugend: die Jugend und ihre Organisation im Dritten Reich*, Hanover: Norddeutsche Verlagsanstalt, 1956. 108pp.

G 757 KOCH, Hannsjoachim, *Geschichte der Hitlerjugend: ihr Ursprünge und ihre Entwicklung, 1922-1945*, Percha: Schulz, 1975. x, 487pp.

G 758 LOEWENBERG, Peter, 'The psychohistorical origins of the nazi youth cohort'. *AM. HIST. REV.*, **76** (5), 1971. pp. 1457-502.

G 759 STACHURA, Peter D., *The German Youth Movement, 1900-1945: an interpretative and documentary history*, London: Macmillan, 1981. x, 246pp. Bib. 217-32.

G 760 STACHURA, Peter D., 'The Hitler Youth in crisis: the case of Reichführer Kurt Gruber, Oct. 1931'. *EUR. STUD. REV.*, **6** (**3**), 1976. pp. 331-56.

G 761 STACHURA, Peter D., 'The ideology of the Hitler Youth in the Kampfzeit'. *J. OF CONTEMP. HIST.*, **8** (**3**), 1973. pp. 155-67.

G 762 STACHURA, Peter D., 'The national socialist Machtergreifung and the German youth movement: coordination and reorganisation, 1933-34'. *EUR. STUD. REV.*, **5** (**3**), 1975. pp. 255-72.

G 763 STACHURA, Peter D., *Nazi Youth in the Weimar Republic*, intro. by Peter H. Merkl, Santa Barbara: Clio Press, 1975. xix, 301pp. Bib. 273-89.

G 764 WALKER, Lawrence D., *Hitler Youth and Catholic Youth, 1933-1936: a study in totalitarian conquest*, Washington, DC: Catholic University of America Press, 1970. x, 203pp.

Nazi Anti-Semitism and the Holocaust

G 765 ADAM, Uwe Dietrich, *Judenpolitik im Dritten Reich*, Düsseldorf: Droste, 1972. 382pp. Bib. 362-75.

G 766 ADLER, Hans-Günther, *Der verwaltete Mensch: Studien zur Deportation der Juden aus Deutschland*, Tübingen: Mohr, 1974. xxxii, 1076pp. Bib.

G 767 *Annals of the American Academy of Political and Social Science*, **450**, July 1980. Special issue on the Holocaust.

G 768 BACHRACH, Walter Zwi, 'Die Ideologie des deutschen Rassenantisemitismus und seine praktischen Folgerungen'. *JAHRB. INST. DTSCH. GESCH.*, **4**, 1975. pp. 369-86.

G 769 BAUER, Yehuda and others, *Guide to unpublished materials of the Holocaust period*, Jerusalem: Hebrew University Inst. of Contemporary Jewry, 1970-9. 5 vols.

G 770 BAUER, Yehuda, *The Holocaust in Historical Perspective*, London: Sheldon Press. Seattle: University of Washington Press, 1978. ix, 181pp.

G 771 BLUMENTHAL, David R., 'Scholarly approaches to the Holocaust'. *Shoah*, 1, Winter 1979. pp. 21-7.

G 772 BROSZAT, Martin, 'Hitler und die Genesis der "Endlösung": aus Anlass der Thesen von David Irving'. *VIERTELJAHRSH. FÜR ZEITG.*, 25 (4), 1977. pp. 739-75.

G 773 BROSZAT, Martin, '"Holocaust" und die Geschichtswissenschaft'. *VIERTELJAHRSH. FÜR ZEITG.*, 27 (2), 1979. pp. 285-98.

G 774 BROSZAT, Martin, 'Holocaust: Literatur in Kielwasser des Fernsehfilms'. *GESCH. IN WISS. IND UNTERR.*, 31 (1), 1980. pp. 21-9.

G 775 BROWNING, Christopher R., 'Zur Genesis der "Endlösung": eine Antwort an Martin Broszat'. *VIERTELJAHRSH. FÜR ZEITG.*, 29 (1), 1981. pp. 97-109.

G 776 CARGAS, Harry James, *The Holocaust: an annotated bibliography*, Haverford, PA: Catholic Library Ass., 1977. 86pp.

G 777 DAWIDOWICZ, Lucy S., *The Holocaust and the Historians*. Cambridge, Mass: Harvard University Press, 1981. x, 187pp.

G 778 DAWIDOWICZ, Lucy S., 'Lies about the Holocaust'. *Commentary*, 70 (6), 1980. pp. 31-7.

G 779 DAWIDOWICZ, Lucy S., *The War against the Jews, 1933-1945*, London: Weidenfeld & Nicolson. New York: Holt, Rinehart & Winston, 1975. xviii, 460pp. Bib. 437-50.

G 780 FLEMING, Gerald, *Hitler und die Endlösung: 'es ist des Führers wunsch'*, Munich: Limes V., 1983. 215pp.

G 781 GENSCHEL, Helmut, *Die Verdrängung der Juden aus der Wirtschaft im Dritten Reich*, Göttingen: Musterschmidt, 1966. 337pp. Bib. 309-21. Göttingen University thesis.

G 782 GILBERT, Martin, *Atlas of the Holocaust*, London: Joseph, 1982. 256pp. Bib. 246-54.

G 783 GOLDHAGEN, Erich, 'Weltanschauung und Endlösung: zum Antisemitismus der nationalsozialistischen Führungsschicht'. *VIERTELJAHRSH. FÜR ZEITG.*, 24 (4), 1976. pp. 379-405.

G 784 HILBERG, Raul, *The Destruction of the European Jews*, Chicago: Quadrangle. London: Allen, 1961. x, 788pp.

G 785   KOCHAN, Lionel, *Pogrom 10 November 1938*, London: Deutsch, 1957. 159pp. Bib. 151-3.

G 786   KREN, George M., and RAPPOPORT, Leon, *The Holocaust and the Crisis of Human behavior*, New York, Meier & Holmes, 1980. 176pp. Bib. 161-72.

G 787   MALINA, Peter, 'Holocaust'. *Zeitgeschichte*, **7**, 1980. pp. 169-91. Review article.

G 788   POLIAKOV, Leon, *Harvest of Hate: the nazi program for the destruction of the Jews of Europe*, foreword by Reinhold Niebuhr, Westport: Greenwood Press, 1971. xiii, 338pp. First pub. Syracuse University Press, 1954. Tr. of *Breviaire de la haine*.

G 789   PRITTIE, Terence and NELSON, Walter Henry, *The Economic War against the Jews*, New York: Random House, 1977. London, Secker & Warburg, 1978. ix, 269pp.

G 790   REITLINGER, Gerald, *The Final Solution: the attempt to exterminate the Jews of Europe*, 2nd edn, London: Vallentine Mitchell. S. Brunswick: Yoseloff, 1968. xii, 668pp. Tr. of *Die Endlösung*, Berlin, 1958.

G 791   REICHMANN, Eva G., *Hostages of Civilization: the social sources of national socialist anti-semitism*, London: Gollancz, 1950. Boston: Beacon Press, 1951. 281pp. Bib. 268-77. Tr. of *Die Flucht in Hass*.

G 792   ROBINSON, Jacob, *The Holocaust and After: sources and literature in English*. Jerusalem: Israel Universities Press, 1973. 353pp.

G 793   ROBINSON, Jacob and FRIEDMAN, Philip, *Guide to Jewish History under Nazi Impact*, New York: Yivo Inst. for Jewish Research, 1960. xxi, 425pp. Repr. Ktav Pub. House, 1973.

G 794   SCHLEUNES, Karl A., *The Twisted Road to Auschwitz: nazi policy towards German Jews, 1933-1939*, Urbana: University of Illinois, 1970. 280pp. Bib. 263-74.

G 795   SCHEFFLER, Wolfgang, *Judenverfolgung im Dritten Reich 1933 bis 1945*, new edn, Berlin: Colloquium V., 1964. 94pp. Bib. 92-4.

G 796   STOKES, Lawrence D., 'The German people and the destruction of the European Jews'. *CENT. EUR. HIST.*, **6** (2), 1973. pp. 167-91.

The Concentration Camp System

G 797   BILLIG, Joseph, *Les Camps de concentration dans l'économie du Reich hitlérien*, pref. by Jacques Droz, Paris: PUF, 1973. 346pp. Bib. 321-8.

G 798   BILLIG, Joseph, *L'Hitlérisme et le système concentrationnaire*, pref. by Henri Michel, Paris: PUF, 1967. xx, 323pp. Bib. 305-9.

G 799   DEVOTO, Andrea, *Bibliografia dell'oppressione nazista fino al 1962*, Florence: Olschki, 1964. ix, 149pp. Mostly on the concentration camps.

G 800   HOESS, Rudolf, *Commandant of Auschwitz: the autobiography of Rudolph Hoess*, intro. by Lord Russell of Liverpool, tr. by Constantine Fitzgibbon, London, Weidenfeld & Nicolson, 1959. New York, World Pub. Co., 1960. 285pp.

G 801   KOGON, Eugen, *The Theory and Practice of Hell: the German concentration camps and the system behind them*, London: Secker & Warburg. New York, Farrar & Strauss, 1950. 307pp. Tr. of *Der SS-Staat*, latest edn. Munich: Heyne, 1979.

G 802   WORMSER-MIGOT, Olga, *Le Système concentrationnaire nazi, 1933-1945*, Paris: PUF, 1968. 660pp. Bib. 605-33.

The NSDAP, Internal Organisation and the State

G 803   BOLLMUS, Reinhard, *Das Amt Rosenberg und seine Gegner: Studien zum Machtkampf im nationalsozialistischen Herrschaftsystem*, Stuttgart: Deutsche Verlags-Anstalt, 1970. 359pp. Bib. 251-350.

G 804   BURDEN, Hamilton Twombley, *The Nuremberg Party Rallies, 1923-1939*, foreword by Adolf A. Berle, London: Pall Mall. New York: Praeger, 1967. xv, 207pp. Bib. 201-2.

G 805   DIEHL-THIELE, Peter, *Partei und Staat im Dritten Reich: Untersuchungen zum Verhältnis von NSDAP und allgemeiner innerer Staatsverwaltung, 1933-1945*, 2nd edn, Munich: Beck, 1971. xiv, 269pp. Bib. 259-65.

G 806   DRESLER, Adolf, *Geschichte des 'Völkische Beobachters' und des Zentralverlages der NSDAP, Franz Eher Nachf*, Munich: Eher, 1937. 210pp.

G 807   HENKE, Josef, 'Die Reichsparteitage der NSDAP in Nürnberg, 1933-1938: Planung, Organisation, Propaganda'. *SCHR. DES BUNDESARCH.*, **25**, 1978. pp. 398-422.

G 808   HORN, Wolfgang, 'Hitler und die NSDAP: neue Untersuchungen zur Geschichte des Nationalsozialismus'. *NEUE POLIT. LIT.*, **13** (4), 1968. pp. 466-84.

G 809   HORN, Wolfgang, 'Zur Geschichte und Struktur des

Nationalsozialismus und der NSDAP'. *NEUE POLIT. LIT.*, **18**, 1973. pp. 194-209.

G 810   HÜTTENBERGER, Peter, *Die Gauleiter: Studie zum Wandel des Machtgefüges in der NSDAP*, Stuttgart: Deutsche Verlags-Anstalt, 1969. 239pp. Bib. 227-31. Bonn University thesis, 1966.

G 811   JORDAN, Rudolf, *Erlebt und erlitten: Weg eines Gauleiters von München bis Moskau*, Leoni am Starnberger See: Drüffel, 1971. 368pp. Memoirs of a former Gauleiter.

G 812   KLENNER, Jochen, *Verhältnis von Partei und Staat, 1933-1945: dargestellt am Beispiel Bayerns*, Munich: Wölfle, 1974. xii, 364pp. Bib. 342-54.

G 813   LAYTON, Roland, 'The 'Völkischer Beobachter'', 1920-1933: the nazi newspaper in the Weimar era'. *CENT. EUR. HIST.*, **3** (4), 1970. pp. 353-82.

G 814   LERNER, Daniel, *The Nazi Élite*, intro. by Franz L. Neumann, Stanford: Hoover Inst., 1951. x, 112pp. Bib. 111-12.

G 815   LINGG, Anton, *Die Verwaltung der Nationalsozialistischen Deutschen Arbeiter-Partei*, 3rd edn, Munich: Eher, 1940. 363pp. Bib. 322-7.

G 816   LÜKEMANN, Ulf, *Der Reichschatzmeister der NSDAP: ein Beitrag zur inneren Parteistruktur*, Berlin: Ernst Reuter-Gesellschaft, 1963. 248pp.

G 817   McKALE, Donald M., *The Nazi Party Courts: Hitler's management of conflict in his movement, 1921-1945*, Lawrence: University Press of Kansas, 1974. xvi, 252pp. Bib. 227-35.

G 818   McKALE, Donald M., *The Swastika Outside Germany*. Kent: Kent State University Press, 1977. xvi, 288pp. Bib. 252-71.

G 819   MEHRINGER, Helmut, *Die NSDAP als politische Ausleseorganisation*, Munich: Deutscher Volksverlag, 1938. 122pp.

G 820   NEESE, Gottfried, *Partei und Staat*, Hamburg: Hanseatische Verlagsanstalt, 1936. 102pp. Bib. 102.

G 821   ORLOW, Dietrich, *The History of the Nazi Party*. Pittsburgh: University of Pittsburgh Press, 1969-73. 2 vols. 1. *1919-33*. Bib. 319-31. 2. *1933-45*. Bib. 505-29.

G 822   PLUM, Günter, *Bibliographie der Gauleiter der NSDAP*, Munich: Inst. für Zeitgeschichte, 1970. 46pp.

G 823   SCHÄFER, Wolfgang, *NSDAP: Entwicklung und Struktur der Staatspartei des Dritten Reiches*, Hanover: Norddeutsche Verlagsanstalt, 1956. 100pp. Bib. 95-9.

G 824   SCHARF, Wilfried, 'Nationalsozialistische Monatshefte, 1930-1944'. *Publizistik (Konstanz)*, **3**, 1973. pp. 409-19.

G 825   WILCOX, Larry Dean, *The National Socialist Party Press in the Kampfzeit, 1919-1933*, University of Virginia thesis, 1970. UM 71-06656. 334pp.

National Socialism and the Third Reich: Local Studies

G 826   BROSZAT, Martin and others (eds), *Bayern in der NS-Zeit*, ed. M. Broszat, Elke Fröhlich, Falk Wiesemann. Munich, Oldenbourg, 1977-1981. 4 vols to date.

G 827   GÖRGEN, Hans-Peter, *Düsseldorf und der Nationalsozialismus: Studie zur Geschichte einer Grossstadt im Dritten Reich*, Düsseldorf: Schwann, 1969. 254pp. Bib. 252-4.

G 828   GRILL, Johnpeter Horst, *The Nazi Party in Baden, 1920-1945*, University of Michigan thesis, 1975. UM 75-20356. 906pp.

G 829   HEYEN, Franz Josef, *Nationalsozialismus in Alltag: Quellen zur Geschichte des Nationalsozialismus vornehmlich im Raum Mainz-Koblenz-Trier*, Boppard am Rhein: Boldt V., 1967. xii, 372pp.

G 830   HORN, Wolfgang, 'Regionale Entwicklung des Nationalsozialismus'. *NEUE POLIT. LIT.*, **21** (3), 1976. pp. 366-76.

G 831   JACOBY, Fritz, *Die nationalsozialistische Herrschaftsübernahme an der Saar: die innenpolitisches Probleme der Rückgliederung der Saargebietes bis 1935*, Saarbrücken: Thinnes & Nolte, 1973. 275pp. Bib. 249-58. Tübingen University thesis, 1971.

G 832   KÜHLING, Karl, *Osnabrück, 1933-1945: Stadt im Dritten Reich*, 2nd edn, Osnabrück: Wenner, 1980. 225pp.

G 833   LEVINE, Herbert S., *Hitler's Free City: a history of the Nazi Party in Danzig, 1925-1939*, Chicago: University of Chicago Press, 1973. xii, 223pp. Bib. 163-81.

G 834   PREIS, Kurt, *München unterm Hakenkreuz: die Hauptstadt der Bewegung: zwischen Pracht und Trümmern*, Munich: Ehrenwirth, 1980. 258pp.

G 835   REBENTISCH, Dieter, 'Frankfurt am Main und das Reich in der NS-Zeit'. *Arch. für Frankfurts Gesch. und Kunst.*, **57**, 1980. pp. 243-67.

G 836   SAUER, Paul, *Württemberg in der Zeit des Nationalsozialismus*, Ulm: Süddeutsche Verlagsanstalt, 1975. 519pp. Bib. 514-18.

G 837   WILHELM, Hermann, *Nationalsozialismus im Münchner Osten,
1919-1945*, Munich: Haidhauser Dokumentationsverlag, 1980. 95pp.

The Nazis and War

G 838   IRVING, David John Cawdell, *Hitler's War*, London:
Hodder & Stoughton. New York: Viking Press, 1977. xxxiii, 926pp.
Bib. 824-8.

G 839   SYDNOR, Charles, 'The selling of Adolf Hitler: David
Irving's Hitler's War'. *CENT. EUR. HIST.*, 12 (2), 1979. pp. 169-99.
Review article.

G 840   IRVING, David John Cawdell, *The War Path: Hitler's
Germany, 1933-1939*, London: Joseph. New York: Viking Press, 1978.
xxv, 301pp.

G 841   HILDEBRAND, Klaus, 'Hitler's war aims'. *J. OF MOD.
HIST.*, 48 (3), 1976. pp. 522-30. Review of Rich, N., G 847.

G 842   HOMZE, Edward L., *Foreign Labor in Nazi Germany*,
Princeton: University Press, 1967. xviii, 350pp. Bib. 313-27.
Pennsylvania State University thesis.

G 843   JACOBSEN, Hans-Adolf, 'Krieg in Weltanschauung und
Praxis des Nationalsozialismus, 1919-1945: eine skizze'. In *Beiträge zur
Zeitgeschichte: Festschrift Ludwig Jedlicka*, St Pölten, 1976. pp. 237-46.

G 844   JANSSEN, Gregor, *Das Ministerium Speer: Deutschlands Rüstung
im Kreig*, Berlin: Ullstein, 1968. 446pp. Bib. 414-29. Bonn University
thesis.

G 845   KOEHL, Robert Lewis, *RKFDV: German resettlement and
population policy, 1939-1945: a history of the Reich Commission for the
Strengthening of Germandom*, Cambridge, Mass: Harvard University
Press, 1957. xi, 263pp.

G 846   Militärgeschichtlichen Forschungsamt, *Das Deutsche Reich und
der Zweiten Weltkrieg*, Stuttgart: Deutsche Verlags-Anstalt, 1979. 10
vols.

G 847   RICH, Norman, *Hitler's War Aims: the establishment of the New
Order*, New York: Norton, 1973. London: Deutsch, 1974. 2 vols. Bib.
vol. 1. pp. 313-42; vol. 2. p. 503-29.

G 848   WRIGHT, Gordon, *The Ordeal of Total War, 1939-1945*,
New York: Harper & Row, 1968. 314pp. Bib. 269-305.

Adolf Hitler (1889-1945)

G 849 AINSZTEIN, Reuben, 'How Hitler died: the Soviet version'. *INT. AFF.*, **43** (**2**), 1967. pp. 307-18.

G 850 ALEXANDER, Edgar, *Der Mythos Hitler*, Munich: Kraus, 1980. 395pp. First pub. 1937.

G 851 AUERBACH, Hellmuth, 'Hitlers politische Lehrjahre und die Münchener Gesellschaft, 1919-1923: Versuch einer Bilanz anhand der neueren Forschung'. *VIERTELJAHRSH. FÜR ZEITG.*, **25** (**1**), 1977. pp. 1-45.

G 852 BANULS, André, 'Das völkische Blatt "Der Scherer": ein Beitrag zu Hitlers Schulzeit'. *VIERTELJAHRSH. FÜR ZEITG.*, **18** (**2**), 1970. pp. 196-203. Response to Daim's book on the source of Hitler's anti-semitism. See G 873.

G 853 BARNES, James John and Patience P., *Hitler's Mein Kampf in Britain and America: a publishing history, 1930-1939*, Cambridge: University Press, 1980. xiii, 158pp.

G 854 BENNECKE, Heinrich, 'Die Bedeutung des Hitlerputsches für Hitler'. *POLIT. STUD.*, **13**, 1962. pp. 685-92.

G 855 BEZYMENSKII, Lev Aleksandrovich, *The Death of Adolf Hitler: unknown documents from Soviet archives*, London: Joseph. New York: Harcourt Brace, 1968. 114pp. Tr. of *Der Tod des Adolf Hitler*, 1968.

G 856 BINION, Rudolph, 'Foam on the Hitler wave'. *J. OF MOD. HIST.*, **46** (**3**), 1974. pp. 522-8. Review article.

G 857 BINION, Rudolph, *Hitler among the Germans*, New York: Elsevier, 1976. xiv, 207pp. Bib. 184-99.

G 858 BINION, Rudolph, 'Hitler and psychohistory'. *J. OF PSYCHOHISTORY.*, **4** (**3**), 1976. pp. 385-8.

G 859 BINION, Rudolph, 'Hitler looks East'. *HIST. OF CHILD-HOOD Q.*, **3** (**1**), 1975. pp. 85-102. *Lebensraum* and anti-semitism.

G 860 BINION, Rudolph, 'Hitler's concept of Lebensraum: the psychological basis'. *HIST. OF CHILDHOOD Q.*, **1** (**2**), 1973. pp. 187-258.

G 861 BOSMAJIAN, Haig A., 'Hitler's twenty-five point program: an exercise in propaganda before *Mein Kampf*'. *Dalhousie Rev.*, **49** (**2**), 1969. pp. 208-15.

G 862 BRACHER, Karl Dietrich, 'Das "Phänomen" Adolf Hitler'.

POLIT. LIT., **1**, 1952. pp. 207-12. Review of biographies of Hitler.

G 863   BRACHER, Karl Dietrich, 'The role of Hitler: perspectives of interpretation'. In LAQUEUR, W., Gn 35. pp. 211-29.

G 864   BREITING, Richard, *Secret Conversations with Hitler: the two newly discovered 1931 interviews*, ed. Edouard Calic, New York: Day, 1971. 191pp. Bib. 180-6.

G 865   BROSSE, Jacques, *Hitler avant Hitler: essai d'interpretation psychoanalytique*, afterword by Albert Speer, Paris: Fayard, 1972. 388pp. Bib. 385-8.

G 866   BROSZAT, Martin, 'Betrachtungen zu "Hitlers zweiten Buch".' *VIERTELJAHRSH. FÜR ZEITG.*, **9** (**4**), 1961. pp. 417-29.

G 867   BUCHHEIT, Gert (ed.), *Der Führer ins Nicht: eine Diagnose Adolf Hitlers: 4 Referäte über Hitler als Politiker, Ideologe, Soldat und Persönlichkeit*, Rastat: Grote, 1960. 88pp.

G 868   BULLOCK, Alan, *Hitler: a study in tyranny*, New York; Harper & Row. London: Odhams Press, 1952. 776pp. Bib. 739-49. Penguin rev. edn, 1962.

G 869   BURKE, Kenneth, *Die Rhetorik in Hitlers Mein Kampf und andere Essays zur Strategie der Überredung*, 2nd edn, Frankfurt/M: Suhrkamp, 1971. 152pp. Bib. 145-52.

G 870   CARR, William, *Hitler: a study in personality and politics*. New York: St Martin's Press, 1979. x, 200pp. Bib. 182-9.

G 871   COHAN, A.S., 'Politics and psychoanalysis: the sources of Hitler's political behaviour'. *BR. J. OF INT. STUD.*, **1** (**2**), 1975. pp. 160-75.

G 872   CRAMER, Erich, *Hitlers Antisemitismus und die Frankfurter Schule: kritische Faschismus-Theorie und geschischtiche Realität*, Düsseldorf; Droste, 1979. 246pp. Bib. 240-4.

G 873   DAIM, Wilfried, *Der Mann der Hitler die Ideen gab: von den religiösen Verirrungen eines Sektierers zum Rassenwahn des Diktators*, Munich: Isar V., 1958. 286pp. Bib. 271-86. On the influence of Jorg Lanz von Liebenfels on Hitler.

G 874   DAVIDSON, Eugene, *The Making of Adolf Hitler*, London: MacDonald & Jane's. New York: Macmillan, 1977. xi, 408pp. Bib. 389-96.

G 875   DEUERLEIN, Ernst, *Hitler: ein politische Biographie*, Munich: List, 1969. 187pp. Bib. 179-87.

301

G 876   DIETRICH, Otto, *Hitler*. Chicago: Regnery, 1955. 277pp. Tr. of *Zwölf Jahre mit Hitler*, Munich, Isar V., 1955, by Richard and Clara Winston. British edn, *The Hitler I Knew*, London: Methuen, 1957.

G 877   DORPALEN, Andreas, 'Hitler: twelve years after'. *REV. OF POLIT.*, **19** (**4**), 1957. pp. 486–506. Review article.

G 878   DUNK, H.W. van der, 'Adolf Hitler en de historici' (Adolf Hitler and the historians). *Kleio*, **18** (**9**), 1977. pp. 749–65.

G 879   FABRY, Philipp, *Mutmassungen über Hitler: Urteile um Zeitgenossen*, Düsseldorf: Droste, 1969. 265pp. Bib. 253–60.

G 880   FAUL, Erwin, 'Hitlers Über-Machiavellismus'. *VIERTEL-JAHRSH. FÜR ZEITG.*, **2** (**4**), 1954. pp. 344–72.

G 881   FEST, Joachim C., *Hitler*, London: Weidenfeld & Nicolson. New York: Harcourt Brace, 1974. vii, 844p. Bib. 819–29. Tr. of *Hitler: eine Biographie*. Berlin, Propyläen V., 1973, by Richard and Clara Winston.

G 882   FEST, Joachim C., 'On remembering Adolf Hitler'. *Encounter*, **41** (**4**), 1973 pp. 19–34.

G 883   GRAML, Hermann, 'Probleme einer Hitler-Biographie: kritische Bemerkungen zu Joachim C. Fest'. *VIERTELJAHRSH. FÜR ZEITG.*, **22** (**1**), 1974. pp. 76–92.

G 884   FISHMAN, Sterling, 'The rise of Hitler as a beer hall orator'. *REV. OF POLIT.*, **26**, 1964. pp. 244–56.

G 885   FOX, John P., 'Adolf Hitler: the continuing debate'. *INT. AFF.*, **55** (**2**), 1979. pp. 252–64. Review of some psychohistories of Hitler.

G 886   GISEVIUS, Hans-Bernd, *Adolf Hitler: Versuch einer Deutung*, Munich: Rütten & Loening, 1963. 565pp. Bib. 545–59.

G 887   GÖRLITZ, Walter, *Adolf Hitler*, Göttingen: Musterschmidt, 1960. 145pp. Bib. 145.

G 888   GOSSET, Pierre and Renée, *Adolf Hitler*, Paris: Julliard, 1961–2. 2 vols.

G 889   GREINER, Josef, *Das Ende des Hitler-Mythos*, Vienna: Amalthea V., 1947. 343pp.

G 890   HAFFNER, Sebastian, *The Meaning of Hitler*, London: Weidenfeld & Nicolson. New York: Macmillan, 1979. 165pp. Tr. of *Anmerkungen zu Hitler*, Munich: Kindler, 1978.

G 891   HAMMER, Hermann, 'Die deutschen Ausgaben von Hitlers

"Mein Kampf".' *VIERTELJAHRSH. FÜR ZEITG.*, **4** (**2**), 1956. pp. 161–78.

G 892   HAMMER, Wolfgang, *Adolf Hitler: Dialog mit dem Führer*, Munich: Delp, 1970–4. 3 vols. Bibs.

G 893   HANFSTAENGEL, Ernst Franz, *Hitler: the missing years*, ed. Brian Connell, London, Eyre & Spottiswoode, 1957. 299pp. US edn, *Unheard Witness* pub. by Lippincott.

G 894   HARTMANN, Wolf-Rüdiger, 'Berwältungsversuche der unbewältigten Vergangenheit: Adolf Hitler im Spiegel neuerer Literatur'. *SCHWEIZ. Z. FÜR GESCH.*, **26** (**4**), 1976. pp. 679–94.

G 895   HAUNER, Milan, 'Did Hitler want a world dominion?' *J. OF CONTEMP. HIST.*, **13** (**1**), 1978. pp. 15–32.

G 896   HAUNER, Milan, *Hitler: a chronology of his life and time*. London: Macmillan, 1983. xi, 221pp.

G 897   HEER, Friedrich, *Der Glaube des Adolf Hitler: Anatomie einer politischen Religiosität*, Munich: Bechtle, 1968. 751pp. Bib. 719–31.

G 898   HEIBER, Helmut, *Adolf Hitler: eine Biographie*, Berlin: Colloquium V., 1960. 159pp.

G 899   HEIDEN, Konrad, *Der Führer: Hitler's rise to power*, tr. by Ralph Manheim, London: Gollancz. Boston: Houghton Mifflin, 1944. 614pp.

G 900   HEIDEN, Konrad, *Hitler: a biography*, London: Constable, 1936. viii, 416pp. Tr. of *Adolf Hitler: eine Biographie*, Zürich, Europa-V., 1936/7. Repr. by AMS Press, 1975.

G 901   HEUSS, Theodore, *Hitlers Weg: eine Schrift aus dem Jahre 1932*, new edn by Eberhard Jäckel, Tübingen: Wunderlich V., 1968. xliv, 167pp. First pub. 1932.

G 902   HEYL, John D., 'Hitler's economic thought: a reappraisal'. *CENT. EUR. HIST.*, **6** (**1**), 1973. pp. 83–96.

G 903   HILDEBRAND, Klaus, 'Der Fall Hitler: Bilanz und Wege der Hitler-Forschung'. *NEUE POLIT. LIT.*, **14** (**3**), 1969. pp. 375–86.

G 904   HILDEBRAND, Klaus, 'Hitlers "Mein Kampf": Propaganda oder Programm? zur Frühgeschichte der nationalsocialistischen Bewegung'. *NEUE POLIT. LIT.*, **14** (**1**), 1969. pp. 72–82.

G 905   HILDEBRAND, Klaus, 'Hitlers Ort in der Geschichte des preussischdeutschen Nationalstaates'. *HIST. Z.*, **217**, 1973. pp. 584–632.

G 906 HILLGRUBER, Andreas, 'Tendenzen, Ergebnisse und Perspektiven der gegenwärtigen Hitler-Forschung'. *HIST. Z.*, **226** (3), 1978. pp. 600–21.

G 907 HITLER, Adolf, *Adolf Hitler: Monologe im Führerhauptquartier 1941–1944: die Aufzeichnungen Heinrich Heims*, ed. Werner Jochmann, Hamburg: Knaus, 1980. 491pp.

G 908 HITLER, Adolf, *Adolf Hitlers drei Testamente: ein Zeitdokument*, ed. Gert Sudholt, Leoni am Starnberger See: Druffel, 1977. 107pp.

G 909 HITLER, Adolf, *'Es spricht des Führer': 7 exemplarische Hitlers-Reden*, ed. Hildegard Von Kotze and Helmut Krausnick, Gütersloh: Mohn, 1966. 378pp.

G 910 HITLER, Adolf, *Hitler: sämtliche Aufzeichnungen, 1905–1924*, ed. Eberhard Jäckel with Axel Kuhn, Stuttgart: Deutsche Verlags-Anstalt, 1980. 1315pp.

G 911 HITLER, Adolf, *Hitler's Table-talk; his private conversations*, 2nd edn intro. by H.R. Trevor-Roper, London: Weidenfeld & Nicolson, 1963. xxxix, 746pp. US edn, *Secret Conversations, 1941–1944*, Octagon Books, 1972. Tr. of *Hitlers Tischgespräche im Führerhauptquartier*, by Norman Cameron and R.H. Stevens.

G 912 HITLER, Adolf, *Hitler's Letters and Notes*, ed. Werner Maser, tr. by Arnold Pomerans, London: Heinemann, 1974. 390pp. Bib. 388. Tr. of *Hitlers Briefe und Notizen*, Düsseldorf: Econ.-V., 1973.

G 913 AUERBACH, Hellmuth, 'Hitlers Handschrift und Masers Lesefehler: eine notwendige Berichtigung'. *VIERTELJAHRSH. FÜR ZIETG.*, **21** (3), 1973. pp. 334–36. Critique of Maser's errors in his ed. of Hitler's letters. See G 912.

G 914 HITLER, Adolf, *Hitler's Secret Book*, intro. by Telford Taylor, New York: Grove Press, 1961. xxv, 229pp. Tr. of *Hitlers zweites Buch*, Stuttgart: Deutsche Verlags-Anstalt, 1961, by Salvator Attanasio.

G 915 HITLER, Adolf, *Mein Kampf*, intro. by D.C. Watt, tr. by Ralph Manheim, London: Hutchinson, 1973. xlviii, 629pp. Bib. xliii. First edn. 1925/7, pub. by Eher V.

G 916 HITLER, Adolf, *Reben des Führers: Politik und Propaganda Adolf Hitlers 1922–1945*, ed. Erhard Klöss, Munich: Deutscher Taschenbuch V., 1967. 334pp. Bib. 327–9.

G 917 HITLER, Adolf, *Hitler: Reden und Proklamationen, 1932–1945, kommentiert von einem deutschen Zeitgenossen*, [ed. Max Domarus], 2nd edn, Munich: Suddeutscher V., 1965. 2 vols.

G 918   HITLER, Adolf, *The Speeches of Adolf Hitler, April 1922-August 1939*, ed. Norman H. Baynes, London: Oxford University Press, 1942. 2 vols. Repr. by Fertig, 1969.

G 919   HITLER, Adolf, *The Testament of Adolf Hitler: the Hitler-Bormann documents, Feb.-April 1945*, ed. Francois Genoud, tr. by R.H. Stevens, intro. by H.R. Trevor-Roper, 2 edn, London: Cassell, 1961. 115pp.

G 920   HITLER, Adolf, defendant, *The Hitler Trial before the People's Court in Munich*, tr. Frenière H. Francis, Arlington: University Pubs of America, 1976. 3 vols.

G 921   HOFFMANN, Peter, *Die Sicherheit des Diktators: Hitlers Leibwachen, Schutzmassnahmen, Residenzen, Hauptquartiere*, Munich: Piper, 1975. 328pp.

G 922   HORN, Wolfgang, 'Ein unbekannter Aufsatz aus dem Frühjahr 1924'. *VIERTELJAHRSH. FÜR ZIETG.*, **16** (3), 1968. pp. 280-94.

G 923   IRVING, David John Cawdell, *Adolf Hitler: the medical diaries: the private diaries of Dr. Theo Morrell*, London: Sidgwick & Jackson, 1983. 240pp. US edn, *The Secret Diaries of Hitler's Doctor*, Macmillan.

G 924   JÄCKEL, Eberhard, *Hitler's Weltanschauung: a blueprint for power*, Middletown: Wesleyan University Press, 1969. 140pp. Tr. of *Hitlers Weltanschauung*, Tübingen: Wunderlich V. 1969, by Herbert Arnold.

G 925   JÄCKEL, Eberhard, 'Literaturbericht: Rückblick auf die sogenannte Hitler-Welle'. *GESCH. IN WISS. UND UNTERR.*, **28**, 1977. pp. 695-710.

G 926   JENKS, William A., *Vienna and the Young Hitler*, New York: Columbia University Press, 1960. 252pp. Bib. 237-41. Repr. by Octagon Books, 1976.

G 927   JETZINGER, Franz, *Hitler's Youth*, foreword by Alan Bullock, Westport: Greenwood Press, 1976. 200pp. First pub. by Hutchinson, 1958. Tr. of *Hitlers Jugend*, Vienna, 1956, by Lawrence Wilson.

G 928   JOCHMANN, Werner, *Im Kampf und die Macht: Hitlers Rede vor dem Hamburger National-Klub von 1919*, Frankfurt/M: Europäische Verlagsanstalt, 1960. 120pp.

G 929   JOCHMANN, Werner and NELLESSEN, Bernd, *Adolf Hitler: Persönlichkeit, Ideologie, Taktik*, Paderborn: Schöningh, 1960. 64pp.

G 930   JONES, J. Sydney, *Hitler in Vienna, 1907-13*, New York: Stein

& Day, 1983. xi, 350pp. Bib. 337–42. Tr. of *Hitlers Weg begann in Wien*, Wiesbaden: Limes V., 1980.

G 931   KERN, Erich (pseud.) [Erich Kernmeyr], *Adolf Hitler*, Göttingen: Schutz, 1970–8. 3 vols. **1**. . . . *und seine Bewegung*. **2**. . . . *und das Dritte Reich*. **3**. . . . *und der Krieg*.

G 932   KUBIZEK, August, *The Young Hitler I Knew*; tr. by E.V. Anderson, intro. by H.R. Trevor-Roper, London: Wingate, 1954. Boston: Houghton Mifflin, 1955. xiv, 204pp. US edn, *Young Hitler*. repr. by Greenwood Press, 1976.

G 933   LANGE, Karl, *Hitlers unbeachtete Maximen: 'Mein Kampf' und die Öffentlichkeit*, Stuttgart: Kohlhammer, 1968. 211pp. Bib. 171–207.

G 934   LANGE Karl, 'Der Terminus "Lebensraum" in Hitlers "Mein Kampf".' *VIERTELJAHRSH. FÜR ZEITG.*, **13** (**4**), 1965. pp. 426–37.

G 935   LANGER, Walter C., *The Mind of Adolf Hitler*, afterword by Robert L. Waite, New York: Basic Books, 1972. London, Secker & Warburg, 1973. ix, 269pp. Bib. 250–63.

G 936   MANNZMANN, Annelise (ed.), *Hitlerwelle und historische Fakten: mit einer Literaturübersicht und einer Materialsammlung zum Neonazismus*, Königstein: Scriptor, 1979. 188pp. Bibs.

G 937   MASER, Werner, *Adolf Hitler: das Ende der Führer-Legende*, Düsseldorf: Econ. V., 1980. 447pp.

G 938   MASER, Werner, *Hitler:* [*legend, myth and reality*], London, Allen & Unwin. New York: Harper and Row, 1973. viii, 433pp. Tr. of *Adolf Hitler: Legende, Mythos, Wirklichkeit*, Munich: Bechtle, 1971, by Peter and Betty Ross.

G 939   MASER, Werner, *Hitler's Mein Kampf: an analysis*, London: Faber, 1970. 272pp. Bib. 244–58. Tr. of *Hitlers Mein Kampf*, Munich, Bechtle, 1966, by R.H. Barry.

G 940   MICHALKA, Wolfgang, 'Hitler im Spiegel der Psycho-History: zu neueren interdisziplinären Deutungsversuchen der Hitler-Forschung'. *Francia*, **8**, 1980. pp. 595–611.

G 941   Nationalsozialistische Deutsche Arbeiter-Partei, *Die Reden des Führers nach der Machterübernahme: eine Bibliographie*, Berlin: Eher, 1939. 192pp.

G 942   NEEDLER, M.C., 'Hitler's anti-semitism: a political appraisal'. *Public Opinion Q.*, **24**, 1960. pp. 665–9.

G 943   NOLTE, Ernst, 'Eine frühe Quelle zu Hitlers Antisemitismus'. *HIST. Z.*, **192**, 1961. pp. 584–606.

G 944   OERTEL, Helmut, '"Mein Kampf" als Quelle im Geschichtsunterricht der Mittelstufe'. *GESCH. IN WISS. UND UNTERR.*, **16** (4), 1965. pp. 237–41.

G 945   OLDEN, Rudolph, *Hitler the Pawn*, London, Gollancz, 1966. 439pp. Tr. of *Hitler*, Amsterdam: Querido, 1935.

G 946   ORLOW, Dietrich, 'Totalitarian politics and sexual perversion: the case of Adolf Hitler'. *J. OF INTERDISC. HIST.*, **9** (3). 1979. pp. 509–15. Review article.

G 947   PAPELEUX, L., 'Psychanalyse d'Hitler'. *REV. D'HIST. DEUX. GUERRE MOND.*, **24** (**96**), 1974. pp. 105–8.

G 948   PAYNE, Robert, *The Life and Death of Adolf Hitler*, London: Cape. New York: Praeger. 1973. xiii, 623pp. Bib. 607–12.

G 949   PESE, Walter Werner, 'Hitler und Italien, 1920–1926'. *VIERTELJAHRSH. FÜR ZEITG.*, **3** (**2**), 1955. pp. 113–26.

G 950   SCHRAMM, Percy Ernst, *Hitler: the man and the military leader*, tr., ed. and with an intro. by Donald S. Detwiler, Chicago: Quadrangle Books, 1971. viii, 214pp.

G 951   RAUSCHNING, Hermann, *Hitler Speaks: a series of political conversations with Hitler on his real aims*. London: Butterworth, 1939. New York: Putnam, 1940. 287pp. US edn, *Voice of destruction*. Tr. of *Gespräche mit Hitler*.

G 952   SCHMIDT, Paul, *Hitler's Interpreter*, ed. R.H.C. Steed, London: Heinemann. New York: Macmillan, 1951. 286pp. Tr. of second half of *Statist auf diplomatischer Bühne*.

G 953   SMITH, Bradley F., *Adolf Hitler: his family, childhood and youth*, Stanford: Hoover Inst. Press, 1967. 180pp. Bib. 168–76.

G 954   SANDVOSS, Ernst, *Hitler und Nietzsche*, Göttingen: Musterschmidt, 1969. 208pp.

G 955   SCHEURIG, Bodo, 'Hitlers Weltanschauung'. *Jahrb. Wittheit Bremen.*, **17**, 1973. pp. 149–62.

G 956   STERN, Joseph Peter, *Hitler: the Führer and the people*. Hassocks: Harvester Press. Berkeley: University of California Press. 1975. 254pp.

G 957   STIERLIN, Helm, *Adolf Hitler: a family perspective*. New York: Psychohistory Press, 1976. 163pp. Tr. of *Adolf Hitler: Familienperspektiven*, Frankfurt/M: Suhrkamp, 1975.

G 958   STONE, Norman, *Hitler*, intro. by J.H. Plumb, London,

Hodder & Stoughton. Boston: Little, Brown, 1980. xii, 195pp. Bib. 182–5.

G 959 THIES, Jochen, *Architekt der Weltherrschaft: die 'Endziele' Hitlers*, 2nd edn, Königstein: Athenäum, 1980. 221pp. Bib. 194–219. Freiburg University thesis, 1975.

G 960 TOLAND, John, *Adolf Hitler*, New York: Doubleday, 1976. xx, 1035pp. Bib. 906–23.

G 961 TOLAND, John, *The Last Hundred Days*, London: Barker. New York: Random House, 1966. 622pp. Bib. 595–609.

G 962 TREVOR-ROPER, Hugh Redwald, 'Hitlers Kriegsziele'. *VIERTELJAHRSH. FÜR. ZEITG.*, **8** (2), 1960. pp. 121–33.

G 963 TREVOR-ROPER, Hugh Redwald, *The Last Days of Hitler*, new edn, London: Pan, 1968. 285pp. First pub. Macmillan, 1947.

G 964 WAGENER, Otto, *Hitler aus nächster Nähe: Aufzeichnungen eines Vertrauten 1929–1932*, ed. H.A. Turner, Frankfurt/M: Ullstein, 1978. xviii, 508pp. Diary of a one-time leader of the SA.

G 965 WAITE, Robert G.L., 'Adolf Hitler's guilt feelings: a problem in history and psychology'. *J. OF INTERDISC. HIST.*, **1** (2), 1971. pp. 229–49.

G 966 WAITE, Robert G.L., *The Psychopathic God: Adolf Hitler*, New York: Basic Books, 1977. xx, 482pp.

G 967 WILKIE, Richard W., 'The self-taught agitator: Hitler, 1907–1920'. *Q. J. OF SPEECH.*, **52** (4), 1966. pp. 371–7.

G 968 WINDELL, George G., 'Hitler, national socialism and Richard Wagner'. *J. OF CENT. EUR. AFF.*, **22**. 1962/3. pp. 479–97.

G 969 WINKLER, Hans-Joachim, *Legende um Hitler: 'Schöpfer der Autobahnen', 'Kraft durch Freude für den Arbeiter', 'Überwinder von Versailles', 'Vorkämpfer Europas gegen den Bolschewismus'*, Berlin: Colloquium V., 1961. 80pp. Bib. 78–9.

G 970 ZENTNER, Christian (ed.), *Adolf Hitlers 'Mein Kampf': eine kommentierte Auswahl*, Munich: List, 1974. 255pp.

G 971 ZIEGLER, Hans Severus (ed.), *Wer war Hitler? Beiträge zur Hitler-Forschung*, Tübingen: V. des Deutschen Hochschullehrer-Zeitung, 1970. 375pp. Bib. 371–5.

Martin Bormann (1900-45)

G 972 BEZYMENSKII, Lev Aleksandrovich, *Die letzten Notizen von Martin Bormann: ein Dokument und sein Verfasser*, Stuttgart: Deutsche Verlags-Anstalt, 1974. 345pp.

G 973 BORMANN, Martin, *The Bormann Letters: the private correspondence between Martin Bormann and his wife from January 1943 to April 1945*, ed. H.R. Trevor-Roper, London: Weidenfeld & Nicolson, 1954. xxiii, 200pp.

G 974 LANG, Jochen von and SIBYLL, Claus, *Bormann: the man who manipulated Hitler*, New York: Random House. London: Weidenfeld & Nicolson, 1979. x, 430pp. Tr. of *Der Sekretär: Martin Bormann*, Stuttgart: Deutsche Verlags-Anstalt, 1977, by Christa Armstrong and Peter White.

G 975 McGOVERN, James, *Martin Bormann*, London: Barker. New York: Morrow 1968. 237pp. Bib. 217-23.

G 976 WULF, Josef, *Martin Bormann: Hitlers schatten*, Gütersloh: Mohn 1962. 254pp. Bib. 241-9.

Adolf Eichmann (1906-62)

G 977 ARENDT, Hannah, *Eichmann in Jerusalem: a report on the banality of evil*, rev. edn, New York: Viking Press, 1964. 312pp. Bib. 299-303.

G 978 BRAHAM, Randolph L., *The Eichmann Case: a source book*. New York: World Federation of Hungarian Jews, 1969. xi, 186pp.

G 979 WUCHER, Albert, *Eichmanns gab es wiele: ein Dokumentarbericht über die Endlösung der Judenfrage*, Munich: Droemersche Verlagsanstalt, 1961. 286pp.

Joseph Goebbels (1897-1945)

G 980 BAIRD, Jay W., 'Goebbels, Horst Wessel, and the myth of resurrection and return'. *J. OF CONTEMP. HIST.*, 17 (4), 1982. pp. 633-50.

G 981 BRAMSTED, Ernest Kohn, 'Goebbels and his newspaper Der Angriff'. In *On the Track of Tyranny*, ed. Max Beloff, London: Vallentine Mitchell, 1959. pp. 45-65.

G 982 BRAMSTED, Ernest Kohn, *Goebbels and National Socialist*

Propaganda, 1925–1945, E. Lansing; Michigan State University Press, 1965. xxxvii, 488pp. Bib. 469–71.

G 983   GOEBBELS, Joseph, *Aufsätze aus der Kampfzeit*, Munich: Eher, 1935–9. 2 vols. Repr. from *Der Angriff*.

G 984   GOEBBELS, Joseph, *The Early Goebbels Diaries: the journal of Joseph Goebbels, 1925–1926*, pref. by Alan Bullock, ed. Helmut Heiber, London: Weidenfeld & Nicolson, 1962. New York: Praeger, 1963. 156pp. Tr. of *Das Tagebuch 1925/26*, Stuttgart, 1961, by Oliver Watson.

G 985   GOEBBELS, Joseph, *The Goebbels Diaries, 1939–1941*, tr. and ed. Fred Taylor, New York: Putnam, 1983. xiii, 490pp. Tr. of *Tagebücher 1939–1941*.

G 986   GOEBBELS, Joseph, *The Goebbels Diaries*, ed., tr. and intro. by Louis P. Lochner, New York: Popular Lib., 1965. 638pp. Also Greenwood Press, 1970. Covers 1942–3.

G 987   GOEBBELS, Joseph, *The Goebbels Diaries: the last days*, ed. Hugh Trevor-Roper, London: Secker & Warburg, 1978. xli, 368pp. Tr. of *Tagebücher, 1945*, Hamburg, Hoffmann & Campe, 1977, by Richard Barry.

G 988   GOEBBELS, Joseph, *Goebbels-Reden*, ed. Helmut Heiber, Düsseldorf: Droste, 1971–2. 2 vols.

G 989   GOEBBELS, Joseph, *My Part in Germany's Fight*, New York: Fertig, 1979. 253pp. Repr. of Hurst & Blackett edn, 1940, tr. of *Vom Kaiserhof zur Reichskanzlei* (first pub. 1934), by Kurt Fiedler.

G 990   HEIBER, Helmut, *Goebbels*, London: Hale. New York: Hawthorn, 1972, v. 387pp. Bib. 367–72. Tr. of *Joseph Goebbels*, Berlin: Colloquium V., 1962, by John K. Dickinson.

G 991   KESSEMEIER, Carin, *Der Leitartikler Goebbels in den NS-Organen 'Der Angriff' und 'Das Reich'*, Münster: Fahle, 1967. 348pp. Bib. 338–48.

G 992   MANVELL, Roger and FRAENKEL, Heinrich, *Doctor Goebbels: his life and death*, London: Heinemann. New York: Simon & Schuster, 1960. xiii, 329pp.

G 993   OVEN, Wilfred von, *Finale furioso: mit Goebbels bis zum Ende*, Tübingen: Grabert, 1974. 662pp.

G 994   REIMANN, Viktor, *The Man who Created Hitler: Joseph Goebbels*, London: Kimber, 1977. Garden City: Doubleday, 1976. 352pp. Bib. 338–40. US edn, *Dr. Joseph Goebbels*. Tr. of *Dr. Joseph Goebbels*, Vienna, Molden, 1971, by Stephen Wendt.

G 995   SCHAUMBURG-LIPPE, Friedrich Christian, Prince zu, *Dr. G.: ein Porträt des Propagandaministers*, 2nd edn, Wiesbaden: Limes V., 1964. 288pp.

Hermann Goering (1893-1946)

G 996   BEWLEY, Charles Henry, *Hermann Goering and the Third Reich: a biography based on family and official records*, New York: Devin-Adair, 1962. xvi, 517pp. Bib. 505-7.

G 997   FRISCHAUER, Willi, *Goering*, London: Odhams, 1950. 304pp. Bib. 304. US edn, *The Rise and Fall of Hermann Goering*, Boston: Houghton Mifflin, 1951.

G 998   GOERING, Emmy, *An der Seite meines Mannes: Begebenkeiten und Bekenntnise*, Göttingen: Schutz, 1967. 337pp.

G 999   GOERING, Hermann, *Germany Reborn*, London: Elkin, Matthews & Marrot, 1934. viii, 160pp. Tr. of *Aufbau einer Nation*, Berlin, 1934.

G 1000   MANVELL, Roger and FRAENKEL, Heinrich, *Hermann Goering*, London: Heinemann. New York: Simon & Schuster, 1962. 429pp.

G 1001   MOSLEY, Leonard, *The Reich's Marshall: a biography of Hermann Goering*, London: Weidenfeld & Nicolson. New York: Doubleday, 1974. xiii, 394pp.

Reinhard Heydrich (1904-42)

G 1002   ARONSON, Shlomo, *Reinhard Heydrich und die Frühgeschichte von Gestapo und SD*, Stuttgart: Deutsche Verlags-Anstalt, 1971. 339pp. Bib. 331-5. Free University of Berlin thesis, 1967.

G 1003   CALIC, Edouard, *Reinhard Heydrich: Schlüsselfigur des Dritten Reiches*, Düsseldorf: Droste, 1982. 577pp.

G 1004   DESCHNER, Günther, *Heydrich: the pursuit of total power*, London: Orbis, 1981. 351pp. Bib. 329-55. US edn, *Reinhard Heydrich: a biography*, New York: Stein and Day, 1981. Tr. of *Reinhard Heydrich*, Esslingen: Bechtle, 1977.

G 1005   GRABER, G.S., *The Life and Times of Reinhard Heydrich*, New York: McKay, 1980. London: Hale, 1981. 245pp.

G 1006   HEYDRICH, Lina, *Leben mit einem Kriegsverbrecher*, commentary by Werner Maser, Pfaffenhofen: Ludwig, 1976. 211pp.

G 1007   PAILLARD, Georges and ROUGÉRIE, Claude, *Reinhard Heydrich (Protecteur de Bohême et Moravie): le violiniste de la mort*, Paris: Fayard, 1973. 316pp. Bib. 309–12.

Heinrich Himmler (1900–45)

G 1008   ACKERMANN, Josef, *Heinrich Himmler als Ideologe*, Göttingen: Musterschmidt, 1970. 317pp. Bib. 307–10.

G 1009   ANGRESS, Werner T., and SMITH, Bradley F., 'Diaries of Heinrich Himmler's early years'. *J. OF MOD. HIST.*, **31** (**3**), 1959. pp. 206–24.

G 1010   FRISCHAUER, Willi, *Himmler: the evil genius of the Third Reich*, Boston: Beacon Press, 1953. 269pp.

G 1011   HEIBER, Helmut (ed.), *Reichsführer . . . Briefe an und von Himmler*, Stuttgart: Deutsche Verlags-Anstalt, 1968. 319pp. Bib. 318–19.

G 1012   HIMMLER, Heinrich, *Geheimreden 1933 bis 1945 und andere Ansprachen*, eds. Bradley F. Smith and Agnes F. Peterson, intro. by Joachim C. Fest, Berlin: Propyläen V., 1974. 319pp. Bib. 313–19. Speeches of Himmler.

G 1013   KERSTEN, Felix, *The Kersten memoirs, 1940–1945*, intro. by H.R. Trevor-Roper, London: Hutchinson, 1956. New York, Macmillan, 1957. 314pp. Tr. of *Totenkampf und Treue*, Hamburg, Molisch, 1952, by Constantine Fitzgibbon.

G 1014   LOEWENBERG, Peter, 'The unsuccessful adolescence of Heinrich Himmler'. *AM. HIST. REV.*, **76** (**3**), 1971. pp. 612–41.

G 1015   MANVELL, Roger and FRAENKEL, Heinrich, *Heinrich Himmler*, London: Heinemann. New York: Putnam, 1965. xvii, 285pp. Bib. 275–8.

G 1016   MEISLER, Y., 'Himmler's doctrine of the SS leadership'. *JAHRB. INST. DTSCH. GESCH.*, **8**, 1979. pp. 389–432.

G 1017   SMITH, Bradley F., *Heinrich Himmler: a nazi in the making, 1900–1926*, Stanford: Hoover Inst. Press. 1971. ix, 211pp. Bib. 201–3.

G 1018   SPEER, Albert, *The Slave State: Heinrich Himmler's masterplan for SS supremacy*, London: Weidenfeld & Nicolson, 1981. ixv, 384pp. Bib. 331–71. Tr. of *Die Sklavenstaat*, Stuttgart, 1981, by Joachim Neugroschel.

G 1019   WYKES, Alan, *Himmler*, London: Pan, 1973. 159pp.

Ernst Röhm (1887–1934)

G 1020   BENNECKE, Heinrich, 'Die Memoiren des Ernst Röhm: ein Vergleich der verschiedenen Ausgaben und Auflagen'. *POLIT. STUD.*, **14**, 1963. pp. 179–88.

G 1021   BENNECKE, Heinrich, *Die Reichswehr und der 'Röhm-Putsch'*, Munich: Olzog, 1964. 93pp. Bib. 93.

G 1022   RÖHM, Ernst, *Die Geschichte eines Hochverräters*, 8th edn, Munich: Eher, 1934. 367pp. Autobiography.

Alfred Rosenberg (1893–1946)

G 1023   BILLIG, Joseph, *Alfred Rosenberg dans l'action idéologique, politique et administrative du Reich hitlérien: inventaire commenté*, etc., Paris: Éd. du Centre de Documentation Juive Contemporaine, 1963. 354pp. Bib. 344–5.

G 1024   CECIL, Robert, *The Myth of the Master Race: Alfred Rosenberg and nazi ideology*, New York: Dodd Mead. London: Batsford, 1972. x, 266pp. Bib. 249–56.

G 1025   KAISER, Wilhelm Jakob, *Das Rechts- und Staatsdenken Alfred Rosenbergs*, Cologne: Wasmund, 1964. xiv, 161pp. Bib. vi–xiv. Cologne University thesis.

G 1026   ROSENBERG, Alfred, *Der Mythus des 20. Jahrhunderts: eine Wertung der seelisch-geistigen Gestaltenkämpfe unserer Zeit*, Munich: Hoheneichen-V., 1944. xxi, 712pp. First pub. 1930.

G 1027   ROSENBERG, Alfred, *Das politische Tagebuch Alfred Rosenbergs, 1934/35 und 1939/40*, ed. Hans-Günther Seraphim, Munich: Deutsche Taschenbuch V., 1964. 265pp.

G 1028   ROSENBERG, Alfred, *Selected writings*, ed. and intro. by Robert Pois, London: Cape, 1970. 204pp. Bib. 197–204.

G 1029   RÜDIGER, Karlheinz (comp.), *Das Werk Alfred Rosenbergs: eine Bibliographie*, Munich: Eher, 1942. 32pp.

Albert Speer (1905–81)

G 1030   BILLSON, Marcus K., 'Inside Albert Speer: secrets of moral evasion'. *Antioch Rev.*, **37** (**4**), 1979. pp. 460–74. Interview with Speer.

G 1031 BRACHER, Karl Dietrich, 'Die Speer Legende'. *NEUE POLIT. LIT.*, **15** (4), 1970. pp. 429-31.

G 1032 O'DONNELL, James P., 'Conversations with Speer'. *Encounter*, **47** (4), 1976. pp. 6-16.

G 1033 REIF, Adalbert (ed.), *Albert Speer: Kontroversen um ein deutsches Phänomen*, Munich: Bernard & Graefe, 1978. 501pp.

G 1034 SPEER, Albert, *Inside the Third Reich: memoirs*, tr. by Richard and Clara Winston, intro. by Eugene Davidson. London: Weidenfeld & Nicolson. New York: Macmillan, 1970. xviii, 596pp.

G 1035 SPEER, Albert, *Spandau: the secret diaries*, London: Collins. New York: Macmillan, 1976. xii, 463pp. Tr. of *Spandauer Tagebücher*, by Richard and Clara Winston.

Julius Streicher (1885-1946)

G 1036 BAIRD, Jay W., 'Das politische Testament Julius Streichers: ein Dokument aus den Papieren des Hauptmanns Dolibois'. *VIERTELJAHRSH. FÜR ZEITG.*, **26** (4), 1978. pp. 660-93.

G 1037 BYTWERK, Randall, 'Julius Streicher and the impact of Der Stürmer'. *WIENER LIB. BULL.*, **29** (**39/40**), 1976/7. pp. 41-6.

G 1038 BYTWERK, Randall, *Julius Streicher: the rhetoric of an antisemite*, Northwestern University thesis, 1975. UM 76-11877. 220pp.

G 1039 EHLERS, Carol Jean, *Nuremberg, Julius Streicher and the Bourgeois Transition to Nazism, 1918-1924*, University of Colorado thesis, 1965. xxi, 698pp.

G 1040 LENMAN, Robin, 'Julius Streicher and the origins of the NSDAP in Nuremburg, 1918-1923'. In NICHOLLS, A.J. and MATTHIAS, E., G 345. pp. 129-59.

G 1041 KIPPHAN, Klaus, 'Julius Streicher und der 9. November 1923'. *Z. FÜR BAYERISCHE LANDESG.*, **39** (1), 1976. pp. 277-88.

Other Personalities

G 1042 DIETRICH, Valeska, *Alfred Hugenberg: ein Manager in der Publizistik*. Free University of Berlin thesis, 1960. 124pp. Hugenberg (1865-1951), tycoon, Nationalist, and supporter of the nazis.

G 1043 DÖNITZ, Karl, *Memoirs: ten years and twenty days*, London: Weidenfeld & Nicolson. Cleveland: World Pub. Co., 1959. 500pp. Tr.

of *Zehn Jahre und zwantig Tage*, Bonn: Athenäum V., 1958. Karl Dönitz (1891-1980), Hitler's successor as Head of State.

G 1044 ENGELMAN, Ralph Max, *Dietrich Eckart and the Genesis of Nazism*, Washington University thesis, 1971. UM 72-09330. 266pp.

G 1045 PLEWNIA, Margarete, *Aus dem Weg zu Hitler: der 'völkische' Publizist Dietrich Eckart*, Bremen: Schünemann, 1970. 155pp. Bib. 138-49. Münster University thesis.

G 1046 FRANK, Hans, *Hans Frank's Diary*, ed. Stanislaw Piotrowski, Warsaw: Panstwowe Wydawn. Naukowe, 1961. 320pp. Abridged English edn of *Sprawy polskie przed Miedzynarodowym Trybunalem Wojeneym w Norymberdze*. 1957. Frank (1900-1946), leading jurist and Governor-General of occupied Poland.

G 1047 LEASOR, James, *Rudolf Hess: the uninvited envoy*, London: Allen & Unwin. New York: McGraw Hill, 1962. 239pp. Bib. 243-6.

G 1048 MANVELL, Roger and FRAENKEL, Heinrich, *Hess: a biography*, London: MacGibbon & Kee, 1971. 256pp. Bib. 219-20.

G 1049 PAPEN, Franz von, *Memoirs*, London: Deutsch, 1952. Repr. by AMS Press. Notes 393-404. Tr. of *Vom Scheitern einer Demokratie*, by Brian Connell.

G 1050 PENTZLIN, Heinz, *Hjalmar Schacht: Leben und Wirken ein umstrittenen Persönlichkeit*, Berlin: Ullstein, 1980. 295pp. Bib. 283-91.

G 1051 SCHACHT, Hjalmar, *My First Seventy-six Years: an autobiography*, London: Wingate, 1955. Tr. of *76 Jahre meines Lebens*, Bad Wörishofen, 1953.

G 1052 PODGÓRECZNY, Marian, *Albert Forster: Gauleiter i oskarzony*, Gdansk: Wyd. Morskie, 1977. 435pp. Bib. 428-33. Albert Forster (1902-54), Danzig Free State Reich Governor.

G 1053 SCHIRACH, Baldur von, *Ich glaubte an Hitler*, Hamburg: Mosaik V., 1967. 367pp.

G 1054 WORTMANN, Michael, *Baldur von Schirach: Hitlers Jugendführer*, Cologne: Böhlau, 1982. 272pp.

G 1055 TYRELL, Albrecht, 'Gottfried Feder und die NSDAP'. In STACHURA, P.D., G 163. pp. 48-87.

G 1056 WAHL, Karl, *Patrioten oder Verbrecher: aus fünfzigjähriger Praxis davon siebzehn Jahre als Gauleiter*, 3rd edn, Heusenstamm: Orion-Heimreiter V., 1975. 243pp. Author Gauleiter of Swabia, 1928-45.

Index

This personal name index lists names of authors, editors, translators, etc., as well as names as subject mentioned in the body of the entry or in the note, or, where the book is concerned with an individual even if not mentioned in entry or note.

BAUMONT, Maurice, G 158
BAYLE, François, G 528
BAYNES, Norman, G 177, G 918
BEAU DE LOMÉNIE, Emmanuel, Fr 43, Fr 98, Fr 148
BEAUFAYS, Jean, Bl 1-2, Bl 10
BECHTEL, Guy, Fr 431
BECK, Yoram, Fr 229
BECKARS, Peter, G 318
BECKENBACH, Ralf, G 601
BECKER, Josef, G 392
BECKERATH, Erwin von, It 53
BEEGLE, J. Allen, G 451
BEETHAM, David, Gn 163-164
BEGNAC, Ivon de, It 200, It 565-567
BELCI, Franco, It 485
BELEMACE, Doru, Rm 24
BELIN, René, Fr 439
BELLOTTI, Felice, It 673
BELOFF, Max, Fr 270, G 62, G 439, G 981
BEN- AMI, Shlomo, Sp 18-20
BENDA, Julien, Fr 230
BENDERSKY, Joseph William, G 694
BENDIX, Reinhard, G 445
BENEDETTI, Ulisse, It 380
BENEDIKT, Heinrich, Au 60
BENEDIKT, Ursula, Au 77
BENET, Juan, Sp 170
BENINI, Zenone, It 674
BENN, Gottfried, G 693, G 699
BENNECKE, Heinrich, G 529, G 854, G 1020-1021
BENNETT, R.J., Gn 164
BENTELI, Marianne, Gn 42
BENVENUTI, Sergio, It 244
BENZE, Rudolf, G 178
BEREGFY, Károly, H 26
BERG, Frederick, Au 1
BERGHAHN, Volker R., G 97, G 265, G 564
BERGOUNIOUX, Alain, Fr 326
BERLE, Adolph A., G 804
BERLUTTI, Giorgio, It 2
BERMANI, Cesare, It 245
BERNABEI, Marco, It 426
BERNADEC, Christian, Fr 345
BERNADINI, Gene, It 414
BERNANOS, Georges, Fr 44, Fr 131, Fr 487-492, Fr 539, Sp 96
BERNBAUM, John A., Au 165-66, G 179
BERNERI, Camillo, It 568
BERNETT, Hajo, G 720
BERNING, Cornelia, G 280
BERSTEIN, Serge, Fr 271, It 93
BERTELE, Aldo, It 324
BERTELLI, Sergio, It 148
BERTH, Edouard, Fr 41, Fr 256
BERTI, Giuseppe, It 449
BERTOLDI, Silvio, It 132, It 569, It 679
BERTOLO, Gianfranco, It 460
BERTRAND, Charles Lloyd, It 201
BESSEL, Richard J., G 464, G 530-531
BESSON, Waldemar, Gn 64, G 225
BETHLEN, Istvan, Count, Au 69, H 23-24
BETHOUARD, Marie Émile, Général, Fr 479
BETIN, Gianfranco, Gn 253
BETZ, Werner, G 280
BEWLEY, Charles Henry, G 996
BEYERSCHEN, Alan D., G 732
BEYME, Klaus von, Sp 173
BEZYMENSKII, Lev Aleksandrovich, G 855, G 972
BIANCHI, Bruna, It 450
BIANCHI, Gianfranco, It 137, It 365, It 680
BIANCINI, Bruno, It 570
BIBER, Dušan, Y 9, Y 39
BIBES, Geneviève, It 21

BIBL, Viktor, Au 24
BIELECKI, Tadeusz, Pl 5
BIERNAT, Karl Heinz, G 434
BIÉTRY, Pierre, Fr 53
BIGLER, Robert M., H 14
BILLIG, Joseph, Fr 363, G 797-798, G 1023
BILLSON, Marcus K., G 1030
BINAZZI, A., It 471
BINCHY, Daniel A., It 486
BINDER, Gerhart, G 226
BINDSLØV- FREDERIKSEN, L., D 12
BINION, Rudolph, G 856-860
BIONDI, Dino, It 571
BIRKELAND, Bjorte, No 74
BIRKENFELD, Wolfgang, G 602
BITELLI, Giovanni, It 572
BLAICH, Fritz, G 609
BLANK, A.S., Gn 193
BLANKE, Bernhard, Gn 191, Gn 194, G 520
BLANKE, Thomas, G 520
BLATT, Joel Richard, Fr 99, Fr 231
BLAYE, Édouard de, Sp 174
BLEUEL, Hans Peter, G 637, G 742
BLINDHEIM, Svein, No 38
BLINKHORN, Martin, Sp 42
BLIT, Lucjan, Pl 29
BLOCH, Charles, G 532
BLOCH, Ernst, Gn 243
BLOKZIJL, Max, Ne 9-10
BLOM, Ida, No 11
BLOND, Georges, Fr 414
BLUM, Léon, It 194
BLUMENKRANZ, Bernhard, Fr 1
BLUMENTHAL, David R., G 771
BOBBIO, Norberto, It 362
BOBERACH, Heinz, G 181, G 639
BOCCA, Giorgio, It 75, It 681
BODENSIECK, Heinrich, G 227-228
BOEGNER, Marc, Fr 453
BOEHME, Inge, G 70
BÖHNKE, Wilfried, G 319
BOENERT, Gunnar Charles, G 155, G 533
BOER, Piet, Ne 34
BOESCH, Joseph, G 229
BÖSZÖRMÉNY, Zoltán, H 31, H 71
BÖTTICHER, Paul Anton, See LAGARDE, Paul de
BOGDAN, Ivo, Y 12
BOGYAY, Tamas, H 74
BOHBOT, David, Fr 331
BOHM, R.P.S.M., Ne 42
BOIADZHIEVA, Elena, E 4
BOISDEFFRE, Pierre de, Fr 191
BOLHUIS, J.J. van, Ne 50
BOLITHO, Hector, Rm 63
BOLLAND, G.J.P.J., Ne 45
BOLLMUS, Reinhard, G 803
BONDY, François, It 184
BONNARD, Abel, Fr 232-233
BONNEFOIS, Max, Fr 336
BONNEVAY, Laurent Marie Benoit, Fr 272
BONO, Emilio de, It 289
BONOMI, Ivanoe, It 214-215
BORCH, Herbert von, G 505
BORDEAUX, Henry, Fr 100
BOREJSZA, Jerzy W., Gn 5, E5-8, Bs 1, It 573
BORGESE, Giuseppe Antonio, It 292
BORGESE, Junio Valerio, It 592
BORGHI, Armando, It 574
BORKENAU, Franz, Gn 254
BORMANN, Martin, G 919, G 972-976
BORRAS Y BERMEJO, Tomas, Sp 147
BORST, Gert, G 111
BOSL, Karl, C 84
BOSMAJIAN, Haig S., G 861

BOSSAN DE GARAGNOL, E., Fr 218
BOSSLE, Lothar, Gn 255
BOSWORTH, Richard J.B., It 22-23, It 447
BOTTAI, Giuseppe, Gn 14, It 205, It 373, It 650-659
BOTZ, Gerhard, Gn 65, Gn 195, Au 2, Au 50-54, Au 99-100, Au 114, Au 120, Au 127, Au 137, Au 153-155, Au 167-169
BOUDIN, Janine, Fr 313
BOUHLER, Philipp, G 199
BOULANGER, Georges -Ernest-Jean-Marie, Général, Fr 69-70
BOURDERON, Roger, Gn 66, Fr 440-441
BOURDREL, Philippe, Fr 344
BOURGEOIS, Daniel, Sw 6
BOURGET, Pierre, Fr 364, Fr 415
BOUSQUET, G.H., Gn 165
BOUSSARD, Isabel, Fr 442
BOUTHILLIER, Yves, Fr 443
BOVERI, Margaret, G 654
BOWEN, Ralph, Gn 290
BOZZETTI, Gherardo, It 575, It 645
BOZZI, Carlo, It 576
BRAATZ, Werner, G 115
BRACALE, Carlo, It 16
BRACHER, Karl-Dietrich, Gn 68, Gn 250, G 67-68, G 393-394, G 439, G 862-863, G 1031
BRADESCO, Faust, Rm 25
BRADY, Robert Alexander, G 69
BRÄCKEL, Thomas, G 375
BRÄUNSCHE, Ernst Otto, G 320
BRAHAM, Randolph L., G 978, H 75-76
BRAHM, Heinz, Gn 196
BRAJOVIĆ, Petar, Y 50, Y 53
BRAMSTED, Ernest Kohn, G 981-982
BRANDENBURG, Hans Christian, G 748
BRANDES, Detlef, C 99
BRANDT, C.D.J., Ne 50
BRANICA, Vinko, Y 58
BRASILLACH, Robert, Fr 131, Fr 249, Fr 493-504, Fr 541, Bl 54
BRAVO, Gian Mario, It 545
BRAVO MARTÍNEZ, Francisco, Sp 54, Sp 111-112
BRÉDOW, Wilfried von, G 230
BREEN, Catherine Müller-Bapst, Fr 234
BREITING, Richard, G 864
BREITLING, Rupert, G 281
BRESNAHAN, William, Gn 288
BRETSCHER, Willy, Sw 7
BREUNING, Klaus, Au 82
BREVIG, Hans Olaf, No 9
BREZZI, Camillo, It 132, It 487
BRINON, Fernand de, Fr 365-366
BRISSAUD, André, Fr 444-445, It 577, It 675
BRIX, Knud, D 1
BROCK, John Joseph, R 2
BROCK, Peter, Pl 2
BROCKDORF, Werner, Gn 321
BRØNDSTED, Johannes, D 13
BROGAN, Denis William, Fr 101, Fr 149
BRONDER, Dietrich, G 30
BRONGERSMA, Edward, Pl 6
BROSSE, Jacques, G 865
BROSZAT, Martin, E9, Y15, Rm 26, Rm 64, Pl 49, C 81, Bs 36, G 70-71, G 146, G 182, G 231, G 282-283, G 321. G 435, G 465, G 509, G 546, G 772-775, G 826, G 866
BROWDER, George Clark, G 183, G 534-535
BROWN, MacAlister, E 10
BROWNING, Christopher R., G 775
BROWNJOHN, J. Maxwell, G 637

317

318

319

322

323

LÖNNE, Karl Egon, G 338
LÖWE, Heinz- Dietrich, R 5
LOEWENBERG, Peter, G 259, G 758, G 1014
LOEWENSTEIN, Bedrich, Gn 106, C 13
LOHALM, Uwe, G 138
LOMBARDINI, S., It 519
LONGCHAMP, Jean Paul de, Rm 34
LOOCK, Hans-Dietrich, No. 21-22, G 296
LOOGMAN, P., Ne 20
LOOMIS, Charles P., G 451
LOPEZ MEDEL, Jesus, Sp 120
LOPUKHOV, Boris Ramovich, It 43
LORENTZEN, Svein, No 11
LOSSOWSKI, Piotr E., E 11, Bs 4
LOUBET DEL BAYLE, Jean-Louis, Fr 242, Fr 517
LOUGEE, Robert W., G 42
LOUSTAUNAU- LACAU, Georges, Fr 351
LOVIN, Clifford R., G 626
LOW, Alfred, Au 94
LOZEK, Gerhard, G 260-261
LUBASZ, Heinz, Gn 39
LUCCHINI, Pierre, Fr 222
LUCCHINI, Riccardo, Gn 265
LUCENA, Manuel, P 1, P 28
LUCHAIRE, Corinne, Fr 398
LUCHAIRE, Jean, Fr 366, Fr 396, Fr 398
LUCHINI, Alberto, Sp 67
LUDENDORFF, Erich, Au 115, G 111-114
LUDWIG, Eduard, Au 117
LUDWIG, Emil, It 602
LUEGER, Karl, Au 40-42, Au 162
LÜKEMANN, Ulf, G 816
LÜTTWITZ, Walter, Freiherr von, G 125
LUIRARD, Monique, Fr 384
LUKÁCS, György, Gn 232
LUNA, Giovanni, It 603
LUNDBERG, Erik, S 7
LUNDE, Gulbrand, No 23
LUTI, Giorgino, It 405
LUTKIE, Wouter, Ne 47
LUTZHÖFT, Hans- Jürgen, G 297
LUŽA, Radomir V., Au 174
LYTTLETON, Adrian, It 44, It 281, It 308, It 333
LYUBOSH, S.B., R 6

MAAMÄGI, V.A., Bs 5
MAASING, Richard, Bs 13
MAASS, Walter B., Au 118, Au 175
MABIRE, Jean, Fr 380, Fr 518
MACARTNEY, Carlyle Aylmer, H 5
MACCEARNEY, James, Fr 164
MACCIOCCHI, Maria Antonietta, Gn 107, It 434
McCLELLAND, J.S., Fr 18
McGOVERN, James, G 975
McGRATH, William J., Au 43
MACGREGOR-HASTIE, Roy, It 89
MACEK, Vladko, Y 27
MACH, A., C 27
MACHEFER, Philippe, Fr 19, Fr 307, Fr 312-317
MACIPE LOPEZ, Antonio, Sp 150
MACK SMITH, Dennis, It 45, It 90-91, It 139, It 226, It 385, It 604
McKALE, Donald M., G 817-818
McKIBBIN, R.I., G 452
MACLEOD, Alexander, Fr 519
McLOUGHLIN, Barry, Ir 4
MACMILLAN, Kathleen, It 312
McRANDLE, James Harrington, G 86
MADAJCZYK, Czeslaw, Gn 204, Pl 51
MADARO, Luigi, It 12
MADAULE, Jacques, Fr 197

MADDEN, James Paul, G 483
MADIRAN, Jean, Fr 500
MAEZTU Y WHITNEY, Ramiro, Conde de, Sp 35-36
MAGOSSI, Robert, C 110
MAHÉ, André, Fr 352
MAIER, Charles S., Gn 108, It 46, It 309
MAIER, Karl- Hanns, Sw 4
MAINER, José Carlos, Sp 94
MAISTRE, Joseph Marie de, Fr 18
MAJCHROWSKI, Jacek M., Pl 22-23
MAJOR, Robert, H 6
MAKANEC, Julije, Y 28
MAKLER, Harry M., P 1
MALAPARTE, Curzio, It 390-391, It 402
MALATYNSKI, Antoni, Pl 34
MALINA, Peter, G 787
MALLET, Alfred, Fr 437
MALNASI, Ödön, H 57
MALUSARDI, Eduardo, It 205
MAMERS, Oskar, pseud., Bs 20-21
MAN, E. de, Bl 80
MAN, Hendrik de, Bl 72-81
MAN, J. de, Bl 80
MANACORDA, Gastone, It 275
MANACORDA, Giuliano, It 386
MANGONI, Luisa, Gn 109-110, It 406
MANHEIM, Ralph, G 81, G 899, G 915
MANN, Reinhard, No 20, D 6, Au 100, G 466, G 469, G 477, G 484, G 547, G 556
MANN, Rosemarie, G 339
MANNING, Maurice, Ir 5-6
MANNZMANN, Annelise, G 936
MANOILESCU, Mihail, Gn 292-293
MANSILLA, Hugo Celso Felipe, Gn 233
MANTICA, Paolo, It 92
MANUNTA, Ugo, It 690
MANVELL, Roger, G 411, G 992, G 1000, G 1015, G 1048
MARCHANT, Hendrik Pieter, Ne 21
MARCUSE, Herbert, Gn 188
MARHEFKA, Edmund, Gn 28
MARIANO, Emilio, It 181
MARIN, Vasile, Rm 35
MARINETTI, Filippo Tommaso, It 193-197, It 402, It 566
MARINO, Valerio E., It 663
MARINUS, B., Ne 8
MARION, Paul, Fr 296
MARITAIN, Jacques, Fr 131, Fr 165, Fr 214-217
MARJANOVIĆ, Jovan, Y 53
MARKMANN, Charles Lam, It 85
MARRUS, Michael Robert, Fr 467
MARSCHALKO, Lajos, H 37
MARTENS, Erika, G 659
MARTIĆ, Milos, Y 47
MARTIGNONI, Angiolo, Sw 18
MARTIN, Bernd, Gn 111
MARTIN, Claude, Sp 189
MARTIN, Dirk, Bl 87
MARTIN, Rául, Sp 68
MARTIN DU GARD, Maurice, Fr 116, Fr 468
MARTINELLI, Franco, It 357
MARTINEZ, José, Sp 76
MARTINEZ CARRASCO, Alfonso, Sp 86
MARTINEZ VAL, José Maria, Sp 69
MARTINS, Herminio, P 2
MARTY, Albert, Fr 117
MARUCCO, Dora, It 348
MARX, Fritz Morstein, G 512
MARX, Karl, It 619
MARZIO, Cornelio di, It 2
MASELLA, Luigi, It 461
MASER, Werner, G 308, G 912-913, G 937-939

MASI, Giorgio, It 302
MASINI, Pier-Carlo, It 568
MASON, Henry Lloyd, Ne 55
MASON, Timothy W., G 155, G 262-263, G 340, G 485, G 665-666
MASSING, Paul W., G 11
MASSIS, Henri, Fr 118, Fr 166, Fr 198, P 41
MASTNY, Vojtech, C 102
MATTEI, Roberto de, Fr 90
MATTEOTTI, Giacomo, It 289-291
MATTHEIER, Klaus, G 12
MATTHES, Reinar, Au 143
MATTHIAS, Erich, G 309, G 340, G 345, G 412, G 1040
MATZERATH, Horst, G 155, G 264, G 341, G 513
MAU, Hermann, G 159
MAUGENDRE, Louis- Alphonse, Fr 373
MAUGER, Gilles, Sp 121
MAULNIER, Thierry, Fr 131, Fr 243
MAURER, Ilse, G 342
MAURIAC, François, Fr 362
MAURICIO, Artur, P 19
MAURRAS, Charles, Fr 18, Fr 41, Fr 70, Fr 89-93, Fr 96-121, Fr 123-126, Fr 130, Fr 133-135, Fr 137-138, Fr 141-143, Fr 145-185, Fr 238, Fr 453, Fr 484, Fr 489, Fr 550, Bl 13-14, Rm 18
MAURRAS, Hélène, Fr 147
MAURRAS, Nicole, Fr 147
MAXENCE, Jean-Pierre, pseud. Fr 244
MAXWELL, Brigid, It 607
MAYDA, Giuseppe, It 419
MAYER, Anton, P 29
MAYER, Arno J., Gn 156
MAYER, Domenico, It 676
MAYER-TASCH, Peter C., Gn 294
MAYOR, Andreas, It 660
MAZGAJ, Paul, Fr 119, Fr 245
MAZIÈRE, Georges, Fr 257
MAZZATOSTA, Teresa Maria, It 371
MEDINA, João, P 42, P 50
MEGARO, Gaudens, It 605
MEHRINGER, Helmut, G 819
MEIJER, Jaap, Ne 3
MEINCK, Gerhard, G 613
MEINCK, Jürgen, G 413
MEINECKE, Friedrich, G 87, G 265
MEISSLER, Y., G 1016
MEISSNER, Hans Otto, G 414
MEIXNER, A., Au 119
MELDINI, Piero, It 45
MELEIRO, Fernando, Sp 97
MELIS, Renato, It 206
MELOGRANI, Piero, It 13, It 358, It 442, It 520-521, It 606
MENEGHELLO- DINČIĆ, Kruno, Y 29
MENGHIN, Oswald, Au 84
MENZE, Ernest A., G 40
MERGLEN, Albert, Fr 381
MERKL, Peter H., Gn 112-113, G 486, G 552-556
MERLI, Stefano, It 552, G 763
MERLIN, Gianni, It 522
MERMANS, Antoon, Bl 48
MERMEIX, pseud., Fr 137
MERRILL, Frances and Mason, Gn 214
MERSCH, Carole, L 4
MESKÓ, Zoltán, H 71
MEŠTROVIĆ, Ivan, Y 30
METAXAS, Ioannēs, Gr 1-4, Gr 8-10
MEYER, Alice, Sw 9
MEYER, Håkon, No 40
MEYER, Henry Cord, G 45
MEYER, Wolfgang, Au 179
MEYERS, J., Ne 22, Ne 36
MEYERS, Peter, G 266
MEYERS, Willem C.M., Bl 49, Bl 88